W9-CNV-933

FOREST VEGETATION MANAGEMENT FOR CONIFER PRODUCTION

FOREST VEGETATION MANAGEMENT FOR CONIFER PRODUCTION

Edited by

JOHN D. WALSTAD

College of Forestry
Oregon State University

and

PETER J. KUCH

Office of Pesticide Programs
U.S. Environmental Protection Agency

A WILEY-INTERSCIENCE PUBLICATION

JOHN WILEY & SONS
NEW YORK   CHICHESTER   BRISBANE   TORONTO   SINGAPORE

Library of Congress Cataloging in Publication Data:
Forest vegetation management for conifer production.

"A Wiley-Interscience publication."
Includes index.
1. Conifers—Weed control—United States.
2. Conifers—Weed control—Canada. 3. Forests
and forestry—Weed control—United States.
4. Forests and forestry—Weed control—Canada.
5. Forest management—United States. 6. Forest
management—Canada. I. Walstad, John D. (John
Daniel), 1944–. II. Kuch, Peter J. (Peter
Jacob), 1940–.
SB608.C7F67 1987   634.9'75   86-28913
ISBN 0-471-85098-5

Printed in the United States of America
10 9 8 7 6 5 4 3 2 1

Contributors

BRADFORD L. BARBER, PH.D., School of Forestry, Auburn University, Auburn, Alabama

RAYMOND J. BOYD, JR., PH.D., USDA Forest Service, Moscow, Idaho

J. DOUGLAS BRODIE, PH.D., College of Forestry, Oregon State University, Corvallis, Oregon

HAROLD E. BURKHART, PH.D., Department of Forestry, Virginia Polytechnic Institute and State University, Blacksburg, Virginia

DEAN H. GJERSTAD, PH.D., School of Forestry, Auburn University, Auburn, Alabama

GLENN R. GLOVER, PH.D., School of Forestry, Auburn University, Auburn, Alabama

PETER J. KUCH, PH.D., Office of Pesticide Programs, U.S. Environmental Protection Agency, Washington, DC

MAXWELL L. MCCORMACK, JR., PH.D., College of Natural Resources, University of Maine, Orono, Maine

MICHAEL NEWTON, PH.D., College of Forestry, Oregon State University, Corvallis, Oregon

LOGAN A. NORRIS, PH.D., College of Forestry, Oregon State University, Corvallis, Oregon

KATHERINE OSTERYOUNG, M.S., Department of Botany, University of California, Davis, California

STEVEN R. RADOSEVICH, PH.D., College of Forestry, Oregon State University, Corvallis, Oregon

CLARK ROW, PH.D., Consulting Resource Economist, Dunkirk, Maryland

ROBERT L. SAJDAK, M.S., School of Forestry, Michigan Technological University, Houghton, Michigan

PETER T. SPRINZ, PH.D., Department of Forestry, Virginia Polytechnic Institute and State University, Blacksburg, Virginia

ALBERT R. STAGE, PH.D., USDA Forest Service, Moscow, Idaho

RONALD E. STEWART, PH.D., USDA Forest Service, Berkeley, California

JOHN C. TAPPEINER II, PH.D., College of Forestry, Oregon State University, Corvallis, Oregon

ROBERT G. WAGNER, M.S., College of Forestry, Oregon State University, Corvallis, Oregon

JOHN D. WALSTAD, PH.D., College of Forestry, Oregon State University, Corvallis, Oregon

SHEPARD M. ZEDAKER, PH.D., Department of Forestry, Virginia Polytechnic Institute and State University, Blacksburg, Virginia

Foreword

Weeds have been defined as plants growing where we do not want them. Plants that compete with commercially desirable species or individuals for space, light, nutrients, and moisture are weeds and may seriously impede the establishment and growth of commercially important conifer forests. Foresters intuitively recognize the need to manage weeds (competing vegetation), but they receive little formal education on these topics. The technical information in this area has not been systematically collected and rigorously interpreted. As a consequence, it has been exceedingly difficult for foresters to select and implement efficient strategies for managing competing vegetation. Controversy and uncertainty about the effectiveness of weed control in promoting forest productivity have led to difficult policy and regulatory decisions. Even research has suffered because it often lacked the integrated approach needed to solve vegetation management problems.

This volume addresses many of these problems. It was prepared by an interdisciplinary team of scientists who are national leaders in their fields. They evaluated and interpreted current concepts and practices relating to the biology and economics of forest vegetation management in the major commercial conifer zones of the United States and Canada. Although the focus is vegetation management, it integrates well with other aspects of silviculture. The three most important contributions of this text are:

1. It provides a solid conceptual and technical foundation for educational purposes, including university curricula for forestry students, continuing education courses for professionals, and information programs for the public.
2. It provides an extensive quantitative data base for decision making at both the stand and regional level, thereby reducing reliance on subjective judgments.
3. It provides guidance for research and future progress in the field of forest vegetation management.

This volume is an important contribution to solving some of the problems that have made it so difficult to implement effective integrated vegetation management practices in the United States and Canada.

LOGAN A. NORRIS

Head, Department of Forest Science
College of Forestry
Oregon State University
Corvallis, Oregon

Preface

The major goal of this text is to consolidate the information available concerning the silvicultural aspects of forest vegetation management. Such a synthesis is needed for a variety of purposes. Forest managers can use the information to evaluate investment decisions and opportunities related to vegetation management. Regulatory officials can apply the information to risk/benefit analysis of specific weed control techniques. Biometricians and forest planners can utilize the data and models presented for growth and yield prediction, thereby improving forecasts of forest productivity. Educators can use the information in the training of forestry students and professionals. In short, a better understanding of the techniques and benefits of forest vegetation management should be useful to numerous individuals and organizations concerned with a number of aspects of commercial forest land management.

A document of this scope is an ambitious undertaking. Therefore, some constraints had to be imposed on the endeavor. As the title implies, the thrust of this text is directed at conifers. Although many of the principles and concepts apply equally well to hardwood management, wildlife habitat manipulation, rights-of-way maintenance, and other uses of vegetation management in forest settings, this text concentrates on its application to softwoods—the major commodity produced by forest land throughout North America.

As the title also implies, this text emphasizes the *production* side of forestry; that is, how vegetation management can be used to enhance the performance of conifer stands and plantations. It does not evaluate potential side effects of various techniques, tools, or approaches to vegetation management. Assessments of the *risk* aspect of vegetation management are more appropriately done by experts in the health and environmental sciences. Certain sections of the text do address the comparative advantages, disadvantages (including potential adverse effects), and limitations of various vegetation management alternatives, but no one method or approach is recommended over another. Such determinations can only be made in the context of specific situations by the individuals responsible for weighing the social, economic, and environmental trade-offs inherent in forest resource management. In short, this text is not designed to be a comprehensive environmental impact assessment of forest vegetation management, although it is hoped that the information it contains will make a major contribution to such evaluations.

The scope of this document is further constrained by practical limitations of time, effort, and support. Rather than attempting an exhaustive analysis of forest vegetation management as it pertains to every region, timber type, vegetation complex, site class, management strategy, and so on, a more generic approach has been taken. The major vegetation problems in the primary conifer production regions are described along with the methods available for managing these problems. General principles and analytical procedures for evaluating vegetation management requirements and options are described and demonstrated.

Chapter 1 introduces the subject of weeds and their influence. It briefly traces the history of weed control in agriculture and forestry—practices that have evolved into a more comprehensive concept known as vegetation management.

Chapters 2 to 4 portray the current forest vegetation management setting. Major weed problems in the Northwest, South, Northeast, Lake states, and adjacent Canadian provinces are described in terms of their past origin as well as their future trajectory under various management scenarios.

Chapter 5 examines the adaptive characteristics and interactions among plants as they compete for limited site resources. The sequence of events in natural and managed forest ecosystems is compared in order to understand the functional responses of plants to environmental conditions.

An overview of vegetation management techniques and approaches is provided in Chapter 6. The methods currently available are described and illustrated and are discussed in qualitative terms with respect to effectiveness and limitations.

The general principles and patterns of conifer growth and yield are introduced in Chapter 7. These concepts are extended in Chapters 8 to 10 to provide specific examples of conifer response to control of competing vegetation. Current biometrical models are described and used to forecast yields under a range of conditions pertinent to the management of loblolly pine in the South, Douglas-fir in the Pacific Northwest, and mixed conifers in the Inland Northwest.

Chapter 11 specifies the kinds of costs and product values associated with vegetation management. Ranges and trends in costs and product values are discussed. Emphasis is placed on identifying all the applicable costs and product values, so that comprehensive stand- and forest-level economic analyses like those presented in Chapter 12 can be performed.

Chapter 13 provides guidance for conducting forest vegetation management programs. It describes the logical prescription process that a forest manager should go through, beginning with identifying problem areas and ending with an ex-post evaluation of treatment results.

Chapter 14 summarizes the key biological concepts and biometrical patterns established by forest vegetation management research. It also highlights the opportunities for enhancing forest productivity and economic returns through the intelligent application of current knowledge about vegetation management. Finally, several recommendations are made for sustaining technological progress in this critical discipline of silviculture.

Key supporting information can be found in the bibliographies associated with each chapter and in the appendixes. Appendix 1 provides scientific names for the plant species mentioned in the text. Appendix 2 provides conversion factors for metric equivalents. A number of financial formulas are presented in Appendix 3 to facilitate the economic analyses described in Chapter 12.

JOHN D. WALSTAD
PETER J. KUCH

Corvallis, Oregon
Washington, DC
January 1987

Acknowledgments

This text is the culmination of 6 years of effort by those directly involved in preparing and editing the various chapters. The task would not have been accomplished, however, without the expert assistance of numerous individuals who provided key services along the way. Principal among them are Lois C. Schuldt and Mary Beth Kemp, who provided proficient secretarial support during the preparation of this manuscript. Ingrid A. McCutcheon and Allan H. Doerksen provided the artistic talent necessary to prepare most of the illustrations. Dr. Julie K. Gorte, formerly of EPA and currently with the Office of Technology Assessment, was instrumental during the formative stage of this project. Dr. John Neisess of the USDA Forest Service helped secure additional financial support during a critical stage of the work. Finally, we are deeply indebted to the careful scrutiny, technical criticisms, and suggestions for improvement provided by the following professionals who reviewed individual chapters pertinent to their respective specialties:

Mr. R. Edward Bailey, *Nova Scotia Department of Lands and Forests*
Dr. Enoch F. Bell, *USDA Forest Service*
Mr. John W. Benzie, *USDA Forest Service*
Dr. John H. Beuter, *Oregon State University*
Dr. Thomas E. Burk, *University of Minnesota*
Dr. Robert A. Campbell, *Ontario Ministry of Natural Resources*
Mr. Rick L. Cantrell, *Auburn University*

Dr. Susan G. Conard, *USDA Forest Service*
Dr. Fred C. Cubbage, *University of Georgia*
Dr. Richard F. Daniels, *Westvaco Corporation*
Mr. John N. Fiske, *USDA Forest Service*
Dr. Charles H. Fitzgerald, *University of Georgia*
Dr. Richard W. Guldin, *USDA Forest Service*
Dr. David E. Hibbs, *Oregon State University*
Dr. Stephen D. Hobbs, *Oregon State University*
Dr. John D. Hodges, *Mississippi State University*
Dr. David M. Hyink, *Weyerhaeuser Company*
Mr. Rick Iverson, *University of Minnesota*
Dr. James E. King, *Weyerhaeuser Company*
Mr. Walter H. Knapp, *USDA Forest Service*
Dr. Robert F. Lowery, *Weyerhaeuser Company*
Dr. Daniel L. Miller, *Potlatch Corporation*
Dr. Don Minore, *USDA Forest Service*
Dr. Peyton W. Owston, *USDA Forest Service*
Dr. David A. Perry, *Oregon State University*
Dr. Leon V. Pienaar, *University of Georgia*
Mr. Richard N. Pierson, *Weyerhaeuser Company*
Mr. Russell A. Ryker, *USDA Forest Service*
Mr. Robert L. Sajdak, *Michigan Technological University*
Mr. G. Richard Schaertl, *Monsanto Agricultural Products Company*
Dr. Greg L. Somers, *International Paper Company*
Dr. Mike R. Strub, *Weyerhaeuser Company*
Mr. Robert F. Tarrant, *Oregon State University*
Dr. Thomas A. Terry, *Weyerhaeuser Company*
Mr. Thomas C. Turpin, *USDA Forest Service*
Dr. Kenneth A. Wearstler, Jr. *Boise-Cascade Corporation*
Mr. Charles A. Wellner *USDA Forest Service*

    Partial financial support for compiling the information in this text was provided to Oregon State University by federal funds from the U.S. Environmental Protection Agency under Cooperative Assistance Agreement No. CR809002 and from the National Agricultural Pesticide Impact Analysis Program of the U.S. Department of Agriculture under Supplement No. PNW-84-357. The contents do not necessarily reflect the views and policies of these agencies, nor does mention of trade names or commercial products constitute endorsement or recommendation for use.

J.D.W.
P.J.K.

Contents

FOREST VEGETATION MANAGEMENT FOR CONIFER PRODUCTION

I

FOREST VEGETATION MANAGEMENT PERSPECTIVES

1

Introduction to Forest Vegetation Management

JOHN D. WALSTAD
PETER J. KUCH

INTRODUCTION

How important are competing plants in the development of commercial forests? When do they exert their maximum influence? How long do the effects persist? What methods can be used to control them, and what trade-offs are involved? These are a few of the questions surrounding the topic of vegetation management in forestry. Before attempting to address these questions, however, it is appropriate to clarify some important concepts about weeds, vegetation management, economic thresholds, and the like. This definition of concepts is followed by a brief historical overview of the development of vegetation management. The chapter concludes with a discussion of previous efforts to analyze the needs and benefits of vegetation management in forestry.

WEEDS IN CONTEXT

Weeds are commonly defined as undesirable plants, plants growing in situations where they are not wanted, or plants out of place (Klingman 1966). Certain plants fall into these categories for a variety of reasons. They can be poisonous to humans (e.g., poison oak) or toxic to livestock (e.g., tansy ragwort). They can interfere with crop establishment or production (e.g., quackgrass in soybeans). They can contaminate seed crops and vegetable produce (e.g., toxic nightshade berries in peas). They can create hazardous conditions (e.g., brush encroaching along roadsides or power lines). They can simply be aesthetically displeasing (e.g., dandelions and crabgrass growing in residential lawns).

It is important to recognize, however, that plants may be considered weeds in one situation and not in another. For example, poison oak—a noxious plant to most humans—is sometimes browsed by deer, and its berries are eaten by birds. Highly competitive grasses can be beneficial in stabilizing disturbed sites, thereby reducing erosion. Fanciers of dandelion wine and salad would protest the unequivocal classification of dandelions as weeds. Indeed, the poet Ella Wheeler Wilcox has gone so far as saying that "a weed is but an unloved flower!"

Therefore, whether or not a plant is a weed depends on the context in which one finds it and on the prespectives and objectives of the people involved. This is particularly true with respect to many forest plants, which can have a diverse array of beneficial and detrimental characteristics. Vine maple, for example, is a favored shrub for deer browse in the spring and a spectacular source of coloration in the Cascade Mountains of Oregon and Washington during autumn. However, it also is known to seriously compete with young conifers for sunlight, moisture, and nutrients, thereby hampering forest regeneration. Likewise, species of alder and ceanothus are known for their capacity to suppress young conifer stands in the Northwest. Yet these species are capable of fixing atmospheric nitrogen under certain circumstances, thereby improving long-term soil fertility. A variety of hardwood species in the South, Northeast, and Lake states are capable of dominating valuable pine sites. Nevertheless, these same species are prized for furniture, firewood, and composite wood products. Thus the characterization of specific forest plants as weeds requires a thorough assessment of their potential impacts on timber production as well as careful consideration of their intrinsic values for other purposes.

CONCEPT OF VEGETATION MANAGEMENT

The practice of reducing the effects of undesirable plants has been historically called "weed control." This practice, with its origins in agriculture, has frequently been aimed at completely eliminating the presence of weeds, insofar as is practical. In recent years, however, the practice has become more appropriately focused on simply reducing the influence of weeds. Indeed, *forest vegetation management* has been defined as the practice of efficiently channeling limited site resources into usable forest products rather than into noncommercial plant species (Walstad and Gjerstad 1984). Any given site is capable of producing a finite amount of biomass in a given period of time, and only through management will such capabilities be optimized with respect to crop tree production. Otherwise, other species may usurp site resources at the expense of the preferred crop trees.

In its broadest sense, forest vegetation management includes manipulation of both crop and noncrop species populations. Customarily, however, the term is usually restricted to activities directed at competitive noncrop species and does not include thinning and other silvicultural treatments that involve only crop trees. It is not uncommon, however, to have certain vegetation management treatments performed in conjunction with such practices. The cutting of undesirable hardwoods at the time of precommercial thinning is one example.

Forest vegetation management embodies a broader array of management considerations than simply killing or suppressing undesirable plants. It includes a variety of cultural treatments that are integrated in a fashion that:

1. Inhibits or retards the initial establishment of weeds, thereby precluding the necessity for subsequent control measures.
2. Reduces the size or number of weeds to a level corresponding to an economic threshold.
3. Maintains the presence of as diverse a population of plant species (including weeds) as is practical in order to reduce other pest problems and to maintain ecological integrity over the long term.
4. Recognizes that a plant species considered a weed in one case may be a desirable species in another situation or at another time.
5. Is compatible with other components of the management system.

Vegetation management is analogous to integrated pest management in many respects. Just as the concept of pest control has developed to include a variety of direct and indirect and natural and artificial means of suppressing economically important pest populations (Stern et al. 1959), the concept of weed control has evolved in a similar fashion. It now includes an array of preventive and corrective measures that are linked to other cultural practices in order to optimize the crop production system as a whole.

Consequently, the strategic concept of vegetation management has replaced the more tactical discipline of weed control. Vegetation management recognizes the importance of suppressing the influence of weeds only to the extent that they *significantly* interfere with beneficial plants, crops, or other uses of the land. It also recognizes the value inherent in having the flexibility to choose from a variety of techniques to efficiently manipulate competing vegetation. Furthermore, vegetation management entails a careful consideration of the advantages and disadvantages of any given technique or prescription in order to facilitate selection of the most appropriate treatment and ensure that the probable consequences of implementation are adequately understood. Finally, sound vegetation management programs require efficient integration with other cultural activities, so that the production system as a whole is optimized.

CONCEPTS OF ECONOMIC INJURY LEVEL AND ECONOMIC THRESHOLD

Central to the discussion of vegetation management are the concepts of economic injury level and economic threshold. It is important to know the point at which the influence of weeds becomes great enough to justify control measures. The concepts of economic injury level and economic threshold were originally developed by entomologists in an effort to optimize the economic efficiency of insect control operations (Stern et al. 1959). The basic premise behind these concepts is that the degree of crop damage or yield reduction is directly related to the size or density of the pest population affecting it. For example, a crop infested with a large pest population will incur more damage than one infested with a small pest population.

Both the economic injury level and economic threshold concepts require knowledge of four basic parameters: (1) the relationship between pest population size and corresponding crop damage; (2) treatment efficacy; (3) treatment costs; and (4) crop value. Thus these concepts integrate biological and economic factors. The most difficult parameter to establish is the relationship between pest population size and corresponding crop damage. Because of the short-term and relatively uniform nature of agronomic crop production, agronomists have been able to establish the importance of various levels of pest populations in their crop systems. For example, it is known that a quackgrass density of 160 shoots/m^2 will reduce the yield of soybeans by only 1%, whereas a density of 520 shoots/m^2 will reduce the yield by 55% (Young et al. 1982). Zimdahl (1980) summarizes similar information for a variety of other agronomic crops, and Table 1-1 has been reproduced from that text to illustrate the relationships. Similar information is being developed in forestry, and some examples are given in Chapters 8 to 10 of this text.

With information on the pest population-crop response system in hand, along with a knowledge of control costs, treatment efficacy, and crop value, it is possible to determine the economic injury level and economic threshold for given situations. The *economic injury level* is defined as the lowest density or size of a pest population that will cause economic damage (Poston et al. 1983). In other words, it represents the actual number of pests (or size of such pests) capable of inflicting damage worthy of control.

The *economic threshold* refers to the level of pest population at which control measures should be initiated to prevent an increasing pest pop-

TABLE 1-1. The Effect of Increasing Weed Density on Crop Yield—Selected Studies

Crop	Weed	Weed Density	Percentage Yield Reduction from Check Plot
Sugarbeet	Kochia	0.04/ft of row	14
		0.1	26
		0.2	44
		0.5	67
		1.0	79
Soybean	Wild mustard	1/ft of row	30
		2	36
		4	42
		8	50
		16	51
	Common cocklebur	1335/acre	10
		2671	28
		5261	43
		10522	52
Wheat	Wild oat	70/yd^2	22
		160	39
	Green foxtail	721/m^2	20
		1575	35
Cotton	Prickly sida	2/ft of row	27
		4	40
		12	41
Rice	Barnyardgrass	1/ft^2	57
		5	80
		25	95
Corn	Giant foxtail	1/2/ft of row	4
		1	7
		3	9
		6	12
		12	16
		54	24

Source: Adapted from Zimdahl (1980).

ulation from reaching the economic injury level (Stern et al. 1959). Thus the economic threshold is usually a more practical and conservative benchmark than the economic injury level in that it specifies the level at which control measures should be implemented in order to *prevent* a pest population from reaching the economic injury level. In situations involving explosive pest populations (e.g., many herbaceous weeds) and those involving pest species capable of rapid growth in size (e.g., sprouting shrubs and hardwoods), the time at which control measures are most affordable may be long before adverse effects on crop development are manifest. In these situations the economic threshold occurs at a preventive level. In cases where weeds develop more slowly (e.g., slow-growing hardwoods germinating from seed) or must reach a certain stage of development before control measures are effective (e.g., adequate foliation or canopy development), it may be more economical to delay treatment until later in the life of the crop. In these latter cases, the economic threshold may closely approximate the economic injury level.

Economic injury and threshold levels have been established for a number of agricultural situations, ranging from insect pest management to weed control (e.g., Marra and Carlson 1983). Efforts are underway to extend these concepts to forestry. However, the complex biological interactions, diverse management strategies, long rotation periods, and uncertain financial scenarios involved in forestry make it difficult to establish these critical pest population levels. Consequently, it is likely that most decisions in the near future regarding forest vegetation management options will continue to be made largely on the basis of practical experience and professional judgment, rather than on empirical data and mathematical models. Nevertheless, attempts are being made to acquire the quantitative data and predictive information needed to establish economic thresholds and injury levels. This text describes the current state of such knowledge.

HISTORICAL PERSPECTIVE OF VEGETATION MANAGEMENT

There is a preponderance of evidence, much of it based on agricultural experience, that justifies efforts to control or manage competing vegetation. The limited availability of environmental resources, such as moisture, nutrients, sunlight, and growing space, inevitably leads to competition among plants for these often scarce resources. Thomas Malthus commented on this in 1798 in "An Essay on the Principle of Population:"

> It is observed...that there is no bound to the prolific nature of plants or animals but what is made by their crowding and interfering with each other's means of subsistence...

> This is incontrovertibly true. Through the animal and vegetable kingdoms Nature has scattered the seeds of life abroad with the most profuse and liberal hand; but has been comparatively sparing in the room and the nourishment necessary to rear them. (Malthus 1826, p.2)

Certain plant species are well known for their "competitive edge" in this perpetual struggle for existence and dominance. Through aggressive colonization of disturbed sites and rapid juvenile growth habits, pioneer species are capable of dominating sites for long periods of time. When such plant species occur on sites being managed for crops, competition for scarce resources can occur. If the competition is severe enough, substantial reductions in crop yield are likely to occur.

The detrimental impact of weeds on crop yield has been recognized in agriculture for centuries. There are even biblical references to the liabilities of permitting the unchecked growth of weeds. *Genesis* 3:18 states that "cursed is the ground because of you; in toil you shall eat of it all the days of your life; thorns and thistles it shall bring forth to you;"

In the first century A.D. a Roman agricultural writer named Columella observed that "but it seems to me the mark of a very poor farmer to allow grass to grow among his crops, for it detracts greatly from the yield if weeding is neglected" (As quoted in Smith and Secoy 1981, p. 30).

And William Shakespeare alluded to the nuisance of weeds in a line from his play *Richard II:* "I will go root away the noisome weeds which, without profit, suck the soil's fertility from wholesome flowers."

Although the detrimental impact of weeds has been recognized for centuries, it was not until the first half of the 18th century that Jethro Tull conducted the experiments that recorded the first scientific evidence that weed competition depressed crop yields (Smith and Secoy 1976). Prior to that time, prescriptions for weed control were based on empirical observations that, without adequate weed control measures, reduced crop yields or outright failure was a common outcome.

With the advent of modern weed science in the 20th century, there has been a concerted effort to identify the threshold levels at which interspecific competition becomes intolerable. Most of this research has been confined to agronomic crops (Zimdahl 1980), but work is also underway to provide analogous information in forestry (Walstad 1981).

Much of the attention in agriculture given to weed control has been focused on methods. This basically evolved from a conviction that certain plants were indeed a problem in crops and that it was imperative to find ways of controlling them in order to avoid significant economic loss. Thus the historical record of agronomic weed control is primarily an evolution of techniques (Table 1-2). It began in antiquity, when magic and superstition were the only recourses available (Secoy and Smith 1978; Smith and Secoy 1981). Primitive hand- and animal-powered implements provided the first reliable means of controlling weeds. These were eventually replaced by mechanized equipment that permitted large acreages to be efficiently cultivated. More recently, the discovery of plant growth regulators has permitted the development and use of organic chemicals as an adjunct to the manual, mechanical, and thermal methods of controlling weeds. As our knowledge of plant ecology, physiology, and biochemistry grows, one can anticipate additional advances in the practice of vegetation management.

TABLE 1-2. Chronological Perspective of Progress in Vegetation Management

Period	Significant Accomplishments
6000 B.C.–1800 A.D.	Magic and superstition gradually discarded. Primitive hand- and cattle-drawn implements used. Early documents written about weeds.
1801–1900	Improved plows, cultivators, mowers and disks developed during horse-drawn era. Prototype sprayers invented for applying inorganic pesticides. Weed control "proved" beneficial in crop production. Scientific publications on weeds and weed control appeared.
1901–1940	Transition to mechanized implements occurred. Inorganic herbicides developed. Research and extension programs established.
1941–1968	Plant growth regulators discovered. Organic herbicides synthesized and marketed. Research and extension rapidily expanded. Major increases achieved in crop production, attributable in part to weed control.
1969–Present	Major breakthroughs in plant physiology, biochemistry, and genetics continued to occur. Organic herbicides further developed and refined for operational use. Regulatory activities expanded and strengthened. Concept of vegetation management adopted. Energy efficiency and environmental impacts became important parameters for evaluating techniques.

Source: Adapted from Timmons (1970).

Similar historical patterns can be found in forestry, although the record is not as long. It was not until the turn of the twentieth century that forest management in the United States developed to the point where foresters became concerned about weeds. As expressed by Filibert Roth in 1902 in his *First Book of Forestry:*

> In a garden we should hardly tolerate these bushes, but would rather grub them out as weeds; and yet they are hardly more useful here in the woods, for surely they will never grow into trees, and in all cases may hinder young trees from starting or choke off the seedlings of our useful trees. They are forest weeds, and while we could hardly afford to grub them out, yet we shall try to keep them down; but how?

Roth's question about how to conduct weeding in the forest went basically unanswered for 40 years. Like agriculture, practical solutions had to await the development of cultural techniques such as mechanical cultivation, prescribed burning and chemical herbicides. In the 1940s and 1950s the importance of site preparation became apparent. By the 1960s site preparation was a standard practice in most regions of the United States where even-aged stands were being managed (Smith 1962). The concommitant development of phenoxy herbicides made it possible to selectively control forest weeds subsequent to site preparation (Fitzgerald 1980). These three developments—mechanical techniques of site preparation, prescribed burning, and selective herbicides for stand release— permitted a quantum leap in the forester's ability to efficiently enhance the productivity of commercial timberland (Walstad 1982).

PREVIOUS ANALYSES OF THE SILVICULTURAL BENEFITS OF VEGETATION MANAGEMENT

It has been estimated that opportunities to enhance forest productivity through vegetation management exist on over 40% of the commercial forest land base (Walker et al. 1973). Results from a number of studies suggest that volume growth can be doubled where weed trees and shrubs are competing with conifers (Stewart et al. 1984). Nevertheless, the information on the scope and magnitude of these opportunities is incomplete. Quantitative data and predictive models are needed that relate anticipated yields to specific levels of competition, treatment cost, and inherent site productivity (Stewart and Row 1981).

Attempts have been made to forecast the benefits of forest vegetation management on local, regional, and national scales. However, such efforts have been hampered by the paucity of data to accurately estimate the acreage amenable to treatment and gains likely to accrue. The complexity of forest management, coupled with long rotation periods, accounts for the scarcity of definitive studies that evaluate the ultimate benefits of forest vegetation management over the long run. For example, the report titled "Biologic and Economic Assessment of 2,4,5-T," prepared by the 2,4,5-T Assessment Team (1979), and the revised supplement to that report prepared by the team's Timber Commodity Group (1983) had to primarily rely on a panel of experienced forest managers in order to estimate the impact of losing 2,4,5-T as a management tool. Limited quantitative data were available at the time that documented the importance of this treatment in maintaining forest yields. That is not to say the collective judgment of experienced foresters is likely to be inaccurate. It simply means that quantitative data would have made a stronger case.

Other efforts to consolidate the information on the benefits of forest vegetation management have been handicapped by lack of expertise or access to the current information available on the subject. For example, the report titled "An Economic Analysis of Alternative Vegetation Management Practices in Commercial Forests of the Pacific Coast Region" (Stavins et al. 1981) uses the antiquated Bulletin 201 (McArdle et al. 1961) to predict yields of Douglas-fir under various weed control scenarios. Access to more current biometrical models, such as DFIT (Bruce et al. 1977) and DFSIM (Curtis et al. 1981), would have ensured a more accurate and contemporary analysis.

A text by Green (1983) on the use of phenoxy herbicides in forestry does utilize one of the latest simulation models (DFIT) for projecting the growth and yield of Douglas-fir under various vegetation management regimes. However, her analysis, like the others cited before, is still constrained by a lack of definitive data on the impact of competing vegetation on timber yield. As a result, the analysis had to rely on subjective estimates of what the yield impacts would be of implementing various vegetation management alternatives. Green's book has also been criticized on a number of technical points (Goetzl 1983). These criticisms raise questions about its utility for analytical purposes.

Despite their limitations, the aforementioned reports provide a basis for extending our understanding of forest vegetation management. They are thorough and explicit with respect to the approach, assumptions, and logic encompassed in the scenarios they present. The information assembled in the chapters that follow builds on these previous reports by incorporating quantitative data into current biometrical and economic models. It also consolidates the silvicultural knowledge of forest vegetation management that has been acquired during the past several decades.

REFERENCES

Bruce, D., D.J. DeMars, and D.C. Reukema. 1977. Douglas-fir managed yield simulator—DFIT user's guide. USDA Forest Service, Pacific Northwest Forest and Range Experiment Station, Portland, OR. Gen. Tech. Rep. PNW-57. 26 p.

Curtis, R.O., G.W. Clendenen, and D.J. DeMars. 1981. A new standard simulator for coast Douglas-fir: DFSIM user's guide. USDA Forest Service, Pacific Northwest Forest and Range Experiment Station, Portland, OR. Gen. Tech. Rep. PNW-128. 79 p.

Fitzgerald, C.H. 1980. Chemical vegetation control in forest stands: the past half century. Paper presented at DuPont Forest Herbicides Seminar. Univ. Georgia, Athens, GA. 11 p.

Goetzl, A. 1983. A critical review of Council on Economic Priorities report on phenoxy herbicides. National Forest Products Assoc., Washington, DC. 11 p.

Green, K. 1983. Forests, herbicides and people. A case study of phenoxy herbicides in western Oregon. Council on Economic Priorities. New York, NY. 203 p.

Klingman, G.C. 1966. Weed control: as a science. John Wiley and Sons, Inc. New York, NY. 421 p.

Malthus, T.R. 1826. An essay on the principle of population. 6th ed. Ward, Lock and Co., Ltd. New York, NY. 614 p.

Marra, M.C. and G.A. Carlson. 1983. An economic threshold model for weeds in soybeans (*Glycine max*). Weed Sci. 31:604–609.

McArdle, R.E., W.H. Meyer, and D. Bruce. 1961. The yield of Douglas-fir in the Pacific Northwest. U.S. Dept. Agr. Tech. Bull. 201. 72 p.

Poston, F.L., L.P. Pedigo, and S.M. Welch. 1983. Economic injury levels: reality and practicality. Bull. Entomol. Soc. Amer. 29(1):49–53.

Secoy, D.M. and A.E. Smith. 1978. Superstition and social practices against agricultural pests. Environ. Rev. 5:2–18.

Shakespeare, W. Richard II. Act 3, Scene 4, Lines 37–39.

Smith, A.E. and D.M. Secoy. 1976. Early chemical control of weeds in Europe. Weed Sci. 24:594–597.

Smith, A.E. and D.M. Secoy. 1981. Weed control through the ages. Weeds Today. Late Spring ed. p. 30–31.

Smith, D.M. 1962. The practice of silviculture. 7th ed. John Wiley and Sons, Inc. New York, NY. 578 p.

Stavins, R.N., D.L. Galt, and K.L. Eckhouse. 1981. An economic analysis of alternative vegetation management practices in commercial forests of the Pacific Coast region. Cooperative Extension and Giannini Foundation of Agricultural Economics, Univ. California, Berkeley, CA. Project Rep. 2. 66 p.

Stern, V.M., R.E. Smith, R. van den Bosch, and K.S. Hagen. 1959. The integrated control concept. Hilgardia 29:81–101.

Stewart, R.E., L.L. Gross, and B.H. Honkala. 1984. Effects of competing vegetation on forest trees: a bibliography with abstracts. USDA Forest Service, Washington, DC. Gen. Tech. Rep. WO-43. 260 p.

Stewart, R.E. and C. Row. 1981. Assessing the economic benefits of weed control in forest management, p. 26–53. *In* Holt, H.A. and B.C. Fischer (eds.) Weed control in forest management. John S. Wright Forestry Conf. Proc., Dept. Forestry and Nat. Resour., Purdue Univ., West Lafayette, IN. 305 p.

Timmons, F.L. 1970. A history of weed control in the United States and Canada. Weed Sci. 18:294–307.

2,4,5-T Assessment Team. 1979. The biologic and economic assessment of 2,4,5-T. Cooperative Impact Assessment Report, U.S. Dept. Agr. Tech. Bull. 1671. 445 p.

2,4,5-T Assessment Team, Timber Commodity Group. 1983. Supplement to the biologic and economic assessment of 2,4,5-T. Cooperative Impact Assessment Report, U.S. Dept. Agr. Tech. Bull. 1671. 244 p.

Walker, C.M. et al. 1973. Rehabilitation of forest lands. J. Forestry 71:136–162.

Walstad, J.D. 1981. Forest vegetation management: a new discipline for an old ethic, p. 10–13. *In* Holt, H. A. and B. C. Fischer (eds.) Weed control in forest management. John S. Wright Forestry Conf. Proc., Dept. Forestry and Nat. Resour., Purdue Univ., West Lafayette, IN. 305 p.

Walstad, J.D. 1982. Increasing fiber production through intensive forest management: opportunities through vegetation management, p. 46–50. *In* Increasing forest productivity. Soc. Amer. Foresters Proc., 1981 Nat. Conv. Orlando, FL. SAF Publ. 82-01. 368 p.

Walstad, J.D. and D.H. Gjerstad. 1984. Concepts of forest vegetation management, p. 21–24. *In* Branham, S.J. and G.D. Hertel (eds.) Integrated Forest Pest Management Sympos. Proc. Center for Continuing Education, Univ. Georgia, Athens, GA. 281 p.

Wilcox, E.W. 1905. The Weed, first stanza. *In* Poems of Love. M. A. Donohue. Chicago. 114 p.

Young, F.L., D.L. Wyse, and R.J. Jones. 1982. Influence of quackgrass (*Agropyron repens*) density and duration of interference on soybeans (*Glycine max*). Weed Sci. 30:614–619.

Zimdahl, R.H. 1980. Weed-crop competition: a review. International Plant Protection Center, Oregon State Univ., Corvallis, OR. 197 p.

2

Forest Vegetation Problems in the Northwest

JOHN D. WALSTAD
MICHAEL NEWTON
RAYMOND J. BOYD, JR.

INTRODUCTION

The Northwest is the nation's leading source of forest products. Over one-third of the domestic supply of lumber, plywood, pulp, paper, and related products comes from this region annually (Phelps 1980). The Northwest is also a major supplier of logs, chips, and finished wood products to international markets, offsetting a substantial portion of the balance-of-payments deficit created by imports of oil, gas, and manufactured goods. Thus the sustained production of wood products from this region is an important contributor to national and international welfare.

Although much of the current harvest from the Northwest is attributable to the presence of large, old-growth timber, the inherent productivity of the region is derived from the fertile soils and favorable climatic conditions. Ranging from the luxuriant rain forest conditions of the Coast and Olympic ranges to the deep volcanic soils found along the Cascades and the Inland Northwest area (Figure 2-1), the region encompasses some of the most productive forest land to be found anywhere in the world. Sound silvicultural practices and economic forest management will ensure the continued production of forest products and amenities from this region.

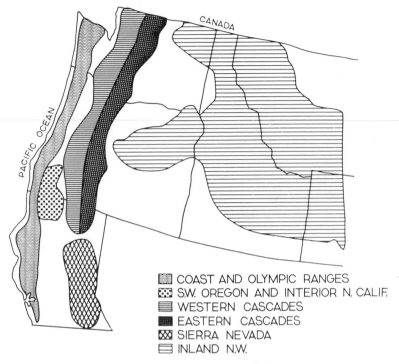

Figure 2-1. Subregions of the Northwest.

EXTENT OF VEGETATION PROBLEMS

The basic goal of commercial forest management is to promptly establish full stocking following harvest and maintain sufficient growth rates so that the production of wood products is assured within a reasonable time. Adequate control of competing vegetation has become a cornerstone in achieving this end. Even though conifers are the natural climax form of vegetation in the commercial forest types of the Northwest, a variety of hardwoods, shrubs, and herbaceous vegetation is capable of seriously delaying or interrupting the process whereby well-stocked stands of conifers eventually become dominant following disturbance. Therefore, vegetation management practices ranging from site preparation to release and timber stand improvement are key requirements in the economical production of conifer forests in this region.

Many of these practices have been used by foresters for decades, but much remains to be done to fully utilize the productive capacity of the Northwest. Surveys conducted in the early 1970s indicated that more than 9 million acres were then dominated by noncommercial brush species or were so poorly stocked with conifers that they were essentially non-productive with respect to wood products (Gratkowski et al. 1973). This is about 10% of the commercial forest acreage in this region.

Considerable progress has been made during the past decade to re-habilitate the backlog of underproductive acreage (Dimock et al. 1976). However, more current resource surveys suggest that the earlier surveys may have underestimated the extent of these vegetation management problem areas. A detailed ground inventory completed in the late 1970s in western Oregon (MacLean 1980a) indicated that about 2.7 million acres, equivalent to 20% of the commercial forest land in the survey area, would benefit from some form of forest vegetation management (Table 2-1). Rehabilitation of brushfields through site preparation and planting and conversion of red alder and other low-value hardwood stands to con-ifer plantations were identified as the major opportunities for improving forest productivity in this area. Similar opportunities exist in northern California (Bolsinger 1980).

Recent "snapshots" of the Northwest using LANDSAT imagery provide further evidence of the large amount of acreage needing attention. A study by Fox et al. (1983) revealed that 10% of the acreage of the McCloud Ranger District of the Shasta-Trinity National Forest in northern Cali-fornia was occupied by brush and hardwoods. Another 9% was in some phase of transition between bare ground, grass, brush, and conifers. Sim-ilar LANDSAT analyses in northwest Oregon showed 22% of a 100,000 acre area to be covered by red alder and another 10% covered by herbs and shrubs (Bright 1984). Even though some of the land covered by herbs and shrubs may also contain acceptable stocking of young conifers, there is still a substantial proportion of the area that is only producing at a fraction of its potential.

Another analysis (McCreight 1984) of forest land conditions in a 270,000 acre area of the central Oregon Coast Range shows that 38% of the potential conifer site land is dominated by low-value hardwoods and noncommercial brush (Figure 2-2). Thus it is not surprising to find state-ments like the following made by resource specialists:

> The greatest opportunity to increase timber production through silvicultural treatment [in western Oregon and Washington] is to regenerate areas now growing weeds, brush, and low-value hardwoods. Further increases may be realized by replacing stands of red alder and poorly stocked conifer with new conifer regeneration stands. (MacLean 1980b, p. 14)

In short, the proper application of forest vegetation management can do much to reclaim and improve the inherent economic productivity of forest lands in this region.

TABLE 2-1. Opportunities for Forest Vegetation Management Treatments in Western Oregon

Stand Category (age, size, or condition)	Treatment	Northwest Oregon Acreage (thousand)	Northwest Oregon Proportion of Commercial Forest Land Base (%)[a]	West-Central Oregon Acreage (thousand)	West-Central Oregon Proportion of Commercial Forest Land Base (%)[a]	Southwest Oregon Acreage (thousand)	Southwest Oregon Proportion of Commercial Forest Land Base (%)[a]	Total for Western Oregon Acreage (thousand)	Total for Western Oregon Proportion of Commercial Forest Land Base (%)[a]
Intermediate	Improvement cut (TSI)	28	0.8	5	0.1	64	1.0	97	0.7
Regeneration	Improvement cut (TSI)	39	1.0	48	1.2	103	1.7	190	1.4
	Site preparation	155	4.2	215	5.4	518	8.4	888	6.4
	Release (cleaning)	40	1.0	18	0.5	174	2.8	232	1.7
Rehabilitation (replacement)	Alder conversion	256	6.9	219	5.5	137	2.2	612	4.4
	Other type conversion	201	5.4	138	3.5	338	5.5	677	4.9
Total opportunity		719	19.4	643	16.2	1334	21.6	2696	19.5

Source: Data are derived from a Renewable Resources Evaluation survey completed by the USDA Forest Service, Pacific Northwest Forest and Range Experiment Station in the late 1970s (MacLean 1980b).

[a]Percentages are based on a total commercial forest area of 3.7 million acres for northwest Oregon, 4 million acres for west-central Oregon, 6 million acres for southwest Oregon, and 13.8 million acres for western Oregon as a whole.

Figure 2-2. Black-and-white reproduction of a color infrared aerial photograph of a 16 mi^2 portion of the Oregon Coast Range showing a large proportion of the landscape dominated by (1) brush and (2) low-value hardwoods compared to (3) mature conifer. (*Source:* Courtesy of R.W. McCreight, Recon Research Inc., Bend, OR)

ORIGIN OF VEGETATION PROBLEMS

Much of the area currently occupied by competing vegetation is a legacy of past practices and natural events. Although many western conifer species are naturally adapted to regenerate after wildfire and other forms of disturbance (cf. Burns 1983), this only occurs if the interval between disturbances is sufficiently long for the conifers to reach maturity (Oliver 1981). Unfortunately, the frequency of disturbance in much of the Northwest has been too great for this to occur. Periodic wildfires (both natural and human caused) and excessive grazing destroyed the natural regeneration of conifers in many areas.

Little attention was given to artificial methods of reforestation by early settlers, loggers, and miners who cleared or burned the land for various purposes. Initial attempts at planting and seeding were limited by inadequate knowledge and cultural practices. Use of low-quality nursery stock, off-site planting or seeding of poorly-adapted seed sources, and careless or untimely planting operations are but a few of the factors that contributed to failures of conifer regeneration.

Several other factors have modified the natural pattern of succession so that nonconiferous species are favored. Specifically, introduced plants such as gorse and scotchbroom, small harvest units with an abundance of surrounding weed sources, and burgeoning populations of animal pests capable of destroying conifer seeds and seedlings or distributing weed seeds are some of the additional factors responsible for poor conifer regeneration. Consequently, tenacious and resilient shrub, hardwood, and herbaceous species having one or more of the following capabilities have been best suited for the adverse conditions:

1. They are able to survive the various disturbances in a relatively intact form and thereby are in a position to rapidly capture the space previously occupied by conifers,
2. They are able to sprout from established stumps, rootstocks, rhizomes, and stolons,
3. They are able to germinate from seeds buried in the soil or litter layer,
4. They are able to seed in from nearby stands or be deposited by birds and mammals.

As a result, much of the landscape that was once covered by productive conifer stands is now occupied by low-value hardwood stands and noncommercial brushfields. In western Oregon alone, hardwoods (principally red alder) occupy 32% of the prime timberland that is currently more profitable for growing conifers (Poppino and Gedney 1984). Adequate regeneration in other areas throughout the Northwest is hindered by dense grass sods and other herbaceous vegetation. Over the long run these seral plant communities are replaced by taller growing conifer species. However, because of the ability of these seral species to usurp limited site resources and create harsh microenvironments, many have remained dominant for decades, slowing the successional process and precluding any financial return from forestry within a reasonable time. For example, the Oregon Coast Range contains the remnants of several old wildfires and clearings that are still dominated by brush and low-value hardwoods (Figure 2-2).

Despite efforts by forest managers to reforest problem sites, only a fraction of the area amenable to treatment has been dealt with. A survey by Dimock et al. (1976) indicated that about 14% of the commercial forest land in western Oregon and Washington was still completely occupied by brush and low-value hardwoods, despite concerted efforts during the previous two decades to convert such areas to conifers. Indeed, the acreage affected by competing vegetation has increased in recent years (particularly on federal lands) as restrictions on prescribed burning and herbicides have been imposed. The problem has been further compounded by delays in treatment as a result of litigation and lengthy administrative procedures (Walstad 1982). For example, many of the initial environmental impact statements dealing with vegetation management were deemed inadequate by federal courts, delaying or preventing implementation of vegetation management programs by federal agencies in the Northwest.

Additional factors have limited the capacity of foresters to contend with the problem of competing vegetation. Much of the terrain in the Northwest is too steep for mechanized equipment that could otherwise be used to control the shrubs, hardwoods, and herbaceous vegetation. Certain harvesting practices, such as multiple-entry shelterwood cutting, have frequently accelerated the growth of hardwood understory species as the conifer overstory is removed, thereby hampering subsequent conifer regeneration (Hobbs and Owston 1985). Clearcutting followed by inadequate site preparation or regeneration delays has likewise led to vegetation problems. Diverse ownership patterns and objectives make it more difficult to implement broad-scale forestry programs designed to reclaim nonproductive areas. Finally, the capital expense required to conduct stand conversion and rehabilitation projects is substantial. In some instances, a full rotation must elapse before any financial return from the original investment occurs.

Thus the challenge facing foresters as they attempt to reclaim these problem areas is substantial. The task is particularly difficult because it must be accomplished while continuing to manage existing conifer stands and reforest newly harvested areas each year. Nevertheless, opportunities for enhancing the productivity of idle and underproductive forest land in the Northwest are attractive, and many organizations are aggressively pursuing the task of controlling unwanted vegetation.

PHYSIOGRAPHIC SUBREGIONS AND VEGETATION

For purposes of classification according to vegetation management problems, the Northwest can be divided into six general subregions (Figure 2-1):

1. Coast and Olympic ranges of California, Oregon, and Washington
2. Southwest Oregon and interior northern California
3. Western Cascades of Oregon, Washington, and northern California
4. Eastern Cascades of Oregon, Washington, and northern California

5. Northern Sierra Nevada of California

6. Inland Northwest area of Idaho, western Montana and Wyoming, northeastern Washington, and the Blue Mountains of northeastern Oregon and southeastern Washington.

Although these subregions are confined to the northwestern United States, conditions comparable to the Coastal and Cascade ranges also occur in British Columbia, Canada. Therefore, much of the information pertinent to these subregions can be extrapolated to western British Columbia.

Each subregion is delineated by reasonably distinct geological, climatic, and botanical characteristics. The main timber species and competing vegetation (including both common and scientific names) are shown for each subregion in Tables 2-2 and 2-3. The principal means by which the competing species reproduce are also shown in Table 2-3.

Several major reference documents are available that describe the ecological features of the Northwest in considerable detail. For example, Whittaker (1960), Daubenmire and Daubenmire (1968), Critchfield (1971), Franklin and Dyrness (1973), Hall (1973), Barbour and Major (1977), and Pfister et al. (1977) have provided comprehensive descriptions of the physiography, environmental conditions, and vegetation types for much of the region. The historical origin of the flora has been recounted by Detling (1968), and the present distribution of forest cover types is displayed in the compilation edited by Eyre (1980), and soils have been described by Heilman et al. (1979). Silvical characteristics for the important timber species of the region are available in the handbook edited by Fowells (1965) and the literature review by Minore (1979). Management guides containing recommended practices for vegetation management and other aspects of silviculture are available in publications edited by Cleary et al. (1978), Barrett (1980), and Burns (1983). However, the following overview should be sufficient for a general understanding of the various conditions encountered in this region.

Coast and Olympic Ranges

The Coast and Olympic ranges are typified by cool, wet maritime conditions throughout the year. Average annual rainfall ranges from 40 to 160 in., and moderate temperatures prevail throughout the year.

Soils derived from basalt and sedimentary deposits are deep and fertile in most of the Coast Range and the western edge of the Olympic Mountains. The interior portion of the Olympic Range also has reasonably productive granitic soils. Glaciated U-shaped valleys and broad alluvial terraces occur in the Olympics, whereas steep slopes, sharp ridges, and narrow valleys characterize much of the Coast Range. Both ranges are sharply dissected by coastal streams and rivers.

TABLE 2-2. Major Coniferous Timber Species on Commercial Forest Land in the Northwest

Scientific Name[a]	Common Name	Subregion[b]
Abies amabalis	Pacific silver fir	WC
A. concolor	White fir	WC, EC
A. concolor var. *lowiana*	California white fir	SWONC, NSN
A. grandis	Grand fir	COR, SWONC, INW
A. lasiocarpa	Subalpine fir	WC, EC, INW
A. magnifica	Red fir	NSN
A. magnifica var. *shastensis*	Shasta red fir	SWONC, WC
A. procera	Noble fir	WC
Chamaecyparis lawsoniana	Port-Orford-cedar	COR, SWONC
C. nootkatensis	Alaska cedar	WC
Larix occidentalis	Western larch	INW
Libocedrus decurrens	Incense-cedar	SWONC, WC, EC, NSN
Picea engelmannii	Engelmann spruce	WC, EC, INW
P. sitchensis	Sitka spruce	COR, SWONC
Pinus contorta	Lodgepole pine	EC, INW
P. contorta ssp. *murrayana*	Lodgepole pine	NSN
P. jeffreyi	Jeffrey pine	SWONC, NSN
P. lambertiana	Sugar pine	SWONC, WC, EC, NSN
P. monticola	Western white pine	SWONC, WC, NSN, INW
P. ponderosa	Ponderosa pine	SWONC, WC, EC, NSN, INW
Pseudotsuga menziesii	Douglas-fir	COR, SWONC, WC, EC, INW
P. menziesii var. *glauca*	Douglas-fir	NSN
Sequoia sempervirens	Coast redwood	COR
Thuja plicata	Western redcedar	COR, SWONC, WC, INW
Tsuga heterophylla	Western hemlock	COR, SWONC, WC, INW
T. mertensiana	Mountain hemlock	WC, NSN, INW

Source: Table 2-2 is primarily derived from Walstad et al. (1982).

[a]Species are arranged in alphabetical order according to scientific name within each subregion. No priority of importance is intended by the order of listing.

[b]Subregion code: COR = Coast and Olympic ranges; SWONC = Southwest Oregon and Interior Northern California; WC = Western Cascades; EC = Eastern Cascades; NSN = Northern Sierra Nevada; and INW = Inland Northwest.

TABLE 2-3. Principal Species of Competing Vegetation on Commercial Forest Land in the Northwest

Scientific Name[a]	Common Name	Subregion[b]	Primary Means by Which Competing Plants Originate or Develop[c]
			Shrubs and Hardwoods
Acer circinatum	Vine maple	COR, SWONC, WC	RS, S, IS
A. glabrum	Rocky Mountain maple	EC, INW	RS, S, IS
A. macrophyllum	Bigleaf maple	COR, SWONC, WC, NSN	RS, S, IS
Alnus rubra	Red alder	COR, WC	S, IS
A. sinuata	Sitka (thinleaf) alder	INW	RS, S, IS
Amelanchier alnifolia	Western serviceberry	INW	RS,S, IS
Arbutus menziesii	Pacific madrone	COR, SWONC, WC, NSN	RS, S, IS
Arctostaphylos columbiana	Hairy manzanita	SWONC, WC	S, BS, IS
A. patula	Greenleaf manzanita	SWONC, EC, NSN	BS, IS
A. viscida	Whiteleaf manzanita	SWONC, NSN	S, BS, IS
Artemisia spp.	Sagebrush	EC, INW	IS
A. tridentata	Big sagebrush	NSN	IS
Baccharis pilularis	Baccharis (chaparral broom)	COR, SWONC	IS
Berberis repens	Oregon grape	INW	IS
Betula papyrifera var. subcordata	White birch	INW	S, IS
Castanopsis chrysophylla	Golden chinkapin	SWONC, WC, EC	RS, S
C. sempervirens	Sierra (bush) chinkapin	SWONC, NSN	RS, S
Ceanothus cordulatus	Mountain whitethorn	SWONC, NSN	S, BS
C. cuneatus	Buckbrush (wedgeleaf) ceanothus	SWONC	S, BS
C. integerrimus	Deerbrush ceanothus	SWONC, WC, NSN	S, BS
C. parvifolius	Littleleaf ceanothus	NSN	S, BS

C. prostratus	Squaw carpet	NSN	BS
C. sanguineus	Redstem ceanothus	SWONC, INW	S, BS
C. thyrsiflorus	Blueblossom ceanothus	SWONC	S, BS
C. velutinus var. *laevigatus*	Varnishleaf ceanothus	COR, SWONC, WC	S, BS
C. velutinus var. *velutinus*	Snowbrush (slickleaf) ceanothus	WC, EC, NSN, INW	S, BS
Cercocarpus ledifolius	Mountain mahogany	INW	S, IS
Chamaebatia foliolosa	Bearmat (bear clover, mountain misery)	SWONC, NSN	S, IS
Chrysothamnus nauseosus	Rabbit brush	INW	IS
Cornus nutallii	Pacific dogwood	SWONC, WC	RS, S, IS
Corylus cornuta	Beaked (western) hazel	COR, WC	S, IS
C. cornuta var. *californica*	California hazel	SWONC	S, IS
Cytisus scoparius	Scotch broom	COR, WC	IS
Gaultheria shallon	Salal	COR, SWONC, WC	S
Holodiscus discolor	Oceanspray	COR, SWONC, WC, INW	S, IS
Juniperus communis	Juniper	INW	RS, IS
Lithocarpus densiflorus	Tanoak	COR, SWONC, NSN	RS, S
Lonicera utahensis	Red twinberry (honeysuckle)	INW	S, IS
Menziesia ferruginea	False huckleberry	COR, INW	S, IS
Pachistima myrsinites	Boxwood	INW	S, BS
Physocarpus malvaceus	Mallow ninebark	INW	S, IS
Populus tremuloides	Quaking aspen	INW	S, IS
P. trichocarpa	Black cottonwood	COR, INW	S,IS
Prunus emarginata	Bitter cherry	COR, WC, EC, NSN	RS, S, IS
P. spp.	Cherry	INW	RS, S, IS
Purshia tridentata	Bitterbrush	EC, NSN, INW	S, IS
Quercus chrysolepis	Canyon live oak	SWONC, NSN	RS, S
Q. garryana	Oregon white oak	SWONC, WC	RS, S, IS

TABLE 2-3. Principal Species of Competing Vegetation on Commercial Forest Land in the Northwest (Continued)

Scientific Name[a]	Common Name	Subregion[b]	Primary Means by Which Competing Plants Originate or Develop[c]
Q. kelloggii	California black oak	SWONC, NSN	RS, S, IS
Q. sadleriana	Sadler oak	SWONC	RS, S, IS
Rhamnus purshiana	Cascara buckthorn	COR	RS, S, IS
Rhododendron macrophyllum	Pacific rhododendron	SWONC, WC	S
Rhus diversiloba	Poison oak	COR, SWONC, WC	S, IS
Ribes roezlii	Sierra gooseberry	NSN	S, BS, IS
R. spp.	Currant and gooseberry	SWONC, NSN, INW	S, BS, IS
R. viscosissimum	Sticky currant	NSN	S, BS, IS
Rosa spp.	Rose	INW	S
Rubus parviflorus	Thimbleberry	COR, WC, INW	S, BS, IS
R. procerus	Himalayan blackberry	COR	S, IS
R. spectabilis	Salmonberry	COR	S, BS
R. ursinus	Trailing blackberry	COR, INW	S, IS
Salix scouleriana	Scouler's (upland) willow	NSN, INW	RS, S, IS
S. spp.	Willows	SWONC, WC, EC	S, IS
Sambucus callicarpa	Pacific red elderberry	COR	S, IS
S. cerulea	Blue elderberry	COR, WC, INW	S, IS
Shepherdia canadensis	Buffalo berry	INW	S, IS
Sorbus scopulina	Greene mountain ash	INW	RS, S, IS
Spiraea betulifolia	Spirea	INW	S, BS
Symphoricarpos spp.	Snowberry	SWONC, WC, NSN, INW	S, IS

Taxus brevifolia	Pacific yew	INW	S
Umbellularia californica	California-laurel	COR, SWONC	RS, S
Vaccinium membranaceum	Big huckleberry	WC	S, IS
V. ovatum	Evergreen huckleberry	COR, SWONC	S, IS
V. parvifolium	Red huckleberry	COR	S, IS
V. spp.	Huckleberries	INW	S, IS
Herbs			
Calamagrostis rubescens	Pine grass	INW	S, IS
Carex spp.	Sedges	SWONC, WC, EC, INW	S
Cirsium spp.	Thistle	INW	IS
Dicots	Forbs (annual and perennial)	COR, SWONC, WC,	S, IS
Epilobium spp.	Fireweed	WC	S, IS
Graminae spp.	Grasses	All	S, IS
Polystichum munitum	Sword fern	COR	S, IS
Pteridium aquilinum	Bracken fern	COR, SWONC, WC, NSN, INW	S
Xerophyllum tenax	Common beargrass	SWONC, WC, EC, INW	S, BS, IS

Source: Table 2-3 is primarily derived from 2,4,5-T Assessment Team (1982) and Walstad et al. (1982).

[a]Woody species are arranged in alaphabetical order according to scientific name within each subregion. No priority of importance is intended by the order.

[b]Subregion code: COR = Coast and Olympic ranges; SWONC = Southwest Oregon and Interior Northern California; WC = Western Cascades; EC = Eastern Cascades; NSN = Northern Sierra Nevada; INW = Inland Northwest; All = all subregions.

[c]Although various plant species may have several ways of capturing or colonizing forest sites, the classification used in this table only pertains to the *principal* means whereby they become a *threat* to conifer regeneration. It does not necessarily include all methods of propagation and establishment for any given species. Code is as follows:

RS = Competing plants that originate from residual stems that have resilient boles, stems, and branches and are capable of surviving overstory removal and other physical disturbances and quickly dominating a site shortly thereafter.

S = Sprouting plants that originate from stumps, persistent rootstocks, rhizomes, or stolons that quickly generate new shoots or stems when existing ones are cut or damaged.

BS = Plants that arise from buried seed and are adapted to catastrophic disturbance such as fire or scarification that stimulates germination.

IS = Plants that arise from introduced seed disseminated by wind currents or animals.

Major coniferous vegetation consists of extensive stands of Douglas-fir intermingled with western hemlock, western redcedar, Sitka spruce, grand fir, and, in northern California, coast redwood. The dominant broadleaf vegetation in the northern portion primarily consists of deciduous hardwoods capable of rapid growth from seed (e.g., red alder) or established rootstocks (e.g., bigleaf maple) following disturbance. Resilient sclerophyllous evergreen hardwoods such as tanoak and California laurel predominate in southwestern Oregon and northern California. Undisturbed hardwoods are also capable of rapid development following the harvest of overstory conifers. In all cases, hardwood species can quickly occupy a site after logging and burning, thereby delaying or precluding the establishment of conifer regeneration (Stubblefield and Oliver 1978, Knapp et al. 1984). Herbaceous and shrubby vegetation (e.g., ferns, grasses, salmonberry, thimbleberry, elderberry, vine maple) can also quickly colonize disturbed sites at the expense of conifer regeneration (Newton 1964, Newton and Overton 1973, Stewart 1978).

Because sunlight is frequently occluded by fog and overcast in this coastal zone, overtopping of conifers by any of the woody and herbaceous species can kill or suppress even the most shade tolerant conifer seedlings (Ruth 1956, 1957, Chan 1984, Howard and Newton 1984). In the study by Howard and Newton (1984), for example, the height and diameter of overtopped Douglas-fir seedlings after 7 years was only about 70% of that for seedlings that only had to contend with surrounding vegetation. Had the study included trees free of surrounding and overtopping vegetation, it is likely that even greater differences would have occurred. Preest (1977) found that control of herbaceous understory vegetation (there was no overtopping vegetation) for a 3-yr period increased height growth of Douglas-fir seedlings by 50%.

Competing vegetation in the Coast and Olympic ranges also provides food and cover for a variety of animal pests that damage or destroy conifer regeneration. High populations of deer, elk, and mountain beaver are responsible for a substantial portion of the seedling mortality in this subregion (Crouch 1969, Hooven 1977, Black et al. 1979, Evans et al. 1981).

Southwest Oregon and Interior Northern California

In contrast, southwestern Oregon and interior northern California are in a droughty Mediterranean-type climate. Summer rainfall is negligible except at high elevations or along the coast. The interior portion of this forested subregion receives less than 40 in. of annual precipitation on the average (Froehlich et al. 1982), and summers are hot and dry (McNabb et al. 1982, Minore and Kingsley 1983).

Traversed by the rugged Siskiyous and other ranges of the Klamath Mountains, many of the soils are rocky, shallow, and less fertile than those of the adjacent Coast and Cascade ranges. They are derived from a variety of parent materials ranging from volcanic tuffs to granitics and sedimentary sandstones, siltstones, and shales, intermingled with ultrabasic peridotites and serpentines. Geological processes such as erosion, folding, intrusion, peneplanation, and metamorphism have created a complex array of soil conditions. Productivity is good along the coast and inland at midelevations where adequate soil moisture and moderate temperatures prevail. Summer drought, skeletal soils, and ultrabasic bedrock create marginal growing conditions on many interior sites, rendering some of them unsuitable for timber production.

Vegetation consists of mixed conifers (e.g., Douglas-fir, pines, true firs, cedars) in the overstory and broadleaf sclerophyll shrubs and hardwoods in the understory. Competition from established shrubs and hardwoods is a serious problem facing young conifers (Hayes 1959, Gratkowski 1959, 1975, Bassett 1979, Minore and Kingsley 1983, Tappeiner et al. 1984). For example, the basal area growth over a 10-year period of Douglas-fir saplings competing with mature tanoak and Pacific madrone was only about 25% of that where these hardwoods had been controlled (Radosevich et al. 1976).

Many of the broadleaf sclerophylls are capable of sprouting from well-developed underground burls and rootstocks (e.g., tanoak, Pacific madrone) as well as germinating from buried seed following fire (e.g., *Ceanothus*, manzanita). With soil moisture at a premium in this xeric habitat, the presence of hardwood sprout clumps and woody shrubs greatly reduces the survival and growth of young conifers. For example, tanoak sprouts are known to be serious competitors to conifer seedlings. Roy (1981) reported on a study involving Douglas-fir seedlings planted at the same time as sprouting of tanoak stumps began. After 22 years, Douglas-fir trees growing among the tanoak clumps were only about 60% as tall as those growing in the open. Roy projected this differential to eventually lead to a loss of 10,000 bd ft/acre over a 100-year rotation.

Adverse impacts on conifer development have also been attributed to manzanita shrubs in this droughty subregion of the Northwest. In a study in the interior portion of the Coast Range of northern California, Oliver (1984) found that brush-free ponderosa pine saplings grew 45 to 140% faster in diameter and 62 to 170% faster in height than similar trees growing in dense brush for the 5-year period following the release treatment. The range in response was primarily associated with initial tree spacing—the response was greatest for trees spaced widest apart. Furthermore, brush cover had to be reduced to 30% or less in order for the pines to respond, regardless of spacing. Based on this study and one by Powers and Jackson (1978), Oliver suggests that investments in silvicultural treatments such as fertilization and thinning may be wasted unless brush is controlled.

A variety of forbs, grasses, and sedges can also seriously impair conifer regeneration on the droughty sites characteristic of the subregion. In one case, Gratkowski et al. (1979) found that survival of Douglas-fir competing with grasses and forbs was less than half that where these herbs were controlled. Numerous additional studies conducted in southwestern Oregon have verified the importance of herbaceous and woody weed control in this subregion if conifer regeneration is to be successful (Baron 1962, Newton 1981, Hobbs 1983).

In some instances competing vegetation can have an indirect, adverse effect on conifer regeneration by providing a habitat for pest animals such as rodents, pocket gopher, mountain beaver, rabbit, hare, deer, and elk (Baron 1962, Evans et al. 1981). One means of reducing the damage to conifer seedlings is to manipulate animal habitat through vegetation control.

Western Cascades

Topographically, the Western Cascades consist of long, relatively gentle slopes that are deeply dissected by rivers and streams. Evidence of glaciation (e.g., U-shaped valleys, glacial till) and recent volcanic activity (e.g., ash and pumice deposits, lava and mudflows) can be found at middle and high elevations. The soils are almost exclusively derived from volcanic parent materials, although areas in the northern portion of the range are typified by glaciated granitics. Weathering of pyroclastic parent materials such as tuffs and breccias has produced deep, fine-textured soils throughout much of the subregion. Coarser textured soils are derived from igneous deposits and flows of andesite and basalt. In general, the soils of this subregion provide moderate to high productivity site conditions for many conifer species.

Soil moisture and ambient air temperatures are suitable for growth throughout most of the year, although droughty conditions often occur during late summer at the lower elevations, and frost-free growing seasons are short at the higher elevations.

The western slopes of the Cascades are characterized by an elevational gradient of plant communities. Relatively homogeneous stands of Douglas-fir are prevalent below 3000 ft, except that ponderosa pine becomes a frequent stand component in the southern portion of the Cascade Range. At midelevations (3000-5000 ft), the stands are comprised of Douglas-fir, western hemlock, western white pine, sugar pine, and true firs. Subalpine forests (5000-6500 ft) contain mixtures of true firs, western hemlock, mountain hemlock, and Engelmann spruce.

Like the conifers, species of competing vegetation vary along the elevational gradient. Grasses, ferns, and a variety of broadleaf species (e.g., oaks, Pacific madrone, dogwood, hazel, poison oak) occupy the foothills of interior valleys. Hardwoods such as bigleaf maple, vine maple, chinkapin, cherry, and red alder are common in the midelevation zone. Broadleaf evergreen and deciduous shrubs such as *Ceanothus*, rhododendron, huckleberry, willows, and *Ribes* characterize much of the understory landscape at middle to higher elevations. Virtually all of the woody species are capable of sprouting vigorously following cutting or disturbance. A few species such as *Ceanothus* and manzanita also germinate from buried seed immediately following burning or scarification and depend on these disturbances for survival and rejuvenation.

In the Cascades, problems arising from herbaceous competition are particularly crucial during plantation establishment. Numerous studies have recorded losses in survival where such species have not been controlled (Zavitkovski et al. 1969, Gratkowski et al. 1979, Dimock 1981). The study by Dimock (1981), for example, found that western white pine, noble fir, Englemann spruce, and Shasta red fir were all adversely affected by beargrass and sedge communities characteristic of the subalpine portions of the Cascades. In every case, survival of unweeded conifers was less than half that where the best weed control treatments were applied. Petersen and Newton (1982, 1985) found that Douglas-fir saplings competing with herbaceous weeds contained only about 60% of the stem volume of trees that had been freed from such competition 4 years earlier.

Problems with herbaceous vegetation in the Cascades stem not only from competition for moisture but from animal damage as well. The dense grass sods and herbaceous ground cover provide ideal refuge for a variety of animals (e.g., mice, voles, pikas, pocket gophers, rabbits, and hares) that are capable of damaging conifer seedlings (Borrecco 1975, Minore 1978, Black et al. 1979, Crouch 1979, 1982, Teipner et al. 1983).

Competition from germinating and sprouting shrubs is also a significant deterrent to conifer regeneration in this subregion. Species such as snowbrush and manzanita are capable of reducing the survival as well as the growth of a variety of conifers (Zavitkovski et al. 1969, Bentley et al. 1971, Gratkowski and Lauterbach 1974, Petersen and Newton 1982). In the study by Petersen and Newton (1982, 1985), snowbrush competition over a 4 year period was shown to reduce the stem volume of Douglas-fir saplings by up to about 60% compared to saplings that were free to grow.

In yet another study, this one spanning 19 years, Roy (1981) and McDonald and Oliver (1983) observed about a 70% decline in height and diameter of ponderosa pine saplings growing in the middle of manzanita and snowbrush near Mount Shasta in northern California. Losses in height alone were estimated to be equivalent to 10 years of normal growth, and trees with heavy understory competition showed no signs of escaping severe stress.

Eastern Cascades

The eastern side of the Cascades tends to be a warm, dry habitat in the summer as a result of the rain shadow effect caused by the mountains. Low temperatures prevail during the winter months as cold continental air masses move down from Canada. In addition, the soils are inherently droughty because of the geologically recent, coarse pumice component. As a result of these climatic and edaphic extremes, there is a sharp elevational gradient of coniferous vegetation, ranging from mountain hemlock, true firs, spruce, and lodgepole pine near the crest of the Cascades, to a narrow zone of Douglas-fir and sugar pine at upper slope elevations, and finally to relatively pure stands of ponderosa or lodgepole pine merging with western juniper at the base of the range. In the absence of fire, grand fir is a common associate throughout much of the elevational span. Most of the competing vegetation consists of evergreen or ericaceous shrubs such as *Ceanothus*, manzanita, golden chinkapin, bitterbrush, and sagebrush scattered throughout openings and understories (Barrett et al. 1983). However, these subordinate species, along with any grasses that might be present, are still capable of preempting what little soil moisture is available. They are also able to rapidly colonize disturbed sites by sprouting or seeding, forming dense and long-lived brushfields.

Examples of the adverse impact of such vegetation on environmental conditions and conifer development can be found in publications by Dahms (1950), Tarrant (1957), Barrett (1973), Christensen et al. (1974), Daniels and Bridgewater (1976), Crouch and Hafenstein (1977), Crouch (1979), and Barrett (1982). With respect to seedling survival, Crouch (1979) observed that the presence of predominantly herbaceous vegetation cut the survival of planted ponderosa pine seedlings in half over a 10-year period. Most of the mortality was attributed to damage by pocket gophers, which were favored by the presence of herbaceous vegetation. However, the fact that pine height after 10 years in the herbaceous plots was only 60% of that for trees where the vegetation was controlled suggests that plant competition for moisture and nutrients was also important.

The long term effects of brush competition in this subregion have also been studied (Barrett 1973, 1982). In a 20-year study involving ponderosa pine, Barrett (1982) found that understory competition from bitterbrush, snowbrush, and manzanita reduced the growth of the pine "saplings" (they were actually 60 or more years old) by 15 to 50%, depending on the initial tree spacing. The influence of competing vegetation was strongest at the wider spacings. For example, pines spaced at a density of 62 trees/acre and growing in the midst of brush contained only 50% of the volume of pines growing without brush after 20 years. At a density of 250 trees/acre, the volume of pines growing in plots with brush competition was about 70% of similar plots without brush. At 1000 trees/acre, there was virtually no difference in yields over the 20-year period because the pines were sufficiently crowded to affect the brush (as well as themselves). However, the authors suggest that pine densities in this area should be kept at no more than 125 to 250/acre in order to obtain marketable products. Thus control of competing brush is an important consideration in this subregion if maximum yields are to be obtained.

Northern Sierra Nevada

The more southern latitude of the Sierra Nevada creates warmer and drier summer conditions in this subregion of the Northwest than those encountered in the Cascade and Coastal zones. However, the relatively long growing season, moderate topography, deep and well-developed granitic soils, and adequate soil moisture throughout most of the year (much of it from snow melt and warm winter precipitation, contributing to a total precipitation of 30 to 90 in. per year) make the western slope of the Sierra Nevada a productive area for growing timber.

The vegetation of the northern Sierra Nevada is similar in many respects to the southern Cascades. The western slopes of both ranges are characterized by (1) ponderosa pine forests at low elevations; (2) mixed conifer forests (e.g., white fir, ponderosa and sugar pines, Douglas-fir, and incense-cedar) at midelevations; (3) red fir forests containing lodgepole and western white pines, and white fir at the montane level; and (4) subalpine forests dominated by mountain hemlock, whitebark pine, and lodgepole pine at the crest. The drier eastern slopes are typified by mixed stands of ponderosa pine, Jeffrey pine, incense-cedar, and white fir. Sparsely stocked stands of western juniper occupy elevations near the floor of the Great Basin.

Understory vegetation likewise follows an elevational gradient. Vegetation on the west side changes from an oak woodland/chaparral in the foothills to broadleaf deciduous and sclerophyllous evergreens (e.g., deerbrush, snowbrush, bearmat, and manzanita) and other fire-adapted shrubs as one climbs in elevation. Pacific madrone, tanoak, and golden chinkapin are frequently found in the mixed conifer zone. Areas burned by hot fires in this zone and the red fir zone above it are often covered by competitive species of *Ceanothus*, manzanita, gooseberry, and currant. Little shrub cover of economic importance occurs in the upper montane and subalpine zones. Herbaceous grasses and forbs are found throughout the western slope of the Sierra Nevada but especially in the ponderosa pine and true fir zones. They tend to provide relatively sparse cover, however, except on the most mesic sites. Understory vegetation on the eastern slope primarily consists of grasses and shrubby species of *Ceanothus*, manzanita, bitterbrush, and sagebrush that are sparsely distributed because of limited soil moisture.

As in the Cascades, southwestern Oregon, and interior northern California, many of the shrub species prevalent in the Sierra Nevada are adapted to disturbance. Some species have long-lived seed buried in the soil that are capable of rapid germination following fire. Most species also sprout vigorously from established rootstocks left after burning or other forms of disturbance.

Although conifers dominate the landscape throughout the northern Sierra Nevada, understory vegetation presents serious competition for young conifers during the regeneration phase (Conard and Radosevich

1982, McDonald 1983, Laake and Fiske 1983a, 1983b, McDonald and Oliver 1983). Bearmat alone has reduced ponderosa pine survival to 9%, compared to 90% for plots where it was controlled (Tappeiner and Radosevich 1982). Its influence on height growth is equally dramatic, restricting trees to less than 6 ft in height after 19 years, compared to almost 20 ft for released trees. The authors estimate that the bearmat competition could reduce net wood production by 75% over a 50-year rotation.

Another study in the Sierra Nevada of northern California indicated that the diameter and height of ponderosa pine growing in the middle of deerbrush and manzanita were only 60 to 90% of that for trees free to grow over the 16-year time span of the study (Oliver 1979, McDonald and Oliver 1983). As in the study by Barrett (1982), the suppression of pine growth was most pronounced at the widest tree spacings.

A variety of herbaceous grasses and forbs are also able to colonize disturbed areas, capturing soil moisture otherwise available to conifer regeneration. Such competition has resulted in less than 4% of planted ponderosa and Jeffrey pine seedlings surviving after 4 years, compared to 41 to 86% survival where herbaceous species were controlled (Eckert 1979). Many of the understory vegetation types also harbor animals such as pocket gophers, hares, rabbits, grasshoppers, and deer that are occasional pests of conifer regeneration.

Inland Northwest

The Inland Northwest subregion is an extremely diverse area from the standpoint of climate, geology, topography, elevation, soils, and vegetation. West of the continental divide, the climate is dominated by Pacific maritime influences with moderate to abundant precipitation (25 to 60 in.) except for the dry summer months. To the east, total precipitation is less, but summer precipitation is more abundant as the continental climatic pattern tends to prevail. Precipitation is highest in the Idaho Panhandle and adjacent areas, and declines to the south, east, and west. Geology of the area is complex, encompassing a number of local mountain ranges and highlands characteristic of the northern Rockies. Topography varies from steep, stream-cut valleys to gently rolling hills to broad glacial valleys of continental glacial origin in the north. Soils in the Blue Mountain section (northeastern Oregon), northern Idaho, northeastern Washington, and portions of western Montana are mantled by deposits of ash, pumice, or loess up to 2 ft in depth over basalt, granite, or metamorphosed sedimentary rock. Elsewhere, soils are derived primarily from granitic parent material. In the extreme north where continental glaciation occurred, the lacustrine valley floor surface material is often underlain by compacted glacial till or alluvial deposits resulting from massive flooding.

Mixtures of subalpine fir, spruce, mountain hemlock, subalpine larch, whitebark pine, and lodgepole pine are found at the cool, wet end of the moisture-temperature gradient determined by elevation and topography. Western white pine, lodgepole pine, western larch, western redcedar, western hemlock, and grand fir are dominant species in the center of the moisture-temperature gradient. Douglas-fir is ubiquitous throughout the subregion but is most prevalent on xeric sites, along with ponderosa pine. Limber pine occurs at the dry end of the moisture-temperature gradient in the eastern and southeastern part of the subregion and also replaces whitebark pine at high elevations in the southeastern part.

There are about 25 species of deciduous and evergreen hardwoods that seriously compete with conifer regeneration in this subregion. Sitka alder, willow, birch, aspen, mountain maple, snowbrush, redstem ceanothus, ninebark, and cherry can impede the slower growing conifers for many years and may enhance the regeneration of less desirable shade-tolerant species such as grand fir and western redcedar. Other species of smaller stature but capable of severe interference with conifer establishment and early growth include ninebark, false huckleberry, snowberry, boxwood, thimbleberry, elderberry, oceanspray, currants, trailing blackberry, huckleberry, and mountain ash. Studies by Hall and Curtis (1970), Hall (1971), Kittams and Ryker (1975), and Ross et al. (1986) have shown increasing height growth and survival of ponderosa pine and Douglas-fir where brush competition has been controlled.

Equally important competitors are the wide variety (both annual and perennial) of herbaceous species, especially pinegrass, beargrass, elk sedge, fireweed, bracken fern, coneflower, thistles, and alien species such as goatweed and spotted knapweed. Herbaceous competition can form a pure cover or be mixed with understory shrubs. In the early postharvest years, herbaceous vegetation is often the dominant competitor, even where the seedling shrub component is large.

Several studies in the Inland Northwest have documented substantial enhancement of seedling survival and growth when grass and forb competition was reduced (Loewenstein et al. 1968, Larson and Schubert 1969, Hall 1971, Stewart and Beebe 1974, Kittams and Ryker 1975, Gratkowski et al. 1979, Dimock and Collard 1981, Boyd 1982, Peterson 1982, Tonn and Graham 1982, Dimock et al. 1983, Eissenstat and Mitchell 1983, Barber 1984). At one Blue Mountain location, effective control of grass sod doubled the survival of ponderosa pine (Dimock and Collard 1981). At other locations where summer precipitation was higher and competition was sparser, survival was not improved, but untreated seedlings suffered a significant 40% reduction in height growth after 2 years. A study in northeastern Washington by Barber (1984) found that survival of Douglas-fir seedlings was dramatically improved by several types of site preparation, especially herbicide treatment. Without site preparation, grass competition caused a substantial increase in plant moisture stress and poor seedling survival. Dimock et al. (1983) reported that 2 years of herbaceous vegetation control increased height and diameter of ponderosa pine and Douglas-fir by about 70% over a 6-year period. This was equivalent to a threefold increase in stem volume production. In western Montana, Peterson (1982) significantly increased the stem wood production of ponderosa pine seedlings up to 300% during the first year with adequate herbaceous weed control. In a 3-year study by Boyd (1986), ponderosa pine stem wood production per unit of planted trees was increased 4.5 times through weed control. In a summary of studies throughout the West (most in this subregion), an average increase in tree survival of 23% was attained by reducing herbaceous competition (Boyd 1982).

As in other subregions, the presence of competing vegetation provides cover and food for animals that can damage or destroy conifer regeneration. Pocket gophers and hares are species that have caused extensive damage to young seedlings in herbaceous and shrub communities in the Inland Northwest subregion (Hoppe 1977, Dimock and Collard 1981, Tonn and Graham 1982). If not done properly, however, the effects of competition control can be counterproductive. Abrupt reductions in normal food sources may cause greatly increased use of conifers by herbivores occurring on these sites. Removal of such vegetation should be done gradually or well in advance of conifer reforestation.

BENEFICIAL ASPECTS OF ASSOCIATED VEGETATION

Although competing vegetation often has a detrimental effect on conifers, there are certain stages or specific situations in which such vegetation may be beneficial. Among the potential benefits of competing vegetation are the following:

1. Prevention of soil erosion on disturbed or unstable sites through the protection provided by canopies and root systems,
2. Uptake, storage, and recycling of nutrients that might otherwise be lost from forest sites after harvesting, site preparation, and other forms of disturbance,
3. Improvement in soil physical and chemical properties through addition of organic matter and nutrients (mainly nitrogen),
4. Amelioration of excessively hot, dry, or cold (frost) conditions in new plantations through shading and mulching effects,
5. Protection of conifer seedlings from browsing animals such as deer, elk, and cattle,
6. Reduction or elimination of damage from conifer diseases (e.g., root rots) through effects on soil-borne pathogens.

Thus excessive control or eradication of vegetation associated with conifer regeneration can be undesirable. On the other hand, the detrimental effects of competing vegetation (particularly during the early stages of stand establishment) can more than offset the ecological benefits of such vegetation. Proper vegetation management should consider both the positive and negative aspects of controlling vegetation. Periodic adjustments in the degree of vegetation control may be necessary in order to ensure that the net outcome represents a reasonable balance between relatively short-term production goals and longer term ecological stability.

Of the preceding attributes, the importance of certain nitrogen-fixing species has received the most attention. A variety of legumes, shrubs, and hardwoods are capable of fixing atmospheric nitrogen in a form usable by other plants, including conifers (Akkermans and Houwers 1979, Haines and DeBell 1979, Binkley 1986). *Ceanothus* and *Alnus* are two common N-fixing northwestern genera of potential importance to long-term site productivity (Gordon et al. 1979, Conard et al. 1985). Numerous studies have documented the accretion of soil nitrogen beneath stands of *Alnus* (Tarrant 1961, Tarrant and Miller 1963, Berg and Doerksen 1975, Tripp et al. 1979, Binkley 1981, 1982, 1983, DeBell et al. 1983, Binkley et al. 1984, Helgerson et al. 1984) and *Ceanothus* (Youngberg and Wollum 1976, McNabb and Geist 1979, McNabb et al. 1979, Youngberg et al. 1979, Binkley et al. 1982, Binkley and Husted 1983, McNabb and Cromack 1983) in the Northwest.

In a few cases, the accretion of soil nitrogen has possibly led to greater growth of conifers growing in admixture with the alder and *Ceanothus* species. For example, a study by Miller and Murray (1978) found that the presence of red alder appeared to increase the yield of Douglas-fir in a plantation in southwestern Washington from 2900 ft^3/acre to 3100 ft^3/acre over a 44-year period. Although this apparent increase of 200 ft^3/acre was not statistically significant, the mixed portion of the plantation also contained 2500 ft^3/acre of alder. Thus the mixed portion contained almost twice the wood volume of the pure Douglas-fir portion.

It should be borne in mind, however, that these results reported by Miller and Murray (1978) represent a special case. Early frost damage to the off-site alder that had been planted plus the fact that it was planted 4 years after the Douglas-fir and at a controlled spacing prevented the alder from completely dominating the Douglas-fir. Under more typical conditions where red alder seeds in densely at the same time as or prior to the establishment of Douglas-fir, the alder can essentially exclude Douglas-fir from the stand (Newton et al. 1968, Miller and Murray 1978, 1979, Walstad et al. 1986). More shade-tolerant conifers such as western hemlock and western redcedar may be required if conifer production is desired on such sites (Miller and Murray 1978).

It should also be emphasized that the site involved in the Miller and

Murray (1978) study was severely deficient in nitrogen. Binkley (1983, 1984a) observed an analogous benefit attributable to nitrogen fixation by red alder for a mixed alder-Douglas-fir stand in British Columbia growing on a nitrogen-deficient site. However, similar benefits were not detected on a fertile, nitrogen-rich site in western Washington. In fact, the alder in this case had a detrimental effect on Douglas-fir survival, growth, and yield. Thus the net effect of red alder on Douglas-fir performance depends in part on soil fertility. Because most commercial forest sites in the Pacific Northwest are fertile, the two nitrogen-deficient cases reported by Miller and Murray (1978) and Binkley (1983, 1984a) are probably exceptions to the general rule.

Harrington and Deal (1982) suggest that Sitka alder, which has a lower growth habit than red alder, may be a more viable candidate for mixed plantations. Indeed Binkley (1982, 1984b) and Binkley et al. (1984) have documented one case where the presence of shrubby Sitka alder increased the soil nitrogen availability and stem growth of Douglas-fir on a nitrogen-deficient site in British Columbia.

To summarize the experience to date with alder, there may be instances where carefully managed stands of mixed alder and Douglas-fir, or alternating rotations of alder and Douglas-fir, could be economically attractive (DeBell et al. 1978, Atkinson et al. 1979, DeBell 1979, Miller and Murray 1979, Harrington and Deal 1982, Tarrant et al. 1983, Binkley et al. 1984, Binkley 1986, Murray and Miller 1986). Further research is necessary to identify appropriate sites and develop suitable management prescriptions for alder-conifer combinations. Alternatively, markets for red alder will need to improve dramatically if this species is to be managed in place of Douglas-fir. As Poppino and Gedney (1984) point out, the current stumpage price for red alder would have to increase 250 to 400% before red alder became economically competitive with Douglas-fir.

With respect to *Ceanothus*, Youngberg et al. (1979) noted that Douglas-fir seedlings growing in the open exhibited "foliar nitrogen stress" during the growing season, whereas those situated among snowbrush clumps did not appear to suffer from nitrogen deficiency. Binkley and Husted (1983) reported similar trends in foliar nitrogen concentrations for Douglas-fir saplings growing in association with redstem ceanothus.

In the study by Youngberg et al. (1979), there appeared to be better short-term height growth of the Douglas-fir growing within or along the edge of snowbrush clumps, but the trends were not sufficiently distinct to predict a long-term growth advantage for Douglas-fir growing under these conditions. Indeed, the authors speculated that a release treatment would soon be needed to avoid excessive competition for light and moisture from the snowbrush.

Even though *Ceanothus* species have the ability to fix nitrogen, they do not always do so, at least in significant quantities. For example, several snowbrush sites in the Cascades of western Oregon have failed to show any significant nitrogen accretion over periods of up to two decades or more (Zavitkovski and Newton 1968; Binkley 1986). Thus the net value of *Ceanothus* species as nitrogen-fixers, like that of *Alnus* species, should be assessed on a site by site basis.

There are also other potential attributes of competing species that can sometimes be beneficial to conifers. Several investigators have recorded higher stocking levels and growth rates (at least temporarily) when conifer seedlings are growing in the middle of shrubs and hardwoods (Show 1924, Wahlenberg 1930, Youngberg et al. 1979). Although the improved conifer performance in these studies has been generally attributed to the shade provided by the brush cover, all of the studies are confounded by potential microsite differences between the open areas and areas where the brush became established. The microsites where the brush became established could have been inherently better, thereby fostering not only brush development but better conifer performance as well. It is also conceivable that the conifers in the "open" areas could have suffered higher levels of herbaceous competition, thereby accounting for their poorer performance. Unfortunately, the studies are not described in sufficient detail to discount these possibilities. Thus it is impossible to definitively conclude that the brush cover was responsible for the apparent improvements in conifer performance. Furthermore, no efforts were made in these studies to determine if trees established in dead shade would perform even better than those established in the shade of living plants. Properly designed experiments are needed to resolve these questions.

Nevertheless, it is certainly plausible that brush cover can protect conifer seedlings from excessively hot or cold temperatures and from excessive evapotranspiration under some conditions. Wahlenberg (1930) observed such effects in his study of *Ceanothus velutinus* and ponderosa pine seedlings, and Tappeiner and Helms (1971) recorded lower evaporation and higher surface soil moisture beneath squaw carpet, a low-growing species of *Ceanothus*, when compared to bearmat, another form of ground cover. Survival of Douglas-fir and white fir seedlings was also higher when growing in association with squaw carpet versus other microenvironments. The initial advantages of most vegetative cover, however, are likely to be eventually overcome by its competitive demand for light, soil moisture, and nutrients. Subsequent, if not immediate, release treatments will be necessary in most cases in order to free established conifers from the surrounding brush. Indeed, Isaac (1943), Zavitkovski et al. (1969), and Conard and Radosevich (1982) showed that the presence of dead shade (as opposed to shade provided by living shrubs) provided the best environment for seedlings of a variety of western conifer species.

Protection of seedlings from browsing animals is another prospective benefit of brush cover. For example, Youngberg et al. (1979) noted that about 70% of the Douglas-fir seedlings growing in the open or near the edge of snowbrush ceanothus clumps were damaged, versus only 28%

within the clumps. Fortunately, more effective methods (e.g., repellents, protective tubes) are available for protecting conifer regeneration from browsing animals, thereby obviating the need to plant conifers in difficult spots within brush clumps.

Yet another potentially beneficial role of competing vegetation relates to its stabilizing influence on soil movement and nutrient cycling. Because such plants are naturally adapted to the ecosystems involved, they can play an important role in preventing erosion, landslides, stream siltation, and loss of nutrients until conifers become well established. Several studies have shown that excessive disturbance of previously forested watersheds, particularly unstable ones, can have deleterious effects on ecosystem parameters ranging from slope stability to site productivity and water quality (Vitousek et al. 1979, Ziemer 1981). Fortunately, proper implementation of forest vegetation management treatments does not require excessive soil disturbance and eradication of all forms of plant cover. Most of the techniques are simply designed to reduce the important species of competing vegetation to a subordinate position until the conifer seedlings are successfully established and relatively free to grow.

A final example of prospective beneficial effects of nonconifer vegetation involves disease reduction. There is circumstantial evidence that the presence of red alder reduces the incidence of laminated root rot of Douglas-fir caused by *Phellinus weirii* (Nelson et al. 1978). In addition, excessive control of hardwoods can conceivably lead to subsequent infections of Armillaria root rot as the pathogen (*Armillaria mellea*) spreads from the decaying hardwood roots into the conifer stock. Thus vegetation management programs designed to favor conifers over other forms of vegetation need to be thoroughly evaluated before implementation.

FUTURE TRENDS IN VEGETATION MANAGEMENT

As the demand for forest products continues to grow and as the acreage available for commercial forestry continues to shrink, it is inevitable that forest management practices will intensify. As in agriculture, a number of approaches will be required to increase the productivity of sites designated for commercial wood production:

1. Carefully conducted harvesting and reforestation practices
   a. Proper harvesting procedures
   b. Adequate site preparation
   c. Prompt reforestation following harvest and site preparation
   d. Use of vigorous, well-adapted genotypes for reforestation
   e. Careful planting or seeding
   f. Protection from pests, diseases, and fire

2. Competition control
   a. Anticipation of weed problems before they develop
   b. Selection of appropriate vegetation management strategies
   c. Correct implementation of weed control techniques
   d. Periodic monitoring of treatment results
3. Stand management practices
   a. Stocking control (precommercial and commercial thinning)
   b. Fertilization (natural and artificial)
   c. Protection from pests, diseases, fire, and physical damage
4. Research and development
   a. Refinements in current technology and information
   b. Development of improved silvicultural practices
   c. Advances in predictive capabilities and biometrical models
   d. Integrative systems management

Vegetation management will play a central role in the intensification effort because adequate control of competing vegetation is frequently needed to achieve successful reforestation. It is also needed to protect the large initial investments in newly established forests and maintain satisfactory growth rates. This does not mean that nonconiferous vegetation will be eradicated from forest sites. Such an achievement is hardly desirable, practical, or possible. Instead, ways will be found to contain the influence of competing vegetation within well-established economic thresholds as tempered by environmental and operational considerations.

As the acreage available for forestry becomes more limited, it is likely that vegetation management will increase in importance. This is because the most productive forest sites (where forestry activities will be concentrated) also tend to have the most prolific and complex weed problems. In areas where forestry practices are less intensive because of lower site productivity, vegetation management will be necessary for plantation establishment. Thus sound vegetation management will become even more critical as a means of maintaining and enhancing renewable forest resources.

The principal problem species in the future will primarily consist of the invading types of herbs, shrubs, and hardwoods. Species of grass, forbs, berries, manzanita, alder, maple, cherry, and madrone that are disseminated by wind, animals, or machinery are capable of quickly dominating the cleared areas created for new conifer plantations. Under these conditions, herbaceous weeds can cause serious losses in conifer survival and early growth, whereas competing shrubs and hardwood trees can cause sustained reductions in plantation growth and development throughout the rotation.

Conversely, the more heavy-seeded and slower growing species of oak, tanoak, chinkapin, and laurel will diminish in importance. These species are mainly a problem in natural stands and poorly managed plantations. Careful regulation of stand density will impede the development of all but the most shade tolerant shrub and hardwood species. Preharvest control measures and proper site preparation treatments should prevent these species from becoming serious competitors in the next rotation.

Several developments will facilitate progress in vegetation management. A number of comprehensive research programs are underway to further develop and refine various practices (Walstad 1981, Walstad et al. 1982, Radosevich et al. 1985). Predictive models of vegetation development such as those developed by Tappeiner et al. (1984) will allow foresters to anticipate potential problems from competing vegetation and treat them before they get out of hand. A better understanding of the impact of various types and levels of plant competition will permit precise targeting of control measures to the exact times, places, and degrees necessary. More complete utilization of residual hardwoods and logging slash will enhance site preparation. Improved methods of chemical, mechanical, and manual control of vegetation will reduce the need for multiple treatments of sprouting shrubs and hardwoods. New methods of control employing biological and cultural approaches may also be developed in the future. Finally, ways will be found to further integrate vegetation management treatments with other silvicultural practices. For example, maintaining a closed stand canopy near the end of the rotation will retard the encroachment of competing vegetation that would otherwise pose a problem in the subsequent rotation. However, some trade-offs in the form of reduced diameter growth, lower harvest value, or higher silvicultural cost may be necessary in order to maintain the stocking at crown closure. Careful analyses will be needed to integrate and optimize the silvicultural production system as a whole.

As the backlog of areas needing conversion or rehabilitation is reduced, more emphasis will be placed on vegetation control early in the life of a plantation. Localized spot treatments of forbs, grasses, and low shrubs may preclude the need for subsequent release treatments because the conifers will have gained a competitive advantage over invading hardwood germinants and residual sprouters. Where release treatments are necessary, they will be applied in a highly selective fashion so that only target species are affected. Timber stand improvement and other cleaning operations will primarily be used to prevent the development of problem vegetation in subsequent rotations. Thus the emphasis will be on preventive rather than curative weed control.

SUMMARY

The need for continued advances in forest vegetation management is imperative. Several million acres in the Northwest are currently dominated by competing vegetation at the expense of more valuable conifer species. This backlog of problem areas must be reclaimed while at the same time preventing the development of deleterious levels of competing vegetation on newly harvested areas. Aggressive and effective programs in forest vegetation management and research are needed to accomplish these goals.

Virtually every published study where competing vegetation has been controlled has resulted in increased survival or growth of conifers (Stewart et al. 1984). This trend is remarkably consistent despite the wide range of environmental conditions, vegetation types, and conifer species that have been studied in these experiments. The response is not surprising, however, when one considers that light, moisture, nutrients, and pest animals frequently limit conifer development in the Northwest.

Occasionally, some of the species that are strong competitors of conifers are also beneficial to them. More often than not, however, the benefits are transient or are outweighed by the competitive ability of such species to monopolize site resources. Further work is needed to identify instances where competing vegetation can be tolerated or even encouraged and where control of competing vegetation can have counterproductive side effects.

Silviculturists should always recognize that the relationship between conifers and weeds is not simplistic (i.e., eliminate the weeds and the conifers will do better). Control of competition under some circumstances may have broad ecosystem effects (both positive and negative) on other components of the community such as animals, insects, pathogens, and abiotic conditions. The potential consequences of these side effects on crop trees should be considered in evaluating vegetation problems and prescribing treatments.

Fortunately, the outlook for achieving improvements in forest vegetation management is promising. A number of research, development, and application programs are underway to address vegetation problems and opportunities. These efforts should greatly enhance the ability to manage competing vegetation in a safe, efficient, and economical manner. Someday it may be possible to exploit some of the beneficial attributes of competing vegetation without incurring the negative consequences of competition for site resources.

REFERENCES

Akkermans, A.D.L. and A. Houwers. 1979. Symbiotic nitrogen fixers available for use in temperate forestry, p. 23-35. *In* Gordon, J.C., C.T. Wheeler, and D.A. Perry (eds.) Symbiotic nitrogen fixation in the management of temperate forests. Workshop Proc., April 2-5, 1979. Forest Research Laboratory, Oregon State Univ., Corvallis, OR. 501 p.

Atkinson, W.A., B.T. Bormann, and D.S. DeBell. 1979. Crop rotation of Douglas-fir and red alder: a preliminary biological and economic assessment. Bot. Gaz. 140 (suppl.):S102-S107.

Barber, H.W., Jr. 1984. Effects of site preparation on survival and moisture stress of interior Douglas-fir seedlings planted in grass. Tree Planters' Notes. 35(4):7-10.

Barbour, M.G. and J. Major (eds.) 1977. Terrestrial vegetation of California. John Wiley and Sons, New York, NY. 1002 p.

Baron, F.J. 1962. Effects of different grasses on ponderosa pine seedling establishment. USDA Forest Service, Pacific Southwest Forest and Range Experiment Station, Berkeley, CA. Res. Note PSW-199. 8 p.

Barrett, J.W. 1973. Latest results from the Pringle Falls ponderosa pine spacing study. USDA Forest Service, Pacific Northwest Forest and Range Experiment Station, Portland, OR. Res. Note PNW-209. 21 p.

Barrett, J.W. (ed.). 1980. Regional silviculture in the United States. John Wiley and Sons, New York, NY. 551 p.

Barrett, J.W. 1982. Twenty-year growth of ponderosa pine saplings thinned to five spacings in central Oregon. USDA Forest Service, Pacific Northwest Forest and Range Experiment Station, Portland, OR. Res. Pap. PNW-301. 18 p.

Barrett, J.W., R.E. Martin, and D.C. Wood. 1983. Northwestern ponderosa pine and associated species, p. 16-18. *In* Burns, R.M. (tech. comp.) Silvicultural systems for the major forest types of the United States. USDA Forest Service, Washington, DC. Agr. Hbk. 445. 191 p.

Bassett, P.M. 1979. Timber resources of southwest Oregon. USDA Forest Service, Pacific Northwest Forest and Range Experiment Station, Portland, OR. Resour. Bull. PNW-72. 29 p.

Bentley, J.R., S.B. Carpenter, and D.A. Blakeman. 1971. Early brush control promotes growth of ponderosa pine planted on bulldozed site. USDA Forest Service, Pacific Southwest Forest and Range Experiment Station, Berkely, CA. Res. Note PSW-238. 5 p.

Berg, A. and A. Doerksen. 1975. Natural fertilization of a heavily thinned Douglas-fir stand by understory red alder. Forest Research Laboratory, Oregon State Univ., Corvallis, OR. Res. Note 56. 3 p.

Binkley, D. 1981. Nodule biomass and acetylene reduction rates of red alder and Sitka alder on Vancouver Island, B.C. Can. J. Forest Res. 11:281-286.

Binkley, D. 1982. Nitrogen fixation and net primary production in a young Sitka alder stand. Can. J. Botany 60:281-284.

Binkley, D. 1983. Ecosystem production in Douglas-fir plantations: interaction of red alder and site fertility. Forest Ecol. Manage. 5:215-227.

Binkley, D. 1984a. Importance of size-density relationships in mixed stands of Douglas-fir and red alder. Forest Ecol. Manage. 9:81-85.

Binkley, D. 1984b. Douglas-fir stem growth per unit of leaf area increased by interplanted Sitka alder and red alder. Forest Sci. 30:259-263.

Binkley, D. 1986. Forest nutrition management. John Wiley and Sons, New York, NY. 290 p.

Binkley, D., K. Cromack, Jr., and R.L. Fredericksen. 1982. Nitrogen accretion and availability in some snowbrush ecosystems. Forest Sci. 28:720-724.

Binkley, D. and L. Husted. 1983. Nitrogen accretion, soil fertility, and Douglas-fir nutrition in association with redstem ceanothus. Can. J. Forest. Res. 13:122-125

Binkley, D., J.D. Lousier, and K. Cromack, Jr. 1984. Ecosystem effects of Sitka alder in a Douglas-fir plantation. Forest Sci. 30:26-35.

Black, H., C. E. Dimock II, J. Evans, and J. Rochelle. 1979. Animal damage to coniferous plantations in Oregon and Washington—Part 1. A survey, 1963-1975. Forest Research Laboratory, Oregon State Univ., Corvallis, OR. Res. Bull. 25. 44 p.

Bolsinger, C.L. 1980. California forests: trends, problems, and opportunities. USDA Forest Service, Pacific Northwest Forest and Range Experiment Station, Portland, OR. Resour. Bull. PNW-89. 138 p.

Borrecco, J.E. 1975. The responses of snowshoe hares to herbicide-induced habitat changes and the implications to forest management. Forestry Research, Weyerhaeuser Co., Tacoma, WA. Tech. Rep. 40/4600/75/26. 14 p.

Boyd, R.J. 1982. Chemical site preparation treatments for herbaceous plant communities, p. 49-53. *In* Baumgartner, D.M. (ed.) Site preparation and fuels management on steep terrain. Sympos. Proc., Coop. Ext., Washington State Univ., Pullman, WA. 179 p.

Boyd, R.J. 1986. Conifer performance following weed control site preparation treatments in the Inland Northwest, p. 95–104. *In* Baumgartner, D.M., R.J. Boyd, D.W. Breuer, and D.L. Miller (comps. and eds.) Weed control for forest productivity in the interior west. Sympos. Proc., Coop Ext., Washington State Univ., Pullman, WA.

Bright, L.R. 1984. Assessment of elk habitat for resource management and planning activities from LANDSAT mapping products, p. 101-108. *In* Harding, R.A. and P.A. Murtha (chairmen). Renewable Resources Management: Applications of Remote Sensing. Proc., Renewable Natural Resources Foundation Symposium on the Application of Remote Sensing To Resource Management. May 22-27, 1983. Seattle, WA. Amer. Soc. of Photogram., Falls Church, VA. 774 p.

Burns, R.M. (tech. comp.) 1983. Silvicultural systems for the major forest types of the United States. USDA Forest Service, Washington, DC. Agr. Hbk. 445. 191 p.

Chan, S.S. 1984. Competitive effects of overtopping vegetation on Douglas-fir morphology in the Oregon Coast Range. M.S. thesis, College of Forestry, Oregon State Univ., Corvallis, OR. 49 p.

Christensen, M.D., J.A. Young, and R.A. Evans. 1974. Control of annual grasses and revegetation in ponderosa pine woodlands. J. Range Manage. 27:143-145.

Cleary, B.D., R.D. Greaves, and R.K. Hermann. (eds.) 1978. Regenerating Oregon's forests. Oregon State Univ. Ext. Serv., Corvallis, OR. 287 p.

Conard, S.G., A.E. Jaramillo, K. Cromack, Jr., and S. Rose. (comps.) 1985. The role of the genus *Ceanothus* in western forest ecosystems. Workshop Proc., Nov. 22-24, 1982, Oregon State Univ., Corvallis, OR. USDA Forest Service, Pacific Northwest Forest and Range Experiment Station, Portland, OR. Gen. Tech. Rep. PNW-182. 72 p.

Conard, S.G. and S.R. Radosevich. 1982. Growth responses of white fir to decreasing shading and root competition by montane chaparral shrubs. Forest Sci. 28:309-320.

Critchfield, W.B. 1971. Profiles of California vegetation. USDA Forest Service, Pacific Southwest Forest and Range Experiment Station, Berkeley, CA. Res. Pap. PSW-76. 54 p.

Crouch, G.L. 1969. Animal damage to conifers on national forests in the Pacific Northwest region. USDA Forest Service, Pacific Northwest Forest and Range Experiment Station, Portland, OR. Resour. Bull. PNW-28. 13 p.

Crouch, G.L. 1979. Atrazine improves survival and growth of ponderosa pine threatened by vegetative competition and pocket gophers. Forest Sci. 25:99-111.

Crouch, G.L. 1982. Pocket gophers and reforestation on western forests. J. Forestry 69:662-664.

Crouch, G.L. and E. Hafenstein. 1977. Atrazine promotes ponderosa pine regeneration. USDA Forest Service, Pacific Northwest Forest and Range Experiment Station, Portland, OR. Res. Note PNW-309. 8 p.

Dahms, W.G. 1950. The effect of manzanita and snowbrush competition on ponderosa pine reproduction. USDA Forest Service, Pacific Northwest Forest and Range Experiment Station, Portland, OR. Res. Note 65. 3 p.

Daniels, T.G. and F.E. Bridgewater. 1976. Effects of chemical and mechanical vegetation control on survival and vigor of ponderosa pine. Forestry Research, Weyerhaeuser Co., Tacoma, WA. Tech. Rep. 80/6600/76/14. 8 p.

Daubenmire, R., and J.B. Daubenmire. 1968. Forest vegetation of eastern Washington and northern Idaho. Washington Agricultural Experiment Station, Pullman, WA. Tech. Bull. 60. 104 p.

DeBell, D.S. 1979. Future potential for use of symbiotic fixation in forest management, p. 451-466. In Gordon, J.C., C.T. Wheeler, and D.A. Perry (eds.) Symbiotic nitrogen fixation in the management of temperate forests. Workshop Proc., April 2-5, 1979. Forest Research Laboratory, Oregon State Univ., Corvallis, OR. 501 p.

DeBell, D.S., M.A. Radwan, and J.M. Kraft. 1983. Influence of red alder on chemical properties of a clay loam soil in western Washington. USDA Forest Service, Pacific Northwest Forest and Range Experiment Station, Portland, OR. Res. Pap. PNW-313. 7 p.

DeBell, D.S., R.F. Strand, and D.L. Reukema. 1978. Short-rotation production of red alder: some options for future forest management, p. 231-244. In Briggs, D.G., D.S. DeBell, and W.A. Atkinson (comps.) Utilization and management of alder. USDA Forest Service, Pacific Northwest Forest and Range Experiment Station, Portland, OR. Gen. Tech. Rep. PNW-70. 379 p.

Detling, L.E. 1968. Historical background of the flora of the Pacific Northwest. Univ. Oregon Mus. Natur. Hist. Bull. 13. 57 p.

Dimock, E.J., II. 1981. Herbicide and conifer options for reforesting upper slopes in the Cascade Range. USDA Forest Service, Pacific Northwest Forest and Range Experiment Station, Portland, OR. Res. Pap. PNW-292. 14 p.

Dimock, E.J., II, T.F. Beebe, and E.B. Collard. 1983. Planting-site preparation with herbicides to aid conifer reforestation. Weed Sci. 31:215-221.

Dimock, E.J., II, E. Bell, and R.M. Randall. 1976. Converting brush and hardwoods to conifers on high sites in western Washington and Oregon—progress, policy, success and costs. USDA Forest Service, Pacific Northwest Forest and Range Experiment Station, Portland, OR. Res. Pap. PNW-213. 16 p.

Dimock, E.J., II, and E.B. Collard. 1981. Postplanting sprays of dalapon and atrazine to aid conifer establishment. USDA Forest Service, Pacific Northwest Forest and Range Experiment Station, Portland, OR. Res. Pap. PNW-280. 16 p.

Eckert, R.E., Jr. 1979. Establishment of pine (*Pinus* spp.) transplants in perennial grass stands with atrazine. Weed Sci. 27:253-257.

Eissenstat, D.M. and J.E. Mitchell. 1983. Effects of seeding grass and clover on growth and water potential of Douglas-fir seedlings. Forest Sci. 29:166-179.

Evans, J., D.L. Campbell, G.D. Lindsey, V.G. Barnes, Jr., and R.M. Anthony. 1981. Distribution of animal damage in southwestern Oregon forests. USDI Fish and Wildlife Service, Washington, DC. Wildlife Leaflet 514. 12 p.

Eyre, F.H. (ed.) 1980. Forest cover types of the United States and Canada. Soc. Amer. Foresters, Washington, DC. 148 p.

Fowells, H.A. (comp.) 1965. Silvics of forest trees of the United States. USDA Forest Service, Washington, DC. Agr. Hbk 271. 762 p.

Fox, L., III, K.E. Mayer, and A.R. Forbes. 1983. Classification of forest resources with Landsat data. J. Forestry 81:283-287.

Franklin, J.F. and C.T. Dyrness. 1973. Natural vegetation of Oregon and Washington. USDA Forest Service, Pacific Northwest Forest and Range Experiment Station, Portland, OR. Gen. Tech. Rep. PNW-8. 417 p.

Froehlich, H.A., D.H. McNabb, and F. Gaweda. 1982. Average annual precipitation, 1960-1980, in southwest Oregon. Ext. Serv., Oregon State Univ., Corvallis, OR. Miscell. Publ. EM 8220. 8 p.

Gordon, J.C., C.T. Wheeler, and D.A. Perry (eds.) 1979. Symbiotic nitrogen fixation in the management of temperate forests. Workshop Proc., April 2-5, 1979. Forest Research Laboratory, Oregon State Univ., Corvallis, OR. 501 p.

Gratkowski, H. 1959. Effects of herbicides on some important brush species in southwestern Oregon. USDA Forest Service, Pacific Northwest Forest and Range Experiment Station, Portland, OR. Res. Pap. 31. 33 p.

Gratkowski, H. 1975. Silvicultural use of herbicides in Pacific Northwest Forests. USDA Forest Service, Pacific Northwest Forest and Range Experiment Station, Portland, OR. Gen. Tech. Rep. PNW-37. 44 p.

Gratkowski, H., D. Hopkins, and P. Lauterbach. 1973. Rehabilitation of forest land. The Pacific Coast and Northern Rocky Mountain Region. J. Forestry 71:138-143.

Gratkowksi, H., R. Jaszkowski, and L. Armstrong. 1979. Survival of Douglas-fir seedlings sprayed with atrazine, terbacil, and 2,4-D. USDA Forest Service, Pacific Northwest Forest and Range Experiment Station, Portland, OR. Res. Pap. PNW-256. 8 p.

Gratkowski, H. and P.G. Lauterbach. 1974. Releasing Douglas-fir from varnish-leaf ceanothus. J. Forestry 72:150-152.

Haines, S.G. and D.S. DeBell. 1979. Use of nitrogen-fixing plants to improve and maintain productivity of forest soils, p. 279-303. *In* Leaf, A.L. (program chairman). Impact of intensive harvesting on forest nutrient cycling. Sympos. Proc., Aug. 13-16, 1979. College of Environmental Science and Forestry, State Univ. New York, Syracuse, NY. 422 p.

Hall, D.O. 1971. Ponderosa pine planting techniques, survival, and height growth in the Idaho Batholith. USDA Forest Service, Intermountain Forest and Range Experiment Station, Ogden, UT. Res. Pap. INT-104. 28 p.

Hall, D.O. and J.D. Curtis. 1970. Planting method affects height growth of ponderosa pine in central Idaho. USDA Forest Service, Intermountain Forest and Range Experiment Station, Ogden, UT. Res. Note INT-125. 8 p.

Hall, F.C. 1973. Plant communities of the Blue Mountains in eastern Oregon and southeastern Washington. USDA Forest Service, Portland, OR. Region 6 Area Guide 3-1. 81 p.

Harrington, C.A. and R.L. Deal. 1982. Sitka alder—a candidate for mixed stands. Can. J. Forest Res. 12:108-111.

Hayes, G.L. 1959. Forest and forest-land problems of southwestern Oregon. USDA Forest Service, Pacific Northwest Forest and Range Experiment Station, Portland, OR. 54 p.

Heilman, P.E., H.W. Anderson, and D.M. Baumgartner (eds.) 1979. Forest soils of the Douglas-fir region. Cooperative Extension Service, Washington State Univ., Pullman, WA. 298 p.

Helgerson, O.T., J.C. Gordon, and D.A. Perry. 1984. N$_2$ fixation by red alder (*Alnus rubra*) and scotch broom (*Cytisus scoparius*) planted under precommercially thinned Douglas-fir (*Pseudotsuga menziesii*). Plant and Soil 78:221-233.

Hobbs, S.D. 1983. Even researchers have 20/20 hindsight. College of Forestry, Oregon State Univ., Corvallis, OR. FIR Rep. 5(1): 9-10.

Hobbs, S.D. and P.W. Owston. 1985. Plant competition associated with Douglas-fir shelterwood management in southwest Oregon, p. 17-21. *In* Mann, J.W. and S.D. Tesch (eds.) Workshop Proc., Shelterwood Management System. Forest Research Laboratory, Oregon State Univ., Corvallis, OR. 116 p.

Hooven, E.F. 1977. The mountain beaver in Oregon: its life history and control. Forest Research Laboratory, Oregon State Univ., Corvallis, OR. Res. Pap. 30. 20 p.

Hoppe, J.P. 1977. Manipulating vegetation to control pocket gopher numbers and gopher-caused seedling mortality. Forestry Research, Weyerhaeuser Co., Tacoma, WA. Tech. Rep. 042-4102/77/34. 6 p.

Howard, K.M. and M. Newton. 1984. Overtopping by successional Coast-Range vegetation slows Douglas-fir seedlings. J. Forestry 82:178-180.

Isaac, L.A. 1943. Reproductive habits of Douglas-fir. Charles Lathrop Pack Forestry Foundation, Washington, DC. 107 p.

Kittams, J.A. and R.A. Ryker. 1975. Habitat type and site preparation affect survival of planted Douglas-fir in central Idaho brushfields. USDA Forest Service, Intermountain Forest and Range Experiment Station, Ogden, UT. Res. Note INT-198. 6 p.

Knapp, W.H., T.C. Turpin, and J.H. Beuter. 1984. Vegetation control for Douglas-fir regeneration on the Siuslaw National Forest: a decision analysis. J. Forestry 82:168-173.

Laake, R.J. and J.N. Fiske. 1983a. Red fir and white fir, p. 41-43. *In* Burns, R.M. (tech. comp.) Silvicultural systems for the major forest types of the United States. USDA Forest Service, Washington, DC. Agr. Hbk. 445. 191 p.

Laake, R.J. and J.N. Fiske. 1983b. Sierra Nevada mixed conifers, p. 44-47. *In* Burns, R.M. (tech. comp.) Silvicultural systems for the major forest types of the United States. USDA Forest Service, Washington, DC. Agr. Hbk. 445. 191 p.

Larson, M.M. and G.H. Schubert. 1969. Root competition between ponderosa pine seedlings and grass. USDA Forest Service, Rocky Mountain Forest and Range Experiment Station, Fort Collins, CO. Res. Pap. RM-54. 12 p.

Loewenstein, H., L.P. McConnel, and F.H. Pitkin. 1968. Root development and survival of planted ponderosa pine seedlings as influenced by competing vegetation. Forest, Wildlife and Range Experiment Station, Univ. Idaho, Moscow, ID. Pap. No. 5. 13 p.

MacLean, C.D. 1980a. Opportunities for silvicultural treatment in western Oregon. USDA Forest Service, Pacific Northwest Forest and Range Experiment Station, Portland, OR. Resour. Bull. PNW-90. 35 p.

MacLean, C.D. 1980b. A technique for identifying treatment opportunities from western Oregon and Washington forest survey plots. USDA Forest Service, Pacific Northwest Forest and Range Experiment Station, Portland, OR. Gen. Tech. Rep. PNW-102. 16 p.

McCreight, R.W. 1984. COPE inventory of July 12, 1984. Personal communication, Recon Research Inc., Bend, OR.

McDonald, P.M. 1983. Clearcutting and natural regeneration...management implications for the northern Sierra Nevada. USDA Forest Service, Pacific Southwest Forest and Range Experiment Station, Berkeley, CA. Gen. Tech. Rep. PSW-70. 11 p.

McDonald, P.M. and W.W. Oliver. 1983. Woody shrubs retard growth of ponderosa pine seedlings and saplings, p. 65-89. *In* Proc., 5th Annual Forest Vegetation Management Conf., Nov. 2-3, 1983, Redding, CA. 162 p.

McNabb, D.H., and K. Cromack, Jr. 1983. Dinitrogen fixation by a mature snowbrush stand in the western Oregon Cascades. Can. J. Microbiol. 29:1014-1021.

McNabb, D.H., H.A. Froehlich, and F. Gaweda. 1982. Average dry-season precipitation in southwest Oregon, May through September. Ext. Serv., Oregon State Univ., Corvallis, OR. Miscell. Publ. EM 8226. 7 p.

McNabb, D.H. and J.M. Geist. 1979. Acetylene reduction assay of symbiotic N_2 fixation under field conditions. Ecology 60:1070-1072.

McNabb, D.H., J.M. Geist, and C.T. Youngberg. 1979. Nitrogen fixation by *Ceanothus velutinus* in northeastern Oregon, p. 481. *In* Gordon, J.C., C.T. Wheeler, and D.A. Perry (eds.) Symbiotic nitrogen fixation in the management of temperate forests. Workshop Proc., April 2-5, 1979. Forest Research Laboratory, Oregon State Univ., Corvallis, OR. 501 p.

Miller, R.E. and M.D. Murray. 1978. The effects of red alder on growth of Douglas-fir, p. 283-306. *In* Briggs, D.G., D.S. DeBell, and W.A. Atkinson (comps.) Utilization and management of alder. USDA Forest Service, Pacific Northwest Forest and Range Experiment Station, Portland, OR. Gen. Tech. Rep. PNW-70. 379 p.

Miller, R.E. and M.D. Murray. 1979. Fertilizer versus red alder for adding nitrogen to Douglas-fir forests of the Pacific Northwest, p. 356-373. *In* Gordon, J.C., C.T. Wheeler, and D.A. Perry (eds.) Symbiotic nitrogen fixation in the management of temperate forests. Workshop Proc., April 2-5, 1979. Forest Research Laboratory, Oregon State Univ., Corvallis, OR. 501 p.

Minore, D. 1978. The Dead Indian Plateau: a historical summary of forestry observations and research in a severe southwestern Oregon environment. USDA Forest Service, Pacific Northwest Forest and Range Experiment Station, Portland, OR. Gen. Tech. Rep. PNW-72. 23 p.

Minore, D. 1979. Comparative autecological characteristics of northwestern tree species...a literature review. USDA Forest Service, Pacific Northwest Forest and Range Experiment Station, Portland, OR. Gen. Tech. Rep. PNW-87. 72 p.

Minore, D. and D. Kingsley. 1983. Mixed conifers of southwest Oregon, p. 23-25. *In* Burns, R.M. (tech. comp.) Silvicultural systems for the major forest types of the United States. USDA Forest Service, Washington, DC. Agr. Hbk. 445. 191 p.

Murray, M.D. and R.E. Miller. 1986. Early survival and growth of planted Douglas-fir with red alder in four mixed regimes. USDA Forest Service, Pacific Northwest Station, Portland, OR. Res. Pap. PNW-366. 13 p.

Nelson, E.E., E.M. Hansen, C.Y. Li, and J.M. Trappe. 1978. The role of red alder in reducing losses from laminated root rot, p. 273-282. *In* Briggs, D.G., D.S. DeBell, and W.A. Atkinson (comps.) Utilization and management of alder. USDA Forest Service, Pacific Northwest Forest and Range Experiment Station, Portland, OR. Gen. Tech. Rep. PNW-70. 379 p.

Newton, M. 1964. Seedling survival and vegetative competition, p. 39-42. *In* Western Reforestation Proc., Western Forestry and Conservation Assoc., Portland, OR.

Newton, M. 1981. Chemical management of herbs and sclerophyll brush, p. 50-65. *In* Hobbs, S.D. and O.T. Helgerson (eds.) Reforestation of skeletal soils. Workshop Proc., Nov. 17-19, 1981. Medford, OR. Forest Research Laboratory, Oregon State Univ., Corvallis, OR. 124 p.

Newton, M., B.A. El Hassan, and J. Zavitkovski. 1968. Role of red alder in western Oregon forest succession, p. 73-84. *In* Trappe, J.M., J.F. Franklin, R.F. Tarrant, and G.M. Hansen (eds.) Biology of alder. Symp. Proc., Northwest Scientific Assoc., Fortieth Annual Meeting, April 14-15, 1967, Pullman, WA. USDA Forest Service, Pacific Northwest Forest and Range Experiment Station, Portland, OR. 292 p.

Newton, M. and W.S. Overton. 1973. Direct and indirect effects of atrazine, 2,4-D, and dalapon mixtures on conifers. Weed Sci. 21:269-275.

Oliver, C.D. 1981. Forest development in North America following major disturbances. Forest Ecol. Manage. 3:153-168.

Oliver, W.W. 1979. Early response of ponderosa pine to spacing and brush: observations on a 12-year-old plantation. USDA Forest Service, Pacific Southwest

Forest and Range Experiment Station, Berkeley, CA. Res. Note PSW-341. 7 p.

Oliver, W.W. 1984. Brush reduces growth of thinned ponderosa pine in northern California. USDA Forest Service, Pacific Southwest Forest and Range Experiment Station, Berkeley, CA. Res. Pap. PSW-172. 7 p.

Peterson, T.D. 1982. First year survival and growth of ponderosa pine after postplanting applications of Velpar and Roundup. Research and Development, Rocky Mountain Timberlands, Champion International Corp., Milltown, MT. Res. Note RM-82-1. 15 p.

Petersen, T.D. and M. Newton. 1982. Growth of Douglas-fir following release from snowbrush and forbs—implications for vegetation management of brushfields. Research and Development, Rocky Mountain Timberlands, Champion International Corp., Milltown, MT. Res. Note RM 82-8. 9 p.

Petersen, T.D. and M. Newton. 1985. Growth of Douglas-fir following control of snowbrush and herbaceous vegetation in Oregon. Dow Chemical USA, Midland, MI. Down to Earth 41(1): 21-25.

Pfister, R.D., B.L. Kovalchick, S.F. Arno, and R.C. Presby. 1977. Forest habitat types of Montana. USDA Forest Service, Intermountain Forest and Range Experiment Station, Ogden UT. Gen. Tech. Rep. INT-34. 144 p.

Phelps, R.B. 1980. Timber in the United States economy: 1963, 1967, and 1972. USDA Forest Service, Washington, DC. Gen. Tech. Rep. WO-21. 90 p.

Poppino, J.H. and D.R. Gedney. 1984. The hardwood resource in western Oregon. USDA Forest Service, Pacific Northwest Forest and Range Experiment Station, Portland, OR. Resource Bull. PNW-116. 37 p.

Powers, R.F. and G.D. Jackson. 1978. Ponderosa pine response to fertilization: influence of brush removal and soil type. USDA Forest Service, Pacific Southwest Forest and Range Experiment Station, Berkeley, CA. Res. Pap. PSW-132. 9 p.

Preest, D.S. 1977. Long-term growth responses of Douglas-fir to weed control. New Zealand J. Forest Sci. 7:329-332.

Radosevich, S.R., P.C. Passof, and O.A. Leonard. 1976. Douglas-fir release from tanoak and Pacific madrone competition. Weed Sci. 24:144-145.

Radosevich, S.R., J.D. Walstad, and M. Newton. 1985. CRAFTS. A cooperative research program in forest vegetation management: an updated prospectus. Forest Research Laboratory, Oregon State Univ., Corvallis, OR. 12 p.

Ross, D.W., W. Scott, R.L. Heninger, and J.D. Walstad. 1986. Effects of site preparation on ponderosa pine (*Pinus ponderosa*), associated vegetation, and soil properties in south central Oregon. Can. J. Forest Res. 16:612-618.

Roy, D.F. 1981. Effects of competing vegetation on conifer performance. Paper presented at the 1981 Forest Vegetation Management Workshop, School of Forestry, Oregon State Univ., Corvallis, OR. Paper is also available from USDA Forest Service, Pacific Southwest Forest and Range Experiment Station, Redding, CA. 54 p.

Ruth, R.H. 1956. Plantation survival and growth in two brush-threat areas in coastal Oregon. USDA Forest Service, Pacific Northwest Forest and Range Experiment Station, Portland, OR. Res. Pap. 17. 14 p.

Ruth, R.H. 1957. Ten-year history of an Oregon coastal plantation. USDA Forest Service, Pacific Northwest Forest and Range Experiment Station, Portland, OR. Res. Pap. 21. 15 p.

Show, S.B. 1924. Some results of experimental forest planting in northern California. J. Ecology 5:83-94.

Stewart, R.E. 1978. Origin and development of vegetation after spraying and burning in a coastal Oregon clearcut. USDA Forest Service, Pacific Northwest Forest and Range Experiment Station, Portland, OR. Res. Note PNW-317. 11 p.

Stewart, R.E., and T. Beebe. 1974. Survival of ponderosa pines following control of competing grasses. Western Soc. Weed Sci. Proc. 27:55-58.

Stewart, R.E., L.L. Gross, and B.H. Honkala. 1984. Effects of competing vegetation on forest trees: a bibliography with abstracts. USDA Forest Service, Washington, DC. Gen. Tech. Rep. WO-43. 260 p.

Stubblefield, G. and C.D. Oliver. 1978. Silvicultural implications of the reconstruction of mixed alder/conifer stands, p. 307-320. *In* Briggs, D.E., D.S. DeBell, and W.A. Atkinson (comps.) Utilization and management of alder. Symp. Proc. USDA Forest Service, Pacific Northwest Forest and Range Experiment Station, Portland, OR. Gen. Tech. Rep. PNW-70. 379 p.

Tappeiner, J.C., II, T.B. Harrington, and J.D. Walstad. 1984. Predicting recovery of tanoak (*Lithocarpus densiflorus*) and Pacific madrone (*Arbutus menziesii*) after cutting or burning. Weed Sci. 32:413-417.

Tappeiner, J.C., II, and J.A. Helms. 1971. Natural regeneration of Douglas-fir and white fir on exposed sites in the Sierra Nevada of California. Amer. Midland Naturalist 86:358-370.

Tappeiner, J.C., II, and S.R. Radosevich. 1982. Effect of bearmat (*Chamaebatia foliolosa*) on soil moisture and ponderosa pine (*Pinus ponderosa*) growth. Weed Sci. 30:98-101.

Tarrant, R.F. 1957. Soil moisture conditions after chemically killing manzanita brush in central Oregon. USDA Forest Service, Pacific Northwest Forest and Range Experiment Station, Portland, OR. Res. Note 156. 4 p.

Tarrant, R.F. 1961. Stand development and soil fertility in a Douglas-fir-red alder plantation. Forest Sci. 7:238-246.

Tarrant, R.F., B.T. Borman, D.S. DeBell, and W.A. Atkinson. 1983. Managing red alder in the Douglas-fir region: some possibilities. J. Forestry 81:787-792.

Tarrant, R.F. and R.E. Miller. 1963. Accumulation of organic matter and soil nitrogen beneath a plantation of red alder and Douglas-fir. Soil Sci. Soc. Amer. Proc. 27:231-234.

Teipner, C. L., E.O. Garton, and L. Nelson, Jr. 1983. Pocket gophers in forest ecosystems. USDA Forest Service, Intermountain Forest and Range Experiment Station, Ogden, UT. Gen. Tech. Rep. INT-154. 53 p.

Tonn, J.R. and R.T. Graham. 1982. The effect of brush competition and plastic mulch on moisture stress of planted Douglas-fir. USDA Forest Service, Intermountain Forest and Range Experiment Station, Ogden, UT. Res. Note INT-320. 3 p.

Tripp, L.N., D.F. Bezdicek, and P.E. Heilman. 1979. Seasonal and diurnal patterns and rates of nitrogen fixation by young red alder. Forest Sci. 25:371-380.

2,4,5-T. Assessment Team. 1982. The biologic and economic assessment of 2,4,5-T. USDA Cooperative Impact Assessment Report, Washington, DC. Tech. Bull. 1671. 445 p.

Vitousek, P.M., J. R. Gosz, C.C. Grier, J.M. Melillo, W.A. Reiners, and R.L. Todd. 1979. Nitrate losses from disturbed ecosystems. Science 204:469-474.

Wahlenberg, W.G. 1930. Effect of ceanothus brush on western yellow pine plantations in the northern Rocky Mountains. J. Agr. Res. 41:601-612.

Walstad, J.D. 1981. Forest vegetation management: a new discipline for an old ethic, p. 10-13. In Holt, H.A. and B.C. Fischer (eds.) Weed control in forest management. John S. Wright Forestry Conf. Proc., Dept. Forestry and Nat. Resour., Purdue Univ., West Lafayette, IN. 305 p.

Walstad, J.D. 1982. Increasing fiber production through intensive forest management: opportunities through vegetation management, p. 46-50. In Increasing forest productivity. Soc. Amer. Foresters Proc., 1981 Nat. Conv., Orlando, FL. SAF Publ. 82-01. 368 p.

Walstad, J.D., J.D. Brodie, B.C. McGinley, and C.A. Roberts. 1986. Silvicultural value of chemical brush control in the management of Douglas-fir. Western J. Appl. Forestry 1:69-73.

Walstad, J.D., J.C. Gordon, M. Newton, and L.A. Norris. 1982. CRAFTS: Comprehensive research program in forest vegetation management. Department of Forest Science, College of Forestry, Oregon State Univ., Corvallis, OR. 27 p.

Whittaker, R.H. 1960. Vegetation of the Siskiyou Mountains, Oregon and California. Ecol. Monographs 30(3):279-338.

Youngberg, C.T. and A.G. Wollum II. 1976. Nitrogen accretion in developing *Ceanothus velutinus* stands. Soil Sci. Soc. Amer. J. 40:109-112.

Youngberg, C.T., A.G. Wollum II, and W. Scott. 1979. Ceanothus in Douglas-fir clearcuts: nitrogen accretion and impact on regeneration, p. 224-233. In Gordon, J.C., C.T. Wheeler, and D.A. Perry (eds.) Symbiotic nitrogen fixation in the management of temperate forests. Workshop Proc., Forest Research Laboratory, Oregon State Univ., Corvallis, OR. 501 p.

Zavitkovski, J. and M. Newton. 1968. Ecological importance of snowbrush *Ceanothus velutinus* in the Oregon Cascades. Ecology 49:1134-1145.

Zavitkovski, J., M. Newton, and B. El-Hassan. 1969. Effects of snowbrush on growth of some conifers. J. Forestry 67:242-246.

Ziemer, R.R. 1981. Roots and the stability of forested slopes, p. 343-361. In Internat. Assoc. Hydrol. Sci., Washington, DC. Publ. 132.

3

Forest Vegetation Problems in the South

DEAN H. GJERSTAD
BRADFORD L. BARBER

INTRODUCTION

The South is rapidly becoming the nation's leading producer of forest products. Although the national demand for forest products is predicted to be only slightly greater in 2030 than in 1976, the South will need to supply a larger share of that demand (USDA Forest Service 1982). In 1976 the Pacific Northwest supplied 50% of the nation's softwood products, whereas the South provided 36%. By 2030 much of the commercial old growth timber in the Pacific Northwest will have been cut, and it is projected that the South will supply half of the nation's softwood requirement for both pulpwood and sawtimber. However, an unexpected downturn in the net annual growth of softwood timber in the southern United States has surfaced in recent forest surveys (Knight 1985). Reasons for this occurrence include a decline in the forested land base, increased mortality, inadequate regeneration, and a slowdown in individual tree diameter growth.

Forestry is important to the South's economy. This is demonstrated in Alabama where forestry exceeds all other industries in terms of value added (Flick 1981). When values for roundwood timber products are compared with those for agricultural crops, roundwood values are first in seven southern states and rank from second to fourth in five other states (Vasievich and Schroeder 1985).

The southern forest occupies approximately 188 million commercial acres from Virginia to eastern Texas and Oklahoma (USDA Forest Service 1982), with major subregions consisting of the Lower Coastal Plain (flatwoods), the Upper Coastal Plain, the Piedmont, the Appalachian Highlands, and the Interior Highlands (Wright and Bailey 1982). The main commercial species are the southern pines, and on a much smaller scale, hardwoods in plantations and natural stands predominantly found on bottomland sites (Table 3-1). The importance of pine to the region, as well as the nation, is demonstrated by loblolly pine accounting for 60% of the bare-root seedlings planted in the United States (Boyer and South 1984). In addition, the combined number of loblolly and slash pine bare-root seedlings is more than double all other species planted in the United States.

Because commercial forest acreage is predicted to remain fairly constant over the next 50 years, productivity must be increased if the South is going to meet a larger share of the nation's timber supply needs. One major factor in reducing productivity of pine forests is competition for light, water, and nutrients from low-quality hardwoods (Walstad 1976). Estimates indicate that hardwood encroachment is occurring each year on about 600,000 acres previously considered to be pine-type in the Southeast (Subcommittee on Weeds 1968). Herbaceous weeds are also a significant problem, especially during plantation establishment (Nelson et al. 1981, Knowe et al. 1985). Competition from both woody and herbaceous vegetation can severely limit available moisture, nutrients, and sunlight, resulting in considerable growth loss and up to 30% of a plantation's mortality (Schneider and Stransky 1966, Kozlowski 1969, Fitzgerald et al. 1973).

TABLE 3-1. Major Commercial Pine and Hardwood Species Grown in the Southern Forest Subregions

Scientific Name[a]	Common Name	Subregion[b]
Pines		
Pinus clausa	Sand	LCP
P. echinata	Shortleaf	All
P. elliottii var. *elliottii*	Slash	LCP
P. palustris	Longleaf	LCP, UCP
P. strobus	White	AH
P. taeda	Loblolly	LCP, UCP, P, AH
P. virginiana	Virginia	P, AH
Hardwoods		
Carya spp.	Hickories	All
Fraxinus pennsylvanica	Green ash	All
Liquidambar styraciflua	Sweetgum	All
Liriodendron tulipifera	Yellow-poplar	All
Platanus occidentalis	Sycamore	All
Populus deltoides var. *deltoides*	Cottonwood	UCP, P, IH
Quercus spp.	Oaks	All

[a]Species are arranged in alphabetical order according to scientific name. No priority of importance is intended by the order.
[b]Subregion code: LCP = Lower Coastal Plain, UCP = Upper Coastal Plain, P = Piedmont, AH = Appalachian Highlands, IH = Interior Highlands.

ORIGIN OF VEGETATION PROBLEMS

Few valid records exist of the original vegetation present when the first European settlers arrived. Early observations indicated the occurrence of both hardwood and pine groves (Bartram 1955). Hardwoods were likely dominant on many sites, as they were the climax species and grew well on the fertile soils present in the region at that time. Prior to European influence, wildfires started by lightning and those set by American Indians also facilitated development of large, relatively pure pine stands (Chapman 1932, Hebb and Clewell 1976). The Native American's most probable objectives for burning were to improve visibility for hunting and travel by reducing understory vegetation. Frequent fires not only reduced the understory vegetation but also restricted development of the more fire sensitive hardwoods. Following centuries of planned and accidental fires, much of the southern forest was parklike in appearance, with a pine overstory relatively free of hardwoods and understory shrubs. However, the early European settlers considered the pine forest an obstacle to their primary interest—agriculture. Not long after the arrival of settlers, the virgin stands were eliminated.

Brender (1952) provides an intriguing account of the European settlers' impact on Georgia's forests. As similar patterns of land use occurred throughout the South, this portrayal is representative of land development in much of the region. The frontier advance across Georgia began in 1773 and reached the Alabama border in 1826. Land was so rapidly cleared for farming that one county opened to settlement in 1812 contained only 200 acres of virgin forest by 1847. Following the Civil War, most suitable land was devoted to continuous cotton cultivation, which in a relatively short time resulted in severe erosion and deterioration of soil properties. Except for small, scattered areas, virtually none of the original forest remained. A slump in cotton prices during the 1880s resulted in abandonment of many fields by sharecroppers, which gave pine a chance to invade these areas. With World War I bringing an increased demand for cotton, second-growth pine was cut, as land was again cleared for farming (Brender 1952). A 1935 survey estimated that 87% of the Piedmont had at one time been in cultivation and some areas had been continuously in cotton for more than 60 years. The introduction of the boll weevil in 1920, along with the Great Depression, resulted in abandonment of many farms. Natural seeding from fence row and other adjacent pines, in addition to millions of seedlings planted by the Civilian Conservation Corps in the 1930s, was the beginning of the current southern forests that now cover approximately 65% of the land base.

Pines are currently more desirable than hardwoods as a timber resource on most southern upland sites. This, in part, is a result of a reduction in soil fertility that occurred from erosion of topsoil following improper agricultural practices. In general, hardwoods require more fertile sites than pines to produce quality timber. Hence on most upland sites, hardwoods are slow growers, produce low volumes, and often have defective, short, crooked boles (Karchesy and Koch 1979). Efforts to manage for hardwood production on southern pine sites are further complicated by the wide variety of species encountered, each with different silvical characteristics, wood properties, and commercial uses.

PHYSIOGRAPHIC SUBREGIONS AND VEGETATION

The southern pine region is bounded by Virginia to North Florida on the Atlantic Coast, Kentucky to the north, and eastern Texas and southeastern Oklahoma to the west (Figure 3-1). Topography of the Coastal Plains is generally flat or gently rolling. However, portions of the Upper Coastal Plain and Piedmont are hilly, whereas the Highlands are distinctly hilly or mountainous. Plentiful rainfall, moderate to warm temperatures, and a long growing season provide excellent conditions for tree growth. Precipitation ranges from 45 in. annually in eastern Texas, southeastern Oklahoma, Virginia, and much of South Carolina to more than 60 in. for the Gulf Coast of Louisiana, Mississippi, and Alabama. The frost-free growing season ranges from 180 days in the northern portion of the region to 300 days on the Gulf Coast.

Major physiographic subregions include the Lower Coastal Plain, Upper Coastal Plain, Piedmont, Appalachian Highlands, and Interior High-

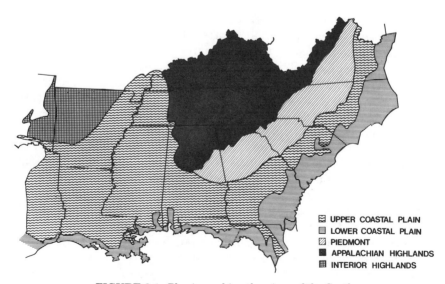

UPPER COASTAL PLAIN
LOWER COASTAL PLAIN
PIEDMONT
APPALACHIAN HIGHLANDS
INTERIOR HIGHLANDS

FIGURE 3-1. Physiographic subregions of the South.

lands. The Appalachian and Interior highlands contain several subdivisions that have been combined. Because of better conditions (e.g., climate, relatively fertile forest soils, and level terrain), the Coastal Plain subregions are the most productive areas. The future of forestry is assured in this region by rapid growth resulting from a warm, humid climate and level terrain leading to easy logging and log transport.

Lower Coastal Plain

The Lower Coastal Plain subregion occupies the area along portions of the Atlantic and Gulf Coast, including the flatwoods and northern Florida (Figure 3-1). The entire region is underlain by limestone, with a sandy soil mantle of variable thickness (Wright and Bailey 1982). Soils in the Upper and Lower Coastal plains have developed from marine sands and clays (Pearson and Ensminger 1957). Upland soils generally have light gray to red sandy surfaces, are 5 to 10 in. deep, and are underlain by yellow-red, friable, sandy clay subsoils. Drainage is poor in the flatwoods and good on upland sites, pH values are approximately 5.0, and organic matter content and nutrient levels are low.

The flatwoods of Florida and parts of the Gulf and Atlantic coasts contain what is generally known as the longleaf-slash pine type. Longleaf pine is drought tolerant and occupies upland sandy sites with good to excessive drainage (Chapman 1944, Fowells 1965). In contrast, slash pine grows best on wet sites that may be seasonally flooded (Chapman 1944, Shoulders 1976). Many natural longleaf and slash pine sites are now being artificially regenerated to loblolly pine. The hardwood and shrub component contains numerous evergreen and wax-leaved species including oaks, magnolias, sweetgum, hollies, red maple, yellow-poplar, white ash, and hickories (Table 3-2) (Garren 1943, Monk 1965, Wright and Bailey 1982).

Pocosin swamps, characterized by poor drainage and fluctuating water tables, are found on the lower plains of North Carolina and South Carolina (Wright and Bailey 1982). The most abundant woody species include southern wax myrtle, gallberry, and pond pine (Garren 1943). These sites are inherently low in pine productivity; however, with proper management (e.g., drainage, fertilization, and vegetation management), they can be among the most productive sites in the region.

Upper Coastal Plain

The Upper Coastal Plain subregion is the major southern pine growing region, extending from Virginia south to Florida, west to eastern Texas, and as far north as western Kentucky (Figure 3-1). Topography is rolling, and in some places, even hilly.

Before the arrival of Europeans, frequent fire allowed longleaf pine to

TABLE 3-2. Principal Species of Competing Vegetation on Commercial Forest Land in the Southern Pine Region

Scientific Name[a]	Common Name	Subregion[b]	Primary Means by Which Competing Plants Originate or Develop[c]
Trees			
Acer rubrum	Red maple	All	RS, S, IS
Aralia spinosa	Devils-walkingstick	UC, IH	S
Carya glabra	Pignut hickory	UC, P, AH, IH	RS, S, BS
C. pallida	Sand hickory	UC, AH	RS, S, BS
C. ovata	Shagbark hickory	UC, P, AH, IH	RS, S, BS
C. texana	Black hickory	IH	RS, S, BS
C. tomentosa	Mockernut hickory	UC, AH, IH	RS, S, BS
Celtis laevigata	Sugarberry	UC, P	S, BS, IS
C. occidentalis	Hackberry	UC	S, BS, IS
Cercis canadensis	Eastern redbud	UC, P, AH, IH	S, BS
Cornus florida	Flowering dogwood	All	S, BS, IS
Crataegus spp.	Hawthorn	UC, P, AH, IH	S
Diospyros virginiana	Common persimmon	UC, P, AH, IH	RS, S, BS, IS
Fagus grandifolia	American beech	IH, P	RS, S, BS
Fraxinus americana	White ash	AH	RS, S, IS
F. pennsylvanica	Green ash	P, IH, AH	RS, S, IS
Liquidambar styraciflua	Sweetgum	All	RS, S, IS
Liriodendron tulipifera	Yellow-poplar	UC, P, AH	RS, S, IS
Morus spp.	Mulberry	UC	S, IS
Magnolia grandiflora	Southern magnolia	LC, UC	S
M. virginiana	Sweetbay magnolia	LC, UC	S
Nyssa sylvatica	Black tupelo (blackgum)	All	RS, S, BS, IS

Scientific name	Common name	Codes	
Oxydendrum arboreum	Sourwood	UC, P, AH	S, IS
Prunus serotina	Black cherry	UC, P, AH, IH	RS, S, BS, IS
Quercus alba	White oak	UC, P, AH, IH	RS, S
Q. coccinea	Scarlet oak	P, AH, IH	RS, S
Q. falcata	Southern red oak	All	RS, S
Q. incana	Bluejack oak	LC, UC	RS, S
Q. laevis	Turkey oak	LC, UC	RS, S
Q. laurifolia	Laurel oak	LC, UC	RS, S
Q. lyrata	Overcup oak	LC, UC	RS, S
Q. marilandica	Blackjack oak	LC, UC, IH	RS, S
Q. nigra	Water oak	All	RS, S
Q. phellos	Willow oak	UC, P, AH, IH	RS, S
Q. prinus	Chestnut oak	P, AH	RS, S
Q. stellata	Post oak	All	RS, S
Q. velutina	Black oak	P, AH, IH	RS, S
Q. virginiana	Live oak	LC	RS, S
Rhus copallina	Winged (shining) sumac	UC, P, AH, IH	S, BS, IS
R. glabra	Smooth sumac	UC, P, AH, IH	S, BS, IS
R. typhina	Staghorn sumac	UC	S, BS, IS
Robinia pseudoacacia	Black locust	UC	S, BS
Sabal palmetto	Cabbage palmetto	LC	S, BS
Salix spp.	Willow	P, AH	S, IS
Sassafras albidum	Sassafras	UC, P, AH, IH	S, IS
Tilia heterophylla	White basswood	AH	RS, S
Ulmus alata	Winged elm	UC, P, AH, IH	RS, S, IS
U. rubra	Slippery elm	P, AH, IH	RS, S, IS

61

TABLE 3-2. Principal Species of Competing Vegetation on Commercial Forest Land in the Southern Pine Region (*Continued*)

Scientific Name[a]	Common Name	Subregion[b]	Primary Means by Which Competing Plants Originate or Develop[c]
Shrubs			
Baccharis halimifolia	Eastern baccharis	LC, UC	S
Callicarpa americana	American beautyberry	All	S, BS, IS
Carpinus caroliniana	American hornbeam	AH, IH	S
Cyrilla racemiflora	Swamp cyrilla (titi)	LC	S, BS
Hamamelis virginiana	Witch-hazel	UC	S, IS
Ilex spp.	Holly	LC, UC	S, BS, IS
I. glabra	Low gallberry	LC	S, BS, IS
I. vomitoria	Yaupon	LC, UC	S, BS, IS
Kalmia latifolia	Mountain-laurel	AH	S
Ligustrum spp.	Privet	UC, P, AH, IH	S
Lyonia spp.	Lyonia	All	S
Myrica cerifera	Southern bayberry (waxmyrtle)	LC, UC	S, BS, IS
Rhododendron maximum	Rosebay rhododendron	AH	S
Vaccinium spp.	Blueberry	All	S, BS, IS
Viburnum spp.	Viburnum	All	S
Vines			
Ampelopsis arborea	Peppervine	All	S, IS
Campsis radicans	Trumpetcreeper	All	S, IS
Ipomoea spp.	Morningglory	All	S, IS
Lonicera japonica	Japanese honeysuckle	All	S, IS
Rubus spp.	Blackberry, dewberry	All	S, IS
Smilax spp.	Greenbriar	All	S, IS
Pueraria lobata	Kudzu	UC, P	S, IS
Rhus radicans	Poison-ivy	All	S, IS

Herbs

Amaranthus spp.	Pigweed	P, IH, UC	IS
Ambrosia artemisifolia	Common ragweed	All	IS
A. trifida	Giant ragweed	UC, P	IS
Andropogon spp.	Bluestems (broomsedge)	All	S, IS
Arundinaria spp.	Switchcane	LC	S, IS
Aster spp.	Aster	All	S, IS
Bromus spp.	Brome	All	S, IS
Carex spp. and *Cyperus* spp.	Sedge	LC, UC, IH	S, IS
Cassia fasciculata	Partridgepea	All	IS
C. obtusifolia	Sicklepod	UC	IS
Chenopodium spp.	Lambsquarters	UC, P, AH, IH	IS
Croton capitatus	Woolly croton	UC	IS
Cynodon dactylon	Bermudagrass	UC	S, IS
Cyperus spp.	Nutsedge	All	S, IS
Conyza canadensis	Horseweed	All	IS
Digitaria spp.	Crabgrass	UC, P, AH	IS
Diodia teres	Poorjoe	LC, UC	IS
Epilobium angustifolium	Fireweed	All	S, IS
Eragrostis spp.	Lovegrass	LC, UC	S, IS
Eupatorium spp.	Thoroughwort	All	S, IS
E. capillifolium	Dogfennel	LC, UC, P	IS
Euphorbia spp.	Spurge	UC, P, AH, IH	S, IS
Festuca spp.	Fescue	P, AH	S, IS
Galium spp.	Bedstraw	LC	S, IS
Lespedeza spp.	Lespedeza	UC, P, AH, IH	S, IS
Oxalis spp.	Woodsorrel	UC, P, AH, IH	S, IS
Panicum spp.	Panic grasses	All	S, IS
Paspalum spp.	Paspalum	LC, UC	S, IS

TABLE 3-2. Principal Species of Competing Vegetation on Commercial Forest Land in the Southern Pine Region (*Continued*)

Scientific Name[a]	Common Name	Subregion[b]	Primary Means by Which Competing Plants Originate or Develop[c]
Phytolacca americana	Common pokeweed	All	S, IS
Polygonum spp.	Smartweed	UC, P, IH, AH	S, IS
Pteridium aquilinum	Brackenfern	LC, UC, IH	S
Rhexia spp.	Meadow-beauty	All	S, IS
Richardia scabra	Florida pusley	All	IS
Rumex spp.	Dock	UC, P, AH, IH	S, IS
Sambucus canadensis	American elder	UC, P, AH, IH	S, IS
Solidago spp.	Goldenrod	All	S, IS
Sorghum halepense	Johnsongrass	UC, AH, IH	S, IS
Vicia spp.	Vetch	All	S, IS
Xanthium spp.	Cocklebur	LC, UC, P, AH	IS

[a]Within categories, species are arranged in alphabetical order according to scientific name. No priority of importance is intended by the order.

[b]Subregion code: LCP = Lower Coastal Plain, UCP = Upper Coastal Plain, P = Piedmont, AH = Appalachian Highlands, IH = Interior Highlands.

[c]Although various plant species may have several ways of capturing or colonizing forest sites, the classification used in this table only pertains to the *principal* means whereby they become a *threat* to conifer regeneration. It does not necessarily include all methods of propagation and establishment for any given species. Code is as follows:

RS = Competing plants that originate from residual boles, stems, and branches and are capable of surviving overstory removal and other physical disturbances and quickly dominating a site shortly thereafter.

S = Sprouting plants that originate from stumps, persistent rootstocks, rhizomes, or stolons that quickly generate new shoots or stems when existing ones are cut or damaged.

BS = Plants that arise from buried seed and are adapted to catastrophic disturbance such as fire or scarification which stimulates germination.

IS = Plants that arise from introduced seed disseminated by wind currents or animals.

dominate much of the area. Loblolly and shortleaf pine thrive where fires occur about every 10 years (Garren 1943, Chapman 1944). Loblolly pine grows best on fine-textured soils (Coile 1940) with poor surface drainage, a deep surface layer, and a firm subsoil (Fowells 1965, Harlow and Harrar 1968). Shortleaf pine grows on coarse-textured and drier soils that are neither highly acidic nor strongly basic. Shortleaf's best development occurs in the Piedmont subregion on sites with friable subsoils (Fowells 1965).

Climax vegetation for the Upper Coastal Plain is the oak-hickory association (Kuchler 1964), with the exception of bottomland hardwoods along river deltas and floodplains (Garren 1943). Species associated with subclimax stands of loblolly and shortleaf pine include Virginia pine, eastern redcedar, black oak, southern red oak, blackjack oak, post oak, chestnut oak, sweetgum, blackgum, mockernut hickory, ash, flowering dogwood, yellow-poplar, and red maple (Table 3-2) (Garren 1943). A mixture of hardwood species generally dominates the understory (Lewis and Harshbarger 1976). In addition, the numerous herbaceous species growing on these sites can exert severe competition for light, water, and nutrients to young pine trees (Fitzgerald et al. 1973, Nelson et al. 1981).

Piedmont

The Piedmont subregion consists of a strip between the Appalachian Mountains and the Atlantic Coastal Plain running through the middle of Virginia and North Carolina, western South Carolina, and northern Georgia to central Alabama (Figure 3-1). Soils, which have developed from igneous rocks, sandstones, and shale, were originally sandy loams and clay loams. However, extensive topsoil erosion has occurred in most areas because of past agricultural practices, leaving the clay subsoil exposed (Pearson and Ensminger 1957).

As oaks and pines dominate much of the Piedmont, the area is commonly referred to as the Oak-Pine Forest Region (Braun 1950). No virgin forests remain in the region as a result of past clearing practices. Successionally, oak and hickory are the dominant climax species. However, because frequent fires have allowed pine to remain prominent in the original forest, the name *Oak-Pine Forest* is appropriate.

Shortleaf and loblolly pine grow best in the Piedmont. Virginia pine and pitch pine can also occur, along with many of the same hardwood species noted for the Upper Coastal Plain subregion (Fowells 1965).

Appalachian Highlands

Major forested areas in this subregion include the Cumberland Plateau and Cumberland Mountains, the southern Appalachian ridges and valleys, and the Blue Ridge Mountains. The Cumberland Plateau is located in east central Tennessee and northeastern Alabama. Elevations range from 1000 ft in the valleys to 2000 ft on the ridgetops. The terrain is deeply dissected sandstone and shale plateaus with steep slopes separated by narrow, level valleys.

The southern Appalachian ridges and valleys located in eastern Kentucky and Tennessee, northwestern Georgia, and northeastern Alabama are approximately 50% forested, with elevations ranging from 600 to 3000 ft. The valleys are oriented from northeast to southwest and are underlain by limestone and shale. The steep ridges are underlain by sandstone and shale.

The natural forests of the Cumberland Plateau and Cumberland Mountains and the southern Appalachian ridges and valleys are composed primarily of mixed hardwood stands with a small component of Virginia, loblolly, and shortleaf pine (Table 3-2). Industrial forest companies are converting some mixed hardwood stands to loblolly pine plantations. Successful conversions require intensive mechanical or chemical site preparation methods to prepare planting spots; otherwise, hardwood competition in the subsequent stand will severely reduce pine survival and growth.

The Blue Ridge Mountains are located in northern Georgia, the western Carolinas, and western Virginia. The mountains rise to 6500 ft, with valley floors as low as 1000 ft elevation. The mountains have steep slopes with sharp crests and are dissected by steep, narrow valleys. More hardwood species are found in this area than anywhere in the eastern United States, as both southern and northern hardwood species occur in the Blue Ridge Mountains. Eastern white pine, Fraser fir, and red spruce are commonly found at higher elevations in the Carolinas and Virginia. Although some eastern white pine in North Carolina as well as loblolly pine in North Georgia are artificially regenerated, forestry mainly consists of extensive management of natural hardwood stands.

Interior Highlands

This subregion is located in northwestern Arkansas and eastern Oklahoma. Major forested areas include the Ouachita Mountains and the Arkansas Valley and Ridge. The Ouachita Mountains are located in west central Arkansas and southeastern Oklahoma. The area is 80% forested, with elevations ranging from 300 to 2700 ft. The steep mountains are underlain by folded and faulted shales, slates, quartzites, sandstones, and novaculite. The Arkansas Valley and Ridge border the Ouachitas to the north. The area is 50% forested, with elevational extremes of 300 to 2800 ft. Underlying materials are slightly folded to level beds of sandstone and shales. Ridge slopes are steep with narrow crests. Valleys are broad and smooth.

The Interior Highlands are part of the oak-hickory forest region. However, as shortleaf pine is abundant, the Ouachita Mountains and the Arkansas Valley and Ridge are often mapped as oak-pine (Table 3-2) (Braun 1950). The rugged terrain makes mechanical operations difficult; hence the conversion of low-grade pine-hardwood stands to pine is somewhat difficult. Nevertheless, with the use of intensive mechanical and chemical site preparation methods, loblolly pine plantation establishment is extending the species range into the southern portion of this subregion.

EXTENT OF VEGETATION PROBLEMS

Low-quality hardwoods now dominate many areas previously occupied by pine. Georgia forest surveys conducted in 1972 and 1982 indicate trends in pine and hardwood stocking that are considered typical for other southeastern states as well (Sheffield and Knight 1984). These surveys showed that the area classified as pine forest type dropped from 12.4 to 11.4 million acres, and they also detected a sharp decline in the number of pine trees in smaller diameter classes. Between 1972 and 1982, some 3.2 million acres of pine stands were harvested, whereas only 1.0 million acres were artificially regenerated to pine. Of the remaining 2.2 million acres, only 41% is now considered pine type.

Without fire, the Lower Coastal Plain would be dominated by the southern mixed hardwood forest (Oosting 1956, Monk 1965, Hebb and Clewell 1976), whereas oak-hickory-pine would be the primary type on the Upper Coastal Plain and Piedmont (Kuchler 1964). In both areas, pine would comprise only a small portion of the climax vegetation (Wright and Bailey 1982). As late as the 1930s, some 38 million forest acres burned each year (White 1984). However, through fire control and preventive measures, annual acreage affected by wildfires has now been reduced to approximately 3 million acres (USDA, Cooperative Fire Protection 1982). Wildfires are particularly devastating to young pine stands (Cooper 1965, Langdon 1971). As pines develop thicker bark and reach 20 ft tall, carefully prescribed burns can be used to top-kill small hardwoods while causing negligible pine injury.

Natural succession, aided by the reduction in fire frequency and increased pine harvesting, favors hardwood development (Wahlenberg 1949). Barrett and Downs (1943) summarized the successional pattern in the Piedmont as follows: (1) the proportion of climax species (oaks and hickories) in hardwood understories increases with the age of the pine overstory; and (2) the number of understory climax hardwoods also increases with the age of the pine stand. Neither the density nor the site index of the pine stand has significant influence upon these trends. This same successional trend is dramatically demonstrated in an uneven-aged loblolly-shortleaf pine stand in southern Arkansas where 12 consecutive annual mechanical and chemical treatments only temporarily removed the hardwoods (Cain and Yaussy 1983). Eighteen years after treatments ended, more hardwood and woody shrubs were present than were counted prior to the initial treatment.

A critical phase in southern pine management occurs following harvest cuts because most hardwoods have the ability to sprout prolifically from stumps and roots. The extensively established hardwood root systems have the capacity to produce vigorous, rapidly growing sprouts that overtop pine seedlings. If residual hardwoods are not controlled in these situations, pine stocking and growth will be greatly reduced.

Pine growth response is greatest when hardwood control is accomplished either during the site preparation phase or no more than 2 years after pine establishment. A somewhat reduced but significant pine growth response occurs when hardwood competition is reduced later in the rotation. A common misconception is that hardwoods are most competitive when pines are young and that pines will eventually over-top and suppress the hardwoods. Glover and Dickens (1985) found that percentage of hardwood basal area did not vary with stand age. That is, if a stand had 40% of hardwood basal area at age 10, it would still have 40% of hardwood basal area at age 25. They concluded that although pines grow faster than hardwoods, pine mortality and hardwood ingrowth tend to maintain a constant proportion. Burkhart and Sprinz (1984) developed a yield model incorporating the concept of a constant hardwood basal area over time. When using the model to generate yield tables at age 30 for 800 trees/acre planted on site index$_{25}$ 60 ft land, a 40% basal area in hardwood decreased the number of pine trees, basal area, and sawlog volume by 36, 64, and 81%, respectively, below those predicted when no hardwoods were present.

Although better growth response is obtained when hardwoods are controlled at or prior to stand establishment, releasing young pine stands from hardwood competition also yields dramatic growth responses when compared with unreleased stands. Balmer et al. (1978) examined 20-year growth and yield effects of controlling hardwoods and pine stocking in young loblolly stands. Pine yields doubled when large hardwoods were controlled and tripled when precommercial thinning and control of small hardwoods were added. Michael (1980) found volumes increased 40% 20 years after releasing grass-stage longleaf pine seedlings. Boyer (1985) reported even more dramatic results from a 30-year-old longleaf pine release study. At age 31, releasing pine at a young age from overtopping hardwoods increased total volume yields by more than 650%. Clason (1978) reported a 45% volume growth increase 5 years after removing hardwood vegetation from a 7-year-old natural loblolly pine stand in Louisiana. Ten years following hardwood removal, total merchantable volume in the treated plots was about 30% greater than in the control

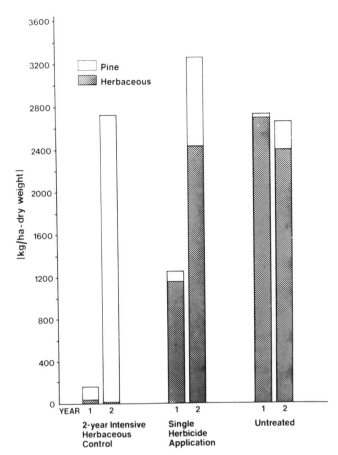

FIGURE 3-2. Total aboveground standing biomass production 1 and 2 years after planting loblolly pine seedlings and (1) 2 years of intensive herbaceous weed control; (2) partial herbaceous weed control resulting from a single herbicide treatment at the beginning of the first year; and (3) no treatment. Hardwoods were eradicated from all plots.

plots; sawtimber volumes were measured a year later and indicated almost a twofold increase for treated plots versus controls (Clason 1984).

Historically, foresters have not considered herbaceous competition as a major growth or survival impediment when regenerating pine. However, recent studies on Upper and Lower Coastal Plain sites indicate that rapid initial growth and crown closure of pines occur when herbaceous weeds are eliminated (Gjerstad 1981, Nelson et al. 1981, Knowe et al. 1985). Although the herbaceous problem is most obvious in the Lower Coastal Plain where dense stands of panicum grasses occupy pine plantations following intensive mechanical site preparation (Swindel et al. 1983), pine growth response can be expected throughout the region when

FIGURE 3-3. Comparison of 3-year-old loblolly pine development: (A) without herbaceous weed control; and (B) with 2 yr of intensive herbaceous weed control near Auburn, AL. Height growth for each year is indicated by the standard.

the herbaceous component is eliminated. Zutter et al. (1986) measured biomass production following 2 years of intensive herbaceous weed control, partial herbaceous weed control, and no control. Greatest first-year biomass production was found on the untreated area, with herbaceous plants comprising more than 98% of the total biomass (Figure 3-2). In contrast, the intensive herbaceous weed control plots had produced only 5% of the total biomass found on the untreated area. By the second year, total biomass production was about equal among treatments; however, 99% of the biomass on the intensive herbaceous weed control plots was pine, whereas only 10% was pine on the untreated plots (Figure 3-3).

Increased availability of soil water is the primary reason pines or any remaining vegetation grow much faster following herbaceous weed control. Because water loss by evaporation exceeds gains from precipitation during the growing season (April to October) (Figure 3-4), reducing evapotranspiration by eliminating competing vegetation will result in greater soil water availability to pines. Nelson et al. (1981) found a direct effect of weed competition for soil water availability, as reflected by plant water stress readings (Figure 3-5). Trees on weeded plots had predawn moisture stress levels of 4 to 5 bars, whereas pines in the nonweeded areas increased to 15 bars within 12 days following a 2-in. rainfall. Although water stress levels of 4 to 5 bars can inhibit height growth, stress levels of 14 bars have been shown to induce seedling dormancy (Cannell et al. 1978).

SUMMARY

Pine is the desired commercial species in the South because growth rates are more rapid than upland hardwoods and the wood is generally of

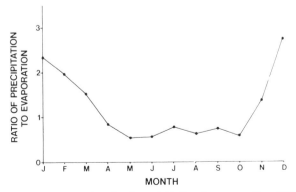

FIGURE 3-4. Average seasonal ratio of precipitation to evaporation (1957-1977) for Auburn, AL. (*Source:* Compiled from U.S. Dept. of Commerce/NOAA 1983)

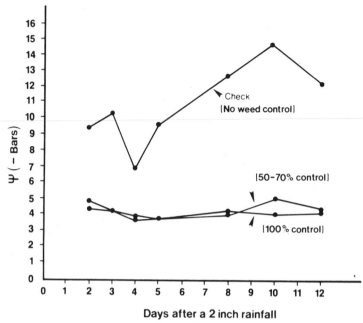

FIGURE 3-5. Predawn xylem pressure potentials of loblolly pine seedlings established for 3 mo with various levels of weed control. (*Source:* From Nelson et al. 1981. Impacts of herbaceous weeds in young loblolly pine plantations. South. J. Appl. Forestry 5:153-158. First published in the *Southern Journal of Applied Forestry*, August 1981. Copyright © by the Society of American Foresters)

greater value. However, foresters must implement proper cultural techniques if vigorous pine stands are to become established and maintain a competitive advantage over hardwoods.

Various surveys have indicated that from 40 to 70% of managed forest lands in the South have weed problems (Nelson 1957, Fitzgerald et al. 1973). These estimates are based on general impressions of experienced foresters. Unfortunately, these foresters did not have weed-free stands for comparison. Thus these estimates are probably conservative. In recent years numerous studies have been initiated by forest researchers that include weed-free treatments. Although most of these studies are less than 10 years old, twofold or greater differences in height and diameter are frequently observed (Gjerstad 1981, Nelson et al. 1981). Glover and Dickens (1985) remeasured several studies that included total competition control during the first and second seasons following planting. By age 10, the treated plots were approximately 3 years ahead in total volume production. Indications are that all but very poorly drained sites in the South will respond to competition control. On most sites, herbaceous species are most important in restricting pine growth and development in plantations up to 4 years old, with hardwood and shrub competition being most important after age 5. The dramatic growth responses shown in various studies suggest that most forest lands have a weed problem and that appropriate weed control technology must be developed and implemented if future demand for softwood forest products is to be met.

REFERENCES

Balmer, W.E., K.A. Utz, and O.G. Langdon. 1978. Financial returns from cultural work in natural loblolly pine stands. South. J. Appl. Forestry 2:111-117.

Barrett, L.I. and A.A. Downs. 1943. Hardwood invasion in pine forests of the Piedmont Plateau. J. Agr. Res. 67:111-128.

Bartram, W. 1955. Travels of William Bartram. Van Doren, M. (ed.) Dover Publication, Inc. New York, NY. 414 p.

Boyer, J.N. and D.B. South. 1984. Forest nursery practices in the South. South. J. Appl. Forestry 8:67-75.

Boyer, W.D. 1985. Timing of longleaf pine seedling release from overtopping hardwoods: a look 30 years later. South. J. Appl. Forestry 9:114-116.

Braun, E.L. 1950. Deciduous forests of eastern North America. The Blakiston Company. Philadelphia, PA. 596 p.

Brender, E.V. 1952. From forest to farm to forest again. Amer. Forests 58:24, 25, 40, 41, 43.

Burkhart, H.E. and P.T. Sprinz. 1984. A model for assessing hardwood competition effects on yields of loblolly pine plantations. School of Forestry and Wildlife Resources, Virginia Polytechnic Institute and State Univ., Blacksburg, VA. FWS-3-84. 55 p.

Cain, M.D. and D.A. Yaussy. 1983. Reinvasion of hardwoods following eradication in an uneven-aged pine stand. USDA Forest Service, Southern Forest Experiment Station, New Orleans, LA. Res. Pap. SO-188. 8 p.

Cannell, M.G.R., F.E. Bridgewater, and M.S. Greenwood. 1978. Seedling growth rates, water stress response, and root-shoot relationships related to eight year volumes among families of *Pinus taeda* L. Silvae Genetica 27:237-248.

Chapman, H.H. 1932. Is the longleaf type a climax? Ecology 13:328-334.

Chapman, H.H. 1944. Fire and pines. Amer. Forests 50:62-64, 91-93.

Clason, T.R. 1978. Removal of hardwood vegetation increases growth and yield of a young loblolly pine stand. South. J. Appl. Forestry 2:96-97.

Clason, T.R. 1984. Hardwood eradication improves productivity of thinned loblolly pine stands. South. J. Appl. Forestry 8:194-197.

Coile, T.S. 1940. Soil changes associated with loblolly pine succession on abandoned agricultural land of the Piedmont Plateau. School of Forestry, Duke Univ., Durham, NC. Bull. 5:1-85.

Cooper, R.W. 1965. Prescribed burning and control of fire, p. 131-137. *In* Wahlenberg, W.G. (ed.) A guide to loblolly and slash pine plantation management in southeastern U.S.A. Georgia Forest Res. Council Rep. 14. 360 p.

Fitzgerald, C.H., F.A. Peevy, and D.E. Fender. 1973. Rehabilitation of forest land—the southern region. J. Forestry 71:148-153.

Flick, W.A. 1981. Forestry's economic contribution to Alabama. Highlights of Agricultural Research, Auburn University, Auburn, AL. 28(2):9.

Fowells, H.A. (comp.) 1965. Silvics of forest trees of the United States. USDA Forest Service, Washington, DC. Agr. Hbk. 271. 762 p.

Garren, K.H. 1943. Effects of fire on vegetation of the southeastern United States. Bot. Rev. 9:617-654.

Gjerstad, D.H. 1981. Chemical weed control in southern forests, p. 116-120. *In* Holt, H.A. and B.C. Fischer (eds.) Weed Control in Forest Management. Proc., 1981 John S. Wright Forestry Conference. Purdue Univ., West Lafayette, IN. 305 p.

Glover, G.R. and D.F. Dickens 1985. Impact of chemical vegetation control on yield of the southern pines. Georgia Forestry Commission, Research Div., Macon, GA. Forest Res. Pap. 59. 14 p.

Harlow, W.M. and E.S. Harrar. 1968. Textbook of dendrology. 5th ed. McGraw-Hill Book Co., Inc., New York, NY. 512 p.

Hebb, E.A. and A.F. Clewell. 1976. A remnant stand of old-growth slash pine in the Florida Panhandle. Bull. Torrey Bot. Club 103:1-9.

Karchesy, J. and P. Koch. 1979. Energy production from hardwoods growing on southern pine sites. USDA Forest Service, Southern Forest Experiment Station, New Orleans, LA. Gen. Tech. Rep. SO-24. 59 p.

Knight, H.A. 1985. Recent survey findings and growth rates in the Southeast, p. 44-52. *In* Proc., 1985 Southern Forest Economics Workshop, Athens, GA. 212 p.

Knowe, S.A., L.R. Nelson, D.H. Gjerstad, B.R. Zutter, G.R. Glover, P.J. Minogue, and J.H. Dukes, Jr. 1985. Four-year growth and development of planted loblolly pine on sites with competition control. South. J. Appl. Forestry 9:11-15.

Kozlowski, T.T. 1969. Soil water and tree growth, p. 30-37. *In* Proc., 17th Annu. Louisiana State Univ. Forestry Symp., Baton Rouge, LA. 203 p.

Kuchler, A.W. 1964. Potential natural vegetation of the conterminous United States. Manual to accompany the map. Amer. Geogr. Soc. Spec. Pub. 36. (With map, rev. ed., 1965, 1966).

Langdon, O.G. 1971. Effects of prescribed burning on timber species in the southeastern Coastal Plain, p. 34-44. *In* Proc., Prescribed Burning Symp. USDA Forest Service, Southeastern Forest Experiment Station, Asheville, NC. 160 p.

Lewis, C.E. and T.J. Harshbarger. 1976. Shrub and herbaceous vegetation after 20 years of prescribed burning in the South Carolina Coastal Plain. J. Range Manage. 29:13-18.

Michael, J.L. 1980. Long-term impact of aerial application of 2,4,5-T to longleaf pine (*Pinus palustris*). Weed Sci. 28:255-257.

Monk, C.D. 1965. Southern mixed hardwood forest of northcentral Florida. Ecol. Monogr. 35:335-354.

Nelson, L.R., R.C. Pedersen, L.L. Autry, S. Dudley, and J.D. Walstad. 1981. Impacts of herbaceous weeds in young loblolly pine plantations. South. J. Appl. Forestry 5:153-158.

Nelson, T.C. 1957. The original forests of the Georgia Piedmont. Ecology 38:390-397.

Oosting, H.J. 1956. The study of plant communities. An introduction to plant ecology. 2nd ed. W.H. Freeman and Co., San Francisco, CA. 440 p.

Pearson, R.W. and L.E. Ensminger. 1957. Southeastern uplands, p. 579-594. *In* Soil: The Yearbook of Agriculture. U.S. Dept. Agr., Washington, DC. 784 p.

Schneider, G. and J.J. Stransky. 1966. Soil moisture and soil temperature under a post oak-shortleaf pine stand. School of Forestry, Stephen F. Austin College, Nacogdoches, TX. Forestry Bull. 8. 24 p.

Sheffield, R.M. and H.A. Knight. 1984. Georgia's Forests. USDA Forest Service, Southeastern Forest Experiment Station, Asheville, NC. Resour. Bull. SE-73. 92 p.

Shoulders, E. 1976. Site characteristics influence relative performance of loblolly and slash pine. USDA Forest Service, Southern Forest Experiment Station, New Orleans, LA. Res. Pap. SO-115. 16 p.

Subcommittee on Weeds. 1968. Weed control. Principles of plant and animal pest control. Vol. 2. Committee on Plant and Animal Pests, Agr. Board, Nat. Res. Counc., Nat. Acad. Sci., Washington, DC. 471 p.

Swindel, B.F., W.R. Marion, L.D. Harris, L.A. Morris, W.L. Pritchett, L.F. Conde, H. Riekerk, and E.T. Sullivan. 1983. Multi-resource effects of harvest, site preparation, and planting in pine flatwoods. South. J. Appl. Forestry 7:6-15.

USDA, Cooperative Fire Protection. 1982. Wildfire statistics. USDA Forest Service, State and Private Forestry, Washington, DC. 51 p.

USDA Forest Service. 1982. Projected trends in domestic timber resources, p. 147-199. *In* An analysis of the timber situation in the United States, 1952-2030. USDA Forest Service, Washington, DC. Forest Resour. Rep. 23. 499 p.

U.S. Dept. of Commerce/NOAA. 1983. 1982 Auburn University micrometeorological data. Agr. Weather Series 22. Auburn Univ., AL. 60 p.

Vasievich, J.M. and P.D. Schroeder. 1985. Southern timber study: economic opportunities for intensive forest management. USDA Forest Service, Southeastern Forest Experiment Station, Research Triangle Park, NC. Preliminary Rep. 100 p.

Wahlenberg, W.G. 1949. Forest succession in the southern Piedmont region. J. Forestry 47:713-715.

Walstad, J.D. 1976. Weed control for better southern pine management. Southern Forestry Research Center, Weyerhaeuser Company, Hot Springs, AR. Weyerhaeuser Forestry Pap. 15. 44 p.

White, Z.W. 1984. Loblolly pine—with emphasis on its history, p. 3-16. *In* Karr, B.L., J.B. Baker, and T. Monaghan (eds.) Proc., Sympos. on the Loblolly Pine Ecosystem (West Region). Mississippi State Univ., MS.

Wright, H.A. and A.W. Bailey. 1982. Southeastern forests, p. 363-387. *In* Fire Ecology: United States and Southern Canada. John Wiley and Sons, Inc., New York, NY. 501 p.

Zutter, B.R., G.R. Glover, and D.H. Gjerstad. 1986. Effects of herbaceous weed control using herbicides on a loblolly pine plantation. Manuscript on file, Alabama Agr. Exper. Sta. J. Series 9-85867. 26 p.

4

Forest Vegetation Problems in the Northeast and Lake States/Provinces

MICHAEL NEWTON
MAXWELL L. McCORMACK, JR.
ROBERT L. SAJDAK
JOHN D. WALSTAD

INTRODUCTION

For purposes of this chapter, the Northeast and Lake states/provinces include the forested areas of New England, New York, Michigan, Wisconsin, Minnesota, and the adjacent Canadian provinces (Figure 4-1). Within the region, it is largely the glaciated northern portion that involves conifer production. Although there are exceptions, the coniferous zone is characterized by shallow, coarse-textured, and acidic soils and by relatively cool, moist summers and cold winters in contrast to the central hardwood zone further south. Annual precipitation averages 24 to 52 in. and is evenly distributed throughout the year, except for the Lake States that tend to have a higher proportion in the summer months, frequently in the form of thunderstorms.

Principal conifer species of commercial value in the Northeast and Lake states/provinces are listed in Table 4-1. Noncommercial or low-value species frequently found competing with conifers are listed in Table 4-2. Additional climatic, physiographic, and botanical information about this region can be found in the works of Loucks (1962), Rowe (1972), Merz (1978), Barrett (1980a), Hansen (1980), and Kingsley (1985).

Timber Types

The greatest expanse of conifer type occurs in the spruce-fir forested areas of the Maritime provinces, central and northern Ontario and Quebec,

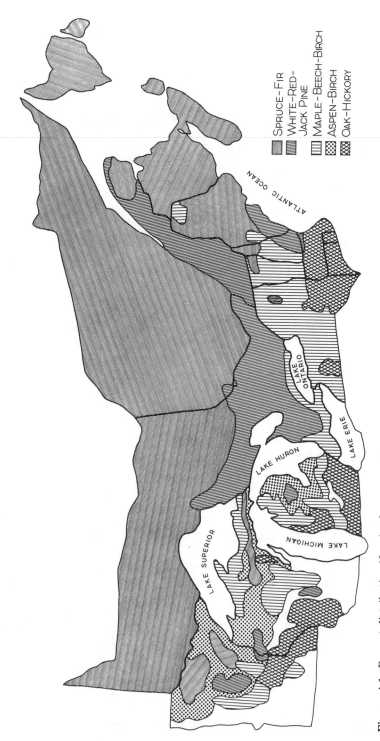

Figure 4-1. Present distribution if major forest types in the Northeast and Lake states/ provinces of the United States and Canada. (*Source:* Adapted from Rowe 1972, Merz 1978, Barrett 1980b, and Kingsley 1985)

SPRUCE-FIR
WHITE-RED-
JACK PINE
MAPLE-BEECH-BIRCH
ASPEN-BIRCH
OAK-HICKORY

ATLANTIC OCEAN

LAKE ONTARIO

LAKE ERIE

LAKE HURON

LAKE MICHIGAN

LAKE SUPERIOR

TABLE   4-1. Major Commercial Conifer Species in the Northeast and Lake States/Provinces

Scientific Name[a]	Common Name
Abies balsamea	Balsam fir
Larix laricina	Eastern larch (tamarack)
Picea glauca	White spruce
P. mariana	Black spruce
P. rubens	Red spruce
Pinus banksiana	Jack pine
P. resinosa	Red pine
P. strobus	Eastern white pine
Thuja occidentalis	Northern (eastern) white-cedar
Tsuga canadensis	Eastern hemlock

[a]Species are arranged in alphabetical order according to scientific name. No priority of importance is intended by the order.

northern Maine, New Hampshire and Vermont, the Adirondack Mountains of New York, and northern portions of the Lake states (Figure 4-1). Even in these areas, however, hardwoods are often prevalent. For example, extensive stands of aspen, birch, and other hardwoods occur in the central and northern portions of Ontario, Quebec, New Hampshire, Vermont, and the Lake states.

South of the spruce-fir forest type is a discontinuous band of red, white, and jack pines interrupted by mixed hardwood stands of maple, birch, beech, oak, and other hardwoods. Jack pine predominates in the northern portion of this band, whereas white pine is more common near the southern extremity. Eastern hemlock, tamarack, and northern white-cedar are other conifers frequently found within this zone. Southward is the beginning of the oak-hickory forests of the central United States, but pine plantations and natural conifer stands can be found from southern New York and Pennsylvania well down the chain of Appalachian Mountains.

Prominent among conifer stands in the northeastern United States are white pine and spruce occupations of abandoned fields that originated during times of economic recession and as settlers moved westward. For instance, Vermont was less than 40% forested a century ago but was 76% forested in 1973 (Kingsley 1977). New York, less than 25% forested in 1880, is now 61% forested, and this pattern is repeated elsewhere in the northeastern United States (Considine 1984). Many of the old fields were also colonized by heavy-seeded hardwoods and now contain a high proportion of poor-quality timber and low merchantable volume per acre.

The northern portions of Maine and the Canadian provinces, on the other hand, have never been cleared to any great extent except by logging and until recently there were few plantations. Where complete harvesting

TABLE 4-2. Principal Species of Competing Vegetation on Commercial Forest Land in the Northeast and Lake States/Provinces

Scientific Name[a]	Common Name	Primary Means by Which Competing Plants Originate or Develop[b]
Trees		
Acer rubrum	Red maple	RS, S, IS
A. saccharinum	Silver maple	RS, S, IS
A. saccharum	Sugar maple	RS, S, IS
Betula alleghaniensis	Yellow birch	S, IS
B. lenta	Sweet (black) birch	S, IS
B. papyrifera	Paper birch	S, IS
B. populifolia	Gray (wire) birch	S, IS
Fagus grandifolia	American beech	RS, S
Fraxinus americana	White ash	RS, S, IS
F. nigra	Black ash	RS, S, IS
Populus balsamifera	Balsam poplar	S, IS
P. grandidentata	Bigtooth aspen	S, IS
P. tremuloides	Quaking (trembling) aspen	S, IS
Prunus pensylvanica	Pin cherry	RS, S, BS, IS
P. serotina	Black cherry	RS, S, IS
Quercus rubra	Northern red oak	RS, S
Salix spp.	Willows	S, IS
Tilia americana	American basswood	RS, S
Shrubs		
Acer pensylvanicum	Striped maple	S
A. spicatum	Mountain maple	S
Alnus rugosa	Speckled alder	S, IS
Comptonia peregrina	Sweet-fern	S
Corylus americana	American hazel	S, IS

C. cornuta	Beaked hazel	S, IS
Crataegus spp.	Hawthorn	S
Hamamelis virginiana	Witch-hazel	S, IS
Rhus spp.	Sumac	IS
Rubus spp.	Raspberry	S, BS, IS
Salix spp.	Willows	S, IS
Vaccinium spp.	Blueberries	S, IS
Herbs		
Asclepias spp.	Milkweed	IS
Aster spp.	Aster	S, IS
Brachelytrum erectum	Short husk grass	S, IS
Calamagrostis canadensis	Blue-joint	S, IS
Carex spp.	Misc. sedges	S
Cinna latifolia	Wood reedgrass	S
Dennstaedtia punctilobula	Hayscented fern	S
Dicots	Misc. forbs	S, IS
Epilobium spp.	Fireweed	S, IS
Graminae spp.	Misc. grasses	S, IS
Pteridium aquilinum	Bracken fern	S
Solidago spp.	Goldenrod	S, IS
Dryopteris noveboracensis	New York fern	S

[a] Within categories, species are arranged in alphabetical order according to scientific name. No priority of importance is intended by the order.
[b] Although various plant species may have several ways of capturing or colonizing forest sites, the classification used in this table only pertains to the *principal* means whereby they become a *threat* to conifer regeneration. It does not necessarily include all methods of propagation and establishment for any given species. Code is as follows:

RS = Competing plants that originate from residual stems that have resilient boles, stems, and branches capable of surviving overstory removal and other physical disturbances and quickly dominating a site shortly thereafter.

S = Sprouting plants that originate from stumps, persistent rootstocks, rhizomes, or stolons that quickly generate new shoots or stems when existing ones are cut or damaged.

BS = Plants that arise from buried seed and are adapted to catastrophic disturbance such as fire or scarification which stimulates germination.

IS = Plants that arise from introduced seed disseminated by wind currents or animals.

TABLE 4-3. Area of Commercial Forest Land Presently Occupied or Potentially Suitable for Conifers in the Northeast and Lake States/ Provinces

Subregion	Conifer[a]	Conifer-Hardwood[b]	Hardwood[c]	Total
	In thousands of acres			
New England and New York	15,667	10,602	—	26,269
Lake states	12,878	—	11,145	24,023
Maritime provinces[d]	27,168	10,652	3,812	41,632
Quebec and Ontario	125,640	50,323	30,879	206,842
Total	181,353	71,577	45,836	298,766

Source: Data for New England and New York are from Lull (1968); data for the Lake states are from Merz (1978); and data for the Canadian provinces are from Bonnor (1982).
[a]Predominantly spruce-fir and white/red/jack pine forest types.
[b]Predominantly white pine/hemlock-mixed hardwood forest types.
[c]Predominantly aspen-birch forest types. Some of the acreage presently dominated by aspen and birch was previously occupied by conifers and is, therefore, included as acreage potentially suitable for conifer production.
[d]Includes Newfoundland, Nova Scotia, New Brunswick, and Prince Edward Island.

(i.e., clearcutting) has occurred, natural regeneration has created mixtures of hardwoods and conifers, sometimes with severe overstocking of one group or the other. Where partial harvesting has occurred—a practice commonly used prior to 1950—the high grading has left species of relatively low quality and vigor. High natural mortality, suppressed juvenile growth, and damage by spruce budworm (*Choristoneura fumiferana*) outbreaks also have had major impacts on stand growth and quality. As a consequence, inferior species composition and extremes in stocking level are widespread problems in this northeastern area.

Altogether the area occupied by conifers or mixtures of conifers and hardwoods in this region is about 250 million acres (Table 4-3). However, the acreage presently in conifers may not reflect the potential area suitable for conifers. In much of New York, and presumably elsewhere in the Northeast, conifers were once much more abundant than now, particularly where Native Americans practiced some form of shifting agriculture involving fire (Considine 1984). A 200-year period of settlement and exploitation has generally obscured the nature of both the original forest composition and the potential productivity under forest management. For example, much of the 11 million acres in aspen-birch in the Lake states (Merz 1978) once supported conifers in the past. About 7 million acres of red-pine type once existed in this region, of which about 1.2 million acres remain (Benzie 1982); and there used to be an even larger acreage of white pine type that now occupies considerably less area. These statistics indicate that much of the landscape in the Northeast and Lake states/

provinces is capable of supporting conifer types, even though pure hardwoods or mixed conifer/hardwoods dominate at the present time. Thus an area approaching 300 million acres of potentially productive conifer-type land is encompassed within this region (Table 4-3). Some of this land is also suitable for producing high-quality hardwoods.

Productivity and Value

Productivity of the Northeast and Lake States/Provinces is currently considered low to medium, with most sites growing 50 to 85 ft³/acre/year. These estimates are based largely on growth of naturally regenerated, unmanaged stands. Complex mixtures of species are the rule, and the incidence of nonmerchantable or low-value hardwoods is high.

Growth and yield data from managed conifer stands and plantations indicate that this region has a much greater capacity for wood production than is generally realized (Bailey n.d., Frothingham 1914, Gevorkiantz and Zon 1930, Ferree and Hagar 1956, Gunter and Rudolph 1968, MacLean and Morgan 1983). Normal yield tables for spruce/fir and white/red/jack pines indicate that a wide range of sites should be able to grow more than 80 ft³/acre/year (Stiell 1964). The failure of existing stands to achieve such production is primarily attributable to poor or excessive stocking and competing vegetation (Fisher 1918, Wilde et al. 1968). In the Maritimes, for example, Ker (1981) recorded growth rates of 116 ft³/acre/year over a 20-year period after stocking control and shrub removal in balsam fir regeneration.

Elsewhere, slow juvenile growth rates may mask site potential for conifer production. Site index curves for much of the spruce-fir type are based on height-over-age relationships derived from measurements taken at or above breast height (4.5 ft). However, the average tree may have taken 15 years to reach breast height due to excessive competition or other factors (Vicary et al. 1984). Yet Newton et al. (1986) have shown that conifers free of dead shade or brush should achieve heights of 13 to 21 ft by age 16. Thus potential yields of conifers in this region, particularly those growing on good sites and free of competing vegetation, tend to be greatly underestimated by current yield forecasts.

Fully 10% of the commercial forest area in the northeastern United States and 25% in the Lake states is poorly stocked (Benzie et al. 1973). Most commercial forest stands east of the Lake states are of natural origin, and very few have had silvicultural treatments to improve spacing, composition, and juvenile growth. Consequently, less than 1% of the forest land in Maine is considered well stocked (Ferguson and Kingsley 1972). Where commercial plantations exist, they are primarily situated on sandy, impoverished sites near the Great Lakes; those on better sites often encounter severe competition from herbaceous and woody species (Coffman 1982, Sajdak and Kotar 1985).

In the Canadian provinces there is an estimated 22 million acres of nonstocked, productive land amenable to commercial timber management (Bonner 1982). Fully 25% of the forest land in Nova Scotia is not economically harvestable because of inadequate stocking (Anonymous 1977). In discussing the long-term prospects for Canada's timber supply, Honer and Bickerstaff (1985, p. 26, 41) highlight the importance of reclaiming the "not satisfactorily restocked" forest land:

> The most serious long-term losses are not in volume but in the continued erosion of the stocked productive land base. Available estimates indicate that 20% of the areas logged, burned or killed by insects and disease annually are not regenerated and go out of production... These lands are generally covered with vegetation such as alder, willow, mountain maple, striped maple or pin cherry and other shrubs which provide strong competition to the regeneration of commercial tree species. Only intensive silvicultural treatments will bring this land back to a productive state.

Thus a history of land clearing and abandonment, overcutting, high grading, inadequate establishment and protection of regeneration, and natural disasters have greatly reduced the current timber value and productivity of forest land in the Northeast and Lake states/provinces. The average growth of commercially valuable species is less than half its potential.

The aforementioned problems notwithstanding, the value of well-managed conifer sites in the Northeast and Lake states/provinces is considerable. In Minnesota, for example, the forest-based sector is the third largest manufacturing industry and accounted for 3.6% of the gross state output of $81 billion in 1982 (Lewis 1984). Except for northern Ontario and Quebec, most forests are within 500 mi of major metropolitan areas and are easily accessible by highway, rail, and water. Mills producing veneer, chipboard, particleboard, pulp, boiler fuel, and lumber are prevalent throughout the region. Furthermore, much of the forested terrain is gentle and suitable for mechanized harvesting and site preparation. This combination of factors should continue to provide incentives for intensive forest management in the region.

The current growing stock ranges in value from firewood or boiler fuel at the lowest level, to pulpwood at an intermediate level, to veneer and solid-wood products at the upper level. With a projected wood shortage in the region shortly after the year 2000 (Sewall 1983), careful harvest planning will be required to prolong the use of older age-class timber, and intensive silviculture will be needed to accelerate the development of young growing stock (McCormack 1985).

Ownership Patterns and Objectives

Over 90% of the commercial forest land in the northeastern United States and over 60% in the Lake states is in private ownership. This is in marked contrast to the Canadian provinces, where only about 14% of the commercial forest land is in private ownership (Bonnor 1982). Forest products companies manage large blocks of land in New Brunswick, northern New England, and in the northern Lake states. For example, the 9 million acres of forest-industry land in northern Maine is the largest concentration of industrial ownership in the United States. Elsewhere, private individuals and small organizations own the majority of forest land, about half of it in parcels of 100 acres or less. Forest lands managed by public agencies comprise less than 10% of the base in the northeastern United States and less than 40% in the Lake states.

A high percentage of nonindustrial, private owners in the northeastern United States and Lake states/provinces do not regard their lands as a sustained timber resource, although two-thirds are willing to cut timber to generate revenue (Considine 1984). Instead, they value the land primarily for recreational or investment purposes. Consequently, it is estimated that only 60% of the potential commercial forest land is managed for timber production, most of which is in units of 100 acres or more. Vegetation competing with conifers may not be considered much of a problem to present owners unconcerned about enhancing forest productivity. Future owners may think otherwise, however, particularly if opportunities for investment in forestry improve. From a management standpoint, future silvicultural prospects are largely determined by vegetative conditions today. Therefore, this chapter will focus on the origin, extent, and types of current vegetation problems affecting conifer production in this region, regardless of present owners' concerns or objectives.

HISTORICAL DEVELOPMENT OF CURRENT FOREST CONDITIONS

Benzie et al. (1973), Barrett (1980a), and Hansen (1980) have summarized the historical development of forest conditions and weed problems in the Northeast and Lake states/provinces. Briefly, many of the eastern states and provinces were heavily logged in the 1700s and early 1800s to provide lumber, fuelwood, and farmland for the two developing nations. Large white pines growing in the middle of hardwoods were the preferred source of lumber, although other species were harvested eventually. Much of the favorable land was cleared for farms and pastures and later abandoned as the early settlers moved west. White pine, other conifers, and a variety of hardwoods were quick to invade these old fields. Other forest areas were coppiced several times for firewood at 25- to 40-year intervals until coal began replacing firewood in the 1850s. Slash accumulations from logging operations led to extensive wildfires in the early 1900s, destroying much of the natural conifer regeneration. These activities and events left a residue of poorly stocked, low-quality stands throughout the Northeast.

Furthermore, much of the poorly stocked land was occupied by woody species of low commercial value, and these situations now comprise the most extensive forest-weed problem. Winter logging and the practice of leaving uncut birches and red maples in Maine and the Maritimes have led to severe problems with overstocking of conifers suppressed by a canopy of poor-quality hardwoods (Ker 1981, Piene 1981, Powell and Dickson 1984).

Wildfires and hurricanes have likewise affected the landscape in many areas of the Northeast. Fernow et al. (1912) and Loucks (1962) have described the forest regeneration problems associated with shrub-dominated "fire barrens" in western Nova Scotia. Elsewhere, pioneer species of poplar and birch have been quick to colonize burned-over conifer sites. Where conifer stands have emerged in this coastal Province, they are sometimes vulnerable to windthrow by hurricanes.

Inland toward the Lake states and adjacent Canadian provinces, the logging of white, red, and jack pines reached a peak at the turn of the century as agricultural expansion occurred in the Midwest. Lack of natural seed sources, poor seedbed conditions, excessive competition from herbs and hardwoods, adverse weather, and frequent wildfires in the late 1800s and early 1900s destroyed or precluded the natural reestablishment of pine. Consequently, vast areas are now occupied by aspen, birch, and other pioneer species of hardwoods. It was not until the 1930s and 1940s that site preparation and planting of pines and other conifers began in earnest, principally on old fields.

Natural events have also helped shape the current forest conditions in the Northeast and Lake states/provinces. Periodic outbreaks of the spruce budworm in northern Maine and the Canadian provinces have devastated many stands of spruce and balsam fir. The openings in the forest canopy have allowed shrubs and hardwoods to dominate the landscape. Although the shift toward hardwood species tends to make the forest more resistant to budworm attack, the industry in this region is largely based on softwood utilization (Blais 1983). Consequently, the emphasis has been placed on protecting, replanting, and releasing the more valuable balsam fir and spruce, further increasing the vulnerability of the forest to subsequent outbreaks of the budworm. As Blais indicates, this present dilemma over species preference will not be easy to resolve.

The aforementioned factors notwithstanding, the major influence on forests of the region has been selective harvesting (usually high grading) without any follow-up reforestation activities. The natural progression of secondary succession has led to the gradual replacement of conifers by more shade-tolerant, but less valuable, hardwoods. In some instances, the exclusion of fire has favored the successional trend toward climax vegetation, thereby eliminating fire-adapted, seral species such as white, red, and jack pines. As Benzie et al. (1973, p. 156) state: "When only the merchantable or most valuable portion of the stand is harvested without providing suitable conditions to regenerate the desirable species, defective trees and weed species are left to form a large part of the next stand." They go on to describe how logging a pure, well-stocked stand of black spruce in Ontario led to rapid occupancy of the site by more than 25,000 speckled alder stems/acre. Sutton (1985, p. 6) summarizes the situation throughout much of Canada as follows:

> The extent of the weed problem is influenced greatly not only by the nature of the stand that was cut but also by the season and method of harvesting, the intensity of utilization, and the time that has been allowed to elapse between harvesting and the attempt to regenerate. Such factors are ignored in exploitation forestry, which strives to minimize the unit cost of extracted wood and maximize immediate profits. The result has been the virtually complete separation of harvesting and regeneration operations in Canadian forestry. This separation, together with the inadequacy of the regeneration effort by industry and governments alike, has produced weed problems on a vast scale.

These conditions are not unique to Canada. After the logging of moist, relatively fertile conifer sites in the Lake states, it is customary to find the areas dominated by speckled alder, willow, mountain maple, dogwood, *Ribes* species, and raspberries. This unintentional conversion of conifer type to less desirable brush and hardwoods is no small matter. Benzie (1982) has estimated that there are 6 million acres less of red pine today than in the "old growth" forests.

As a consequence of this conversion process, many landowners have abandoned conifer production as an objective. The abundant supply of hardwood raw material in the Lake states has caused the manufacturing emphasis to shift from a softwood economy based on lumber to a low-grade hardwood economy dependent on chips. Consequently, low-value but abundant hardwoods (primarily aspen) have become the production goal. The opportunity to grow conifers has been foregone, even though the intrinsic value of the land in the long run may be much higher for softwood species. Thus it is generally agreed that many forested areas of this region could produce more valuable timber under intensive management regimes targeted for conifer production (Benzie et al. 1973).

The occurrence of over 45 million acres of predominantly aspen-birch type (Table 4-3), much of which was previously in conifer cover, represents a major opportunity for stand conversion back to conifers. Some of this land is owned by the forest industry that has manufacturing facilities designed to utilize the low-grade hardwoods; this capital investment probably excludes use of their land for conifer production. Still, there are over 11 million acres of aspen-birch type in the Lake states (Merz 1978) on which the existing growing stock is of negligible value to owners and where rehabilitation to conifers is possible. For example, over 873 thousand acres in Michigan have been identified as candidates for conversion to red pine (Smith and Spencer 1985). This survey also identified an additional 1 million acres of maple-birch type and 534 thousand acres of oak-hickory type growing less than 50 ft³/acre/year of low quality wood that would be much more likely to produce economically viable crops if converted to softwoods. Similar opportunities exist in the adjacent Canadian provinces.

There are also large tracts, primarily on industry land in the spruce-fir type of the Northeast and Maritimes, where clearcut harvesting has led to dense hardwood cover suppressing medium- to overstocked conifer regeneration. This provides opportunities for large scale release and stocking control programs. Finally, it should be noted that much of the commercial forest land in the Northeast will produce a good yield of softwoods, despite a history of hardwood occupation (Raup and Carlson 1941). Coupled with the preponderance of low-grade logs in hardwood stands, even of high-value species, there are many economically viable opportunities for converting poor hardwood stands to conifers throughout the region. However, such conversion activities should be restricted to relatively poor sites where hardwood growth rates are slow. Fertile hardwood sites should continue to be managed for production of high-quality hardwood lumber and veneer.

Recently mechanical harvesting of biomass for a mixture of pulp and fuel products has created opportunities to reverse this trend toward low-grade hardwood forests. Several companies in the Northeast have developed power co-generation facilities run on biomass harvests and are using this conversion opportunity to reestablish conifer stands (T. Sawyer 1985, personal communication).

IMPORTANT SILVICAL RELATIONSHIPS BETWEEN CONIFERS AND COMPETING VEGETATION

On many sites in the region, hardwoods have an inherent advantage over conifers, because they (1) produce abundant seed crops at frequent intervals; (2) are capable of rapid juvenile growth from either seed or sprouts; (3) are often tolerant of shade; and (4) can germinate in either hardwood or softwood litter. For example, birch and aspen species can quickly invade disturbed sites through wind-blown seed dispersal. These same species, along with maples, oaks, cherries, and beech can also sprout prolifically from established rootstocks. Aspen is particularly troublesome because of the tendency to produce numerous, fast-growing root suckers. Juvenile growth rates often exceed 1 to 3 ft/year, quickly overtopping the slower growing conifer regeneration. The relative shade tolerance of species like maples and beech, coupled with their ability to germinate on thick duff, allows these species to develop in the understory until conifers are harvested, at which point they assume dominance. Germination of persistent seeds of pin cherry, raspberry, and other woody species add to the competitive environment. Finally, animals residing in dense, young hardwood thickets may also selectively remove the more desirable conifers (Murray 1984, Newton et al. 1986).

Although certain conifer species in the region are also tolerant (e.g., balsam fir, red spruce, and eastern hemlock), it may take a century or more for them to become a significant component of a stand. Fluctuating environmental conditions generally lead to all-or-nothing results in natural conifer regeneration (McCormack 1985). When seed crops of conifers are abundant and fall on freshly logged or burned areas or where dense reproduction of conifers exists before harvest (as with spruce-fir), overstocked stands can be expected. These will eventually need to be thinned to avoid stand stagnation. When seed crops or site preparation is inadequate, aggressive woody vegetation can dominate slower growing conifers such as white pine, balsam fir, and spruce. Consequently, few coniferous forests in this region can be expected to reach maturity in a productive, economical fashion without silvicultural assistance.

Jack and red pines, like birch and aspen, are well suited for colonizing disturbed areas where woody competitors are sparse. Jack pine has serotinous cones that require the heat from wildfires to facilitate cone opening and subsequent seed dispersal. These pine species have relatively fast juvenile growth. On the lightest sandy and gravelly soils, competition from hardwoods and brush is not a serious problem. On better sites, however, brush and grass problems can develop that prevent reestablishment of the conifer species after harvesting. Many brushfields in the Lake states owe their present existence to such circumstances. Thus the inherent productivity of the forest land has been obscured.

White pine, although more tolerant of shade than other pines found in the Northeast and Lake states/provinces, is also well adapted to openings created by site disturbances. It is capable of colonizing freshly burned, scarified, or impoverished areas such as old fields but can also persist as isolated dominants in mixed hardwood or spruce-fir forests due to its longevity and ability to achieve great size. Successful regeneration and early development in stands, however, usually require some form of hardwood control, particularly on good sites (Raup and Carlson 1941).

White spruce is tolerant of some shading (Nienstadt 1957), and deciduous cover may be beneficial to young trees by decreasing frost damage on new leaders (Nienstadt and Jeffers 1976). Nevertheless, white spruce 4 to 6 years old seems to grow better in low- rather than high-brush densities (Jordon and Posner 1984).

Some of the principal shrub competitors in the Northeast and Lake states/provinces are species of *Rubus*. Following overstory removal, they can dominate a site for 10 to 25 years unless advanced conifer regeneration is present or measures are taken to control them. Otherwise, prolonged rotations are inevitable.

TABLE 4-4. Relative Degree of Competition Likely to be Encountered by Young Red Pine Plantations Established in Various Habitat Types in the Lake States. The Determination of Competitive Condition and Habitat Type Is Based on the Relative Abundance of Indicator Species

Degree of Competition	Indicator Species	PVD PVC	QAE	AQV	TMV	TM	AQVib	ATD	AVO	AOC
				Relative Abundance of Indicator Species[b]						
Slight	Blueberries	A	A	C	C					
	Wintergreen	C	C	A	C	S	S			
	Starflower		C	C	C	S	S			
	Hazel		S	C	C	A	C	S		
	Wild lily-of-the-valley			S	C	C	S	S	S	
	Wild sarsaparilla			S	C	A	C	S	S	
Moderate	False Solomon's seal				S	S	C	C	C	S
	Spinulose shield fern				S	S	S	A	C	S
	Twisted stalk					S	C	C	C	C
	Trillium					S	C	C	A	A
	Elderberry					S	S	C	C	S
	Sugar maple seedlings					S	S	A	A	A

90

Severe				
Sweet Cicely	S	C	A	A
Hairy solomon's seal	S	C	C	C
Violets	S	C	C	C
Jack-in-the-pulpit	S	S	C	C
Blue cohosh	S	S	C	A
Maidenhair fern	S	S	C	A

Source: Adapted and condensed from Kotar and Coffman (1984).

[a]Habitat types and corresponding site index range for red pine are as follows:

Code	Habitat type	Site index range (ft, Base Age 50)
PVD	*Pinus-Vaccinium-Deschampsia*	40-59
PVC	*Pinus-Vaccinium-Carex*	40-59
QAE	*Quercus-Acer-Epigaea*	40-59
AQE	*Acer-Quercus-Vaccinium*	64-68
TMV	*Tsuga-Maianthemum-Vaccinium*	72-82
TM	*Tsuga-Maianthemum*	72-82
AQVib	*Acer-Quercus-Viburnum*	72-82
ATD	*Acer-Tsuga-Dryopteris*	78-82
AVO	*Acer-Viola-Osmorhiza*	78-82
AOC	*Acer-Osmorhiza-Caulophyllum*	78-82

[b]Relative abundance code: A = abundant, C = common, S = sparse.

Various species of grasses and sedges can also become a serious problem for artificial reforestation. Dense stands of grass often develop where hardwoods and brush have been removed by mechanical or chemical means.

Competing vegetation can also contribute to the development of insect and disease problems in conifer stands. Generally, any vegetation that reduces conifer vigor can influence the stand's susceptibility to damage by forest pests (Heyd 1982, Nicholls et al. 1984). For example, sweet-fern, goldenrod, asters, and oaks serve as alternate hosts for several serious rust diseases on red and jack pine. Sweet-fern is also the primary alternate host for the Saratoga spittlebug (*Aphrophora saratogensis*), a serious pest of red and jack pine. Several insect and disease problems are most prevalent on trees less than 10 ft tall. By maximizing seedling growth, the period of susceptibility to damage is reduced.

Recognition of the importance of competing vegetation to conifer performance in the Lake states has led to the development of indicator species for use in identifying habitat types that are likely to be difficult to regenerate (Kotar and Coffman 1984, Sajdak and Kotar 1985). For example, the presence of violets or sweet Cicely in a stand indicates that strong hardwood competition is likely to reduce the success of pine regeneration efforts unless special measures are taken (Table 4-4).

RESPONSE OF CONIFERS TO CONTROL OF COMPETING VEGETATION

Numerous studies have documented the necessity of controlling competing vegetation in order to secure successful establishment and satisfactory growth of conifer stands in the Northeast and Lake states/provinces. Many of these have been summarized in the bibliography prepared by Stewart et al. (1984). Therefore, only a few examples will be given here to illustrate the general patterns and magnitudes of conifer response to control of competing vegetation in the region.

Site Preparation

The Northeast and Lake states/provinces contain a number of areas where herbaceous weeds inhibit plantation and natural stand establishment. Several studies have shown that thorough site preparation is often necessary in order to obtain adequate survival of conifer stock in the region. For example, McLeod (1964) obtained 73% survival of white spruce seedlings planted in furrows that eliminated competition from grass sod in a rehabilitated area in New Brunswick. Survival in nonfurrowed plots was only 37%. Stoeckler and Limstrom (1950), Cayford (1961), and Cayford and Jarvis (1963) reported analogous results of furrowing in northern Wisconsin and southeastern Manitoba for white spruce, black spruce, jack pine, and red pine. Care must be exercised in using such mechanical techniques, however. The most fertile topsoil is often removed and, in the case of furrowing, the trees are planted in less fertile subsoil where they can become easily overtopped by vegetation colonizing the berm. Seedlings are also prone to damage from rodents that utilize the furrow for habitat.

In Ontario, Von Althen (1972) obtained the highest survival of white pine and white spruce following plowing, disking, and herbicide application to an abandoned hayfield. Mullin (1972) recorded gains in both survival and height growth for red pine seedlings planted in southeastern Ontario where a dense sod was removed by scalping. Survival after 10 years was 59 to 85% in scalped plots compared to only 24 to 31% in untreated plots; tree heights in the scalped plots were about double those in the unscalped plots, despite removal of surface soil and litter.

Historically, much research has been conducted on the value of mechanical and other methods of site preparation to reduce the competition from grasses and forbs. Nevertheless, newly established forests in this region seldom fail because of herbaceous weeds, unless pest animals utilizing herbaceous cover for habitat are present. Reductions in stocking level, growth, and yield can be substantial, however.

One of the best examples of the long-term value of site preparation involves red pine plantations established in Wisconsin during 1935. Wilde et al. (1968) found that a plantation established following cultivation (plowing and disking, followed by hand weeding for two springs after planting) produced almost three times the merchantable volume of an adjacent plantation established without such cultivation. After 31 years the cultivated plantation contained trees that averaged 45 ft tall, 5.4 in. in diameter at breast height (DBH), and a merchantable volume to a 3-in. top of 27.5 cords/acre. The uncultivated plantation contained trees that averaged only 29.5 ft tall, 4.1 in. DBH, and merchantable volume of 10.8 cords/acre.

Release

Long-term documentation of conifer response to release treatments in the Northeast and Lake states/provinces is limited. However, the few studies that have been conducted indicate a consistently positive response to treatment. For example, measurements taken after 32 years in a balsam fir plantation in northwestern New Brunswick indicated that manually clearing mountain maple sprouts to a 3-ft radius around the seedlings increased balsam-fir volume by 64% compared to unreleased seedlings (MacLean and Morgan 1983). Broadcast herbicide release treatments in a similar plantation more than tripled the volume of balsam fir over unreleased stands after 28 years.

In another long-term study, Lehela (1981) examined several operationally released and unreleased balsam fir plantations in northern Ontario. Using stem analysis procedures, he was able to reconstruct the periodic height increments for balsam fir seedlings since the time of herbicide treatment. Over a 20-year period following release on a relatively fertile silt-loam site, he observed a 66% increase in height and a doubling in volume compared to unreleased trees.

Several release studies of shorter duration have also detected positive growth responses of conifers to vegetation control. For instance, a study in Maine involving the release of natural conifer regeneration 7 years after establishment showed that a variety of herbicide treatments maintained the stocking and dominance of red spruce, balsam fir, and white pine over red maple and other hardwoods (McCormack 1985). Height growth patterns for balsam fir and red spruce for the first 4 years following treatment are shown in Figure 4-2. Threefold increases in radial growth have also been recorded for released trees in this study. Baskerville (1961) noted that spruce and fir expressed greatly increased height growth after release, with greatest growth observed in the largest trees. Numerous other examples of conifer release studies can be found in the bibliography by Stewart et al. (1984).

Some conifer species may respond more effectively to release treatments than others. For example, Baskerville (1961) found that balsam

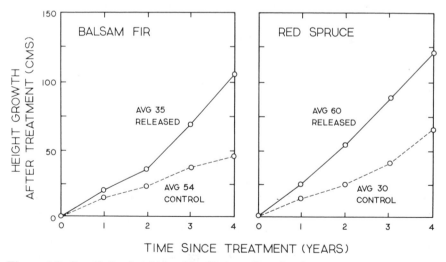

Figure 4-2. Cumulative height growth of balsam fir and red spruce over a 4-year period following release treatments. Each plotted line is based on the average number of trees measured in the treatment indicated. (*Source:* From McCormack 1985)

fir responded more rapidly than spruce following shrub or aspen removal in New Brunswick. Similar observations of poor spruce response have been made by others (Plice and Hedden 1931, Day 1974, Bunce 1979), but there have been instances where the response of spruce has been good (Westveld 1937, Waldron 1959, Baskerville 1961, Sutton 1975, Willocks 1979, McCormack and Newton 1980, Richardson 1982), sometimes exceeding that of fir (Mulloy 1941). Newton et al. (1986) have observed stocking of both spruce and fir to decline sharply under hardwood competition. Diameter growth of surviving trees of both species was also reduced.

The variation in species response alluded to before may be attributed to conifer size at the time of treatment. Lehela (1981) reexamined the data of Bunce (1979) and detected a positive height growth response of spruce to release when trees under 20 in. tall (presumably those of less vigor) were excluded from the analysis. Thus conifers should be well established and vigorous in order to respond quickly before competing vegetation recovers (Engle 1951, Baskerville 1961, Sutton 1985). This implies that release treatments should be performed early in the life of a stand before suppression is severe if conifer growth and development are to be maximized.

Some of the eastern conifers are tolerant enough to survive in the understory of stands for decades. When the overstory is removed, they are capable of eventually responding to the open conditions. In northern Minnesota, for example, the cutting of an aspen-birch overstory doubled the volume growth of a 19-year-old understory of red pine (compared to an untreated stand) over a 25-year period (Buckman and Lundgren 1962). Berry (1982) reported successful release of white pine, red pine, and white spruce that had been suppressed for 27 years by an aspen-pine overstory in Ontario. Cayford (1957) observed that suppressed white spruce up to at least 100 years old were still capable of responding to release from an aspen overstory. Thus although free-to-grow conditions are advantageous throughout the life of a stand (Wilde et al. 1968, McCormack 1985), the opportunity for conifer release in this region persists for an extended period after the development of woody competitors.

FUTURE VEGETATION MANAGEMENT CONCERNS AND OPPORTUNITIES

Information is scarce on the performance of free-to-grow stands on good sites previously in forest cover. Most plantations have been established on abandoned farmland occupied by little woody vegetation, and site preparation treatments have focused on herbs and low shrubs. Much of the future site preparation in this region will be done on productive forest land after timber harvesting. In these instances, sprouting hardwoods, raspberry thickets, grass sods, and occasional overstocking of conifers will constitute the primary problems—a major change from past experiences. Conventional wisdom has been that bare mineral soil is good for natural regeneration; hence there has been a tendency to expose mineral soil while logging. In addition to leaving sprouting root stocks of aspen and other species, this procedure leads to prompt invasion of birches, pin cherry, and raspberry. The conifers also regenerate, but in random patterns, usually with overstocking in some locations and gaps in others. Winter logging in the northern portion of the spruce-fir type can leave dense stands of conifer regeneration beneath the snow pack. When the growing season begins in the spring, the seedlings must contend with

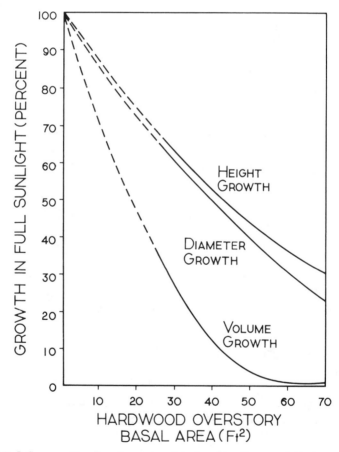

Figure 4-3. Influence of hardwood overstory basal area on the growth of planted red pine. Based on red pine release studies in nine plantations ranging from 2 to 40 yr old on medium to good sites in Lower Michigan. (*Source:* From Benzie 1977)

unmerchantable hardwoods left after logging. Both release and stocking control are required to achieve successful conifer stand development.

Burkhart et al. (see Chapter 8) have noted that growth of southern pines is less vigorous on cutover forest lands than on old field sites of equivalent site quality, and this decline has been linked to the presence of hardwoods. The same relation may hold in the Northeast and Lake states/provinces. In this region there is ample evidence of compositional problems on cutover lands. A small number of stands of well-spaced northern conifers grown in comparative freedom from woody competitors provides a glimpse of the rapid growth that may be achieved (McCormack 1985). Certainly one of the most important areas of research will be in developing methods whereby conifer plantations can be grown relatively free of both inter- and intraspecific plant competition in this region.

Thus stocking control, combined with vegetation management treatments both early and late in the development of conifer forests of the Northeast and Lake states/provinces, can be highly beneficial and is considered to be one of the better investments in forestry (Fisher 1918, Buckman and Lundgren 1962). Ground covers of ferns, grass, and forbs can reduce seedling survival and early growth as well as increase pest problems. Dense thickets of *Rubus* species, speckled alder, beaked hazel, and other shrubs can, likewise, retard early stand development, as can sprouting maples and suckering beech and aspen. Overstories of aspen, birch, maple, and beech are particularly strong competitors of conifer seedlings and saplings, and early suppression or removal of such species can greatly accelerate the height and diameter growth rates of conifers. Benzie (1977) has used such information to predict the yield of red pine stands growing under different degrees of hardwood cover (Figure 4-3). Additional unifying work of this type would greatly facilitate the application of vegetation management to conifer stands in the Northeast and Lake states/provinces.

SUMMARY

Throughout the Northeast and Lake states/provinces, harvesting without deliberate reforestation has been the pattern for the 100 to 200 year period of forest exploitation. The systematic removal of valuable species and of high-quality specimens of all species without removing low-value trees has left the forest with poor-quality growing stock. Standard practices have involved (1) partial cutting that left defective and low-value species; (2) clearcutting that relied on natural coppice or seeding for regeneration; and (3) abandonment of fields and pastures by farmers, resulting in the random invasion of low-quality or noncommercial tree species. As a consequence, most of the area amenable to conifer production in this region has a serious weed problem. The current condition is one of poor species composition and stand structure, and few stands are growing at more than 50% of capacity. Conventional harvesting and regeneration practices, coupled with natural disturbances such as spruce budworm outbreaks, tend to perpetuate such conditions.

Even where shrubs and hardwoods are adequately controlled, competition from grass and forbs seriously impedes conifer development. The problem is most critical on the relatively dry, infertile soils of the Lake states, but such competition can also affect early plantation survival and growth in the wetter, more productive areas of the Northeast and Canadian provinces.

The degree to which the 300 million acres of potential conifer type is likely to be reclaimed or intensively managed for conifer production is difficult to assess. Of all the forested regions of North America, the Northeast and Lake states/provinces have the lowest proportion of private owners who seem to be motivated to use their land in an active forest management capacity. Even industrial lands have been largely managed on a custodial basis because of the tendency for much of the land to regenerate naturally (albeit to nonconifer type) and still produce marketable chips and fuelwood.

Despite these features, the Northeast and Lake states/provinces remain an attractive region for forestry investment. Well-established manufacturing facilities, readily accessible transportation networks, and proximity to population centers give the region a logistical advantage not enjoyed elsewhere. The application of forest vegetation management can do much to enhance the inherent productivity of forests in this region, thereby sustaining its importance as a wood basket. The penetration of such practices into normal silvicultural use is just beginning, however, and much developmental work is needed to refine local prescriptions and make them compatible with environmental, recreational, and aesthetic goals.

REFERENCES

Anonymous. 1977. How do our forest grow? Highlights of the 1965-71 Nova Scotia Provincial Forest Inventory. Nova Scotia Department of Lands and Forests, Truro, NS. 7 p.

Bailey, R.E. (n.d.). Forestry field handbook. Nova Scotia Department of Lands and Forests, Truro, NS. 25 p.

Barrett, J.W. 1980a. The Northeast Region, p. 25-65. In Barrett, J.W. (ed.) Regional silviculture of the United States. John Wiley and Sons, Inc., New York, NY. 551 p.

Barrett, J.W. (ed.) 1980b. Regional silviculture of the United States. John Wiley and Sons, Inc. New York, NY. 551 p.

Baskerville, G.L. 1961. Response of young fir and spruce to release from shrub competition. Canada Department of Forestry, Ottawa. Forest Res. Div. Tech. Note 98. 14 p.

Benzie, J.W. 1977. Manager's handbook for red pine in the north central states. USDA Forest Service, North Central Forest Experiment Station, St. Paul, MN. Gen. Tech. Rep. NC-33. 22 p.

Benzie, J.W. 1982. Red pine, p. 134-141. *In* Mroz, G.D. and J.F. Berner (comp.) Proc., Artificial Regeneration of Conifers in the Upper Great Lakes Region. Michigan Technological University, Houghton, MI. 435 p.

Benzie, J.W., S. Little, and R.F. Sutton. 1973. Rehabilitation of forest land: the Northeast and Boreal Region. J. Forestry 71:136-137.

Berry, A.B. 1982. Response of suppressed conifer seedlings to release from an aspen-pine overstorey. Forestry Chron. 58:91-92.

Blais, J.R. 1983. Trends in the frequency, extent, and severity of spruce budworm outbreaks in eastern Canada. Can. J. Forest Res. 13:539-547.

Bonnor, G.M. 1982. Canada's forest inventory—1981. Forestry Statistics and Systems Branch, Canadian Forestry Service, Department of the Environment, Chalk River, Ontario. 79 p.

Buckman, R.E. and A.L. Lundgren. 1962. Three pine release experiments in northern Minnesota. USDA Forest Service, Lake States Forest Experiment Station, St. Paul, MN. Pap. 97. 9 p.

Bunce, P.M. 1979. Effect of aerial applications of 2,4-D on the height growth of *Picea glauca* (Moench) Voss and *Picea mariana* (Mill.) B.S.P. B.Sc.F. thesis. School of Forestry, Lakehead University, Thunder Bay, Ontario.

Cayford, J.H. 1957. Influence of the aspen overstory on white spruce growth in Saskatchewan. Canada Department of Northern Affairs and National Resources, Forestry Branch, Sault Ste. Marie, Ontario. Forest Res. Div. Tech. Note 58. 12 p.

Cayford, J.H. 1961. Furrowing improves first-year survival of planted spruce and pine in Manitoba. Tree Planters' Notes. 48:13-14.

Cayford, J.H. and J.M. Jarvis. 1963. Furrowing and sheltering to improve early survival of planted red pine on dry sites, southeastern Manitoba. Tree Planters' Notes. 59:21-24.

Coffman, M.S. 1982. Regeneration prescriptions: the need to be holistic, p. 190-208. *In* Mroz, G.D. and J.F. Berner (comps.) Proc., Artificial Regeneration of Conifers in the Upper Great Lakes Region. Michigan Technological University, Houghton, MI. 435 p.

Considine, T.J., Jr. 1984. An analysis of New York's timber resources. USDA Forest Service, Northeastern Forest Experiment Station, Upper Darby, PA. Resour. Bull. NE-80. 70 p.

Day, R.J. 1974. An evaluation of the effectiveness of aerial spraying with 2,4-D for the release of coniferous reproduction. M.S. thesis. School of Forestry, Lakehead University, Thunder Bay, Ontario. 17 p.

Engle, L.G. 1951. Releasing white pine from oak and aspen. USDA Forest Service, Lake States Forest Experiment Station, St. Paul, MN. Tech. Notes 346. 2 p.

Ferguson, H. and P. Kingsley. 1972. The timber resources of Maine. USDA Forest

Service, Northeastern Forest Experiment Station, Upper Darby, PA. Resour. Bull. NE-26. 129 p.

Fernow, B.E., C.D. Howe, and J.H. White. 1912. Forest conditions of Nova Scotia. Commission of Conservation, Ottawa, Ontario. 93 p.

Ferree, M.J. and R.K. Hagar. 1956. Timber growth rates for released forest stands in New York State. State University of New York, College of Forestry, Syracuse, NY. Tech. Pub. 78. 56 p.

Fisher, R.T. 1918. The yield of volunteer second growth as affected by improvement cutting and early weeding. J. Forestry 16:493-506.

Frothingham, E.H. 1914. White pine under management. U.S. Department of Agriculture, Washington, DC. Bull. 13. 70 p.

Gevorkiantz, S.R. and R. Zon. 1930. Second growth white pine in Wisconsin. Wisconsin Agricultural Experiment Station, Madison, WI. Bull. 98. 40 p.

Gunter, J.E. and V.J. Rudolph. 1968. Economics of red pine release on the Fife Lake State Forest. Michigan Agricultural Experiment Station, East Lansing, MI. Quart. Bull. 50(4):507-519.

Hansen, H.L. 1980. The Lake States region, p. 67-105. In Barrett, J.W. (ed.) Regional silviculture of the United States. John Wiley and Sons, Inc., New York, NY. 551 p.

Heyd, R.L. 1982. Insects versus artificial regeneration of conifers, p. 358-374. In Mroz, G.D. and J.F. Berner (comps.) Proc., Artificial Regeneration of Conifers in the Upper Great Lakes Region. Michigan Technological University, Houghton, MI. 435 p.

Honer, T.G. and A. Bickerstaff. 1985. Canada's forest area and wood volume balance 1977-1981: an appraisal of change under present levels of management. Pacific Forestry Centre, Canadian Forestry Service, Victoria, BC. BC-X-272. 84 p.

Jordon, P.A. and S. Posner. 1984. Effects of deciduous shrubs on young planted white spruce, with references to moose, in northeastern Minnesota. Department of Fisheries and Wildlife, College of Forestry, Univ. of Minnesota, St. Paul, MN. Final Report to Superior National Forest. 62 p.

Ker, M.F. 1981. Early response of balsam fir to spacing in northwestern New Brunswick. Maritimes Forest Research Centre, Canadian Forestry Service, Fredricton, NB. Information Rep. M-X-129. 36 p.

Kingsley, N.P. 1977. The forest resources of Vermont. USDA Forest Service, Northeastern Forest Experiment Station, Upper Darby, PA. Resour. Bull. NE-46. 58 p.

Kingsley, N.P. 1985. A forester's atlas of the Northeast. USDA Forest Service, Northeastern Forest Experiment Station, Broomall, PA. Gen. Tech. Rep. NE-95. 96 p.

Kotar, J. and M.S. Coffman. 1984. Site selection based on ecosystem classification, p. 101-108. In Marty, R. (ed.) Managing red pine. Proc., Second Soc. Amer. Foresters Region 5 Technical Conference, Marquette, MI. Department of Forestry, Michigan State Univ., East Lansing, MI. SAF Publ. 85-02. 273 p.

Lehela, A. 1981. Benefits of herbicide control of unwanted vegetation in the boreal mixedwood forest, p. 221-233. In Proc., Boreal Mixedwood Symposium. Great

Lakes Forest Research Centre, Canadian Forestry Service, Sault Ste. Marie, Ontario. No. 0-P-9. 278 p.

Lewis, B.J. 1984. Minnesota forest industry as a force in economic development: options for the future. Paper presented at Governor's Conference, Dec. 17, 1984, Minneapolis, MN. College of Forestry, St. Paul, MN. 51 p.

Loucks, O.L. 1962. A forest classification for the Maritime Provinces. Proc., Nova Scotia Institute of Science 25 (Pt. 2):85-167.

Lull, H.W. 1968. A forest atlas of the Northeast. USDA Forest Service, Northeastern Forest Experiment Station, Upper Darby, PA. 46 p.

MacLean, D.A. and M.G. Morgan. 1983. Long-term growth and yield response of young fir to manual and chemical release from shrub competition. Forestry Chron. 59:177-183.

McCormack, M.L., Jr. 1985. Vegetation problems and solutions—Northeast, p. 315-326. *In* Proc., Southern Weed Sci. Soc., 38th Annu. Mtg., Houston, TX. 562 p.

McCormack, M.L., Jr. and M. Newton. 1980. Aerial applications of triclopyr, phenoxys, picloram, and glyphosate for conifer release in spruce-fir forests of Maine. Abstr., Weed Sci. Soc. Amer. p. 47-48.

McLeod, J.W. 1964. Planting white spruce on wet brush land. Forest Research Branch, Canada Department Forestry, Ottawa. Publ. 1067. 4 p.

Merz, R.W. (comp.) 1978. Forest atlas of the Midwest. USDA Forest Service, North Central Forest Experiment Station, St. Paul, MN. 48 p.

Mullin, R.E. 1972. Machine planting of red pine. Forestry Chron. 48:37-38.

Mulloy, G.A. 1941. Cleaning of scattered young balsam fir and spruce in cut-over hardwood stands. Lake Edward-Project No. 7. Dominion Forest Service, Ottawa, Canada. Silvic. Res. Note 67. 19 p.

Murray, T.S. 1984. Site preparation in the Maritime Provinces. *In* Sympos. Proc., Reforestation in the Maritimes. Canadian Forestry Service, New Brunswick Department of Natural Resources, Nova Scotia Department of Lands and Forests, and Prince Edward Island Department of Energy and Forestry. Monocton, NB.

Newton, M., M.L. McCormack, Jr., E.C. Cole, and D.E. White. 1986. Response of young spruce-fir forests to aerial release sprays. Unpublished manuscript on file, Department of Forest Science, College of Forestry, Oregon State Univ., Corvallis, OR.

Nicholls, T.H., A.J. Prey, and D.H. Hall. 1984. Red pine diseases and their management in the Lake states, p. 230-264. *In* Marty, R. (ed.) Proc., Managing Red Pine. Soc. Amer. Foresters Publ. 85-02. 273 p.

Nienstadt, H. 1957. Silvical characteristics of white spruce (*Picea glauca*). USDA Forest Service, Lake States Forest Experiment Station, St. Paul, MN. Station Pap. 55. 23 p.

Nienstadt, H. and R.M. Jeffers. 1976. Increased yields of intensively managed plantations of improved jack pine and white spruce, p. 51-59. *In* Intensive planation culture. USDA Forest Service, North Central Forest Experiment Station, St. Paul, MN. Gen. Tech. Rep. NC-21. 117 p.

Piene, H. 1981. Early growth responses to operational spacing in young balsam fir stands on the Cape Breton Highlands, Nova Scotia. Maritimes Forest Research Centre, Canadian Forestry Service, Fredricton, N.B. Information Rep. M-X-125. 29 p.

Plice, M.J. and G.W. Hedden. 1931. Selective girdling of hardwoods to release young growth of conifers. J. Forestry 29:32-40.

Powell, D.S. and D.R. Dickson. 1984. Forest statistics for Maine. USDA Forest Service, Northeastern Forest Experiment Station, Broomhall, PA. Resour. Bull. NE-81. 194 p.

Raup, H.M. and R.E. Carlson. 1941. The history of land use in the Harvard Forest. Harvard Forest, Petersham, MA. Bull. 20. 64 p.

Richardson, J. 1982. Release of young spruce and pine from alder competition. Newfoundland Forest Research Centre, Canadian Forestry Service, Environment Canada, St. Johns, Newfoundland. Information Rep. N-X-211. 13 p.

Rowe, J.S. 1972. Forest regions of Canada. Department of Environment, Canadian Forestry Service, Ottawa, Ontario. Publ. 1300. 172 p.

Sajdak, R.L. and J. Kotar. 1985. Vegetation management problems and solutions—Lake States, p. 327-336. In Proc., Southern Weed Sci. Soc., 38th Annu. Mtg., Houston, TX. 562 p.

Sawyer, T. 1985. Personal communication. Chadbourne Lumber Co., Bethel, ME.

Sewall, J.W., Co. 1983. Spruce-fir wood supply/demand analysis. Contract report for Maine Department of Conservation. 94 p. appendixes.

Smith, W.B. and J.S. Spencer, Jr. 1985. Forest management opportunities for Michigan, 1981-1990. USDA Forest Service, North Central Forest Experiment Station, St. Paul, MN. Res. Pap. NC-264. 31 p.

Stewart, R.E., L.L. Gross, and B.H. Honkala. 1984. Effects of competing vegetation on forest trees: a bibliography with abstracts. USDA Forest Service, Washington, DC. Gen. Tech. Rep. WO-43. 260 p.

Stiell, W.M. 1964. Twenty-year growth of red pine planted at three spacings. Canada Department of Forestry, Ottawa. Publ. 1045. 24 p.

Stoeckeler, J.H. and G.A. Limstrom. 1950. Reforestation research findings in northern Wisconsin and Upper Michigan. USDA Forest Service, Lake States Forest Experiment Station, St. Paul, MN. Pap. 23. 34 p.

Sutton, R.F. 1975. Nutrition and growth of white spruce outplants: enhancement by herbicidal site preparation. Can. J. Forest Res. 5:217-223.

Sutton, R.F. 1985. Vegetation management in Canadian forestry. Great Lakes Forest Research Centre, Canadian Forestry Service, Sault Ste. Marie, Ontario. Information Rep. O-X-369. 34 p.

Vicary, B.P., T.B. Brann, and R.H. Griffin. 1984. Base-age invariant polymorphic site index curves for even-aged spruce-fir stands in Maine. Univ. Maine Agr. Exp. Sta. Bull. 802. 33 p.

Von Althen, F.W. 1972. Eight-year results of an afforestation study. Forestry Chron. 48:325-326.

Waldron, R.M. 1959. Hazel foliage treatments to reduce suppression of white spruce reproduction. Forestry Branch, Canada Department of Northern Affairs and National Resources, Ottawa. Forest Res. Div. Tech. Note 75. 17 p.

Westveld, M. 1937. Increasing growth and yield of young spruce pulpwood stands by girdling hardwoods. U.S. Department of Agriculture, Washington, DC. Circ. 431. 20 p.

Wilde, S.A., B.H. Shaw, and A.W. Fedkenheuer. 1968. Weeds as a factor depressing forest growth. Weed Res. 8:196-204.

Willcocks, A.J. 1979. Growth studies on a twenty-eight-year-old plantation at Moonbeam, Ontario. Ontario Ministry of Natural Resources, Kapuskasing. Unpub. rep. on file.

5

Principles Governing Plant-Environment Interactions

STEVEN R. RADOSEVICH
KATHERINE OSTERYOUNG

INTRODUCTION

A fundamental goal of forest regeneration is to stock a site with desirable trees following natural or human-caused disturbance. To most effectively accomplish this goal, the manner in which trees interact and respond to their environments must be known. Knowledge of the ecological principles that govern plant growth and distribution is essential for vegetation management, for it is through the study and application of ecological concepts that the problems of forest regeneration will be solved.

ECOLOGICAL CONCEPTS

Environmental Resources and Conditions

Plants exist in a wide array of environments. The survival, growth, and distribution of plants is a function of the environment to which they are exposed. The environment is usually considered from two perspectives: macroenvironment and microenvironment. The *macroenvironment* is broadscale, often regional, and includes many aspects of climate and soil. The *microenvironment* is local in scale and is influenced by physical characteristics (rocks, debris, soil type, plants) and topography (slope and aspect). The microenvironment is modified whenever trees are cut and forests are replanted.

The resources available to an individual tree and the physical conditions it faces make up its microenvironment. *Resources* are environmental factors that are directly consumed by plants. They include light, water, nutrients, and the gases necessary for photosynthesis and respiration. *Conditions* are factors that influence the survival and growth of plants but are not directly consumed by them. Temperature, soil compaction (aeration), soil penetrability, and animal grazing are examples of environmental conditions. Table 5-1 lists the important environmental resources and conditions necessary for plant growth. The manner by which plants experience and respond to the microenvironment determines species distribution patterns, size, and abundance on a site. People can also influence vegetative patterns and relative species abundance by direct manipulation of vegetation. Activities such as clearing or cultivation modify the microenvironment of a site and thereby influence the appearance and composition of vegetation that follows the disturbance. Therefore, forest regeneration is based on the physiological and morphological responses of tree seedlings to the available resources and suitability of conditions that occur on a site following disturbance.

TABLE 5-1. Important Factors of the Environment

Factors	Important Aspects	Component
	Climatic Factors	
Light	Intensity	Resource
	Quality	or
	Duration or photoperiod	Condition
Temperature	Degree	Condition
	Fluctuation	
	Duration	
Precipitation	Amount	Resource
	Frequency	
	Seasonal distribution	
Humidity	Degree	Resource
	Duration	or
		Condition
Wind	Velocity	Condition
	Duration	
Gases	Oxygen	Resource
	Carbon dioxide	
	Pollutants (sulfur dioxide, halogens, smog, etc.)	Condition

TABLE 5-1. Important Factors of the Environment (*Continued*)

Factors	Important Aspects	Component
	Edaphic Factors	
Origin and classification of soil		Condition
Topography, slope, and exposure of soil		Condition
Physical properties of soil	Structure	Condition
	Texture	Condition
	Aeration	Condition
	Moisture	Resource
	Temperature	Condition
	Slope	Condition
Chemical properties of soil	pH	Condition
	Minerals	Resource
	Organic compounds	Resource or Condition
	Base exchange capacity, etc.	Condition
Biotic properties of soil	Organic matter	Condition
	Plants	Condition
	Animals	Condition
	Biotic Factors	
Humans	Clearings	Resource
	Drainage	or
	Fire	Condition
	Cultivation and other cultural treatments (fertilization, pruning, thinning, weeding, girdling, irrigation, vegetative reproduction, etc.)	
Insects	Defoliation	Condition
	Stem and root feeding	Condition
	Disease transmission	Condition
	Pollination, etc.	Condition
Plants	Competition (light, water, minerals, space)	Resource or
	Parasitism	Condition
	Symbiosis, etc.	
Animals	Grazing by animals, rodents birds, etc.	Condition
	Mechanical damage	Condition

Source: Adapted from Kramer, P.J. and T.T. Kozlowski. 1960. Physiology of Trees. McGraw-Hill Book Co., Inc., New York, NY. Copyright © 1960 by the McGraw-Hill Book Co., Inc. Reproduced by permission of the McGraw-Hill Book Co., Inc.

Theory of Tolerances

Because the surface of the earth is a network of microenvironments that vary in both space and time, scientists have attempted to correlate environmental variations with apparent patterns of species evolution and distribution. During the last century, agriculturalists, plant geographers, and ecologists have proposed a *theory of tolerances* to account for plant species distribution. The components of this theory as summarized by Good (1931, 1974) and later by Barbour et al. (1980) are as follows:

1. Each and every plant species is able to exist and reproduce successfully only within a definite range of environmental factors.

2. In general order of importance, the environmental factors are climatic, edaphic, and biotic.

3. Tolerance ranges may be broad for some factors and narrow for others, and they may change in their relative importance with the phenological stage, size, and age of the species.

4. Tolerance ranges cannot be determined from an examination of morphological features; instead, they are related to physiological features that can only be measured experimentally.

5. Tolerance ranges may change in the process of natural selection; however, this process is so slow that environmental change is typically accompanied by plant migration rather than a change in the plants' tolerance.

6. The relative distribution of species with similar tolerance ranges for physical factors is determined finally by the result of competition (or other biotic interactions) among the species.

Some ecologists disagree with the order of importance for the environmental factors just listed (Harper 1964, Ellenberg 1958). They cite evidence suggesting that biotic factors are more important than climatic ones for species distribution. Certainly, human-caused disturbance, competition among plant species existing together, fire, and animal grazing can be very important in determining plant distribution. The range of factors under which a plant species can exist and grow best in isolation is its potential range and potential optimum, respectively (Barbour et al. 1980) (Figure 5-1). However, the actual range and actual ability to grow are influenced by human activities and the presence and abundance of other plant and animal species also present on the site. In regard to forest regeneration, these biotic factors ultimately influence the microenvironment of trees directly or the ability of the trees to respond to their environment.

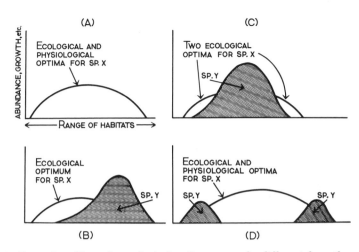

Figure 5-1. Examples of how the ecological optimum may be different from the physiological optimum due to competition. In (A), Species X grows alone, and laboratory experiments determine that its physiological optimum lies in the center of the curve. In nature, it faces competition from other species that displace it from habitats it could grow in alone; consequently, its ecological optimum is shifted far to the left of its physiological optimum, as shown in (B). In (C), Species X competes poorly and is displaced from the middle of its range; it appears to have two ecological optima. In (D), Species X competes poorly at the range extremes, with a result that the ecological optimum still coincides with the physiological optimum, but the range is shortened. (*Source:* From Walter, H. 1973. Vegetation of the Earth in Relation to Climate and the Eco-physiological Conditions. By permission of Springer-Verlag)

Evolutionary Strategies of Plants

According to Grime (1979), all of the external factors that limit the amount of plant material on any site fall into the categories of stress and disturbance. *Stress* relates to factors that limit production such as the limitations of light, water, mineral nutrients, or extremes in temperature. *Disturbance* is the total or partial destruction of plant biomass. It arises from the activities of pathogens, herbivores, people, or physical phenomena like fire, wind, snow, or landslide. When the spectra of habitats occupied by plants are examined, it is obvious that the levels of stress and disturbance vary considerably. However, if only the extremes of stress and disturbance are considered (high and low), four situations emerge with which plants must contend:

| | Stress | |
Disturbance	High	Low
High	Mortality	Ruderal
Low	Stress tolerator	Competitor

The combination of high disturbance (i.e., severe and frequent) and high stress does not result in a tenable strategy because plant mortality is the outcome of such a harsh environment. Plants have adapted to the remaining three situations in a variety of ways. These have been grouped into three general strategies to explain the temporal and spatial distribution of plants: ruderals, competitors, and stress tolerators.

Ruderal plants have a short life span and high seed production. They are most prevalent in severely or frequently disturbed but potentially productive habitats. Ruderal species also have been termed colonizers, pioneers, and invaders because they usually appear rapidly on newly or frequently disturbed sites. Annual or short-lived perennial grasses and forbs that occupy recent clearcuts would be examples of ruderal species. *Stress tolerators* are adapted toward the other extreme. Such species maintain relatively low vegetative and reproductive effort and exhibit adaptations that ensure endurance of relatively mature individuals in difficult environments. It is important to note that a limiting environment can be caused by physical or climatic factors (e.g., drought or flood) or biotic factors, such as other vegetation. Species with stress-tolerant characteristics usually are most abundant in late stages of succession or unproductive habitats and are termed *climax species*. *Competitors* depend on characteristics that maximize the capture of environmental resources in productive but relatively undisturbed habitats, such as the early stages of reforestation. They may be herbs, but shrubs or trees that produce an abundance of vegetative growth are more common. Competitors occupy the early to middle stages of succession. Once they inhabit a site they often remain there for long periods.

These evolutionary strategies represent an array of plant adaptations for individual species survival over time and constitute the means for continual site occupation by vegetation. A complete list of characteristics describing these three important categories of vegetation is presented in Table 5-2. It is important to note, however, that most plant species probably do not fall into any single category. Rather, it is more common for the strategies to merge, with characteristics of each category often represented in a given species. Thus Grime (1979) indicated that composites of two or more of the extremes in evolutionary strategies are more usual.

It appears that many shrub and tree species that occur on moderately disturbed forest lands follow a combined strategy of competition and stress tolerance (Figure 5-2). These species are capable of dominating early and intermediate seral communities following a disturbance to the forest. As competitors, these species possess early and rapid rates of vegetative growth, especially if sprouting occurs following top removal. They are also shade tolerant and long lived, often existing for decades. Furthermore, they tend to allocate a significant amount of their resources (primarily carbon) to canopy development and support, thereby utilizing

TABLE 5-2. Some Characteristics of Competitive, Stress-Tolerant, and Ruderal Plants

	Competitive	Stress Tolerant	Ruderal
Morphology			
1. Life forms	Herbs, shrubs, and trees	Lichens, herbs, shrubs, and trees	Herbs
2. Morphology of shoot	High, dense canopy of leaves Extensive lateral spread above- and belowground	Extremely wide range of growth forms	Small stature, limited lateral spread
3. Leaf form	Robust, often meso-morphic	Often small or leathery, or needle-like	Various, often mesomorphic
Life History			
4. Longevity of established phase	Long or relatively short	Long—very long	Very short
5. Longevity of leaves and roots	Relatively short	Long	Short
6. Leaf phenology	Well-defined peaks of leaf production coinciding with period(s) of maximum potential productivity	Evergreens, with various patterns of leaf production	Short phase of leaf production in period of high potential productivity
7. Phenology of flowering	Flowers produced after (or, more rarely, before) periods of maximum potential productivity	No general relationship between time of flowering and season	Flowers produced early in the life history
8. Frequency of flowering	Established plants usually flower each year	Intermittent flowering over a long life history	High frequency of flowering

111

TABLE 5-2. Some Characteristics of Competitive, Stress-Tolerant, and Ruderal Plants (*Continued*)

	Competitive	Stress Tolerant	Ruderal
9. Proportion of annual production devoted to seeds	Small	Small	Large
10. Perennation	Dormant buds and seeds	Stress-tolerant leaves and roots	Dormant seeds
11. Regenerative strategies[a]	V, S, W, B$_s$	V, B$_r$	S, W, B$_s$
Physiology			
12. Maximum potential relative growth rate	Rapid	Slow	Rapid
13. Response to stress	Rapid morphogenetic responses (root-shoot ratio, leaf area, root surface area) maximizing vegetative growth	Morphogenetic responses slow and small in magnitude	Rapid curtailment of vegetative growth, diversion of resources into flowering
14. Photosynthesis and uptake of mineral nutrients	Strongly seasonal, coinciding with long continuous period of vegetative growth	Opportunistic, often uncoupled from vegetative growth	Opportunistic, coinciding with vegetative growth

15. Acclimation of photosynthesis, mineral nutrition, and tissue hardiness to seasonal change in temperature, light, and moisture supply	Weakly developed	Strongly developed	Weakly developed
16. Storage of photosynthate and mineral nutrients	Most photosynthate and mineral nutrients are rapidly incorporated into vegetative structure, but a proportion is stored and forms the capital for expansion of growth in the following growing season	Storage systems in leaves, stems, and/or roots	Confined to seeds
Miscellaneous			
17. Litter	Copious, often persistent	Sparse, sometimes persistent	Sparse, not usually persistent
18. Palatability to unspecialized herbivores	Various	Low	Various, often high

Source: Grime, J.P. 1979. Plant Strategies and Vegetation Processes. Copyright © 1979 by John Wiley and Sons, Ltd. Reprinted by permission of John Wiley and Sons, Ltd.

[a]Key to regenerative strategies: V—vegetative expansion, S—seasonal regeneration in vegetation gaps, W—numerous small wind-dispersed seeds or spores, B_s—persistent seed bank, B_s—persistent seedling bank.

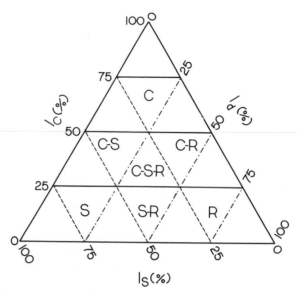

Figure 5-2. Model describing the various equilibria between competition, stress, and disturbance in vegetation and the location of primary and secondary strategies. I_c, relative importance of competition (——); I_s, relative importance of stress (----); I_d, relative importance of disturbance (—·—·). C, R, and S refer to competitor, ruderal, and stress-tolerator strategies, respectively. (*Source:* From Connell and Slatyer 1977. Reproduced from American Naturalist, 111:1119-1144, by permission of the University of Chicago Press. Copyright © 1977 by the University of Chicago Press)

considerable physical space and site resources. Because of these traits, the succession of later, more stress-tolerant species can be very slow.

Succession

The concept of *succession* has long been central to ecological thinking. It is the process of community change over time. Barbour et al. (1980, p. 10) state that

> Vegetation which does not change with time is in equilibrium with its environment and is said to be mature, stable, or in a *climax* state. In contrast, vegetation which is changing is said to be *seral*. In the process of succession, one seral community replaces another until a climax community is established and perpetuates itself. This path of succession through time is called a *sere*.

The colonization of a new substrate that has never supported plant life before is termed *primary succession*. However, *secondary succession* is of most concern to foresters and other land managers. This is the pattern of change after a disturbance whereby a patch in the physical environment is recolonized by plants. Horn (1974) states that secondary succession often is the result of interspecific competition, with pioneer species (ruderals) beating later dominant species to openings and sometimes outcompeting them. However, the ruderal species usually diminish as later species (competitors or stress tolerators) become more dominant on the site. Figure 5-3 depicts several stages of secondary succession following removal of conifers by logging. Early, intermediate, and late seral stages are evident. A forest resembling the original should eventually result if the area is not disturbed.

Examples of Forest Succession

The occurence of succession following partial or complete overstory removal of a forest is well substantiated by observation and scientific study. Dyrness (1973) documented over a 7-year period the vegetative changes that occurred on several clearcut sites in the western Cascade Mountains of Oregon. Total plant cover was 15, 49, and 79% in the first, second and fifth years, respectively, after logging and slash burning. Invading herbaceous (ruderal-like) species dominated from the second through fourth growing seasons following burning; thereafter, residual herbaceous and woody species (competitor-like) gained dominance. Dyrness also observed that differences in the level of disturbance from logging and burning

Figure 5-3. Secondary succession after logging activity. Various stages of community development are evident depending on the time (years) after conifer canopy removal.

influenced the species composition on the sites. In areas of undisturbed soil, residual species such as vine maple and salal predominated. These species probably would conform to Grime's (1979) competitors. Areas that were both logged and burned were occupied by seedling snowbrush or fireweed, which Dyrness termed *invaders* (ruderal-like species). Both "residual" and "invader" species occupied logged but unburned areas.

Similar successional trends were reported by Isaac (1940) in an 8-year study following logging and slash burning in the Douglas-fir region of western Washington and Oregon. Isaac indicated that a large number of species were found, but the major proportion of the cover in each plot comprised 28 herbaceous and brush species. Isaac found a tendency for herbaceous cover to decline (62 to 42%) during the study, but brush cover increased (26 to 42%) over the same period. On some plots, brush species had eliminated all other cover within 5 years. Isaac observed that when Douglas-fir became established early, that is, when the cover from other species was light, the trees continued to live, even after the shrub cover grew dense. When herbs or shrubs became established first, Douglas-fir abundance and growth were reduced. Thus eventual forest regeneration depended on the ability of Douglas-fir to establish quickly following disturbance and for that species to grow, close its canopy, and eventually suppress the associated brush species.

The fact that succession occurs and species are replaced over time is certain. However, the manner by which the early and intermediate species are replaced by climax species as secondary succession proceeds varies considerably. After logging, fire (slash burning), and other physical disturbances, it appears that ruderal- or competitor-like species with either broad dispersal powers or rapid growth rates are the first to occupy the site. These species may "invade" the area or may be "residual" on the site as a result of localized disturbance of the original overstory. In cases where disturbances are less severe, the development of established competitive-type and stress tolerant-type plants is favored.

Mechanisms of Succession

Connell and Slatyer (1977) have proposed three mechanisms (models) by which the earliest occupants of a site may be replaced by other plant species (Figure 5-4). In the *"facilitation"* model, the establishment and growth of the later species are dependent on a modification of the microenvironment by early species. As a result, the site becomes more suitable for colonization by later species. This model is the traditional assistance concept of Clements and his followers. According to Connell and Slatyer, evidence in support of this mechanism mainly applies to certain primary successions. The *"tolerance"* model suggests that a predictable sequence is exhibited by species that have evolved different strategies for exploiting environmental resources. Later species will be those able to tolerate lower levels of certain resources than earlier ones. Thus

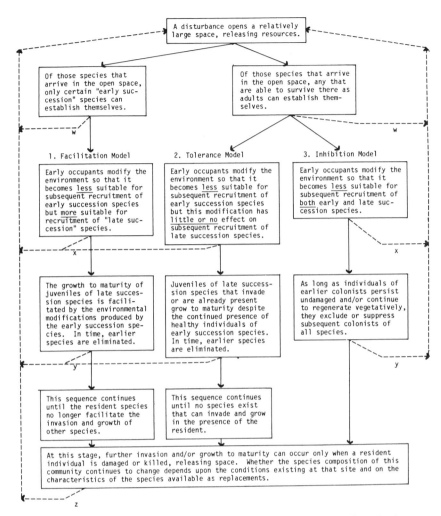

Figure 5-4. Three models of the mechanisms producing the sequence of species in succession. The dashed lines represent interruptions of the process, in decreasing frequency in the order w, x, y, and z. (*Source:* Adapted from Connell and Slatyer 1977, American Naturalist 111:1119-1144. Copyright © 1977 by the University of Chicago Press)

they can invade and grow to maturity in the presence of those that preceded them. In the "*inhibition*" model, all species, even the earliest, retard invasions of other species. The first occupants preempt the space and will continue to exclude or inhibit later colonists until the former die or are damaged, thus releasing environmental resources. Only then can later colonists become established and eventually reach maturity. The latter model of Connell and Slatyer might be the ideal for intensively managed forest stands where wood production is the primary goal. Although such models are generally instructive to assist in our understanding of plant change over time, Oliver (1978) and Hibbs (1983) point out several common examples of succession that do not fit strictly any of the proposed models of Connell and Slatyer (1977). It is possible, however, that composite processes exist in such cases.

The shrub, tree, and vine species that appear early in forest succession on productive sites often possess similar characteristics. These traits include rapid dry matter production (compared to other trees and shrubs), rapid stem extension, leaf production through most of the growing season, and rapid phenotypic responses of leaf or stem morphology to shade. Grime (1979) indicates that such features are particularly conspicuous among deciduous trees (e.g., *Ailanthus, Betula, Populus*) and shrubs that occur in the early phases of natural reforestation in disturbed woodlots of the Northeast and Lake states. Species that assume a similar role in the forested areas of the Northwest occur in the genera *Arctostaphylos, Ceanothus, Rubus, Alnus, Arbutus*, and *Acer* (Radosevich and Holt 1984). Early successional stages in much of the South are comprised of a variety of herbs, vines, pines, and light-seeded hardwoods (e.g., *Acer, Fraxinus, Liquidambar, Nyssa*, and *Populus*) (Oosting 1956).

Most of the species that colonize an area following disturbance by fire or logging do so by immigration from other sites or from long-term seed reserves in the soil. Initial seedling growth is usually slow, but once the seedling is established, extensive and rapid vegetative growth follows. In addition, many species (e.g., manzanitas, *Ceanothus* spp., maples, Pacific madrone, tanoak in the Northwest, and oaks, hickories, and maples in the South and Northeast) sprout readily from root crowns or stumps if the disturbance only removes top growth. Total canopy coverage can approach the predisturbance levels in only a few years. Maximum photosynthate production and usually vegetative growth coincide with periods of low moisture stress. Some of these species are notably shade intolerant, however, and the ultimate dominance of more shade-tolerant trees is assured once the trees emerge above the canopy.

Secondary succession occurs, at least in part, as a result of interactions among the species that occupy a site after disturbance. The outcome of these interactions is affected by differences in carbon allocation patterns among the species (Table 5-2), which influence successional (competitive) tactics. Thus some species assume dominance, whereas others may be suppressed or even displaced. The factors that determine success, in terms of ultimate dominance, are the availability of environmental resources and the relative ability of the species to capture (usurp) resources or tolerate low levels of them. Plant species that can occupy a site in large numbers or can quickly occupy a large volume of space by rapid growth will initially dominate and may persist for a long period of time.

Newton (1973, p. 159) has proposed the term *dominance potential* to signify the ability of individual species to preempt resources. In defining this process, he states:

> Dominance potential (DP)...is the summation of all features of a species relating to its ability to assume dominance (over a specific length of time, DP_t) in a limited system. For a given site, a species with high local DP will tend to replace or suppress a species with a lower DP but an equal start. A species with lower DP may prevail if it is established first, but a species with high "long-term" DP_t will eventually displace a species with high "short-term" DP_t.

Because of the rapid occupation of sites by certain shrub or tree species, some form of brush suppression often has been desirable for adequate conifer regeneration. However, once conifers assume dominance, they should remain because of their high long-term dominance potential, especially in the absence of other constraining factors like animals, insects, or disease. The need for brush suppression often is dependent on the conifer and shrub species involved and effectiveness and timeliness of site preparation in relation to planting (Schubert and Adams 1971).

Whatever the outcome of succession, it is determined by differences in physiological and reproductive strategies and in morphological characteristics among the species involved. The fact that some level of coexistence among species in a community is possible suggests that these strategies are highly refined by natural selection, so that competition is minimized and optimum overall site utilization is ensured. In the context of artificial forest regeneration (where conifer production is desired), it is instructive to examine the competitive strategies of young conifers in relation to those species with which they are associated.

Succession and Implications for Management

As will be discussed later, the physiological and morphological characteristics affecting the competitive interactions between individual plants account for the successional sequences that invariably occur in the natural environment following a disturbance. The fact that one species outcompetes another at some point in succession does not mean it will continue to dominate indefinitely. As plant senescence occurs or resource availability and other factors become modified over time, those species with adaptations more suitable to the changing environment will gain a competitive edge and succession will proceed, even if slowly. Thus the goal of vegetation management may be viewed as shortening the time between initial and later stages of secondary succession by providing conditions that favor growth of desirable tree species until they can naturally outcompete less desirable colonizers of the site. Vegetation management also can be used to delay the encroachment of later successional species (e.g., a variety of hardwood species in the South) that may be of less economic value than conifers.

TABLE 5-3. A Complete List of All Biologically Possible Types of Interactions

Name of Interaction	On[a]		Off[a]	
	A	B	A	B
Neutralism	0	0	0	0
Competition	−	−	0	0
Mutualism, symbiosis	+	+	−	−
Unnamed	+	+	−	−
Protocooperation	+	+	0	0
Commensalism	+	0	−	0
Unnamed	+	0	0	0
Amensalism	0	−	0	0
Parasitism, predation, herbivory	+	−	0	0

Source: Adapted from Burkholder (1952).

[a]When organisms A and B are close enough to participate in the interaction, the interaction is "on"; otherwise it is "off." Stimulation is symbolized as +, no effect as 0, and depression as −.

INTERFERENCE AND COMPETITION

Plants rarely exist in isolation; association with members of the same or other species is more common. Burkholder (1952) and later Odum (1971) have categorized the possible interactions that may occur among plants growing together (Table 5-3). These interactions are symbolically described in terms of their effect on two populations. When the two populations are in contact, the interaction is "on"; otherwise it is "off." The term *interference* has been used to describe interactions caused by the presence of a plant in the environment of a neighbor. Interference can be neutral (e.g., no effect), positive (e.g., stimulation), or negative (e.g., depression or antagonism). The actual causes of interference may include production or consumption of resources, production of growth stimulants or toxins, parasitism, predation, or protection. Each of the possible interactions listed by Burkholder probably is important for some species in the forest ecosystem.

As indicated in Chapter 2, numerous examples of both positive and negative interference exist for forest species. In this chapter we are primarily concerned about negative interactions between small (seedling) conifers and early successional vegetation. Therefore, only a few examples of positive interference are presented. Other positive associations between conifers and associated vegetation also are possible, such as protection from predators or by acting as a decoy, and some examples are given in Chapter 2. Also note that positive and negative interference may be temporally separated and, thus, are not necessarily mutually exclusive when succession is considered in its entirety.

Positive Interference

The importance of natural or artificial shade to the survival of conifer seedlings has been reported numerous times. In many instances, it appears that first-year survival after germination or planting often is enhanced by the shade of a shrub or tree that may in other ways be competing with the seedling (Wahlenberg 1930, Isaac 1938, Maguire 1955, Gordon 1970). The most common cause for the increased early survival of conifer seedlings under shade appears to be the moderation of environmental factors such as moisture, temperature, or light. Wahlenberg (1930) reported that increased survival of seedling ponderosa pine under natural shrub canopies may have been due to greater soil moisture and relative humidity or lower evaporation rates than in open areas. Isaac (1938) observed that mortality of Douglas-fir seedlings, except in the first year, was inversely related to the degree of shade provided by brush species. Excessive heat was considered to be the cause of mortality in open/burned areas the first year. However, insect, rodent, and mechanical damage to conifers accounted for considerable loss in brush-covered areas in subsequent years. The presence of dead rather than living shade increased coniferous survival in Isaac's study. Maguire (1955) found that shading 2-year-old nursery seedlings of ponderosa pine resulted in 80% survival. In contrast, only 20% survival occurred when seedlings were unshaded. Maguire believed the mortality of unshaded seedlings was caused by very high soil surface temperatures. However, shade also may have decreased the evaporative demand on ponderosa pine and thus water stress. Although initial conifer survival may be enhanced by shrub association, it appears that once the seedling trees become established (approximately 1 year), the benefits derived from shade diminish as the requirements for soil moisture and light increase.

A type of mutualistic relationship involving higher plants is symbiotic nitrogen fixation. This process, which only certain prokaryotic organisms can accomplish, involves the conversion of nitrogen gas to ammonium ions. Species of the nitrogen-fixing blue-green algae *Nostoc* and *Anabaena* are found in symbiotic association with certain liverworts, cycads, and *Azolla*—a genus of small aquatic ferns. Many legumes are found associated with the nitrogen-fixing bacterium *Rhizobium*. Symbionts in the genus *Frankia* are found in association with *Alnus*, *Ceanothus*, *Purshia*, and *Cercocarpus*—which are important early successional constituents of coniferous forests in the West. Generally, the nitrogen-fixing symbiont is localized in morphologically specialized structures on the host plant—for example, in root nodules (Peters 1978). Frequently, the symbiont is morphologically and physiologically distinct from free-living species of the same genus.

The nitrogen-fixing ability of red alder and certain species of *Ceanothus* has particularly important implications for forest regeneration because those species also are believed to compete with conifer seedlings for available resources. To reiterate some of the findings presented in Chapter 2, possible increases in coniferous biomass have been observed from association with nitrogen-fixing broadleaf species (Miller and Murray 1978). Tarrant (1961) observed that 25- to 27-year-old Douglas-fir in Oregon were similar in height and diameter in both mixed red alder-Douglas-fir and pure Douglas-fir stands, despite increased competition in the mixed stand. Approximately 10% more stems/acre were present in the mixed than in the pure stand. The total volume of wood in the mixed stand was more than twice that in the pure stand (2368 vs. 1103 ft^3/acre). However, the wood volume of Douglas-fir alone was somewhat less in the mixed stand because it had fewer Douglas-fir stems/acre than the pure stand. The rates of height and diameter increase of the dominant Douglas-fir were greater in the mixed stand at age 25 to 27 (the differences became significant at age 25 for height growth and age 20 for diameter growth). Total height of felled dominants of Douglas-fir was significantly greater in the mixed stand. Soil nitrogen was 65% greater beneath the mixed stand, and Douglas-fir had higher foliar nitrogen content in the alder association. However, the Douglas-fir in Tarrant's study was planted 4 years earlier than the alder, and the alder was repeatedly frost damaged in the juvenile stages. These factors may have reduced competitive interactions between the species or allowed a greater positive expression of the association (Murray and Miller, 1978). Nonetheless, the Douglas-fir volume by age 48 was 3100 ft^3/acre in the mixed stand as compared to 2900 ft^3/acre in the pure stand; the difference was not statistically significant, however. Red alder volume was about 2500 ft^3/acre. These observations have led Murray and Miller (1978) to conclude that the maintenance of a red alder component in Douglas-fir stands can increase merchantable yields on nitrogen-deficient sites. However, controlling stand density at an early age is necessary to maintain both Douglas-fir and red alder in dominant and codominant positions, respectively.

Youngberg and Wollum (1976) measured nitrogen accretion in snowbrush stands that developed following a wildfire and salvage logging in a second-growth Douglas-fir stand. They concluded that soil nitrogen could be restored to preburn levels after 7 years. However, Zavitkovski (1966) estimated that over 35 years would be required for the replenishment of nitrogen to predisturbance levels. Zavitkovski and Newton (1968) observed a significant correlation in a greenhouse study between the fresh weight of Douglas-fir and western hemlock seedlings and the dry weight of litter collected from beneath snowbrush stands. They concluded that nitrogen fixation by snowbrush did not add much nitrogen to the soil but formed a nitrogen-rich litter layer. Binkley (1986) found that the sites studied by Zavitkovski and Newton (1968) had not accumulated measurable amounts of nitrogen after 16 years, despite shrub nodulation and full occupancy of the site by snowbrush.

Cromack (1981) indicates that a number of soil properties can be altered by the addition of nitrogen from biological fixation. These properties include soil bulk density, soil pore size and distribution, cation exchange capacity, and soil aggregate size and strength. Thus the water-holding capacity and the availability of inorganic nitrogen and other nutrients in the soil solution could be enhanced by the added soil organic matter from the decomposition of nitrogen-fixing and other plant species. These studies suggest that on nitrogen-deficient sites, there may be considerable value in maintaining a nitrogen-fixing component of succession during forest regeneration. However, it appears that the greatest value from these associations arises upon death and decomposition of the nitrogen-fixing associate. It also is apparent that potential benefits may not be realized quickly by conifers but may be evident relatively late in succession. The relationship between this phenomenon and possible negative impacts on initial conifer survival and growth represents an important area for further study.

Negative Interference

Of the 10 possible interactions listed in Table 5-3, only three result in a negative influence on one or both of the interacting populations. These are competition, amensalism, and parasitism. *Competition* is the mutually adverse effects of two plants that utilize the same resource. *Amensalism* refers to the interaction in which only one of the plants is depressed, whereas the other is not. Allelopathy, the inhibition of one plant by another via the release of a selective toxicant, is a form of amensalism. *Parasitism* is a special form of negative interference because one plant derives its resources directly from the other. Parasitism of forest trees by microorganisms and higher plants (e.g., dwarf mistletoe, *Arceuthobium* spp.) is an important aspect of forest pest management but is beyond the scope of this chapter.

Amensalism and competition are often considered together because in both forms of interaction one species usually is depressed more than the other by the association. In addition, many "competition" experiments only measure the response of one of the species in the study, which makes any differentiation between competition and amensalism impossible. Thus competition often is poorly defined but generally refers to the suppression of one plant species by another. Herbaceous, shrub, or undesirable tree species are considered to be competitors of conifer seedlings. Often increased mortality and reduced growth rates of the conifers result from the association with these plants.

Stewart et al. (1984) have summarized over 260 studies that report the effects of weed competition or response of commercial tree species to weed control. In most of the studies, the trees responded positively to reduced weed competition, with substantial increases in growth. Stewart routinely observed that the largest gains in tree growth occurred when young trees never experienced, or were released early from, the presence of overtopping species. These studies demonstrate the relative aggressiveness of weed species in competition with tree seedlings. However, sufficient information usually is not provided to determine the levels of weed suppression necessary (i.e., economic thresholds) for optimum tree response or to assess times in stand development when competition is most critical. In addition, few studies have attempted to identify the environmental resource(s) for which competition was occurring.

Competition

At some point in development after germination, the seedling exhausts its parental supplies and must become independent of them if it is to survive. Further growth then depends on the seedling's ability to extract the resources it needs from the environment. The supply of resources may be unrestricted in certain environments, but limitation is more common. Resource limitation can be caused by unavailability, inadequate supply, or consumption by neighboring plants. The presence of neighbors can aggravate an already insufficient condition or create a deficiency where there is ample resource for a single individual (Radosevich and Holt 1984).

Harper (1977) describes three distinct classes of neighbors that may occur in the field: parts of the same plant (roots, leaves, branches, clones, etc.), neighbors of the same species but from different seed, and neighbors of different taxa. All are of interest to plant population biologists; however, the last two are of most importance to applied ecologists, agronomists, foresters, and other land managers. *Intraspecific competition* is the negative interaction between plants of the same species. It is necessarily very intense because closely related individuals must exist in similar, if not identical, microenvironments.

Interspecific competition involves adverse interference among plants of different species. Current evolutionary theory holds that selection pressure drives species within a community to utilize different parts of the environment, with the result that competition is minimized (i.e., niche separation). For example, Yeaton et al. (1977) demonstrated that differences in rooting depth among three desert species reduced competition for water among them. Niche separation may occur over time as well as in space. Flowering and seed production of understory species in eastern deciduous forests often occur before the trees are in full leaf, so that required amounts of light and other resources needed by the understory and overstory plants are separated in time (Whittaker 1975). If partitioning of environmental resources or access to them did not occur, coexistence among different plant species within a community would not be possible.

Because of niche separation, most natural systems are typified by a high degree of species diversity. That situation would be satisfactory in managed systems as well, if multiple species success was the only goal. However, when single species productivity is of primary concern, most environmental potential (resources) must be directed toward the desired species. Often the niche separation between seedling conifers and associated vegetation is not distinct enough to allow maximum productivity of conifers. However, some spatial and temporal specialization among particular coniferous species and other vegetation is naturally evident, and coexistence may be possible without diminishing crop wood production appreciably.

Space Capture

Because resource use is integrated within an individual and among plants in association, some workers have chosen to consider the space utilized as an index of the impact of resources on growth. Thus space is an indicator of the composite of all resources necessary for plant growth. The concept of space, as an integrative resource, allows scientists to study the effect of proximity among individuals without concern for the actual cause of the interaction. In this manner, the mutual effects of individuals sharing the same environment can be measured because each individual must act as the biological indicator of "space" utilization by the other. However, whether to consider resource availability as a composite factor such as space or to consider resources independently depends on the information desired. There are certainly situations in which the identification and supplementation of a single limiting resource has corrected a growth deficiency that may have been aggravated by the presence of neighboring plants. At times it is advantageous to consider space and its implied resources as the object of competition, whereas at others the influence of individual resources must be considered.

In most plant populations, a size distribution arises in which most plants are suppressed and small, but a few are large and dominant. The place that an individual occupies within this hierarchy of size classes is apparently determined at a very early stage of development. A model developed by Ross (1968) and later presented by Harper (1977) demonstrates this point. Figure 5-5 illustrates the effect of the sequence of seedling emergence on space capture. In this figure, the space occupied by 10 grass seedlings placed randomly in a flat over 10 consecutive days is shown. The space each seedling preempted was proportional to its weight, which was, in turn, a function of when the seedling was planted. It is apparent that each plant in Figure 5-5 stopped growth when its space was restricted by its neighbors. Therefore, the last seedlings to be planted (numbers 7, 8, 9, and 10) were able to grow very little. The experiment by Ross as well as actual field observations in which the plants that emerge early appear to be the most competitive plants indicates that the

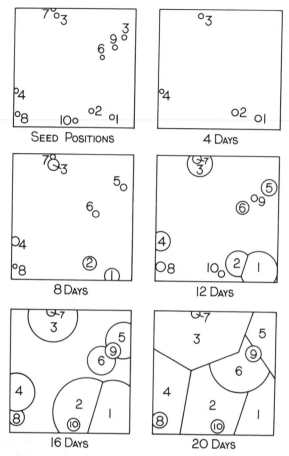

Figure 5-5. Diagrammatic model of the preemption of space (i.e., resources) by developing seedlings. The seedlings are numbered according to planting date; that is, 1 = planted first; 10 = last. (*Source:* Adapted from Ross 1968)

timing of emergence or initial occupancy of a site is more important than the spatial arrangement of the plants.

Effect of Density

Density is the number of individuals per unit of area. Common units of measure are plants/m^2, plants/acre or ha, or plants per plot. Density is often used to describe the number of plants in a crop or tree stand. As density increases or the size of individuals increases, a certain level of stocking is reached at which interference will occur between neighboring plants. Plants respond to density in two ways: through a plastic response of growth and/or an altered risk of mortality. Both types of responses may occur as a consequence of either intraspecific or interspecific competition.

Figure 5-6A represents the typical growth response of a plant population at increasing density. With the passage of time, plants growing at high density quickly meet the stress created by the proximity of neighbors, whereas plants at low density do so only as the neighboring plants get bigger. The result is that for a fully occupied site, total yield per unit of area is independent of density. Thus foresters often observe that cubic volume yield is relatively constant over a broad range of forest stand densities or stocking levels (see Chapter 7). The yield per unit area is equivalent over a broad range of densities because the amount of growth by individual plants (i.e., plant size) decreases as density increases. In its initial phase or at very low densities, the yield of the population is determined by the number of individuals. Eventually, however, the resource-supplying power of the environment becomes limiting, thereby determining ultimate yield. Such a relationship between density and productivity is similar for all plant species and mixtures of species. It is called the *law of constant final yield.*

As seen in Figure 5-6B, either increasing or decreasing the amount of resource may determine the ultimate amount of biomass production but does not affect its relationship to density. Furthermore, under high initial density, the ultimate yield may be determined by many small plants, or because of density-dependent mortality, fewer larger ones. In either case,

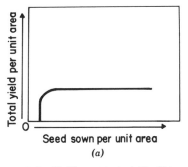
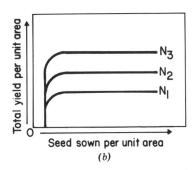

Figure 5-6. (A) Theoretical yield of biomass per unit area as a function of density of seed sown. (B) Influence of increasing the amount of a resource on the relationship of total yield per unit area to density of seed sown. N_1, N_2, and N_3 represent increasing increments of a limiting resource, for example, nitrogen fertility. (*Source:* Adapted from Radosevich and Holt 1984. By permission of John Wiley and Sons, Inc. Copyright © 1984)

the yield per unit area is a relatively constant feature of the environment for a given association of plant species.

Plant populations self-thin as space (or resources) available becomes more and more limited. This may be viewed as a lowered probability of survival as plant numbers increase. In fact, growth suppression (or stagnation) and loss of vigor are responses to less severe cases of the conditions that lead to self-thinning because death is the most extreme response to stress. The fact that self-thinning is an important phenomenon is reflected in numerous agricultural and forest management studies. Thus agronomists often recommend certain seeding rates of annual crops, and foresters suggest wide spacing between planted conifers and stocking control to avoid self-thinning or growth suppression. For example, Oliver and Powers (1978) have predicted that 50% suppression in ponderosa pine growth will occur in 40 yr if trees are planted on 3.9 m^2 versus 11 m^2 spacings. They also found that tree mortality was significantly greater as the trees became more confined due to close planting. Further ramifications of such intraspecific competition are discussed in standard mensurational texts. Examples of the effect of interspecific competition on forest growth and yield can be found in other chapters in this book.

Earlier we stated that in a competitive struggle for limited resources, there is an apparent premium on early establishment (site occupancy) and rapid growth. The growing plant must preempt space (i.e., resources) for its own use, thereby denying them to a neighbor via competition). Thus successful capture of resources by an individual depends on rapid colonization, adequate distance from neighbors, and rapid juvenile growth (plant size). Increased size can result from either a faster intrinsic rate of growth or a longer period of initial growth than a neighbor. When two species are grown together, delaying the time of establishment of one will influence markedly the relative contribution of each to the total output (dominance). However, differences in planting time, emergence, or establishment will not affect the final total yield if the contributions of both species are considered together and enough time elapses for full site occupancy to be achieved.

METHODS OF COMPETITION STUDY

Study Designs

In the study of competition, it is important to consider three factors: total density of plants, the proportion of each species involved, and the spatial arrangement of the species relative to each other. There are several experimental designs employed in agriculture and forestry to study competitive interactions that utilize the previously mentioned factors to varying degrees. These generally are termed the *additive, substitutive,* and *systematic* designs.

Additive Designs

In experiments using the additive design, two species are grown together, for example a crop and a weed. In this case the density of one species, usually the crop, is held constant, whereas that of the other, the weed, is varied. Basically, this experimental approach is a form of bioassay with the crop species acting as the indicator of the aggressive ability of the weed species. This approach is used widely because of its relevance to many field situations in which one species (the crop) is established in an area at a fixed density and the area is then invaded by another (weeds).

Numerous experiments have been conducted using this design to assess the impact of weeds on crop yields. In general, a sigmoidal relationship (Figure 5-7) exists between crop yield and weed density. Little loss in crop yield usually is observed at very low weed densities. Further increases in weed density cause sharp decreases in crop yield. Finally, a point is reached where additional increases in weed density do not proportionally decrease crop yields. Zimdahl (1980) and Stewart et al. (1984) have reviewed numerous studies in which the yield losses of various crops and trees associated with density of certain weeds were derived from additive experiments. In every case a clear pattern of diminishing returns

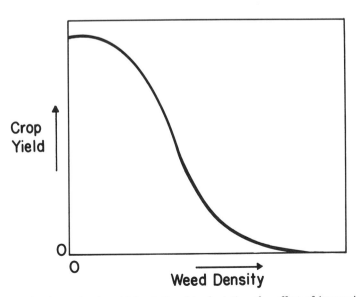

Figure 5-7. A schematic sigmoidal relationship depicting the effect of increasing weed density on crop yield. (*Source:* Redrawn from Zimdahl 1980, by permission of the International Plant Protection Center, Oregon State University, Corvallis, OR)

existed; that is, as weed density increased, crop yield decreased to a point at which no further addition of weeds substantially decreased crop or tree yields.

McDonald (1980) reported an additive experiment in which a constant density of seedling ponderosa pine (0.1 tree/m² = 1000 trees/ha) was subjected to various shrub densities (0 to 3.5 shrubs/m²). Canopy cover of the shrubs at the sixteenth year ranged from 0 to 4100 m²/ha. A strong relationship was found between ponderosa pine growth (tree diameter and height) and the degree of shrub density and cover. During the 16 years of this study, the increase in tree productivity in the shrub-free versus the heavy brush stand was 9.5 cm in diameter and 3.2 m in height.

A similar study was conducted by Oliver (1979) on a more productive experimental site. In this study various spacings of ponderosa pine were subjected to either a constant level of shrubs (14,100 m³/ha canopy) or to no shrubs. After 12 years, the absence of brush had significantly increased stem diameter, height, and live crown ratio of the ponderosa pine relative to trees growing in shrubs. The effects of shrub association were most pronounced at wide tree spacings. Similar observations have been made in other experiments with other herbaceous, shrub, or tree species (e.g., Fritz and Rydelius 1966, Gratkowski and Lauterbach 1974, Radosevich et al. 1976, Allan et al. 1978, Balmer et al. 1978, Nelson et al. 1981, Conard and Radosevich 1982, Petersen and Newton 1982).

Although this approach is used widely to assess competition and often can provide insight into the cost of competition in terms of yield loss, it is difficult to determine the degree of interaction either between species or among individuals of the same species. The value of the additive approach is the ability to determine directly the impact (yield loss) that is associated with the absence of weed control.

Substitutive Designs

De Wit (1960) has proposed another design to assess competitiveness between species. This approach examines the implication of a deviation from density-independent yield (the law of constant final yield) and the relative proportionality between the species involved. The basic premise of this approach is that yield in a mixture can be predicted from the yield of each species when grown separately. The substitutive design, or replacement series, examines the interactive relationship between the two species when grown together. It requires that total density or biomass (species A + species B) is held constant and that the two species are established in varying proportions. Each species also must be grown alone to assess intraspecific competition.

According to Harper (1977), four basic models of interference are possible (Figure 5-8). Model I describes a situation in which two possibilities exist: (1) the density of the mixed population is so low that individuals

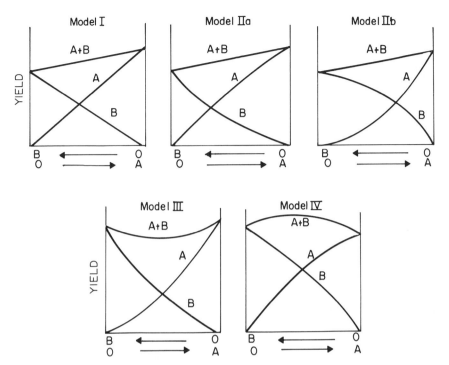

Figure 5-8. A variety of models for results of replacement series experiments for interference study. The vertical axis indicates some measure of plant yield, and the horizontal axis represents the proportion (ranging from none to all) of each species in the mixture. See text for explanation of models. (*Source:* Modified from Harper 1977, Population Biology of Plants. Copyright © 1977 by John L. Harper)

do not interfere with each other (in this case the requirement for density-independent yield has not been met); or (2) the density is great enough for interference, but the ability of the two species to interfere with each other is equivalent. Results depicted in Model I are interpreted to mean that both species make identical demands on environmental resources defined by the experiment and can, therefore, substitute for one another.

The responses in Model II are more usual. In this situation, one species provides more than expected to the total yield, whereas the other provides less than expected. This is the model for competition. In Model IIa, species A is more aggressive (competitive) for a resource than species B, and it eventually will dominate or even replace species B under the existing environmental constraints. In Model IIb, species B is more competitive.

In Model III, neither species contributes its expected share to the total yield. This is the case of mutual antagonism. Harper indicates that if each species damages the environment of the other more than its own, such a situation would exist. For example, species A might luxuriantly consume water and thus hinder B, but species B might produce a toxin that inhibits the growth of A and thus prevents A from fully exploiting its advantage.

In Model IV, both species provide more to the total yield than either one alone. This could be the result of symbiosis (mutual gain by each species). It also could indicate the escape of each species from competition with the other. For example, the major growth of species A could occur during a period when species B was dormant or absent, so that neither interfered markedly with the demands of the other.

Few studies have been reported that utilize this approach to examine the competitive relationship between conifers and shrubs. However, a study by Radosevich (1984), which examines interference between seedling ponderosa pine and sprouting greenleaf manzanita, is well underway. Initially, after the proportions were established (1980), both trees and shrubs grew as if unrestricted (Figure 5-9A). However, by the end of the third growing season (1982), a significant competitive interaction emerged (Figure 5-9B) because decreases in ponderosa pine aboveground biomass were observed in all mixtures that contained shrubs. Average aboveground biomass of ponderosa pine grown in pure stand was only 5 kg/plot in comparison to 167 kg/plot for the pure stand of greenleaf manzanita. Furthermore, no difference in shrub aboveground biomass was observed in 1982 between the shrub proportions of 0.5 to 1.0, whereas density independence was not achieved for the conifers at this point of the study. These data indicate that shrubs have a significant competitive impact on early seedling growth of ponderosa pine (the proportion 0.25 shrub:0.75 tree reduced pine growth by almost three times its potential in pure stand during the first three growing seasons). It appears from these initial data that a nearly 90% or more reduction in shrub canopy volume must be maintained for maximum growth of the pine. It is uncertain, however, whether such a low level of shrub volume would be necessary throughout the entire rotation of the pine stand.

It must be emphasized that the study by Radosevich (1984) was established as a long-term experiment, and the criterion for an independent density-to-yield relationship does not exist for the conifers in the early phase of this experiment. Thus densities of shrub and tree individuals do not reflect equivalency of biomass levels at this time. However, it is expected as the experiment progresses and trees become larger that this criterion will be met and equivalent "substitution" of tree biomass for shrub biomass should occur, eventually. Data collected in 1985 indicate that tree biomass in plots without shrubs has increased to levels similar to the shrub biomass in pure stands.

The value of replacement series experiments is their predictiveness. In this respect, several calculations can be made. A particularly valuable calculation is the *relative yield total* (RYT) that predicts whether the two

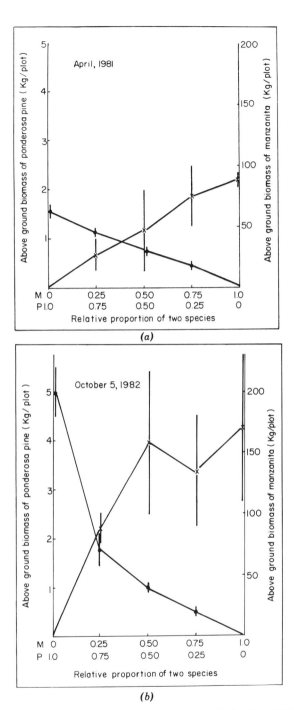

Figure 5-9. Biomass accumulation in (a) April 1981 and (b) October 1982, of ponderosa pine (.) and greenleaf manzanita (x) when grown in a replacement series experiment. (*Source:* From Radosevich 1984)

species are making demands on the same resource(s):

$$RYT = \frac{\text{yield of Species A in mixture}}{\text{yield of A in pure stand}} + \frac{\text{yield of Species B in mixture}}{\text{yield of B in pure stand}}$$

RYT values of about 1.0 indicate the same resource is being utilized. RYT values less than 1.0 imply mutual antagonism, whereas an RYT greater than 1.0 suggests that the species avoid competition, make different demands on resources, or maintain a symbiotic relationship. The RYT value in 1982 for the species in the study just described was 1.04 for the 0.50:0.50 proportion of trees to shrubs. This indicates that both species were competing for the same resource(s).

Systematic Designs

Systematic designs were first considered by Nelder (1962) for spacing studies involving single species (Figure 5-10). In such designs the plant density is considered as well as the arrangement (rectangularity) of individuals in relation to each other. Plants are grown in a circular grid

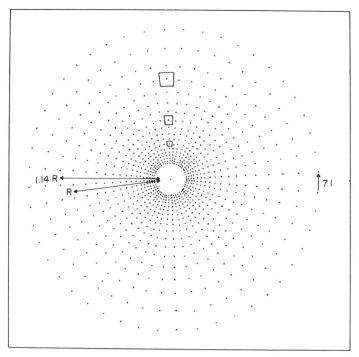

Figure 5-10. Diagram of 48-spoke Nelder plot with a rectangularity of 1 and a 30% increase in area per plant per arc. (*Source:* From Zedaker 1981)

pattern so the area per plant (position) changes in some consistent fashion over the different parts of the grid (i.e., as one moves outward along the spoke of the wheel).

Although Nelder designs have been used in a number of studies to determine the influence of intraspecific competition on tree yields, they have not been used widely to study interspecific interactions. They appear to be most useful to account for influences of spatial arrangement within a given plant species. However, it is also possible to consider the effect of total plant density and single or multiple proportions of both species with this design. Unfortunately, few studies using a systematic design exist that examine interference between seedling conifers and potential competitors.

Zedaker (1981) and Cole (1984) explored the effect of competitor type and density on the growth of Douglas-fir seedlings in the Oregon Coast Range using a systematic design. Nelder plots, encompassing a range of 300 to 15,000 cm^2 per plant along the spokes of the wheel, were established on three sites. Each plot was split into six pie-shaped sections. Two sections were planted with 1-year-old Douglas-fir seedlings; two sections had alternating spokes of Douglas-fir and 1-year-old red alder wildlings; and two sections were planted with Douglas-fir and broadcast seeded with grass. Observations of soil moisture, plant moisture stress, light attenuation in the seedling canopy, tree height, diameter and volume growth, and dry matter accumulation were taken at the end of the second and third growing seasons.

Zedaker found that Douglas-fir growth was inhibited by competition with itself or with either red alder or grass. Significant interactions between site and competitor type also were found. Differences in soil moisture depletion and plant moisture stress were indicative of the site-competitor-density interactions. Tree growth was correlated best with area (space) per tree, reaching an upper asymptote within the range studied. Moisture did not appear to be a limiting factor for growth in the range of sites studied as long as Douglas-fir had no competitors. Foliage, root, and total biomass per tree were positively correlated with the amount of space available. These observations generally were substantiated by Cole.

Measurement of Competition

In order to measure competition, some quantification of growth (e.g., yield) of the species must occur. Depending on the objectives of the study and type of design, it is sometimes enough to measure only yield of one species (usually the desirable tree species) and to express yield loss as due to the other species. Yield may be measured as vegetative production, seed, or as total biomass. Of most value are studies that determine yields for each species present in the experiment. Regardless of how yield is measured, the data are usually collected once. This single measurement of competition is particularly useful in the competition studies performed in the field and in many situations may be the only practical method of data collection. It provides a direct assessment of the abundance of harvestable material in the presence or absence of competitor interference. However, a series of observations are usually needed in studies involving woody species, where changes in species dominance may occur over time.

Other studies of competition are concerned with the relative attributes of species that allow one species to dominate over another. In these experiments, determination of growth (dry matter accumulation) differences between the species is used to assess the effects of competition within a specified environment. This procedure requires smaller and more frequent harvests or estimates of yield than the single harvest approach. It is most applicable for greenhouse or controlled environment (e.g., growth chamber) studies but does not preclude field experimentation. This experimental approach lends itself to the use of mathematical growth analysis, which has been described by Ledig (1974) for forest environments.

Growth analysis is a dynamic technique, focusing on growth rates rather than final yields. In growth analysis, periodic harvests or estimates of dry weight, leaf area, or proportions of various plant tissues are made to partition growth among plant components. In agriculture, it is most common to use several periodic destructive harvests of biomass throughout the growing season to derive the parameters of growth analysis. In forestry, frequent destructive harvests are usually impractical, and growth is estimated by linear regressions relating canopy or wood volume to probable biomass. This process is called *production* or *dimension* analysis (Ledig 1974).

In mathematical growth analysis, relative growth rate (RGR) is the most important index of productivity. It is an overall growth index for comparing the rate of growth at different times, among different populations, or among different environments (e.g., treatments). Because absolute growth depends, in part, on the amount of growing material, Ledig indicates that it would be meaningless to compare absolute growth rates among populations of individuals that differed in size (Figure 5-11). Therefore, growth rate should be expressed relative to the amount of growing material already present. RGR, the change in dry weight (dW) per unit time (dt) per unit of growing material (W) is given by the differential equation:

$$RGR = (d\mathrm{W}/dt)(1/\mathrm{W})$$

The value of examining species interactions (competition) through growth analysis can be seen in the substitutive experiment (Radosevich 1984) that was described earlier. In that study, ponderosa pine and green-

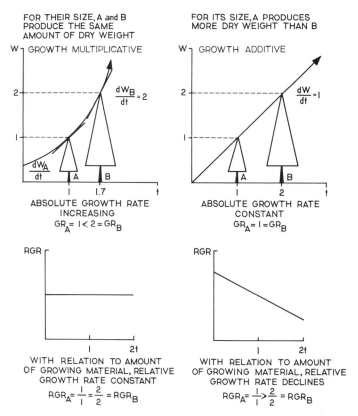

Figure 5-11. The relationship between growth rate (GR) and relative growth rate (RGR) for the opposing cases of multiplicative and additive dry weight (W) growth in time (t).

leaf manzanita were grown at a constant density comprised of various proportions. A significant depression in ponderosa pine yield was observed whenever the two species were grown in mixture. The RGR values of ponderosa pine growing in pure stand and at various proportions of shrubs are presented in Figure 5-12 for the 1982 growing season. No differences in relative growth rates between treatments (shrub/tree proportions) were observed for the entire growing season when trees and shrubs were grown together. This contrasts with marked increases in RGR of ponderosa pine without shrub interference. Clearly, growth of ponderosa pine is inhibited by association with the shrub species, and competition is most critical during the spring and summer portions of the growing season. Radosevich also has measured soil moisture and light abundance in this study. Neither resource was limiting in the pure stand of ponderosa pine, in contrast to the shrub-tree associations. However, the fact that RGR of the pure stand of ponderosa pine declined dramatically during the latter

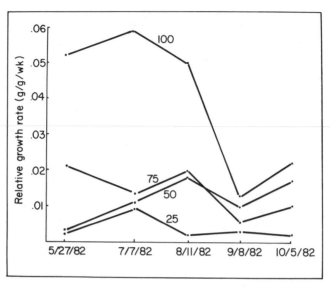

Figure 5-12. Relative growth rates (RGR) during 1982 of seedling ponderosa pine growing in pure stand and associated with greenleaf manzanita. 100, 75, 50, and 25 refer to relative proportions of all trees, 0.75 trees and 0.25 shrubs, 0.50 trees and shrubs, and 0.25 trees and 0.75 shrubs, respectively. (*Source:* From Radosevich 1984)

portion of the growing season suggests that competition for available resources is not the only factor determining ponderosa pine growth.

Relative growth rate can be further partitioned into physiological and morphological components of growth:

$$\text{RGR} = \underset{\substack{\text{physiological} \\ \text{component}}}{\text{NAR}} \times \underset{\substack{\text{morphological} \\ \text{component}}}{\text{LAR}}$$

The index of physiological activity is the net assimilation rate (NAR); that for the morphological component is represented by the leaf area ratio (LAR). The NAR is the rate of increase in total dry weight (dW/dt) per unit of leaf area (LA). Thus

$$\text{NAR} = (d\text{W}/dt)(1/\text{LA})$$

It is a measure of the efficiency of energy capture and conversion and of carbon allocation. Productivity also is influenced by the overall architecture of a plant as it proceeds through its life cycle. The leaf area ratio (LAR) is the important structural component of growth analysis because it relates the degree of assimilatory surface (LA = total leaf area) to biomass (total weight, W):

$$LAR = LA/W$$

Further partitionings of these various components of growth are possible, and the value and implications of these calculations have been described in several other texts (Evans 1972, Ledig 1974, Hunt 1978, Patterson 1982, Radosevich and Holt 1984). It would be most instructive for experiments to be conducted, similar to the one done by Radosevich (1984), in which the various components of growth could be separated and mathematically derived. Through such study, it should be possible to determine features of tree and shrub physiology and morphology that are most influenced by competition. Once such factors are identified, it should be possible to develop or alter management practices so as to allow optimum conifer growth and perhaps a level of coexistence with other species.

PHYSIOLOGICAL BASIS OF COMPETITION

As indicated earlier, the supplying power of the environment nearly always becomes limited at some point during a plant's development. This limitation of environmental resource(s) may be aggravated by proximity to neighboring plants. Most studies of negative interference indicate that such interactions occur. However, the outcome of competition is determined by the physiological responses to the resources and conditions that characterize the microenvironment of the interfering plants. Thus the greatest understanding of the mechanisms underlying competitive interactions arise when the limiting factors are identified and the plant responses to those factors are elucidated.

Light Availability

Light—the driving force in photosynthesis—is a fundamental requirement for plant growth. In forest environments, low light availability severely restricts the growth of tree species. Competition for light occurs when one species, because of more rapid growth, taller stature, or established presence, casts shade on another, thereby limiting its growth.

Plants with an ability to grow rapidly will be able to preempt resource supplies, produce more photosynthetic tissue, and perhaps shade out competitors. The maximum potential for growth will be partly determined by the maximum photosynthetic capacity, which varies among species. Jarvis and Jarvis (1964) report that photosynthetic rates are 5 to 10 mg CO_2 dm^{-2} hr^{-1} in temperate zone conifers and 10 to 20 mg CO_2 dm^{-2} hr^{-1}

in deciduous broadleaved trees and shrubs. Conard and Radosevich (1981) measured light-saturated photosynthetic rates of 13.6 and 34.8 mg CO_2 dm^{-2} hr^{-1} in white fir and snowbrush, respectively. Light-saturated rates in conifers comparable to those found in broadleaved trees also have been measured by Kramer and Clark (1947) and Kreuger and Ruth (1969).

In the natural environment, conifers are probably limited in their productivity by self-shading resulting from the orientation and density of their needles and branches. This possibility was demonstrated by Kramer and Clark (1947). These researchers found that photosynthetic rates in fully exposed individual loblolly pine needles reached saturation at one-third of full sunlight but increased gradually for the entire seedlings up to about 90% of full sunlight.

Shirley (1929) observed that plant species vary in their ability to maintain a positive carbon balance (i.e., photosynthesis exceeds respiration) in low light. Species with high photosynthetic capacities generally do not grow as well in dim light as those with lower capacities. The term *tolerance* has been used by silviculturists to describe the ability to survive and grow under conditions of low light. Bates and Roeser (1928) found that the minimum light requirements in a variety of conifer species ranged from 0.62 to 6.3% of full sunlight in ascending order for redwood, Engelmann spruce, Douglas-fir, and several pine species. This order corresponds to the shade-tolerance rating shown in Table 5-4 for some of the western species.

Photosynthetic efficiency in low light also has been correlated with the degree of shade tolerance. In addition to low light compensation points discussed before, shade-tolerant species generally exhibit lower photosynthetic rates at light saturation and higher photosynthetic rates at very low light levels than do intolerant species. They also retain their leaves longer and, therefore, require less light for the production of new photosynthetic tissue (Daniel et al. 1979). These characteristics are summarized in Figure 5-13. Low light requirements account for the ability of some species to compete successfully under the canopies of others. In general, it appears that shade-tolerant species can withstand a higher degree of light competition from other plants.

Only light impinging on a photosynthetically active organ is available for plant growth. Thus the surface area and orientation of the leaves are important for the assimilation of carbon by the plant. Allocation of carbohydrate to new photosynthetic surface area will result in an exponential increase in growth (Brix 1967), if other factors are not limiting. Increased growth may allow the development of a canopy that will shade a competitor, thereby reducing its growth and ability to exploit available resources. Allocation to belowground structures, although necessary for water and nutrient uptake, increases the respiratory demand and decreases the carbohydrate available for canopy development (Schulze 1982). Allocation patterns could, therefore, significantly affect the light-capturing ability and ultimate success of competing species.

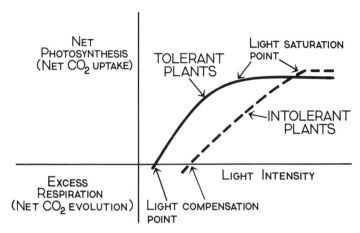

Figure 5-13. Effect of increasing light intensity on fully exposed foliage of tolerant and intolerant plants.

Environmental conditions can strongly influence the physiological parameters involved in photosynthesis. In a comprehensive review, Bjorkman (1981) cited a number of studies in which herbaceous plants adapted to high-light habitats had lower maximum photosynthetic rates and lower light compensation points when preconditioned under low light than clones of the same species grown under high light. However, the shade-grown plants still had light compensation points considerably higher than shade-adapted plants grown in deep shade. Shade-adapted plants do not appear to have a similar capacity for acclimation to high light. Some shade-adapted species have lower maximum photosynthetic rates when grown in the sun than when grown in shade. The same responses to light shown for sun- and shade-adapted species (Figure 5-13) probably apply to "sun" and "shade" foliage on a single plant.

Shade-tolerant tree species have photosynthetic characteristics that closely resemble those of shade-adapted herbs; that is, at low light, tolerant tree species can maintain a net carbon gain and are relatively efficient at light utilization (Kramer and Kozlowski 1960). However, shade-tolerant tree species often cannot acclimate readily to a sudden change in the light environment such as that following a complete competition release treatment or heavy thinning operation. This phenomenon is called *release shock* or *thinning shock*, and shade-tolerant species may respond with loss of foliage, slowed growth or even death where drastic changes in the light environment occur rapidly. In open situations, less shade-tolerant species would be expected to perform better (Daniel et al. 1979).

Growth patterns can also be affected by the light regime. Brix (1967) found that although photosynthetic capacity in Douglas-fir seedlings increased with increasing light intensity, allocation of photosynthate to leaf

TABLE 5-4. Relative Tolerance of Western Conifers and Hardwoods

Western Conifers

Very tolerant
Western hemlock (*Tsuga heterophylla*)
Alpine fir (*Abies lasiocarpa*)
Western red cedar (*Thuja plicata*)
Pacific yew (*Taxus brevifolia*)
California torreya (*Torreya californica*)

Tolerant
Sitka spruce (*Picea sitchensis*)
Engelmann spruce (*Picea engelmannii*)
Mountain hemlock (*Tsuga mertensiana*)
Pacific silver fir (*Abies amabilis*)
Grand fir (*Abies grandis*)
White fir (*Abies concolor*)
Redwood (*Sequoia* spp.)
Incense-cedar (*Libocedrus decurrens*)
Port-Orford-cedar
   (*Chaemacyparis lawsoniana*)
Alaska yellow cedar[a]
   (*Chaemacyparis nootkatensis*)

Intolerant
Limber pine (*Pinus flexilis*)
Pinyon pine[a] (*Pinus edulis*)
Ponderosa pine (*Pinus ponderosa*)
Jeffrey pine (*Pinus jeffreyi*)
Lodgepole pine (*Pinus contorta*)
Coulter pine (*Pinus coulteri*)
Knobcone pine (*Pinus attenuata*)
Bishop pine (*Pinus muricata*)
Big-cone spruce (*Pseudotsuga macrocarpa*)
Noble fir (*Abies procera*)
Junipers (*Juniperus* spp.)

Very intolerant
Whitebark pine (*Pinus albicaulis*)
Foxtail pine (*Pinus balfouriana*)
Bristlecone pine (*Pinus aristata*)
Digger pine (*Pinus sabiniana*)
Western Larch (*Larix occidentalis*)
Alpine larch (*Larix lyallii*)

Intermediate
 Western white pine (*Pinus monticola*)
 Sugar pine (*Pinus lambertiana*)
 Monterey pine (*Pinus radiata*)
 Blue spruce (*Picea pungens*)
 Douglas-fir (*Pseudotsuga menziesii*)
 Red fir[a] (*Abies magnifica*)

Western Hardwoods

Very tolerant
 Vine maple (*Acer circinatum*)

Tolerant
 Tan oak (*Lithocarpus densiflorus*)
 Canyon live oak (*Quercus chrysolepis*)
 Bigleaf maple (*Acer macrophyllum*)
 Pacific madrone[a] (*Arbutus menziesii*)
 California laurel[a] (*Umbellularia californica*)

Intermediate
 Red alder (*Alnus rubra*)
 Golden chinquapin[a]
  (*Castanopsis chrysophylla*)
 Oregon ash (*Fraxinus latifolia*)
 California white oak[a] (*Quercus lobata*)
 Oregon white oak[a] (*Quercus garryana*)

Very intolerant
 Quaking aspen (*Populus tremuloides*)
 Cottonwoods (*Populus* spp.)

[a]Cases of great uncertainty.

143

surface area decreased, whereas leaf thickness increased. High light can also result in an increased root/shoot ratio in conifers, increased root and shoot (total) dry weight (Kramer and Kozlowski 1960), increased leader elongation (Emmingham and Waring 1973), and increased root elongation (Barney 1951).

Water Availability

Water is a major limiting resource in many timber-producing regions of the western United States. It is an important limiting factor in other forested regions as well, even though sustained periods of drought are not as prevalent as in the West. Experimental evidence indicates that interspecific competition for available soil moisture may pose a greater limitation to tree growth than light availability. For example, in a recent study in the Sierra Nevada, the effect of brush competition was greatly reduced when the roots of shrubs competing with white fir were killed, but the shrub canopy was left in place (Conard and Radosevich 1982). The removal of the shrub canopy without also killing the root system did not stimulate white fir growth. Measurements of soil moisture indicated that the death of the shrub roots significantly enhanced the availability of soil moisture. In another study, Lanini and Radosevich (1986) demonstrated that soil moisture availability at a depth of 100 cm and subsequent growth of three coniferous species were inversely correlated with shrub canopy volume. Carter et al. (1984) also observed that elimination of competing vegetation around 5-year-old loblolly pine significantly lowered moisture stress of the pines when compared to a no-elimination treatment. Similar effects of vegetation and moisture availability on tree growth have been found for numerous tree species (Nelson et al. 1981, Eissenstat and Mitchell 1983, Cole 1984).

A variety of processes contribute to a plant's ability to compete successfully for a limited supply of water. Perhaps the most important is root growth. Because rare summer rains infrequently and incompletely replenish soil moisture in drought-prone regions, the roots must continually explore new soil horizons as the moisture supply in their immediate vicinity becomes depleted. Differences in the allocation of photosynthate to root growth could, therefore, affect the relative competitive abilities of different species.

Although a vigous root system is undoubtedly necessary in areas experiencing a summer drought, data on a variety of species from xeric habitats (10-26 in./year) indicate a poor relationship between precipitation, depth of root penetration, presence of taproot, and root-to-shoot biomass ratio. These rooting patterns appear to be responses to soil characteristics rather than genetic adaptations to drought conditions (Kummerow 1980). However, plants can exhibit considerable plasticity in root development and morphology because different root structures have been observed in the same species under different soil moisture conditions (Kummerow 1980). Because water is absorbed most efficiently at the root tips, root branching may be most closely related to a plant's ability to exploit available water resources. Peterson (1969) observed that Douglas-fir roots usually were more dense and extensive when the water supply was adequate than when trees experienced some level of water stress. The success of pine in an area that could not support Pacific silver fir or spruce has been attributed to a 24-fold greater number of root branches and an 8-fold greater absorbing surface area in the pines than in the fir or spruce (Kramer and Kozlowski 1960). This observation also may indicate temporal differences in root development among tree species.

The need for water uptake by the roots is influenced by the rate at which water is lost through the stomata in the leaves. Stomatal control of transpiration in response to unfavorable environmental conditions is crucial to plant survival. The mechanisms governing stomatal opening and closing are complex and are not thoroughly understood but are influenced by several factors including light, temperature, humidity, plant water status, and internal CO_2 concentration.

Stomatal responses to environmental conditions differ among species and affect their competitive interactions. In a study on the stomatal responses of 3-year-old conifer seedlings to increasing soil drought, lodgepole pine, ponderosa pine, and Engelmann spruce exhibited a more rapid decline in transpiration than grand fir or Douglas-fir (Lopushinsky 1969). The rapid transpiration decline in the pines and spruce, which probably involved increases in both stomatal and mesophyll resistances, resulted in lower moisture stress levels than in the firs at the end of the transpiration decline. The more gradual decline and higher stress levels in the firs suggest that these species may be more tolerant of high water stress and can continue to photosynthesize under more adverse conditions than pines. Conard and Radosevich (1981) concluded that the higher leaf conductances late in the summer in two shrub species, coupled with their ability to recover from low xylem sap potentials (high water stress), enabled them to maintain a nearer-to-maximum photosynthetic rate for a longer period each season than white fir was able to maintain. Although rapid growth of the shrubs suppressed white fir growth for many years, the water-conserving stomatal response of the fir ensures its survival under the low soil moisture conditions created by the presence of the shrub competition. The ability of white fir to photosynthesize at very low light levels may also account for its eventual emergence and dominance over shrubs that occur with natural succession.

Nutrient Availability

Chapin (1980) reviewed the physiological characteristics that influence the ability of plant species to successfully exploit soil nutrients. Different characteristics may be distinguished in plants exhibiting the ruderal, competitive, or stress-tolerant strategies described by Grime (1979).

In habitats of moderate to high fertility such as a recently disturbed area in which a release of nutrients and other resources has occurred, an exploitive strategy allowing rapid uptake and assimilation of nutrients confers a competitive advantage over less exploitive species. This type of strategy is found in ruderals and competitors. The physiological traits that allow rapid exploitation of soil nutrients include high absorption capacity by roots (nutrient absorption rate per unit of root), high photosynthetic rate, and high respiration rate, which result in rapid growth. Maximum advantage is gained under high light conditions that sustain maximum photosynthetic rates. In plants with these characteristics, photosynthesis is sensitive to leaf nitrogen level, and depletion of soil nitrogen results in a declining growth rate. Also, photosynthesis and root absorption decline with tissue age. High nutrient uptake levels must, therefore, be maintained to support the continued rapid production of new tissue that assures occupancy of the site. Other things being equal, as long as nutrient levels remain high in the soil, ruderal and competitive species usually will outcompete other plants and maintain dominance. However, as soil nutrients become depleted over time, or other successional changes occur, these species will show signs of deficiency and nutrient stress and will become less vigorous. Stress-tolerant species may then gain a competitive advantage and eventually succeed the earlier colonizers of the site (Chapin 1980).

The physiological attributes that allow stress-tolerant species to compete successfully on infertile soils include high root absorption capacity, low photosynthetic capacity, low rate of tissue production and growth, and low rate of nutrient loss through senescence or leaching. Nutrient reserves that build up in nonphotosynthetic tissues of stress-tolerant species enable plant survival during periods of very low nutrient availability because requirements for production of new tissue are not high. Stress-tolerant species occupying infertile sites are usually perennial because nutrients can be stored in their tissues. Other adaptations that maximize nutrient retention include long-lived evergreen leaves, long-lived roots, effective translocation of nutrients between tissues, and traits that minimize foliar leaching by reducing water contact with leaves such as a well-developed smooth cuticle, certain types of pubescence, and vertical leaf angle (Chapin 1980). The characteristics that enable plant species to compete successfully under conditions of low or high nutrient availability are summarized in Figure 5-14.

Chapin points out that many of the characteristics adaptive for nutrient-poor habitats (i.e., slow metabolic rates) also are adaptive for habitats deficient in other resources. For instance, nutrient and water deficiency often develop concurrently on a site. In addition, as the canopy becomes progressively more dense in the years following a disturbance,

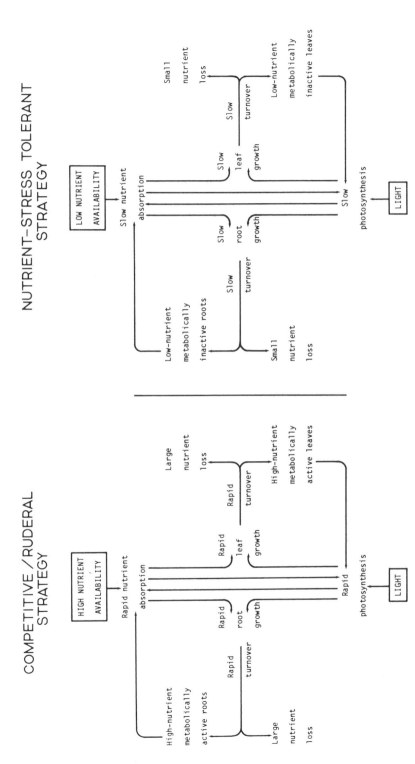

Figure 5-14. Interacting characteristics of plant strategies that are adaptive under conditions of high or low nutrient availability. (*Source:* From Chapin 1980. Reproduced, with permission, from the Annual Review of Ecology and Systematics, Volume 11, Copyright © 1980 by Annual Reviews, Inc.)

light availability in the understory becomes reduced. Shade-tolerant species, which exhibit many of the conservative traits adaptive to infertile sites, gain a competitive advantage and eventually dominate (Grime 1979).

Excess Environmental Factors

Excesses in environmental resources can sometimes exert a detrimental influence on plant growth and can affect species distribution patterns. For example, continuous exposure to high light has been shown to cause chlorosis and injury to Engelmann spruce, although lodgepole pine remains healthy under the same conditions (Ronco 1975). In a study of the natural distribution of red fir seedlings in the northern Sierra Nevada, Ustin et al. (1984) found that the species regenerated only on sites that did not receive long exposures to midday sun. They postulated that excessive soil temperatures were the major factors preventing red fir regeneration on sunny sites. Excess water (flooding) also can inhibit growth and is lethal in many instances (Kramer 1951, Kramer and Kozlowski 1960). Many pine species, for example, are intolerant of flooding (Daniel et al. 1979). Nutrient excesses characterize some soil types and restrict the number of species able to compete successfully on them. One example is serpentine soil, which contains high concentrations of magnesium, nickel, and chromium. Species inhabiting serpentine soils are able to tolerate levels of these minerals that would be toxic to other species (Whittaker 1975). Dominance of incense-cedar at low elevations of the western Sierra Nevada is partially due to the presence of serpentine in these regions (Daniel et al. 1979). In Oregon, Douglas-fir is restricted to nonserpentine soils, whereas pines (especially Jeffrey pine) are more serpentine tolerant (Whittaker 1975).

INTERACTIVE FEATURES OF ENVIRONMENTAL RESOURCES

Although various components of the environment have been described in terms of their individual effects on plant growth and competition, it is the interactive effects of all environmental factors, coupled with the adaptive characteristics of plant species, that ultimately influence plant survival and growth in the natural setting. Greaves et al. (1978, p. 19) provide the following example of the interactive nature of environmental factors and plant growth.

> The amount of available [soil] moisture is influenced by temperature; as temperature increases, evaporation and transpiration rates increase and deplete available moisture more quickly. Temperature is affected by the intensity of

and duration of solar radiation. Solar radiation indirectly influences moisture because of the interdependency between temperature and moisture. Soil moisture and temperature influence nutrient supply by regulating the rate of decomposition.

The specific responses of plant species to the totality of environmental factors ultimately determine the success or failure of those plants in competition with their neighbors. Several models of forest growth rely heavily on the assumption that the environmental factors controlling growth can be treated as multiplicative nonlinear functions; that is, the factors interact to control plant growth. This concept has been tested by Reed et al. (1983) by studying Douglas-fir under three regimes of light and four levels of fertility. Growth increased with increasing nitrogen and light, but low nitrogen caused severe chlorosis in the high light treatment. Reed et al. concluded that (1) Douglas-fir growth responds strongly to nitrogen and light availability; (2) light was the dominant factor; and (3) the effect of environmental factors on growth can be modeled better by multiplicative nonlinear functions than simple linear regression models.

SITE MODIFICATION, RESOURCE AVAILABILITY, AND FOREST REGENERATION

The same environmental resources and conditions (light, heat, CO_2, nutrients, and water) are fundamental to every forest system. Therefore, the relative success of any species in a seral stage will depend on its ability to survive environmental site conditions and to preempt limited resources. Success of a species will depend on the resource requirements of that species, the availability of resources during periods of demand, and adaptations to partitioning of resources in time and space relative to other species in the community.

Several studies have examined the growth responses of conifers to site preparation (e.g., Plass and Green 1963, Waldron 1964, Kittams and Ryker 1975, Stransky 1980). Numerous other studies have reported increased conifer growth in response to specific competition release treatments that resulted in little tree injury but significant shrub suppression (e.g., Atkins 1956, Ferguson 1958, Wilde et al. 1968, Schultz 1975, Radosevich et al. 1976, Preest 1977, Balmer et al. 1978, Nelson et al. 1981, Conard and Radosevich 1982, Petersen and Newton 1982, Swindel et al. 1983). Few experiments concerning either site preparation or herbicide application for competition release of young conifers have examined the effects on environmental resources or the physiological responses of the trees to the treatments.

Lanini and Radosevich (1986) measured the microenvironmental changes and shrub responses that resulted from three methods of site preparation (rotary chopper, brushrake, or controlled burn) and subsequent shrub suppression by herbicide application. The relative value of vegetative manipulation was also examined by evaluating conifer growth in relation to site resource status. Among the treatments that received only site preparation, the brushrake resulted in the greatest delay in shrub reinvasion, whereas the rotary chopper allowed the least delay. After 4 years 2000 m^3/ha and 7200 m^3/ha of shrub canopy volume were observed on the brushraked and rotary chopped plots, respectively. The controlled burn was intermediate in response (5500 m^3/ha). However, herbicide application after any method of site preparation maintained shrub canopy volumes below 1000 m^3/ha for the 4-year study period. Resource availability varied with the level of shrub suppression. Both soil moisture and light were most plentiful when shrub canopy volumes were lowest. However, water abundance was the resource most improved by the absence of shrubs.

In the same study, growth and water potential of ponderosa pine, sugar pine, and white fir were related to the shrub canopy volumes (SCV). Water potentials of the conifers were always highest (i.e., low stress) when SCV was low. The difference in water potential between high and low SCV subplots was greatest during the latter part of summer. Low water potentials (high stress) in the high SCV plots resulted in an earlier cessation of seasonal growth. Height, stem diameter, and canopy volume growth of each conifer species were greatest on the low SCV plots and least on the high SCV plots. High conifer water potentials (low stress) on low SCV plots are believed to have resulted in higher first year levels of carbohydrate production or accumulation than on plots with high SCV. Tree growth responses lagged behind treatments by 1 or more years. The delayed response was probably due to the cyclic nature of conifer growth, in which the current season's growth is substantially dependent on carbohydrate produced the year before.

The relative contribution of soil moisture and light to growth was evaluated for the three species of conifers (Lanini 1983). Cumulative seasonal totals for light and soil moisture were calculated for 3 separate years. Stepwise regression was used to select the most important resource variables for predicting three aspects of growth (height, stem diameter, or canopy volume) of each species. Path analysis was then utilized to evaluate the relative contribution of the previously chosen resource variables to conifer growth. Ponderosa pine growth responded similarly to increases in both light and soil moisture. These factors interacted significantly to increase growth of ponderosa pine when shrub canopy volumes were low. Increases in soil moisture were more beneficial for sugar pine and white fir height and canopy volume growth than was increased light. However, an increase in white fir stem growth resulting from an increase in soil moisture at low shrub canopy volumes was offset by increased light abundance that had a negative influence.

Studies similar to that of Lanini and Radosevich (1986) have been conducted by others (e.g., Zedaker [1981], Preest [1975] and Ross et al. [1986]). In essence, these studies have found a quantitative linkage between the availablity of resources, physiological processes, and subsequent morphological development. Gains in growth rate of crop conifers have generally been greatest when the competing vegetation has been well controlled and when the operations were performed very early in the life of the conifers.

SUMMARY

The primary goal of vegetation management in forestry is to alter the competitive balance of early successional vegetation to favor conifer establishment and growth. Such alteration can result in early and long-term dominance by conifers. Because the same environmental resources are common to all forests but at different levels of availability, it is the ability of individual species to outcompete their neighbors in a limited system that determines success. Conifers, brush, and herbaceous species respond in a predictable manner to changes in environmental conditions. Lack of knowledge about these relationships limits our ability to predict responses. It is important for researchers to characterize intra- and interspecific interactions among species, identify limiting resources, characterize microenvironments, and elucidate the physiological controls for growth and development of both coniferous and competing vegetation. In this way, predictive and effective management tactics can be developed for forest vegetation management and conifer production.

REFERENCES

Allan, G.G., J.W. Beer, and M.J. Cousin. 1978. Growth enhancement of a juvenile conifer forest six years after application of a controlled release herbicide. Internat. Pest Control 20(2):6-13.

Atkins, E.S. 1956. The use of chemicals to release white fir reproduction. Can. Dept. North. Afforest. and Natur. Resour., Forestry Branch, Technol. Note 37. 9 p.

Balmer, W.E., K.E. Utz, and O.G. Langdon. 1978. Financial returns from cultural work in natural loblolly pine stands. South. J. Appl. Forestry 2:111-117.

Barbour, M.G., J.H. Burkand, and W.D. Pitts. 1980. Terrestrial plant ecology. Benjamin/Cummings Publ. Co., Inc., Menlo Park, CA. 604 p.

Barney, W.C. 1951. Effects of soil temperature and light intensity on root growth of loblolly pine seedlings. Plant Physiol. 26:146-163.

Bates, C.J. and J. Roeser. 1928. Light intensities required for growth of coniferous seedlings. Amer. J. Bot. 15:185-195.

Binkley, D. 1986. Forest nutrition management. John Wiley and Sons, New York, NY. 290 p.

Bjorkman, O. 1981. Responses to different quantum flux densities, p. 57-107. *In*: Lange, O.L., P.S. Nobel, C.B. Osmond, and H. Ziegler (eds.) Physiological plant ecology I. Responses to the physical environment. Springer-Verlag, New York, NY. Encyclopedia of Plant Physiology. New Ser. 12A. 625 p.

Brix, H. 1967. An analysis of dry matter production of Douglas-fir seedlings in relation to temperature and light intensity. Can. J. Bot. 45:2063-2072.

Burkholder, P.R. 1952. Cooperation and conflict among primitive organisms. Amer. Sci. 40:601-631.

Carter, G.A., J.H. Miller, D.E. Davis, and R.M. Patterson. 1984. Effect of vegetative competition on the moisture and nutrient status of loblolly pine. Can. J. Forest Res. 14:1-9.

Chapin, F.S., III. 1980. The mineral nutrition of wild plants. Annu. Rev. Ecol. Syst. 11:233-260.

Cole, E.C. 1984. Fifth year growth responses of Douglas-fir to crowding and other competition. M.S. thesis, College of Forestry, Oregon State Univ., Corvallis, OR. 321 p.

Conard, S.G. and S.R. Radosevich. 1981. Photosynthesis, xylem pressure potential, and leaf conductance of three montane chaparral species in California. Forest Sci. 27:627-639.

Conard, S.G. and S.R. Radosevich. 1982. Growth responses of white fir to decreased shading and root competition by montane chaparral shrubs. Forest Sci. 28:309-320.

Connell, J.J. and R.O. Slatyer. 1977. Mechanisms of succession in natural communities and their role in community stability and organization. Amer. Natur. 111:1119-1144.

Cromack, K., Jr. 1981. Below-ground processes in forest succession, p. 361-373. *In* West, D.C., H.H. Shugart, and D.B. Botkin (eds.) Forest succession: concepts and application. Springer-Verlag, New York, NY. 517 p.

Daniel, T.W., J.A. Helms, and F.S. Baker. 1979. Principles of silviculture. 2nd ed. McGraw-Hill Book Co., Inc., New York, NY. 500 p.

Dyrness, C.T. 1973. Early stages of plant succession following logging and burning in the western Cascades of Oregon. Ecology 54:57-69.

Eissenstat, D.M. and J.E. Mitchell. 1983. Effect of seedling grass and clover on growth and water potential of Douglas-fir seelings. Forest Sci. 29:166-179.

Ellenberg, H. 1958. Bodenreaktion (einschlieplich Kalfrage), p. 638-708. *In*: Ruhland, W. (ed.) Hanbuch der Pflanzenphysiologie. Springer-Verlag, Berlin. Vol. 4.

Emmingham, W.H. and R.H. Waring. 1973. Conifer growth under different light environments in the Siskiyou Mountains of southwestern Oregon. Northwest Sci. 47:88-99.

Evans, G.C. 1972. The quantitative analysis of plant growth. Univ. California Press, Berkeley, CA. 734 p.

Ferguson, E.R. 1958. Response of planted loblolly pines to reduction of competition. J. Forestry 56:29-32.

Fritz, E. and J.A. Rydelius. 1966. Redwood reforestation problems. An experimental approach to their solution, p. 97-l04. Foundation for American Resource Management. San Francisco, CA.

Good, R.D. 1931. A theory of plant geography. New Phytologist 30:149-203.

Good, R.D. 1974. The geography of the flowering plants. 4th ed. Longman, London. 557 p.

Gordon, D.T. 1970. Shade improves survival rate of outplanted 2-0 red fir seedlings. USDA Forest Service, Pacific Northwest Forest and Range Experiment Station, Portland, OR. Res. Note PNW-210. 4 p.

Gratkowski, H. and P. Lauterbach. 1974. Releasing Douglas-firs from varnishleaf ceanothus. J. Forestry 72:150-152.

Greaves, R.D., R.K. Hermann, and B.D. Cleary. 1978. Ecological principles, p. 7-26. *In* Cleary, B.D., R.D. Greaves, and R.K. Hermann (eds.) Regenerating Oregon's forests. Ext. Serv., Oregon State Univ., Corvallis, OR. 286 p.

Grime, J.P. 1979. Plant strategies and vegetation processes. John Wiley and Sons, Chichester. 222 p.

Harper, J.L. 1964. The individual in the population. J. Ecol. 52 (suppl.): 149-158.

Harper, J.L. 1977. Population biology of plants. Academic Press, New York, NY. 892 p.

Hibbs, D.E. 1983. Forty years of forest succession in central New England. Biology 64:1394-1401.

Horn, H.S. 1974. The ecology of secondary succession. Annu. Rev. Ecol. Syst. 5:25-37.

Hunt, R. 1978. Plant growth analysis. Edward Arnold Publishers, London. 67 p.

Isaac, L.A. 1938. Factors affecting establishment of Douglas-fir seedlings. U.S. Dept. Agr., Washington, DC. Cir. 486. 45 p.

Isaac, L.A. 1940. Vegetative succession following logging in the Douglas-fir region with special reference to fire. J. Forestry 38:716-721.

Jarvis, P.G. and M.S. Jarvis. 1964. Growth rates of woody plants. Physiol. Plant. 17:654-666.

Kittams, J.A. and R.A. Ryker. 1975. Habitat type and site preparation affect survival of planted Douglas-fir in central Idaho brushfields. USDA Forest Service, Intermountain Forest and Range Experiment Station, Ogden, UT. Res. Note INT-198. 6 p.

Kramer, P.J. 1951. Causes of injury to plants resulting from flooding of the soil. Plant Physiol. 26:722-736.

Kramer, P.J. and W.S. Clark. 1947. A comparison of photosynthesis in individual pine needles and entire seedlings at various light intensities. Plant Physiol. 22:51-57.

Kramer, P.J. and T.T. Kozlowski. 1960. Physiology of trees. McGraw-Hill Book Co., Inc. New York, NY. 642 p.

Krueger, K.W. and R.H. Ruth. 1969. Comparative photosynthesis of red alder, Douglas-fir, Sitka spruce, and western hemlock seedlings. Can. J. Bot. 47:519-527.

Kummerow, J. 1980. Adaptation of roots in water-stressed native vegetation, p. 57-73. *In* Turner, N.C. and P.J. Kramer (eds.) Adaptation of plants to water and high temperature stress. John Wiley and Sons, Inc., New York, NY. 482 p.

Lanini, W.T. 1983. The interaction of site preparation and secondary release treatment on conifer survival and growth. Ph.D. dissertation. Univ. California, Davis, CA. 89 p.

Lanini, W.T. and S.R. Radosevich. 1986. Response of three conifer species to site preparation and shrub control. Forest Sci. 32:61-77.

Ledig, F.T. 1974. Concepts of growth analysis, p. 166-182. *In* Reid, C.P.P. and G.H. Fechner (eds.) Proc., Third North Amer. Forest Biol. Workshop. College of Forestry and Natur. Resour., Colorado State Univ., Fort Collins, CO. 388 p.

Lopushinsky, W. 1969. Stomatal closure in conifer seedlings in response to leaf moisture stress. Bot. Gaz. 130:258-263.

Maguire, W.P. 1955. Radiation, surface temperature, and seedling survival. Forest Sci. 1:277-285.

McDonald, P. 1980. Brushfield ecology and growth of planted pines. USDA Forest Service, Pacific Southwest Forest and Range Experiment Station, Redding, CA. Unpublished data on file.

Miller, R.E. and M.D. Murray. 1978. The effect of red alder on growth of Douglas-fir, p. 283-306. *In* Briggs, D.G., D.S. DeBell, and W.A. Atkinson (eds.) Utilization and management of alder. USDA Forest Service, Pacific Northwest Forest and Range Experiment Station, Portland, OR. Gen. Tech. Rep. PNW-70. 379 p.

Nelder, J.A. 1962. New kinds of systematic designs for spacing studies. Biometrics 18:283-307.

Nelson, L.R., R.C. Pedersen, L.L. Autry, S. Dudley, and J.D. Walstad. 1981. Impact of herbaceous weeds in young loblolly pine plantations. South. J. Appl. Forestry 5:153-158.

Newton, M. 1973. Forest rehabilitation in North America: some simplifications. J. Forestry 71:159-162.

Odum, E.P. 1971. Fundamentals of ecology. 3rd ed. W.B. Saunders Co., Philadelphia, PA. 574 p.

Oliver, C.D. 1978. The development of northern red oak in mixed stands in central New England. School of Forestry and Environmental Studies, Yale Univ., New Haven, CT. Bull. 91. 63 p.

Oliver, W.W. 1979. Early response of ponderosa pine to spacing and brush: observations on a 12-year-old plantation. USDA Forest Service, Pacific Southwest Forest and Range Experiment Station, Berkeley, CA. Res. Note PSW-341. 7 p.

Oliver, W.W. and R.F. Powers. 1978. Growth models for ponderosa pine: I. Yield of unthinned plantations in northern California. USDA Forest Service, Pacific

Southwest Forest and Range Experiment Station, Berkeley, CA. Res. Pap. PSW-133. 21 p.

Oosting, H.J. 1956. The study of plant communities. 2nd ed. W.H. Freeman and Co., San Francisco, CA. 440 p.

Patterson, D.T. 1982. Effect of light and temperatures on weed/crop growth and competition, p. 407-421. *In* Hatfield, J.L. and I.J. Thomason (eds.) Biometeorology in integrated pest management. Academic Press, New York, NY. 491 p.

Peters, G.A. 1978. Blue-green algae and algal associations. BioScience 28:580-585.

Petersen, T. and M. Newton. 1982. Growth of Douglas-fir following control of snowbrush and herbaceous vegetation in Oregon. Dow Chemical USA, Midland, MI. Down to Earth 41(1): 21-25.

Peterson, C.A. 1969. Some physiological effects of atrazine on Douglas-fir seedlings. M.S. thesis, School of Forestry, Oregon State Univ., Corvallis, OR. 44 p.

Plass, W.T. and A.W. Green. 1963. Preplanting treatments for brush old fields in southern Illinois. USDA Forest Service, Central States Forest Experiment Station, Columbus, OH. Res. Pap. CS-1. 8 p.

Preest, D.S. 1975. Effects of herbaceous weed control on Douglas-fir moisture stress and growth. Ph.D. thesis, School of Forestry, Oregon State Univ., Corvallis, OR. 111 p.

Preest, D.S. 1977. Long-term growth response of Douglas-fir to weed control. N. Z. J. Forest Sci. 7:329-332.

Radosevich, S.R. 1984. Interference between greenleaf manzanita (*Arctostaphylos patula*) and ponderosa pine (*Pinus ponderosa*), p. 259-270. *In* Duryea, M. and G.N. Brown (eds.) Seedling physiology and reforestation success. Martinus Nijhoff/Dr. W. Junk Publ., Boston, MA. 326 p.

Radosevich, S.R. and J.S. Holt. 1984. Ecology of weeds. John Wiley and Sons, Inc. New York, NY. 265 p.

Radosevich, S.R., P.C. Passof, and O.A. Leonard. 1976. Douglas-fir release from tanoak and Pacific madrone competition. Weed Sci. 24:144-145.

Reed, K.L., J.S. Shumway, R.B. Walker, and C.S. Bledsoe. 1983. Evaluation of the interaction of two environmental factors affecting Douglas-fir seedling growth: light and nitrogen. Forest Sci. 29:193-203.

Ronco, F. 1975. Diagnosis: "sunburned trees." J. Forestry 73:31-35.

Ross, D.W., W. Scott, R.L. Heninger, and J.D. Walstad. 1986. Effects of site preparation on ponderosa pine (*Pinus ponderosa*), associated vegetation, and soil properties in south central Oregon. Can. J. Forest Res. 16:612-618.

Ross, M.A. 1968. The establishment of seedlings and the development of patterns in grassland. Ph.D. thesis, University of Wales.

Schubert, G.H. and R.S. Adams. 1971. Reforestation practices for conifers in California. Div. Forestry, Calif. Resour. Agency, Sacramento, CA. 359 p.

Schultz, R.P. 1975. Intensive culture of southern pines: maximum yields on short rotations. Iowa State J. Res. 49:325-337.

Schulze, E.D. 1982. Plant life forms and their carbon, water and nutrient relations, p. 615-676. *In* Lange, O.L., P.S. Nobel, C.B. Osmond, and H. Ziegler (eds.) Physiological plant ecology II. Springer-Verlag, New York, NY. Encyclopedia of Plant Physiology, New Ser. 12B. 747 p.

Shirley, H.L. 1929. The influence of light intensity and light quality upon the growth of plants. Amer. J. Bot. 16:354-390.

Stewart, R.E., L.L. Gross, and B.H. Honkala. 1984. Effects of competing vegetation on forest trees: a bibliography with abstracts. USDA Forest Service, Washington, DC. Gen. Tech. Rep. WO-43. 260 p.

Stransky, J.J. 1980. Vegetation response to various methods of site preparation. Feb. 1980 Progress Report Summary. On file, USDA Forest Service, Southern Forest Experiment Station, Nacogdoches, TX.

Swindel, B.F., L.F. Conde, and J.E. Smith. 1983. Plant cover and biomass response to clear-cutting, site preparation, and planting in *Pinus ellottii* flatwoods. Science 219:1421-1422.

Tarrant, R.F. 1961. Stand development and soil fertility in a Douglas-fir—red alder plantation. Forest Sci. 7:238-246.

Ustin, S.L., R.A. Woodward, M.G. Barbour, and J.L. Hatfield. 1984. Relationships between sunfleck dynamics and red fir seedling distribution. Ecology 65:1420-1428.

Wahlenberg, G.M. 1930. Effect of *Ceanothus* brush on western yellow pine plantations in the northern Rocky Mountains. J. Agr. Res. 41:601-612.

Waldron, R.M. 1964. The effect of preplanting ground treatment on early survival and growth of planted white spruce. Tree Planters' Notes 65:6-8.

Walter, H. 1973. Vegetation of the earth in relation to climate and the ecophysiological conditions. Springer-Verlag, London. 237 p.

Whittaker, R.H. 1975. Communities and ecosystems. 2nd ed. Macmillan Publ. Co., New York, NY. 385 p.

Wilde, S.A., B.H. Shaw, and A.W. Fedkenheuer. 1968. Weeds as a factor depressing forest growth. Weed Res. 8:196-204.

Wit, C.T. De. 1960. On competition. Verslagen van landbouwkundige onderzoekingen. No. 66.8.

Yeaton, R.I., J. Travis, and E. Gilinsky. 1977. Competition and spacing in plant communities: the Arizona upland association. J. Ecol. 65:587-595.

Youngberg, C.T., and A.G. Wollum, II. 1976. Nitrogen accretion in developing *Ceanothus velutinus* stands. Soil Sci. Soc. Amer. J. 40:109-112.

Zavitkovski, J. 1966. Snowbrush, *Ceanothus velutinus* Dougl., its ecology and role in forest regeneration in the Oregon Cascades. Ph.D. thesis, School of Forestry, Oregon State Univ., Corvallis, OR. 102 p.

Zavitkovski, J. and M. Newton. 1968. Ecological importance of snowbrush *Ceanothus velutinus* in the Oregon Cascades. Ecology 49:1134-1145.

Zedaker, S.M. 1981. Growth and development of young Douglas-fir in relation to intra- and interspecific competition. Ph.D. thesis, School of Forestry, Oregon State Univ., Corvallis, OR. 112 p.

Zimdahl, R.L. 1980. Weed crop competition: a review. International Plant Protection Center, Oregon State Univ., Corvallis, OR. 197 p.

6

Overview of Vegetation Management Alternatives

JOHN D. WALSTAD
MICHAEL NEWTON
DEAN H. GJERSTAD

INTRODUCTION

Vegetation management is an integral part of silviculture and must be practiced if commercial forests are to be effectively and economically managed. Vegetation management is also used to enhance wildlife habitat, stabilize soil, maintain rights-of-way, and facilitate recreational use. The latter four uses are beyond the scope of this text, but they involve many of the same principles and techniques.

The diversity of forest conditions and resource management objectives throughout the United States and Canada has led to a variety of approaches to vegetation management. The purpose of this chapter is to describe the principal methods in use, identify the problems for which they are suited, and provide a general picture of their advantages, disadvantages, limitations, and costs (1986 basis). Table 6-1 provides a brief synopsis of the major attributes of the various techniques employed in forest vegetation management. A bibliography at the end of the chapter lists additional sources of information on pertinent topics.

VEGETATION MANAGEMENT PRACTICES

Silvicultural vegetation management practices include harvesting, site preparation, stand (plantation) release, and timber stand improvement.

TABLE 6-1. Summary of Major Attributes Associated with Various Forest Vegetation Management Practices

Practice	General Method	Specific Technique	Applicable Region	Principal Advantages	Principal Disadvantages
Harvesting	Clearcutting	Conventional	All	Facilitates efficient even-aged management Removes overstory competition Disturbs residual shrubs and hardwoods Most economical method of logging Most reliable method of reforestation if planting is done Beneficial to many wildlife species	Seedling stock may not be adapted to the site Aids pioneering vegetation Promotes sprouting May cause erosion and associated adverse impacts Habitat changes may alter composition of wildlife species Asthetically less pleasing
		Minimum disturbance	Northwest	Same as preceding plus: 1. Hinders pioneering vegetation 2. Helps protect site quality	Same as preceding except: 1. Aids residual rather than pioneering vegetation 2. Logging more costly than conventional clearcutting
	Seed-tree and shelterwood systems		South and Northwest	Ameliorates harsh environmental conditions for seedlings Less expensive natural regeneration possible Ensures seedling adaptation to site (unless planted) Aesthetically more pleasing (at least temporarily) than clearcutting	Difficult and costly to perform on steep terrain Difficult to control number and distribution of seedlings Aids understory shrubs and hardwoods Multiple entries can damage advanced regeneration and remaining trees Unsuitable for thin-barked species susceptible to stem decay from logging damage

Method	Region	Advantages	Disadvantages
Selection harvesting	South, Northeast, and Inland Northwest	Facilitates all-aged or uneven-aged management; Provides a relatively continuous stream of revenue; Inexpensive natural regeneration possible; Ensures seedling adaptation to site; Helps protect site quality and maintain stable environmental conditions; Aesthetically more pleasing than clearcutting; Perpetuates stable habitat for some wildlife species; Reduces the chances of catastrophic losses from fire and natural agents	Increases incidence of root rot and dwarf mistletoe diseases; Damage possible to high value residuals from lightning, windthrow, and insects; Logging more costly than clearcutting; Succession can lead to gradual dominance by low-value hardwoods; Generally less profitable and more complicated than even-aged management; Multiple entries can damage advanced regeneration and disturb soils; Increases incidence of root rot diseases; Logging more costly than clearcutting; Precludes opportunities to use genetically improved stock or change species
Site preparation — Prescribed burning — Broadcast burning	All	Reduces risk of subsequent wildfire; Provides suitable environment for seeding and planting; Facilitates access for planting and other silvicultural activities; Provides some control of residual shrubs and hardwoods	Requires precise weather and site conditions to ensure: 1. Adequate disposal of slash 2. Minimum risk of escape 3. Compliance with smoke management regulations; Occupational hazards are inherent in any technique utilizing fire

159

TABLE 6-1. Summary of Major Attributes Associated with Various Forest Vegetation Management Practices (*Continued*)

Practice	General Method	Specific Technique	Applicable Region	Principal Advantages	Principal Disadvantages
				Successional patterns similar to that caused by natural wildfires Reasonably inexpensive when done under suitable conditions Improves forage for wildlife and livestock (Note: This may lead to seedling damage in some situations)	Can be detrimental to soils and site quality Aggravates sprouting and germination problems with fire-adapted species Generally requires pretreatment via mechanical or chemical means Exposed environment for new seedlings can be too harsh
		Burning of piles and windrows	All	Same as preceding plus: 1. Minimizes risk of escape during burning 2. Weather and fuel conditions do not have to be quite so stringent 3. Makes entire area suitable for planting or seeding	Same as preceding plus: 1. Requires costly mechanical or manual methods to pile or windrow the material 2. Piling or windrowing operations must be carefully done to ensure that material is burnable and that soils are not adversely impacted 3. Terrain must be suitable for operation of mechanical equipment
	Mechanical methods	Various types of heavy equipment	All	Reduces risk of subsequent wildfire Residual vegetation frequently uprooted or damaged Provides suitable environment for seeding or planting	Expensive, energy-intensive approach Not applicable on steep slopes or excessively wet soils Can cause serious soil damage and loss of site productivity

Method	Application		Advantages	Disadvantages
Chemical methods	Broadcast application (usually aerial application)	All	Facilitates access for planting and other silvicultural activities Occupational safety is reasonable if work is done carefully Sensitive areas can be treated with little controversy or risk of off-site damage Provides effective control of many residual species Applicable to steep slopes and difficult sites Generally the safest, most efficient, and most cost-effective mode of application, especially for large, remote areas; indirect costs can be substantial, however	Follow-up burning generally required to dispose of material Does not control sprouting vegetation unless it is uprooted Creates ideal conditions for invasion of pioneering vegetation Can aggravate problems with pest animals Exposed environment for new seedlings can be too harsh Adequate training and precautions are required for proper application Follow-up burning or mechanical treatment generally required Treatments are confined to specific seasons of the year and vegetation conditions Efficacy often dependent upon weather conditions Legal impediments and regulatory restrictions can be limiting Can be a controversial form of treatment
	Ground application (usually spot, band, or individual stem treatments)	All	Same as preceding plus: 1. Efficacy tends to be greater 2. Treatments can often be applied yearround 3. Can be tailored to small areas, boundaries, and buffer strips 4. Environmental precautions required tend to be less restrictive	Same as preceding plus: 1. Frequency of occupational injuries associated with labor-intensive methods is inherently greater 2. Occupational exposure to chemicals is greater 3. Not feasible on adverse terrain or in brushy conditions

TABLE 6-1. Summary of Major Attributes Associated with Various Forest Vegetation Management Practices (*Continued*)

Practice	General Method	Specific Technique	Applicable Region	Principal Advantages	Principal Disadvantages
	Manual methods	Slashing	Northwest	Can be used when or where machines are inoperable and chemicals are unsuitable Relatively small areas can be treated High-value trees or plants can be saved	4. Costs tend to be higher 5. Production rates are lower Primarily restricted to brushfield reclamation and stand conversion projects Hazardous occupational practice even after extensive safety training (involves power saws and machetes) Expensive, labor-intensive approach Does not control sprouting species Adjunct treatment with fire, mechanical, or chemical treatment usually required
		Mulching and scalping	Northwest	Same as preceding plus: 1. Done in conjunction with planting 2. Can improve soil moisture conditions and seedling survival	Only effective on forbs and grasses Careful installation of mulching material (paper or plastic) required Not stable on excessively steep ground Scalping less effective than mulching Expensive, labor-intensive approach

Release					
	Chemical methods	Broadcast application (usually aerial application)	All	Same as for broadcast chemical site preparation plus: 1. Use of broad-spectrum, selective herbicides can provide adequate control of competing vegetation without damaging conifers 2. Most widely tested and used method of release	Same as for broadcast chemical site preparation except: 1. Follow-up burning or mechanical treatments are inappropriate 2. Correct timing is critical to avoid damage to conifers
		Ground applications (usually directed foliar or basal sprays)	All	Same as for ground chemical site preparation plus: 1. Generally the most effective and selective treatment, provided the conditions are practical and economical	Same as for ground chemical site preparation except: 1. Follow-up burning or mechanical treatments are inappropriate 2. Conifers can be damaged unless care is taken during application
	Manual methods	Various types of hand tools and power saws	All	Highly selective treatment Minimizes potential for adverse environmental impacts Reasonably efficient means of treating small, sensitive areas where other methods are inappropriate Can be done in conjunction with precommercial thinning	Highly hazardous occupational practice Expensive, labor-intensive practice Difficult to perform on adverse sites and under brushy conditions Multiple treatments may be required to control resprouting vegetation Conifers can be accidentally cut or set back by "thinning shock" Silvicultural benefits largely undocumented, except when done in conjunction with precommercial thinning

163

TABLE 6-1. Summary of Major Attributes Associated with Various Forest Vegetation Management Practices (Continued)

Practice	General Method	Specific Technique	Applicable Region	Principal Advantages	Principal Disadvantages
	Biological methods	Livestock grazing	South and Northwest	Can be an effective, efficient, and inexpensive means of controlling herbs and shrubs Can generate supplemental revenue Promotes multiple-use management	Livestock must be adapted to forest conditions Conifer seedlings can be damaged, killed, or eaten Careful herd management required Stream pollution, disease transmission, and displacement of wildlife are possible Implementation of effective grazing programs can be complex Silvicultural benefits largely undocumented
Timber stand improvement	Chemical methods	Broadcast application (aerial and mist blower application)	South	Same as for broadcast chemical release	Same as for broadcast chemical release except: 1. Aerial application restricted to treatment of intermediate to codominant-sized hardwoods 2. Ground treatment with mist blowers restricted to treatment of understory species on gentle topography 3. Some herbicide applications may affect desirable hardwoods

Method	Region	Advantages	Limitations
Individual treatments (usually tree injection)	South and Northeast	Provides both maximum degree of control and selectivity. Treatments can be applied year-round. Can be tailored to small areas, boundaries, and buffer strips. Reduces need for vegetation control measures in subsequent rotations. Tree spacing can be adjusted at the same time	Same as for ground chemical release except conifer damage is likely if "backflash" (translocation of herbicide from hardwoods to conifers via the root systems) occurs
Manual methods — Power saws	All	Same as for manual site prep and release plus: 1. Merchantable material can be harvested 2. Tree spacing can be adjusted at the same time 3. Conifer damage can generally be avoided	Same as for manual release plus: 1. Stumps capable of sprouting may become serious competitors in the subsequent rotation
Prescribed burning — Broadcast understory burning	South and Northwest	Same as for site prep broadcast burning except: 1. Provisions for regeneration are not an important consideration except for shelterwood reforestation in the Northwest 2. Normal plant successional sequence is delayed 3. Need for vegetation control measures in subsequent rotations is reduced 4. An inexpensive silvicultural practice, particularly in the South	Same as for site prep broadcast burning except: 1. Neither mechanical nor chemical treatment is required as adjunct measures 2. Valuable hardwood stems may be adversely affected 3. Danger of crown scorch or bole damage to conifers if fire becomes too hot 4. Restricted in Northwest to shelterwood system of reforestation, where even here it is a risky proposition due to the chance of fire escape

Harvesting, by its very nature, affects existing plants and also sets the stage for subsequent development of vegetation. Site preparation disposes of previous logging slash and residual woody vegetation and prepares the land for reforestation. Release treatments, which include cleanings and liberation cuts, are used to reduce competition from weeds so that establishment of the new stand or plantation is assured and satisfactory growth rates are attained. Timber stand improvement, sometimes referred to as *cull timber removal*, is designed to reduce the proportion of unmerchantable or low-quality trees and brush in an established stand. Competition is thereby reduced, and the overall quality of the stand is improved. Timber stand improvement also can be used prior to harvest as a means of minimizing the development of vegetation problems in the next rotation.

All four vegetation management practices are founded on basic ecological principles described in Chapter 5:

1. Vegetation control improves the availability of site resources for the benefit of desirable tree species. This may come about through harvesting of mature timber, removal of residual brush and low-quality hardwoods, prevention of colonization by pioneering weeds, or suppression of established weeds.

2. The more resources that are made available by reducing the level of competing vegetation, the greater the survival and growth of the timber stand are likely to be, provided other factors (e.g., nutrients, pests, disease) are not limiting. That is, if desirable species are present, a decrease in weed growth is usually accompanied by a corresponding increase in the survival and growth of desirable species.

3. Although vegetation management treatments are often singular events during the life of a forest stand, they cause changes in plant community structure, composition, and stand density that determine the pattern of ensuing successional stages. Proper application of vegetation management treatments will help ensure the dominance of commercially valuable timber species throughout the rotation period.

INFLUENCE OF HARVESTING PRACTICES

Even-aged silvicultural management regimes generally produce the most profitable yield of desirable wood volume per acre. This approach involves clearcutting, seed-tree, or shelterwood systems of harvesting and reforestation. It is particularly suited for species naturally adapted to even-aged conditions. The southern pines, most eastern conifers, and many western conifers fall into this category.

Of the three systems, clearcutting followed by seeding or planting has generally proven to be the simplest, most reliable, and economical way to reforest average or better sites. There are instances, largely restricted to below-average sites and certain timber types of the Inland Northwest, where natural regeneration by seed-tree and shelterwood systems of harvest is preferred. One important consideration in choosing which system to use is its influence on competing vegetation (Figure 6-1). The condition of the stand, quality of the site, and understory development at the time it is logged, coupled with the degree of disturbance during logging, de-

Figure 6-1. Clearcut (foreground) and shelterwood (background) harvesting systems; half of the clearcut has been burned. Each area will produce a different set of problems with competing vegetation.

termine the type of site preparation and release measures required later to control competing vegetation.

Conventional methods of clearcutting involve removal of all merchantable wood from a site. Depending on stand history and the site quality, various amounts of herbaceous weeds, understory shrubs, and hardwoods will have developed prior to harvest. These are capable of rapidly expanding following overstory removal. Consequently, they are the prime targets for pre- or postharvest weed control. Even though they may be seriously disturbed or severed by the logging, many of these species sprout, making them difficult to control. Site preparation under these conditions is intended to keep sprouts and residual stems from attaining dominance over new conifer regeneration.

In parts of the Northwest, there has been a trend toward utilizing minimum-disturbance methods of clearcutting (as well as seed-tree and shelterwood-type harvests) instead of conventional clearcutting, particularly on harsh sites or those where aesthetic and other nontimber considerations are paramount. Each of these alternatives is likely to increase the problem with preexisting understory vegetation, especially noncommercial hardwoods, unless steps are taken to contain it. Minimum-disturbance methods of logging, however, will limit the ability of invading weeds to colonize the area.

Minimum-disturbance logging entails the use of aircraft (balloons or helicopters) or cable systems with complete suspension of logs during the yarding operation. In the process, understory shrubs are left largely intact, and they will have a corresponding advantage over newly established conifers. Conversely, more conventional cable yarding or tractor skidding will increase the degree of surface soil disturbance, thereby increasing the damage to residual brush and hardwood stems. Although such operations help reduce the cover and sprouting capacity of many of the residual plants, they may enhance invasion by species with airborne seed such as red alder. Alternatively, the disturbance may stimulate germination of buried seed of species like snowbrush and manzanita, or emergence of shoots from underground stolons of species like salmonberry and thimbleberry.

In the South, Northeast, and Lake states regions, it is common to have mixed pine-hardwood stands that have developed from a history of selective logging and natural succession where fire has been excluded. Although these stands may have been predominantly pine at one time, the openings created by periodic removal of high-quality pine poles and sawtimber gradually become occupied by less valuable hardwoods and noncommercial shrubs and vines. Meticulous implementation of the selection process of an all-aged management system, coupled with timber stand improvement and release treatments, will generally avoid such encroachment, but they are difficult to achieve on a large enough scale to be practical. Furthermore, the all-aged system is suitable only for shade tolerant species.

Thus seed-tree, shelterwood, and selection systems of reforestation sometimes constitute a weeding for the benefit of the weeds. The strongest competitor of understory vegetation is a dense overstory. When the stand canopy is opened up, understory plants respond rapidly. Repeated entries to harvest trees can further increase the abundance and dominance potential of residual understory species. Therefore, from a vegetation management standpoint, seed-tree, shelterwood, and selection systems of reforestation should only be used where understory nonconiferous vegetation is relatively sparse or where it can be easily controlled before or immediately after harvest.

In general, then, the net effect of a logging operation on competing vegetation is determined by:

1. The type and abundance of vegetation present before logging,
2. The frequency and intensity of the logging disturbance,
3. The presence of adjacent seed sources, seed stored in the soil, or residual plants capable of exploiting the unoccupied site.

Clearcutting a dense conifer stand with little understory is likely to provide excellent conditions for reforestation. On the other hand, harvesting methods that minimize disturbance in sparsely stocked stands, and multiple-entry harvesting of conifer or mixed conifer-hardwood stands are both likely to create postharvest problems with residual vegetation. Furthermore, harvesting methods that physically disturb the surface soil, although providing some control of sprouting species, can lead to rapid colonization by pioneering grasses, forbs, vines, shrubs, and hardwoods— all of which can impede or suppress conifer regeneration. Thus some additional treatment of vegetation is generally needed following harvest operations in order to achieve successful reforestation.

SITE PREPARATION

Effective site preparation accomplishes four basic objectives, but only the last two are directly related to vegetation management goals:

1. Logging slash is reduced or removed, thereby reducing the danger of subsequent wildfire.
2. Suitable access and microsites for planting and seeding operations are provided.

3. Newly established conifers obtain a head start over potentially competing nonconiferous vegetation. This is particularly important in freshly logged areas where a variety of woody and herbaceous species are capable of rapidly dominating the site.

4. Undesirable vegetation such as hardwood brush and herbaceous weeds is removed, thereby facilitating conversion of the site to preferred timber species. Examples of such rehabilitation opportunities include nonmerchantable brushfields, low-quality hardwood stands, and nonforested grasslands that were previously occupied by productive conifer stands.

The foregoing objectives must be achieved without exceeding various economic and environmental constraints—factors that limit the choices to some extent. For example, the degradation of long-term site productivity through excessive removal of topsoil and organic material is of particular concern.

Methods of site preparation fall into four basic categories: prescribed fire, mechanical, chemical, and manual. Many of the methods must be used in combination to obtain satisfactory results. The following general descriptions summarize the salient features of each method.

Prescribed Burning

Prescribed burning after logging fulfills many of the requirements of effective site preparation. Historically, fire was "Nature's way" of preparing sites for a new stand of conifers. In fact, many of the most valuable conifer species owe their present abundance to past wildfires. However, because wildfires are often destructive to standing timber and soils, they are rarely tolerated in modern forest management. Instead, prescribed burning is used to eliminate or reduce logging slash and understory vegetation so that they no longer constitute a fire hazard or impede access (Figure 6-2). Prescribed burning also provides a suitable environment for planting or seeding and enhances the uniformity of the subsequent stand. Follow-up management activities such as stocking surveys, animal damage control, and release operations are also facilitated by the improved accessibility it affords. Prescribed burning can lead to improved forage for wildlife and livestock utilizing forest land. Finally, prescribed burning is an effective means of controlling the subsequent development of shrub and hardwood species. Many are killed outright by the fire, and, for others, the sprouting vigor is reduced.

There are several disadvantages to prescribed burning that limit the applicability of this technique in many instances. Conditions must be suitable for burning, both from the standpoint of safety as well as efficacy. Broadcast burning is particularly vulnerable to escape unless precautions are taken to keep the fire contained. Weather conditions and fuel moisture

Figure 6-2. Prescribed burning for slash disposal and vegetation control is widely practiced in forestry.

levels must be adequate to carry the fire, yet not so critical that the risk of wildfire becomes serious. Many of these problems can be minimized by piling the material in windrows before burning, but terrain and soil conditions must be suitable for such mechanized operations.

All of these factors tend to make the cost of prescribed burning highly variable. Where conditions are relatively ideal such as the gently rolling topography of the Atlantic Coastal Plain, burns can cost as little as $8/ acre. Under more difficult circumstances of heavy slash accumulation and steep topography characteristic of the Northwest, direct costs of $300/ acre or more are common. Indirect costs associated with planning, obtaining permits, litigation, and compensation for damage caused by escaped burns can drive the total cost of a prescribed burn substantially higher.

In some states, atmospheric conditions must be within certain parameters in order to avoid smoke intrusions into populated or environmentally sensitive areas. Waiting for proper conditions to burn can sometimes delay reforestation activities by a year or two or preclude them altogether.

Prescribed burning is occasionally detrimental to certain soil types where thin upper horizons are subject to loss of organic matter and nutrients or vulnerable to structural changes caused by excessive heat (e.g., hydrophobic properties). Burning on steep topography can potentially lead to eventual soil losses through erosion and mass movement (slumps, landslides, and creep).

Species with substantial sprouting vigor such as maples, tanoak, Pacific madrone, oaks, hickories, and vines will not be controlled by fire even though they are burned to the ground. Furthermore, prescribed burning frequently aggravates problems caused by fire-adapted shrubs such as snowbrush and manzanita. A variety of herbaceous and hardwood species are also capable of rapidly invading recently burned sites, thereby hampering conifer regeneration.

Thus prescribed burning as a method of site preparation has important benefits, but it also has limitations. As a general rule, it is best suited for level to moderately steep terrain where slash accumulations are great and understory vegetation is dense. Weather and fuel conditions must be suitable, and numerous safety and environmental precautions must be taken. Prescribed burning frequently is applied after chemical and mechanical treatments to further ensure adequate site preparation. In some instances, prior chemical or mechanical treatments are needed in order to reduce the risk of the fire spreading beyond the area intended to be burned.

Methods of conducting prescribed burning range from hand-held drip torches to aerial ignition techniques utilizing helicopters. Mass ignition techniques using jellied gasoline cannisters spaced at strategic intervals along the contour and connected by primacord have also been effective. This latter method is particularly useful for burning large areas in a short period of time, although the "heli-torch" technique is even more efficient in this respect.

Mechanical Methods

The use of mechanized equipment to prepare sites for reforestation is a common practice in all forest regions of the United States and Canada. A variety of heavy duty machinery is used (Figure 6-3). Crawler-type tractors equipped with shearing blades or toothed brush rakes are the most prevalent kinds of equipment used. Also employed are crushing devices, rolling drum choppers, rotary shredders, and specialized disking and bedding plows, trenchers, and spot scarifiers. Prescribed burning of piled or crushed material is usually required to maximize the area suitable for reforestation. Chemical treatments may also be necessary to contain sprouting and germinating weeds. In extreme cases, mechanical site preparation is analogous to agricultural cultivation.

Key advantages of mechanical site preparation are the following:

1. Disposal of the slash and residual vegetation after logging is an effective technique for abating the hazard of subsequent wildfire.

Figure 6-3. Equipment commonly used to prepare sites for reforestation: (a) brush crusher; (b) rolling chopper; (c) V-blade; and (d) toothed brush rake. (*Source:* Photo d courtesy of USDA Forest Service)

2. Stems and root stocks of residual vegetation are often removed or damaged, thereby reducing their competitive influence.
3. Accessibility for planting and related activities is improved, particularly if the debris is burned. This results in better quality planting, more uniform spacing, and lower planting costs.
4. Suitable and relatively uniform conditions aboveground are provided for establishment of the new conifer seedlings.
5. Relatively small and sensitive areas near homesteads and other populated areas can be treated with little or no controversy.

On some sites, mechanical site preparation is all that is required to establish and maintain a new crop of conifers. Usually, however, additional silvicultural treatments are needed to protect the conifers from encroachment of vegetation and animal pests.

Like prescribed burning, mechanical methods of site preparation have limitations. The most important constraints are related to topography and soil conditions. Operating machinery on slopes greater than 25 to 30% is not only dangerous and inefficient but also greatly increases the risks of serious soil erosion and water pollution. Operating heavy equipment on wet soils and steep slopes can cause compaction and subsequent declines in site productivity. Excessive disturbance or removal of topsoil may lead to an overall degradation of site quality. Careless piling of debris mixed with topsoil can concentrate nutrients in places where they are largely unavailable to the new crop of trees.

Mechanical site preparation can aggravate several pest and vegetation problems. Piled debris can occupy up to 10% of an area unless it is burned. This not only restricts planting and seeding operations, but it also provides a haven for animal pests such as rodents, rabbits, and mountain beaver. Excessive clearing, however, can increase the damage from other pests such as deer, cattle, and pine tip moths. If residual vegetation capable of sprouting is not uprooted or controlled with fire or chemicals, it will rapidly reoccupy the cleared site, posing a serious problem for conifer regeneration. On the other hand, if the site is extensively cultivated or scarified, an ideal seedbed is created for a host of invading herbaceous species, woody vines and shrubs, and low-quality hardwoods such as red alder, aspen, sweetgum, maple, ash, birch, and elm. The stage is essentially set for natural secondary succession to begin, which may not be the best environment for young conifer regeneration. For example, Douglas-fir seedlings will not survive beneath the canopy of a dense stand of red alder saplings. The growth of loblolly pine seedlings will be severely restricted by surrounding herbaceous and woody vegetation. Dense thickets of aspen and birch have precluded the development of white pine, red pine, and jack pine on conifer sites in the Northeast and Lake states.

Finally, the use of mechanized equipment for site preparation is expensive. The equipment itself is high priced, and the costs of operating it are also high. Therefore, mechanical site preparation is a capital- and energy-intensive approach to vegetation management. Direct costs ranging from $60/acre to $300/acre are typical for most sites amenable to mechanized treatment. Ancillary burning or chemical treatments further add to the cost of site preparation. Thus the use of mechanical site preparation is generally confined to the best forest sites where sufficient timber revenues are anticipated to defray the high initial costs.

Chemical Methods

The use of herbicides as a site preparation tool is generally for the sole purpose of controlling competing vegetation. This is in contrast to other site preparation methods, which often accomplish multiple objectives ranging from slash disposal to facilitating planting. Although some herbicides are also used as foliage and twig desiccants to enable prescribed burning to be done, such preparatory uses tend to be uncommon.

The efficacy of herbicides in controlling weeds makes them ideally suited for many site preparation situations where competing vegetation poses a threat to conifer reforestation efforts. No other methods are capable of providing comparable control of both sprouting residuals and invading germinants without considerable soil disturbance. The survival and growth response of conifer regeneration can be greatly enhanced by such treatments.

There are several other advantages of chemical site preparation. It can be used on steep slopes, fragile soils, or under other adverse site conditions where alternative mechanical and burning methods would be destructive, unsafe, or impractical. Because chemical site preparation does not physically disturb the site, there are no significant long-term impacts on inherent site productivity associated with its use as long as the recommended application rates are used. Some treatments can also be applied prior to harvesting, thereby providing advanced control of sprouting hardwoods. However, such preharvest applications need to be scheduled properly so that enough time is allowed for the chemical to work but not so much time that the killed hardwoods endanger loggers during subsequent harvest operations.

On sites where clearing of residual vegetation and disposal of slash are necessary and appropriate, herbicide treatments are often a cost-effective adjunct to burning and mechanical treatments. Herbicides are sometimes applied prior to such operations as a way of maximizing the control of sprouting brush and hardwoods. In both the South and Northwest, for example, herbicides are an occasional precursor to broadcast burning in order to desiccate the vegetation so it will carry the fire. There are also instances, particularly on bedded flatwood sites in the South and on certain scarified sites in the Northwest and Lake states, where herbicide treatments are applied after or concurrent with mechanical site preparation in order to prevent the development of dense herbaceous vegetation.

A final attribute of herbicides is their versatility. They can be applied to large and small areas in a number of ways, at many times of the year, and at a wide range of costs, depending on the vegetation involved and the financial resources of the land manager. Options range from aerial-broadcast applications to individual stem treatments, and from seasonal time frames to yearround operations. The materials can be economically applied using low-cost, hand-held equipment if labor costs are reasonable, or they can be efficiently distributed by tractors and aircraft if relatively large, inaccessible areas must be covered quickly. Thus the use of herbicides can be tailored to fit particular situations.

The major drawback of herbicide use for site preparation is that other means must frequently be used to clear the area of logging slash and other woody biomass and provide a suitable environment for planting or seeding. In areas that have been cleanly logged, these latter conditions are not a problem, and chemical site preparation alone is sometimes enough to adequately prepare the sites for restocking. But this is more the exception than the rule, and the addition of prescribed burning or mechanical methods is usually required to create suitable conditions for establishing the new crop. In addition, it is frequently necessary to wait for the shrubs and hardwoods to sprout before applying herbicides in order to maximize chemical uptake and translocation. Thus substantial delays in reforestation may be incurred when chemical site preparation is employed.

Herbicides are sometimes limited by their efficacy. They are not always effective against all the species of problem vegetation that might be encountered in a given area. Follow-up release treatments with other chemicals or alternative methods may be necessary to provide adequate vegetation control. Vegetation may need to be of a certain size or at a specific stage of development before herbicides are effective. Weather conditions must also be suitable before, during, and after application in order to ensure adequate herbicidal activity. Finally, difficulties in securing uniform application (e.g., skips, double dosing) can sometimes reduce the overall efficacy and selectivity of herbicide treatments.

Reasonable care in the use of herbicides will minimize the potential for adverse side effects. However, damage to nearby crops and ornamental plants, contamination of streams and ponds, modification of wildlife habitat, residual soil toxicity, and occupational injury are some of the possible consequences if herbicides are not applied properly. Adequate education and training, strict compliance with appropriate regulations and label precautions, and careful attention to detail during application are necessary to ensure proper use of these materials. Also a variety of protective apparel and a number of drift control systems are available to further facilitate the safe use of herbicides.

The occasional misuse of herbicides in the past, coupled with considerable misinformation and perceived uncertainty about their safety, has led to a substantial degree of public anxiety over the use of herbicides in forestry. This concern exists in spite of (1) the relatively small amount of forest acreage treated with herbicides each year (in comparison with agricultural, industrial, and urban uses); (2) the general remoteness of the treated areas with respect to residential populations; (3) the fact that the chemicals used are designed to affect certain plant physiological functions, not animal systems; and (4) the exceptional record of safe use that has been compiled over the years by forestry applicators (there have been no documented cases of adverse health effects associated with the proper use of these materials in forestry). Nevertheless, the public's concern has prompted a variety of laws, regulations, legal injunctions, and other actions that have restricted the use of herbicides, especially on federal forest lands.

Many of the aforementioned restrictions are attributable to difficulties in preparing environmental impact statements (EISs) that meet the requirements of the National Environmental Policy Act (NEPA) of 1969 as interpreted by the courts. The problems have been largely procedural in nature, questioning whether federal agencies have prepared adequate EIS documents covering their planned actions. The question of whether herbicide use is likely to be safe or harmful usually has not been a direct issue. Indeed, where this issue has been directly addressed in litigation to date, herbicides have been acquitted. Presumably, the NEPA requirements can be satisfied, and herbicide applications will proceed on federal lands where appropriate. Meanwhile, efforts to improve our understanding of herbicide exposure, toxicology, and environmental impacts should continue. Better means of educating the public about the safety of herbicides are also in order so as to reduce unwarranted apprehensions over the use of these materials in forestry.

Several different herbicides are used for site preparation. The phenoxy herbicides such as 2,4-D and dichlorprop (and 2,4,5-T and silvex before they were canceled) have had the longest history of use. They are effective against a wide array of woody and herbaceous broadleaf species. Their ability to translocate downward into the root system makes them effective deterrents against certain sprouting species. Herbicide combinations are frequently used to broaden the spectrum of control. Dicamba, glyphosate, hexazinone, picloram, and triclopyr have also gained widespread use on woody species since the loss of 2,4,5-T and silvex. These materials as well as dinoseb are sometimes used to desiccate twigs and foliage prior to burning. The granular formulation of hexazinone has proven effective against a variety of deciduous hardwood species. Atrazine, glyphosate, hexazinone, oxyfluorofen, simazine, and sulfometuron have been used effectively for herbaceous weed control in intensively site-prepared areas, particularly in the South and Lake states.

As mentioned earlier, herbicides can be applied in a variety of ways, depending upon the vegetation involved, the time available for completing the task, the expertise of the applicator, and the financial resources available. Aerial application of broad-spectrum herbicides via helicopters equipped with boom-type sprayers is the most common method of application, particularly for managers of large forest acreages (Figure 6-4). Relatively large, inaccessible areas can be treated quickly and effectively at direct costs (chemical plus application) ranging from $20/acre to $80/acre.

Ground-based methods of herbicide application are also used where terrain is accessible, target vegetation is suitable, and aerial application is inappropriate. In the South and Lake states, broadcast, band, and spot applications of soil-active preemergence herbicides such as atrazine, hexazinone, oxyfluorofen, simazine, and sulfometuron are probably the most common ground treatments. They are generally applied by backpack or tractor equipment to relatively flat sites that have been intensively cultivated and where a dense cover of invading woody and herbaceous weeds is anticipated. Injection of nonmerchantable hardwood trunks with 2,4-D, triclopyr, or a combination of 2,4-D and picloram is practiced where

Figure 6-4. Aerial application of herbicides to forest land is usually done by helicopter. (*Source:* Photo courtesy of USDA Forest Service)

the residual trees are sparse or difficult to control by other means. Foliar applications of glyphosate, phenoxy, and picloram herbicides using tractor-mounted sprayers for control of hardwood saplings have also been used in the South and Lake states where topography is flat to gently rolling.

Individual stem treatments such as trunk injection, hack-and-squirt, cut-stump applications, and basal stem sprays are the most prevalent forms of ground application (Figure 6-5). However, broadcast, low-volume backpack spray applications are increasing in use. Picloram, triclopyr, and 2,4-D are the herbicides most commonly used in these individual stem treatments and backpack spray operations.

Costs of ground application vary considerably, depending upon the actual method used, the herbicide involved, and the conditions under which it is applied. Treatment costs as low as $10 to 50/acre are possible for stem injection treatments applied to light- to moderately stocked residuals. Banding of preemergence herbicides for herbaceous weed control costs about $15/acre or less, whereas spot treatments around individual conifer seedlings can cost $16/acre or less. Backpack basal sprays directed at hardwood sprout clumps in dense brushfields can cost in excess of $100/acre. Broadcast sprays using backpack equipment can be applied for as

Figure 6-5. Injection of herbicide into cull hardwoods is done with hatchets or tubular injectors.

little as \$20 to 40/acre, provided the terrain is accessible and the vegetation is of suitable size and density for this method of treatment.

Attention to the precautions and concerns associated with herbicide application has added substantial indirect costs (especially for federal agencies) to chemical methods of forest vegetation management in recent years. Requirements for environmental impact statements on federal lands, applicator training, water quality monitoring, special research studies, security measures, educational programs, and litigation are some of the indirect cost items currently associated with applying herbicides. However, as a consequence of these activities, the use of herbicides has been thoroughly analyzed as an approach to forest vegetation management.

Manual Methods

Manual methods of site preparation are largely restricted to brushfield reclamation and stand conversion projects. They are virtually always used in combination with herbicides, mechanical treatments, and/or prescribed burning. This approach to site preparation is most commonly used in the Northwest to convert thickets of red alder and other low-value hardwoods back to conifer stands. Chainsaws and occasionally other hand-held cutting tools are used to fell the woody stems in preparation for prescribed burning or mechanical removal. Prior treatment with herbicides is sometimes done to minimize sprouting. Otherwise, follow-up release treatments are generally required.

The main advantage of this method of site preparation is that relatively small areas can be treated. The technique is also selective, permitting the retention of high-value trees or plant species where fire is not used. There is generally no direct physical impact on the soil, and sensitive areas can be easily excluded.

If the topography is not too steep nor the vegetation too dense, felling can be done for about $100/acre. Where conditions are more severe, the felling operation can cost more than $250/acre.

The main disadvantages of this method are related to cost, efficacy, and worker safety. The use of power saws and sharp cutting tools is an expensive, hazardous activity, particularly on steep, brushy terrain. The treatments often need to be repeated, due to the prolific sprouting potential of most of the hardwood species when cut. Conceivably, the exhaust emissions from the power equipment can be injurious to workers under the dense canopy conditions frequently encountered in brushfields and hardwood thickets. Extensive safety training and careful implementation are advisable for all manual operations.

Finally, there are few data available that describe the survival and long-term growth responses of conifers to manual site preparation. The data collected from short-term studies indicate that the overall efficacy of manual cutting is poor unless combined with other measures.

Mulching and Scalping

Mulching and scalping treatments represent special cases of manual weed control. They are done in conjunction with tree-planting operations and are specifically aimed at controlling herbaceous vegetation. Primarily confined to interior regions of the Northwest where prolonged summer droughts frequently occur, scalping and mulching are designed to secure seedling survival.

Scalping involves clearing the duff and herbaceous vegetation in a circular spot as trees are planted. The radius of the spot rarely exceeds 2 ft. In reality, the main benefit of the treatment is to ensure that seedlings are planted in bare mineral soil, although some transient control of grasses and forbs may be provided.

Mulching usually entails the use of kraft paper or plastic sheets from 2 to 3 ft on a side, with the seedling located in the middle of the square sheet (Figure 6-6). They are effective at excluding herbaceous weeds around the base of the seedlings for 6 months to 2 years, depending on the material used. Careful installation (usually burying of the sides or corners) is required to avoid movement of the mulch and damage to the seedling.

Both scalping and mulching are labor-intensive techniques, and costs are comparatively high. Paper mulching, in particular, is an expensive treatment, amounting to $100 to 200/acre once the costs of materials and installation have been incorporated. Thus this technique should be restricted to high-value sites where herbaceous competition threatens seedling survival and more economical methods of control are not available.

RELEASE

Release treatments in forestry are analogous to postemergence weed control in farm crops. As in agriculture, the techniques are designed to *selectively* control competing vegetation without damaging the crop. Several practical constraints, however, limit the options available for conducting release operations in forestry. For example, mechanical cultivation is not practical in most forest plantations due to the difficulties of maneuvering on steep terrain and avoiding physical damage to the young conifers. Prescribed burning is not feasible because it would destroy the conifer regeneration as well as the competing vegetation. Therefore, only chemical, manual, and occasionally biological methods are suitable for performing release operations in young conifer plantations. Of these three options, the use of herbicides has been the most thoroughly tested and widely practiced approach. Efficacy data for manual and biological methods of release are scarce and mostly of very short duration.

Release treatments are most beneficial when applied during the first 8 years after plantation establishment. Control of competing vegetation during this period enhances survival and early growth of conifer regeneration. Benefits are greatest where serious competition is never permitted to develop. Release treatments can be performed at a later date but are generally limited to cleanup activities during precommercial thinning. Timely release treatments also enhance the utility, efficiency, and value of later silvicultural treatments such as fertilization and commercial thinning. Finally, effective release treatments will shorten the period

Figure 6-6. Paper mulches are sometimes used to suppress herbaceous weeds around recently planted seedlings.

during which young conifer plantations are vulnerable to destruction by fire and certain pests.

The purpose of release is to ensure that the preferred crop is the dominant species in the stand. Eradication of competing vegetation is not economically feasible or environmentally desirable. Simply reducing the weeds to a subordinate position is sufficient in most instances. In other cases, only temporary removal is required, and reinvasion can be allowed once the conifers are established.

Chemical Methods

Many of the advantages, disadvantages, and technical details discussed for chemical site preparation treatments apply to release treatments as well. There are some notable differences, however, and these are covered in the following discussion.

The use of selective herbicides has been the mainstay of postemergence weed control in forestry just as it has in agriculture. The materials are generally applied as broadcast applications by helicopter. However, helicopter treatments of individual clumps of bigleaf maple sprouts are conducted in the Northwest, and tractor-mounted sprayers are used on occasion for control of sapling-sized hardwoods in the South. Backpack applications of foliar or basal sprays are sometimes used near sensitive areas and where other methods are impractical. Individual stem applications (trunk injection, hack-and-squirt, cut-stump treatments) are rarely used because of the small size and vast number of stems usually involved in release operations.

Several herbicide formulations have been developed over the years to provide effective control of woody vegetation without damaging coniferous species. Prior to their cancellation, 2,4,5-T and silvex were the major herbicides used to release conifer plantations. Other phenoxy herbicides such as 2,4-D and dichlorprop have been substituted for many of the applications. However, 2,4-D is phytotoxic to southern pines, so its use for this purpose in the South is confined to directed applications where treatment of pines can be avoided (e.g., individual stem treatments, basal sprays). Amitrole-T can be safely applied over Douglas-fir and western hemlock (provided the dosage and season of application are correct), but it is only useful where elderberry and salmonberry are major components of the target vegetation.

Recently, several new herbicides have been developed for plantation release. Fosamine, glyphosate, hexazinone, and triclopyr have all been registered for specific release conditions. Although these materials are often more effective than the phenoxies at controlling particular problem species, they are generally not capable of affecting as broad a spectrum of plant species. In the Northwest, for example, glyphosate provides excellent control of salmonberry and thimbleberry but is erratic against the maple species frequently found in the same area. It is not effective at all on broadleaf evergreen species such as snowbrush and manzanita. Consequently, multiple treatments or herbicide combinations may be necessary to adequately suppress all the species of competing vegetation.

Some of the new soil-active herbicides are ideally suited for spot or band applications. However, their success is often dependent on proper soil conditions. Hexazinone, for instance, is best suited for coarse-textured soils. High rates of application are required for fine-textured soils and soils high in organic matter in order to achieve adequate hardwood control. These high rates of application are not only expensive but can also damage established conifers.

Some of the other herbicides can also be phytotoxic to conifers. Glyphosate, for example, will kill the leader growth of western hemlock, and triclopyr can cause complete mortality of pines. In short, the use of herbicides for plantation release is a sophisticated silvicultural practice, requiring careful prescription and implementation. Correct timing and rates of application are critical.

Despite these shortcomings, the use of herbicides for plantation release is an important silvicultural treatment. In many instances, it is the only practical method of controlling competing vegetation under the difficult ground conditions characteristic of most forest sites. At direct costs ranging from \$30 to 80/acre and production rates ranging from 100 to 300 acres/hr, aerial application is by far the most efficient method of releasing plantations from brush competition. Thus this method offers the special advantage of being able to complete relatively large projects quickly, while the target weeds are still susceptible to the herbicide and conifers are still resistant.

Manual Methods

The restrictions on the use of herbicides on federal forest lands have stimulated efforts to find alternative means of performing release operations. One approach involves the use of manual labor to cut or pull unwanted brush. Other than the fact that this approach does not rely on controversial chemical technology, the principal advantage is related to the selectivity of the treatment. It is possible to treat only the serious competing vegetation immediately surrounding individual crop conifers, leaving innocuous vegetation in intervening areas intact. However, this is an advantage common to all selective, nonbroadcast methods of release, including certain types of herbicide applications. Unless the manual cutting operation is performed carefully, though, it is easy to accidentally damage many of the desired conifers due to the difficulty of distinguishing them from the surrounding vegetation when the conifers are small. Physiological "thinning shock" to young conifers is also a potential problem associated with the sudden removal of overtopping vegetation. These problems notwithstanding, the use of spot manual control methods will generally minimize any potential adverse impacts on site quality, species diversity, and wildlife populations. It can also be done in conjunction with precommercial thinning, although delaying release until this time can sacrifice considerable conifer growth and perhaps survival. Nevertheless, cutting unwanted hardwoods at the time of precommercial thinning is a viable option, particularly in the South, and can be accomplished with virtually no damage to the residual pine stand.

The major dilemma with most manual methods conducted prior to precommercial thinning age (5 to 15 years old) is that they only provide transient release for the conifers. In most instances, the species involved quickly sprout and regain their former stature before the conifers have had a chance to respond. Edge effects from untreated vegetation surrounding the cleared area can also be a serious problem. These problems can be avoided by applying a herbicide such as 2,4-D, picloram, or triclopyr to the freshly cut stubs and to the perimeter of the cleared area. However, a safe, inexpensive, and practical means of performing such applications has not been developed yet. Consequently, manual treatments may need to be repeated several times before the conifers adequately capture the site.

Another possible solution to the sprouting problem involves pulling or grubbing the root systems of the target plants (Figure 6-7). Limited trials with hand pulling of seedling snowbrush on the light-textured volcanic soils of the Cascade Mountains in Oregon have shown that plants may be removed this way when small. Preliminary observations suggest that the treatment can be performed at costs as low as $50/acre when the snowbrush plants are young. However, the silvicultural and environmental impacts of this approach remain to be determined. Furthermore, the technique is not applicable to most release situations where the sprouting plants are well established and the soils are dense or where a significant proportion of the vegetation is comprised of other species.

Other disadvantages of manual methods have been described previously in the site preparation section. The key difficulties are the hazardous nature of the work, the large labor force required to cover the acreage needing treatment each year, and the high cost associated with the work, generally ranging from $50 to 300/acre or more for a single treatment, except when done in conjunction with precommercial thinning. Further developmental work on manual techniques and more thorough evaluations of the silvicultural and safety aspects are needed.

Biological Methods

Weed control through the use of natural biological agents such as microorganisms, insects, and livestock is theoretically attractive for release situations in forestry. Prospective advantages of this approach include (1) selective control of particular target weed species; (2) ability to be self-sustaining; (3) energy efficiency; (4) comparatively inexpensive once developed; and (5) in the special case of livestock, potential for generating supplemental revenue. However, the development of suitable and successful control agents involves considerable time, testing, and expense. Thus with the possible exception of controlled livestock grazing, there have not been any successful attempts at applied biological control of forest weeds. The applications of this approach to date have been largely confined to agricultural and aquatic situations, particularly those involving introduced weeds lacking natural enemies. The use of chrysomelid beetles (*Chrysolina quadrigemina*) to control the toxic Klamath weed in California, Idaho, and Washington is a classic example. In the Northwest, the cinnabar moth (*Tyria jacobea*) and a flea beetle (*Longitarsus jacobea*) have been introduced to control the spread of tansy ragwort—another weed poisonous to livestock.

The primary feature that makes most biological control agents so attractive, however, also limits their utility, particularly for forestry purposes. Because most biological control agents (e.g., insects, pathogens) are highly host specific, this approach is not very practical for controlling the wide array of weed species capable of affecting forest stands and plantations. Even if promising organisms are found that have broad host

Figure 6-7. Manual grubbing of small shrubs is a promising technique on light-textured volcanic soils.

ranges, care will need to be taken during implementation in order to assure that conifers and other desirable vegetation are not vulnerable. Potential adverse side effects of introduced biological control agents will also need to be carefully assessed.

As mentioned earlier, the use of livestock represents one promising instance where animals can be used to suppress competing vegetation in young conifer plantations. The record is ambiguous and controversial, though. Historically, excessive grazing by cattle, sheep, and goats has actually destroyed young conifer plantations rather than helped them. Damage from trampling, rubbing, soil compaction, and feeding has been observed time and again in such situations. Nevertheless, cattle have successfully grazed in open, pole-sized stands of southern pines for decades, and recent efforts in Oregon indicate that both cattle and sheep can forage in young conifer plantations, provided the livestock is properly managed (Figure 6-8). Key recommendations include:

1. Use only livestock accustomed to forest conditions,
2. Regulate the number of animals to avoid excessive grazing and soil compaction, yet maintain adequate vegetation control,
3. Defer grazing until conifer seedlings are no longer vulnerable to browsing or trampling,
4. Restrict the grazing period to times when the forage is more palatable than the conifer seedlings,
5. Have herders or wranglers on site to control distribution of the animals,

Figure 6-8. Carefully managed cattle grazing is an effective means of suppressing competing vegetation in pine plantations.

6. Strategically locate water sources, supplemental feeding areas, and bedding grounds to prevent aggregation near seedlings vulnerable to damage,
7. Keep livestock out of riparian zones and other ecologically sensitive areas,
8. Establish and maintain cordial, businesslike relations with cooperating livestock owners.

The aforementioned guidelines notwithstanding, much remains to be learned about effective use of livestock for vegetation management purposes in forestry. There are only a few published articles describing this approach, and many of the studies are still in their infancy. Furthermore, issues such as management complexity, availability of suitable livestock, interactions with wildlife, pollution and disease transmission, and economics need to be explored. In short, the use of livestock is a promising approach for certain situations in forest vegetation management. However, it is not a panacea for the vast array of vegetative problems facing forest managers. Indeed, such an approach will likely add another dimension of complexity to silvicultural prescriptions.

TIMBER STAND IMPROVEMENT

Timber stand improvement for vegetation management purposes involves the reduction of competition any time between release and final harvest. In the Northwest, the practice usually coincides with commercial thinning operations; special entry just for the purpose of cleaning the stand is generally not warranted nor economical in this region. Most western coniferous species are capable of maintaining long-term control of a site once they have passed the sapling stage in a dominant position.

In the South amd Northeast, timber stand improvement is often referred to as *cull timber removal*. As such, it involves the selective harvest or control of low-value woody vegetation that is encroaching on or dominating the stand. Defective or low-quality hardwoods and understory brush are the usual target species in these operations.

Although timber stand improvement is generally not necessary in stands established with good vegetation control, it can greatly boost the growth and value of the residual trees where stands have been neglected for one reason or another. Furthermore, improvements conducted near the time of final harvest can reduce the need for vegetation management in the subsequent rotation.

The principal methods of timber stand improvement include manual, chemical, and prescribed burning techniques. Manual control methods are employed during conventional thinning and harvesting operations. Nonmerchantable material is simply cut and left on site to decompose. Where practical, merchantable logs are harvested and transported to the mill for processing. The costs are usually absorbed by the thinning or logging operation and are not tallied as a separate charge.

Chemical methods of timber stand improvement are generally used when the material to be controlled has no merchantable value. Large tracts can often be efficiently treated with broadcast applications of selective herbicide sprays, granules, or pellets. Either helicopters or ground-based equipment can be used for this purpose. Smaller tracts or those with scattered cull hardwoods are more amenable to individual stem treatments such as trunk injection, cut-stump application, and basal sprays. The herbicides most frequently used in these operations are 2,4-D, hexazinone, picloram, triclopyr, and combinations thereof. Herbicide treatment costs largely depend on stand conditions but range from a low of $30/acre for aerial application to more than $80/acre for some manual applications.

Understory burning as a method of timber stand improvement is used extensively across the South and in parts of the Inland Northwest where fire-resistant timber types occur. Not only does it help contain the encroachment of undesirable hardwoods, but it also reduces the risk of wildfire in highly flammable situations. To be safe, the conifers must be beyond the sapling stage, and the burn has to be conducted under appropriate weather conditions. To effectively control the understory hardwoods, several burns at 3- to 5-year intervals are usually required. Hardwoods greater than 6 in. diameter at breast height (DBH) are rarely killed by prescribed burning. Instead, they are gradually degraded by the fire scars and subsequent decay fungi that develop. Alternatively, the weed trees may be individually treated with herbicides.

Adverse topographic and climatic features make understory burning a difficult and risky proposition in most of the Northwest. About the only place where the technique has been used with some success is in conjunction with the shelterwood system of reforestation. Here broadcast burns are conducted after partial removal of the overstory to facilitate seedbed preparation for the ensuing seedfall. Some control of competing vegetation is provided, although fire-adapted species such as tanoak and snowbrush can become even more of a problem under certain conditions. If piling of slash and debris is necessary in order to conduct a safe, effective, understory burn, then the potential for adverse impacts of mechanical treatment (e.g., high cost, soil compaction, erosion, damage to residual trees) needs to be considered.

Prescribed burning of understory vegetation is one of the cheapest silvicultural practices available, particularly in the South. The initial burn within a stand of pines in this region may cost $30 to 50/acre, but subsequent burns can be accomplished at costs as low as $4/acre. The considerable risk associated with understory burning in the Northwest necessitates elaborate precautionary measures ranging from extensive fire trails to standby fire suppression equipment. Consequently, direct costs ranging from $100 to 750/acre are customary.

The advantages and disadvantages of the various methods of timber stand improvement are analogous to those described for their counterparts in site preparation and release. However, there are a few key stand attributes that largely determine which method to use. Where the material to be removed has merchantable value, then a manual method of cutting is appropriate, often with a follow-up herbicide treatment to the cut stump. Where the material is unmerchantable and has a high potential of sprouting, then a chemical stem injection treatment is preferable. If fire hazard reduction or seedbed preparation for regeneration are primary considerations, then prescribed burning of the understory vegetation is in order.

SUMMARY

The major attributes associated with the various approaches to forest vegetation management are summarized in Table 6-1. As can be seen, a variety of options are available for dealing with competing vegetation at a number of stages in forest management. Vegetation problems can be prevented from arising in the first place by employing certain preharvest, logging, and site-preparation measures. Selective treatments can be used to release young stands from encroaching or overtopping weeds. Timber stand improvement can be used to maximize value growth toward the end of the rotation and to minimize vegetation problems in the next one. A number of mechanical, chemical, manual, biological, and burning techniques are available to choose from at most of the stages.

Which general approach to take and which specific technique to use for any given site depends on a careful weighing of the anticipated consequences. Each method has advantages and disadvantages associated with it, which depend on the forest and site conditions where the treatment is planned to be employed. The ultimate decision should be based on the development of a thorough silvicultural prescription that integrates all of the management treatments necessary to meet the timber production goals while safeguarding environmental and other forest values (see Chapter 13). Thus, forest vegetation management practices are selected within the context of other silvicultural practices such as harvesting, reforestation, thinning, fertilization, and protection. This ensures that vegetation management activities contribute to achieving the overall goals of forest management.

BIBLIOGRAPHY*

Silviculture Texts

Barrett, J.W. (ed.) 1980. Regional silviculture of the United States. 2nd ed. John Wiley and Sons, Inc., New York, NY. 551 p.

Burns, R.M. (tech. comp.) 1983. Silvicultural systems for the major forest types of the United States. USDA Forest Service, Washington, DC. Agr. Hbk. 445. 191 p.

Cleary, B.D., R.D. Greaves, and R.K. Hermann (eds.) 1978. Regenerating Oregon's forests. Ext. Serv., Oregon State Univ. Corvallis, OR. 286 p.

Fowells, H.A. (comp.) 1965. Silvics of forest trees of the United States. USDA Forest Service, Washington, DC. Agr. Hbk. 271. 762 p.

Smith, D.M. 1986. Practice of silviculture. 8th ed. John Wiley & Sons, Inc., New York, NY. 620 p.

Wahlenberg, W.G. (ed.) 1965. A guide to loblolly and slash pine plantation management in Southeastern USA. Georgia Forest Res. Counc., Macon, GA. Rep. 14. 360 p.

Wenger, K.F. 1984. Forestry handbook. 2nd ed. John Wiley & Sons, Inc., New York, NY. 1,335 p.

General Descriptions of Alternative Methods of Forest Vegetation Management

Benzie, J.W., S. Little, and R.F. Sutton. 1973. Rehabilitation of forestland: the Northeast and Boreal region. J. Forestry 71:154-158.

Dingle, R.W. 1976. Principles of site preparation, p. 107-116. *In* Baumgartner, D.M. and R.J. Boyd (eds.) Tree planting in the Inland Northwest. Conf. Proc., Coop. Ext. Serv., Washington State Univ., Pullman, WA. 311 p.

Fitzgerald, C.H., F.A. Peevy, and D.E. Fender. 1973. Rehabilitation of forestland: the Southern region. J. Forestry 71:148-153.

Gjerstad, D.H. and P.J. Minogue. 1985. Vegetation problems and solutions—Southeast, p. 305-312. *In* Proc., 38th Annu. Mtg., South. Weed Sci. Soc., Houston, TX. SWSPBE 38. 562 p.

Gratkowski, H., D. Hopkins, and P. Lauterbach. 1973. Rehabilitation of forestland: the Pacific Coast and Northern Rocky Mountain region. J. Forestry 71:138-143.

Greaves, R.D. 1978. Competing vegetation, p. 190-192. *In* Cleary, B.D., R.D. Greaves, and R.K. Hermann (eds.) Regenerating Oregon's forests. Ext. Serv., Oregon State Univ., Corvallis, OR. 287 p.

*This bibliography includes key references and reviews dealing with various subject areas pertinent to forest vegetation management. It is not an exhaustive compilation of published information. Instead, it is intended to provide guidance for obtaining more detailed information on topics of interest to prospective readers.

Holt, H.A. and B.C. Fischer (eds.) 1981. Weed control in forest management. Proc. 1981 John S. Wright Forestry Conf., Purdue Univ., West Lafayette, IN. 305 p.

Johnson, T.N., Jr., G.H. Schubert, and D.P. Almas. 1973. Rehabilitation of forestland: the Rocky Mountain-Intermountain region. J. Forestry 71:144-147.

McCormack, M.L., Jr. 1985. Vegetation problems and solutions—Northeast, p. 315-326. In Proc., 38th Annu. Mtg., South. Weed Sci. Soc., Houston, TX. SWSPBE 38. 562 p.

Newton, M. and C.A. Roberts. 1979. Brush control alternatives for forest site preparation. 28th Annu. Oregon Weed Control Conf., Salem, OR. Proc. and Res. Prog. Rep. 10 p.

Newton, M. and J.D. Walstad. 1985. Vegetation problems and solutions— Northwest, p. 313-314. In Proc., 38th Annu. Mtg., South. Weed Sci. Soc., Houston, TX. SWSPBE 38. 562 p.

Ross, D.W. and J.D. Walstad. 1986. Vegetative competition, site preparation, and pine performance: a literature review with reference to southcentral Oregon. Forest Research Laboratory, College of Forestry, Oregon State Univ., Corvallis, OR. Res. Bull. 58. 21 p.

Sajdak, R.L. and J. Kotar. 1985. Vegetation management problems and solutions—Lake states, p. 327-336. In Proc., 38th Annu. Mtg., South Weed Sci. Soc., Houston, TX. SWSPBE 38. 562 p.

Stewart, R.E. 1978. Site preparation, p. 99-129. In Cleary, B.D., R.D. Greaves, and R.K. Hermann (eds.) Regenerating Oregon's forests. Ext. Serv., Oregon State Univ., Corvallis, OR. 287 p.

Sutton, R.F. 1985. Vegetation management in Canadian forestry. Great Lakes Forestry Research Centre, Department of the Environment, Canadian Forestry Service, Sault Ste. Marie, Ontario. Information Rep. 0-X-369. 34 p.

Walker, C.M. 1973. Rehabilitation of forest land. J. Forestry 71:136-137.

Walstad, J.D. 1976. Weed control for better southern pine management. South. Forestry Res. Ctr., Weyerhaeuser Co., Hot Springs, AR. Weyerhaeuser Forestry Pap. 15. 44 p.

Williston, H.L. 1977. Release cutting in southern forests: economical and effective stand conversion. USDA Forest Service, Southeastern Area, State and Private Forestry, Atlanta, GA. Forest Manage. Bull. 4 p.

Williston, H.L. 1977. Tips on improvement cutting. USDA Forest Service, Southeastern Area, State and Private Forestry, Atlanta, GA. Forest Manage. Bull. 4 p.

Prescribed Burning

Baumgartner, D.M. (ed.) 1982. Site preparation and fuels management on steep terrain. Sympos. Proc., Coop. Ext., Washington State Univ., Pullman, WA. 179 p.

Cooper, R.W. 1975. Prescribed burning. J. Forestry 73:776-780.

Crow, A.B. 1973. Use of fire in southern forests. J. Forestry 71:629-632.

Fischer, W.C. 1978. Planning and evaluating prescribed fires—a standard procedure. USDA Forest Service, Intermountain Forest and Range Experiment Station, Ogden, UT. Gen. Tech. Rep. INT-43. 19 p.

Grano, C.X. 1970. Eradicating understory hardwoods by repeated prescribed burning. USDA Forest Service, Southern Forest Experiment Station, New Orleans, LA. Res. Pap. SO-56. 11 p.

Hooven, E.F. and H.C. Black. 1978. Prescribed burning aids reforestation of Oregon Coast Range brushlands. School of Forestry, Oregon State Univ., Corvallis, OR. Forest Res. Lab. Res. Pap. 38. 14 p.

Hurley, C. and D.J. Taylor. 1974. Brown and burn site preparation in western Washington. Washington State Dept. Natur. Resour., Olympia, WA. DNR Note 8. 9 p.

Lotan, J.E., M.E. Alexander, S.F. Arno, R.E. French, O.G. Langdon, R.M. Loomis, R.A. Norum, R.C. Rothermel, W.C. Schmidt, and J.W. van Wagtendonk. 1981. Effects of fire on flora. USDA Forest Service, Washington, DC. Gen. Tech. Rep. WO-16. 71 p.

Loucks, D.M., S.R. Radosevich, T.B. Harrington, and R.G. Wagner. 1986. Prescribed burning in Pacific Northwest forests: an annotated bibliography. Forest Res. Lab., College of Forestry, Oregon State Univ., Corvallis, OR. CRAFTS Rep. 185 p.

Martin, R.E. 1976. Prescribed burning for site preparation in the Inland Northwest, p. 134-156. *In* Baumgartner, D.M. and R.J. Boyd (eds.) Tree planting in the Inland Northwest. Conf. Proc., Coop. Ext. Serv., Washington State Univ., Pullman, WA. 311 p.

Martin, R.E. and J.D. Dell 1978. Planning for prescribed burning in the inland northwest. USDA Forest Service, Pacific Northwest Forest and Range Experiment Station, Portland, OR. Gen. Tech. Rep. PNW-76. 68 p.

McRae, D.J. 1980. Preliminary fuel consumption guidelines for prescribed burning in Ontario slash fuel complexes. Great Lakes Forest Research Centre, Department of the Environment, Canadian Forestry Service, Sault Ste. Marie, Ontario. Information Rep. 0-X-316. 25 p.

McRae, D.J. 1985. Prescribed burning of boreal mixedwood slash in the Ontario Clay Belt Region. Great Lakes Forest Research Centre, Department of the Environment, Canadian Forestry Service, Sault Ste. Marie, Ontario. Information Rep. 0-X-367. 18 p.

McRae, D.J., M.E. Alexander, and B.J. Stocks. 1979. Measurement and description of fuels and fire behavior on prescribed burns: a handbook. Great Lakes Forest Research Centre, Department of the Environment, Canadian Forestry Service, Sault Ste. Marie, Ontario. Information Rep. 0-X-287. 60 p.

Mobley, H.E. (sen. comp.) 1976. Southern forestry smoke management guidebook. USDA Forest Service, Southeastern Forest Experiment Station, Asheville, NC. Gen. Tech. Rep. SE-10. 140 p.

Mobley, H.E., R.S. Jackson, W.E. Balmer, W.E. Ryziska, and W.A. Hough. 1973. A guide for prescribed fire in southern forests. USDA Forest Service, Southeastern Area State and Private Forestry-2, Atlanta, GA. 40 p.

Mechanical Methods

Burns, R.M. and E.A. Hebb. 1972. Site preparation and reforestation of droughty, acid sands. USDA Forest Service, Washington, DC. Agr. Hbk. 426. 61 p.

Froehlich, H.A. 1984. Mechanical amelioration of adverse physical soil conditions in forestry, p. 507-521. *In* Proc., Symposium on Site and Productivity of Fast Growing Plantations, Internat. Union Forest Res. Organ., Pretoria and Pietermaritzburg, South Africa, April 30-May 11, 1984.

Gent, J.A., Jr., R. Ballard, and A.E. Hassan. 1983. The impact of harvesting and site preparation on the physical properties of lower coastal plain forests. Soil Sci. Soc. Amer. J. 47:595-598.

Gorman, J.R. (comp.) 1985. Procedings of the 1984 mechanized silviculture workshop. Northern Forestry Research Centre, Canadian Forestry Service, Edmonton, Alberta. Information Rep. NOR-X-272. 47 p.

Haines, L.W., T.E. Maki, and S.G. Sanderford. 1975. The effects of mechanical site preparation treatments on soil properties and tree (*Pinus taeda* L. and *P. elliottii* Englem. var. *elliottii*) growth, p. 379-395. *In* Proc., Bernier, B. and C.H. Winget (eds.) Forest soils and forest land management. Fourth North Amer. Forest Soils Conf., Laval Univ. Press, Quebec. 675 p.

Hedin, I.B. 1986. Mechanical site preparation trials in coastal British Columbia. Forest Engineering Research Institute of Canada, Vancouver, B.C. Tech. Rep. TR-69. 25 p.

Hughes, R.H. 1965. Cultivation in pine plantations, p. 287-291. *In* W.G. Wahlenberg (ed.) A guide to loblolly and slash pine plantation management in southeastern USA. Georgia Forest Res. Counc., Macon, GA. Rep. 14. 360 p.

Moehring, D.H. 1970. Forest soil improvement through cultivation. J. Forestry 68:328-331.

Schultz, R.P. 1976. Environmental changes after site preparation and slash pine planting on a flatwood site. USDA Forest Service, Southeastern Forest Experiment Station, Asheville, NC. Res. Pap. SE-156. 20 p.

Shoulders, E. and T.A. Terry. 1978. Dealing with site disturbances from harvesting and site preparation in the lower coastal plain, p. 85-97. *In* Tippin, T. (ed.) Proc., Symposium on principles of maintaining productivity on prepared sites. USDA Forest Service, Southern Forest Experiment Station, New Orleans, LA. Publ. 78-9.

Terry, T.A. and R.G. Campbell. 1981. Soil management considerations in intensive forest management, p. 98-106. *In* Forest regeneration. Proc., Amer. Soc. Agr. Eng. Symposium on Engineering Systems for Forest Regeneration. ASAE Publ. 10-81.

Terry, T.A. and J.H. Hughes. 1975. The effects of intensive management on planted loblolly pine (*Pinus taeda* L.) growth on poorly drained soils of the Atlantic Coastal Plain, p. 351-377. *In* Proc., Bernier, B. and C.H. Winget (eds.) Forest soils and forest land management. Fourth North Amer. Forest Soils Conf., Laval Univ. Press, Quebec. 675 p.

Wilhite, L.P., and T.A. Harrington. 1965. Site preparation, p. 22-31. *In* W.G. Wahlenberg (ed.) A guide to loblolly and slash pine plantation management in Southeastern USA. Georgia Forest Res. Counc., Macon GA. Rep. 14. 360 p.

Chemical Methods

Ayling, R.D., and B. Graham. 1978. A survey of herbicide use in Canadian forestry. Forestry Chron. 54:302-308.

Bentley, J.R. and K.M. Estes. 1978. Control of brush regrowth with herbicides on pine plantations in Northern California. USDA Forest Service, Pacific Southwest Forest and Range Experiment Station, Berkeley, CA. Res. Pap. PSW-134. 13 p.

Bovey, R.W. 1977. Response of selected woody plants in the United States to herbicides. U.S. Dept. Agr., Washington, DC. Agr. Hbk. 493. 101 p.

Bovey, R.W., and J.D. Diaz-Colon. 1978. Selected bibliography of the phenoxy herbicides. VIII. Effects on higher plants. MP-1388. Texas Agr. Exper. Sta., College Station, TX. 59 p.

Bovey, R.W. and A.L. Young. 1980. The science of 2,4,5-T and associated phenoxy herbicides. John Wiley and Sons, Inc., New York, NY. 462 p.

Boyd, R.J. 1982. Chemical site preparation treatments for herbaceous plant communities, p. 49-53. *In* Baumgartner, D.M. (ed.) Site preparation and fuels management on steep terrain. Sympos. Proc., Coop. Ext., Washington State Univ., Pullman, WA. 179 p.

Boyd, R.J., D.L. Miller, F.A. Kidd, and C.P. Ritter. 1985. Herbicides for forest weed control in the Inland Northwest: a summary of effects on weeds and conifers. USDA Forest Service, Intermountain Research Station, Ogden, UT. Gen. Tech. Rep. INT-195. 66 p.

Cain, M.D. and D.A. Yaussy. 1984. Can hardwoods be eradicated from pine sites? South. J. Appl. Forestry 8:7-13.

Cantrell, R.L. 1985. A guide to silvicultural herbicide use in the Southern United States. School of Forestry, Auburn Univ., Auburn, AL. 482 p.

Conard, S.G. and W.H. Emmingham. 1983. Herbicides for shrub control on forest sites in northeastern Oregon and northern Idaho. Oregon State Univ., Corvallis, OR. Forest Res. Lab. Spec. Pub. 5. 8 p.

Conard, S.G. and W.H. Emmingham. 1984. Herbicides for forest brush control in southwestern Oregon. Oregon State Univ., Corvallis, OR. Forest Res. Lab. Spec. Pub. 6. 8 p.

Conard, S.G. and W.H. Emmingham. 1984. Herbicides for grass and herbaceous weed control in Oregon and Washington. Oregon State Univ., Corvallis, OR. Forest Res. Lab. Spec. Pub. 7. 8 p.

Conard, S.G. and W.H. Emmingham. 1984. Herbicides for brush and fern control on forest sites in western Oregon and Washington. Oregon State Univ., Corvallis, OR. Forest Res. Lab. Spec. Pub. 8. 8 p.

Conard, S.G. and W.H. Emmingham. 1984. Herbicides for clump and stem treatment of weed trees and shrubs in Oregon and Washington. Oregon State Univ., Corvallis, OR. Forest Res. Lab. Spec. Pub. 9. 8 p.

Dimock, E.J., II. 1981. Herbicide and conifer options for reforesting upper slopes in the Cascade Range. USDA Forest Service, Pacific Northwest Forest and Range Experiment Station, Portland, OR. Res. Pap. PNW-292. 14 p.

Dimock, E.J., II, T.F. Beebe, and E.B. Collard. 1983. Planting-site preparation with herbicides to aid conifer reforestation. Weed Sci. 31:215-221.

Elwell, H.M. 1967. Herbicides for release of shortleaf pine and native grasses. Weeds 15:104-107.

Fitzgerald, C.H. and J.C. Fortson. 1979. Herbaceous weed control with hexazinone in loblolly pine (*Pinus taeda*) plantations. Weed Sci. 27:583-588.

Gratkowski, H. 1975. Silvicultural use of herbicides in Pacific Northwest forests. USDA Forest Service, Pacific Northwest Forest and Range Experiment Station, Portland, OR. Gen. Tech. Rep. PNW-37. 44 p.

Grakowski, H. 1976. Herbicides for grass and forb control in Douglas-fir plantations. USDA Forest Service, Pacific Northwest Forest and Range Experiment Station, Portland, OR. Res. Note PNW-285. 7 p.

Gratkowski, H.J. 1977. Seasonal effects of phenoxy herbicides on ponderosa pine and associated brush species. Forest Sci. 23:2-12.

Gratkowski, H. 1978. Herbicides for shrub and weed tree control in western Oregon. USDA Forest Service, Pacific Northwest Forest and Range Experiment Station, Portland, OR. Gen. Tech. Rep. PNW-77. 48 p.

Hamel, D.R. 1981. Forest management chemicals: a guide to use when considering pesticides for forest management. USDA Forest Service, Washington, DC. Agr. Hbk. 585. 512 p.

Hamel, D.R. and C.I. Shade. 1985. Weeds, trees, and herbicides—a public forest and rangeland survey. USDA Forest Service, Forest Pest Management, Washington, DC. 52 p.

Haymond, J.L. and K.F. Ray. 1983. Herbicides for forestry. Coop. Ext. Serv., Clemson Univ., Clemson, SC. Forestry Notes 20 (rev.) 30 p.

Haywood, J.D. 1979. Combinations of foliar- and soil-applied herbicides for controlling hardwood brush. USDA Forest Service, Southern Forest Experiment Station, New Orleans, LA. Res. Note SO-247. 3 p.

Heidmann, L.J. 1969. Use of herbicides for planting site preparation in the Southwest. J. Forestry 67:506-509.

Heidmann, L.J. 1984. Using herbicides for reforestation in the Southwest. USDA Forest Service, Rocky Mountain Forest and Range Experiment Station, Fort Collins, CO. Gen. Tech. Rep. RM-103. 12 p.

Kossuth, S.V., J. Young, J. Voeller, and H.A. Holt. 1978. Four season herbicide injection of hardwoods. Weed Res. 18:161-167.

Mann, W.F., Jr. and M.J. Haynes. 1978. Status of some new herbicides. USDA Forest Service, Southern Forest Experiment Station, Pineville, LA. Gen. Tech. Rep. SO-21. 18 p.

Miller, D.L. 1982. Herbicides: guidelines for use and site preparation prescriptions in the Inland Northwest, p. 55-62. *In* Baumgartner, D.M. (ed.) Site preparation and fuels management on steep terrain. Sympos. Proc., Coop. Ext., Washington State Univ., Pullman, WA. 179 p.

Miller, D.L. and F.A. Kidd. 1983. Shrub control in the Inland Northwest—a summary of herbicide test results. Wood Products, Western Div., Potlatch Corp., Lewiston, ID. Forestry Res. Note RN-83-4. 49 p.

Nelson, L.R., D.H. Gjerstad, and P.J. Minogue. 1983. Use of herbicides for industrial forest vegetation management in the southern United States. p. 11-25. *In* Garner, W.Y. and J. Harvey, Jr. (eds.) Chemical and biological controls in forestry. ACS Sympos. Ser. 238. Amer. Chem. Soc., Washington, DC.

Nelson, L.R., S.A. Knowe, and D.H. Gjerstad. 1982. Use of effective herbicide treatments for artificial regeneration of longleaf pine. Georgia Forestry Commission, Macon, GA. Georgia Forest Res. Pap. 40. 7 p.

Nelson, L.R., B.R. Zutter, and D.H. Gjerstad. 1985. Planted longleaf pine seedlings respond to herbaceous weed control using herbicides. Southern J. Appl. Forestry 9:236-240.

Newton, M. 1975. Constructive use of herbicides in forest resource management. J. Forestry 73:329-336.

Newton, M. 1984. Herbicides in forestry, p. 90-103. *In* Whitson, T.D. and R.D. William (comps.) Oregon weed control handbook. Ext. Serv., Oregon State Univ., Corvallis, OR. 189 p.

Newton, M. and F.B. Knight. 1981. Handbook of weed and insect control chemicals for forest resource managers. Timber Press, Beaverton, OR. 213 p.

Peevy, F.A. 1972. Injection treatments for killing bottomland hardwoods. Weed Sci. 20:566-568.

Peevy, F.A. and H.A. Brady. 1968. Mist blowing versus other methods of foliar spraying for hardwood control. Weed Sci. 16:425-426.

Radosevich, S.R., E.J. Roncoroni, S.G. Conard, and W.B. McHenry. 1980. Seasonal tolerance of six coniferous species to eight foliage-active herbicides. Forest Sci. 26:3-9.

Romancier, R.M. 1965. 2,4-D, 2,4,5-T, and related chemicals for woody plant control in the Southeastern United States. Georgia Forest Res. Counc., Macon, GA. Rep. 16. 46 p.

Starr, J.W. 1964. The use of the mist blower for control of undesirable hardwoods. Miss. State Univ., Agr. Exp. Sta. Bull. 692. 15 p.

Stewart, R.E. 1976. Chemical site preparation in the Inland Empire, p. l58-l7l. *In* Baumgartner, D.M. and R.J. Boyd (eds.) Tree planting in the Inland Northwest. Conf. Proc., Coop. Ext. Serv., Washington State Univ., Pullman, WA. 311 p.

Stewart, R.E. 1978. Origin and development of vegetation after spraying and burning in a coastal Oregon clearcut. USDA Forest Service, Pacific Northwest Forest and Range Experiment Station, Portland, OR. Res. Note PNW-317. 11 p.

Sutton, R.F. 1967. Selectivity of herbicides. Forestry Chron. 43:265-268.

Sutton, R.F. 1970. Chemical herbicides and forestation. Forestry Chron. 46:458-465.

Sutton, R.F. 1984. Plantation establishment in the boreal forest: glyphosate, hexazinone, and manual weed control. Forestry Chron. 60:283-287.

Williston, H.L., W.E. Balmer, and L.P. Abrahamson. 1976. Chemical control of vegetation in southern forests. USDA Forest Service, Southeastern Area, State and Private Forestry, Atlanta, GA. Forest Manage. Bull. 6 p.

Manual Methods

Beebe, T. 1982. Are handscalps an effective method of site preparation in central Washington? p. 45-48. *In* Baumgartner, D.M. (ed.) Site preparation and fuels management on steep terrain. Sympos. Proc., Coop. Ext., Washington State Univ., Pullman, WA. 179 p.

Bernstein, A. 1978. Using a chainsaw to control brush. J. Forestry 80:474-475.

Flint, L.E. and S.W. Childs. 1987. Effects of shading, mulching, and vegetation control on Douglas-fir seedling growth and water use. Forest Ecol. Manage. (in press).

Forest Service Equipment Development Center. 1985. Better handtools for site preparation. USDA Forest Service, Equipment Development Center, Missoula, MT. Equip Tips. 2 p.

Harrington, C.A. 1984. Factors influencing initial sprouting of red alder. Can. J. Forest Res. 14:357-361.

Hermann, R.K. 1964. Paper mulch for reforestation in southwest Oregon. J. Forestry 62:98-101.

Hobbs, S.D. and K.A. Wearstler, Jr. 1985. Effects of cutting sclerophyll brush on sprout development and Douglas-fir growth. Forest Ecol. Manage. 13:69–81.

Hoyer, G.E. and D. Belz. 1984. Stump sprouting related to time of cutting red alder. Washington State Dept. Natur. Resour., Olympia, WA. DNR Rep. 45. 17 p.

Hunt, L.O. 1963. Evaluation of various mulching materials to improve plantation survival. Tree Planters' Notes 57:19-22.

Roberts, C.A. 1980. Cooperative brush control study: second year report. Unpublished report by C.A. Roberts, Reforestation Consultant, Corvallis, OR. 29 p.

Walker, L.C. 1961. Black plastic "mulch" for pine planting. Tree Planters' Notes 45:1.

Biological Methods

Grelen, H.E. 1978. Forest grazing in the South. J. Range Manage. 31:244-250.

Huffaker, C.B. 1971. Biological control. Plenum Press, New York, NY. 511 p.

Krueger, W.C. 1983. Cattle grazing in managed forests, p. 29-41. In Forestland Grazing. Symposium Proc., Washington State Univ., Pullman, WA.

Krueger, W.C. 1983. Forest grazing—growing trees, grass and livestock together, p. 233-245. In Mosher, W. (ed.) Foothills for food and forests. Timber Press, Beaverton, OR. 350 p.

Sharrow, S.H., and W.C. Leininger. 1983. Sheep as a silvicultural tool in coastal Douglas-fir forests, p. 219-232. In Mosher, W. (ed.) Foothills for food and forests. Timber Press, Beaverton, OR. 350 p.

Sharrow, S.H. and W.C. Leininger. 1983. Forest grazing—growing trees, grass and livestock together. 2. Western Oregon, p. 247-257. In Mosher, W. (ed.) Foothills for food and forests. Timber Press, Beaverton, OR. 350 p.

Syntheses of Conifer Growth and Yield Response to Forest Vegetation Management

Burkhart, H.E. and P.T. Sprinz. 1984. A model for assessing hardwood competition effects on yields of loblolly pine plantations. School of Forestry and Wildlife

Resour., Virginia Polytechnic Institute and State Univ., Blacksburg, VA. Publ. No. FWS-3-84. 55 p.

Ffolliott, P.F. and W.P. Clary. 1982. Understory-overstory vegetation relationships: an annotated bibliography. USDA Forest Service, Intermountain Forest and Range Experiment Station, Ogden, UT. Gen. Tech. Rep. INT-136. 39 p.

Glover, G.R. and D.F. Dickens. 1985. Impact of competing vegetation on yield of the southern pines. Georgia Forestry Commission, Macon, GA. Georgia Forest Res. Pap. 59. 14 p.

Schultz, R.P. 1975. Intensive culture of southern pines: maximum yields on short rotations. Iowa State J. Res. 49(3):325-337.

Stewart, R.E., L.L. Gross, and B.H. Honkala. 1984. Effects of competing vegetation on forest trees: a bibliography with abstracts. USDA Forest Service, Washington, DC. Gen. Tech. Rep. WO-43. 260 p.

Walstad, J.D. 1982. Increasing fiber production through intensive forest management: opportunities through vegetation management, p. 46-50. *In* Increasing forest productivity. Soc. Amer. Foresters Proc., 1981. Nat. Conv., Orlando, FL. SAF Publ. 82-01. 368 p.

Economic Analyses of Forest Vegetation Management

American Paper Institute/National Forest Products Association. 1978. Benefits of 2,4,5-T in forest management. Amer. Paper Inst./Nat. Forest Prod. Assoc., Washington, DC. 139 p.

Anderson, W.C. 1974. An economist's view of the pine-site hardwood problem. Forest Products J. 24(4):14-16.

Balmer, W.E., K.A. Utz, and O.G. Langdon. 1978. Financial returns from cultural work in natural loblolly pine stands. South. J. Appl. Forestry 2:111-117.

Guldin, R.W. 1984. Economic returns from spraying to release loblolly pine, p. 248-254. *In* Proc., Biotechnology and Weed Science, 37th Annual Meeting of Southern Weed Science Soc., January 17-19, 1984, Hot Springs, AR. Weed Sci. Soc. Amer., Champaign, IL.

Knapp, W.H., T.C. Turpin, and J.H. Beuter. 1984. Vegetation control for Douglas-fir regeneration on the Siuslaw National Forest: a decision analysis. J. Forestry 82:168-173.

Stavins, R.N., D.L. Galt, and K.L. Eckhouse. 1981. An economic analysis of alternative vegetation management practices in commercial forests of the Pacific Coast region. Coop. Ext. and Giannini Found. Agr. Econ., Univ. California, Berkeley, CA. Project Rep. 2. 66 p.

Stewart, R.E. and C. Row. 1981. Assessing the economic benefits of weed control in forest management, p. 26-53. *In* Holt, H.A. and B.C. Fischer (eds.) Weed control in forest management. John S. Wright Forestry Conf. Proc., Dept. Forestry and Natur. Resour., Purdue Univ., West Lafayette, IN. 305 p.

2,4,5-T Assessment Team. 1979. The biologic and economic assessment of 2,4,5-T. U.S. Dept. Agr., Washington, DC. Tech. Bull. 1671. 445 p. plus supplement.

Walstad, J.D., J.D. Brodie, B.C. McGinley, and C.A. Roberts. 1986. Silvicultural value of chemical brush control in the management of Douglas-fir. Western J. Appl. Forestry 1:69-73.

Health and Environmental Risk Evaluations of Forest Vegetation Management

Bovey, R.W. and J.D. Diaz-Colon. 1978. Selected bibliography of the phenoxy herbicides. IV. Ecological effects. MP-1360. Texas Agr. Exper. Sta., College Station, TX. 28 p.

Dost, F.N. 1978. Toxicology of phenoxy herbicides and hazard assessment of their use in reforestation. USDA Forest Service, California-Pacific Region. San Francisco, CA. 134 p.

Ghassemi, M., S.Quinlivan, and M. Dellarco. 1982. Environmental effects of new herbicides for vegetation control in forestry. Environment Internat. 7:389-401.

Kimmins, J.P. 1975. Review of the ecological effects of herbicide usage in forestry. Canadian Forestry Service, Victoria, British Columbia. Information Rep. BX-X-139. 44 p.

Loucks, D.M., S.R. Radosevich, T.B. Harrington, and R.G. Wagner. 1986. Prescribed burning in Pacific Northwest forests: an annotated bibliography. Forest Res. Lab., College of Forestry, Oregon State Univ., Corvallis, OR. CRAFTS Rep. 185 p.

Mobley, H.E. 1974. Fire—its impact on the environment. J. Forestry 72:414-417.

Newton, M. and F.N. Dost. 1984. Biological and physical effects of forest vegetation management. Washington State Dept. Natur. Resour., Olympia, WA. Final Report. 426 p.

Newton, M. and J.A. Norgren. 1977. Silvicultural chemicals and protection of water quality. Region X, U.S. Environmental Protection Agency, Seattle, WA. EPA Rep. 910/ 9-77-036. 224 p.

Norris, L.A. 1971. Chemical brush control: assessing the hazard. J. Forestry 69:715-720.

Norris, L.A. 1985. Implementing forest pest management practices in the USA: problems and solutions. Forestry Chron. 61:243-246.

Norris, L.A. 1986. Accuracy and precision of analyses for 2,4-D and picloram in streamwater by ten contract laboratories. Weed Sci. 34:485-489.

Richter, D.D., C.W.Ralston, and W.R. Harms. 1982. Prescribed fire: effects on water quality and forest nutrient cycling. Science 215:661-663.

Sandberg, D.V., J.M. Pierovich, D.G. Fox, and E.W. Ross. 1979. Effects of fire on air: a state-of-knowledge review. USDA Forest Service, Washington, DC. Gen. Tech. Rep. WO-9. 40 p.

Sassman, J., R. Pienta, M. Jacobs, and J. Cioffi. 1984. Pesticide background statements. Vol. 1. Herbicides. USDA Forest Service, Washington, DC. Agr. Hbk. 633. 48 p. plus Herbicide Background Statements.

U.S. Department of Agriculture and U.S. Environmental Protection Agency. 1978. Symposium on the use of herbicides in forestry. Office of the Secretary, U.S. Dept. Agr., Washington, DC. 213 p.

Walstad, J.D. and F.N. Dost. 1984. The health risks of herbicides in forestry: a review of the scientific record. College of Forestry, Oregon State Univ., Corvallis, OR. Forest Res. Lab. Spec. Pub. 10. 60 p.

Walstad, J.D. and F.N. Dost. 1986. All the king's horses and all the king's men: the lessons of 2,4,5-T. J. Forestry. 84(9):28-33.

II

CONIFER RESPONSE TO
VEGETATION MANAGEMENT

7

General Principles and Patterns of Conifer Growth and Yield

SHEPARD M. ZEDAKER
HAROLD E. BURKHART
ALBERT R. STAGE

INTRODUCTION

Understanding how vegetation management affects conifer production requires a basic knowledge of how forest productivity is expressed and predicted. Foresters evaluate productivity through the analysis of growth and yield. *Growth* is an increase in size with time and is accompanied by a corresponding increase in weight. *Yield* refers to the total amount of harvestable product available at a given time. Therefore, the growth accumulated over time is yield. In this chapter, we will discuss the general patterns of conifer tree and stand growth and review the basic principles of growth and yield projection.

INDIVIDUAL TREE GROWTH

The growth of individual trees is a summation of the division, elongation, and thickening of plant cells. Although the specific rates and activities involved in the growth process vary widely among different tree species, the general pattern of growth is remarkably consistent. When expressed as a cumulative function, the increase in size of a plant part or a whole plant takes on the characteristic "S" or sigmoid-shaped curve shown in Figure 7-1A. All tree dimensions (height, diameter, basal area, volume, and weight), when plotted over age, will exhibit various forms of this shape. This curve can be expressed as an equation in the generalized form of the *logistic growth curve*, commonly referred to as the *Chapman-Richards function* (Causton and Venus 1981):

$$W = \{n/k - [n/k - W_0^{(1-m)}]e^{-(1-m)kt}\}^{1/(1-m)}$$

where W = plant dimension
t = time or age
W_0 = dimension at $t = 0$
n = an anabolic constant
k = a catabolic constant
m = an allometric constant
e = base of natural logarithm

When plotted as a derivative (Figure 7-1B), the pattern of tree growth becomes more apparent. Young conifers grow relatively slow at first, increasing their growth rate to the point of inflection of the cumulative

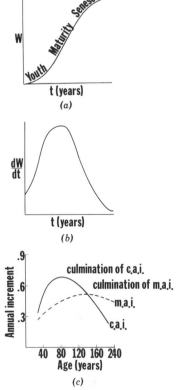

Figure 7-1. Generalized growth curves for conifers: (A) sigmoid shaped curve of increase in size or weight with time; (B) derivative of change in size over time showing the growth rate curve or current annual increment (CAI); (C) CAI, periodic annual increment (PAI), and mean annual increment (MAI) curves

growth curve. When trees are mature, the growth rate declines and approaches zero as they become senescent. Foresters call the point at which the growth is maximized, the peak of Figure 7-1B, the *culmination of current annual increment* (c.a.i.). Thus Figure 7-1B is a plot of current annual increment if the units of time used to determine the change in size are single years. The changes in tree dimension over time can also be expressed as *mean annual increment* (m.a.i.) (Figure 7-1C). Mean annual increment is found by dividing the cumulative size by the age. Mean annual increment culminates when it is equal to current annual increment.

The Chapman-Richards equation can also be used to determine other growth attributes that are important to foresters. The maximum size the tree can reach, the upper asymptote of Figure 7-1A, is

$$W_{max} = (n/k)^{1/(1-m)}$$

The maximum growth rate is

$$G_{max} = W_{max}km^{m/(1-m)}$$

The size at the maximum growth rate is

$$W_{Gmax} = W_{max}m^{1/(1-m)}$$

All tree dimensions can be affected by the growth of competing vegetation. Height and diameter, and subsequently volume, can be different from what might be expected if the trees had been growing alone in the open. Biologists often express this change as an increase or decrease in the relative growth rate of the individual. The absolute growth rate of a tree is not always a reliable indicator of its performance or vigor because growth changes with tree size and age. A better growth rate parameter is *relative growth rate* (RGR) (see Chapter 5):

$$RGR = (1/W)*(dW/dt).$$

Relative growth rate is a measure of the efficiency of production of a given unit of plant size (Harper 1977). The value of relative growth rate decreases as trees get older because the absolute growth approaches zero as the size approaches W_{max} (Figure 7-2). Because dW/dt is not directly observable, the average growth rate over a specified time is commonly used (Fisher 1921):

$$\frac{dW}{dt} \simeq \overline{G} = \frac{\log W_{t_2} - \log W_{t_1}}{t_2 - t_1}$$

where $\overline{G}$ = average growth rate
W_t = size or weight at time t
log = logarithm base 10

Height Growth

The height growth patterns of North American conifers are dependent on genetics and the environment in which they are grown. Species vary widely in height growth and maximum height (Figure 7-3). Western conifers with long life spans, like Douglas-fir and redwood, grow to heights exceeding 200 ft and maintain relatively rapid height growth for over 100 years. In contrast, loblolly pine, a southeastern species, rarely exceeds 140 ft in height and completes most of its height growth before the age

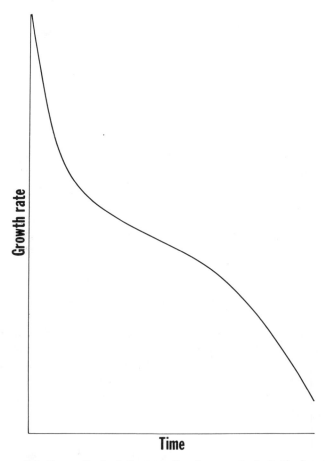

Figure 7-2. Generalized relative growth rate curve for individual conifers

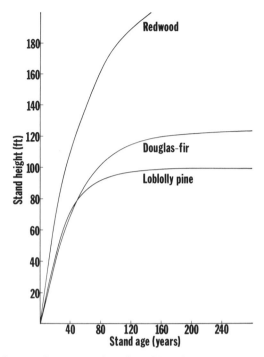

Figure 7-3. Height growth patterns for selected North American conifers. (*Data source:* Lindquist and Palley 1961, Brickell 1968, and U.S. Department of Agriculture 1976)

of 50. Regardless of this extreme variation, certain patterns seem consistent in conifer height growth.

Trees are often classified by their stage of development relative to height growth. These classes are *seedlings, saplings, poles, thrifty-mature,* and *mature* (Figure 7-4). Both planted and natural seedlings exhibit slow initial height growth. The first year after outplanting, most conifers experience a condition called *planting shock* that results from damage and stress caused during lifting, handling, and planting of the seedlings. This shock, combined with a reduced ability to absorb nutrients and water through a limited root system, restricts first-year height growth. Thus newly planted trees may have slow relative growth rates when compared to natural trees of the same age or size growing under similar conditions. Trees are considered seedlings until the period of slow initial height growth is completed. Intolerant pioneer conifers grow out of this stage rapidly in the absence of competition. Some tolerant species tend to prolong the seedling stage regardless of the level of competition, whereas others have the same growth pattern as intolerants in the absence of competition.

The sapling stage is characterized by an acceleration of height growth.

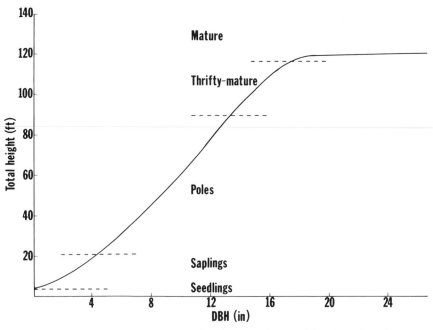

Figure 7-4. Height growth stages of forest trees. (*Source:* After Daniel et al. 1979)

As in the seedling stage, some tolerants tend to lag behind intolerants in this acceleration. Intense competition will also retard the acceleration of growth and in the case of intolerant species can lead to mortality. Conifers intermediate in tolerance often maintain height growth and may even increase height growth under moderate levels of competition (Zedaker 1981). However, this usually results in decreased diameter and root growth.

The pole stage is characterized by an almost linear increase in tree height. Growth rates from 2 to 5 ft/year are common during this stage. No consistent difference between tolerants and intolerants is evident. Dominant and codominant conifer height growth in the pole stage is generally not affected by competing vegetation.

In the thrifty-mature stage, conifers are still increasing their height, but height growth begins to decelerate. The relative height growth rate declines sharply. This period can span several decades, as is usually the case with long-lived tolerants or may be only a few years in short-lived intolerants.

The rate of height growth during the mature stage approaches that of the seedling stage. In some cases, tree height may actually decline due to top dieback or damage. In this stage, tree height approaches an asymptote thought to represent the upper limit of height possible for a given set of site conditions. Physiological controls of moisture transport, interacting with soil moisture availability and atmospheric demand, are thought to be the major determinants of the height asymptote.

The growth environment, dictated in part by the site conditions, influences not only the absolute height attainable but also the growth rate of conifers. In general, the better the growth environment, the faster a tree will reach a particular height on a given site. The availability of moisture, light, and nutrients, as influenced by competing vegetation, can have profound effects on height growth. The availability of moisture affects height growth through two different processes. Height growth is dependent on the size and number of cells produced by the apical meristem of the terminal shoot. When conifers are under moisture stress, their stomata close, reducing the uptake and fixation of carbon, thus reducing the amount of material available for the production of new cells and thickening of existing cell walls. The second and perhaps more profound effect of moisture stress is in reducing cell elongation. A positive turgor pressure is necessary for cell elongation. When trees are stressed, turgor pressure is reduced, and height growth declines.

Light and nutrients affect height growth mainly through their influence on the efficiency and amount of photosynthesis. Increasing light intensities increase the amount of photosynthate produced per unit of chlorophyll or leaf area per unit time. Increasing nutrient availability increases the chlorophyll content of individual leaves and increases the leaf area of individual trees of a given size. Both conditions lead to an increase in photosynthate produced and thus more material available for cell production and individual cell growth.

There are two basic patterns in the seasonal height growth of conifers. Some conifers, like eastern white pine, complete all of their height growth within the first few weeks of the growing season. Others such as loblolly pine complete much of their height growth in the first few weeks but may continue to grow through repeated flushes throughout the growing season if conditions are right. These patterns are called *fixed* and *free growth* and will be discussed in detail in the section on crown development.

Results from thinning and spacing studies have shown that, within fairly broad limits for many conifers, height growth is not greatly affected by manipulation of stand density (Clutter et al. 1983). The extent to which this generalization applies depends on the species and site conditions. Most species show decreased height growth at very low and at very high densities, with relatively little effect from variations in density over a fairly broad range of "moderate" densities. However, Lynch (1958) found that height increment of ponderosa pine is reduced by increasing stand density on land of extremely low site quality. A similar effect was observed for lodgepole pine by Alexander et al. (1967).

Diameter Growth

Diameter growth is a result of cell division and thickening in the cambium. In temperate forest conifers, a distinct ring of wood cells is grown around the entire tree each year. The thickness of this ring is determined by genetics, tree age, the position along the bole, and the growth environment. As is the case with height, different coniferous species have widely varying diameter growth rates.

In conifers, diameter growth begins just after bud break and progresses downward from the top to the bottom of the bole. Diameter growth is determined by the number and diameter of individual cells produced. The largest cells are produced in the spring and early summer and make up the *early wood*. Cells produced later in the season are thick walled, generally smaller in diameter, and constitute the *late wood* of the annual ring. Individual cell diameter is inversely proportional to moisture stress and directly proportional to nutrient and light availability. Unlike height, diameter growth is more evenly distributed throughout the growing season in all conifers.

Although the general pattern of diameter growth follows the sigmoid shape, diameter increment decreases rapidly with age. Even though the same amount or more total wood may be produced each year during the pole stage, it is distributed over an ever-increasing surface area. For convenience, *DBH* or diameter growth at breast height (4.5 ft) is of major interest for growth and yield projection. However, the longitudinal distribution of diameter increment varies considerably and has a dramatic effect on stem taper. The distribution of diameter increment follows *Pressler's* (1864) *hypothesis*: the cross-sectional area of a tree ring is proportional to the quantity of foliage above it. Thus diameter increment is maximized at a point in the lower crown and decreases downward because the same cross-sectional area must be spread over a larger initial diameter. In addition, vertical distribution of diameter increment also responds to mechanical stress. As a consequence, tree boles closely approximate beams of uniform stress.

Competition from other trees affects the size and vigor of conifer crowns and thus influences longitudinal diameter distribution (Figure 7-5). For the average forest-grown conifer that is not overcrowded, the annual sheath is small at the top and increases to a point that coincides with the most productive part of the crown. The sheath area remains fairly constant below the crown to a point just above the ground where it increases slightly. In an open-grown tree, the pattern in the crown is the same, whereas below the crown the sheath area continues to increase rather than remain constant. In a suppressed tree with a marginally productive crown, the pattern in the bole along the crown is the same, whereas below the crown the sheath area decreases. In some extremely

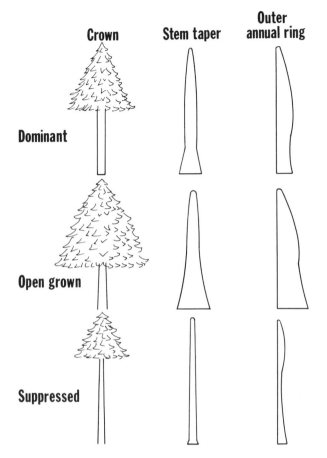

Figure 7-5. Tree taper forms for forest-grown, open-grown, and suppressed conifers. (*Source:* After Wilson 1970)

suppressed trees, there may be no growth at all along the middle portion of the bole (Wilson 1970).

Spacing and thinning experiments have consistently shown increases in DBH growth with decreasing stand density (Clutter et al. 1983). Although part of this increase may be because of a redistribution of growth in response to mechanical stress, the majority is a result of increases in the resources available for individual tree growth. Intertree competition affects diameter growth at very low stand densities, particularly in the case of intolerant species. Consequently, for maximum diameter growth, stand densities must be kept very low, both in terms of the species of interest and in terms of the competing vegetation.

Crown Development

The shape, size, and development of conifer crowns are important determinants of height and diameter growth. The crown provides the photosynthate necessary for cell growth. Conifer crowns develop a conical form
with the strong apical dominance of a single leader. This type of crown
form is called *excurrent* and is different from the *deliquescent* crown form
that most hardwoods exhibit. As conifers approach the mature stage, their
excurrent crown form breaks down. Terminals become stunted, and adjacent laterals turn upward. Although the reasons are not clear, conifers
that lose their excurrent form, whether mature or not, are less vigorous
and more susceptible to attack from insect and disease. Conifers growing
under extreme moisture stress develop small shrub-like crowns that are
the result of early loss of apical control (Brown 1977). In contrast, conifers
stressed by low light intensities typically increase apical control to the
point of producing columnar crowns. Nutrient stress has no consistent
effect on crown form but greatly reduces the density and distribution of
leaves in the crown. Increased nutrient availability aids in the retention
and continued function of needles 2 or more years old. Tolerants, by
definition, tend to maintain their crown form and needle density under
stress better than intolerants.

Two distinct patterns of crown development in conifers have been identified. These are *fixed growth* in which preformed primordia overwinter
in the bud and elongate the following spring, and *free growth* in which
primordia elongate the same growing season that they are formed. Most
conifers exhibit only free growth as first- and sometimes second-year
seedlings. Some species, most of which are southern yellow pines, carry
out both fixed and free growth during their entire life span. They set an
overwintering bud that breaks dormancy in the early spring but will set
buds and flush as many as six times during the summer. For other conifers, like Douglas-fir, true firs, red pine, white pines, ponderosa pine,
and lodgepole pine, fixed growth is the norm. Species exhibiting fixed
growth will, under highly favorable conditions, produce a second flush.
However, this second flush is considered *lammas growth*, rather than free
growth, because it will normally result in reduced shoot growth from the
overwintering bud the following year (Lanner 1976).

These differences in crown development have important ramifications
in the response of conifers to competition, particularly where moisture
stress is the most limiting factor for growth. The annual shoot growth of
conifers exhibiting fixed growth is closely related to the competition and
growth environment of the previous year. The number of cells and the
amount of carbohydrate allocated to cell expansion were determined during the previous growing season. The moisture necessary for cell elongation is readily available in the early spring due to the recharge of soil
moisture during the winter. For fixed-and-free-growth conifers, a large

proportion of the annual shoot growth often comes from the free-growth portion. Therefore, crown development in these species is most influenced by the competition and growth environment during the concurrent growing season. Fixed-and-free-growth conifers may be more responsive, in terms of relative height growth, than fixed-only species to control of competition under conditions of late summer moisture stress. Such differences may have led to significant adaptive advantages for these patterns of crown development. Fixed-growth conifers predominate in regions with hot, dry, summer climates, whereas fixed-and-free-growth conifers are most common in humid, wet, summer climates.

As trees mature and the crowns begin to touch in a forest canopy, the point of *stand closure* is reached. The crown development of individual trees after stand closure is altered by competition from adjacent trees and controlled by the tolerance of the species. Lower branches receive less and less light as stand height and shade increase. Light levels fall below the compensation point at which carbohydrate can be assimilated. These branches then become sinks rather than sources of carbohydrates and are shed by the tree, causing the crown to recede up the tree bole. Tolerant species have lower light compensation points than do intolerants and are able to retain lower branches longer. The ratio of the length of the live crown to the total tree height, called *live crown ratio*, is an indicator of tree vigor. Conifers are most vigorous when live crown ratios exceed 30%.

Competition in the stand canopy causes a differentiation of individual trees into crown classes. The most vigorous individuals occupy superior positions in the canopy, whereas less vigorous trees succumb to competition and begin to drop out of the main canopy. Trees are classified as (1) *dominants*—trees with crowns extending well above the general level of the canopy, receiving full sunlight from above and partly from the sides; (2) *codominants*—trees with crowns forming the general canopy level, receiving light only from above; (3) *intermediates*—trees with crowns extending into the main dominant canopy but receiving little direct sunlight; and (4) *suppressed*—trees with crowns entirely below the main canopy, receiving no direct sunlight (Smith 1962). The live crown ratio of conifers is greatest for dominants and least for suppressed individuals.

Height-Diameter Relationships

Separately, height and diameter growth are important in assessing the productivity of forest stands. However, because the end product of value is the volume, weight, or quality of fiber produced, height and diameter must be considered together. Knowledge of the relationship between tree height and diameter is necessary for the construction of taper tables and local, or single-entry, volume tables. Height-diameter curves can be de-

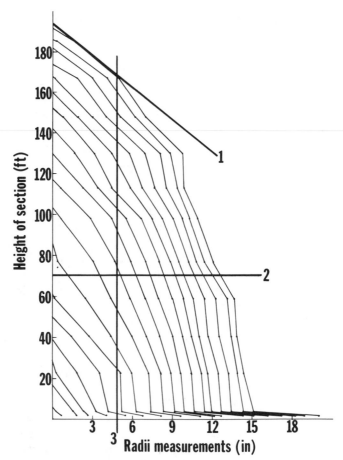

Figure 7-6. Stem analysis curves showing (1) oblique, (2) horizontal, and (3) vertical sequences. (*Source:* After Duff and Nolan 1953)

veloped in two different ways. Detailed stem analysis can be performed on individual trees, or samples of trees in a stand can be measured for their diameters and corresponding heights.

Stem analysis is a method of obtaining detailed information about the accumulated height, diameter, and volume of individual trees. Trees are felled, cut into sections along the bole, and the inside-the-bark diameter of the rings and the number of rings are measured. A plot of the height and diameter of the stem for all the years it grew can be constructed (Figure 7-6). From these data, an analysis of three different growth patterns is possible: (1) an oblique sequence where the widths of rings within each annual sheath of wood are compared at each internode; (2) a sequence where ring widths are a function of ring number from the pith; and (3) a vertical sequence where ring widths at a fixed number of rings away from the pith are compared from each internode (Duff and Nolan 1953). These patterns can be used to separate systematic (genetic) from random (environmental) effects on tree growth and have been used to study the competitive relationships between individual trees.

Because height and diameter are both correlated with age, it is not surprising that they are related to each other. Like the height-age, and diameter-age relationships, the height-diameter relationship is generally sigmoid in shape. However, when the lower end of the relationship is ignored, the curve takes the shape illustrated in Figure 7-7. A model that has been used extensively to describe the height-diameter relationship in pure, even-aged stands is (Avery and Burkhart 1983)

$$\log H = b_0 + b_1 D^{-1}$$

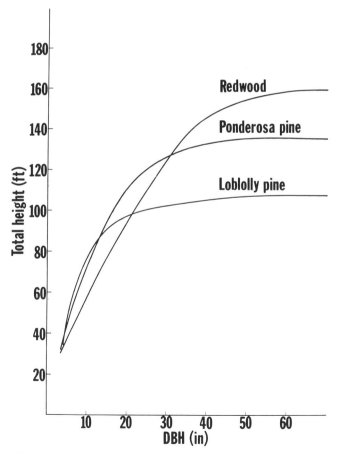

Figure 7-7. Height-diameter curves for selected North American conifers. (*Data source:* Meyer 1938, Hasel 1950, and U.S. Department of Agriculture 1976)

where H = height
         D = diameter at breast height
b_0, b_1 = constants

Age, site index, and stand density influence the height-diameter relationship of stands. Burkhart and Strub (1974) found the level of the curve, or intercept (b_0), to be closely related to site quality, whereas the slope (b_1) was dependent on age and number of trees per unit area in loblolly pine plantations.

Tree Volume and Taper Relationships

Stem taper is the rate of change of diameter with increasing height in the tree. Conifer taper varies by species, size, age, and growth environment of the trees. Because taper changes with height, even within the same tree, boles do not fit a single form of a geometric solid perfectly (Husch et al. 1982).

Excurrent tree stems are best described as a composite solid consisting of a frustum of a neiloid at the base, a frustum of a parabaloid in the center, and a cone or parabaloid at the top (Figure 7-8). Adjustments to this idealized shape are categorized as form factors, form quotients, taper tables, and taper equations.

A *form factor* is the ratio of the actual bole volume to that of an idealized geometric solid. The utility of form factors is limited because upper stem diameters must be known. *Form quotients* are easier to apply and are simply the ratio of some upper stem diameter to the diameter at breast height. The *Girard Form Class* is the most commonly used form quotient for conifer volume estimation and is determined by dividing the diameter inside the bark at 17.3 ft aboveground by the diameter outside the bark at breast height and expressing the ratio as a percentage.

Taper tables can be constructed by computing the average taper rate for specified upper stem lengths. The most common method used is to average upper-log taper rates for standard 16-ft logs and arrange them according to diameter at breast height and merchantable height in logs.

Many different functions have been used in attempts to describe upper stem diameters using *taper equations*. No single equation is in common use, but most are in the form of polynomials in which

$$d = f(D,h,H)$$

where d = stem diameter at some height, h, above the ground
      D = diameter at breast height
      H = stem total height

Although tree volumes can be computed from taper relationships, di-

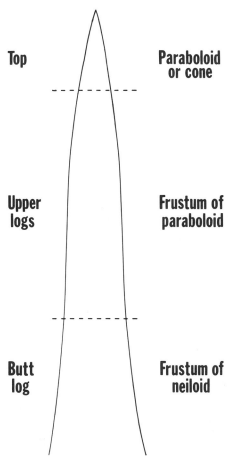

Top

Paraboloid or cone

Upper logs

Frustum of paraboloid

Butt log

Frustum of neiloid

Figure 7-8. Geometric shapes assumed by different portions of conifer boles. (*Source:* After Husch et al. 1982)

rect prediction of tree bole volume is commonly practiced. The most widely used tree volume equation is the so-called *combined variable function*:

$$V = b_0 + b_1 D^2 H$$

where
V = tree volume (or weight)
D = diameter at breast height
H = tree height (total or merchantable)
b_0, b_1 = regression coefficients

The combined variable equation usually accounts for 97% or more of the observed variation in tree volume, and there has been little success at incorporating additional tree or stand variables into the prediction equation (Burkhart 1977, Lohrey 1983).

SITE QUALITY ASSESSMENT

The concept of forest site refers to a specific area of land and its associated environment for growing trees. *Site quality* is a measure of the productive capacity of that environment. Because the primary objective of conifer management for timber production is to economically grow the greatest amount of usable wood possible in a given time, knowledge of the potential productivity of forest sites is essential. A direct method of determining site quality is to grow a fully stocked stand of the desired species on the site for a designated period. The actual productivity would then be the amount of volume or weight of wood or fiber produced per year over the rotation. Unfortunately, productivity data like these do not exist for most forest sites, and actual yield can be affected by such nonsite factors as genetic composition, stand density, competing vegetation, pests, diseases, and the climate experienced during the period over which growth was measured. Consequently, indirect methods of evaluating site quality are most common and can be classified as causal factor or bioassay techniques. *Causal factor techniques* rely on the identification of physical factors of the site that are correlated with site quality. A *bioassay*, or *phytometer technique* in the case of plants, is the use of a living organism to measure the quantity or quality of physical or chemical factors that are difficult to measure directly. The two primary bioassay techniques used for site quality estimation are the indicator plant approach and the calculation of site index. Readers are referred to Carmean (1975) for a review of forest site quality evaluation in the United States.

Physical Factors Approach

Available moisture, light, nutrients, and temperature are the primary environmental factors affecting growth of trees. However, measurement of the quality and quantity of these factors available for tree growth on a site over an entire rotation is not possible. Instead, foresters have used secondary factors such as local climate, topography, and soil attributes that influence the primary factors and are much easier to measure.

There are many ways that climate can influence conifer growth, but the most obvious are through precipitation and temperature. Precipitation determines the total amount of water potentially available for growth, whereas temperature influences water loss through evapotranspiration and the rates of photosynthesis, metabolism, and respiration. Good relationships between rainfall and conifer growth have been established for many areas, particularly those regions subject to periodic droughts. For example, McClurkin (1953) found that site quality for longleaf pine in the South was highly correlated with the amount of rainfall received between January and June.

Because the net amount of water available is more important than the gross amount received on a site, the effects of precipitation and temperature are often confounded. The water balance, precipitation minus evapotranspiration, is well correlated with the site quality for western conifers. However, changes in elevation further complicate the relationship. In the West, precipitation normally increases with increasing elevation while temperature decreases. Although the net water balance may improve, growth may be limited by low temperatures (Spurr and Barnes 1980).

Topography affects site quality through its influence on temperatures and soil development. Aspect can be equally as important as elevation in determining a site's water balance. South- and west-facing slopes are generally warmer and thus have higher water deficits than north- and east-facing slopes. The result can be lower site quality on southwest slopes, irrespective of other conditions, in areas of periodic drought. However, southwest slopes may also have longer growing seasons at high elevations, resulting in better productivity. Thus the optimum aspect depends on the interaction of moisture and heat deficits in relation to the adaptations of different species.

Increasing steepness of slopes tends to accentuate the effects of aspect but may also have an independent effect acting through soil depth and soil moisture recharge. Slope percentage and slope position are highly correlated with soil development and thus influence moisture stress and nutrient availability. Steep slopes erode quickly, preventing the development of deep soils. Soils on shoulders and backslopes are more shallow than foot slope and terrace soils.

Soil characteristics have been used to determine site quality. Total soil depth, depth of various horizons, texture, drainage, nutrient content, cation exchange capacity, and pH are the major soil features that have been related to site productivity (Carmean 1975). Depth, texture, and drainage dictate moisture availability and rooting depth. Greater soil depths improve total water holding capacity of the soil profile and the root development potential. Soils that are excessively coarse will not hold sufficient water for tree growth after the gravitational water has drained. Fine soils may hold large amounts of water throughout the growing season but at potentials too low for tree roots to extract. Nutrient content, cation exchange capacity, and pH affect the availability of essential nutrients for tree growth.

The most successful attempts to use physical site factors to predict site quality have been those that combine a number of factors in equations predicting volume or height growth. For example, Shoulders and Walker (1979), were able to explain 82% of the variation in loblolly pine height growth and 94% of longleaf pine growth on dry sites using rainfall, slope, and soil texture variables. Mader (1976) explained 80% of the variation in total board foot volume yield and 88% of the variation in the height growth of eastern white pine using age, slope percentage, drainage class, and physical and chemical properties of the A and B horizons.

Indicator Plant Approach

The presence, abundance, and size of understory plants can serve as useful indicators, or phytometers, of forest site quality (Carmean 1975). Many shrubs and herbs have a relatively narrow ecological tolerance and thus may serve as better indicators of growing conditions than the existing trees on a site. Understory plants are more apt to be affected by overstory density and composition, site history, and localized disturbance than overstory trees, but they also recover from disturbance much more quickly. Thus understory plants have been used successfully to predict productivity, particularly in northern coniferous forests.

In boreal and subalpine forests, where the dominant conifers are spruce and fir, overstory density is usually low, and the tree species are widely distributed over many different site types. Species diversity in the understory is low, and understory communities are distinct. Human-caused disturbance is relatively rare, and there is little history of fertility changes due to agricultural use. In contrast, southern and coastal forests are more diverse and have been subject to frequent disturbance. For these reasons, the use of plant indicators for site quality evaluation has focused on high-latitude coniferous forests and forests of the Inland Pacific Northwest (Spurr and Barnes 1980).

Species complexes, rather than single species, have been most useful in evaluating site quality. *Habitat type classification*, a habitat type representing a complex of overstory and understory species dominant during climax, seems most promising of the indicator plant approaches. Differences in the height growth of ponderosa pine can be clearly detected when sites are delineated by their habitat type (Daubenmire 1961). Hodgkins (1960) was somewhat successful at developing an indicator plant assessment technique for longleaf pine. Working in Alabama, Hodgkins calculated the average actual site quality for stands in which longleaf pine and individual associate species occurred. The site quality of unknown sites was then calculated by determining the presence and dominance of the indicator species on sample plots.

Site Index Approach

Site index is defined as the average total height of the dominant and codominant trees on a site at a particular base age. It is the most common indirect bioassay, or phytometer, technique used to determine potential

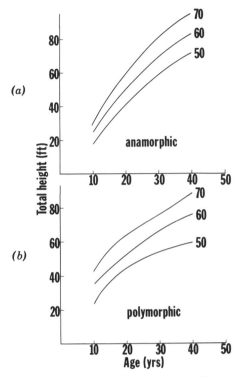

Figure 7-9. (a) Idealized anamorphic and (b) polymorphic site index curves for conifers, base age 25. (*Source:* After Clutter et al. 1983)

productivity of forest sites. A base age of 25 years is most commonly used for southern pines, whereas 50 or 100 years is used for northern and western conifers. Age at breast height, or total tree age, is used for natural stands, and age from planting is used for plantations. Total height is used because it is known to be highly correlated with site quality and volume production, whereas being relatively insensitive to stand density and species composition. In addition to the density and species composition relationships to height, other assumptions are implied in the use of site index. The site index of a stand must not change during a stand's life, and the height of dominant and codominant trees must not have been influenced by disease, insects, storm damage, or competition (Jones 1969).

To use site index, height-over-age curves are constructed for a range of site qualities. The most common type of site index curves in use are *anamorphic*, meaning that all curves have the same shape (Figure 7-9a). Frequently, a linear equation of the form

$$\log H_d = b_0 + b_1 A^{-1}$$

where H_d = height of dominants and codominants
        A = age
     b_0, b_1 = regression constants

is used to construct a guide curve from which all other site index curves are derived. Age and height data are required from an unbiased sample of site qualities. Because, by definition, site index is equal to the height at the base age, site index curves are generated by substitution and rearranging the equation such that

$$\log S = \log H_d - b_1 (A^{-1} - A_i^{-1})$$

where S = site index
      A_i = base age

Anamorphic site index curves work well for some conifers but have several drawbacks that preclude them from universal acceptance. The technique is sound only if the average site quality is the same for all age classes sampled for curve construction. Unfortunately, younger age classes are often associated with better sites, whereas older trees exist only on poor sites left to harvest last. In addition, height growth patterns cannot always be assumed to be similar on all sites. Differences in the quality of deeper soil horizons, soils with restricted layers, and various topographic features often cause differences in the height growth pattern between poor and good sites. The reduction in height growth rate tends to be greater during the thrifty-mature stage, and the pole stage is generally shorter in duration on poor sites. For these reasons, the use of polymorpic site index curves is increasing. *Polymorphic* site index curves can exhibit a different shape for each site quality (Figure 7-9b). Whereas temporary plot data are often used for the construction of anamorphic curves, the height-age pairs needed for polymorphic curves can only be obtained by repeated measurement of permanent plots or through detailed stem analysis.

Combined Approach

Even when all the assumptions of the site index approach are satisfied, height growth patterns may not account for effects of all the factors controlling site productivity. Within a given site index, the actual productivity, or the total carrying capacity, of forest stands may vary considerably. This variation seems most apparent on very dry sites or in regions where growth is limited by a lack of heat. Species that have a wide ecological amplitude such as Douglas-fir in the Inland Northwest can have low site indexes induced by short, cool growing seasons at high elevations and by droughty conditions at low elevations. However, for the same site index, high-elevation stands can carry more basal area, or more total volume, than low-elevation stands at the same age. This concept has been recognized elsewhere and represented by *yield classes* within site index class (Hamilton and Christie 1973). Combining an indicator plant approach with site index has provided an additional way to classify sites on the basis of productivity (Daubenmire and Daubenmire 1968, MacLean and Bolsinger 1973, Pfister et al. 1977, Hall 1983).

STAND GROWTH AND DEVELOPMENT

Although conifer forests are made up of individual trees, it is the growth of stands that is of primary interest to foresters. A *stand* is defined as a contiguous group of trees sufficiently uniform in species composition, arrangement of age classes, and condition to be a homogeneous and distinguishable unit (Smith 1962). Stands are populations of trees that, as individuals, change in size, die, or are cut. The sum of the changes in individual trees makes up stand growth. The basic components of stand growth are ingrowth, accretion, mortality, and cut and are applied to a specified period between measurements of the stand. *Ingrowth* is the number, basal area, or volume of trees growing into a measurable (or merchantable) size. *Accretion* is the growth occurring on all trees that were measured at the beginning of the growth period. The number or volume of trees that die during the period is *mortality* and the trees or volume removed during a harvest is the *cut*.

As with individual trees, the growth and development of stands are dependent on the site conditions. Growth is also dependent on the stand structure and stocking or density. *Stand structure* is the size, age, and species composition of the stand. *Stand density* refers to the number of trees or basal area of trees on a unit area. It is a measure of crowding that can be expressed as an absolute number or in relative terms. *Stocking* is most often regarded as the relative density of a stand based on a specified density for some particular management objective. For example, a loblolly pine stand at age 20 with a density of 550 trees/acre may be considered fully stocked for pulpwood but overstocked if the stand is being managed for sawlogs. More recently, stocking in young conifer plantations has also been defined as the percentage of the stand area occupied by trees at the specified density (Cleary et al. 1978).

Stand Structure

The population of trees in a stand can consist of many different species, different ages, and a wide range of tree sizes. The species composition of conifer stands is usually broken down into two classes: pure and mixed species stands. A *pure stand* is one that contains a large proportion of one species, and the management is directed at maintaining that single species. Pure stands are most common for the management of Douglas-fir in the Pacific Northwest, red, white, and jack pines in the Lake states, and yellow pines in the Southeast (Barrett 1980). Mixed species stands are prevalent in the Inland Northwest and spruce-fir in the Northern Boreal Forest.

It would be ideal, from the standpoint of inventory and harvesting ease, if all trees in a stand were exactly the same size. Unfortunately, they are not and determining the distribution of tree sizes in a stand is a major problem in growth and yield estimation. Tree-size distribution is most often described in terms of the number of trees in each DBH class for the range of diameters in the stand. *Diameter distributions*, as they are called, can take on many different forms, but two general shapes are common and are related to the range of tree ages in stands. Even-aged stands, those in which all trees are the same age or age class, have a characteristic unimodal, bell-shaped distribution that may be skewed toward the high or low diameter classes (Figure 7-10A). The limits of the age class may be 1 year, as is generally the case with plantations, or several years, which is common for natural stands. Tree diameters in even-aged stands are clustered around the average, with decreasing num-

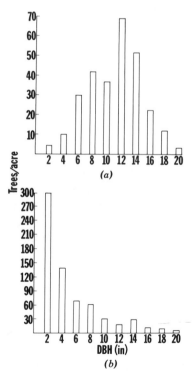

Figure 7-10. Idealized diameter distributions for (A) even-aged and (B) uneven-aged conifer stand. (*Source:* After Clutter et al. 1983)

bers of very large or small trees. Although even-aged stands of intolerants are more common, tolerants can also form even-aged stands.

Diameter distributions of uneven-aged stands depend on frequency of harvests and the abundance of regeneration. In frequently harvested selection-cut forests, stands often exhibit an inverse J-shaped diameter distribution with large numbers of small trees and decreasing numbers of trees in larger diameter classes (Figure 7-10B). The wide range of tree sizes is a result of generally continuous reproduction. In the case of tolerant conifers, large numbers of seedlings may germinate every few years, and their numbers diminish rapidly as competition increases mortality. Intolerants can form uneven-aged stands, but reproduction is more sporadic and dependent on large-scale disturbance to create openings in the stand. Thus uneven-aged stands of intolerant conifers may actually consist of small groups of even-aged trees. Diameter distributions for such stands may be multimodal or highly irregular.

Stand Density/Stocking Relationships

Density and stocking are important determinants of productivity in forest stands and are the major factors that foresters can easily manipulate. Stand density, measured in terms of number of trees or basal area per unit area, changes with age and is dependent on species tolerance. In even-aged stands, the number of trees per unit area decreases as the stand ages because of the mortality of individual stems. The basal area, however, increases as the stand gets older and may approach an asymptote. In general, basal area development in stands of intolerant conifers is rapid, and the asymptote is reached at relatively young ages. Tolerant conifers can carry much higher stand basal areas, and basal area growth continues even at advanced ages (Figure 7-11). If regeneration is blocked, the same pattern of basal area and number of stems per unit area (density) would be evident in uneven-aged stands. When regeneration continues and uneven-aged stands are manipulated such that the periodic cut plus mortality is equal to the accretion plus ingrowth, both number of stems and basal area remain fairly constant. In the ideal case, such stands are considered "perfectly balanced."

Site quality also influences stand-density relationships. Within an individual species, the basal area on good sites typically exceeds that on poor sites at the same age. The difference in good and poor sites can be quite large. For example, ponderosa pine growing on poor sites has less than 50% of the basal area commonly encountered on the best sites for stands of the same age. Although increasing species tolerance seems to decrease the differences in stand density on poor and good sites for some conifers, there are enough exceptions to preclude a definite tolerance relationship (Daniel et al. 1979). For example, intolerant jack pine and

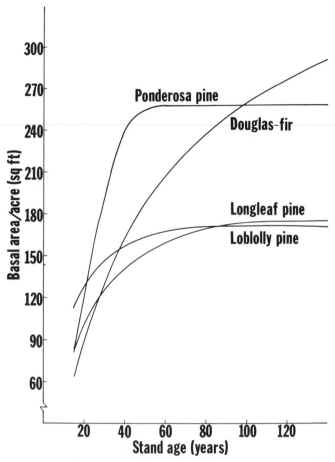

Figure 7-11. Basal area growth for pure stands of selected North American conifers. (*Data source:* Meyer 1938, McArdle et al. 1949, and U.S. Department of Agriculture 1976)

tolerant western hemlock both maintain over 85% of the basal area they typically carry on good sites when growing on poor sites.

Stand density affects mean tree diameter in a consistent pattern. Reineke (1933) found that in pure, even-aged, fully stocked conifer stands the number of trees per unit area was similar for a given mean stand tree diameter. The number of trees for a given diameter varied considerably between species but was generally consistent within a species regardless of age or site quality (Figure 7-12). Trees growing on better sites simply reached the same average diameter and corresponding density at an earlier age than trees growing on poor sites. Consistent with the relationship between basal area and tolerance, tolerant conifers gen-

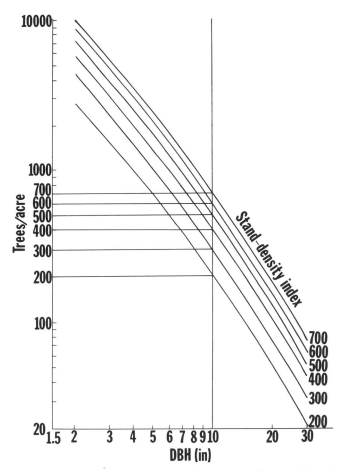

Figure 7-12. Stand density index chart for ponderosa pine. (*Source:* After Reineke 1933 and Meyer 1938)

erally carry higher densities for a given average stand diameter than intolerants. Reineke used this concept to develop a *stand density index* to determine stocking. He defined the maximum stocking curve or reference curve as

$$\log N = -1.605 \log D + k$$

where N = number of trees/acre
$\quad\quad D$ = diameter (in.) of tree of average basal area
$\quad\quad k$ = a constant varying with species

The stand density index or reference stocking level was then defined as the number of trees/acre when D equals 10 in. and is determined by

$$\log SDI = \log N + 1.605 \log D - 1.605$$

where SDI = stand density index

This relationship of plant size or weight to density has been recognized in many species and is known as the *law of self-thinning* (Yoda et al. 1963). As a linear equation, the self-thinning law is expressed as

$$\ln W = \ln C - a(\ln p)$$

where W = mean tree weight or volume
$\quad\;\; C$ = a constant for a species
$\quad\;\; p$ = density in trees per unit area
$\quad \ln$ = natural logarithm
$\quad\;\; a$ = slope constant

When weight or volume versus density data are regressed against one another for many different species, the intercept, $\ln C$, varies, but the slope constant, a, is usually close to $-3/2$. The density-mean tree size relationship has also been used to determine management strategies and thinning schedules for Monterey pine and Douglas-fir (Drew and Flewelling 1977, 1979).

Stand growth and yield are highly dependent on stand density. The relationship between stand growth and density was described by Langsaeter in 1941 (Smith 1962). He determined that volume growth increased as density increased to a point where a relatively broad plateau was reached and then growth declined at extreme densities (Figure 7-13). Although the actual values for the curve differ by site, species, and age, the form of the curve is consistent for a particular site and age. Density can be expressed as number of trees, basal area, or volume per unit area, and growth is usually expressed in terms of basal area or volume per unit area per unit time. These plots are commonly referred to as *growth-over-growing stock curves*. Although Langsaeter used five, four distinct zones in the growth-over-growing stock are generally recognized (Daniel et al. 1979). In the isolated zone, trees are growing independent of each other such that growth increases directly as growing stock increases. The wide-spaced zone is characterized by the beginning of competition between trees. Annual growth continues to increase but at a decreasing rate. In the well-spaced zone, large changes in growing stock density have little effect on growth. Tolerants tend to have broader and flatter plateaus in the growth-over-growing stock curves. In stands that are crowded, individual trees tend to be smaller, and the stands may carry less merchantable volume per unit area. Stands in the crowded zone are considered

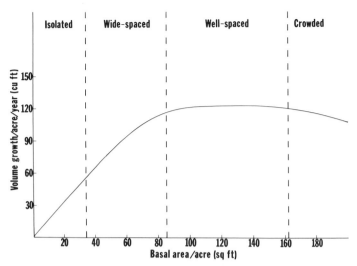

Figure 7-13. Idealized growth-over-growing stock curve showing relative density regions. (*Source:* After Langsaeter 1941, data from U.S. Department of Agriculture 1976)

overstocked and are more susceptible to decline caused by insects and disease. Although they are relatively rare in nature, such stands are considered stagnated and occur most frequently in fire-adapted, intolerant conifers regenerated naturally on poor sites.

Conifer stands that receive some density control treatment often exhibit accelerated growth. This accelerated growth is a response to the release of site resources that were previously controlled by the vegetation removed (Newton 1973). The density can be reduced by removing conifers, as is the case with thinning, or by removing noncommercial species through release. Accelerated stand height growth occurs in intolerants in the seedling and sapling stage but diminishes rapidly with age. Tolerants, by definition, have a much better ability to respond to release even at an advanced age. Accelerated height growth is generally less conspicuous than mean tree basal area or diameter growth. The acceleration in mean tree basal area growth may not be immediate. Trees respond to the release of site resources first by building their crowns and increasing their diameters just above the ground in response to increased mechanical stress. Increased diameter growth, at breast height, may not be evident for several years after density is reduced. Older trees, especially those that have been suppressed for some time, may even display slower growth rates. This deceleration, called *thinning shock* or *release shock*, is generally thought to be caused by the failure of the shade-grown foliage to adapt fast enough to increased light intensities and atmospheric moisture demands. Stand basal area growth may not change dramatically after thinning as long as the original and residual growing stock levels remain on the plateau of the Langsaeter curve for that species. The rate and duration of accelerated growth are dependent on the amount of growing stock reduction from the optimum growth-over-growing stock ratio.

GROWTH AND YIELD PREDICTION

Decisions on vegetation management strategies for conifer production are predicated on knowledge of stand growth and yield. Efficient methods of predicting growth and yield are essential because conifer forests are not static, vegetation treatments are costly, and detailed data collection of treatment effects over an entire rotation may be impossible. Conifer stand dynamics can be predicted through direct or indirect methods (Avery and Burkhart 1983).

Approaches to Growth and Yield Prediction

The most common direct method is *stand-table projection*. To use this method, a present stand table showing the number of trees in each diameter class must be obtained. Future growth is predicted from past growth obtained from increment cores, and a future stand table is developed from the predicted accretion, ingrowth, and expected mortality. Although useful for many different purposes, stand-table projection is not suitable for predicting growth and yield response from vegetation management. Inferences from past growth are limited to the conditions under which that growth occurred; conditions can change dramatically as a result of vegetation control. Indirect methods are more suitable and are made through the use of yield tables, equations, and computer simulations.

   The indirect approaches to growth and yield prediction can be divided into three classes of models that differ in their level of resolution. These are, in order of increasing detail, whole stand models, size-class distribution models, and individual-tree models.

   Whole-stand models consist of yield tables and functions that do not directly account for variation of individual tree size within stands. A *yield table* is a tabular presentation of the volume per unit area by age, site index, and other stand characteristics for even-aged stands. Volume is assumed to be dependent on whole stand attributes such as age, site index, species, and density. Three types of yield tables are identified by the assumed stand characteristics. *Normal yield tables* (Table 7-1) are developed by deliberately locating plots for their construction in fully stocked or "normal" density portions of stands. Thus normal yield tables represent the optimal relationship between volume, age, and site but one that rarely exists in nature. Consequently, *empirical* or *"average stand" yield tables* have been developed. Because empirical yield tables have

TABLE 7-1. Normal Yield Table for Douglas-Fir in the Pacific Northwest, Board Feet per Acre, Scribner Rule[a]

Age (years)	Site Index, Ft (Base Age 100)				
	80	110	140	170	200
30	0	0	300	2,600	8,000
40	0	200	4,500	11,900	24,400
50	30	3,300	12,400	27,400	44,100
60	1,100	8,100	23,800	42,800	62,000
70	2,400	14,000	35,200	57,200	78,200
80	4,400	20,100	45,700	70,000	92,500
90	6,900	26,000	55,000	81,000	104,800
100	9,600	31,400	62,800	90,400	115,100
110	12,200	36,300	69,400	98,300	123,700
120	14,700	40,700	75,000	105,100	131,100
130	17,000	44,700	80,000	111,000	137,700
140	19,200	48,300	84,500	116,300	143,500
150	21,300	51,600	88,600	121,200	148,700
160	23,300	54,600	92,400	125,700	153,500

Source: From McArdle et al. 1961.
[a]Volume of all trees 11.6-in. DBH and larger. Assumed stump height is 2 ft, minimum top diameter is 8 in., trimming allowances is 0.3 ft for each 26-ft log.

been developed for stands representing average stocking, it is believed that these tables more closely approximate typical yields. *Variable-density yield tables* and functions are a further refinement and include a density measure as a predictor variable. This eliminates the need to correct volume estimates from normal or empirical yield tables for nonnormal or nonaverage stocking.

Variable-density growth and yield equations employ multiple regression techniques to derive equations that best express the relationship between the dependent variable (yield) and the independent variables of stand and site attributes. An example of a variable-density yield equation for conifers is Clutter's (1963) prediction model for loblolly pine

$$\ln Y = b_0 + b_1 A^{-1} + b_2 S + b_3 \ln B$$

where Y = yield (cubic volume per unit area)
A = stand age
S = site index
B = basal area
b_i = regression constants (i = 0, 1, 2, 3)

Growth and yield equations are termed *compatible* if the growth equation can be derived from the yield equation and vice versa. As previously defined, growth and yield are related biologically but can also be related mathematically by

$$Y = \int_0^A G \, du$$

where Y = yield
A = stand age
G = instantaneous growth
u = unit of time

Thus the preceding yield equation, developed by Clutter (1963) for loblolly pine, can be differentiated with respect to age to give the growth equation

$$G_v = dY/dA = b_3 YB^{-1}(dB/dA) - b_1 YA^{-2}$$

where G_v = instantaneous volume growth

Growth and yield models based on the size-class distribution of trees in conifer stands provide more detail and flexibility for use in vegetation management decision making. A notable advantage is the ability to predict the stand volume by tree size-class. Larger stems that can be sawed for lumber and peeled for plywood veneer command a premium price, making the ability to differentiate volume by tree size very important.

A number of models have been developed that consider the stand in terms of the distribution of the number of trees per unit area by size/ class. In most cases, DBH classes have been used. The most common stand models in this general category are based on a *diameter distribution analysis procedure*. In this approach, the number of trees per unit area in each diameter class is estimated through the use of a *probability density function* (PDF) that provides the relative frequency of trees by diameters. Mean total tree heights are predicted for trees of given diameters growing under given stand conditions. Volume per diameter class is calculated by substituting the predicted mean tree heights and the diameter class midpoints into tree volume equations. Yield estimates are obtained by summing the diameter classes of interest. Although only overall stand values (such as age, site index, and number of trees per unit area) are needed as input, detailed stand distributional information is obtainable as output. An example of output from a diameter distribution based growth and yield model for loblolly pine is shown in Table 7-2.

The various diameter-distribution models differ chiefly in the function used to describe the diameter distribution. The *Weibull distribution* has been most widely used. Regardless of the PDF used, the *parameter prediction method* involves estimating the PDF parameters for each plot in the data set (usually by the method of moments or maximum likelihood) and then developing regression equations to relate these parameter es-

TABLE 7-2. Predicted Diameter Distribution and Yield for Loblolly Pine Plantations Age 25, Site Index 60 Ft (Base Age 25 Years), 720 Trees per Acre Planted on Site-Prepared Areas in the South

DBH Class (inches)	Density (trees/acre)	Average Height (ft)	Basal Area (ft²/acre)	Total Volume (ft³/acre)
3	2.7	35.1	0.1	2.9
4	17.3	43.1	1.5	33.8
5	41.3	48.7	5.6	131.1
6	65.9	52.8	12.9	313.9
7	80.4	56.0	21.5	539.8
8	77.8	58.5	27.2	702.9
9	60.1	60.5	26.6	704.6
10	36.8	62.2	20.1	544.3
11	17.7	63.6	11.7	321.7
12	6.5	64.8	5.1	143.8
13	1.8	65.8	1.7	47.9
Totals	408.5		134.0	3,486.7

Source: From Amateis et al. 1984.

timates to a unit area basis. Alternatively, a *parameter recovery method* may be used that consists of forecasting overall stand attributes (e.g., total cubic volume, total basal area) and solving for the parameters of a theoretical diameter distribution model (such as the Weibull) that will give rise to the overall stand attributes. Such an approach provides a direct mathematical link between the overall stand values and the distribution of those values.

Approaches to predicting stand yields that use individual trees as the basic unit are commonly referred to as *individual-tree models.* The components of tree growth in these models are linked together through a computer program that simulates the growth of each tree and then sums these to provide estimates of stand growth and yield.

Individual-tree models are generally divided into two classes, distance-dependent and distance-independent, depending on whether or not individual tree locations are required tree attributes. *Distance-independent models* project tree growth either individually or by size-classes, usually as a function of present size, vigor, and stand level variables such as site index and basal area per unit area.

Distance-dependent models that have been developed vary in detail but are similar in overall concept and structure. Initial stand data are input or generated, and each tree is assigned a coordinate location. The growth of each tree is simulated as a function of its attributes, the site quality, and a measure of competition from neighbors. The *competition index* varies from model to model but in general is a function of the size of the subject tree and the size of, and distance to, competitors. Tree growth is commonly adjusted by a random component representing genetic and/or microsite variability, and survival is controlled either stochastically or deterministically as a function of competition and/or individual tree attributes. Yield estimates are obtained by summing the individual tree volumes (computed from tree taper or volume equations) and multiplying by appropriate expansion factors.

Applying Growth and Yield Models

Choosing an Appropriate Model

A wide variety of growth and yield models—ranging from whole-stand models that provide only a specified aggregate stand volume to models with information about individual trees—have been developed. In choosing a growth and yield model, one must be concerned with the stand detail needed for a particular decision and the efficiency in providing the information required (Daniels et al. 1979). Obviously, no single growth and yield model can be best for all possible problems.

Although advantages and disadvantages cannot be ascribed to different modeling approaches except in the context of specific uses, general characteristics of the various alternatives can be briefly described. Whole-stand models can generally be applied with existing inventory data and are computationally efficient. However, whole-stand models do not provide size-class information needed to evaluate various utilization options and product breakdowns and usually cannot be used to analyze a wide range of stand treatments.

Diameter-distribution models require only overall stand values as input but provide detailed size-class information as output. Thus alternative utilization options can be evaluated. Computationally, these models are somewhat more expensive to apply than whole-stand approaches, and they may not be flexible enough to evaluate a broad range of stand treatments.

Individual-tree models provide maximum detail and flexibility for evaluating alternative utilization options and stand treatments. They are, however, more expensive to develop, require a more detailed data base to implement, and are much more expensive to apply, requiring sophisticated computing equipment and greater execution time for comparable stand estimates than the whole-stand or diameter-distribution models (Avery and Burkhart 1983).

Modifying Growth and Yield Models for Silvicultural Treatments

When modifying a model to reflect various silvicultural treatments, it is necessary to develop biological paradigms of how the treatment might affect growth, specify mathematical models of those paradigms, and evaluate the resultant predictions against conventional wisdom and experimental data. As additional data from treated stands become available, this information can be used to evaluate the appropriateness of the original models and to estimate coefficients in growth and yield models.

The approach to incorporating silvicultural treatment effects in growth and yield models will be determined by the type of model(s) and the extent and nature of data on treatment effects that are available. Treatments may affect many different aspects of tree growth and stand development. Changes in any one factor are not necessarily independent of the other factors. Thus it would not be realistic to assume a simple change in diameter or height growth with no corresponding change in factors such as tree form and mortality rates. In many instances, models are structured such that a change in one factor will affect many other factors. For example, if height growth is increased without any increase in diameter growth and both DBH and height are used to estimate tree volume, then an improvement in form is implied even if the coefficients in the tree volume or taper equation are not modified (Burkhart and Matney 1981).

As a further example, consider how the effects of vegetation control might be used to predict the performance of a given conifer plantation. If the growth and yield model involved is simply expressed as a function of the initial number of conifer trees planted and stand age, then effects of competing vegetation are not explicitly incorporated in the model. Thus the degree of vegetation control provided by a given treatment cannot be used to predict the subsequent survival, growth, and yield of the plantation. If, on the other hand, the influence of competing vegetation has been incorporated into the model as a variable affecting conifer survival or growth, then the degree of vegetation control provided by a given treatment can be used to predict survival, growth, and yield of the plantation. Such a model has been developed by Burkhart and Sprinz (1984) and is illustrated in Chapter 8.

Effects of vegetation control treatments on conifer growth and yield will usually be positive. However, negative effects may also occur and need to be modeled. Chemicals used for conifer release may kill some trees and adversely affect the height growth of others. Direct and indirect effects of vegetation-control treatments can influence survival and growth of conifers in confounding ways. For example, Newton and Overton (1973) evaluated the direct and indirect effects of atrazine, 2,4-D, and dalapon on Douglas-fir and grand fir in western Oregon. Using a technique called *analysis of causal paths*, they were able to separate the positive indirect effects of weed control from the negative direct effects of dalapon.

In cases where the model components are interrelated, a change in only one component may affect all other components. When the components are not interrelated, it may be necessary to modify several functions to appropriately reflect a change in a single factor. Model architecture also influences the way that vegetation management treatments are incorporated. Modelers have generally been more successful in incorporating silvicultural treatment effects using models that estimate growth (i.e., *growth architecture models*). *Yield architecture models* (i.e., models that estimate yield) are difficult to use for treatment effects that cause changes in growth (e.g., weed control) because growth is usually determined by comparing yield estimates. The approach necessary and the likelihood of success in incorporating silvicultural treatment effects in growth and yield models depend on the model architecture, the components of the model, the predictor variables used, and the interdependence of the model components.

Estimating Yields on an Area Basis

Growth and yield models are often used to estimate the expected differences between alternative management strategies, such as thinned versus unthinned stands and released (from competing vegetation) versus unreleased stands. To be useful, estimates of differences in growth and yield per unit area must be expanded to a stand or forest basis. Unfortunately, vegetation management treatments are rarely applied uniformly to all areas in a stand. For example, during site preparation, brush may be piled in windrows that may or may not be planted and may contain much higher levels of competing vegetation than the open areas if not burned. Areas of skips in the spray pattern from aerial release with herbicides would grow as if not released. It is not uncommon for 10% or more of a tract to essentially remain unchanged after a vegetation control treatment is applied. Due to this lack of uniformity, yield improvement on a stand- or forest-level basis is rarely as good as the results from small experimental research plots might predict (Bruce 1977).

When the estimates of yield per unit area are expanded to a stand or forest basis, the following precautions should be taken (Avery and Burkhart 1983):

1. If there are significant differences in predictor variables such as site, species composition, treatment effectiveness, or stand density for a given area, the area should be stratified into reasonably homogeneous units and predictions made separately for each of these units to ensure accurate results.

2. Nonproductive areas (e.g., roads, landings, and other voids in plantations) should be deducted before expanding yield estimates to an area basis. It is important that net area, not gross area, be used in order to avoid overestimates.

3. Allowance should be made for logging breakage and other losses incurred before or during harvest. Adjustments to predicted values from growth and yield models must often be made in order to approximate volumes that are likely to be realized under actual conditions.

SUMMARY

Determining the benefits of vegetation management in conifer stands requires an understanding of how trees and stands grow and how growth and yield are estimated. Trees change in diameter, height, and volume over time in consistent patterns that vary widely in magnitude depending on the species, their silvical characteristics, and site conditions. The effects of competing vegetation on individual tree growth can only be determined if the inherent patterns of growth are known. More detailed discussions of the patterns of individual tree growth can be found in Wilson (1970) and in Zimmermann and Brown (1971).

Although conifer stands are comprised of individual trees, they have characteristics and developmental patterns that are not readily apparent from studying the individual trees themselves. Individual tree growth, stand attributes, and site characteristics are interrelated. Stand density influences the growth of individuals as well as the total growth rate of the stand. Site quality can be estimated in many different ways but always determines the total carrying capacity or the maximum basal area density a stand can develop. Carmean (1975) should be referred to for an excellent discussion of site quality estimation, and Daniel et al. (1979) should be consulted for more detail on stand dynamics.

There are many different techniques and models that can be used to estimate the growth and yield of conifer stands. The technique used depends greatly on the data available, the objectives for, or use of, the estimates, and the resolution desired. Success in incorporating responses to vegetation management in growth and yield estimation is dependent on the ability to determine the model architecture and components that will best describe the biological effects of weed control on crop trees and stands. Growth and yield literature for the Pacific Northwest can be obtained by using Hann and Riitters (1982), and Williston (1975) and Farrar (1979) can be useful for literature on southeastern forests.

REFERENCES

Alexander, R.R., D. Tackle, and W.G. Dahms. 1967. Site indexes for lodgepole pine, with corrections for stand density: methodology. USDA Forest Service, Rocky Mountain Forest and Range Experiment Station, Fort Collins, CO. Res. Pap. RM-29. 19 p.

Amateis, R.L., H.E. Burkhart, B.R. Knoebel, and P.T. Sprinz. 1984. Yields and size class distributions for unthinned loblolly pine plantations on cutover site-prepared lands. School of Forestry and Wildlife Resources, Virginia Polytechnic Institute and State Univ., Blacksburg, VA. Publ. FWS-2-84. 69 p.

Avery, T.E. and H.E. Burkhart. 1983. Forest measurements. 3rd ed. McGraw-Hill Book Co., Inc., New York, NY. 331 p.

Barrett, J.W. 1980. Regional silviculture of the United States. John Wiley and Sons, Inc., New York, NY. 551 p.

Brickell, J.E. 1968. A method for constructing site index curves from measurements of tree age and height—its application to inland Douglas-fir. USDA Forest Service, Intermountain Forest and Range Experiment Station, Ogden, UT. Res. Pap. INT-47. 23 p.

Brown, C.L. 1977. Growth and form, p. 125-168. *In* Zimmerman, M.H. and C.L. Brown (eds.) Trees: structure and function. Springer-Verlag, New York, NY. 336 p.

Bruce, D. 1977. Yield differences between research plots and managed forests. J. Forestry 75:14-17.

Burkhart, H.E. 1977. Cubic-foot volume of loblolly pine to any merchantable top limit. South. J. Appl. Forestry 1:7-9.

Burkhart, H.E. and T.G. Matney. 1981. Growth and yield modeling—a place for genetic improvement effects, p. 6-17. *In* Proc., Sixteenth Southern Forest Tree Improvement Conference, Blacksburg, VA, May 27-28, 1981. Sponsored by USDA Forest Service, Southeastern Forest Experiment Station, Forestry Sciences Laboratory, Athens, GA. 363 p.

Burkhart, H.E. and P.T. Sprinz. 1984. A model for assessing hardwood competition effects on yields of loblolly pine plantations. School of Forestry and Wildlife Resources, Virginia Polytechnic Institute and State Univ., Blacksburg, VA. Publ. FWS-3-84. 55 p.

Burkhart, H.E. and M. R. Strub. 1974. A model for simulation of planted loblolly pine stands, p. 128-135. *In* Growth Models for Tree and Stand Simulation. Royal College of Forestry, Stockholm, Sweden. p. 128-135.

Carmean, W.H. 1975. Forest site quality evaluation in the United States. Adv. Agron. 27:209-269.

Causton, D.R. and J.C. Venus. 1981. The biometry of plant growth. Arnold Press, London. 307 p.

Cleary, B.D., R.D. Greaves, and R.K. Hermann. (eds.) 1978. Regenerating Oregon's forests—a guide for the regeneration forester. Oregon State Univ. Ext. Serv., Corvallis, OR. 286 p.

Clutter, J.L. 1963. Compatible growth and yield models for loblolly pine. Forest Sci. 9:354-371.

Clutter, J.L., J.C. Fortson, L.V. Pienaar, G.H. Brister, and R.L. Bailey. 1983. Timber management: a quantitative approach. John Wiley and Sons, Inc., New York, NY. 333 p.

Daniel, T.W., J.A. Helms, and F.S. Baker. 1979. Principles of silviculture. McGraw-Hill Book Co. New York, NY. 500 p.

Daniels, R.F., H.E. Burkhart, and M.R. Strub. 1979. Yield estimates for loblolly pine plantations. J. Forestry 77:581-583, 586.

Daubenmire, R.F. 1961. Vegetative indicators of rate of height growth in ponderosa pine. Forest Sci. 7:24-34.

Daubenmire, R. and J.B. Daubenmire. 1968. Forest vegetation of eastern Washington and northern Idaho. Washington Agricultural Experiment Station, Pullman, WA. Tech. Bull. 60. 104 p.

Drew, T.J. and J.W. Flewelling. 1977. Some recent Japanese theories of yield-density relationships and their application to Monterey pine. Forest Sci. 23:517-534.

Drew, J.T. and J.W. Flewelling. 1979. Stand density management: an alternative approach and its application to Douglas-fir plantations. Forest Sci. 25:518-532.

Duff, G.H. and N.J. Nolan. 1953. Growth and morphogenisis in the Canadian forest species. 1. The controls of cambial and apical activity in *Pinus resinosa* Ait. Can. J. Bot. 31:471-513.

Farrar, R.M., Jr. 1979. Status of growth and yield information in the south. South. J. Appl. Forestry 3:132-137.

Fisher, R.A. 1921. Some remarks on the methods formulated in a recent article on "The quantitative analysis of plant growth." Annals Appl. Biol. 7:367-372.

Hall, F.C. 1983. Growth basal area: a field method for appraising forest site potential for stockability. Can. J. Forest Res. 13:70-77.

Hamilton, G.J. and J.M. Christie. 1973. Construction and application of stand yield models. British Forestry Commission Res. and Develop. Pap. 96. 14 p.

Hann, D.W. and K. Riitters. 1982. A key to the literature on forest growth and yield in the Pacific Northwest: 1910-1981. Forest Research Laboratory, Oregon State Univ., Corvallis. Res. Bull. 39. 77 p.

Harper, J.L. 1977. Population biology of plants. Academic Press, London. 892 p.

Hasel, A.A. 1950. Board-foot and cubic-foot volume tables for second growth redwood. USDA Forest Service, California Forest and Range Experiment Station, Berkeley, CA. Res. Note PSW-66. 14 p.

Hodgkins, E.J. 1960. Estimating site index for longleaf pine through quantitative evaluation of associated vegetation. Proc., Soc. Amer. Foresters 1960:28-32.

Husch, B., C.I. Miller, and T.W. Beers. 1982. Forest mensuration. John Wiley and Sons, Inc., New York, NY. 402 p.

Jones, J.R. 1969. Review and comparison of site evaluation methods. USDA Forest Service, Rocky Mountain Forest and Range Experiment Station, Fort Collins, CO. Res. Pap. RM-51. 27 p.

Langsaeter, A. 1941. Om tynning i enaldret gran-og furuskog. Meddel. f.d. Norske Skogforsoksvesen 8:131-216.

Lanner, R.M. 1976. Patterns of shoot development in pines and their relationship to growth potential, p. 223-243. *In* Cannell, M.G.R. and F.T. Last (eds.) Tree Physiology and Yield Improvement. Academic Press, New York, NY. 567 p.

Lindquist, J.L. and M.N. Palley. 1961. Site curves for young-growth coastal redwood. California Forestry and Forest Products Note 29:1-4.

Lohrey, R.E. 1983. Stem volume prediction and crown characteristics of thinned longleaf pine plantations, p. 338-343. *In* Jones, E.P., Jr. (ed.) Proc., Second Biennial Southern Silvicultural Research Conference, Nov. 4-5, 1982, Atlanta, GA. USDA Forest Service, Southeastern Forest Experiment Station, Asheville, NC. Gen. Tech. Rep. SE-24. 514 p.

Lynch, D.W. 1958. Effects of stocking on site measurement and yield of second-growth ponderosa pine in the Inland Empire. USDA Forest Service, Inter-mountain Forest and Range Experiment Station, Ogden, UT. Res. Pap. INT-56. 39 p.

MacLean, D.C. and C.L. Bolsinger. 1973. Estimating productivity on sites with a low stocking capacity. USDA Forest Service, Pacific Northwest Forest and Range Experiment Station, Portland, OR. Res. Pap. PNW-152. 18 p.

Mader, D.L. 1976. Soil-site productivity for natural stands of white pine in Massachusetts. Soil Sci. Soc. Amer. J. 40:112-115.

McArdle, R.E., W.H. Meyer, and D. Bruce. 1949. The yield of Douglas-fir in the Pacific Northwest. U.S. Dept. Agr., Washington, DC. Tech. Bull. 201. (1st rev.) 74 p.

McArdle, R.E., W.H. Meyer, and D. Bruce. 1961. The yield of Douglas-fir in the Pacific Northwest. U. S. Dept. Agr., Washington, DC. Tech. Bull. 201 (2nd rev.) 74 p.

McClurkin, D.C. 1953. Soil and climatic factors related to the growth of longleaf pine. USDA Forest Service, Southern Forest Experiment Station, New Orleans, LA. Occ. Pap. 132. 12 p.

Meyer, W.H. 1938. Yield of even-aged stands of ponderosa pine. U.S. Dept. Agr., Washington, DC. Tech. Bull. 630. 60 p.

Newton, M. 1973. Forest rehabilitation in North America: some simplifications. J. Forestry 71:159-162.

Newton, M. and W.S. Overton. 1973. Direct and indirect effects of atrazine, 2,4-D, and dalapon mixtures on conifers. Weed Sci. 21:269-275.

Pfister, R.D., B.L. Kovalchik, S.F. Arno, and R.C. Presby. 1977. Forest habitat types of Montana. USDA Forest Service, Intermountain Forest and Range Experiment Station, Ogden, UT. Gen. Tech. Rep. INT-34. 174 p.

Pressler, M.R. 1864. Das Gesetz der Stamanbildung. Arnoldische Buchhandlung, Leipzig. 153 p.

Reineke, L.H. 1933. Perfecting a stand density index for even-aged forests. J. Agr. Res. 46:627-628.

Shoulders, E. and F.V. Walker. 1979. Soil, slope and rainfall affect height and yield in 15-year-old southern pine plantations. USDA Forest Service, Southern Forest Experiment Station, New Orleans, LA. Res. Pap. SO-153. 52 p.

Smith, D.M. 1962. The practice of silviculture. 7th ed. John Wiley and Sons, Inc., New York, NY. 578 p.

Spurr, S.H. and B.V. Barnes. 1980. Forest ecology. 3rd ed. John Wiley and Sons, Inc., New York, NY. 687 p.

U.S. Department of Agriculture. 1976. Volume, yield, and stand tables for second growth Southern pines. U.S. Government Printing Office, Washington, DC. Misc. Publ. 50. (rev.) 202 p.

Williston, H.L. 1975. Selected bibliography on growth and yield of the four major southern pines. USDA Forest Service, Southeastern Area State and Private Forestry, Athens, GA. S&PF-5. 27 p.

Wilson, B.F. 1970. The growing tree. Univ. Massachusetts Press, Amherst, MA. 152 p.

Yoda, K., T. Kira, H. Ogawa, and K. Hozumi. 1963. Intraspecific competition among higher plants. XI. Self-thinning in over-crowded pure stands under cultivated and natural conditions. Osaka City Univ. J. Biol. 14:107-129.

Zedaker, S.M. 1981. Growth and development of young Douglas-fir in relation to intra- and interspecific competition. Ph.D. thesis. Oregon State Univ., Corvallis, OR. 175 p.

Zimmermann, M.H. and C.L. Brown. (eds.) 1971. Trees: structure and function. Springer-Verlag, New York, NY. 336 p.

8

Loblolly Pine Growth and Yield Response to Vegetation Management

HAROLD E. BURKHART
GLENN R. GLOVER
PETER T. SPRINZ

INTRODUCTION

Loblolly pine is the primary commercial species in the South. It grows well from Maryland, south to Florida, and west to eastern Texas. A major problem with growing loblolly pine is competition from hardwood and herbaceous vegetation for moisture, nutrients, and light. Competing vegetation can reduce survival and growth of the desired pines.

The purpose of this chapter is to present information on loblolly pine response to vegetation management. This presentation is divided into two primary parts. The first part provides a summary of data from field studies of loblolly pine response to hardwood or herbaceous vegetation control. In the second part, a model of hardwood competition effects on loblolly pine survival and growth is presented.

VEGETATION CONTROL FIELD STUDIES

The paucity of data for evaluating loblolly pine growth response to weed control prompted an effort to locate existing areas where this information could be obtained. Southern forestry and related organizations were asked to identify areas where replicated studies, paired plots, or operational comparisons of chemical vegetation control versus other methods or no control had been installed. For a comparison to be considered, an untreated or mechanically treated area had to be present within the same stand as the treated area. Stands that were treated entirely with chemicals and thus had no check area for comparison were not measured. Forty comparisons 4 to 36 years old were located. Twenty-two of these comparisons involved hardwood control, whereas the other 18 primarily involved herbaceous vegetation control. A description of location, establishment information, and treatments for each measured comparison is available from Glover and Dickens (1985) and Glover (1986). Geographic distribution of the studies is shown in Figure 8-1.

The following data were recorded for pines on each measurement plot: diameter at breast height (DBH) to the nearest 0.1 in., total height of a subsample of trees (minimum 10) to the nearest 1.0 ft, crown class, merchantable height in 16-ft logs to the nearest one-half log for trees 9.5 in. DBH and larger, damage or disease incidence and type, and the Virginia Division of Forestry's Free-to-Grow classification (Zutter et al. 1985) for trees 8 years old and younger. Data collected for each hardwood tree 0.6 in. DBH and larger included DBH to the nearest 1.0 in., total height to the nearest 10 ft, and species. Because of the age of most comparisons, herbaceous vegetation samples were not collected. Site information, such as slope and aspect, was recorded at each measurement plot. Additional information on measurement procedures and a complete summary of data for 25 of the comparisons are given in Glover and Dickens (1985).

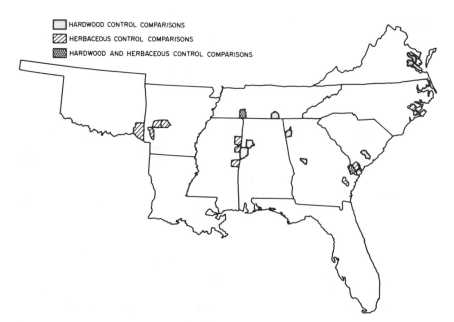

Figure 8-1. Map showing location of measured hardwood and herbaceous vegetation control comparisons in loblolly pine plantations.

Hardwood Control Comparisons

A summary of data comparing loblolly pine response to hardwood control by chemical, mechanical, hand, and no hardwood control is given in Table 8-1. There was high variability in pine and hardwood response to herbicide application. In some comparisons there were fewer, smaller hardwood stems on herbicide treated plots and a corresponding greater pine yield. In other cases, herbicide application had either no effect or decreased pine yield. All but one of the comparisons showing no response or negative response of pine yield to herbicide application were operational comparisons using 2,4,5-T, where initial conditions, herbicide rates, and application techniques were often not closely controlled.

Due to the inherent variability in operational comparisons and the fact that several of the research comparisons were installed as tests of rates, timing, soil interactions, and the like, the basic effect of hardwoods on pine yield is not revealed if one looks solely at treatment means. A more important relationship is pine yield versus the amount of hardwood present in the stand, regardless of treatment. One relationship that can be examined is pine yield (basal area or volume) versus percentage of total basal area in hardwoods. Figure 8-2 shows examples of this relationship for three studies. Pine yield appears to be related to the relative proportion of hardwood basal area irrespective of other site and stand effects.

Although pines tend to grow faster than hardwoods, apparently pine mortality and hardwood ingrowth can combine to maintain a constant proportion of hardwood basal area over time (Burkhart and Sprinz 1984). This indicates that once hardwoods become established in a loblolly pine stand, the pines do not generally completely dominate and eliminate the hardwoods; instead, the hardwoods remain as competition adversely affecting pine yield. In instances where an assumption of constant proportion of hardwood basal area over time is reasonable, the percentage of basal area in hardwoods can be measured in a stand several years after treatment and still provide an indication of initial relative hardwood density and/or treatment effectiveness (assuming hardwood stocking was equivalent across plots at time of treatment, which is not always a good assumption). The apparent lack of effectiveness of treatment in some operational comparisons may be due to the violation of the assumption of equivalent hardwood stocking at the time of treatment. This points out that a comparison of treatment means alone may not be sufficient to accurately interpret the response of loblolly pine to past hardwood control measures.

Herbaceous Vegetation Control Comparisons

The ability to control herbaceous vegetation in loblolly pine plantations is a relatively recent development. Herbicides that gave broad spectrum

TABLE 8-1. Summary of Information on Loblolly Pine Response to Various Hardwood Vegetation Control Treatments

Study (Treatment Age; Measurement Age)	Treatment[a]	Trees per Acre	Measurement Parameters[b]				
			Basal Area per Acre (ft²)	Volume per Acre (ft³)	Mean DBH (in.)	Mean Total Height (ft)	Basal Area in Hardwood (%)
Fayette (0;24)	CHC	418	142.9	3758	7.7	56	11
	MHC	474	167.2	4393	7.9	57	9
	HHC	212	70.5	1764	7.5	52	46
	NHC	204	16.9	359	3.6	31	86
Floyd County (6;11)	CHC	901	32.5	554	2.4	16	33
	NHC	588	22.8	317	2.2	15	49
Grass Creek (5;9)	CHC	772	51.1	551	3.3	20	22
	NHC	760	43.6	474	3.1	21	37
Hobbs-Western (6;18)	CHC	432	51.5	1147	4.8	31	43
	NHC	227	34.1	648	5.4	35	60
Marston (5;10)	CHC	458	22.8	252	2.8	15	37
	NHC	774	22.1	313	2.1	14	52
North End (5;10)	CHC	1122	50.5	664	2.5	16	13
	NHC	942	42.9	643	2.7	17	28
Pickens (5;20)	CHC	356	108.6	2984	7.2	52	14
	NHC	331	112.3	3150	7.7	56	24
Piedmont (4;9)	CHC	810	44.2	513	2.9	16	4
	NHC	768	38.9	479	2.8	17	22
Pineville (0,1,2; 36)	CHC	257	115.7	3940	9.0	66	6
	HHC	226	30.0	4821	9.8	76	4
	NHC	230	115.6	3899	9.0	63	16

Rochelle	CHC	460	26.0	283	3.1	17	13
(2;7)	NHC	510	19.3	258	2.5	16	47
Sewanee	CHC	523	20.8	229	2.6	15	26
(0;6)	NHC	529	11.6	175	1.8	13	57
Shannon	CHC	375	6.3	99	1.7	12	58
(0;5)	MHC	580	4.2	45	1.1	9	28
	NHC	680	0.4	7	0.4	4	99
Summerville-1	CHC	294	156.4	5234	9.8	72	5
(3;25)	NHC	318	171.1	5970	9.9	75	5
Summerville-2	CHC	294	144.0	4540	9.3	66	5
(3;25)	NHC	282	158.2	5418	10.0	72	8
Summerville-3	CHC	196	138.1	4651	11.1	72	19
(4;26)	NHC	144	123.7	4626	12.3	78	27
Summerville-6	CHC	192	159.1	5865	12.2	78	19
(8;30)	NHC	208	160.0	5804	12.1	79	18
Summerville-8	CHC	232	167.8	6423	11.2	82	2
(5;27)	NHC	164	144.4	5496	12.5	82	24
Summerville-9	CHC	146	108.3	3799	11.4	73	10
(5;27)	NHC	124	93.7	3359	11.9	74	31
Summerville-10	CHC	342	168.9	5416	9.3	69	4
(1;23)	NHC	220	137.1	4204	10.4	65	11
Summerville-11	CHC	142	135.4	4966	13.1	79	11
(6;28)	NHC	230	170.2	6466	11.4	82	5
Upson	CHC	736	78.5	1857	4.1	30	27
(6;22)	NHC	409	86.1	1878	6.1	42	32
Waddels	CHC	620	37.8	374	3.2	15	18
(3;6)	NHC	430	22.5	225	3.0	15	51

[a]CHC = Chemical hardwood control
MHC = Mechanical hardwood control
HHC = Hand (manual) hardwood control
NHC = No hardwood control
[b]Basal area, volume, and DBH parameters are based on outside bark measurements.

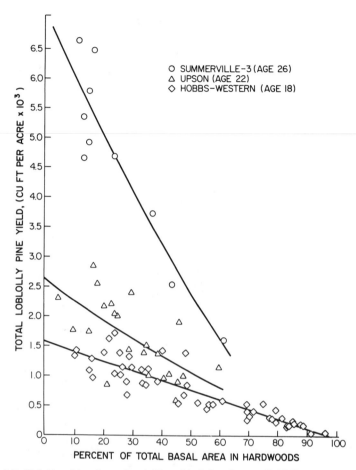

Figure 8-2. Relationship of merchantable cubic-foot volume of loblolly pine to percentage of total basal area in hardwoods for three example studies.

control of herbaceous vegetation commonly found in loblolly pine plantations, without excessive pine damage, were not available until the mid-1970s and were not fully developed until the early 1980s. Applications of this technology have increased rapidly though because of the interest resulting from large growth increases observed in treated versus untreated plots. Silvicultural benefits from controlling herbaceous vegetation during the early years of loblolly pine development have been documented by Smith and Schmidtling (1970), Holt et al. (1975), Fitzgerald (1976), Nelson et al. (1981), Knowe et al. (1985), and Michael (1985). For example, Knowe et al. (1985) reported a 97% increase in groundline diameter and a 115% increase in total height of 4-year-old loblolly pines that received 2 years of broadcast herbaceous weed control compared to the check. Seventy-six percent of the variation in groundline diameter and 70% of the variation in total height at age 4 could be explained by herbaceous biomass (weight) from clipped plots in June of the second growing season.

In the effort to locate existing herbaceous vegetation control comparisons not reported in the literature, 18 research studies (no operational comparisons) were found and measured. Table 8-2 summarizes weed control effects on pine survival, basal area, volume, DBH, and total height. Four studies were installed as fertilization/weed control comparisons, with two also including different site preparation treatments. The oldest studies of loblolly pine response to herbaceous vegetation control located, which were suitable for measurement, were 11 years old (Dubberly and Savannah Town). These studies utilized herbicides that gave only limited vegetation control. In 1974 one study (Mingo Bottom) and in 1975, three studies (Dierks, Mountain Pine, and Old Plant Site) were initiated using hand-hoeing of the vegetation to maintain weed-free plots. Some herbicides were used during the second and subsequent years of the studies. Various herbicides that are currently available and will give excellent weed control on most loblolly pine sites were used in the remaining 12 studies.

Treated plots in the 18 herbaceous vegetation control studies show a per study average increase of 70% in basal area and 67% in volume yield (44 ft³/acre/year compared to untreated plots). Figure 8-3 shows total volume production (residual stems plus thinnings) over time for three hand-hoed studies through age 10. The weed control versus no weed control volume curves are still diverging at age 10 for all three studies, although volume differences at Old Plant Site (high site index) appear to be stabilizing.

Evaluation of harvest yields of loblolly pine plantations following herbaceous weed control will not be possible until present studies mature. If current growth trends continue, the trees will reach harvestable size several years earlier on plots that received weed control. Conventional planting densities and thinning regimes may have to be reconsidered if herbaceous weed control becomes widely practiced.

Many of the earlier herbaceous weed control studies involved broadcast control of vegetation over the entire plot, often for more than 1 year. Due to economic and environmental considerations, many current studies and operational applications of herbicides for herbaceous weed control are being made the first year after planting only as 3- to 5-ft bands over pine rows or as 2- to 3-ft radius plots around individual pine trees. Although studies designed to evaluate weed-control effects on early loblolly pine survival have not been reported, control of herbaceous weeds should increase moisture availability to young pine seedlings and increase survival in years where moisture stress is a major cause of seedling mortality.

Numerous field studies have shown that both herbaceous and hardwood vegetation can have a negative impact on loblolly pine growth and yield. Evaluation of the full range of possible impacts and benefits from vege-

TABLE 8-2. Summary of Information on Loblolly Pine Response to Various Herbaceous Vegetation Control Treatments

Study (Treatment Age; Measurement Age)	Treatment[a]	Trees per Acre	Basal Area[b] per Acre (ft²)	Volume[b] per Acre (ft³)	Mean DBH[c] (in.)	Mean Total Height[c] (ft)
Amity (0;6)	WC	710	28.0	270	2.8	14
	NWC	746	22.1	230	2.3	12
Burks Road (1;10)	WC	457	91.8	1459	6.0	33
	NWC	490	68.4	876	5.0	25
Central Arkansas (0;7)	WC	350	10.4	106	2.2	11
	NWC	262	4.9	60	1.7	10
Craven 35 (0,1;7)	WC	477	105.2	1473	6.2	29
	NWC	518	86.2	1118	5.4	27
Dierks (0;10)	WC	345[d]	124.1	1878	7.7	34
	NWC	635	73.1	1051	4.5	28
Dubberly (0;11)	WC	579	93.2	1686	5.2	34
	NWC	640	78.6	1386	4.5	30
Mingo Bottom (0;11)	WC	347[e]	140.2	2372	7.5	40
	NWC	351	77.8	1271	6.0	35
Mississippi Velpar (0;6)	WC	685	48.9	159	3.4	17
	NWC	821	37.4	95	2.8	15

Measurement Parameters

Mount Ida	WC	799	47.2	473	3.3	17
(0;6)	NWC	817	37.8	386	2.9	16
Mountain Pine	WC	348[f]	92.1	1150	6.3	27
(0;10)	NWC	350	46.7	509	4.3	21
Oklahoma Velpar	WC	579	44.4	460	3.7	18
(0;7)	NWC	514	37.0	376	3.6	18
Old Plant Site	WC	341[g]	141.3	2366	7.4	41
(0,1,3;10)	NWC	349	76.6	1173	5.7	31
Ritter Extension	WC	647	27.1	271	2.7	14
(0;4)	NWC	527	5.5	92	1.3	8
Ritter Hill	WC	883	95.4	1399	4.4	28
(0,1; 7)	NWC	748	81.7	1104	4.3	26
Ritter Road	WC	783	95.9	1238	4.7	26
(0,1; 7)	NWC	766	68.6	785	4.0	21
Ritter-Williams	WC	437	52.6	625	4.6	22
(1;7)	NWC	438	36.9	408	3.8	19
Ross	WC	509	12.3	111	2.0	12
(0;4)	NWC	596	5.7	50	1.3	9
Savannah Town	WC	586	98.9	1799	5.4	36
(0;11)	NWC	530	80.5	1381	5.2	34

[a]WC = Weed Control; NWC = No Weed Control.
[b]Basal areas and volumes (outside bark) for thinned plots are total production; that is, residual stems plus thinnings. Plots were thinned by specified rules, but thinning and competition control effects may be confounded.
[c]Mean DBH (outside bark) and total height for thinned plots are for residual stand only.
[d]WC thinned in 1980, 627 trees/acre before thinning.
[e]Thinned in 1980, WC 923, NWC 785 trees/acre before thinning.
[f]WC thinned in 1982, NWC in 1983; WC 578, NWC 592 trees/acre before thinning.
[g]Thinned in 1980, WC 727, NWC 785 trees/acre before thinning.

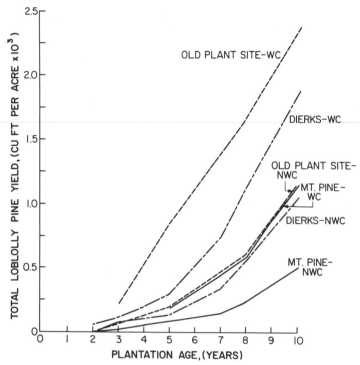

Figure 8-3. Total cubic-foot volume production (thinnings plus residual stems) for loblolly pine in hoed plot herbaceous weed control studies by treatment. WC = weed control; NWC = No weed control.

tation management practices, however, requires that the growth and yield of loblolly pine stands with varying levels of competing vegetation are modeled. Models cannot be completed and validated without suitable data. Many of the past vegetation control studies, including the majority of those summarized here, were not designed for modeling purposes. Some of the studies, particularly those with herbaceous vegetation control, are presently too young for most modeling applications. There are data, albeit somewhat limited from a yield modeling standpoint, that can be used to assess hardwood competition effects on loblolly pine growth and yield. In the next section, a model for hardwood competition effects on growth and yield of loblolly pine plantations is described and implications from the model predictions are presented.

MODEL OF HARDWOOD COMPETITION EFFECTS

A model that predicts pine survival, growth, and yield for stands with varying levels of competing vegetation can be used to assess the feasibility of various vegetation management strategies. In this section, a model is presented for predicting growth and yield of unthinned loblolly pine plantations with varying levels of hardwood competition. This model represents the effects of persistent competitors, which, once established, remain a part of the stand throughout the rotation. Although the model discussed is for loblolly pine, the general conceptual framework may be applicable to other species as well. The inputs required, outputs obtained, data base used, modeling methods employed, assumptions made, and limitations of the model are discussed briefly. A detailed explanation of the modeling methods employed and the computer programs developed to implement the model can be found in Burkhart and Sprinz (1984).

Model Inputs/Outputs

A diameter distribution approach (see Chapter 7) was taken to modeling growth and yield of unthinned loblolly pine plantations with varying levels of hardwood competition. To operate the model, called *HDWD*, the user must specify the following:

Number of loblolly pine trees planted per unit area
Site index for loblolly pine
Percentage of hardwood basal area in the main canopy of the stand
Ages at which output is desired

From these input parameters, the model computes estimates for the pine component, by 1-in. DBH classes, of the following:

Number of trees surviving per unit area
Total height
Basal area
Total stem cubic volume plus merchantable volumes of the pulpwood
   and sawtimber components

In addition to the values by DBH class, total numbers of trees, basal area and volumes, and arithmetic mean DBH, are also shown.

With the complete stand table (numbers of trees by DBH class) provided, one can evaluate the impact of competing vegetation on product yields as well as on overall survival and volume. Such information is needed when performing economic analyses of vegetation management alternatives.

Data Base

Three primary data sources were used to construct a model designed to quantify hardwood competition effects on loblolly pine yields:

1. Data from sample plots in unthinned loblolly pine plantations es-

tablished on abandoned agricultural land (called "old fields") were used to establish an "upper limit" on hardwood competition control effectiveness for site-prepared lands that were supporting forests before being cut and regenerated to loblolly pine plantations. Because these old-field plantations developed essentially free of competition from hardwood species, the survival and growth can be regarded as an upper limit for plantations established on cutover, site-prepared areas, which are the areas of primary concern in contemporary plantation management in the South. (Pine seedlings for many of these old-field plantations experienced considerable herbaceous competition in the early years; however, because of limitations in data bases, it was not possible to model its effect.)

2. Measurements from sample plots in unthinned loblolly pine plantations on cutover, site-prepared areas were used, where possible, to estimate the effects of competing hardwoods on pine survival and growth. The data available included a wide variety of site preparation methods, with varying degrees of effectiveness and thus varying levels of competing vegetation.

3. Observations from a site conversion study were used to develop basic relationships and evaluate various assumptions. Although this study (commonly referred to as the "Fayette Study") was not designed for the objectives of this analysis, it was the only designed-experiment type data available for this modeling effort. The old-field and cutover-site plantation data came from sample plots in operationally established plantations.

These data sets, which include a wide range of ages and site conditions, were used to construct an initial model of hardwood competition effects on the growth and yield of loblolly pine plantations.

Old-Field Plantation Plots

Selected old-field loblolly pine plantations were sampled in the Piedmont and Coastal Plain regions of Virginia and in the Coastal Plain region of Delaware, Maryland, and North Carolina. Of the 189 sample plots, 129 were located on Coastal Plain sites, whereas 60 were in the Piedmont region of Virginia. Temporary 0.1-acre, circular sample plots were randomly located in selected stands. To be sampled, plantations were required to be unthinned, free of severe insect or disease damage, unburned and unpruned, relatively free of wildlings, and contain no interplanting.

On each plot, DBH was recorded to the nearest 0.1 in. for all trees in the 1-in. DBH class and above. Total height was recorded to the nearest 1.0 ft for at least one, but usually two trees per 1-in. DBH class. Six to eight dominant and codominant trees were selected as sample site trees, and total age of the stand was determined from planting records or increment borings.

A summary of the sample plot characteristics is shown in Table 8-3; the geographic distribution of the plots is displayed in Figure 8-4. Ad-

TABLE 8-3. Summary of Characteristics of Sample Plot Data Used to Model Hardwood Competition Effects on Loblolly Pine Plantation Yields

Data	Number Plots	Mean	Minimum	Maximum
Old-field plantation plots	189			
Site index$_{25}$ (ft)[a]		67.0	47.4	92.3
Age		16.6	9.0	35.0
Surviving pine (trees/acre)		751.9	300.0	2900.0
Basal area in pine (ft^2/acre)		151.8	72.0	277.3
Cutover-site plantation plots	186			
Site index$_{25}$ (ft)[a]		62.8	33.5	97.3
Age		15.2	8.0	25.0
Surviving pine (trees/acre)		558.3	275.0	950.0
Basal area in hardwood (%)		4.8	0.0	27.8
Basal area in pine (ft^2/acre)		150.1	22.9	230.9
Site-conversion study plots				
Age 11				
Surviving pine (trees/acre)	25[b]	486.5	40.8	673.5
Basal area in hardwood (%)	25	39.7	3.7	100.0
Basal area in pine (ft^2/acre)	25	40.4	0.0	90.6
Age 24				
Site index$_{25}$ (ft)[a]	29	58.8	44.3	69.1
Surviving pine (trees/acre)	33	316.0	0.0	531.0
Basal area in hardwood (%)	33	33.1	0.0	100.0
Basal area in pine (ft^2/acre)	33	97.6	0.0	174.9

[a]All site index values (base age = 25 years) were computed using the equation for combined Coastal Plain and Piedmont data from Amateis and Burkhart (1985).
[b]The number of usable observations for each characteristic varied somewhat between measurement times. Two of the original 35 plots were cut in early 1980 during a southern pine beetle salvage operation, leaving a maximum of 33 plots for measurement.

ditional information about these plots can be obtained from Burkhart et al. (1972).

Cutover-Site Plantation Plots
During the 1980-1981 and 1981-1982 dormant seasons, permanent plots were established in cutover, site-prepared plantations throughout the native range of loblolly pine. The initial measurement data from these permanent plots were available for use in this study. To be included in the sample, the plantations had to meet the following specifications: be at least 8 years in age (defined as years since planting), unthinned, free of evidence of severe disease or insect attack, not heavily damaged by ice storms or windstorms, free of interplanting, unpruned, not fertilized within the last 4 years, not planted with genetically improved stock,

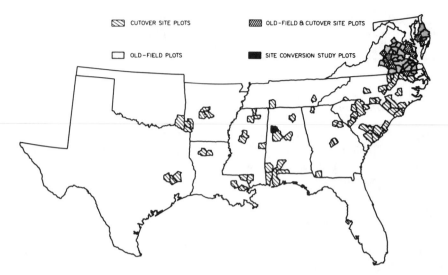

Figure 8-4. Map showing distribution of sample plots used to model hardwood competition effects on loblolly pine plantation yields.

contain a minimum of 200 to 300 planted pine stems per acre that appear "free to grow," have not more than 25% of the main canopy composed of volunteer pines, and be established on a cutover area that received conventional site preparation treatment for the site conditions and time at which the plantation was established.

The following data were recorded for all planted pines: DBH to the nearest 0.1 in., total height to the nearest 1.0 ft, height to the base of the live crown, crown class, and a stem quality assessment. In addition, the number of trees planted and the ages were determined.

The following information was recorded for natural pines and hardwoods that were in the main canopy: DBH to the nearest 0.1 in., total height to the nearest 1.0 ft, and species. Natural pine and hardwood trees not in the main canopy, but greater than 0.5 in. in DBH, were tallied by 1-in. DBH classes only.

Summary information on these plots is contained in Table 8-3, and the geographic location is shown in Figure 8-4. Additional detail can be obtained from Burkhart et al. (1985).

Conversion-Study Plots

In January 1959, a hardwood conversion/site preparation study was installed at the Fayette Experimental Forest of the Auburn University Agricultural Experiment Station in Fayette County, Alabama, which is in the Upper Coastal Plain soils region. The objective of this study was to test effects of seven methods of conversion on survival and early growth of planted loblolly pine on a cutover site.

A randomized block design, consisting of seven treatments (including an untreated check) with five replications per treatment, was installed on a relatively uniform site. Treatment plots were square, 132 ft on each side, with a 46.2-x-46.2 ft permanent sample plot located in the center of each treated plot. The treatments were (1) check; (2) scarification by bulldozer; (3) injector-applied herbicide; (4) girdle without herbicide; (5) axe frill and herbicide; (6) chain girdle and herbicide; and (7) foliage spraying plus axe frill and herbicide. These treatments varied widely in effectiveness, resulting in sample plots that ranged from essentially pure pine to pure hardwood. A detailed description of the study area, methods, treatments, and results at the end of the first 6 yr has been given by Whipple and White (1965). Glover et al. (1981) gave a summary of data at age 22.

Measurements on both the pine and the hardwood components at ages 11 and 24 were used in these analyses. The age 11 information was on a plot basis with details on the number of surviving trees and average DBH and basal area per acre of the pine and hardwood components provided. The following individual-tree information for the pines was provided with the age 24 measurements: DBH to the nearest 0.1 in., total stem cubic volume, crown class, and, on a subsample of trees, total height to the nearest 1.0 ft. Hardwood information at age 24 included the number of trees by species in 2-in. DBH classes and 10-ft total height classes. Table 8-3 gives summary statistics for the age 11 and 24 measurements; Figure 8-4 shows the study location.

Model Structure

Approach

The approach taken to modeling hardwood competition effects on yield was to regard values observed in old-field plantations as upper limits and to compute reduction factors based on the level of hardwood competition. As a first step, the effects of hardwood competition on various stand components were assessed. These assessments were made by (1) computing regression equations with the data from cutover-site plantations and determining if hardwood variables significantly reduced the error sum of squares; and by (2) comparing regression equations fitted to the old-field data with those fitted to the cutover-site data. Because the level of hardwood competition was relatively low in most of the cutover-site plots (see Table 8-3), attempts to incorporate hardwood competition variables using these data were generally not successful. Comparisons between regressions fitted to the old-field versus the cutover-site data showed significant differences, however. These differences were examined on the following stand components of the pine portion of the stands:

1. Height over age development (for dominants and codominants)
2. Height over diameter curves
3. Individual tree volume relationships
4. Diameter distribution
5. Survival relationships

Height-Age Development

Comparisons of height-age (site index) curves for old-fields versus cutover sites were made by using data from stem analysis trees collected at the time of plot installation. These comparisons were for dominant and co-dominant trees only; that is, for trees occupying positions in the upper canopy and above much of the competing vegetation. There were statistically significant differences between the two data sets. The differences were not overly large from a practical standpoint, however, and they could not be related to level of hardwood competition. This lack of a significant relationship to level of hardwood in the stand is consistent with the generally small effect of stand density—over a fairly broad range—on dominant height growth of loblolly pine. Because the primary purpose of this model was to assess the effect of hardwood competition on the yields of loblolly pine plantations on cutover, site-prepared land, the site index curves from Amateis and Burkhart (1985), which were derived from stem analysis trees taken on the cutover-site plantation plots described previously, were adopted. The equation for the height-age relationship as well as for other model components can be found in Burkhart and Sprinz (1984).

Height-Diameter Curves

Height-diameter curves were significantly different for the old-field and cutover-site data. The large sample sizes (2452 trees from old fields and 56,989 from cutover sites) resulted in a powerful test that was almost certain to indicate a significant difference if one existed. Differences could not be related to levels of hardwood competition, however, and comparisons of the two curves showed predicted values to be almost identical. Because the primary objective was to model yields for cutover-site areas, the height-diameter curve fitted to the cutover-site data was incorporated into the model.

Individual Tree Volume Relationships

Data from the stem analysis trees were used to compare individual tree volume relationships for old fields with those from cutover sites. Again,

significant differences were detected, but the differences were not sufficiently large to be of practical importance, and they could not be related
to hardwood variables. All stem-analysis trees from cutover-site plantations were in the dominant or codominant crown classes, whereas the
data set from old-field plantations contained all crown classes. (When
comparing volume relationships between the two data sets, only data
from dominant and codominant trees in old fields were used.) Because of
the small differences between the two data sets and because volume
predictions are needed for all crown classes, the volume equations from
Burkhart (1977), which were fitted to the old-field data from all crown
classes, were used.

Diameter Distribution

Comparisons of DBH distributions in old-field and cutover-site plantations showed substantial differences. In general, cutover-site plantations
had a smaller mean diameter and less basal area per unit area than old-
field plantations with the same age, average height of dominants and
codominants, and number of pines surviving. Differences in the two data
sets may be partially due to a number of factors, but the most important
factor is probably the level of hardwood competition. The relatively large
impact of hardwood competition on diameter growth as opposed to height
growth is consistent with the fact that the general trend of competition
effects are more pronounced on diameter than height development (Chapter 7). We ascribed all differences in diameter distribution to differences
in hardwood competition and developed adjustment factors to account for
varying hardwood levels. As hardwood competition level increases, both
the mean diameter and the mean squared diameter (and hence basal
area) are decreased in the model.

Pine Survival

Hardwood competition effects were most pronounced on pine diameter
growth and pine survival. Seventy-five of the 186 cutover-site plantations
had valid observations on the numbers of trees planted per acre in addition to the number surviving at the time of plot installation. None of
the old-field plots contained information on the number of trees planted.
Thus the literature was searched for an appropriate survival curve for
old-field plantations. After evaluating several alternative functions, the
survival curve from Coile and Schumacher (1964) was selected. The predicted number of trees surviving on an old field was modified as a function
of the amount of hardwood competition by fitting a modifier function to
data from the cutover-site plantation plots. Figure 8-5 shows survival
curves for 800 pines/acre planted and various levels of hardwood competition.

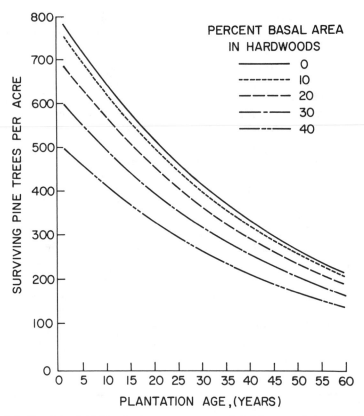

Figure 8-5. Surviving loblolly pine trees per acre as related to percentage of basal area in hardwoods. Figure is for 800 trees per acre planted.

Projection of Stand Composition

The percentage of total basal area in hardwood in the main canopy is a required input for Model HDWD. When making projections through time, the behavior of the stand composition in terms of pine and hardwood basal areas needed to be considered. Both pines and hardwoods were measured at ages 11 and 24 in the Fayette Study. These data provided information on stand composition relationships in loblolly pine plantations after crown closure.

Plotting the percentage of basal area in hardwood at age 24 versus percentage at age 11 showed a straight-line relationship with a slope near 1.0 (Figure 8-6). A simple linear regression was fitted to the data to predict percentage of basal area in hardwoods at age 24 from the percentage at age 11. The slope coefficient (0.97) for the fitted equation was not significantly different from 1.0. Thus the hypothesis that the stand composition by basal area does not change after crown closure was accepted. A constant ratio of hardwood basal area to total basal area should be

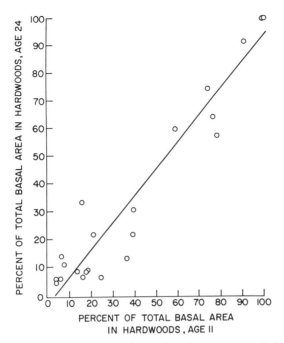

Figure 8-6. Relationship between percentage of basal area composed of hardwoods in the main canopy of loblolly plantations at ages 11 and 24 in a hardwood conversion/site preparation study, Fayette County, Alabama.

reasonable for many sites and for projection periods of interest for loblolly pine plantations. The stability of this ratio can be observed in data presented in other studies (e.g., Lange 1951).

In Model HDWD, the user must specify the percentage of basal area in hardwood in the main canopy at any point after crown closure. This percentage is then assumed to remain constant.

Model Validation and Use

Plot observations from the hardwood conversion/site preparation study in Fayette County, Alabama, were used to validate model predictions. The Fayette Study plots are an independent data set (none of the information from that study was used in fitting any of the components of the model) that covers the full spectrum of hardwood competition. Thus these data provided a rigorous evaluation of model adequacy. Figure 8-7 is a graph of the total cubic-foot volume in loblolly pine on the Fayette Study plots at age 24 versus percentage of total basal area in hardwood. Superimposed on the data points plotted in Figure 8-7 is a line showing the model behavior for site index 60 ft (base age 25 years), 714 trees per acre

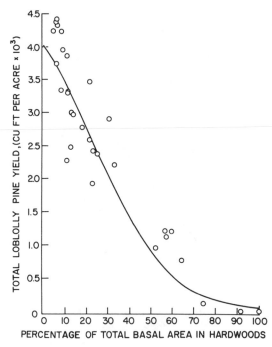

Figure 8-7. Total yield of loblolly pine versus percentage of total stand basal area in hardwoods from plot observations in a hardwood conversion/site preparation study in Fayette County, Alabama. The line represents predictions from program HDWD.

planted, age 24 years, and percentage of hardwood 0 to 100. The Fayette Study was planted with 714 trees per acre on an area that averaged 58.8 ft site index. Overall, there is close agreement between the observed values and the model predictions.

In addition to validation with the Fayette data, various combinations of the input variables were specified, and model behavior was observed. Somewhat extreme values of some of the independent variables were used to illustrate the behavior of the model over a wide range of conditions. Figure 8-8 shows model response in terms of total cubic-foot volume at ages 10, 30, and 50 years versus percentage of basal area in hardwood for site index 60 ft with 800 trees per acre planted. In general, the predicted trends conform to trends observed in field studies (compare with Figure 8-2).

Program HDWD was used to generate yield tables at age 30 for 800 trees per acre planted on site index 60 land with 0, 20, and 40% of the total stand basal area in hardwood (Table 8-4). From Table 8-4, one can note that with 20% of the basal area in hardwood, the number of trees, basal area, and sawlog volume decrease 12, 28, and 40%, respectively, from the values for 0 percentage of basal area in hardwood. At 40% of the total basal area in hardwood, the decreases in number of trees, basal area, and sawlog volume are 36, 64, and 81%, respectively, below that of the figures for 0% hardwood. Thus, as the proportion of the total stand basal area in hardwood increases, the decline in pine basal area and volume is even more marked because there are losses in both numbers of pine and in the average diameter of the pine that survive. The decline in sawlog volume is especially dramatic because the entire pine DBH distribution is shifted to the left as a result of hardwood competition (Figure 8-9). As the percentage of basal area in hardwood increases, the variance of the pine DBH distribution remains the same, but the mean shifts to the left, resulting in a somewhat more skewed distribution with relatively few trees in the larger diameter classes (Figure 8-9).

To further evaluate the "reasonableness" of model predictions, we computed the *relative yield total* (RYT) using data from the Fayette Study. The RYT is defined as (see Chapter 5)

$$\text{RYT} = \frac{\text{Yield of Species A in mixture}}{\text{Yield of A in pure stand}} + \frac{\text{Yield of Species B in mixture}}{\text{Yield of B in pure stand}}$$

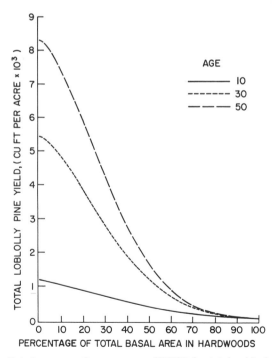

Figure 8-8. Predicted response from program HDWD for total cubic foot yield of loblolly pine plantations, site index (base age 25) 60 ft, 800 trees per acre planted at ages 10, 30, and 50 years versus percentage of total basal area in hardwoods.

TABLE 8-4. Stand and Stock Tables for the Planted Component of Unthinned Loblolly Pine Plantations at Age 30 with 800 Trees per Acre Planted on Site Index 60 (Base Age 25) Land

Percentage of Basal Area in Hardwood = 0
(Arithmetic Mean DBH for Pine = 8.78 in.)

DBH Class (in.)	Trees/Acre (no.)	Total Height (ft)	Basal Area (ft²/acre)	Volumes (ft³ per acre)		
				Total[a]	Pulpwood[b]	Sawlog[c]
3	0.0	37.7	0.0	0.1		
4	1.9	47.0	0.2	4.3		
5	10.4	53.7	1.5	37.9	25.5	
6	29.0	58.7	5.8	156.5	125.2	
7	56.0	62.5	15.2	424.0	368.1	
8	81.8	65.5	28.7	830.6	754.4	556.5
9	91.3	68.0	40.4	1199.8	1119.8	912.1
10	76.1	70.0	41.3	1255.7	1192.8	1029.4
11	45.2	71.7	29.5	915.7	880.3	788.3
12	18.1	73.2	14.0	441.1	427.7	392.7
13	4.6	74.4	4.1	131.6	128.4	120.0
14	0.7	75.5	0.7	22.6	22.1	21.0
Totals	414.9		181.4	5419.9	5044.3	3819.9

TABLE 8-4. (*Continued*)

				Percentage of Basal Area in Hardwood = 20 (Arithmetic Mean DBH for Pine = 7.90 in.)		
				Volumes (ft³ per acre)		
DBH Class (in.)	Trees/Acre (no.)	Total Height (ft)	Basal Area (ft²/acre)	Total[a]	Pulpwood[b]	Sawlog[c]
3	1.3	37.6	0.1	1.7		
4	7.9	47.2	0.7	17.8		
5	23.0	54.1	3.2	83.3	56.0	
6	46.0	59.2	9.2	248.7	198.9	
7	69.5	63.2	18.7	528.3	458.7	
8	80.3	66.3	28.1	820.2	745.0	549.6
9	69.5	68.8	30.5	918.3	857.1	698.1
10	43.0	70.9	23.2	714.4	678.6	585.7
11	18.0	72.7	11.7	366.3	352.1	315.3
12	4.7	74.2	3.6	116.0	112.4	103.2
13	0.7	75.5	0.6	21.0	20.5	19.2
Totals	364.0		129.7	3836.2	3479.5	2271.1

TABLE 8-4. (*Continued*)

DBH Class (in.)	Trees/Acre (no.)	Total Height (ft)	Basal Area (ft²/acre)	Volumes (ft³ per acre)		
				Total[a]	Pulpwood[b]	Sawlog[c]
			Percentage of Basal Area in Hardwood = 40 (Arithmetic Mean DBH for Pine = 6.53 in.)			
2	0.8	23.3	0.0	0.5		
3	8.1	37.6	0.4	10.2		
4	23.8	47.8	2.2	52.9		
5	42.9	55.2	5.9	155.4	104.4	
6	56.1	60.8	11.1	306.5	245.1	
7	55.6	65.1	14.8	429.9	373.2	
8	41.7	68.5	14.4	434.5	394.7	291.1
9	23.2	71.3	10.1	313.9	293.0	238.7
10	9.3	73.6	5.0	159.0	151.0	130.3
11	2.6	75.5	1.7	55.0	52.8	47.3
Totals	264.0		65.7	1917.8	1614.4	707.5

[a]Total values include the total volume of all stems in the 1-in. DBH (outside bark) class and larger.
[b]Pulpwood values include the volume of all stems in the 5-in. DBH (outside bark) class and larger up to a 4-in. diameter (outside bark) top.
[c]Sawlog values include the volume of all stems in the 8-in. DBH (outside bark) class and larger up to a 6-in. diameter (outside bark) top.

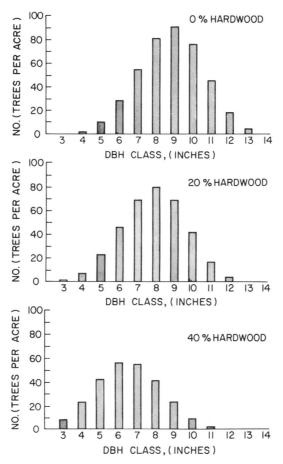

Figure 8-9. Loblolly pine DBH distribution for 0, 20, and 40% of the total stand basal area in hardwoods. These histograms are for age 30 with 800 trees per acre planted on site index (base age 25 years) 60 ft land.

Plots with pure pine and pure hardwood in the Fayette Study were used to estimate yield of Species A and B in pure stands, respectively. A RYT value was then computed for all other plots with a pine-hardwood mixture. The average RYT value for the data at age 11 was 0.75; at age 24 the average was 0.80. Because these RYT values are less than 1.0, they imply mutual antagonism. Consequently, the model characteristic of pine basal area and volume decreases being greater than a proportional increase in hardwood basal area seems plausible. Langdon and Trousdell (1974) observed impacts of competing hardwoods on the growth of loblolly pine in natural stands that were of the same general order of magnitude as those predicted by model HDWD for loblolly pine plantations.

Limitations

Model HDWD can be used to analyze the biological and economic implications of controlling hardwood competition to various levels prior to crown closure in loblolly pine plantations. There are, however, several limitations regarding the types of analyses that can be performed. Specifically they are as follows:

1. The levels of hardwood competition are not related to specific treatments. The proportion of basal area in hardwoods must be input by the users based on past experience, judgment, and local data if available.

2. The model does not account for any differences in competitive effects attributable to variation in hardwood species composition. The differential effects of various species of competing hardwoods have not been studied in sufficient detail to incorporate them into the model at the present time.

3. The model applies only to unthinned stands. If thinnings were carried out, some of the assumptions of the model (such as a constant ratio of hardwood basal area to total stand basal area) may not be valid.

4. Only analyses of hardwood competition in the main canopy can be performed. The effects of controlling understory vegetation and of controlling grasses and herbs at the time of seedling establishment cannot be evaluated. (It may be possible to model these effects through a shift in stand age, but more data are needed before recommendations can be made.)

5. Release treatments cannot be evaluated unless they are performed early in the life of the stand so that development of the released stand can be assumed to be the same as an unreleased plantation having the same level of hardwood competition. If the release treatment has a direct effect on the pine—such as causing mortality, a loss of a portion of a season's growth, or acting as a growth stimulant—then adjustment in the pine variables (trees surviving, age, site index) should be made to reflect these effects.

Although Model HDWD should be satisfactory for a wide range of analyses of the effects of hardwood competition on the growth and yield of loblolly pine plantations, for many vegetation treatments, plot data are too few in number or too short in duration to be adequate for modeling purposes. In these situations, observations from field studies can be used to provide insight into vegetation management effects.

SUMMARY

Based on data collected from numerous field studies, increasing levels of hardwood vegetation are strongly correlated with reductions in loblolly pine yield. One can logically conclude that competition from hardwoods is a major factor in these yield reductions. Nevertheless, high variability and inconsistent treatment effects were noted in several comparisons involving operational control of competing hardwoods. More consistent trends in pine response were evident in the research studies because of more uniform initial stand conditions and better control of competing hardwoods.

The relationship between the presence of hardwoods and subsequent pine performance permitted the development of a model to predict survival, growth, and yield for unthinned loblolly pine plantations with varying levels of hardwood competition in the main canopy. Inputs for the model are number of loblolly pine trees planted per acre, site index for loblolly pine, percentage of hardwood basal area in the main canopy of the stand, and age(s) at which output is desired. From these inputs the model computes, by 1-in. DBH classes, the number of pines surviving, basal area, and volumes per acre. Validation of the model with an independent data set revealed close agreement between the observed values and the model predictions. Stand simulations using the model indicate that the relative influence of hardwood competition on pine yield is greater than its proportional occupancy of the stand basal area, thereby implying mutual antagonism as the form of interference (see Chapter 5).

Studies on competition from herbaceous vegetation are not sufficiently advanced to permit modeling of its effects on loblolly pine growth and yield. However, the information that has been collected to date indicates a substantial and consistently positive growth response whenever herbaceous weeds are controlled. For example, total cubic volume of loblolly pine at age 10 has been doubled in some studies where good herbaceous weed control was maintained for the first 2 years. Thus control of herbaceous vegetation promises to accelerate young plantation development, thereby potentially shortening the time to harvest.

REFERENCES

Amateis, R.L. and H.E. Burkhart. 1985. Site index curves for loblolly pine plantations on cutover site-prepared lands. South. J. Appl. Forestry 9:166-169.

Burkhart, H.E. 1977. Cubic-foot volume of loblolly pine to any merchantable top limit. South. J. Appl. Forestry 1:7-9.

Burkhart, H.E., D.C. Cloeren, and R.L. Amateis. 1985. Yield relationships in unthinned loblolly pine plantations on cutover, site-prepared lands. South. J. Appl. Forestry 9:84-91.

Burkhart, H.E., R.C. Parker, M.R. Strub, and R.G. Oderwald. 1972. Yields of old-field loblolly pine plantations. Division of Forestry and Wildlife Resources, Virginia Polytechnic Institute and State Univ., Blacksburg, VA. Publ. FWS-3-72. 51 p.

Burkhart, H.E. and P.T. Sprinz. 1984. A model for assessing hardwood competition effects on yields of loblolly pine plantations. School of Forestry and Wildlife Resources, Virginia Polytechnic Institute and State Univ., Blacksburg, VA. Publ. FWS-3-84. 55 p.

Coile, T.S. and F.X. Schumacher. 1964. Soil-site relations, stand structure, and yields of slash and loblolly pine plantations in the southern United States. T.S. Coile, Inc., Durham, NC. 296 p.

Fitzgerald, C.H. 1976. Post-emergence effects of Velpar in a Piedmont pine plantation. *In* Proc., South. Weed Sci. Soc. 19:299.

Glover, G.R. 1986. Location, establishment, and treatment information for measured comparisons of loblolly pine response to various methods and degrees of weed control. Unpublished information on file at School of Forestry, Auburn Univ., Auburn, AL.

Glover, G.R. and D.F. Dickens. 1985. Impact of competing vegetation on yield of the southern pines. Georgia Forestry Commission, Macon, GA. Res. Pap. 59. 14 p.

Glover, G.R., S.A. Knowe, and D.H. Gjerstad. 1981. Fayette site preparation study—22 year results. Dept. Forestry, Auburn Univ., Auburn, AL. Silvicultural Herbicide Cooperative Res. Note 1. 8 p.

Holt, H.A., J.E. Voeller, and J.F. Young. 1975. Herbaceous vegetation control as a forest management practice. *In* Proc., South. Weed Sci. Soc. 18:219.

Knowe, S.A., L.R. Nelson, D.H. Gjerstad, B.R. Zutter, G.R.Glover, P.J. Minogue, and J.H. Dukes, Jr. 1985. Four-year growth and development of planted loblolly pine on sites with competition control. South. J. Appl. Forestry 9:11-15.

Langdon, O.G. and K.B. Trousdell. 1974. Increasing growth and yield of natural loblolly pine by young stand management, p. 288-296. *In* Proc., Symposium on Management of Young Pines, Alexandria, LA, and Charleston, SC. USDA Forest Service; Southeastern Area, State and Private Forestry; and Southern and Southeastern Forest Experiment Stations. 349 p.

Lange, K.D. 1951. Effects of clearcutting understory hardwoods on the growth of a shortleaf-Virginia pine stand. J. Forestry 49:176-177.

Michael, J.L. 1985. Growth of loblolly pine treated with hexazinone, sulfometuron methyl, and metsulfuron methyl for herbaceous weed control. South. J. Appl. Forestry 9:20-26.

Nelson, L.R., R.C. Pedersen, L.L. Autry, S. Dudley, and J.D. Walstad. 1981. Impacts of herbaceous weeds in young loblolly pine plantations. South. J. Appl. Forestry 5:153-158.

Smith, L.F. and R.G. Schmidtling. 1970. Cultivation and fertilization speed growth of planted southern pines. Tree Planters' Notes 21(1):1-3.

Whipple, S.D. and E.H. White. 1965. Response of planted loblolly pine following various conversion methods. Auburn Univ. Agr. Exper. Sta. Bull. 362. 26 p.

Zutter, B.R., G.R. Glover, and D.F. Dickens. 1985. Competing vegetation assessment systems in young southern pine plantations, p. 279-286. *In* Proc., Third Biennial Southern Silvicultural Research Conference, Atlanta, GA. USDA Forest Service, Southern Forest Experiment Station, New Orleans, LA. Gen. Tech. Rep. SO-54. 589 p.

9

Douglas-fir Growth and Yield Response to Vegetation Management

J. DOUGLAS BRODIE
JOHN D. WALSTAD

INTRODUCTION

Douglas-fir is the major timber tree species growing in both mixed and relatively pure stands throughout much of British Columbia, northern California, northern Idaho, Oregon, and Washington. The great commercial importance of this species has led to substantial investments in research and management, including the subject of Douglas-fir growth response to control of competing vegetation.

Vegetation control is an important part of Douglas-fir management because competition can greatly reduce the survival, growth, and development of this species. Individual Douglas-fir trees follow a relatively steep sigmoid growth curve characteristic of intolerant species grown in the absence of competition (see Chapter 7, Figure 7-4). Under competition, however, height growth of Douglas-fir may continue for many years but at the expense of crown development, root expansion, and diameter growth (Cole 1984). Suppressed Douglas-fir saplings have sparse crowns, spindly stems, and shade-adapted needles susceptible to sun damage when suddenly exposed to open growing conditions. Several years may pass before such trees respond to release treatments.

In this chapter, we will discuss the general pattern of Douglas-fir growth and development. This summary is based on information developed from several decades of research in the heart of the commercial range of Douglas-fir—western Oregon and Washington. We focus on *stand* development because the collective performance of Douglas-fir trees as a relatively even-aged stand usually determines the yield of this species.

Noncommercial forest sites and those of relatively low site quality are not considered here because management for timber production is generally of less importance on those sites. In addition, available stand simulation models, yield tables, and other biometric information are most reliable for the more productive Douglas-fir forest sites.

We offer several case-study examples to illustrate the response of young Douglas-fir stands to various degrees and types of competing vegetation. The response ranges from slight reductions in stocking and growth rate to virtual replacement of Douglas-fir by competing species. The case studies represent the kinds of competitive situations encountered throughout much of the range of Douglas-fir.

PARAMETERS AFFECTING DOUGLAS-FIR GROWTH AND YIELD

Site quality and silvicultural practices are the driving forces that affect the growth and yield of conifer forests (Figure 9-1). These parameters determine which species will colonize a particular site, their stocking and growth rate, their ultimate yield, and the time required for the stand to reach maturity.

Site quality, a large determinant of Douglas-fir productivity, is a function of soil properties and climatic conditions. Site quality thus varies from area to area, depending on such site characteristics as geological history, weathering rates of parent material, soil depth and texture, topography, rainfall patterns, and length of growing season.

Yield tables for natural stands of Douglas-fir are based on the yields of fully stocked, "normal," natural stands growing on sites of widely varying quality (McArdle 1961). Anticipated yields for natural stands of Douglas-fir range in site quality from I (high) to IV (low) (Table 9-1).

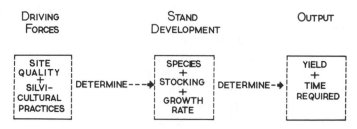

Figure 9-1. Conceptual relationship among the factors determining stand yield and rotation length.

TABLE 9-1. Yield of Natural and Managed Stands of Douglas-fir at Age 60 on Various Sites

Management Regime[a]	Site Class: Site Index$_{50}$:	IV 85	III 105	II 125	I 145
		Total cubic feet per acre			
Natural		6,121	8,612	11,357	14,416
Planted		6,007	8,832	12,031	15,426
Planted + commercial thinning		6,149	8,946	12,000	15,426
Precommercial and commercial thinning		6,724	9,675	13,038	16,767
Precommercial and commercial thinning + fertilization		8,375	11,744	15,149	18,916

Source: Site class is from McArdle et al. (1961). Site index (in ft at age 50) is from Curtis et al. (1982) and is converted from site index$_{100}$ given by McArdle et al. (1961) to site index$_{50}$ by King (1966).

[a]These management regimes are given in Curtis et al. (1982), and the total yield associated with each regime (exclusive of mortality) is derived from the following tables in their report for all trees 1.6 in. DBH and larger:

Regime	Table
Natural	1
Planted	2
Planted + commercial thinning	7
Precommercial and commercial thinning	9
Precommercial and commercial thinning + fertilization	12

Managed stand yield tables and simulation models for Douglas-fir have also been developed (Bruce et al. 1977, Curtis et al. 1981, 1982). Like natural stands, managed stand yields are strongly affected by site quality (Table 9-1). In addition, these mensurational guides show the importance to stand development of management practices such as planting, precommercial and commercial thinning, and fertilization.

Vegetation management treatments also affect tree growth rate. For example, conifer growth can be greatly accelerated by appropriately timed release treatments that reduce the size and competitiveness of surrounding weeds (Walstad 1982, Howard and Newton 1984, Stewart et al. 1984). Failure to control competing vegetation can prolong the time required for conifers to develop or can lead to mixed conifer-hardwood stands of comparatively low economic value (see Chapters 2 and 12).

Thus site quality, vegetative conditions, and management practices have an important bearing on both individual tree growth as well as stand development and yield. These parameters interact to form a matrix of outcomes as displayed in Figure 9-2. Where conifer stocking is dense and weeds are controlled, growth of individual conifer trees will be relatively slow, but stand yields will be high. Where propensities for veg-

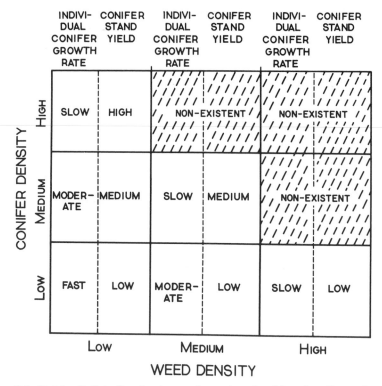

Figure 9-2. Matrix of silvicultural outcomes for various densities of conifers and weeds.

etative development are high, such as might be encountered on highly productive sites, failure to contol the weeds can lead to poor conifer stocking, slow growth, and low yields. In extreme cases, species such as red alder and bigleaf maple can exclude conifer development for extended periods of time, rendering conifer management nonexistent for all practical purposes. In more moderate cases, shrubs such as salmonberry and snowbrush can reduce the stocking and retard the growth of conifers.

The aforementioned factors ultimately determine the time required to grow a stand of merchantable timber. Without effective vegetation management, a century or more may pass before a merchantable stand of Douglas-fir and other conifers can develop. On the other hand, rotation lengths can be shortened to 60 yr or less and can be controlled more accurately where appropriate steps have been taken to reduce competing vegetation. Economic returns also can be enhanced by channeling most of the site productivity into a stand of well-distributed conifers rather than into species of less economic value or those having slower growth rates.

APPROACHES TO GROWTH AND YIELD ANALYSIS

Competing vegetation can influence the survival and growth of conifer stands long before they mature, so the economic impacts of weed competition must be projected for long periods of time. Such projections require a knowledge of long-term stand growth and yield with and without weed competition.

Failure to control competing vegetation in conifer stands can have four long-term consequences, three of which imply economic loss:

1. Low stocking levels resulting in reduced yields (the extreme case is complete displacement of the intended conifer crop by less valuable or noncommercial species).
2. Slow stand development, leading to delayed yield (or lower yield at any time before the end of the planned rotation).
3. Both low stocking levels and slow stand development, leading to reduced yields and longer rotations.
4. Temporary reductions in the rate of stand development which are offset by faster development later in the rotation, resulting in no loss in total yield or the time required to reach rotation age.

Growth and yield trajectories for the four situations are displayed in Figure 9-3. The first three scenarios lead to a loss in yield or an extended time required for the stands to reach silvicultural maturity (i.e., culmination of mean annual increment [MAI]). The fourth scenario is probably not realistic because stands suppressed in their initial development tend to continue to grow more slowly than those free to grow throughout the rotation.

The impact of competing vegetation on stand development may be forecast, given knowledge of the anticipated growth trajectory of a stand. There are two basic approaches to Douglas-fir yield forecasting. The first approach entails the use of yield tables based on empirical data gathered from fully stocked natural or managed stands. The second approach involves the use of dynamic models in which simulated stand development is based on established biometric relationships and sample plot data from managed stands.

The principal advantage of the yield table approach is its relative simplicity. One simply consults standard yield tables (e.g., McArdle et al. 1961) in the case of natural stands or analogous yield tables derived from biometrical simulators (e.g., Curtis et al. 1982) in the case of intensively managed stands and reduces the MAI by a fixed percentage, based on an estimate of the loss attributable to weed competition. The result is a yield estimate less than that for a stand that has developed relatively

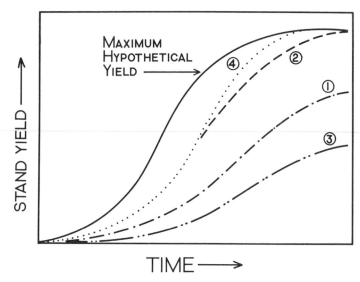

Figure 9-3. Possible scenarios for the growth and yield of conifer stands developing under the influence of competing nonconiferous vegetation. (1) lower stocking; (2) slower growth; (3) lower stocking and slower growth; and (4) slower initial growth that is later compensated for by faster growth. The "maximum hypothetical yield" is that for a fully stocked stand developing free of competing nonconiferous vegetation.

free of weed competition, the presumed basis for the natural and managed stand yield tables. Given the anticipated reduction in MAI, one alternatively can calculate the extra time required for the stand to reach merchantable size. In either case, the yield table approach is primarily a simple, straightforward way of comparing hypothetical outcomes. However, to accurately estimate the reduction in yield attributable to weeds, it is necessary to know how the competition affects specific stand parameters such as stocking, diameter growth, and height growth.

Thus a better approach to growth and yield analysis is to use models to project the development of stands through time, with the outcome dependent on variables such as initial stand conditions and silvicultural treatments. In this fashion, it is possible to simulate the development of weeded and unweeded stands under various management regimes. Managed stand simulators (models) that accurately project stand development through time are available for Douglas-fir (e.g., Bruce et al. 1977, Curtis et al. 1981).

Despite the availability of yield tables and simulation models for Douglas-fir, only recently could either be used confidently to forecast stand yields with and without vegetation management. Previously, quantitative information was not available on which to assess the long-term impact of competing vegetation on growth of western conifer species. Past assessments were forced to rely on assumptions of certain percentage reductions in yield due to weed competition, coupled with sensitivity tests of the outcomes of various scenarios to estimate where the greatest gains in vegetation management were likely to occur (e.g., 2,4,5-T Assessment Team [1979], Stavins et al. [1981], Green [1983]). This approach was the best that could be taken when the cited studies were done because there was no long-term quantitative information. Now, however, a data base is available to more accurately predict the long-term effects of vegetation management.

CASE STUDIES

In this section we present results from several case studies and describe how they can be used in conjunction with conventional yield tables and simulation models to predict the benefits of vegetation management in Douglas-fir silviculture. These case studies are less precise than the specially designed experiments now underway, but they do illustrate the general patterns and consequences likely to occur as a result of interspecific competition.

Competing vegetation can reduce conifer stand yields by reducing stocking, reducing growth rate, or by reducing both stocking and growth rate. Reduced stocking occurs when competing vegetation either (1) dominates developing conifer seedlings to the point where mortality ensues; or (2) prevents seedling establishment in the first place. Reduced stocking can result in stands ranging from only marginal stocking to virtual elimination or displacement of conifers by less desirable species such as red alder. Alternatively, encroaching and overtopping vegetation can retard the growth of developing conifers, thereby delaying stand maturity relative to one free to grow. The following case studies illustrate the effects of vegetative competition on conifer stocking and growth rate.

Siuslaw National Forest (Impact: Reduced Stocking)

An analysis by Knapp et al. (1984) of Douglas-fir plantations on the Siuslaw National Forest in western Oregon provides an example of the impact of competing vegetation on conifer stocking level. A combination of plantation records and professional experience was used to develop stocking outcomes from various methods of controlling competing vegetation.

The Siuslaw National Forest, centered in the Oregon Coast Range, occupies 568,000 acres. Site index for Douglas-fir—the main conifer species—is 135 ft, 50-year basis. Western hemlock, western redcedar, and Sitka spruce are common conifer associates of Douglas-fir in this area. Competing vegetation consists primarily of red alder but includes several other shrubs such as salmonberry, thimbleberry, and vine maple. Competition from these species occurs primarily on north- and east-facing slopes, which constitute about 10% (58,000 acres) of the Forest where mixed conifer-hardwood types occur.

In the absence of vegetation control on north- and east-facing slopes of the Forest, where mixed conifer-hardwood types prevail, the expected MAI volume growth for conifers will decline from 250 ft^3/acre/year to 157 ft^3/acre/year over a 75-year rotation, a 37% reduction primarily as a result of reduced stocking. Over the past several decades, experience with these areas of the Forest indicates that adequate site preparation, good planting techniques, and well-timed release treatments will produce "fully stocked" stands of well-distributed conifers (i.e., 260 trees/acre) within 5 to 7 years. Without release, the best that can be expected is a "low stocking" of conifers (150 trees/acre) or conversion to essentially pure hardwoods of comparatively low economic value.

The difference in yield between "full conifer stocking" (18,750 ft^3/acre) and "low conifer stocking" (11,775 ft^3/acre) is 6975 ft^3/acre at rotation age 75 years. This loss in yield due to competition does not take into account the additional economic loss associated with lengthening the rotation of poorly stocked stands to achieve the culmination of MAI before harvest; it simply takes longer for sparsely spaced trees growing in the middle of competing vegetation to reach their maximum rate of growth.

Toledo Cutoff Unit (Impact: Species Displacement)

The Toledo Cutoff Unit is located in southwestern Washington on gently sloping clay loam soil at an elevation of about 600 ft. Site index for Douglas-fir is estimated to be 125 ft, 50-year basis.

The unit was logged and burned in 1944 and left to regenerate naturally. When examined in the mid 1950s, Douglas-fir stocking was amply distributed throughout the unit but under competition from sapling-sized red alder. In June 1957, most of the unit was aerially sprayed with a herbicide. The eastern and southern portions of the unit were not sprayed because of nearby property lines. Posttreatment evaluation indicated that red alder was effectively controlled in the treated portion of the unit (Lauterbach 1967). No other silvicultural treatments have been applied to the unit since it was treated.

A 1982 survey showed that the treated area of the unit consisted largely of Douglas-fir (75% canopy cover), but the untreated portion was dominated by red alder (75% cover). When the unit was remeasured in 1983 (Walstad et al. 1986), there were significant differences between treated and untreated areas in Douglas-fir stocking and basal area (Table 9-2). Dominance of red alder in the untreated area virtually excluded the development of Douglas-fir, with the exception of a few isolated trees.

DFSIM, a growth and yield model for Douglas-fir (Curtis et al. 1981),

TABLE 9-2. Age, Stocking Level, Basal Area, and DBH of Douglas-fir in the Treated and Untreated Areas within Each Study Unit at the Time of Measurement[a]

Unit	Stand Age (years)[b]	Treatment	Stocking Level (no. trees/acre)	Mean Basal Area (ft²/acre)	Mean DBH (in.)
Toledo Cutoff	30-39	Treated	200*	132*	10.3
		Untreated	16	9	10.2
Oxbow Burn	12-18	Treated	223[c]	20*	4.0*
		Untreated	223[c]	17	3.1

[a]Where marked by an asterisk (*), differences between treated and untreated areas within each unit are statistically significant at the 95% level, according to Student's t-statistic.

[b]Range based on period of time required for stand regeneration.

[c]Although no differences in stocking were detected between the treated and untreated areas at the Oxbow Burn unit, the treated area was precommercially thinned 2 years before these measurements were taken. No precommercial thinning of the untreated area was performed, suggesting that excessive competition from varnishleaf ceanothus had already reduced the stocking such that thinning was not required.

was used to estimate the anticipated yields at rotation age for the treated area as a function of the assumptions given in Table 9-3. For the untreated area, age-based normal yield tables (Worthington et al. 1960) were used to forecast the volume of red alder at rotation age. The differential yields projected for the treated and untreated areas are shown in Table 9-3. The treated area is expected to provide a typical yield of high-value Douglas-fir for this site index, whereas the untreated area will be limited to red alder.

Alder/Douglas-fir Mixture (Impact: Reduced Growth)

A few Douglas-fir survived dense competition from red alder in the un-treated portion of the Toledo Cutoff Unit. Detailed stem analysis of these trees (Walstad et al. 1986) and of similar dominants growing in the adjacent Douglas-fir area revealed distinctly different patterns of height and diameter growth (Figure 9-4). Diameter increment at breast height for the Douglas-fir growing in competition with codominant red alder was substantially reduced. Height growth was not reduced because height growth of intolerant conifer species must at least equal the growth of competing vegetation if the conifers are to survive and develop. Numerous studies have shown that diameter growth is usually the parameter most sensitive to competition, whether interspecific or intraspecific.

The impacts of such competition at the stand level can be forecast with DFSIM simulations for two hypothetical stands—one of pure Douglas-fir, and the other a mixture of Douglas-fir and red alder. The yield forecast that follows is only for the Douglas-fir component in the respective stands because yield simulators for the development of red alder were unavailable at the time the analysis was performed. Several assumptions are also required in order to run the DFSIM simulations. First an equivalent number of Douglas-fir trees per unit area must be assigned to each stand at a specified age. In the simulations described in Table 9-4, 200 trees/acre at age 33 have been used as a standard reference point. This stocking level approximates that for the relatively pure Douglas-fir stand in the Toledo Cutoff Unit. Differential in quadratic mean diameter must also be specified for the Douglas-fir growing in the pure and mixed stands. In the example given in Table 9-4, the Douglas-fir in the pure stand have been assigned an average of 10.0 in. DBH, similar to the average diameter of the relatively pure Douglas-fir area. Douglas-fir in the mixed stand have been assigned an average of 7.0 in. DBH, a reduction proportional to that recorded for the dominant Douglas-fir measured by stem analysis in the Douglas-fir and red alder areas in the Toledo Cutoff Unit at age 33 (Walstad et al. 1986).

A third assumption pertains to the DFSIM specifications for site index, stand origin, thinning, harvest age, and other pertinent management criteria (see Table 9-4 and attendant footnotes).

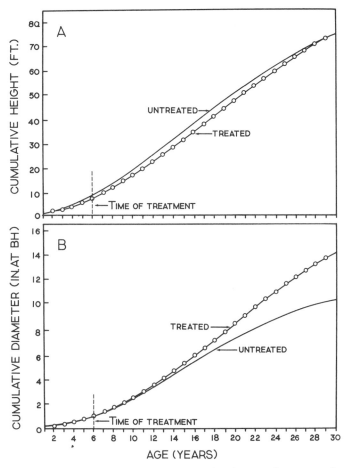

Figure 9-4. (A) Height and (B) diameter at breast height growth patterns for dominant Douglas-fir trees in the treated and untreated areas at the Toledo Cutoff Unit. (*Source:* After McGinley 1984)

A final assumption involves the DFSIM model itself, which was developed for relatively pure stands of Douglas-fir. We have assumed that the model can also be applied to Douglas-fir growing in mixture with red alder. This assumption was necessary pending the refinement and validation of models for mixed stands of Douglas-fir and red alder, such as that recently developed by Arney (1985). In any event, the results projected in Table 9-4 appear to be reasonable and are probably conservative because the competitive impact of red alder beyond age 33 is not considered in the analysis; that is, the two stands are projected beyond age 33 as if both are pure Douglas-fir. One stand starts at an average DBH of 10.0 in., whereas the other starts at 7.0 in. Thus the initial impact of the

TABLE 9-3. Comparison of Stand Development under Simulated Management Regimes with and without a Release Treatment at the Toledo Cutoff Unit. The Released Area Develops into a Douglas-fir Stand, whereas the Untreated Area Becomes a Red Alder Stand[a]

Stand Age[b] (years)	Treatment or Activity[c]	Species	Mean Stand DBH[d] (in.)	Stocking or (Removals)[d] (trees/acre)	Basal Area[d] (ft²/acre)	Merchantable Volume[e] (ft³/acre)
			Treated Area[f]			
0	Site prep & natural seeding	Douglas-fir	—	—	—	—
6	Release	Douglas-fir	—	400	—	—
33	Measurement	Douglas-fir	10.3	200	132	—
45	Stand exam	Douglas-fir	14.0	187	199	7,173
	Commercial thin	Douglas-fir	12.6	(114)	99	3,572
	Residual stand	Douglas-fir	15.9	72	100	3,601
60	Final yield	Douglas-fir	20.6	(72)	166	7,182
	Total yield	Douglas-fir	—	(186)	265	10,754

Untreated Area[f]

Age[b]	Site prep & natural seeding[c]	Species				
0	Site prep & natural seeding	Douglas-fir	—	—	—	—
33	Measurement	Red alder	9.3	272	127	—
50[g]	Final yield	Red alder	13.6	(165)	166	6,680
	Total yield	Red alder	—	(165)	166	6,680

[a]For additional descriptive information on this unit, see Walstad et al. (1986).

[b]Although the actual age of trees within each stand varies (due to the extended period of regeneration), a single stand age has been used at each interval in order to simplify the analyses. It is based on the average age of the trees measured by stem analysis.

[c]For simplicity, only major silvicultural treatments and activities are included in the prescribed management regimes for treated and untreated stands. Furthermore, the treatments have been standardized in order to streamline the analyses. Measurement age represents stand conditions at the time of the most recent survey.

[d]Current stand parameters for Douglas-fir and red alder are derived from regeneration surveys or current measurement data. Future projections to final harvest for Douglas-fir are based on DFSIM stand simulations (Curtis et al. 1981) using current stand parameters and estimated site indexes as projection criteria. Projections are constrained such that 100 ft^2/acre of basal area remains after the commercial thinning of Douglas-fir at age 45. Future projections for red alder at the Toledo Cutoff Unit are derived from normal yield tables (Worthington et al. 1960) using current stand conditions and the estimated site index as projection criteria.

[e]Merchantable volume to a 4-in. diameter top is derived from stand simulations (Douglas-fir), or normal yield tables (red alder). Volumes are based on Douglas-fir 7.6 in. DBH and larger and red alder 5.5 in. DBH and larger.

[f]Projections beyond age 33 are based on current stand conditions as determined from survey data. Site index$_{50}$ is estimated to be 125 ft for Douglas-fir and 110 ft for red alder.

[g]A rotation age of 50 years was used for red alder because natural mortality of merchantable trees of this species commonly begins at age 50 (Worthington et al. 1960).

TABLE 9-4. Comparison of Stand Development under Simulated Management Regimes with and without Release Treatment, Leading to a Relatively Pure Douglas-fir Stand and a Mixed Douglas-fir/Red Alder Stand, Respectively[a-f]

Stand Age[b] (years)	Treatment or Activity[c]	Species	Mean Stand DBH[d] (in.)	Stocking or (Removals)[d] (trees/acre)	Basal Area[d] (ft²/acre)	Merchantable Volume[e] (ft³/acre)
Relatively pure Douglas-fir stand						
0	Site prep & natural seeding	Douglas-fir	—	—	—	—
6	Release	Douglas-fir	—	—	—	—
33	Measurement	Douglas-fir	10.0	200	109	—
45	Stand exam	Douglas-fir	13.5	167	168	6,109
	Commercial thin	Douglas-fir	12.1	(85)	68	2,461
	Residual stand	Douglas-fir	14.9	82	100	3,648
60	Final yield	Douglas-fir	17.9	(92)[g]	162	7,162
	Total yield	Douglas-fir	—	(177)	230	9,623
Mixed Douglas-fir/red alder stand[h]						
0	Site prep & natural seeding	Douglas-fir	—	—	—	—
33	Measurement	Douglas-fir	7.0	200	54	—
45	Stand exam[i]	Douglas-fir	9.4	198	95	3,015
	Final yield	Douglas-fir	13.4	(138)	135	5,995
60	Total yield	Douglas-fir	—	(138)	135	5,995

[a]See Table 9-3 for explanation of footnotes *a–e.*

[f]These simulations are based on hypothetical stands because no *bona fide* study areas or case histories could be found to analyze the effect of reduced Douglas-fir growth as a result of competition from red alder. Consequently, the stand conditions at measurement age (33 years) are derived from stem analysis relationships and current stocking and average diameter for Douglas-fir in the treated area at the Toledo Cutoff Unit (Walstad et al. 1986). Site index $_{50}$ for Douglas-fir is estimated to be 125 ft.

[g]The increase in the number of trees per acre from 82 to 92 over the 15-year period is a result of ingrowth of trees that were present in the stand at age 45 but were not tallied at the time because they were less than 7.6 in. in DBH.

[h]Stand characteristics shown include only the Douglas-fir component because insufficient information exists to project the development of red alder in mixture with Douglas-fir.

[i]Insufficient basal area exists for this stand at age 45 to justify a commercial thinning.

red alder competition is a 3.0 in. difference in Douglas-fir DBH at age 33, and the impact of this differential is projected through to rotation age.

Given these assumptions and conditions, the estimated impact of red alder competition on Douglas-fir yield is shown in Table 9-4. The pure stand of Douglas-fir is expected to yield a total of 9623 ft^3/acre, whereas the Douglas-fir in the mixed stand is forecast to produce only 5995 ft^3/acre over the 60-year rotation. Thus a substantial decline in yield (or a considerably longer rotation for an equivalent yield) is forecast for Douglas-fir growing in competition with red alder.

There is some evidence, based on empirical observations (M. Newton, personal communication), that sparsely scattered Douglas-fir trees greatly accelerate in growth once they emerge through a red alder canopy. However, red alder can maintain its dominant position over Douglas-fir for 30 to 50 years, so it is unlikely that emerging Douglas-fir could overtake their counterparts growing in a relatively pure conifer stand. Certainly more time than rotation periods of 60 to 70 years would be required, and overall softwood yields would still be considerably less due to the low stocking.

If one were to add the volume of red alder to the Douglas-fir yields in the mixed stand, then a case might be made that species mixtures are advantageous. Indeed, Miller and Murray (1978) have recorded a higher total yield (at age 44) for a mixed stand of red alder and Douglas-fir than for a pure stand of Douglas-fir. However, this site represents a special case (see Chapter 2); the more typical situation is for red alder to severely impede the development of young Douglas-fir whenever the two species are established simultaneously. Furthermore, any efforts to manage mixed stands of Douglas-fir and red alder must take their respective economic values into consideration. Historically, stumpage prices for Douglas-fir have been several times those for red alder. Even in the early 1980s when Douglas-fir stumpage prices in coastal Oregon dropped from $350 per thousand board feet (MBF) to less than $200 per MBF, red alder stumpage remained at about $40 per MBF. Such stumpage prices for red alder are often insufficient for an owner to recover the costs of sale preparation, harvesting, and reforestation. Based on existing markets, the wide differential in value between Douglas-fir and red alder is expected to continue into the foreseeable future (Poppino and Gedney 1984). Attractive opportunities do exist, however, for alternating rotations of red alder and Douglas-fir, particularly where soils are deficient in nitrogen (Tarrant et al. 1983).

Oxbow Burn Unit (Impact: Reduced Stocking and Growth)

The Oxbow Burn, located in the interior portion of the Oregon Coast Range, contains a unit that can be used to demonstrate the impact of competing vegetation on both conifer stocking and growth. The unit is situated on a gentle south-facing slope with clay loam soil at about 650 ft elevation. Douglas-fir site index is estimated to be 128-ft on a 50-year basis.

The east side of the unit was logged in the 1960s, as were parts of the west side. In 1966, the entire unit was burned in an extensive wildfire (the Oxbow Burn) that covered 43,000 acres. The unit was aerially seeded with Douglas-fir during the winter of 1966-1967. The seeding resulted in spotty stocking, particularly on the east side. Consequently, the east side was interplanted in 1970 and again in 1971. Timber remaining on the west side of the unit was salvaged in 1968, and that side was aerially seeded again in early 1969 to ensure satisfactory stocking.

Seeds of varnishleaf ceanothus germinated throughout the unit after the fire, and in the early 1970s the east side of the unit was aerially sprayed with herbicides to release the young Douglas-fir. Stand examinations in 1975 indicated that 70% of the trees on the released east side were free to grow, whereas trees on the untreated west side were still largely suppressed by the dense cover of ceanothus. A 1982 survey indicated that conifer canopy cover was about 35% on the treated east side

Figure 9-5. View of the Oxbow Burn site showing treated and untreated areas at the time of measurement. Douglas-fir in the treated area on the right have achieved crown closure, whereas in the untreated area on the left they are still struggling to emerge from a dense canopy of varnishleaf ceanothus.

but only about 5% on the untreated west side. Conversely, ceanothus occupied only about 5% of the canopy of the treated side but more than 75% of that of the untreated side.

The unit was remeasured in 1983 when the trees were 12 to 18 yr old (Walstad et al. 1986). Average DBH of Douglas-fir was 4 in. on the treated area and about 3 in. on the untreated area (Table 9-2), a significant difference presumably caused by competition from ceanothus. Stocking was not different between the two areas, despite the treated area's having been thinned precommercially 2 years before measurements were made, suggesting a possible effect of competition from ceanothus in reducing stocking. Furthermore, visual observations (Figure 9-5) indicated that stocking distribution was much more uniform on the treated side of the unit, which should facilitate future management activities and improve product uniformity and value at harvest.

Projecting the growth (DFSIM) of these two equally stocked portions of the unit to the end of the rotation indicates that the treated side will produce about 1450 ft^3/acre more Douglas-fir than the untreated side (11,378 ft^3/acre, versus 9927 ft^3/acre) (Table 9-5).

EXTENDING CASE STUDIES TO CURRENT AND FUTURE SILVICULTURAL CONDITIONS

The case studies just described have important implications for much of the Northwest because they bracket most of the stand conditions encountered in vegetation management. For example, shrubs and hardwoods of low economic value occupy more than 4 million acres of cut- and burned-over land in this region that were previously occupied by high-value conifers (Gratkowski et al. 1973). Thus conditions such as those encountered at the Toledo Cutoff Unit and the Oxbow Burn Unit are common. Such areas are usually treated in one of two fashions: (1) where conifer stocking is sufficient, one or more applications of selective herbicides is applied to ensure eventual dominance of the conifers, as was done in the case studies; and (2) where conifer stocking is inadequate, foresters often resort to stand conversion or rehabilitation. This entails harvesting, slashing, burning, or otherwise disposing of the unwanted woody vegetation and then restocking the area with conifers. Many nonstocked and poorly stocked areas in the coastal ranges of Oregon and Washington have been reclaimed in this fashion. Efforts to restore conifer stands continue in other highly productive areas of the Northwest where such economic investments are deemed profitable.

With the advent of intensive forest management, the need for multiple release treatments and stand conversion operations has become less frequent. Thorough site preparation, coupled with planting of vigorous conifer stock and protection from animal damage, generally ensures

TABLE 9-5. Comparison of Stand Development under Simulated Management Regimes with and without Release Treatments at the Oxbow Burn Unit. Both the Treated and Untreated Areas Develop into Douglas-fir Stands, but the Untreated Area is Characterized by Lower Initial Stocking and Slower Growth[a]

Stand Age[b] (years)	Treatment or Activity[c]	Species	Mean Stand DBH[d] (in.)	Stocking or (Removals)[d] (trees/acre)	Basal Area[d] (ft²/acre)	Merchantable Volume[e] (ft³/acre)
				Treated Area[f]		
0	Site prep & aerial seeding or plant	Douglas-fir	—	—	—	—
2	Release	Douglas-fir	—	400	—	—
4	Release	Douglas-fir	—	400	—	—
15	Precommercial thin	Douglas-fir	—	—	—	—
	Measurement	Douglas-fir	4.0	223	20	—
45	Stand exam	Douglas-fir	14.5	183	210	7,698
	Commercial thin	Douglas-fir	13.1	(118)	110	4,033
	Residual stand	Douglas-fir	16.9	64	100	3,664
60	Final yield	Douglas-fir	21.9	(64)	167	7,345
	Total yield	Douglas-fir	—	(182)	277	11,378
				Untreated Area[f]		
0	Site prep & aerial seeding	Douglas-fir	—	—	—	—
15	Measurement	Douglas-fir	3.1	223	17	—
45	Stand exam	Douglas-fir	12.7	198	175	6,342
	Commercial thin	Douglas-fir	11.4	(104)	75	2,605
	Residual stand	Douglas-fir	14.0	93	100	3,738
60	Final yield	Douglas-fir	17.9	(92)	161	7,322
	Total yield	Douglas-fir	—	(196)	235	9,927

[a]See Table 9-3 for explanation of footnotes a–e.
[f]Projections beyond age 15 are based on current stand conditions as determined from the survey by Walstad et al. (1986). Site index $_{50}$ for Douglas-fir is estimated to be 128 ft.

successful establishment of a conifer crop. Such practices delay the resurgence of competing shrubs and hardwoods and allow the conifers to gain control of the site at an early age. Restrictions on aerial application of herbicides for release purposes, particularly on federal land, have also led to more emphasis on initial stand establishment, thereby reducing the need for subsequent release treatments.

If release treatments are still needed, they are applied early in the rotation in order to prevent weed development that requires costly corrective action later in the life of the stand. This practice not only promotes seedling survival but also enhances juvenile growth rates. In many instances, early weed control treatments are directed at herbaceous vegetation. This approach fosters rapid conifer development (Figure 9-6), thereby minimizing the chance of overtopping or suppression by hardwood and shrub species.

Recent trends in forest vegetation management have led to a systems approach in which early investments in site preparation, planting, protection, and release reduce the need for expensive remedial actions later in the life of the stand. For when corrective actions are delayed too long, the losses caused by weed competition may never be recovered. Intensive vegetation management procedures during the initial stages of plantation establishment also facilitate other silvicultural practices. Animal damage control is more feasible, adequate stocking levels are easier to maintain,

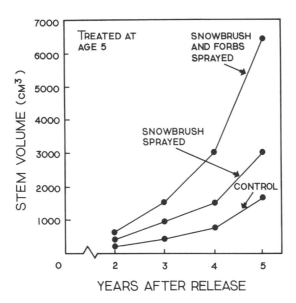

Figure 9-6. Stem volume growth of Douglas-fir saplings after release at age 5. (*Source:* From Peterson and Newton 1985)

stand fertilization and thinning can be done at an earlier age, and yield projections are more reliable due to more uniform stocking and growth.

SUMMARY

The effects of competing vegetation on the growth and yield of Douglas-fir have been considered in this chapter. Several empirical case studies illustrate the major impacts of competing vegetation on conifer stand development. Weeds compete by reducing conifer stocking, conifer growth, or both stocking and growth. The extent of the reductions is a function of the type and severity of competition and the stage of conifer development. For example, a sparse cover of ceanothus sprouts may reduce growth of well-established Douglas-fir saplings only moderately or not at all, whereas a dense red alder thicket can virtually eliminate Douglas-fir seedlings.

Silvicultural outcomes of vegetation management can be predicted. Simulation models can be used to project stand development under different management regimes in a manner similar to that done for the case studies described in this chapter. One simply adjusts the stocking level or the growth rate in order to account for the anticipated effect of competing vegetation.

Research in progress will improve methods of predicting conifer growth and yield associated with vegetation management. As silvicultural practices become more intensive and are implemented earlier in the rotation, the long-term effects of such treatments will need to be accurately projected. Ideally, the relationship between degrees of weed competition and subsequent conifer development will be quantified and included in simulation models in a way analogous to thinning and fertilization effects. Well designed experiments will provide the information needed to construct mensurational guides and the adjustment factors required to accurately forecast stand development under various levels of vegetation management.

REFERENCES

Arney, J.D. 1985. SPS: Stand Projection System for mini- and micro-computers. J. Forestry 83:378.

Bruce, D., D.J. DeMars, and D.L. Reukema. 1977. Douglas-fir managed yield simulator—DFIT user's guide. USDA Forest Service, Pacific Northwest Forest and Range Experiment Station, Portland, OR. Gen. Tech. Rep. PNW-57. 26 p.

Cole, E.C. 1984. Fifth-year growth responses of Douglas-fir to crowding and other competition. M.S. thesis, College of Forestry, Oregon State Univ., Corvallis, OR. 321 p.

Curtis, R.O., G.W. Clendenen, and D.J. DeMars. 1981. A new stand simulator for coast Douglas-fir: DFSIM user's guide. USDA Forest Service, Pacific Northwest Forest and Range Experiment Station, Portland, OR. Gen. Tech Rep. PNW-128. 79 p.

Curtis, R.O., G.W. Clendenen, D.L. Reukema, and D.J. DeMars. 1982. Yield tables for managed stands of coast Douglas-fir. USDA Forest Service, Pacific Northwest Forest and Range Experiment Station, Portland, OR. Gen. Tech. Rep. PNW-135. 182 p.

Gratkowski, H., D. Hopkins, and P. Lauterbach. 1973. Rehabilitation of forest land. The Pacific Coast and Northern Rocky Mountain Region. J. Forestry 71:138-143.

Green, K. 1983. Forests, herbicides and people. A case study of phenoxy herbicides in western Oregon. Council on Economic Priorities. New York, NY. 203 p.

Howard, K.M. and M. Newton. 1984. Overtopping by successional Coast-Range vegetation slows Douglas-fir seedlings. J. Forestry 82:178-180.

King, J.E. 1966. Site index curves for Douglas-fir in the Pacific Northwest. Weyerhaeuser Forestry Research Center, Weyerhaeuser Co., Centralia, WA. Weyerhaeuser Forestry Pap. 8. 49 p.

Knapp, W.H., T.C. Turpin, and J.H. Beuter. 1984. Vegetation control for Douglas-fir regeneration on the Siuslaw National Forest: a decision analysis. J. Forestry 82:168-173.

Lauterbach, P.G. 1967. Chemical weeding and release of conifers in western Oregon and Washington, p. 148-151. *In* Symposium Proc., Herbicides and Vegetation Management in Forests, Ranges, and Non-crop Lands. College of Forestry, Oregon State Univ., Corvallis, OR. 356 p.

McArdle, R.E., W.H. Meyer, and D. Bruce. 1961. The yield of Douglas-fir in the Pacific Northwest. U.S. Dept. Agr., Washington, DC. Tech. Bull. 201. 72 p.

McGinley, B.C. 1984. A statistical analysis of vegetation management effects on Douglas-fir growth. M.F. paper, Forest Management Department, College of Forestry, Oregon State Univ., Corvallis, OR. 42 p.

Miller, R.E. and M.D. Murray. 1978. The effects of red alder on growth of Douglas-fir, p. 283-306. *In* Briggs, D.G., D.S. DeBell, and W.A. Atkinson (comps.) Utilization and management of alder. USDA Forest Service, Pacific Northwest Forest and Range Experiment Station, Portland, OR. Gen. Tech. Rep. PNW-70. 379 p.

Petersen, T.D. and M. Newton. 1985. Growth of Douglas-fir following control of snowbrush and herbaceous vegetation in Oregon. Dow Chemical Co., Midland, MI. Down to Earth 41(1):21-25.

Poppino, J.H. and D.R. Gedney. 1984. The hardwood resource in western Oregon. USDA Forest Service, Pacific Northwest Forest and Range Experiment Station, Portland, OR. Resource Bull. PNW-116. 37 p.

Stavins, R.N., D.L. Galt, and K.L. Eckhouse. 1981. An economic analysis of alternative vegetation management practices in commercial forests of the Pacific Coast region. Cooperative Extension and Giannini Foundation of Agricultural Economics, Univ. California, Berkeley, CA. Project Rep. 2. 66 p.

Stewart, R.E., L.L. Gross, and B.H. Honkala. 1984. Effects of competing vegetation on forest trees: a bibliography with abstracts. USDA Forest Service, Washington, DC. Gen. Tech. Rep. WO-43. 260 p.

Tarrant, R.F., B.T. Bormann, D.S. DeBell, and W.A. Atkinson. 1983. Managing red alder in the Douglas-fir region: some possibilities. J. Forestry 81:787-792.

2,4,5-T Assessment Team. 1979. The biologic and economic assessment of 2,4,5-T. Cooperative Impact Assessment Report, U.S. Dept. Agr., Washington, DC. Tech. Bull. 1671. 445 p. plus supplement.

Walstad, J.D. 1982. Increasing fiber production through intensive forest management: Opportunities through vegetation management, p. 46-50. *In* Increasing forest productivity. Proc., Soc. Amer. Foresters 1981 Nat. Conv., Orlando, FL. SAF Publ. 82-01. 368 p.

Walstad, J.D., J.D. Brodie, B.C. McGinley, and C.A. Roberts. 1986. Silvicultural value of chemical brush control in the management of Douglas-fir. Western J. Appl. Forestry. 1:69-73.

Worthington, N.P., F.A. Johnson, G.R. Staebler, and W.J. Lloyd. 1960. Normal yield tables for red alder. USDA Forest Service, Pacific Northwest Forest and Range Experiment Station, Portland, OR. Res. Pap. 36. 29 p.

10

Evaluation of Growth and Yield Responses to Vegetation Management of the Mixed-Conifer Forests in the Inland Northwest

ALBERT R. STAGE
RAYMOND J. BOYD, JR.

INTRODUCTION

Mixed-conifer forests of the Inland Northwest (northern Idaho, western Montana, and northeastern Oregon and Washington) differ from the forests of the other regions described in corresponding chapters in two important respects for vegetation management. First, the major tree species are all conifers, and all have commercial value. Hardwoods that attain tree sizes—birch, aspen, and cottonwood—occur in limited ecological niches. Therefore, they seldom pose a management problem. Other hardwoods such as cherry and mountain maple are tall shrubs. This life form competes with conifers only during the early stages of development of even-aged conifer stands. Therefore, these latter species, along with other shrubs, forbs, and grasses, comprise the major competitors of young conifers in this region (see Chapter 2).

The second difference is that most stands in this region consist of rich mixtures of conifer species. Depending on the habitat type, a single stand may contain as many as 7 of the 11 significant species:

Douglas-fir	(*Pseudotsuga menziesii*)
Engelmann spruce	(*Picea engelmannii*)
Grand fir	(*Abies grandis*)
Lodgepole pine	(*Pinus contorta*)
Mountain hemlock	(*Tsuga mertensiana*)

Ponderosa pine	(*Pinus ponderosa*)
Subalpine fir	(*Abies lasiocarpa*)
Western hemlock	(*Tsuga heterophylla*)
Western larch	(*Larix occidentalis*)
Western redcedar	(*Thuja plicata*)
Western white pine	(*Pinus monticola*)

Habitat types defined by the potential climax community have been developed by Daubenmire and Daubenmire (1968), Pfister et al. (1977), and Steele et al. (1981). Successional pathways to these climax communities depend on the nature of the disturbance. Developmental sequences can involve all of the species except western white pine and western larch in both seral and climax roles, depending on the habitat type. The two exceptions are always seral.

Decisions concerning vegetation management in Inland Northwest forests are of two types: strategic harvest-level decisions and tactical stand-level decisions (see Chapters 11 and 12). Strategic decisions, which usually involve many stands, have seldom considered much detail about silvicultural practices other than the classical regeneration system to be employed (i.e., whether clearcut, seed-tree, shelterwood, or selection) and choice of thinning regime to control conifer competition. Although general costs and effects of vegetation management may have been implicitly included in strategic analyses, lack of definitive data has prevented including specific vegetation management alternatives in these analyses. New data and models of vegetation development and its response to treatment presented in this chapter have the capability to change this situation. The methods we describe are still limited by the scope of the response data. Although the new data represent important situations, many more plant communities and a wider range of climatic conditions still need to be sampled.

Choice among alternative treatments for a particular stand is the second type of decision that can be guided by the methods we describe. Stand-level decisions define materials and methods to be used and timing for treatments of specific stands. Choices should be based on comparisons of estimated effects derived from stand examinations of relevant site and stand conditions (see Chapter 13).

The first step in a rational approach to vegetation management is to define where there is (or is likely to be) a problem. *Hazard analysis*, to borrow a term from forest pest management, can help define the geographic and ecologic scope of the problem within the Inland Northwest. Once the problem has been delineated, specific inventory data should be collected in sufficient detail to allow prediction of responses to treatment alternatives that seem appropriate for the problem. Because vegetation management options at the time of stand establishment can have long-range effects on relative stocking, species composition, and stand development, comparisons should recognize species differences in growth and value when development is projected to the final harvest of the stand.

This chapter describes procedures whereby such projections can be made for the mixed-conifer type of the Inland Northwest. Analytic procedures for summarizing the short-term response data into a form suitable for predicting the longer term responses are also provided.

Several case examples are also presented, illustrating the use of these procedures to forecast responses of mixed-conifer stands to vegetation management practices. To use these procedures requires data from experimental trials of vegetation management practices. Leads to sources of such data, which will be available when sufficient time has passed to assess the growth responses, are also provided.

YIELD FORECAST CONSIDERATIONS

Applicable Models

The Prognosis Model for Stand Development (Stage 1973, Wykoff et al. 1982) can be used to calculate expected yields for management regimes that include vegetation management. Some treatments are represented by response data already codified in the model. Other treatments will require entering short-term response estimates into the modeling system, whereupon the model's internal logic will calculate the long-term effects.

Recent extensions to the Prognosis Model have increased the range of silvicultural treatments that can be evaluated through its use. Regeneration of conifers following harvest is represented by the Regeneration Establishment Model (Ferguson and Crookston 1984, Ferguson et al. 1986). This new component adds planting and site preparation by either burning or mechanical means to the repertoire of treatments that can be compared. Another extension representing the associated understory vegetation is called the COVER and BROWSE extension (Moeur 1985) because its development was motivated by the necessity to link with models of watershed processes and wildlife habitat qualities. The base Prognosis Model represents the influence of thinning and regeneration harvest on the growth of the residual stand and on the new trees passed to it from the Regeneration Establishment Model. Finally, through a direct link with the CHEAPO computer program (Horn et al. 1986), possible yields through a full rotation estimated by the Prognosis Model can be given economic values. In conjunction with cost data for the management regime, CHEAPO can be used to calculate various economic criteria to compare alternative investments. Instructions for compiling cost information and conducting economic analyses are given in Chapters 11 and 12.

These capabilities considerably extend the usefulness of the Stand Prognosis System for evaluating treatments to control weed competition during the establishment and early development of conifer forests in the Inland Northwest. This chapter describes how to use the system to translate data describing short-term responses of conifers to weed control treatments into end-of-rotation effects on timber yield. These long-range projections provide the estimates of responses needed to assess weed control in the decision-making context described by Stewart and Row (1981).

The analyses presented in this chapter are based on the Inland Empire Version 5.1 of the Prognosis Model for Stand Development. Regional variants of the base Prognosis Model have been calibrated for eastern and southwestern Oregon, eastern Washington, eastern Montana, central Idaho, and western Wyoming. Research is under way to calibrate the Regeneration Establishment Model extension to these areas as well.

Management Scope

Vegetation management practices in the Inland Northwest include (1) site preparation by burning, mechanical, and chemical methods; (2) early conifer release from shrub and herb competition; and (3) cleaning and thinning to favor particular conifer species while controlling stand density. Of these vegetation management practices, all except chemical site preparation and conifer release from shrubs are represented in the Prognosis Model for Stand Development. The structure of the model and the facility with which it can be manipulated does, however, permit the evaluation of treatments not explicitly represented in the system.

Time Frame

Biometric and economic analyses of most silvicultural practices require a long time span. Vegetation management is no exception. Although direct effects on stand establishment and growth are limited to about the first quarter of a rotation, economic effects can be evaluated only at the end of the rotation. Hence the analysis may have a time span of 80 to 150 years.

HAZARD ANALYSIS

In the Inland Northwest, if vegetation management is obviously needed, it is almost too late to obtain much benefit. Therefore, anticipating the problem is an essential part of solving it. Inland Northwest forests are so ecologically diverse that few people have sufficient experience to anticipate how successional processes will turn out, especially in a quantitative sense. Collective experience, formulated as quantitative models, can help.

Two components of the Prognosis system help to anticipate problem areas needing vegetation management. One component, the Regeneration Establishment Model, represents effects of silvicultural system, site preparation, and site factors on the probability of stocking, species composition, density, and early height growth of conifer regeneration.

The second component, COVER, includes the SHRUBS extension of the Prognosis system. This model represents the canopy coverage and species distribution and height of the shrubby vegetation as well as some ferns, forbs, and graminoids.

Used together, these two models can show where vegetation management should be considered. To illustrate, we have used the models on a set of locations that characterize the sites in the National Forests of northern Idaho. Inventories of these National Forests were obtained from a random sample of stands (Stage and Alley 1972).

Each of these sample-stand locations has an associated "acre weight" that is proportional to the area in the entire forest that, by sampling inference, is represented by the subject stand and its location. Therefore, by summing the products of any attribute of these locations multiplied by its acre weight, we can estimate the total of that attribute in the entire forest.

We classified these inventory locations into a matrix of cells defined by site attributes that affect the course of development of stands in the Prognosis system. These attributes were geographic location (represented by the identity of the National Forest), elevation, slope percentage, aspect (N or S), and habitat type. When the inventory locations were sorted into the cells of this fiveway table, there were 246 occupied cells representing the diversity of the forest conditions. Cells were deleted that represented habitat types such as in the *Pinus ponderosa* series where the full Prognosis Model is not yet applicable.

Forecasts of early vegetation development were calculated for each of these 246 cells, assuming a clearcut-natural regeneration system with an average mix of mechanical and burning methods of site preparation. From the forecasts produced by the model, two attributes have been selected for display. One is conifer stocking 15 years after harvest. In this model, conifer stocking is represented by the probability that there will be at least one established conifer on a plot of 1/300 acre. To be considered established, the conifer must be at least 1 ft tall for the intolerant species and at least 0.5 ft tall for the tolerant species.

The second attribute is the average shrub cover 5 years after harvest. Total shrub cover can be greater than 100% because of overlapping of shrub canopies of different heights. Note that these two attributes (conifer stocking and shrub cover) represent the vegetation at two times, 10 years apart.

When one compares these two attributes, it is important to understand that the two models were based on exactly the same set of plot locations, although the analyses leading to the estimation equations were the work of different investigators.

Figure 10-1 displays the relationship between the estimates of probability of stocking and total shrub cover. Aggregating the locations into only two aspects—due north versus due south—shows the very important effect of aspect. The upper cluster contains the north-facing locations, and the lower cluster contains the south-facing locations. The gap between the clusters would be filled if the intervening aspects had been included by a finer classification of aspect.

The relationship of stocking to shrub cover differs between the two clusters. On north-facing slopes, conditions favoring more shrub cover also favor better stocking by conifers. But on the south-facing aspects, the opposite relationship is evident: the more shrub cover, the poorer the conifer stocking.

Stocking, however, is not the only indicator of need for vegetation management. Growth of the established conifers is also important. Height development of conifers in this region is significantly related to aspect and hence to the average vegetation found on those aspects. Despite the tendency for northern aspects to have less shrub cover than southerly aspects, the northern aspects produce regeneration of shorter trees at

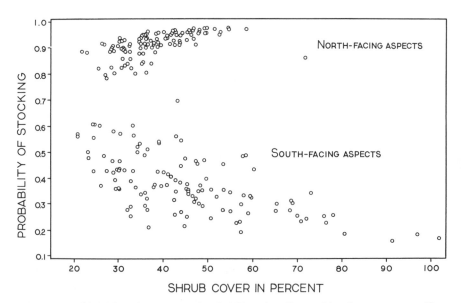

Figure 10-1. Model-based estimates of probability of conifer stocking (one or more conifers per 1/300 acre) 15 years after disturbance compared to estimated shrub cover 5 years after disturbance. The upper cluster of points represents north-facing aspects; the lower cluster of points represents south-facing aspects.

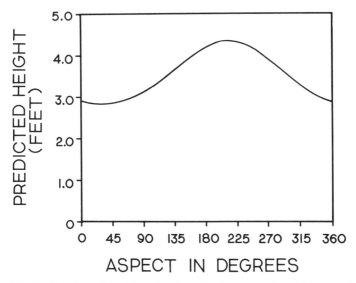

Figure 10-2. Predicted height of Douglas-fir natural regeneration 10 years after establishment as a function of aspect.

comparable stand age than southern aspects within the range of the habitat types in which these species regenerate: Douglas-fir (Figure 10-2), western white pine, lodgepole pine, Engelmann spruce, and western redcedar (Ferguson et al. 1986).

Conceivably, cool temperatures and less sunlight limit height growth of conifers on the north aspects compared to the south aspects. An alternate explanation for the reduced heights on north slopes would be that there is more intraconifer competition as a consequence of the high probabilities of stocking. However, analyses of these same data show just the reverse—trees in dense patches are as tall or taller than trees in less dense patches. Apparently, microsite influences are creating a positive correlation between stocking and height, whereas the direct effect of increased stocking should be the reverse.

Regardless of the interactions between site conditions and conifer performance, north-facing slopes should be considered "hazardous" for height growth where heavy shrub cover is expected. Again, the shrub model can be used to forecast shrub development following disturbance so that problem areas can be identified before the stand is regenerated.

INVENTORY

The model can start either from a stand examination that uses routine inventory methods or from a site description independent of the existing stand.

Site Preparation

To evaluate effects of site preparation requires data describing the site, its location, and proposed treatments. Data required to use the Regeneration Establishment Model in conjunction with the Prognosis Model for Stand Development are obtained from a grid of sampling points within the stand of interest. At each point, habitat type, aspect, slope, and topographic position are recorded. In addition, geographic location and elevation are recorded for the stand as a whole.

Sampling intensity should depend on the loss function for the decision to be made (Hamilton 1979, Stage and Ferguson 1984). However, 25 to 40 points per stand seem to provide reasonable estimates in stands on terrain of average variability.

If the regeneration methods to be compared include any of the partial stand harvesting methods (seed-tree, shelterwood, or selection), then the inventory must also include descriptions of the trees to be left in the vicinity of each sampling point in the grid. Either variable-radius plots or fixed-area plots can be used to obtain a tree list in which each tree is described by species and diameter at breast height (DBH). Additional tree attributes (height, diameter increment, crown ratio, and desirability for retention) can improve the resolution of the yield forecasts.

Conifer Release

Effects of prospective conifer release treatments can be evaluated for situations in which (1) stands have yet to be regenerated or in which (2) stands have already been regenerated.

In the first case, data requirements are the same as for evaluating site preparation. In the second case, additional data describing site preparation used, stocking by recently regenerated conifer seedlings and saplings, and the shrub species' heights and cover are useful but not essential.

In the Regeneration Establishment Model, trees less than 3 in. DBH are sampled on 1/300 acre around each point in the grid. Although all trees within the plot are included in the tally, a few trees are described in greater detail. These trees are selected by the following rules (Ferguson and Crookston 1984):

1. Select the two tallest trees on each 1/300-acre plot, regardless of species.
2. Select the tallest one tree of each additional species represented on the plot.
3. If the first two rules do not total four trees, select in order of descending height from any remaining trees, if present, until four are chosen.

TYPICAL BRUSHFIELD SITUATION

| 7 | | 8 | 7 | 8 | 6 | 2 | 7 | | 6 |

CONIFER CROWN CLASS CODE

1,2 – NOT INFLUENCED BY SHRUB
COMPETITION – OPEN GROWN

6 – FREE TO GROW – LEADER IS
EXPOSED TO NEARLY FULL SUN

7 – WITHIN BRUSH CANOPY

8 – UNDER BRUSH CANOPY

Figure 10-3. Codes used in Northern Region, U.S. Department of Agriculture, Forest Service, for recording conifer crowns in relation to shrub cover. (*Source:* From Stand Examination Handbook; Forest Service Handbook 2409.21, Chapter 300, May 1983. Region-1. Missoula, MT)

On these selected trees, position of the terminal with respect to surrounding shrubs (Figure 10-3), 5-year height increment (on subsample), crown ratio, and diameter at breast height (if taller than 4.5 ft) are recorded.

If the 1/300-acre plot is absolutely unsuitable for tree establishment, such as solid rock or talus, then the point is recorded as nonstockable. As a consequence, the model reduces the growing space available by the proportion of points classified as nonstockable.

REPRESENTING WEED CONTROL EFFECTS

At any given point in a stand's development, its future development depends on its present density, physical size, and vigor. Changes in size and vigor can be expressed as functions of age for even-aged, undisturbed stands. However, when management is imposed upon stand development, the natural relationships of size and vigor to age are vitiated.

Vegetation management treatments have substantial effects on vigor and, hence, increment. Two modeling approaches to estimating yields following vegetation management are available when vigor is not included: (1) assume that height increment after some period of treatment effect will proceed the same as for an older stand of the same height (i.e., the "effective age" of the stand will appear to be older than it actually

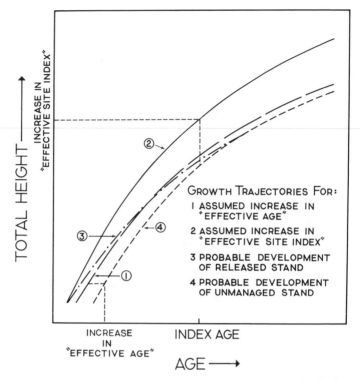

Figure 10-4. Use of "effective age" (Curve 1) or "effective site index" (Curve 2) may overestimate actual growth responses (Curve 3) to vegetation management.

is; Curve 1 of Figure 10-4); (2) assume that the treatment can be represented as an increase in site quality, with height development following the height development pattern for the "effective site index" (Curve 2 of Figure 10-4).

The first assumption ignores the continuing effect of improved vigor and, therefore, underestimates yields at early ages. The second assumption ignores effects of site quality on the upper asymptote of height development and will overestimate yields.

Therefore, simplistic age-driven models of stand development are not convenient for representing effects of such treatments. Instead, the Prognosis Model represents growth as the sum of a series of increments, each of which depends on tree size and vigor as well as the customary decriptors of competition and environmental influences.

To represent weed control treatments, users of the Prognosis Model selectively change some of the variables and increment rates in the model. Although users can interject hypothetical responses to estimate the long-term value of the hypothesis, the more interesting use of the system is to interject estimates of responses based on summaries of relevant experiments.

Weed control responses can be described to the Regeneration Establishment and Prognosis Models in five ways:

1. Change in the expected stocking of established seedlings on an area
2. Change in the species composition of the established seedlings
3. Change in the height of newly established seedlings and saplings
4. Change in periodic height increment of saplings
5. Change in periodic diameter increment of saplings

The first three of these changes are processed by the Regeneration Establishment Model; the last two by the base Prognosis Model. Information to change the operation of the models is entered by adding keywords and their associated parameters into the set of control records that go with the inventory data. Although one should refer to the detailed descriptions of these two models to understand how they operate on the data, a brief summary is provided here.

The Regeneration Establishment Model "sees" the stand as a collection of small, fixed-area plots (1/300-acre). Each plot is characterized by habitat type (Daubenmire and Daubenmire 1968), geographic location, elevation, slope, aspect, topographic position, evidence of site preparation, and overstory basal area and species composition. Shrubs on the plots are described by three sets of values for species, height, and coverage percentage. Thus one can describe coverage of either three species of similar heights, three height layers of a single species, or three combinations of species and height.

Treatments to the stand (harvest, site preparation, or planting) are scheduled by the user. At two intervals following the date of harvest, the model either estimates, or obtains from the inventory data, a tally of the new and advance regeneration. These intervals, which are supplied by TALLYONE and TALLYTWO keyword records, are usually set for 10 and 20 years after date of harvest. The tally describes whether each plot is stocked with at least one established conifer seedling. Stocking, so described, gives more emphasis to distribution of the new trees than to the average density, although the two measures are correlated.

On each stocked plot, the tally also includes the numbers of seedlings and the species and the heights of the four best trees as estimated by the model. For explicit information on the estimating equations, refer to Ferguson et al. (1986). By comparing seedling heights with the shrub heights, their relative competitive status can be approximated, although their spatial proximity within the 1/300-acre circle would be unknown.

Among the keywords available in the Regeneration Establishment

Model, those that can be used to represent vegetation management effects are the following: to modify the proportion of stocked plots, use STOCK-ADJ or PLANT; to change relative species composition, use SPECMULT; and to change the height at the time of the tally, use HTADJ.

At the time of each "tally," records representing the seedlings are passed to the Prognosis Model. There they are added to the list for which incremental changes in height and diameter, crown development, and mortality rates are estimated for each successive interval in time. Height increments for trees less than 3.0 in. DBH are calculated with an expression that changes with habitat type, slope, aspect, geographic location, species, initial tree height, and conifer competition. These periodic increments in height can be modified multiplicatively with the REGHMULT keyword record. Additional response in diameter increment can also be introduced multiplicatively with the REGDMULT keyword record. Each tree record in the list represents a number of trees/acre that are determined by the inventory design. Mortality is represented by reducing this number of trees at each time step by the proportion of trees like the subject trees that are expected to die in the interval. This proportion can be modified by the MORTMULT keyword record.

HOW TO CHOOSE THE STOCKING, GROWTH, AND MORTALITY MODIFIERS

Research on the efficacy of various methods of weed control is not sufficiently advanced to codify treatment results so that the user need only specify the kind and intensity of treatment to the Prognosis Model. Therefore, some insight into both data sources and model operations is required to use the Prognosis modifiers.

Sources of Stocking and Growth Response Data

The Intermountain Research Station, U.S. Department of Agriculture, Forest Service, has extensive data for effects of site preparation and conifer release. Both mechanical and chemical treatments are represented in this data base. Table 10-1 summarizes data available for site preparation treatments by habitat type, conifer species, and targeted competition. Effects on targeted competition have been recorded after treatment as well as seedling survival and growth at annual intervals. Conifer responses have been followed for up to 5 years.

Table 10-2 is a similar summary of data bases concerning effects of conifer release studies. In these studies, the most important responses are height increment and diameter increment.

These data bases are maintained by the Intermountain Research Station's Research Work Unit, Quantitative Analysis of Forest Management Practices, which is located at the Forestry Sciences Laboratory at Moscow, Idaho. In addition, Boyd (1986) has compiled an extensive summary of weed control experiments in the Inland Northwest.

How to Estimate Parameters of Model-Modifying Keywords

Most weed control treatments affect the early development of the crop trees (see Curve 3, Figure 10-4). At this time, incremental growth rates are usually increasing. Furthermore, bigger trees get bigger faster. Therefore, any treatment that modifies increment will have a compounded effect on growth. A growth increase introduced by modifying the model relations in one period will generally be followed by greater increment in subsequent periods even without further benefit from the release from competition. Because of this deviation-amplifying nature of growth, analyses of weed control responses should use the same sequence of time intervals after treatment as will be used in the model.

Duration of the treatment response is as important as the magnitude of the response. All of the ...MULT keywords take effect at a specified date and continue in effect until replaced by another ...MULT keyword record with a subsequent date. Although these dates can be arbitrary, the cycles with which Prognosis steps through time must be made to start on dates on which the modifiers take effect. TIMEINT and INVYEAR keyword records provide this flexibility. Indeed, because cycle and date can be used interchangeably on keyword records, the most direct method is to specify the ...MULT keyword timing using the cycle number. The usual cycle length is 10 yr because that was the period of growth data used to calibrate the model. However, deviations are possible when necessary to accommodate the use of available analyses of weed control responses.

The modifiers of stocking and the addition to initial heights of trees passed from the Regeneration Establishment Model extension are one-time effects, so duration is less critical. However, the interval between the weed control treatment and the dates specified for TALLYONE at which the modifier is to be implemented should match the duration of the measured vegetation response. However, the TALLYONE date should not be later than 18 yr after the date of disturbance.

Increasing heights and height increments by the HTADJ and REGH-MULT keywords also increase tree diameters through correlations internal to the model between height and diameters (for small trees only). Additional effects on DBH can be achieved with the REGDMULT keyword, but its use is beyond the scope of this discussion.

TABLE 10-1. Data Bases Available from the Intermountain Research Station of the USDA Forest Service Concerning Site Preparation

Habitat Type[a]	Conifer Species[a]	Target Competition[a]	Treatment[b]	Initial Year
PIPO/AGSP	PP	AGSP	S; R; V; D; A; AD	1983
PICO/CARU	LPP	CARU	S; R; V; D; A	1982
PSME/CARU	DF	CARU	S; R; V; D; A; AD	1980
PSME/CARU	LPP	CARU	S; R; V; D; A	1982
PSME/CARU	WL	CARU	S; R; V; D; A; AD	1980
PSME/PHMA	PP	CARU, CAREX	S; R; V; D; A; AD	1979
PSME/PHMA	PP	Misc. graminoids, heavily grazed	S; R; V; D; A; AD	1982
ABLA/XETE	DF	CARU, XETE, CAREX	S; R; V; D; A; AD	1979
ABLA/XETE	ES	CARU, XETE, CAREX	S; R; V	1983
ABLA/XETE	LPP	CARU, XETE, CAREX	S; R; V; D; A; AD	1979
ABLA/CARU	LPP	CARU, CAREX	S; R; V; D; A; AD	1979
ABGR/PAMY	DF	CARU, PHMA, HODI, ROSA, SPBE	S; R; V; D; A	1982
ABGR/PAMY	PP	CARU, PHMA, HODI ROSA, SPBE	S; R; V; D; A	1982
ABGR/PAMY	PP	CARU, CAREX	R; V; A	1981
ABGR/PAMY⎫	DF	PTAQ	M	1978
ABGR/PAMY⎪	ES	PTAQ	M	1978
ABGR/PAMY⎬[c]	GF	PTAQ	M	1978
ABGR/PAMY⎪	LPP	PTAQ	M	1978
ABGR/PAMY⎭	WWP	PTAQ	M	1978
THPL/PAMY	DF	CARU, CAREX	R; V	1982
THPL/PAMY	DF	Misc. graminoids	R; V; A; AD	1980
THPL/PAMY	PP	Misc. graminoids	R; V; A; AD	1980

[a]Species codes are:
Conifers
GF/ABGR Grand fir/*Abies grandis*
SAF/ABLA Subalpine fir/*Abies lasiocarpa*
WL Western larch/*Larix occidentalis*
ES Engelmann spruce/*Picea engelmannii*
LPP/PICO Lodgepole pine/*Pinus contorta*
WWP Western white pine/*Pinus monticola*
PP/PIPO Ponderosa pine/*Pinus ponderosa*
DF/PSME Douglas-fir/*Pseudotsuga menziesii*
WRC/THPL Western redcedar/*Thuja plicata*
TSHE Western hemlock/*Tsuga heterophylla*
Understory vegetation
ACGL *Acer glabrum*
AGSP *Agropyron spicatum*
ALSI *Alnus sinuata*
AMAL *Amelanchier alnifolia*
BEPA *Betula papyrifera*
CARU *Calamagrostis rubescens*
CAREX *Carex* spp.

TABLE 10-1 (*Continued*)

CESA	*Ceanothus sanguineus*
CEVE	*Ceanothus velutinus*
HODI	*Holidiscus discolor*
MEFE	*Menziesia ferruginea*
PAMY	*Pachistima myrsinites*
PHMA	*Physocarpus malvaceous*
PTAQ	*Pteridium aquilinum*
ROSA	*Rosa* spp.
SALIX	*Salix* spp.
SPBE	*Spirea betulafolia*
XETE	*Xerophyllum tenax*

[b]Treatment codes are:

S = Scalp
R = Roundup®
D = dalapon
V = Velpar®
A = atrazine
AD = atrazine + dalapon
M = asulam

(Note: In addition to specific "treatments," each test includes an untreated control.)
[c]This study is predominately in a bracken "glade" closely associated with the ABGR/PAMY habitat type.

HTADJ

-The HTADJ keyword adds to the heights assigned to regeneration by the Regeneration Establishment Model at the time specified for TALLYONE, which may be 3 to 15 yr following harvest or site preparation treatments. Therefore, all that is required from the data base is the difference in heights of trees between treated and untreated plots.

PLANT

-The PLANT keyword specifies the density of trees to be planted, their species, and expected survival to the date of the first "tally." Therefore, effects of treatment can be represented by merely changing the specified survival.

STOCKADJ

-Natural regeneration can be expected in most disturbed stands where there is a seed source, whether the area is planted or not. Effects of mechanical site scarification or burning are already represented in the Regeneration Establishment Model. However, increases in survival due to chemical site preparation must be represented by changing the probabilities of stocking. The degree to which the probabilities should be

TABLE 10-2. Data Bases Available from the Intermountain Research Station of the USDA Forest Service Concerning Conifer Release

Habitat Type[a]	Conifer Species[a]	Target Competition[a]	Treatment[b]	Initial Year[c]
PSME/PHMA	PP	PHMA, CARU	C; C/T; R; V	1982
ABLA/MEFE	ES	MEFE, XETE	R; H; C; C/T	1982
ABLA/MEFE	LPP	MEFE, XETE	R; H; C; C/T	1982
ABLA/MEFE	SAF	MEFE, XETE	R; H; C; C/T	1982
ABGR/PAMY	DF	CEVE, SALIX	2,4-D/2,4,5-T; R/G; K; R; G; 2,4-D; C; C/T	1976 (1982)
ABGR/PAMY	DF	CESA, SALIX	2,4-D/2,4,5-T; R; C; C/T	1976 (1982)
ABGR/PAMY	DF	SALIX, ACGL, BEPA, AMAL	2,4,5-T	1964 (1975)
ABGR/PAMY	DF	CEVE, PHMA	2,4-D; H	1982
ABGR/PAMY	DF	ACGL, ALSI, SALIX, PHMA	R; C; C/T	1982
ABGR/PAMY	GF	CEVE, SALIX	2,4-D/2,4,5-T; R/G; K; R; G; 2,4-D; C; C/T	1976 (1982)
ABGR/PAMY	GF	CESA, SALIX	2,4-D/2,4,5-T; R; C/T	1976 (1982)
ABGR/PAMY	GF	SALIX, ACGL, BEPA, AMAL	2,4,5-T	1964 (1975)
ABGR/PAMY	LPP	ACGL, ALSI, SALIX, PHMA	R; C; C/T	1982
ABGR/PAMY	LPP	CEVE, SALIX	R; C; C/T	1982
ABGR/PAMY	LPP	CESA	R; K; G; 2,4-D; C	1979
ABGR/PAMY	LPP	CEVA, PHMA	2,4-D; H	1982
ABGR/PAMY	LPP	ACGL, ALSI, SALIX, PHMA	R; C; C/T	1982
ABGR/PAMY	PP	CEVA, PHMA	2,4-D; H	1982

THPL/PAMY	DF	CESA, SALIX, ACGL	2,4-D/2,4,5-T; R; C; C/T	1976 (1982)
THPL/PAMY	DF	CESA	R; H	1982
THPL/PAMY	GF	CESA, SALIX, ACGL	2,4-D/2,4,5-T; R; C; C/T	1976 (1982)
THPL/PAMY	LPP	CESA	R; H	1982
THPL/PAMY	PP	CESA	R; H	1982
THPL/PAMY	WRC	CESA, SALIX, ACGL	R; C; C/T	1982
TSHE/PAMY	DF	BEPA	R	1982
TSHE/PAMY	DF	SALIX, ALSI	R; K; G; 2,4-D; C	1979
TSHE/PAMY	DF	CESA, SALIX, CEVE, ALSI	R; K; G; 2,4-D; C	1979
TSHE/PAMY	GF	BEPA	R	1982
TSHE/PAMY	GF	CESA, SALIX, CEVE, ALSI	R; K; G; 2,4-D; C	1979
TSHE/PAMY	GF	CEVE, PHMA	2,4-D/2,4,5-T	1976 (1980)
TSHE/PAMY	SAF	SALIX, ALSI	R; K; G; 2,4-D; C	1979
TSHE/PAMY	WRC	BEPA	R	1982

[a]See Table 10-1 for species codes.
[b]Treatment codes:

- H = Hand pulled
- C = Hand cut
- C/T = Cut and stump treatment with Garlon®
- G = Garlon®
- R = Roundup®
- K = Krenite®
- R/G = Roundup® + Garlon®

(Note: In addition to specific "treatments," each test includes untreated controls.)

[c]If study measurements have been discontinued, the last year of measurement is in parentheses.

311

changed to represent the effects of treatment on survival depends on the probabilities experienced in the control (untreated) plots.

Therefore, the user must obtain expected stocking probabilities from the Regeneration Establishment Model for the control (untreated) situation to which the proposed treatment is to be compared. Call this probability P_{cM}. From the data base, survival probabilities are needed for the control (P_c) and the treated (P_t) trees. Then, the average difference between

$$\ln \left(\frac{1 - P_t}{P_t} \right)$$

and

$$\ln \left(\frac{1 - P_c}{P_c} \right)$$

is calculated for the pairs of treated and untreated plots in the data for the treatment being considered. Call the exponential of this difference K. Then, the multiplier for the STOCKADJ keyword is

$$\frac{1}{P_{cM} + K(1 - P_{cM})}$$

For example, if the model for no treatment estimates survival $P_{cM} = 0.75$, but the data base gives $P_c = 0.5$ versus $P_t = 0.8$, then

$$K = \frac{1 - 0.8}{0.8} \times \frac{0.5}{1 - 0.5} = 0.25$$

and the multiplier for the STOCKADJ keyword would be

$$\frac{1}{0.75 + 0.25(1 - 0.75)} = 1.23$$

Therefore, the expected survival on treated areas in the model would be

$$1.23 \, P_{cM} = (1.23)(0.75) = 0.9225$$

Note that the multiplier of 1.23 is considerably less than the 1.6 that a naive ratio of treated to control would provide. But the latter, multiplied by an expected control survival of 0.75, would give an impossible survival probability greater than 1.

REGHMULT

-The parameter on the REGHMULT keyword multiplies the height increment (H) of the small trees (<3.0 in. DBH) in the stand. During this phase of development, growth is exponential. That is

$$\frac{dH}{dt} = kH$$

or, in differential form, the relative growth rate (k) is

$$\frac{dH}{H} = k\ dt.$$

The average relative growth rate $(\bar{k})$ during an interval $t_2 - t_1$ is given by

$$\bar{k} = (\ln H_2 - \ln H_1)/(t_2 - t_1)$$

Therefore, the multiplier for representing treatment effect should be calculated from the trees in the data base as

$$\text{REGHMULT} = \frac{\displaystyle\sum_{\substack{\text{treated}\\\text{trees}}} (\ln H_{2j} - \ln H_{1j})/(t_{2j} - t_{1j})}{\displaystyle\sum_{\substack{\text{control}\\\text{trees}}} (\ln H_{2j} - \ln H_{1j})/(t_{2j} - t_{1j})} \times \frac{n_{\text{control trees}}}{n_{\text{treated trees}}}$$

For example, in the "Superior '79 and '80" studies of chemical site preparation (Boyd 1986), summed increments of treated and control ponderosa pines are as shown in Table 10-3. Then, based on the data in Table 10-3

$$\text{REGHMULT} = \frac{\left(\dfrac{20.391}{3} + \dfrac{34.935}{2}\right) \times 137}{\left(\dfrac{42.660}{3} + \dfrac{48.472}{2}\right) \times 72} = 1.20$$

Although these two studies have been followed for 6 and 5 years, respectively, after planting, the first 3 years of growth have been omitted from this calculation because we use the REGHMULT keyword to accelerate the increment of established trees. Ideally, the interval of observation of the experimental data should match the period during which the keyword parameter will be in effect in the simulation.

TABLE 10-3. Summed Height Increment Multipliers for Treated and Control Ponderosa Pines in Vegetation Management Studies Selected from Boyd (1986)

Study	Years of Increment	Treated		Control	
		No.	$\Sigma(\ln H_2 - \ln H_1)$	No.	$\Sigma(\ln H_2 - \ln H_1)$
Superior '79	3	21	20.391	54	42.660
Superior '80	2	51	34.935	83	48.472

CASE EXAMPLES

Three situations have been selected for analyses that illustrate the techniques for evaluating vegetation management practices. Two of the stands represent natural regeneration following clearcutting and broadcast burning. These two stands were selected from the list represented in Figure 10-1. The third situation represents a plantation of ponderosa pine.

In the description of each case, only the keywords used to represent effects of vegetation management have been listed. How to use the full set of keywords is described in the set of User's Manuals for the Prognosis System (Wykoff et al. 1982, Ferguson and Crookston 1984). Results of the case analyses are shown in Tables 10-4 through 10-6.

Stand #12 (Tables 10-4A and B)

TREATMENT. Site preparation in addition to burning and disturbance accompanying harvesting. Proportion of area burned was 64%; mechanically disturbed, 11%; remainder, undisturbed. Additional benefits of site preparation are represented by increased stocking, increased height of seedlings, and increased periodic increment of conifers.

SITE CONDITIONS. *Abies grandis/Pachistima* habitat type, south-facing slope of 80%, elevation 4500 ft on Clearwater National Forest in northern Idaho. The shrub model predicts 76% cover of shrubs at 5 years, predominantly *Ceanothus* spp. more than 4 ft in height.

Keyword parameters

STOCKADJ 2.6	Increases stocking at 5 yr from 18% to 49%
HTADJ 1.5	Increases heights at 5 yr by 1.5 ft
REGHMULT 1.2	For 5 to 10 yr after harvest
REGHMULT 1.1	For 10 to 15 yr after harvest
MORTMULT 0.8	Reduces mortality by 20% for 5 to 10 yr after harvest

Stand #58 (Tables 10-5A and B)

TREATMENT. Release of natural conifers that regenerated following site preparation in which 64% of the area was affected by broadcast burning and 11% was mechanically disturbed.

SITE CONDITIONS. *Abies grandis/Pachistima* habitat type, north-facing slope of 50%, elevation 3200 ft on Colville National Forest in northeastern Washington. The shrub model predicts 24% shrub cover at 5 yr, predominantly *Physocarpus malvaceus* and *Rubus parviflorus* of 2 to 3 ft in height.
    Keyword parameters:

REGHMULT 1.10   Increases height increment by 10% for 10 yr
                 starting 5 yr after site preparation

Stand "Superior '79" (Tables 10-6A and B)

TREATMENT. Chemical site preparation before planting ponderosa pine at 500 trees per acre. Six-year survival without treatment was 32%.

SITE CONDITIONS. *Pseudotsuga menziesii/Physocarpus malvaceus* habitat type on south-facing slope of 30%, elevation 4000 ft on Lolo National Forest in western Montana. Competition was *Carex* spp.
    Keyword parameters:

PLANT 1979 10 500 87   Plant 500 ponderosa pine (spp. code =
                        10) per acre with 87% survival
HTADJ 1.1   Increases height at 5 yr by 1.1 ft
REGHMULT 1.24   Increases height increment by 24% for
                        5 to 10 yr after planting

ECONOMIC EVALUATIONS

Two procedures are available for economic analyses of projected yields generated by the model just described. These two procedures roughly correspond to whether the scope of the analysis is limited to a single stand as it would be in comparing alternative prescriptions or whether the scope is a broader area as it would be in strategic planning for a large forest ownership (see Chapter 12).

Stand Level

Economic analyses at the stand level can be readily computed with the CHEAPO (Horn et al. 1986) economic model designed to use Prognosis

TABLE 10-4A. Yield Forecast for Stand #12 with Natural Stand Establishment Following Clearcutting and Broadcast Burning[a]

Year	Age (yr)	Trees per Acre (no.)	Volume per Acre Total (ft³)	Merchantable (ft³)	(bd ft)	Basal Area per Acre (ft²)	Crown Competition Factor	Top Ht (ft)	Growth and Mortality per Acre Period (yr)	Accretion (ft³/yr)	Mortality (ft³/yr)
1984	0	0	0	0	0	0	0	0	5	0	0
1989	5	101	0	0	0	0	0	2	5	0	0
1994	10	101	1	0	0	0	1	6	5	1	0
1999	15	100	5	0	0	1	2	11	5	2	0
2004	20	100	17	0	0	2	4	16	10	6	0
2014	30	93	72	0	0	6	10	27	10	13	0
2024	40	83	197	91	304	12	18	41	10	29	1
2034	50	79	483	368	1,391	24	32	53	10	41	1
2044	60	75	881	780	3,161	38	46	61	10	55	3
2054	70	72	1,402	1,311	5,654	53	59	71	10	66	6
2064	80	69	2,006	1,913	8,847	67	70	78	10	73	8
2074	90	66	2,654	2,554	12,504	81	79	86	10	93	14
2084	100	62	3,443	3,333	17,142	96	90	92	10	87	16
2094	110	59	4,157	4,039	21,270	107	98	98	10	95	24
2104	120	55	4,867	4,742	25,303	118	106	104	10	94	28
2114	130	52	5,527	5,397	28,964	126	111	110	10	109	34
2124	140	48	6,276	6,141	32,989	135	117	115	10	102	33
2134	150	45	6,960	6,819	36,648	142	122	120	0	0	0

[a]Summary statistics based on total stand area and derived from the Stand Growth Prognosis System, Version 5.1—Inland Empire.

TABLE 10-4B. Yield Forecast for Stand #12 with Growth and Mortality Rates Modified to Represent Effects of Vegetation Management in Addition to the Treatments Specified in Table 10-4A

Year	Age (yr)	Trees per Acre (no.)	Volume per Acre Total (ft³)	Volume per Acre Merchantable (ft³)	Volume per Acre Merchantable (bd ft)	Basal Area per Acre (ft²)	Crown Competition Factor	Top Ht (ft)	Growth and Mortality per Acre Period (yr)	Growth and Mortality per Acre Accretion (ft³/yr)	Growth and Mortality per Acre Mortality (ft³/yr)
1984	0	0	0	0	0	0	0	0	5	0	0
1989	5	324	0	0	0	0	1	6	5	3	0
1994	10	322	14	0	0	2	5	12	5	5	0
1999	15	321	38	0	0	5	11	18	5	10	0
2004	20	320	88	0	0	10	19	24	10	26	0
2014	30	293	343	126	451	27	41	36	10	50	2
2024	40	266	828	468	1,727	52	71	45	10	80	4
2034	50	247	1,587	1,218	4,701	82	107	54	10	109	10
2044	60	230	2,577	2,253	9,121	114	138	66	10	144	17
2054	70	213	3,848	3,545	15,435	144	161	76	10	172	28
2064	80	194	5,284	5,012	23,212	173	180	85	10	167	41
2074	90	175	6,547	6,278	30,686	191	191	92	10	176	59
2084	100	156	7,717	7,456	37,754	205	199	100	10	189	70
2094	110	140	8,915	8,652	44,774	218	205	107	10	185	76
2104	120	125	10,006	9,742	50,974	228	208	115	10	179	86
2114	130	112	10,938	10,675	56,334	235	210	121	10	188	102
2124	140	100	11,795	11,535	61,077	239	212	126	10	159	97
2134	150	90	12,416	12,161	64,545	241	210	130	0	0	0

[a]Summary statistics based on total stand area and derived from the Stand Growth Prognosis System, Version 5.1—Inland Empire.

317

TABLE 10-5A. Yield Forecast for Stand #58 with Natural Regeneration Following Clearcutting and Broadcast Burning

Year	Age (yr)	Trees per Acre (no.)	Volume per Acre Total (ft³)	Merchantable (ft³)	Merchantable (bd ft)	Basal Area per Acre (ft²)	Crown Competition Factor	Top Ht (ft)	Growth and Mortality per Acre Period (yr)	Accretion (ft³/yr)	Mortality (ft³/yr)
1984	0	0	0	0	0	0	0	0	5	0	0
1989	5	688	0	0	0	1	2	2	5	1	0
1994	10	681	4	0	0	1	4	7	5	3	0
1999	15	1,591	19	0	0	4	12	12	5	10	0
2004	20	1,566	70	0	0	10	24	19	10	29	0
2014	30	1,471	360	11	40	35	65	34	10	71	1
2024	40	1,232	1,059	291	936	80	127	45	10	95	5
2034	50	1,077	1,960	1,154	4,016	121	177	51	10	118	14
2044	60	876	2,997	2,120	7,837	160	219	62	10	134	23
2054	70	719	4,098	3,326	12,805	194	250	69	10	150	36
2064	80	595	5,241	4,549	18,387	221	271	73	10	151	48
2074	90	492	6,266	5,647	23,865	239	279	81	10	148	59
2084	100	410	7,161	6,593	29,093	251	280	86	10	166	71
2094	110	347	8,109	7,583	34,973	261	280	92	10	165	76
2104	120	298	8,997	8,507	40,872	270	279	95	10	159	84
2114	130	259	9,752	9,314	46,094	275	275	101	10	149	91
2124	140	226	10,329	9,925	50,349	276	270	106	10	156	91
2134	150	200	10,985	10,614	54,662	279	266	110	0	0	0

[a]Summary statistics based on total stand area and derived from the Stand Growth Prognosis System, Version 5.1—Inland Empire.

TABLE 10-5B. Yield Forecast for Stand #58 with Heights and Height Increment Modified to Represent Conifer Release Treatment

Year	Age (yr)	Trees per Acre (no.)	Volume per Acre			Basal Area per Acre (ft²)	Crown Competition Factor	Top Ht (ft)	Growth and Mortality per Acre		
			Total (ft³)	Merchantable					Period (yr)	Accretion (ft³/yr)	Mortality (ft³/yr)
				(ft³)	(bd ft)						
1984	0	0	0	0	0	0	0	0	5	0	0
1989	5	674	0	0	0	1	2	2	5	2	0
1994	10	667	10	0	0	3	7	8	5	6	0
1999	15	1,613	40	0	0	8	20	14	5	16	0
2004	20	1,587	122	0	0	18	39	21	10	37	0
2014	30	1,482	492	21	60	49	89	32	10	81	3
2024	40	1,263	1,279	441	1,450	97	153	44	10	117	8
2034	50	1,080	2,377	1,439	5,102	148	210	53	10	130	18
2044	60	876	3,493	2,485	9,362	185	248	64	10	132	30
2054	70	716	4,508	3,663	14,245	211	269	70	10	139	41
2064	80	588	5,488	4,723	19,295	229	278	77	10	171	56
2074	90	484	6,629	5,985	25,896	247	285	84	10	171	65
2084	100	404	7,689	7,104	32,173	260	287	90	10	148	72
2094	110	341	8,457	7,925	37,304	265	281	95	10	157	82
2104	120	291	9,207	8,735	42,297	268	276	99	10	157	85
2114	130	251	9,925	9,489	46,919	271	271	105	10	151	90
2124	140	219	10,541	10,161	51,191	272	265	110	10	151	94
2134	150	193	11,110	10,755	55,127	272	260	114	0	151	0

[a]Summary statistics based on total stand area and derived from the Stand Growth Prognosis System, Version 5.1—Inland Empire.

TABLE 10-6A. Yield Forecast for Ponderosa Pine Plantation of 500 Trees per Acre Having 32% Survival at 5 Years

Year	Age (yr)	Trees per Acre (no.)	Volume per Acre			Basal Area per Acre (ft²)	Crown Competition Factor	Top Ht (ft)	Growth and Mortality per Acre		
			Total (ft³)	Merchantable					Period (yr)	Accretion (ft³/yr)	Mortality (ft³/yr)
				(ft³)	(bd ft)						
1979	0	0	0	0	0	0	0	0	5	0	0
1984	5	160	0	0	0	0	1	2	5	2	0
1989	10	158	9	0	0	1	2	8	5	4	0
1994	15	156	29	0	0	5	6	14	5	12	0
1999	20	155	88	0	0	12	12	21	10	26	0
2009	30	153	348	102	317	27	26	35	10	48	0
2019	40	151	820	510	1,655	45	40	50	10	60	1
2029	50	148	1,412	1,187	4,039	61	53	60	10	79	3
2039	60	144	2,164	2,009	6,980	79	67	70	10	85	6
2049	70	140	2,945	2,785	10,052	94	79	79	10	108	11
2059	80	134	3,920	3,754	14,452	111	90	88	10	127	15
2069	90	128	5,039	4,865	19,678	129	100	97	10	112	20
2079	100	122	5,952	5,773	24,513	142	108	102	10	122	28
2089	110	115	6,894	6,710	28,732	155	115	107	10	92	30
2099	120	109	7,521	7,335	31,984	162	118	111	10	82	42
2109	130	102	7,926	7,742	34,567	165	119	114	10	119	47
2119	140	95	8,648	8,462	39,275	172	122	118	10	109	44
2129	150	89	9,299	9,111	43,835	178	124	123	0	0	0

ᵃSummary statistics based on total stand area and derived from the Stand Growth Prognosis System, Version 5.1—Inland Empire.

TABLE 10-6B. Yield Forecast for Ponderosa Pine Plantation of 500 Trees per Acre with Survival and Early Growth Enhanced by Chemical Site Preparation

Year	Age (yr)	Trees per Acre (no.)	Volume per Acre			Basal Area per Acre (ft²)	Crown Competition Factor	Top Ht (ft)	Growth and Mortality per Acre		
			Total (ft³)	Merchantable (ft³)	(bd ft)				Period (yr)	Accretion (ft³/yr)	Mortality (ft³/yr)
1979	0	0	0	0	0	0	0	0	5	0	0
1984	5	435	0	0	0	1	1	4	5	8	0
1989	10	429	38	0	0	7	9	10	5	18	0
1994	15	427	127	0	0	21	23	17	5	36	0
1999	20	424	306	0	0	38	39	23	10	66	1
2009	30	415	955	240	744	75	71	41	10	108	3
2019	40	398	2,007	1,292	4,228	117	105	53	10	121	10
2029	50	376	3,121	2,521	8,565	148	130	64	10	127	19
2039	60	350	4,202	3,740	12,969	172	148	74	10	143	31
2049	70	322	5,329	4,907	17,909	193	162	82	10	125	35
2059	80	297	6,229	5,832	22,016	206	169	87	10	142	50
2069	90	270	7,155	6,822	26,611	216	173	95	10	129	53
2079	100	246	7,916	7,606	30,818	223	175	99	10	127	62
2089	110	223	8,567	8,269	34,305	227	175	103	10	121	65
2099	120	202	9,127	8,839	37,376	229	174	106	10	93	62
2109	130	185	9,435	9,159	38,841	228	171	110	10	124	76
2119	140	168	9,913	9,646	42,234	228	168	114	10	117	70
2129	150	153	10,387	10,127	45,676	229	166	117	0	0	0

[a]Summary statistics based on total stand area and derived from the Stand Growth Prognosis System, Version 5.1—Inland Empire.

Model output. CHEAPO accepts costs and benefits of the management regime being evaluated. Yield estimates classified according to product size are provided by Prognosis to CHEAPO as machine-readable files specifically formatted for access by CHEAPO. Analysis of the time streams of costs and benefits provides several investment decision indicators that can be used to determine the relative economic feasibility of alternative management regimes. Investment indicators include internal rate-of-return, soil expectation values for regenerated stands, and net present value for existing stands (see Chapter 12).

An alternative procedure for stand-level analyses has been provided by K. Norman Johnson (1985, personal communication). His procedure is convenient if the economic values have already been formatted for use in FORPLAN. If so, he has prepared a special version of Prognosis that reads the FORPLAN economic file and calculates the investment decision indicators in special subroutines imbedded in the base Prognosis Model.

Strategic Planning

Effects of vegetation management should not be evaluated independently of all the other silvicultural options being considered in strategic planning. The dependency follows from the need to estimate the flow of future benefits and costs coming from the management unit taken as a whole. As with any silvicultural option that modifies growth, vegetation management may have an "allowable cut effect" when flows of output are modulated and the forest does not have a uniform distribution of age classes (see Chapter 12 and Schweitzer et al. 1972). Fortunately, vegetation management problems do not diffuse in space. Therefore, their marginal effects can be represented simply by entering alternative "yield tables" into almost any of the strategic planning linear programming models, such as Timber RAM (Navon 1971), MAX-MILLION (Clutter et al. 1968), MUSYC (Johnson and Scheurman 1977), and FORPLAN (Johnson 1986) or strategic planning simulation models, such as SIMAC (Sassaman et al. 1972). If one of the linear programming models is used, then shadow prices can be used to evaluate vegetation management treatments.

Differences between shadow prices of management regimes that differ only by a vegetation management treatment estimate the marginal value of that treatment in the context of the whole program of forest management.

SUMMARY

Vegetation management practices have been shown to affect both initial survival and subsequent growth of conifers in the mixed-species forests of the Inland Northwest. Models are available that land managers in this region can use to evaluate the need for site preparation treatments and early release of conifers from shrub competition in specific combinations of habitat type, aspect, and elevation. A data base containing experimental results is being maintained that can be analyzed by procedures specified in this chapter to provide the current best estimates of quantitative responses. How to use these short-term effects to produce long-term forest yield estimates is explained with examples. Outcomes of the resulting yield forecasts can be evaluated economically at the stand level or used in optimizing models for resource allocation in larger management areas.

REFERENCES

Boyd. R.J. 1986. Conifer performance following weed control site preparation treatments in the Inland Northwest, p. 95–104. *In* Baumgartner, D.M., R.J. Boyd, D.W. Breuer, and D.L. Miller, (comps. and eds.) Weed control for forest productivity in the interior west: Sympos. Proc., Feb. 5-7, 1985, Spokane, WA. Coop. Ext. Serv., Washington State Univ. Pullman, WA.

Clutter, J.L., J.H. Bamping, J.E. Bethune, J.C. Fortson, L.A. Hargreaves, L.S. Shackelford, S.B. Kinne, E.L. Norman, and G.O. Ware. 1968. MAX-MILLION. A computerized forest management planning system. Biometrics-Operations Research Section, School of Forest Resour., Univ. Georgia, Athens, GA. 61 p.

Daubenmire, R.F. and J.B. Daubenmire. 1968. Forest vegetation of eastern Washington and northern Idaho. College Agr., Washington Agr. Experiment Station, Washington State Univ., Pullman, WA. Tech. Bull. 60. 140 p.

Ferguson, D.F. and N.L. Crookston. 1984. User's guide to the Regeneration Establishment Model—a Prognosis Model extension. USDA Forest Service, Intermountain Forest and Range Experiment Station, Ogden, UT. Gen. Tech. Rep. INT-161. 23 p.

Ferguson, D.E., A.R. Stage, and R.J. Boyd. 1986. Predicting regeneration in the grand fir-hemlock ecosystem of the Northern Rocky Mountains. Forest Sci. Monogr. 26. 41 p.

Hamilton, D.A., Jr. 1979. Setting precision for resource inventories: the manager and the mensurationist. J. Forestry. 77:667-670.

Horn, J.E., E.L. Medema, and E.G. Schuster. 1986. User's guide to CHEAPO II—Economic analysis of Stand Prognosis Model outputs. USDA Forest Service, Intermountain Research Station, Ogden, UT. Gen. Tech. Rep. INT-211. 38 p.

Johnson, K.N. 1985. Using the Prognosis Model for stand development in conjunction with FORPLAN. Personal communication, College of Forestry, Oregon State Univ., Corvallis, OR.

Johnson, K.N. 1986. FORPLAN version I: an overview. Land Management Planning Systems Section, USDA Forest Service, Washington, DC. 85 p.

Johnson, K.N. and H.L. Scheurman. 1977. Techniques for prescribing optimal timber harvest and investment under different objectives; discussion and synthesis. Forest Sci. Monogr. 18. 31 p.

Moeur, M. 1985. Cover: a user's guide to the Canopy and Shrubs Extension of the Stand Prognosis Model. USDA Forest Service, Intermountain Research Station, Ogden, UT. Gen. Tech. Rep. INT-190. 49 p.

Navon, D.I. 1971. Timber RAM...a long-range planning method for commercial timber lands under multiple-use management. USDA Forest Service, Pacific Southwest Forest and Range Experiment Station, Berkeley, CA. Res. Pap. PSW-70. 10 p.

Pfister, R.D., B.I. Kovalchik, S.F. Arno, and R.C. Presby. 1977. Forest habitat types of Montana. USDA Forest Service, Intermountain Forest and Range Experiment Station. Ogden, UT. Gen. Tech. Rep. INT-34. 174 p. plus enclosures.

Sassaman, R.W., E. Holt, and K. Bergsvik. 1972. User's manual for a computer program for simulating intensively managed allowable cut. USDA Forest Service, Pacific Northwest Forest and Range Experiment Station, Portland, OR. Gen. Tech. Rep. PNW-1. 50 p.

Schweitzer, D.L., R.W. Sassaman, and C.H Schallau. 1972. Allowable cut effect: some physical and economic implications. J. Forestry 70:415-418.

Stage, A.R. 1973. Prognosis model for stand development. USDA Forest Service, Intermountain Forest and Range Experiment Station, Ogden, UT. Res. Pap. INT-137. 32 p.

Stage, A.R. and J.R. Alley. 1972. An inventory design using stand examinations for planning and programing timber management. USDA Forest Service, Intermountain Forest and Range Experiment Station, Ogden, UT. Res. Pap. INT-126. 17 p.

Stage, A.R. and D.E. Ferguson. 1984. Linking regeneration surveys to future yields, p. 153-157. *In* New forests for a changing world. Proc., Soc. Amer. Foresters Nat. Conv., October 16-20, 1983, Portland, OR. Soc. Amer. Foresters, Washington, DC.

Steele, R., R.D. Pfister, R.A. Ryker, and J.A. Kittams. 1981. Forest habitat types of central Idaho. USDA Forest Service, Intermountain Forest and Range Experiment Station, Ogden, UT. Gen. Tech. Rep. INT-114. 138 p.

Stewart, R.E. and C. Row. 1981. Assessing the economic benefits of weed control in forest management, p. 26-53. *In* Holt, H.A., and B.C. Fischer (eds.) Proc., Weed control in forest management. John S. Wright Forestry Conference, February 3-5, 1981. Purdue Univ., West Lafayette, IN. 305 p.

Wykoff, W.R., N.L. Crookston, and A.R. Stage. 1982. User's guide to the Stand Prognosis Model. USDA Forest Service, Intermountain Forest and Range Experiment Station, Ogden, UT. Gen. Tech. Rep. INT-133. 112 p.

III

EVALUATING FOREST VEGETATION MANAGEMENT OPTIONS

11

Using Costs and Values in Forest Vegetation Management Analyses

CLARK ROW

INTRODUCTION

Treatment costs and timber values are important in several phases of decision making in forest vegetation management. These phases are (1) strategic planning of long-term timber rotations that determine which treatments or combinations of treatments will be used; (2) developing short-term operational plans that select projects, specify how each treatment is to be done, and estimate funds required; and (3) monitoring costs to keep expenses at an appropriate level.

This chapter discusses the cost components that managers should consider, the current cost ranges for vegetation management treatments, recent cost trends, the influence of project-related factors on unit costs, and procedures that can be used to estimate costs for budgeting purposes. It also describes the historical trends in timber values and discusses future projections under various scenarios. Collectively the treatment costs and timber values are important ingredients in economic evaluations of forest vegetation management, such as those presented in Chapter 12.

Available sources of vegetation management cost data show wide variation in costs per unit area for individual projects of the same type. Differences in costs can be partially accounted for by variations in on-the-ground conditions. Variable weather, market fluctuations, and other unpredictable occurrences also contribute to the wide range in vegetation management costs. Finally, several management-related factors such as efficiency, carefulness, and administrative requirements account for some of the variation in costs, particularly when one compares costs reported by different organizations.

Using Costs and Values in Strategic Planning

Chapter 13 emphasizes developing management regimes for entire timber stand rotations. These silvicultural prescriptions may include site preparation, regeneration, release, thinning, and other treatments, and they also should consider potential interactions among the treatments. For example, site preparation intensity may affect planting density and subsequently affect the need for release and precommercial thinning (Guldin 1984b).

Because strategic plans are generally made for broad groups of stands classified by timber type, site productivity, and other factors, the costs used need to be representative of typical conditions within each group. Average costs for recent projects by the classes used in planning may be suitable, with adjustments if necessary. Approximate costs for treatments that could potentially be used but for which there is no immediate operational experience or data may have to be estimated from projected labor, equipment, and material requirements. Using realistic costs in economic analyses of timber growing is critically important. Mills et al. (1976) found that estimates of financial return were more sensitive to errors in estimating costs than to any other factor.

Long-term projections of timber values are also required in strategic planning. These should incorporate rates of value change developed from analyses or assumptions. These value projections should differentiate among species, species groups, or product quality classes when their current values differ substantially.

Using Costs and Values in Operational Planning

Once long-term management regimes are planned, detailed costs and projected values are useful in annual operational planning and budgeting. This planning may involve setting priorities for treatment of individual sites, selecting specfic treatments and methods of application, or deciding whether to contract the projects to an outside firm or use the organization's own crews and equipment. For these uses, cost data should be based on detailed analyses of recent project costs by accounting methods that recognize classes of difficulty and anticipated conditions under which the treatments will be conducted. In some organizations cost-estimating relationships or equations, often supplemented by professional judgment, are used to estimate costs for each project in the work plan. As in long-term strategic planning, projected timber values should be incorporated in the analyses when appropriate.

Using Costs to Monitor Operational Efficiency

Many organizations compare actual costs incurred with estimated or budgeted costs to gauge operational efficiency and to detect problems with treatment prescriptions and implementation. Such cost monitoring may suggest ways costs can be lowered or identify situations that could be handled more efficiently or improve the budgeting process. Cost information is also needed to determine income tax liabilities (Pitsenbarger 1982).

Cost and Value Specifications

Several generally accepted conventions are used in specifying these costs:

1. *Costs Are Net to Management.* Costs include all components that are paid by the organization. If the organization's own crews perform the work, costs include an appropriate share of overhead for administration, personnel, and equipment maintenance and depreciation. Purchased material costs include supplies as well as taxes and transportation charges. If projects are contracted to outside firms, costs include planning, contract administration, and performance monitoring, in addition to the contract price, which is assumed to cover all the contractor's costs.

2. *Costs Are Incremental.* Analysis of treatment costs should consider the costs associated with particular treatments, contrasted to the costs that would be incurred without the treatments. The distinction is important if treating a timber stand reduces or eliminates other costs that would be incurred if the treatment is not done.

3. *Costs Are Adjusted for Inflation.* If the accounting or project records used to estimate costs extend back several years, they may seriously understate current costs if not adjusted for inflation. Frequently used factors for adjusting past values for inflation are the Gross National Product Deflators and the Consumer and Producer Price Indexes. The Gross National Product Deflators (available from the U.S. Council of Economic Advisors, Washington, DC) are often preferred because they represent all sectors of the national economy—not just consumption of final goods or raw and intermediate materials. The adjusted values are called "constant dollars" or "real" values.

Even though many vegetation management treatment costs have increased faster than general inflation and managers expect such trends to continue, "real" costs (and timber values) are almost always used in long-term planning. Expectations that costs or timber values will increase in real value (i.e., faster than inflation) are explicitly stated and incorporated into economic analyses. For short-term budget preparation, however, expected costs are usually estimated in current dollars by assuming that both recent trends in real costs and inflation will continue.

Several conventions are also generally used for timber values. They are:

1. *Timber Is Valued as "Stumpage."* By convention, timber is most often valued as stumpage—the right to cut standing timber. Thus costs of sale preparation and monitoring are costs of timber growing, but logging and associated road construction are not.

2. *Timber Is Valued in the Same Units as Yields Are Measured.* Often timber is sold by commercial units of thousand board feet (MBF), cords, or by a weight unit, whereas growth and yields are measured in volumetric units like cubic feet. Consequently, either the values for commercial units must be converted to values per volume units or the yield volumes converted to commercial units.

3. *Timber Values Are Net to Management.* If the state where the timber is grown levies yield or severance taxes and these are paid by the timber owner (which is subject to negotiation with a purchaser), they should be subtracted from timber values. Such taxes are generally in lieu of property taxes, which are a cost of timber growing. Federal and state income taxes are not usually included because they depend on the owner's current tax situation, though they may be considered in an "after-tax" analysis (see Chapter 12).

4. *Timber Values, Like Costs, Are Adjusted for Inflation.* The same concepts and procedures should be used for values as are used for costs.

COMPONENTS OF TREATMENT COSTS

Variable Costs

Variable costs are for inputs of labor, equipment, and material that are used more or less proportionally to the number or area of units treated. These costs are paid directly by the forest management organization if the organization's crews do the work. If the treatments are done under contract, variable costs are paid by the contractor and are presumably incorporated into the contract price. In some cases, materials such as chemicals or specialized equipment may be furnished to the contractor, and their costs must be included in total cost.

The proportion of each class of variable cost varies widely by type of treatment (Table 11-1). Labor costs in the South, for example, vary from 11 to 69%, and equipment costs vary from 6 to 77%. The treatments that use tractors or aircraft are capital-intensive and have high proportions of equipment cost. For herbicide treatments, about 32 to 73% of the cost

TABLE 11-1. Proportional Components of Total Variable Costs in the South

Treatment	Method	Direct Labor	Equipment	Chemicals
		Percentage of total variable costs		
Mechanical site preparation	Various	23	77	—
Prescribed burning	Hand-held			
	drip torch	69	31	—
	Aerial ignite	56	44	—
Chemical release	Aerial spray	11	16	73
	Backpack spray	38	10	52
	Stem injection	62	6	32
	Mobile ground			
	spray	17	15	68
Precommercial thinning	Power saw	48	52	—

Source: Straka and Watson (1985).

is for chemicals, with the smallest share for stem injection due to heavy labor usage.

Direct Labor Costs

Typical nonsupervisory workers performing vegetation management treatments range from common laborers to semiskilled heavy equipment operators and well-trained, licensed aircraft pilots. Total compensation includes wages or salaries paid directly to them plus mandatory insurance and other fringe benefits. Mandatory insurance includes Social Security for workers' retirement, unemployment insurance in case they are laid off, and workmen's compensation in case they are injured or killed on the job.

Table 11-2 shows the range of wages and representative mandatory insurance rates in 1984 for firms in six representative states whose business is primarily silvicultural contracting. Such firms are classified into different broad groups in each state. Both wages and insurance rates are lower in the South than in the Pacific Northwest, where wages have been affected by unionization and other social factors.

Forest industry firms and large contractors must observe federal wage and hour regulations. Small contractors are usually exempt from overtime or minimum wage requirements under agricultural exemptions but are advised to check the appropriate regulations (consult the U.S. Department of Labor, Washington, DC, or regional offices).

Other benefits vary by type of employer. Small contractors whose work is seasonal pay few, if any, additional benefits (Guldin 1984a). If forest

TABLE 11-2. Ranges of Hourly Wages and Rates of Mandatory Insurance for Selected States in 1984

	Wages		Mandatory Insurance			
State	Machine Operator ($/hour)	Laborer ($/hour)	Social Security[a] (%)	Unemployment[b] (%)	Workmen's Compensation[b] (%)	Total Insurance (%)
Washington	5.60-12.85	3.35-7.80	6.70	4.41	13.63	24.74
Oregon	5.10-13.50	3.35-6.90	6.70	5.23	8.57	20.50
California	6.50-15.40	3.35-7.20	6.70	3.40	8.65	18.75
North Carolina	5.30-13.20	3.50-8.60	6.70	3.51	3.31	13.52
Georgia	6.10- 9.50	3.35-5.20	6.70	2.70	5.12	14.52
Louisiana	5.40-12.50	3.35-6.50	6.70	5.36	4.80	16.86

Source: Unpublished survey of state employment and insurance agencies by the author.

[a]Social Security rate rose to 7.05% for both employers and employees on January 1, 1985.

[b]Unemployment and Workmen's Compensation rates are based on those for new firms entering the business. These rates are normally reduced somewhat after the firms have operated for several years and have established a satisfactory safety record.

product firms are typical of U.S. firms with 100 employees or more, all of them have paid holidays, 90% have partially or wholly paid health insurance, 70% have retirement plans in addition to Social Security, and 40% have other benefits (USDL Bureau of Labor Statistics 1985). Fringe benefits may add as much as one-third of the amount of direct wages to total labor costs.

Wages in forestry firms have been rising along with those in most other sectors. Although statistical series for forest management organizations are lacking, the trends are probably similar to general nonagricultural wages shown in Figure 11-1. Though current wages have increased continually, real wages rose slowly but steadily from the late 1940s to about 1973, at about 1.9% per year. There has been little change since 1973.

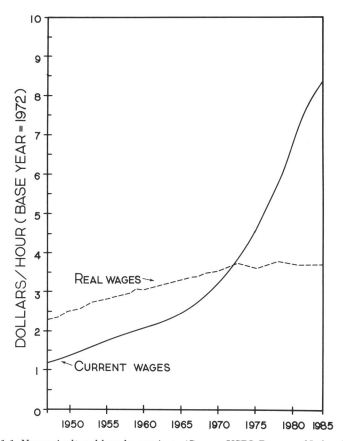

Figure 11-1. Nonagricultural hourly earnings. (*Source:* USDL Bureau of Labor Statistics, Employment and Earnings Statistics)

Vegetation management encounters labor problems in addition to those associated with other forestry operations:

1. Many treatments are not only seasonal but have a narrow and sometimes unpredictable period of time during which they are effective. For example, herbicide applications may have to be completed within a few weeks when the target vegetation is physiologically susceptible and conifers are comparatively resistant. This may cause difficult labor recruitment and scheduling problems, thereby raising labor costs.

2. The limited season for work may cause large per unit costs for job and safety training. By the time workers develop efficient and safe work routines, the treatment season may be over.

3. The work is physically demanding, thereby limiting the labor force willing and able to perform the vegetation management tasks. Crew turnover rates are often high, and injuries and allergies (both real and psychosomatic) associated with certain practices complicate labor problems further.

Equipment Cost

Equipment used in treatments includes the prime movers such as tractors that supply power and mobility, and attachments and other devices (see Chapter 6, Figure 6-3). Helicopters and fixed-wing airplanes used in aerial spraying constitute another major type of equipment; few forestry firms have their own fleet of aircraft used for such purposes. Consequently, costs of such equipment are usually incorporated into the contract price.

Unit costs of ground equipment used in vegetation management are usually expressed as dollars per hour operated. Hourly total costs (without operator) vary widely and depend on original cost of equipment, size and type of prime-mover traction (e.g., crawler or wheel), maintenance and repairs, and level of power (or load factor) required for the specific treatment (Caterpillar Tractor Co. 1984). For crawler-type tractors, site preparation with a shear blade is considered a medium-factor load, and pulling other equipment such as a rolling drum chopper is a light-factor load.

Components of equipment cost (excluding operator) are shown in Table 11-3 for four representative machines: relatively low-power (60 to 90 horsepower) crawler and wheel prime movers (the John Deere models) and medium-power (120 to 160 horsepower) crawler and wheel machines (the Caterpillar models). Owning costs per hour depend on estimated machine life; 10,000 hours over 5 yr is typical. Owning costs include depreciation of original cost (excluding tires), interest, insurance, and taxes (Miller 1973). Operating costs are dominated by fuel costs (which depend on load factors) and on repairs (which vary widely but which average 70 to 90% of the original cost annually).

The cost per hour for a given type of machine increases with horsepower, which is strongly related to size and weight. The work that can

TABLE 11-3. Estimates of Component Costs in 1984 for Selected Prime Movers

	John Deere		Caterpillar	
Cost Component	JD550 (Crawler)	JD540B (Wheel)	D6D (Crawler)	950 (Wheel)
Horsepower	72	90	140	155
Total life (years)	5	5	5	5
Total life (operating hours)	10,000	10,000	10,000	10,000
Delivered price ($)	62,181	56,190	131,000	92,000
Less tires ($)	—	9,707	—	5,240
Net value ($)	62,181	46,484	131,000	86,760
Owning costs ($/operating hour)				
Replacement cost	6.91	5.16	14.56	9.64
Interest, insurance, taxes	2.80	2.09	5.90	3.90
Total owning cost	9.71	7.26	20.45	13.54
Operating costs ($/operating hour)[a]				
Fuel (medium load)	2.81	3.41	7.13	5.24
Oil (engine, hydraulic)	0.16	0.15	0.52	0.56
Grease, lubricants	0.05	0.04	(incl.)	(incl.)
Filters, miscellaneous parts	0.06	0.05	0.13	0.08
Repairs (90% of replacement cost)	6.22	4.65	13.10	8.68
Tires	—	3.88	—	2.10
Total operating cost	9.30	12.18	20.88	16.65
Total owning and operating cost ($/operating hour)	19.01	19.44	41.33	30.19

Source: Computations are based on methods derived from Caterpillar Tractor Co. (1984) and current data from equipment manufacturers. Mention of specific pieces of equipment does not constitute endorsement of use or preference over other brands and models of comparable design.

[a]Operating costs do not include operator wages.

be done per hour also increases with weight and horsepower. The optimal size of tractor for each type of job is determined by maximum size of vegetation to be treated or removed, size of equipment to be pulled or pushed, terrain, and soil conditions. The trade-offs between versatility, work speed, and per hour costs are numerous, and operating experience is the best guide for selecting an appropriate machine and cost record.

Current equipment prices have risen rapidly in recent years (Tufts et al. 1981). Average price indexes for machinery and equipment from 1947 to 1984 are shown in Figure 11-2. Though current costs have risen each year, sometimes rapidly, real costs have had a zigzag pattern. Real costs increased in the 1940s and 1950s, declined until the early 1970s, then increased to 1980, leveling off in recent years. In general, the efficiency of most equipment has been increasing because of technical improvements

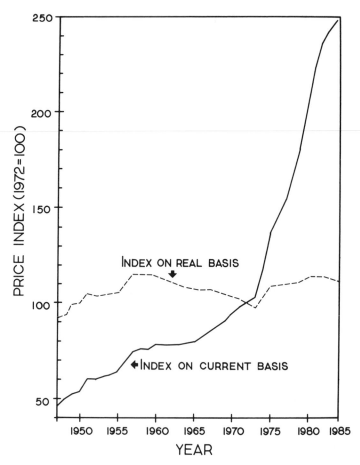

Figure 11-2. Machinery and equipment price indexes. (*Source:* USDL Bureau of Labor Statistics, Producer Prices and Price Indexes)

and increased abilities of new machines. Another factor has been the entry of foreign competitors into the equipment market.

Though prime movers—either crawler or rubber wheeled—differ little between brands within a given horsepower range, they are used with a wide variety of attachments designed especially for site preparation. These include blades, rakes, disks, and crushers. Ground and aerial spray equipment are used for site preparation, release, and timber stand improvement (cull tree removal). Numerous hand- and portable-power tools are used for release and precommercial thinning (Larson and Hallman 1980).

Analyses and decisions must be made concerning whether to invest in specialized equipment adapted to particular sites and conditions or use equipment with a wide range of versatility, though perhaps it is not quite as efficient or effective. Analysis of equipment trade-offs may require projection of program needs for several years.

Herbicide Costs

A major variable cost in herbicide treatments is the chemical. Typical 1985 costs for major forestry herbicides from wholesale suppliers are shown in Table 11-4. Costs per unit area treated are not necessarily proportional to per gallon costs. Applied costs depend on the herbicide

TABLE 11-4. Representative Wholesale Costs of Major Forestry Herbicides Purchased in Minimal Lots in 1985

Herbicide Common Name	Representative Product	Manufacturer	Quantity	Cost[a]
Amitrole	Amitrol T ®	Union Carbide	2.5 gal	$39.90/gal
Amitrole/simazine	Amizine ®	Union Carbide	2.5 gal	19.08/gal
Asulam	Asulox ®	Rhone-Poulenc	2.5 gal	42.50/gal
Atrazine	Aatrex ® 4L	Ciba-Geigy	2.5 gal	9.10/gal
Bromacil	Hyvar ® X-L	DuPont	5 gal	13.80/gal
Dalapon-Na	Dowpon ® M	Dow	10 lb	2.02/gal
Dicamba	Banvel ® 4-W.S.	Velsicol	2.5 gal	58.20/gal
Dichlobenil	Casoron ® G-4	Thompson-Hayward	50 lb	1.15/lb
Fosamine	Krenite ®	DuPont	5 gal	50.50/gal
Glyphosate	Roundup ®	Monsanto	5 gal	91.00/gal
Hexazinone	Velpar ® L	DuPont	5 gal	51.20/gal
MSMA	Trans-Vert ®	Union Carbide	5 gal	24.50/gal
Oxyfluorfen	Goal ® 2EC	Rohm and Haas	2.5 gal	62.10/gal
Picloram	Tordon ® 10K	Dow	50 lb	4.25/lb
Picloram/2,4-D	Tordon ® 101R	Dow	5 gal	17.85/gal
Picloram/2,4-D	Tordon ® 101	Dow	5 gal	33.85/gal
Simazine	Princep ® 80W	Ciba-Geigy	5 lb	3.20/lb
Sulfometuron	Oust ®	DuPont	48 oz	8.20/oz
Tebuthiuron	Spike ® 80W	Elanco	50 lb	21.00/lb
Triclopyr amine	Garlon ® A	Dow	5 gal	53.80/gal
Triclopyr ester	Garlon ® 4	Dow	5 gal	71.50/gal
Trifluralin	Treflan ®	Elanco	2.5 gal	32.80/gal
2,4-D amine	DMA ® 4	DOW	5 gal	13.90/gal
2,4-D ester	Esteron ® 99 ® Concentrate	DOW	5 gal	11.00/gal
2,4-DP	Weedone ® 2,4-DP	Union Carbide	5 gal	22.50/gal

Source: Unpublished survey of three or more distributors for each herbicide by author. Mention of specific trade names does not imply endorsement of these products to the exclusion of other brands. They are simply used to provide representative examples.
[a]Discounts are usually available for purchasing larger quantities.

used and the method and rate of application, which are dictated by the species to be controlled and their size and distribution. Effectiveness on the weed species and resistance or tolerance of the conifers are generally more important in selecting herbicides than relative cost.

Long-term trends in average costs of herbicides used in forestry have been influenced by both prices of specific herbicides and environmental regulations. Some low-cost, broad-spectrum herbicides such as 2,4,5-T and silvex have been withdrawn from use in the United States. Their replacements have generally been more expensive. The cost of 2,4-D, a commonly used forestry herbicide, and price indexes for a constant market basket of agricultural chemicals are shown in Figure 11-3. Prices for oil, the chief feedstock for herbicides, have a major influence on chemical prices. Real costs declined until the early 1970s but increased sharply

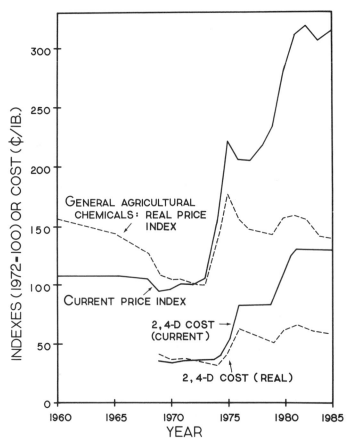

Figure 11-3. General agricultural chemical price index and 2,4-D cost. (*Source:* U.S. Department of Agriculture 1984)

following the oil crises in 1973 and 1978-1979. In addition, some herbicides require petroleum-based carriers or adjuvants whose costs have also risen.

Prices of proprietary pesticides are set by manufacturers. Development of herbicides involves many years of effort and by the time a new pesticide is registered for use and marketed, the manufacturer has invested millions of dollars. Two types of research—efficacy/toxicological testing and marketing research—must go on concurrently and are important factors in decisions to go forward or to terminate development of a product.

On the basis of studies that identify pests for which controls may have adequate markets, firms screen thousands of compounds, pilot testing promising ones on pest plants or organisms to identify their range of effectiveness. Potentially useful chemicals must then undergo a variety of toxicological tests to determine possible human health and environmental hazards. Strengthened safety regulations and potential liability problems have sharply increased these development costs.

While developing a new product, manufacturers must evaluate its effectiveness or cost advantages relative to other chemicals now registered for the proposed applications. They must decide whether potential sales revenues at a competitive price will cover the manufacturing cost, repay the investment in research and development over time, and return a profit.

Even when registration and labeling are accomplished and a new product is put on the market, the uncertainties for the manufacturer are considerable. The length of product life may be shortened by a still newer product that is cheaper or more effective. Manufacturers must also consider the risks of liability and shortened product life if the pesticide causes health or environmental damage not suspected when initially registered.

Fixed Costs

Supervision and administrative overhead costs incurred by vegetation management treatments are considered fixed because they are not proportional to project size. Large projects, for example, may require little more supervision or overhead than small projects. Supervisory costs charged to vegetation management projects in the South range from 4 to 15% of total costs (Table 11-5). Percentages for overhead have a slightly wider range. They include such highly variable items as moving equipment to sites, support services (e.g., personnel, purchasing, contract administration, security, and storage facilities), project planning, training and certification, research, environmental assessments (where required), environmental monitoring, community notification, public relations, and sometimes litigation.

These costs, which firms may or may not include in their tabulations and reporting of treatment costs, are nonetheless incurred. Federal agen-

TABLE 11-5. Fixed Costs as a Percentage of Total Treatment Costs for Selected Vegetation Management Practices in the South in 1984

Treatment	Method	Super-vision	Over-head	Total Fixed
		Percentage of total treatment costs		
Mechanical site preparation	Various	4.3	13.3	17.6
Prescribed burning	Hand-held			
	drip torch	15.0	15.1	30.1
	Aerial ignite	5.3	4.5	9.8
Chemical release	Aerial spray	5.4	1.8	7.2
	Backpack spray	12.7	2.7	15.4
	Stem injection	9.4	11.4	20.8
	Mobile ground			
	spray	10.4	3.4	13.8
Precommercial thinning[a]	Power saw	6.9	2.0	8.9

Source: Straka and Watson (1985).
[a]Includes cutting of unmerchantable hardwoods as well as conifers.

cies, for example, have had to spend large amounts preparing environmental impact statements and defending decisions and operations against lawsuits seeking to restrict vegetation management treatments, particularly those that involve herbicides and prescribed burning. A large environmental impact statement may cost $1 million or more in direct and indirect costs. Increased expenditures on planning, analysis, and environmental assessments may, in some cases, lead to more selective and localized prescriptions, thereby reducing the area requiring treatments and avoiding undesirable environmental damage.

Average Unit Costs for Vegetation Management

The sum of all variable and fixed costs of vegetation management comprises total costs per project. Because almost all forest planning is conducted on a unit area basis, forest managers usually think of costs in terms of total costs per acre treated.

Despite the approximately $1 billion spent each year on forest management, only fragmentary information on unit costs in forestry is available. For the South, the best data are a series of reports published at irregular intervals for more than 30 years (Worrell 1953, Yoho and Fish 1961, Somberg et al. 1963, Yoho et al. 1969, Moak and Kucera 1975, Moak et al. 1977, Moak et al. 1980, Moak 1982, Straka and Watson 1985). This series, which may be called the Worrell-Yoho-Moak reports, also offers some measure of trends in costs. For the Pacific Northwest, the Industrial Forestry Association (1979) has also prepared average cost data, though on a somewhat more limited basis. The only nationwide studies have been of USDA Forest Service silvicultural contracts (Row 1971, Mills et al. 1985), but they cover only two limited periods of time and are not comparable.

A primary difficulty in assembling and reporting costs is the extreme diversity of treatments actually applied. As previously mentioned, foresters tailor all silvicultural operations to specific conditions on the tracts to be treated, season of application, growing conditions expected, and the type of timber stand desired. Treatments in the broad class of site preparation, for example, may include scores of variations in shearing, raking, crushing, disking, herbicide application, and broadcast and windrow burning. Consequently, average costs may be of little use to forest planners. Several broad generalizations may be made, however:

1. In all foresty regions of the United States and Canada, unit costs by tract or by contract vary within broad ranges. This wide variation has important implications for budgeting of vegetation treatments—average costs may not be very useful in operational planning. Cost estimates for individual projects should be based on documented experience in the immediate locality and under conditions to be expected, as tempered by professional judgment.

2. Costs in the western forestry regions are generally higher for the same treatment or combination of treatments than in the South, Northeast, or Lake states. Intensively managed commercial forests are more likely to be on rugged terrain in the West. Labor rates in the West are also higher.

3. Public agencies such as the USDA Forest Service and USDI Bureau of Land Management have higher costs than forest industry and private owners for the same treatment and method. Some attribute the difference to more concern over cost-effectiveness in corporate and private organizations. Comparisons of average costs for broad categories of treatments between public and private forest lands may be deceptive, however, because treatment prescription practices may be quite different (Guldin 1983a). Federal agencies are also subjected to a variety of regulatory and administrative requirements, such as compliance with the National Environmental Policy Act and the National Forest Management Act, which add substantial indirect costs to forestry activities by those agencies.

Representative Vegetation Management Costs

The latest compilation in the Worrell-Yoho-Moak reports (Straka and Watson 1985) subdivides many of the broad silvicultural treatment classes into specific treatment combinations and associated costs. Table 11-6 shows their breakdown for the South and also includes cost ranges for other regions where the information was readily available.

TABLE 11-6. Representative Costs of Vegetation Management Treatments in 1984[a]

	South[b]	Northwest[c]		Northeast and Lake States[d]	
Treatment	Private	Private	Public	Private	Public
	Dollars per acre				
Site Preparation					
Mechanical					
Shear	60	50–80	—	60–90	80–130
Disk or single chop	45	40–100	60–150	—	70–120
Bed	30	—	—	—	—
Double-chop	60	—	80–200	50–75	—
Crush	75	—	—	—	—
Shear, rake, pile	95	80–200	100–250	80–120	—
Shear, rake, pile, bed	155	"	"	"	—
Shear, rake, pile, disk	145	"	"	"	—
Chop, rake, pile, disk	110	"	"	"	—
Slash disposal					
Broadcast burning	10	50–90	100–400	—	—
Windrow burning	5	20	30	—	—
Herbicide application					
Stem injection	55	50–100	—	60–80	—
Aerial spray	50	30–70	50–100	40–60	40–60
Spot ground spray[e]	40	25–60	50–200	—	50–70
Release					
Herbicide application					
Backpack spray	55	50–100	90–180	—	50–70
Aerial spray	40	30–70	70–160	—	40–100
Manual cutting					
Brush cutting	—	—	120–300	—	100–200
Precomm. thinning[f]	45	30–130	100–220	60–200	100–250
Timber Stand Improvement					
Herbicide application					
Stem injection	55	—	—	—	—
Mobile ground spray	80	—	—	—	—
Understory burning	10	—	—	—	—

[a]Cost figures presented should be viewed as broad regional averages. For any particular treatment there is generally a wide range in cost because of factors such as site variation and unit size. Costs shown include both variable and fixed cost components.
[b]Primary source of cost figures is the report by Straka and Watson (1985), supplemented by information obtained from professional contacts by the author.
[c]Primary source of cost figures is the Industrial Forestry Association in Portland, Oregon, coupled with information obtained from USDA Forest Service documents (e.g., environmental impact statements) and from professional contacts by the author.
[d]Primary sources of cost figures are USDA Forest Service documents (e.g., environmental impact statements) coupled with information obtained from contacts by the author.
[e]Involves band and spot sprays of preemergence herbicides to control herbaceous weeds at the time of planting or shortly thereafter.
[f]Includes cutting of unmerchantable hardwoods as well as conifers.

In the South, mechanical site preparation costs range from $30/acre for simple bedding operations where terrain is flat and vegetation is primarily herbaceous, to $155/acre for highly intensive operations where terrain is rugged and woody vegetation is dense. Burning of logging slash and woody debris adds another $5 to $10/acre. Where suitable, chemical site preparation and release can be accomplished for as little as $40 to $55/acre. Manual brush cutting is not generally practiced in the South, but cutting of unmerchantable hardwoods at the time of precommercial thinning has been done for $45/acre. Timber stand improvement activities range from $10/acre for understory burning to $55 to $80/acre for chemical control of cull hardwoods and brush.

Cost information for the Northwest, Northeast, and Lake states regions is less well documented, but broad averages have been derived from a composite of sources (Table 11-6). Except for herbicide applications, the costs in these regions tend to be higher than those in the South, primarily because of more difficult terrain and higher labor costs. Furthermore, the costs for public agencies (which manage large acreages in these regions) are usually much more than for private landowners. As mentioned earlier, a variety of conditions and constraints make management practices more expensive in the public sector. For example, Forest Service land is generally more rugged and less productive than either industrial forest lands or those owned by farmers or other individuals. The average size of project tracts on federal lands is generally smaller because of policy limitations on size of clearcut areas—thus reducing economies of tract size.

Two studies of silvicultural contracts for National Forests have shown marked cost differences for similar treatments by forest type and various other factors (Row 1971, Mills et al. 1985). Data from Mills et al. (1985) are shown in Table 11-7. Each of the silvicultural practice groups are so broad, however, that the information may indicate more about the average treatment intensity than the relationship to cost of any particular treatment or method.

Another compilation averages costs for treatments on nonindustrial private lands assisted by the Forestry Incentives Program in the South (Vasievich 1985). These costs show patterns similar to the other studies, with per acre costs (without planting) of "light" site preparation of $40, "medium" site preparation $70, and "heavy" site preparation $105. Average costs of precommercial thinning, cull tree removal (usually by stem injection), and release are from $40 to $45/acre.

INFLUENCE OF PROJECT AND SITE FACTORS ON COSTS

Information on the effect of project and site factors on costs has come principally from statistical analyses of silvicultural treatments conducted by public agencies. A number of studies made prior to 1970 have developed

TABLE 11-7. Average Costs per Acre of USDA Forest Service Silvicultural Contracts, 1975-1978

Forest-Type Group	Site Preparation	Reforestation	Site Preparation and Reforestation	Intermediate Treatments[a]	Slash Disposal
			Dollars per acre		
Northern conifers	37	50	—	19	—
Southern pines	46	37	—	37	—
Central hardwoods	47	—	—	—	—
Northern hardwoods	20	57	—	18	—
Douglas-fir	63	75	91	53	99
Ponderosa/white pine	48	73	96	32	29
Mixed spruce	61	66	77	66	44
Lodgepole pine	43	71	53	56	—

Source: Mills et al. (1985).
[a]Includes precommercial thinning, release, and timber stand improvement.

the research methodology and determined which factors are significantly associated with cost. Among these are: (1) Wikstrom and Alley (1967) found a consistent influence of tract size and treatment difficulty on USDA Forest Service project costs in Montana, northern Idaho, and eastern Washington; (2) Hilliker et al. (1969) found that site differences were major factors affecting project costs of state lands in Wisconsin; and (3) Conkin (1971) found tract size, measures of difficulty, and type of equipment accounted for significant portions of cost variation in state agency projects in the North. However, the cost levels reported in these studies are dated.

Broad Coverage Analyses

An analysis by Row (1971) of all silvicultural contracts let by the USDA Forest Service from July 1969 through June 1970 indicated that costs of many major treatments were strongly related to measurable on-the-ground factors. Some 773 of the contracts included five broad types of treatment that were suitable for regression analysis: slash disposal, site preparation, hand planting, powersaw thinning, and helicopter spraying. The area in the treated tracts significantly affected cost per unit area for all categories. In all treatments except helicopter spraying, measures of difficulty of work were significant: terrain for all treatments; season of year for slash disposal and site preparation; number and age of trees for planting; and size of trees for powersaw thinning. What is most important, the apparent fixed cost associated with each contract was related to the apparent level of mechanization or capital investment in equipment. Helicopter operations had the highest fixed costs; hand planting had relatively low fixed costs.

Row's (1971) basic cost model for each treatment type was

$$TC = b_f + b_t (NT - 1) + b_a * AC + \sum_{p=1}^{p} (b_{Vp} * V_p * AC)$$

where TC = total cost in dollars
NT = number of tracts
AC = total acres treated
V_p = one of p influencing variables
b_f = coefficient for fixed cost
b_t = coefficient for cost of additional tracts
b_a = coefficient for total area
b_{Vp} = coefficient for p influencing variables.

Data for regions were included in one regression for each treatment. For example, the equation developed for site preparation is

$$TC = 542 + 158 \, (NT - 1) + 30.9 \, AC + 8.2 \, D * AC$$
$$+ 5.5 \, S * AC + 11.0 \, DF * AC + 4.7 \, PP * AC$$

where the additional influencing variables are

D = 1 if more than 1/2 hour travel time from work base; 0 otherwise
S = 1 if treatment in summer; 0 otherwise
DF = 1 if treatment in Douglas-fir forest type; 0 otherwise
PP = 1 if treatment in ponderosa pine forest type; 0 otherwise

A study by Olson et al. (1978) developed equations for six types of treatment—hand planting, machine site preparation, aerial spraying, prescribed burning, manual release, and precommercial thinning—but on public lands in Minnesota and Michigan. In all the equations, costs were related to project acreage. For all treatments except aerial spraying and prescribed burning, intensity of treatment or method used influenced costs also.

Olson et al. (1978) employed a cost model similar to the one used by Row. Examples of the equations they developed, all for the North, are

Site Preparation

$$TC = 86 + 33.9 \, AC - 7.1 \, OP * AC$$

where OP is −1 where a machine-pushing operation, +1 where a machine-pulling operation,

Manual Release

$$TC = 73 + .95 \, BAR * AC$$

where BAR is basal area removed in square feet per acre,

Aerial Spraying

$$TC = 3.4 + 8.7 \, AC$$

In their analysis of 2957 silvicultural contracts let by the USDA Forest Service from 1975 to 1978, Mills et al. (1985) developed cost prediction equations for four broad types of silvicultural treatments: slash disposal, site preparation, reforestation, and intermediate treatments (which included individual stem treatment and broadcast release, precommercial thinning, and timber stand improvement). Per acre costs of slash disposal and site preparation in southern pine, Douglas-fir, and ponderosa/white pine types decreased with size of tract, linkage of multiple areas in the same contract, and several other factors. Reforestation costs (tree planting) were related to slope or elevation above sea level and presence of obstacles, in addition to size of tract. Costs of intermediate treatments were generally related to area treated, linkage of multiple areas in the same contract, and slope in Douglas-fir and ponderosa/white pine types.

The model of Mills et al. (1985) considered each explanatory variable independently; that is, without considering that some variables may affect the fixed cost and some the per acre variable cost. For example, the equation developed for site preparation in southern pine is

$$TC = 846 + 22.8\,AC - 79.8\,MA + 213.6\,DBH$$

where the additional variables are

MA is 1 if multiple tracts, 0 if single tracts;
DBH is average diameter at breast height of treated trees (in inches)

The equation for the Douglas-fir forest type is

$$TC = 3647 + 18.5\,AC - 290.2\,MA.$$

Studies of Specific Treatments

A study by Guldin (1983b) of planting costs for 42 contracts in the South in 1980 and 1981 illustrates the trade-offs between vegetation management and other treatment costs. He found that the cost of planting was significantly reduced by the amount spent on site preparation, particularly on bedding that reduces vegetative competition. Factors that increased costs were the number of parcels into which the tract was divided, slopes over 5%, and machine planting. Similar results have been reported by Gardner (1981).

Other analyses of factors influencing particular silvicultural costs include the studies of cull tree removal in southern pine stands (Balmer et al. 1978), vine removal in the Northeast (Smith and Smithson 1975), planting southern pines (Sundra and Lowry 1975, Weaver and Ostenhous 1976), and prescribed burning in the South (Vasievich 1980). A common factor in all of these studies was the influence of the size of tract on the cost of treatments.

Variation in Costs Encountered

In the Row (1971), Olson et al. (1978), and Mills et al. (1985) studies, the apparent explanatory variables accounted for modest to major proportions of the variation. Planting regressions had the closest fits, with R^2 values from 0.81 to 0.94. Regressions for site preparation, helicopter operations, release, and thinning had R^2 values ranging from 0.38 to 0.95, indicating that in many of the equations important factors may not have been included or that the operations were inherently variable. The standard deviations, or the range within which two-thirds of the predictions using the equations would fall, were from 28 to 81% of the average value.

This degree of accuracy is perhaps sufficient for estimating costs in long range planning but still leaves much to be desired for operational planning. Nevertheless, use of the equations to estimate costs is signif-

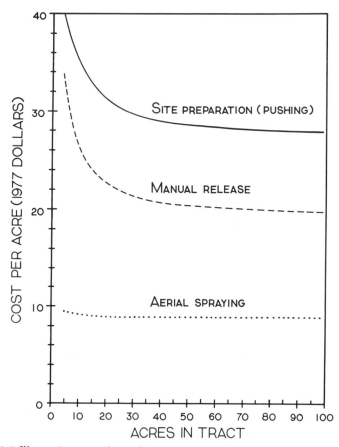

Figure 11-4. Illustrative cost relationships for site preparation, manual release, and aerial spraying as a function of tract size. (*Source:* Olson et al. 1978)

icantly better than using regional or forest-type averages. The accuracy of the relationships suggests that estimation of on-the-ground costs by experienced professionals should be used if they are available and if the treatments have been used in the locality.

Importance of Tract Size

In nearly all studies of influences on cost of silvicultural treatments, tract size has been significant. The most common relationship is the reverse J-shaped curve that would result from a fixed cost per tract being spread over a range of tract sizes. These relationships have been plotted in Figure 11-4 for three of the treatments studied by Olson et al. (1978). Acreage-affected cost relationships have been used to simulate the economies of size in management and harvesting of forest tracts (Row 1978, Cubbage 1983b). Depending on type of treatment, most economies of size are realized in tracts larger than 50 to 100 acres.

The prevalence of this cost relationship has many management policy implications for both public and private forest management (Cubbage 1983a). For industrial forests, it stresses the importance of management of sufficiently large compartments or stands so economies of size are realized. For private, nonindustrial forest ownerships and the programs that assist them, it means that vegetation management and timber growing in general may be unprofitable on small tracts unless costs are carefully controlled (Mills and Cain 1976). For large public agencies such as national forests, it emphasizes the difficult trade-offs between the efficient management of moderate- to large-size units versus the environmental and aesthetic advantages of managing small and irregular parcels of land (Guldin 1984b).

TRENDS IN COSTS OF VEGETATION MANAGEMENT

The trends from long-term cost data such as the Worrell-Yoho-Moak series are subject to considerable qualification. In the 30 years of the series, the nature and intensity of the treatments, and perhaps their definitions, have changed substantially. Nevertheless, Figure 11-5 shows the trends for two representative treatments: mechanical site preparation and chemical release.

None of the trends in current costs shows steady increases, such as might be expected from the continued increases in labor, equipment, and chemical costs. The trends in real costs are irregular but generally upward. Because the differences between successive cost averages may be affected by the mix of respondents and the areas they represent, or other confounding influences, small interval-to-interval changes are not likely to be significant. Despite these qualifications, this evidence of long-term

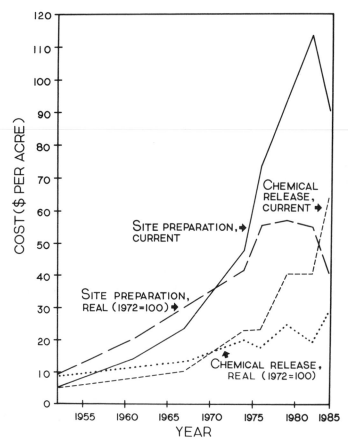

Figure 11-5. Trends in vegetation management costs in the southern United States. (*Source:* Straka and Watson 1985)

increases in real costs is persuasive. The average annual rates of increase, computed from the first 1952 survey data to an average of the 1982 and 1984 survey results (all adjusted for inflation by GNP deflators), are 5.3% for mechanical site preparation; 3.3% for chemical release; and 6.4% for prescribed burning. Even if silvicultural techniques have intensified, these costs trends still indicate actual increases in outlays for firms.

COST ESTIMATION METHODS

The foregoing discussion indicates that forest planners should rely heavily on local sources for estimating costs. In most organizations, analysts should use their recent operational experience. If the financial records have been kept on an individual project-by-project basis, relating project costs to project conditions may be possible. Some organizations have operational data base systems that compile the required information. The methods by which this information may be analyzed are presented in cost accounting texts such as Dopuch et al. (1982). Among these methods are:

1. *Analysis of Historical Cost Data.* Though use of individual project cost data is preferable, average costs per unit accomplished by season or other short period, and by operating unit, can be used. The data should be checked to make sure that operating or accounting policies have not introduced irrelevant or confounding factors and that the data are homogeneous or from similar kinds of projects. Cost data should match accomplishment data by time period and unit. Data over several years old should be adjusted for inflation if appropriate. Plots of average costs by treatment method, period, or operating unit may reveal "outlier" observations that are quite different from the main body of information. They should be investigated to determine whether they are the result of nonrecurring factors or unique conditions (in which case they should be discarded) or are merely instances of extreme but normal behavior (and, therefore, kept in the sample). Analysis by treatment method and year will indicate average costs, the range of costs to be expected, and perhaps trends.

2. *Cost Estimating Equations.* In addition to the preceding approach, costs may be related to explanatory factors (Wikstrom and Alley 1967, Row 1971, Olson et al. 1978, Guldin 1984b, Mills et al. 1985). The methodology is also presented in standard texts and special monographs (Johnson 1960, Dean 1966). Factors that should be particularly considered are acreage in the tracts, grouping of similar tracts in one contract or project, measures of slope, elevation, or distance from work center, and ground conditions inhibiting movement of workers or equipment. However, only factors that can be measured or estimated well in advance of operations should be used. This eliminates using weather or other transitory conditions that cannot be predicted easily, even though they may significantly influence costs.

3. *Engineering Methods or Built-Up Costs.* When experience with the treatment or method to be used is insufficient to develop a record of historical costs, analysts may estimate costs from projected requirements of labor, equipment, and materials. Such an approach is universally used by engineers and architects for structures or transport facilities and has been used for logging costs. Preliminary estimates can be derived from machine time studies and analyses (Anderson 1976). The resources are priced using historical data on cost of labor, equipment, and supplies, supplemented by estimates of supervision and other overhead.

In vegetation management, estimates of requirements can be difficult to make for new treatment alternatives. A factor that should be considered in estimating costs for relatively new treatments or methods is the "learning curve." The first few times a treatment is conducted, it may be relatively expensive because workers may not know routines and may make mistakes. As experience is gained, however, average costs per unit accomplished should decline. The decline in costs experienced in new treatments may be sufficiently significant to suggest that it be taken into account in estimating future costs and in adjusting past project costs. No studies of the "learning effect" in forestry practices have been published.

ESTIMATING TIMBER VALUES

Evaluation of and planning for vegetation management also needs values for the timber to be produced. Prices for timber are usually expressed as values of standing timber ready to be sold and cut, or "stumpage prices." Values for timber vary widely, just as costs do. Among the factors that must be considered are (1) prevailing prices for species or species groups; (2) long-term trends in timber prices; (3) differentials for tree and stand characteristics; and (4) other local factors.

Regional Prices for Timber Species or Species Groups

Fortunately, sources of information on regional timber values for major species are readily available. At a minimum, most states regularly report prices for various species of timber, usually by sawtimber and pulpwood classifications. In some states, this information is a by-product of assessing the timber for yield or severance taxes. In addition, regions of the USDA Forest Service release average bid prices for timber sales and average cut prices for timber harvested (e.g., Ruderman and Warren 1985, Warren 1986).

Table 11-8 shows average bid prices for softwood sawtimber sold from National Forest lands in major regions in the first quarter of 1985. The large differences between species and regions indicate major variations in tree size, wood quality, end use demands, and market competition. In some regions the demand for stumpage from public and private lands is highly competitive, with many firms bidding on most sales. In other areas, there are only a few timber buyers, and competition is somewhat lower, thereby leading to lower prices.

In the South, one regular source of price information is *Timber-Mart South* (published monthly). This service is based on private timber sale transactions in the southern states, and it reports prices by major species groups, size classifications, and geographic provinces. Evaluation of the *Timber-Mart* reporting service has shown it to have little apparent bias (Wallace and Silver 1981). A *Timber-Mart North* service is also being initiated by the same publisher but as yet only covers Michigan.

Effects of Tree and Stand Characteristics on Values

Timber quality has a pronounced effect on timber prices because large trees are cheaper to log, haul, and process, and large and defect-free logs yield high proportions of upper grade and, thus, high priced products. Even though differences often may not be fully recognized in timber markets, they are important in conducting vegetation management programs. Secondary benefits of treatments are improvements in average tree size and quality and accessibility.

In a limited sense, the commercial distinction between pulpwood and sawtimber recognizes an important value difference. Prices for sawtimber, converted to value per cubic feet, are generally several multiples of similarly converted prices for pulpwood. Separate prices for sawtimber and pulpwood should be used in all evaluations of timber-growing investments but analysts differ on the use of price distinctions within the broad classes of sawtimber and pulpwood. In the informal markets for stumpage, a wide variety of other factors, in addition to wood quality differences, seem to affect prices and mask quality premiums.

In the last several decades a number of statistical analyses of individual timber sales have shown that average tree size and grade, stand density, and other factors have major effects on stumpage prices. If the effects of long-term trends and cyclical fluctuations are removed, such quality factors are associated with a high proportion of the variation in prices. Using various factors, Guttenberg (1956), Guttenberg and Row (1961), Holley (1970), Anderson (1973), and Row (1973), developed stumpage price prediction equations for southern pine sold from National Forests. Anderson (1961, 1969) found similar relationships with private southern timber. Typical findings were that timber that averaged 19 in. DBH was twice as valuable per cubic foot as that 12 in. DBH, which was twice as valuable as 8-in. DBH timber (Row 1973). Recent changes in log processing and the trend toward whole tree merchandizing have changed the specific diameter limits but not the general relationships.

In the West, fewer studies of stumpage prices using individual sales have been made. Nevertheless, the existence of stumpage price differentials, at least by average size of tree cut, has been demonstrated, and the effect on the profitability of timber growing has been determined (Darr 1973, Randall and Darr 1974).

Other Price Factors

Among the other factors that forest managers and planners should consider are short-term market cycles, location of timber with respect to mills, difficulty of logging, and temporary competitive situations. All have been shown to influence stumpage price but are primarily local or transient in nature.

TABLE 11-8. Average Bid Prices for Softwood Sawtimber Sold from National Forests, First Quarter 1985

	Forest Service Region[a]							
	1	2	3	4	5	6	8	9
	$/MBF[b]							
Western softwoods								
Cedar								
Incense	—	—	—	—	58	89	—	—
Port-Orford	—	—	—	—	—	266	—	—
Western red	81	—	—	—	—	130	—	—
Douglas-fir[c]								
(east side)	37	7	7	43	—	37	—	—
(west side)	—	—	—	—	64	125	—	—
Fir								
Grand	28	—	—	20	—	56	—	—
Noble	—	—	—	—	—	41	—	—
Shasta red	—	—	—	—	—	62	—	—
Sub-alpine	28	6	—	4	—	—	—	—
White	—	—	—	26	—	33	—	—
Hemlock								
Western	35	—	—	—	—	51	—	—
Larch	39	—	—	17	—	35	—	—
Pine								
Lodgepole	28	14	—	31	26	21	—	—
Ponderosa	50	12	16	26	84	152	—	—
Sugar	—	—	—	—	93	164	—	—
Western white	87	—	—	—	—	140	—	—
Redwood	—	—	—	—	84	77	—	—

Projecting Price Trends

The timber prices of most concern are not current prices but prices that would be received when treated timber stands are ready for sale or harvest, normally 15 to 80 years away. Forecasting trends in real timber prices is controversial. A number of methods have been used—graphic or statistical curve fitting, and single- and multiple-equation econometric models. If quarterly or monthly time series are used, adjustments for seasonal patterns should be made. For all time series, the major problem is to distinguish long-term trends from business cycle fluctuations. Using a series that starts in a timber economic recession and ends in an economic boom period, or vice versa, may lead to erroneous projected rates of increase or decrease.

Trends for major types of stumpage vary markedly. Hardwood timber,

TABLE 11-8. (*Continued*)

	Forest Service Region[a]							
	1	2	3	4	5	6	8	9
Spruce								
Englemann	33	14	—	13	—	17	—	—
Sitka	—	—	—	—	—	91	—	—
Eastern softwoods								
Pine								
Eastern white	—	—	—	—	—	—	71	73
Red	—	—	—	—	—	—	—	29
Southern yellow	—	—	—	—	—	—	51	118
Spruce								
All	—	—	—	—	—	—	—	24

Source: USDA Forest Service, Washington, DC.
[a]Forest Service regions cover, in general:
1.Montana, Northern Idaho
2.Wyoming, Colorado
3.Arizona, New Mexico
4.Utah, Nevada, Southern Idaho
5.California
6.Oregon, Washington
8.Minnesota, Wisconsin, Michigan, Missouri, Illinois, Indiana, Ohio, Kentucky, Pennsylvania, West Virginia, Vermont, New Hampshire
9.Virginia, North Carolina, South Carolina, Georgia, Florida, Alabama, Tennessee, Mississippi, Louisiana, Texas, Arkansas, Oklahoma
[b]MBF = thousand board feet (Scribner scale).
[c]Douglas-fir is separated into that grown east of the crest of the Cascade Mountains and that grown west.

either sawtimber or pulpwood, has not increased in real value (except for fine hardwood species of exceptionally high value). Softwood pulpwood prices have generally increased slowly—at one-half percent a year or less. The irregular upward trends in sawtimber stumpage prices for several softwood species over long periods of time are quite striking (Figure 11-6), however. Simple extrapolation of such trends, depending on the period chosen for the relationship, may suggest that future values of timber are likely to be substantially greater than recently experienced. However, the trends are in some contrast to those of indexes of lumber and wood products, which have increased little in real value in the last 35 years (Figure 11-7).

    Forest sector models, such as the Timber Assessment Market Model (TAMM) by Adams and Haynes (1980), have used spatial market-equilibrium techniques to project timber values (as well as regional production, timber growth, and trade). The recent revision of the model (Haynes

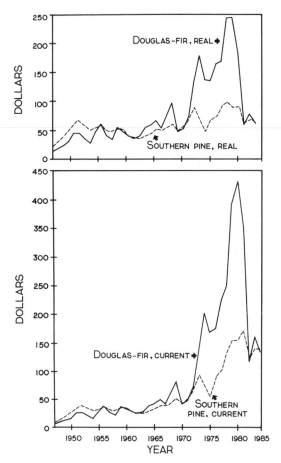

Figure 11-6. Historical stumpage prices of Douglas-fir and southern pine. (*Source:* Ulrich 1984)

and Adams 1985) has sharply reduced the expected rates of timber price increase, and thus future price, anticipated only a few years ago (Table 11-9).

Some analysts, however, believe that the historical trends in prices may be related to nonrecurring historical developments, such as the harvest of most of the western old-growth timber and the failure of new sources of timber to develop in the western United States and Canada—factors that caused much of the rise in this century. They believe that because an increasing proportion of timber used is coming from second-growth forests, the rate of price increase will level off. Thus they suggest that it is unwise to count on future price increases of the magnitude of those in the past. Indeed, many of the simulations using the TAMM model that assume lower than expected growth in housing demand, increased

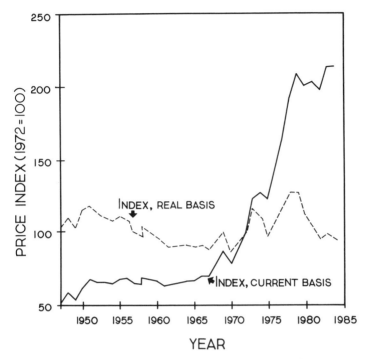

Figure 11-7. Lumber and wood products price indexes. (*Source:* USDL Bureau of Labor Statistics, Producer Prices and Price Indexes)

TABLE 11-9. Currently Expected Relative Price Indexes for Timber Coming from Various Regions of the United States

Year	North	South	Rocky Mts.	Douglas-fir	Ponderosa	California
			Region			
			1982 dollars per MBF[a]			
1980	57	156	60	173	93	114
1990	72	224	119	224	93	87
2000	102	251	108	192	84	117
2010	137	317	153	254	132	165
2020	186	368	213	323	183	224
2030	213	458	257	377	221	287
			Average annual rate of change (%)			
1980–2030	2.67	2.18	2.96	1.56	1.75	1.87

Source: Haynes and Adams (1985). Values converted to 1982 dollars by the Producer Price Index, the index used in the study.
[a]MBF = thousand board feet (Scribner scale).

National Forest harvests, or increasing industrial or nonindustrial private forest productivity (such as that resulting from increased vegetation management) indicate substantially smaller rates of price increases. Whether national and international demand for domestic forest products will offset these assumptions remains to be seen.

DISCOUNT RATE

The rate of discount is another important economic factor in addition to fixed and variable costs and values for timber cut. In some respects, the discount rate is a cost—the payment for the capital used in long-term production of timber. If funds are borrowed by the owner, the interest paid is indeed a cost and must be included in computing the overall profitability of the investment.

In most investment analyses of timber growing, however, measures of financial returns are computed *before* interest payments on borrowed funds (as well as income taxes) are subtracted. The analyses are then on an "internal" basis and measure the economic efficiency of an investment in terms of a present net value (PNV) or an internal rate of return (IRR) (see Chapter 12).

In many computations such as for the PNV, a realistic expected rate of return on the invested capital in alternative investments is needed to represent capital's real or opportunity cost. Many organizations have set a policy on the appropriate discount rate that analyses of long-term investments should use (such as in Row et al. 1981 for the USDA Forest Service). If the analysis is not so constrained, several components should be considered in selecting a discount rate:

1. The current basic return on long-term investments in the economy, which may be approximated by the average returns on "Aaa" corporate bonds reported by investment information services (such as Moody's Investor's Service 1986). Such bonds have virtually no, or minimal, risk.

2. The expected level of inflation, which is usually subtracted from the returns on the corporate bonds to obtain a "real" rate of return. This puts the discount rate on the same real basis as costs and prices.

3. The risk of the investment measured in terms of an expected percentage rate of loss of the capital invested. It is often urged (particularly in federal agencies) that the risks of losses be incorporated into the yield estimates and conservative price increase expectations be used, so that a risk premium does not have to be added to the discount rate. Corporate or other private investors often add such a premium for risk and uncertainty, however.

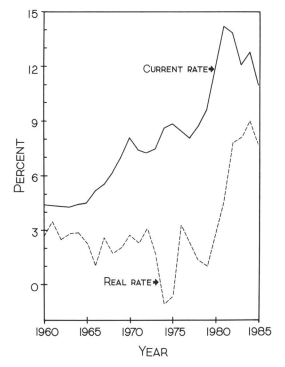

Figure 11-8. Aaa corporate bond interest rates. (*Source:* Moody's Investor's Service)

4. Average income tax rates paid by corporations. The Aaa bond income is *after* corporate taxes are paid, whereas IRR is determined
   before taxes. Consequently, to make the comparison with IRR eq-
   uitable, the bond rate should be adjusted to a pretax basis. This is
   done by dividing the bond rate by one less the average percentage
   of income tax rate on such investments. The relevant tax rate on
   timber is usually the capital gains rate. It should be noted that
   corporate bond income is subject to individual income taxes, and
   thus the discount rate need not be adjusted for that.

In the Forest Service's detailed study of these factors in 1979, it determined that a risk-free real rate of return expected in the corporate investment sector would be at least 4% (Row et al. 1981). So that Forest
Service investments (which draw funds from the private economy) would
not be unfairly competitive with private ones, they set a policy that its
long-term resource investments, after adjustment for risk, should meet
this minimum expectation.

Under the economic circumstances of the mid-1980s, selecting an appropriate discount rate is unusually difficult. As Figure 11-8 shows, the
basic return to capital, as measured by returns on corporate Aaa bonds,

adjusted for inflation, once fluctuated in a moderate range around 2 to 4%. In the inflation crisis of the mid-1970s, interest rates did not climb as fast as inflation, so the real returns from many fixed investments like corporate bonds were actually negative. Subsequently, interest rates stayed high until 1986, despite drastically reduced inflation rates. This may be due to large budgetary deficits of the federal government, accompanied by heavy borrowing from abroad and continued fears of long-term economic instability caused by changes in government policies. Both current and real rates have shown marked signs of coming down and stabilizing. However, what real interest rate is appropriate over the long term for timber investments must be based largely on judgment.

SUMMARY

This chapter has discussed two important factors in economic evaluation of vegetation management—treatment costs and values of yields produced. Costs are particularly important for managers and planners because they are able to control them, at least in part. Both costs and values are crucial factors in strategic planning, and adequate cost information is vital in operational planning and monitoring efficiency.

The components of costs that vary with acreage treated are (1) labor, which has unusual problems in vegetation management in addition to those associated with other forestry operations; (2) equipment costs, which may become dominant in treatments such as mechanical site preparation and aerial spraying; and (3) herbicide costs, which are a significant factor in all chemical site preparation and release treatments.

Average costs for vegetation management treatments vary widely among types of treatments and intensity of treatments. They are generally higher in the North and West than in the South and for public forests than for industrial forest lands. All studies of costs indicate that individual projects have large variations in per acre costs. This increases the importance of carefully estimating costs for individual projects.

Studies of costs of individual projects have produced cost-prediction relationships that are useful in project planning and budgeting. A particularly important conclusion in all studies is that tracts less than 50 to 100 acres in size have significantly higher costs than larger tracts. This stresses the need to organize treatments into economical units.

Values for timber produced used in evaluations of treatments and entire management rotations should recognize species, size, and quality differences in the timber produced because vegetation management may affect these factors. Evaluations should specify and incorporate the financial management assumptions being made about the rate of value increases expected in the future.

REFERENCES

Adams, D.M. and R.W. Haynes. 1980. The 1980 Softwood Timber Assessment Market Model: structure, projections, and policy simulations. Forest Sci. Monogr. 22. 64 p.

Anderson, W.C. 1961. A method of appraising pine sawtimber in South Carolina. USDA Forest Service, Southeastern Forest Experiment Station, Asheville, NC. Res. Pap. 122. 15 p.

Anderson, W.C. 1969. Pine sawtimber price behavior in South Carolina. USDA Forest Service, Southern Forest Experiment Station, New Orleans, LA. Res. Pap. 42. 12 p.

Anderson, W.C. 1973. Pricing sawtimber automatically. Forest Farmer 33(1):13, 18.

Anderson, W.C. 1976. Time study methods in forestry, p. 125-129. *In* Economics of southern forest resources management. Proc. 25th Forestry Symp., Louisiana State Univ., Baton Rouge, LA.

Balmer, W.E., K.A. Utz, and G.O. Langdon. 1978. Financial returns from cultural work in natural loblolly pine stands. South. J. Appl. Forestry 2:111-117.

Caterpillar Tractor Co. 1984. Caterpillar performance handbook. Caterpillar Tractor Co. Peoria, IL. 474 p.

Conkin, M.E. 1971. Cost of timber management for selected areas in the northern region of the United States. M.S. thesis. Iowa State Univ., Ames, IA. 103 p.

Cubbage, F.W. 1983a. Tract size and harvesting costs in southern pines. J. Forestry 81:430-433.

Cubbage, F.W. 1983b. Economics of forest tract size: theory and literature. USDA Forest Service, Southern Forest Experiment Station, New Orleans, LA. Gen. Tech. Rep. SO-41. 21 p.

Darr, D.R. 1973. Stumpage price—does it vary by diameter? Forest Prod. J. 23:58-60.

Dean, J. 1966. Statistical cost estimation. Indiana Univ. Press, Bloomington, IN. 112 p.

Dopuch, N., J.G. Birnberg, and J.S. Demski. 1982. Cost accounting. Harcourt, Brace, and Jovanovich, New York, NY. 726 p.

Gardner, W.E. 1981. Effect of tract size on cost of reforestation. M.S. thesis. North Carolina State Univ., Raleigh, NC. 44 p.

Guldin, R.W. 1983a. Site preparation costs in the southern coastal plain—an update. USDA Forest Service, Southern Forest Experiment Station, New Orleans, LA. Res. Note SO-292. 3 p.

Guldin, R.W. 1983b. Regeneration costs for industrial landowners using hand vs. machine planting. South. J. Appl. Forestry 7:104-108.

Guldin, R.W. 1984a. The silvicultural contractor. J. Forestry 82:28-32.

Guldin, R.W. 1984b. Site characteristics and preparation practices influence costs of hand-planting southern pine. J. Forestry 82:97-100.

Guttenberg, S. 1956. Influence of timber characteristics on timber prices. USDA Forest Service, Southern Forest Experiment Station, New Orleans, LA. Occas. Pap. 146. 14 p.

Guttenberg, S. and C. Row. 1961. Markets, timber quality influence southern pine timber prices. The Timberman 662(10):66-67, 69.

Haynes, R. and D.M. Adams. 1985. Simulations of the effects of alternative assumptions on demand-supply determinants on the timber situation in the United States. USDA Forest Service, Forest Resources Economics Research, Washington, DC. 113 p.

Hilliker, R.L., H.H. Webster, and J.W. Tritch. 1969. Cost relationships for evaluating major timber management opportunities in the Lake states. J. Forestry 67:170-174.

Holley, D.L, Jr. 1970. Factors in the 1959-69 price rise in southern pine timber analyzed. Forest Industry 97(4):40-41.

Industrial Forestry Association. 1979. Industrial tree farm progress report: 1949-1978. Industrial Forestry Association, Portland, OR.

Johnson, J. 1960. Statistical cost analysis. McGraw-Hill, New York, NY. 388 p.

Larson, J. and R. Hallman. 1980. Equipment for reforestation and timber stand improvement. USDA Forest Service, Equipment Development Center, Missoula, MT. 253 p.

Miller, R.K. 1973. Estimating logging equipment replacement costs. Forest Industry 100(2):32-33.

Mills, T.A. and M. Cain. 1976. 1974 Forestry Incentives Program: indications of cost effectiveness. J. Forestry 74:678-683.

Mills, T.J., M.H. Goforth, and T.P. Hart. 1976. Sensitivity of estimated financial returns on timber investments to data errors. USDA Forest Service, Washington, DC. Res. Pap. WO-31. 23 p.

Mills, T.J., P.B. Shinkle, and G.L. Cox. 1985. Direct cost of silvicultural treatments on national forests, 1975-1978. USDA Forest Service, Washington, DC. Res. Pap. WO-40. 22 p.

Moak, J.E. 1982. Forestry practices cost trends in the South. South. J. Appl. Forestry 6:130-132.

Moak, J.E. and J.M. Kucera. 1975. Current costs and cost trends for forestry practices in the South. Forest Farmer 34(5):75-82.

Moak, J.E., J.M. Kucera, and W.F. Watson. 1977. Current costs and cost trends for forestry practices in the South. Forest Farmer 36(5):16-21.

Moak, J.E., W.F. Watson, and P. Van Deusen. 1980. Costs and cost trends for forestry practices in the South. Forest Farmer 39(5):58-66.

Moody's Investor's Service (published monthly). Bond Record. Moody's Investor's Service, New York, NY.

Olson, J.T., A.L. Lundgren, and D. Rose. 1978. Equations for estimating stand establishment, release, and thinning in the Lake States. USDA Forest Service, North Central Forest Experiment Station, St. Paul, MN. Res. Pap. NC-163. 7 p.

Pitsenbarger, P.M. 1982. Book versus tax accounting for forestry costs, p. 8-13. *In* Sizemore, W. (ed.) Accounting for the money that grows on and is spent on trees. School of Forestry and Environmental Studies, Duke Univ., Durham, NC.

Randall, R.M. and D.R. Darr. 1974. Douglas-fir thinning values sensitive to price-diameter relationships. USDA Forest Service, Pacific Northwest Forest and Range Experiment Station, Portland, OR. Res. Note PNW-227. 7 p.

Row, C. 1971. Silvicultural service contract cost study, FY 1970. USDA Forest Service, Washington, DC. Unpublished report. 15 p.

Row, C. 1973. Probabilities of financial returns from southern pine timber growing. Ph.D. dissertation. Tulane Univ., New Orleans, LA. 428 p.

Row, C. 1978. Economics of tract size in timber growing. J. Forestry 76:576-582.

Row, C., H.F. Kaiser, and J. Sessions. 1981. Discount rate for long-term Forest Service investments. J. Forestry. 79:367-369.

Ruderman, F.K. and D.D. Warren. 1985. Production, prices, employment, and trade in Northwest forest industries, first quarter 1985. USDA Forest Service, Pacific Northwest Research Station, Portland, OR. Resource Bull. PNW-126. 49 p.

Smith, H.C. and P.M. Smithson. 1975. Cost of cutting grapevines before logging. USDA Forest Service, Northeastern Forest Experiment Station, Upper Darby, PA. Res. Note NE-207. 4 p.

Somberg, S.I., L.D. Eads, and J.G. Yoho. 1963. What it costs to practice forestry in the South. Forest Farmer 22(3):6-8, 15-17.

Straka, T.J. and W.F. Watson. 1985. Costs of forestry practices. Forest Farmer 44(5):16-22.

Sundra, H.J. and G.L. Lowry. 1975. Regeneration costs in loblolly pine management. J. Forestry 73:406-409.

Timber Mart-South. (published monthly). Timber prices in southern United States. Timber Mart-South, Highland, NC.

Tufts, R.A., B. Izlar, D. Simmons, et al. 1981. Forestry equipment cost index— 1968-1978. South. J. Appl. Forestry 5:201-204.

Ulrich, A.H. 1984. U.S. timber production, trade, consumption, and price statistics. USDA Forest Service, Washington, DC. Misc. Pub. 1442. 83 p.

U.S. Council of Economic Advisors. (Prepared annually). Economic Report of the President. U.S. Council of Economic Advisors, Washington, DC.

U.S. Department of Agriculture. 1984. Agricultural statistics, 1984. U.S. Department of Agriculture, Washington, DC. 558 p.

USDL Bureau of Labor Statistics. (published monthly). Employment and earnings statistics. U.S. Department of Labor, Washington, DC.

USDL Bureau of Labor Statistics. (published monthly). Producer prices and price indexes. USDL Bureau of Labor Statistics, Washington, DC.

USDL Bureau of Labor Statistics. 1985. Employee benefits in medium and large firms. USDL Bureau of Labor Statistics, Washington, DC. Bull. 2213. 56 p.

Vasievich, J.M. 1980. Costs of hazard-reduction burning on southern national forests. South. J. Appl. Forestry 4:12-15.

Vasievich, J.M. 1985. Economic opportunities for intensive forestry: reference data book. Southeastern Center of Forest Economics Research, Research Triangle Park, NC.

Wallace, T.D. and J.L. Silver. 1981. Price variation for southern timber markets. Cooperative research agreement A8-FS-20. USDA Forest Service, Southeastern Forest Experiment Station and Duke Univ., Durham, NC. 148 p.

Warren, D.D. 1986. Production, prices, employment, and trade in Northwest forest industries, fourth quarter 1985. USDA Forest Service, Pacific Northwest Research Station, Portland, OR. Resource Bull. PNW-130. 49 p.

Weaver, G.H. and C.A. Ostenhous. 1976. Economic analysis of planting costs of loblolly pine management. J. Forestry 4:217-219.

Wikstrom, J.H. and J.R. Alley. 1967. Cost control in timber growing on the National Forests in the Northern Region. USDA Forest Service, Intermountain Forest and Range Experiment Station, Odgen, UT. Res. Pap. INT-42. 37 p.

Worrell, A.C. 1953. Costs to practicing forestry in the South. Southern Lumberman 186:43-44.

Yoho, J.G., G.F. Dutrow, and J.E. Moak. 1969. What it costs to practice forestry. Forest Farmer 28(11):20-24, 26, 28, 30-31.

Yoho, J.G. and R.B. Fish. 1961. What it costs to practice forestry in the South. Forest Farmer 21(2):6-8, 19.

12

Economic Analysis of the Silvicultural Effects of Vegetation Management at the Stand and Forest Levels

J. DOUGLAS BRODIE
PETER J. KUCH
CLARK ROW

INTRODUCTION

Economic analyses of forest vegetation management techniques and regimes are needed for a variety of purposes. They are required by forest managers for making strategic investment decisions concerning the selection of optimal forest management regimes. They are needed for making tactical decisions concerning the selection of individual control techniques once weed problems occur. Economic analyses of forest management regimes on public lands are required by federal or state laws such as the National Environmental Policy Act (NEPA). The Federal Insecticide, Fungicide and Rodenticide Act (FIFRA), as amended, requires economic analysis of the benefits provided by pesticides that become the subject of "Special Reviews" as a result of concerns about potential adverse health and environmental effects. Combined risk-benefit analyses are then used by the Environmental Protection Agency (EPA) to make decisions about the continued registration of such pesticides. Herbicides used in forest vegetation management are subject to this regulatory procedure.

These analyses take different forms and include somewhat different data elements, depending on who is doing them and the purpose they are intended to serve. Nonetheless, they should all employ certain basic economic techniques and principles.

BASIC PRINCIPLES AND TECHNIQUES OF ECONOMIC ANALYSIS

All economic analyses use criteria that compare the financial benefits from the use of a control technique or a sequence of control techniques with its costs. Because these benefits and costs are distributed through time, meaningful comparison requires that they all be discounted to a common point in time, usually the present. Hence, the present value of the benefits can be compared to the present value of the costs. Most economists agree that this comparison should take the form of calculating the present value of net benefits, known as present net value (PNV) or present net worth (PNW).

$$\text{PNW} = \sum_{t=1}^{h} \frac{B_t}{(1 + r)^t} - \sum_{t=1}^{h} \frac{C_t}{(1 + r)^t} \tag{1}$$

where B_t = benefits accrued over time
C_t = costs accrued over time
r = chosen discount rate
t = time (years)
h = the time horizon of investments

No regime or technique that gives rise to PNW < 0 is acceptable. Where there is more than one option having PNW > 0, the one with the largest PNW is the most desirable. In order for PNW to be valid in comparing alternatives, the time horizon of the investments must be made comparable.

Alternatively, one can use the benefit-cost ratio (B/C) or the internal rate of return (IRR):

$$B/C = \sum_{t=1}^{h} \frac{B_t}{(1 + r)^t} \bigg/ \sum_{t=1}^{h} \frac{C_t}{(1 + r)^t} \tag{2}$$

$$IRR = r, \text{ where } \sum_{t=1}^{h} \frac{B_t}{(1 + r)^t} = \sum_{t=1}^{h} \frac{C_t}{(1 + r)^t} \tag{3}$$

Use of these latter approaches can lead to less efficient outcomes. They will maximize the return per dollar spent but will not necessarily maximize the return to the total land investment. For example, firewood production requires little investment, thereby yielding a high return *per dollar* invested. However, the return *per acre* may be relatively low compared to that obtained from softwood plantation management. Fraser (1985) provides an in-depth discussion of benefit-cost analysis and the effects of discount rates on the outcome.

The question now arises as to what should be included in the benefits

(B_t) and the costs (C_t). As emphasized in Chapter 11, that will depend on the type of decision to be made (e.g., strategic or tactical) and where the decision maker is situated (e.g., the private or public sector). For the private sector forest manager, the costs are the labor, materials, equipment, and overhead used in the silvicultural regime. The benefits are the market value of products anticipated as a result of the silvicultural regime. For the public land manager or the Administrator of EPA, broader social benefits and costs must be included as well. Any increases in the level of the output of other products or services, or environmental amenities and public health, are benefits; any reductions are costs. For strategic decisions, all costs associated with the silvicultural regime are relevant and should be included. But for tactical decisions, costs incurred before the weed problem arose are considered "sunk costs" and should be omitted because they are irrelevant to the decision.

Where certain benefits or costs cannot be monetized or where there is not general agreement as to how they should be valued, as frequently occurs with decisions involving human health and ecological effects, cost-effectiveness or risk-benefit (R/B) criteria should be used. For example, if one were considering regulatory options for reducing human exposure to a herbicide that posed a chronic health risk, one would compute the ratio of the expected risk reduction (ΔR) and the resulting reduction in PNW for each option:

$$\Delta R/B = \frac{\Delta R}{\Delta \left[\sum_{t=1}^{h} \frac{B_t}{(1 + r)^t} - \sum_{t=1}^{h} \frac{C_t}{(1 + r)^t} \right]} \tag{4}$$

The option yielding the highest risk-benefit ratio is the most desirable and should be selected. This is the formulation of the "Risk-Benefit Analysis" EPA uses when it is considering canceling or restricting the registration of a pesticide. It is expected that curtailing the use of the pesticide will reduce yields $(\Delta B_t < 0)$ and raise production costs $(\Delta C_t > 0)$ but that these sacrifices are justified in order to protect human health or the environment.

A related approach is cost-effectiveness analysis where measurable monetary costs are compared to measurable nonmonetary effects. The effectiveness criterion is a proxy for monetary benefits and should be closely correlated with them. Increases in wood growth or reductions in contamination incidents are examples.

The discount rate (r) used in Equations 1 and 4 represents the "opportunity cost" of funds relevant to the decision-making entity; that is, what the funds to be expended could earn in alternative investments (see Chapter 11). For forest products firms, this might be the real rate of interest they could earn from buying bonds with maturities equal to stand rotations. For public land management agencies, assuming that financing the federal deficit reduces funds available for private sector investment, the appropriate discount rate might be the real cost of public debt. Note that because future inflation rates are so difficult to predict, "real values" are normally used in the measurement of benefits and costs (see Chapter 11). Generally, a real, net-of-inflation rate of interest should be used for the discount rate.

Vegetation management treatments may change the optimal rotation length and the desirability of subsequent silvicultural treatments. It is conventional in forestry to use the PNW of an infinite series of rotations, known as the soil expectation (SE) value, when comparing silvicultural regimes of different lengths (see Equation 2, Appendix 3). The economic objective of forest managers should be to choose the regime that maximizes the value of the site in producing future crops. Generally this comparison is made at year 0 and is often referred to as "bare land analysis." It will often occur that the optimal treatment for a stand already established will differ from what should be done at the bare ground stage. It may be that, retrospectively, vegetation management should have been performed within a given stand at an early stage but that now it should be managed to rotation and then replaced with an optimally treated stand.

Taxation is another important institutional influence on silvicultural decisions. Internal Revenue Service regulations with respect to expensing or capitalizing improvements and capital gains treatment are complex considerations that vary with the individual or corporate taxpayer's situation. Forest land is taxed under ad valorem, yield (severence), and per acre fee bases, depending on the state involved. These taxes can affect marginal evaluations of forestry investments, and their impact also varies with the taxpayer's situation. For those reasons, this chapter analyzes forest vegetation management on a *before-tax* basis. Readers should consult their local tax authority or extension service for pertinent information on after-tax analysis of financial investments.

APPROACHES TO ECONOMIC ANALYSIS OF VEGETATION MANAGEMENT AT THE STAND LEVEL

Vegetation management in forestry is a term applied to a body of chemical and nonchemical methods used to free stands from competing vegetation. Biological evaluations of the need for vegetation management are based on quantitative and qualitative assessments of the type and degree of competition facing such stands. Economic evaluations of the need for vegetation management are subsequently derived by comparing the expected costs and future returns of controlling competition versus letting the stand develop on its own (i.e., determining the economic threshold as described in Chapter 1). Because competing vegetation influences the survival or growth of stands long before they reach commercial size, methods of projecting stand development from establishment to final harvest must be used.

Three methods of doing this will be demonstrated, and background information on each of them can be found in Chapters 7, 8, and 9. The first method will be called the "yield-table assumption method." The advantage of this method is its simplicity and the fact that it can be applied to any species for which yield tables exist. The second method will be called the "simulated managed stand comparison method." A managed stand simulator, a computer model of managed stand growth, is essential for the application of this method, and the treated and untreated stands are independently projected and compared. This method more accurately projects posttreatment stand differences and allows for differing silvicultural prescriptions and comparisons between treated and untreated stands. It can be applied only to those situations and species for which accurate managed stand simulation models exist. This chapter will explain and demonstrate these first two methods using the DFSIM model (Curtis et al. 1981) and a series of control and treatment plot comparisons derived from examples involving Douglas-fir reported by Roberts (1982) and Walstad et al. (1986).

The third method, which has most recently become possible will be called the "optimization method." In addition to a managed stand simulation model, this method requires the development of an optimization algorithm for a particular managed stand simulator. To demonstrate the optimization approach, we will utilize a model described by Valsta and Brodie (1985) using stand models for loblolly pine developed by Burkhart and Sprinz (1984) and Cao et al. (1982).

Yield-Table Assumption Method

The 2,4,5-T Assessment Team (1979), Stavins et al. (1981), and Green (1983) have all used the yield-table assumption method to conduct economic sensitivity analyses for changes in cost, interest rate, and yield assumptions in vegetation management. The latter two studies used the McArdle et al. (1961) or DFIT-derived (Bruce et al. 1977) yield tables, whereas the 2,4,5-T Assessment Team used the general stand simulator structure MULTIPLOY (Row 1976) essentially in yield-table assumption format. Because the preceding studies adequately outline and demonstrate the principles of economic sensitivity analysis, we will confine ourselves to straightforward examples without analyzing the sensitivity to a wide range of variables.

There are three logical outcomes associated with failure to control competing vegetation on productive forest sites:

1. Failure to control vegetation results in an equivalent but delayed yield.
2. Failure to control vegetation results in reduced yield.
3. Failure to control vegetation results in both reduced and delayed yield.

These simplistic outcomes are displayed in Chapter 9, Figure 9-3. A wide range of scenarios exist within these patterns, based on the length of delay and degree of productivity loss; however, the methodology can be adequately demonstrated with a single example for each pattern.

Table 12-1 contains two simulated DFSIM runs headed "Vegetation Base" and "Vegetation Base Less 10% Productivity." Vegetation Base is a simulated plantation on site 115 (ft, 50-year basis at breast height). This is middle Site III, which has about average productivity for Douglas-fir on the west side of the Cascades in the Pacific Northwest. The silvicultural prescription is: Plant 400 trees/acre, commercially thin to 100 ft²/acre of basal area at age 45, and harvest the stand at age 70. Economic assumptions and criteria are noted in the table footnotes. The net stumpage values reflect quality premiums associated with large diameter material and high removals per acre. Initial site preparation costs of $300/ acre reflect any preplanting vegetation control treatments as well as planting cost in both cases.

Using the data from Table 12-1, the impact of each of the three assumptions previously mentioned is evaluated in Table 12-2, and the value of potential release treatments at age 2 or ages 2 and 5 is derived. It is clear that minor delays or productivity losses during regeneration result in substantial value losses and justify considerable expenditures for release treatments (Table 12-2). Single rotation loss in terms of PNW varies from $72 to $185/acre, and the justified treatment expenditure at the time of application varies from $78 to $200/acre if a single treatment at age 2 is required and from $41 to $115/acre if two treatments at ages 2 and 5 are required. These economic threshold values are well in excess of most current release treatment costs (see Chapter 11), and the delay (5 years) and productivity loss (10%) assumptions are modest when compared to the empirical evidence that has been compiled (Stewart et al. 1984).

The "yield-table assumption method" requires the analyst to make a subjective appraisal of the end impact in terms of delay and productivity loss based on a particular or hypothetical stand comparison. This is contrasted later with the "simulated managed stand comparison method" that projects treated and untreated stands based on their current condition. The basic assumption is that the simulation model accurately

TABLE 12-1. A Comparison of Similar Management Regimes for Douglas-fir with a Difference in Productivity of 10%[a]

Age (yr)	Mean Stand DBH (in.)	Treatment or Activity	Stocking or (Removals) (trees/acre)	Basal Area (ft²/acre)	Merchantable Volume (ft³/acre)[b]	Net Stumpage Value ($/MCF)[c]
			Vegetation Base			
0	—	Plant	400	—	—	—
45	10.8	—	303	192	6,158	—
	9.7	Commercial thin	(180)	92	2,878	254
	12.2	Residual	123	100	3,280	—
70	17.5	Final harvest	(117)	197	8,714	1,040
	—	Total harvest	(297)	—	11,592	—

Soil Expectation Value = $435/acre.
Mean Annual Harvest = 166 ft³/acre.

Age (yr)	Mean Stand DBH (in.)	Treatment or Activity	Stocking or (Removals) (trees/acre)	Basal Area (ft²/acre)	Merchantable Volume (ft³/acre)[b]	Net Stumpage Value ($/MCF)[c]
			Vegetation Base Less 10% Productivity[d]			
0	—	Plant	400	—	—	—
45	10.8	—	318	183	5,468	—
	9.7	Commercial thin	(178)	83	2,392	175
	11.4	Residual	140	100	3,076	—
70	16.5	Final harvest	(132)	1976	8,158	950
	—	Total harvest	(310)	—	10,550	—

Soil Expectation Value = $288/acre.
Mean Annual Harvest = 151 ft³/acre.

[a] Analysis assumes a site preparation and regeneration cost of $300/acre, a precommercial thinning cost of $80/acre if applied, and a real interest rate of 4%. Net unit revenue is derived from a pond value (PV) function: PV = 9.91 + 70.81D, where D represents true stand diameter in inches. Logging costs are from Sessions (1979) with a multiplier of 0.66. Hauling cost is set at $75/M ft³.
[b] Merchantable volume of all trees 7.6 in. DBH and larger to a 4-in. diameter top.
[c] MCF = thousand cubic feet.
[d] A 10% productivity loss in the DFSIM model is inserted through formula transformation of site index.

TABLE 12-2. A Comparison of Financial Losses Resulting from Delay in Final Harvest as Well as Productivity Loss and the Justified Expenditure for Each Case Involving Douglas-fir Management Regimes

	SE^a	ΔSE^b	ΔPNW^c	Justified Current Expenditure per Treatment	
				Release at Age 2[d]	Release at Ages 2 and 5[e]
			($/acre)		
Vegetation base	435	—	—	—	—
Vegetation base with a 5-yr delay[f]	358	77	72	78	41
Vegetation base less 10% productivity[g]	288	147	137	148	78
Vegetation base less 10% productivity and with a 5-yr delay[f]	237	198	185	200	115

[a] Soil expectation value (SE) = the PNW/acre of an infinite series of rotations.
[b] ΔSE is the reduction in SE compared with vegetation base.
[c] $\Delta PNW = \Delta SE \dfrac{(1 + i)^{70} - 1}{(1 + i)^{70}}$ (Converts infinite series value to that for a single rotation)
[d] Expenditure $= \Delta PNW(1 + i)^2$
[e] Expenditure $= (\Delta PNW)/[1/(1 + i)^2 + 1/(1 + i)^5]$
[f] A 5 year delay is calculated by $SE - \dfrac{SE}{(1 + i)^5}$
[g] A 10% productivity loss in the DFSIM model is inserted through formula transformation of site index.

projects two dissimilar stands for the remainder of their management regimes. As opposed to a yield table, a growth simulator can be calibrated to more accurately represent and project the differing conditions of existing stands.

Simulated Managed Stand Comparison Method

Four areas in western Oregon and Washington were sampled initially by Roberts (1982) and later by Walstad et al. (1986). Each area had a known history of vegetation control (herbicide release treatment) and a portion of the area left untreated because of nearby property lines or other reasons. The herbicide treatments were applied 10 to 25 years previously, allowing preliminary analysis of long-term differences. The two reports document slope, aspect, site, and vegetation differences for each site and contain measurements of canopy cover and conifer and hardwood size and density. These data are biometrically analyzed in Chapter 9 and will not be repeated here; however, the primary stand structure differences between the treated and untreated areas will be outlined. Logging costs and log values were assumed to be constant for each of the four areas. Thus at least in the simulations presented here, differences among areas and between treated and untreated plots within each area are due to differences in current stand condition and not differing technological and economic conditions. These conditions need not be standardized in practical analysis, but the analyst is then obliged to separate the differences based on stand condition and those due to differing productivity, costs, and regime. The examples presented below in Tables 12-3, 12-4, and 12-5 correspond to the examples in Tables 9-3, 9-4, and 9-5 in Chapter 9. The economic comparisons are standardized at age 0 soil expectation value; however, transformation to any age in the regime is a relatively simple matter (see Appendix 3). These four cases are representative of typical conditions in the Northwest but do not necessarily cover the full range of situations that might be encountered in this region.

Douglas-fir Stand versus Red Alder Stand
The treated stand in this example is estimated to be a 33-yr-old stand stocked with 200 Douglas-fir trees/acre with a quadratic mean diameter at breast height (DBH) of 10.3 in. (Table 12-3). The treated stand was sprayed with herbicide at age 6, whereas the untreated stand was not. The untreated stand is essentially a 33-yr-old red alder stand stocked with 272 trees/acre, 9.3 in. DBH.

The treated stand under our set of assumptions has a soil expectation value of $855/acre assuming a $300/acre regeneration cost and no cost for the herbicide treatment. A $25/acre treatment cost at age 6 in each 60-yr rotation would cause a reduction in soil expectation value of $22/acre, resulting in a value of $833/acre. (The $22/acre reduction in soil expectation value is derived as follows: First, discount the $25/acre treatment cost at 4% for 6 years, giving a value of $19.76 in terms of present net worth. Next, use Equation 2 in Appendix 3 to convert this present net worth amount to a soil expectation value of $22/acre, assuming a 60-year rotation.)

The untreated stand might yield 6680 ft³/acre of natural red alder on a 50-yr rotation, giving a soil expectation value of $219/acre if the stumpage value were $200/MCF (thousand cubic feet) and regeneration costs were zero. On the other hand, if the untreated stand was orginally planted with Douglas-fir at a cost of $300/acre and the plantation lost from neglect of vegetation control, the soil expectation value is $−131/acre. The negative soil expectation value indicates that this regime will not earn a 4% rate of return on costs. The treated regime with a positive $833/acre soil expectation value exceeds this rate substantially, earning nearly 6.5% (internal rate of return) if there are no other management costs.

TABLE 12-3. Comparison of Simulated Regimes for Treated and Untreated Stands, Leading to Douglas-fir and Red Alder Stands, Respectively[a]

Age (yr)	Mean Stand DBH (in.)	Treatment or Activity	Stocking or (Removals) (trees/acre)	Basal Area (ft²/acre)[d]	Merchantable Volume (ft³/acre)[b]	Net Stumpage Value ($/MCF)[c]
		Treated Stand: Douglas-fir[d]				
0	—	Plant	—	—	—	—
33	10.3	Measurement	200	132	—	—
45	14.0	Stand exam	187	199	7,173	—
	12.6	Commercial thin	(114)	99	3,572	600
	15.9	Residual stand	72	100	3,601	—
60	20.6	Final harvest	(72)	166	7,182	1,200
	—	Total harvest	(186)	265	10,754	—

Soil Expectation Value = $855/acre.
Mean Annual Harvest = 179 ft³/acre.

Age (yr)	Mean Stand DBH (in.)	Treatment or Activity	Stocking or (Removals) (trees/acre)	Basal Area (ft²/acre)[d]	Merchantable Volume (ft³/acre)[b]	Net Stumpage Value ($/MCF)[c]
		Untreated Stand: Red Alder[d]				
0	—	Plant[e]	—	—	—	—
33	9.3	Measurement	272	127	—	—
50	13.6	Final Harvest	(165)	166	6,680	200
	—	Total Harvest	(165)	166	6,680	—

Soil Expectation Value = $−131/acre.
Mean Annual Harvest = 134 ft³/acre.

[a]Economic assumptions are given in Table 12-1.
[b]Merchantable volume to a 4-in. diameter top for Douglas-fir 7.6 in. DBH and larger and red alder 5.5 in. DBH and larger.
[c]MCF = thousand cubic feet.
[d]Site index$_{50}$ is 125 (ft) for Douglas-fir and 110 (ft) for red alder.
[e]Assumes that Douglas-fir are planted, but failure to release them at age 6 leads to dominance by natural invasion of red alder.

Douglas-fir Stands That Are Differentially Stocked

The treated stand in this case is estimated to be 15 years old and stocked with 223 Douglas-fir trees/acre with a mean DBH of 4.0 in. after precommercial thinning (Table 12-4). The treated stand received herbicide applications at ages 2 and 4, whereas the untreated stand did not. The untreated stand is also stocked with 223 Douglas-fir trees/acre with a mean DBH of 3.1 in. The control has double the brush canopy of the treated stand. It is assumed that both stands cost $300/acre to establish and that the treated stand has been precommercially thinned (coincidentally) to 223 trees/acre at age 15. A commercial thinning will be made at age 45 in each case to 100 ft²/acre of residual basal area. The final harvest will be at age 60. The soil expectation values for the treated and untreated stands are $1069 and $695/acre, respectively, ignoring the cost of the two vegetation control treatments for the treated stand. The difference in soil expectation value would justify an expenditure of $190/acre on each of these two treatments. This is three to four times current aerial herbicide treatment costs on most private land (see Chapter 11). (The expenditures of $190/acre are derived as follows: First, subtract the soil expectation value of $695/acre for the untreated stand from that of $1069/acre for the treated stand, giving a difference of $374/acre. Next, use Equation 2 in Appendix 3 to convert this differential in soil expectation value to a differential in present net worth of $338/acre. Finally, use Equation 6 in Appendix 3 to determine that $190/acre could be spent on treatments at ages 2 and 4, provided there were no other costs associated with management of this stand.)

Douglas-fir Stand versus Mixed Douglas-fir/Red Alder Stand

The treated stand in this case is estimated to be 33 years old and supports 200 Douglas-fir trees/acre with a mean DBH of 10.0 in. (Table 12-5). At age 6 herbicide was applied. The untreated stand has 200 Douglas-fir trees 7.0 in. DBH and competing noncommercial red alder trees. A thinning to 100 ft²/acre of basal area at age 45 is projected for the treated stand, with final harvest at age 60. A final harvest of Douglas-fir at age 60 is also assumed for the untreated stand, yielding 5995 ft³/acre of Douglas-fir valued at $640/MCF. The soil expectation value of the treated stand is $714/acre versus $73/acre for the untreated stand. The contribution of the herbicide treatments to soil expectation value in this instance is $641/acre. The treatment at age 6 would justify an expenditure of $734/acre—more than 10 times current cost of herbicide application in the private sector. (The expenditure of $734/acre is derived as follows: First, subtract the soil expectation value of $73/acre for the untreated stand from that of $714/acre for the treated stand, giving a difference of $641/acre. Next, use Equation 2 in Appendix 3 to convert this differential in soil expectation value to a differential in present net worth of $580/acre. Finally, use Equation 5 in Appendix 3 to determine that $734/acre

TABLE 12-4. Comparison of Simulated Regimes for Treated and Untreated Stands, Leading to Differentially Stocked Douglas-fir Stands[a]

Age (yr)	Mean Stand DBH (in.)	Treatment or Activity	Stocking or (Removals) (trees/acre)	Basal Area (ft²/acre)	Merchantable Volume (ft³/acre)[b]	Net Stumpage Value ($/MCF)[c]
			Treated Stand[c]			
0	—	Plant	—	—	—	—
15	4.0	Precommercial thin	223	20	—	—
45	14.5	Stand exam	183	210	7,698	—
	13.1	Commercial thin	(118)	110	4,033	511
	16.9	Residual	64	100	3,664	—
60	21.9	Final harvest	(64)	167	7,345	1,360
	—	Total harvest	(182)	277	11,378	—

Soil Expectation Value = $1,069/acre.
Mean Annual Harvest = 190 ft³/acre.

Age (yr)	Mean Stand DBH (in.)	Treatment or Activity	Stocking or (Removals) (trees/acre)	Basal Area (ft²/acre)	Merchantable Volume (ft³/acre)[b]	Net Stumpage Value ($/MCF)[c]
			Untreated Stand[d]			
0	—	Plant	—	—	—	—
15	3.1	Measurement	223	17	—	—
45	12.7	Stand exam	198	175	6,342	—
	11.4	Commercial thin	(104)	75	2,605	397
	14.0	Residual	93	100	3,738	—
60	17.9	Final harvest	(92)	161	7,322	1,080
	—	Total harvest	(196)	235	9,927	—

Soil Expectation Value = $695/acre.
Mean Annual Harvest = 165 ft³/acre.

[a]Economic assumptions are listed under Table 12-1.
[b]Merchantable volume to a 4-in. diameter top for Douglas-fir 7.6 in. DBH and larger.
[c]MCF = thousand cubic feet.
[d]Site index$_{50}$ is 128 (ft) for Douglas-fir.

TABLE 12-5. Comparison of Simulated Regimes for Treated and Untreated Stands, Leading to Pure Douglas-fir and Mixed Douglas-fir/Red Alder Stands, Respectively[a]

Age (yr)	Mean Stand DBH (in.)	Treatment or Activity	Stocking or (Removals) (trees/acre)	Basal Area (ft²/acre)[d]	Merchantable Volume (ft³/acre)[b]	Net Stumpage Value ($/MCF)[c]
			Treated: Douglas-fir Stand[d]			
0	—	Plant	400	—	—	—
33	10.0	Measurement	200	109	—	—
45	13.5	Stand exam	167	168	6,109	—
	12.1	Commercial thin	(85)	68	2,461	500
	14.9	Residual	82	100	3,648	—
60	17.9	Final harvest	(92)[e]	162	7,162	1,080
	—	Total harvest	(177)	230	9,623	—

Soil Expectation Value = $714/acre.
Mean Annual Harvest = 160 ft³/acre.

Age (yr)	Mean Stand DBH (in.)	Treatment or Activity	Stocking or (Removals) (trees/acre)	Basal Area (ft²/acre)[d]	Merchantable Volume (ft³/acre)[b]	Net Stumpage Value ($/MCF)[c]
			Untreated: Douglas-fir/Red Alder Stand[d]			
0	—	Plant	200	—	—	—
33	7.0	Measurement	200	54	—	—
60	13.4	Final harvest	(138)	95	5,995	640
	—	Total harvest	(138)	135	5,995	—

Soil Expectation Value = $73/acre.
Mean Annual Harvest = 100 ft³/acre.

[a]Economic assumptions are listed under Table 12-1. Site index$_{50}$ = 125 ft.
[b]Merchantable volume to a 4-in. diameter top for Douglas-fir 7.6-in. DBH and larger.
[c]MCF = thousand cubic feet.
[d]Site index$_{50}$ is 125 (ft) for Douglas-fir.
[e]Increase in number of trees/acre is due to ingrowth of trees that were below the 7.6-in. DBH diameter limit used in the stand exam at age 33.

could be spent on a treatment at age 6, provided there were no other costs associated with management of this stand.)

Douglas-fir Stands that are Both Differentially Stocked and Have Differential Growth Rates

These two stands are estimated to be 26 years old. The treated stand is stocked with 232 Douglas-fir/acre, 6.0 in. in mean DBH, whereas the untreated stand is stocked with 200 Douglas-fir/acre 4.1 in. in DBH (Table 12-6). Tree vigor is substantially lower in the untreated stand, as indicated by the smaller diameter and a 22% reduction in tree height. The treated stand received applications of herbicide at ages 14 and 19.

The management regime for both stands involved no further treatment, with final harvest at age 70. The soil expectation value for the treated stand is $200/acre, whereas the soil expectation value for the untreated stand is $28/acre. This difference in soil expectation value for the two stands implies that $148/acre could be spent on each of the treatments at ages 14 and 19. (The expenditure of $148/acre is derived as follows: First, subtract the soil expectation value of $28/acre for the untreated stand from that of $200/acre for the treated stand, giving a difference of $172/acre. Next, use Equation 2 in Appendix 3 to convert this differential in soil expectation value to a differential in present net worth of $156/acre. Finally, use Equation 6 in Appendix 3 to determine that $148/acre could be spent on treatments at ages 14 and 19, provided there were no other costs associated with management of this stand.)

Discussion of Douglas-fir Examples

Two methods of evaluating the impacts of vegetation management have been presented for Douglas-fir. The "yield-table assumption method" allows testing of assumptions about productivity losses, harvest delays, or combined harvest delays and productivity losses as they affect financial returns. Base yields can come from either standard empirical yield tables or a simulation model used to derive base yields. The differences in present net worth or soil expectation value can be used to evaluate the cost of failure to apply vegetation control, or they can be transformed to derive justified expenditures for vegetation control.

The "simulated managed stand comparison method" requires a managed stand simulator for the crop species that will accept the differing density and tree size information obtained from paired comparisons of treated and untreated field plots. The simulation comparison method thus requires long-term records of vegetation management treatments and intensive field sampling such as supplied by Roberts (1982) and Walstad et al. (1986). Most managed stand simulators are unreliable for projecting mixed stands or very low conifer density, and so an alternate method or set of assumptions is necessary for projecting the effects of some treatments as in the case involving a mixed stand of Douglas-fir and red alder.

TABLE 12-6. Comparison of Simulated Regimes for Treated and Untreated Stands of Douglas-fir, Leading to Both Differential Stocking and Growth[a]

Age (yr)	Mean Stand DBH (in.)	Treatment or Activity	Stocking or (Removals) (trees/acre)	Basal Area (ft²/acre)	Merchantable Volume (ft³/acre)[b]	Net Stumpage Value ($/MCF)[c]
		Treated[a]				
0	—	Plant	400	—	—	—
26	6.0	Stand exam	232	46	—	—
70	15.0	Final harvest	(169)	208	9,135	830
	—	Total harvest	—	—	9,135	—

Soil Expectation Value = $200/acre.
Mean Annual Harvest = 131 ft³/acre.

Age (yr)	Mean Stand DBH (in.)	Treatment or Activity	Stocking or (Removals) (trees/acre)	Basal Area (ft²/acre)	Merchantable Volume (ft³/acre)[b]	Net Stumpage Value ($/MCF)[c]
		Untreated[a]				
0	—	Plant	400	—	—	—
26	4.1	Stand exam	200	18	—	—
70	13.8	Final harvest	(158)	164.3	7,150	711
	—	Total harvest	(158)	164.3	7,150	—

Soil Expectation Value = $28/acre.
Mean Annual Harvest = 102 ft³/acre.

[a]Economic assumptions are listed under Table 12-1.
[b]Merchantable volume to a 4-in. diameter top for Douglas-fir 7.6-in. DBH and larger.
[c]MCF = thousand cubic feet.
[d]Site index$_{50}$ is 115 (ft) for Douglas-fir.

379

The four case examples were standardized by assuming equivalent cost and value conditions and by evaluating each case at stand initiation. The resulting differences in stand analysis are due to the differences in stand condition between treated and untreated plots and between locations.

The example in Table 12-3 (Douglas-fir versus red alder) is a comparison between a moderately stocked Douglas-fir stand and an untreated stand that developed into pure red alder. Age and current stocking permitted commercial thinning of the treated stand. The value of the control was negative, (assuming a $300/acre cost for the failed planting of Douglas-fir), with the treated stand generating 61% more volume.

The example in Table 12-4 (differentially stocked stands) represents a comparison between an adequately stocked stand and a better stocked, higher vigor stand that has been released. Although both stands are suitable for commercial thinning, the treated stand generates 54% more revenue and 15% more volume.

The example in Table 12-5 (relatively pure Douglas-fir versus a mixture of Douglas-fir and red alder) is a comparison of a well-stocked Douglas-fir stand and a similar stand with some red alder retarding Douglas-fir growth. The Douglas-fir density justifies commercial thinning only in the treated stand. Economic analysis indicates a 10-fold advantage in soil expectation value for the relatively pure stand of Douglas-fir.

The example in Table 12-6 (both differential stocking and growth) is a comparison with an untreated stand whose stocking is only slightly less than the treated stand but whose height and diameter indicate a very substantial difference in vigor. Age and current stocking preclude precommercial or commercial thinning, and the value of either stand is substantially below the well-stocked stands in Table 12-4. Nonetheless, vegetation control appears to have enhanced potential revenues by 600% and volume by 28%.

Although the analyses presented here were standardized at age 0 and calculated in terms of either present net worth for a single rotation or soil expectation value for an infinite series of rotations, transformation to alternate bases or use of different costs, prices, and interest rates is a simple matter. Appendix 3 indicates how the computations were done and how they might be transformed.

Optimization Method

Vegetation management interacts with all other elements in a silvicultural regime and is affected by costs, revenues, tree-size-quality premiums, and precommercial and commercial density control. The silviculturist may react to the early detrimental effects of competing vegetation by lengthening the rotation or varying the commercial thinning density control treatments. Thinning analysis presents a complex problem of timing, intensity, and number of stand entries, and the best or optimum solution can only be approximated by iterative simulations. Dynamic programming is a tool for efficiently searching the large number of stand treatment alternatives and finding the alternative that maximizes a volume or value objective. Using this technique, we can demonstrate how the optimal regime varies as competing vegetation increases, and we can also show how to derive the value reduction arising from different levels of competing vegetation.

Model Structure for Optimizing Vegetation Management in Loblolly Pine

Two basic growth models were grafted together to form the vegetation management optimization model presented by Valsta and Brodie (1985). One model, developed by Burkhart and Sprinz (1984), forecasts future stand development for loblolly pine plantations planted at different densities and resulting in different percentages of hardwood basal area in the main canopy (see Chapter 8). Although this model is an excellent tool for analyzing the effects of various levels of hardwood competition resulting from different site preparation intensities, it does not provide for postregeneration release treatments or thinning. The second model, developed by Cao et al. (1982), is an "old field" plantation model with growth relationships similar to those in the Burkhart and Sprinz (1984) model but differing in that it provides for commercial thinning density control dynamics and is applicable only to pure loblolly pine plantations. Grafting the two models together provides a third model that (1) permits analysis of differing effectiveness of site preparation as reflected in the percentage of hardwood basal area in the juvenile stand; and (2) allows commercial conifer density control beginning at age 10 and potentially every 5 years thereafter until final harvest age.

At the first entry, the hardwood basal area in the stand must be completely controlled to facilitate the transfer from the first to the second model conditions. This complete release treatment is a control variable that can be exercised at any point in the rotation or not at all if an extremely high cost of hardwood removal is used. The optimization model does not permit conifer thinnings without treatment of the hardwoods. In general, hardwood treatment is undertaken at the first opportunity, along with a conifer thinning if the hardwood percentage is low, and without any conifer thinning at higher hardwood basal area levels.

Results of Applying the Optimization Model in Loblolly Pine

Table 12-7 shows the impact of competing hardwoods on loblolly pine growth and value. Table 12-8 gives the details of the optimal regimes with the various hardwood basal area components. The reduction of early growth due to hardwood competition caused the optimal rotation in terms of soil expectation value to lengthen and the yields to decline (Table 12-8). In the loblolly pine examples, we used an 8% discount rate that is

TABLE 12-7. Impact of Hardwood Competition on Loblolly Pine Growth and Value[a]

Hardwood (% of stand basal area)	Mean Annual Increment for Conifers (ft³/acre/yr)	Soil Expectation Value ($/acre)	Basal Area at Age 10		Present Net Worth Reduction Due to Hardwood Competition	
			Conifer (ft²/acre)	Hardwood (ft²/acre)	($/acre)	(%)
0	164.6	220	89.6	0	0	—
10	148.5	175	77.6	8.6	42[b]	20
30	135.7	96	49.5	21.2	116[b]	56
50	117.6	48	25.8	25.8	160[b]	78

[a]Underlying parameter values: Site index—65 (ft, base age 25 years); number of trees planted—725/acre; regular site preparation—cost $135/acre (does not include vegetation control for any treatment); hardwood release treatment at age 10 or later with a cost of $1/ft² of hardwood basal area, with a minimum of $30/acre and a maximum of $50/acre; in every case, it was optimal to remove the hardwoods at the first possible age (10 yr); thinning entry cost—$20/acre; thinning type—"Thinomatic," a modification of thinning from below (Burk et al. 1984); stumpage prices used: pulpwood (DBH 5-7 in.)—$0.17/ft³ = $13 to 15/cord; chip'n saw (DBH 8-10 in.)—$0.48/ft³ = $44/cord; sawlogs (DBH 11-22 in.)—$0.74 to 1.18/ft³ = $160 to 200/MBF (thousand board feet, Scribner); and interest rate = 8%.
[b]In each of these cases, $14/acre of the present net worth difference is due to having to treat hardwoods at age 10. The remainder could be spent on additional site preparation or other silvicultural activities.

consistent with the behavior of private managers who prescribe rotation lengths of 20 to 35 yr. (The 4% rate used earlier in the Douglas-fir examples reflects the longer rotations and higher costs in the West and the influence of public management.)

The optimal rotation is 30 years with perfect site preparation and 0% hardwood basal area achieved. The optimal rotation lengthens to 35 yr with 10, 30, or 50% hardwood basal area. Conifer thinnings are taken at ages 10 and 15 in the 0% hardwood basal area case and in the 10% case along with a hardwood treatment. In the 30 and 50% hardwood cases, only the hardwoods are removed early in the rotation, indicating that mortality and slower growth of the pines would not justify early thinning. Where applicable, the age 10 hardwood removal cost was $30/acre, equivalent to $14/acre when discounted to the present. Thus in the case of the 10% hardwood, the $42/acre difference in present net worth could be partitioned, with $14 of it due to the necessity of spending $30/acre on release at age 10 and $28 due to site preparation treatments not achieving perfect hardwood control (Table 12-7). The pine mortality and basal area reduction from light hardwood competition (10% of stand basal area) for the first 10 years resulted in a 5-year extension of the rotation, a 10% reduction in volume growth, and a 20% reduction in soil expectation value

(Tables 12-7 and 12-8). The expenditure on release permitted higher pine yields and larger diameter harvests in later entries. The adverse impacts of hardwood competition on pine yields and values are considerably greater at higher hardwood basal areas.

The hardwood component is directly influencing the stand in these examples for only the first 10 years, and yet its impact is substantial. The average annual growth reductions over a rotation are 10, 18, and 29%, whereas the reductions in present net worth are 20, 56, and 78% for the 10, 30, and 50% hardwood cases (Table 12-7). These figures indicate that even at a high real interest rate of 8%, vegetation management treatments for site preparation and release are likely to be cost-effective even when the hardwood component appears to be minor.

One of the advantages of optimization analysis by dynamic programming is the large number of alternatives that can be examined. Figure 12-1 displays the manner in which soil expectation value varies with percentage of hardwood basal area and rotation length. The four optimal regimes presented previously are circled, but there are a large number of near optimal regimes involving shorter or longer rotations. Figures 12-2A and 12-2B compare the diameter profiles of loblolly pine plantations at age 30 for the 0 and 50% hardwood basal area examples with and without thinning and release. Clearly, site preparation and subsequent release and thinning treatments can concentrate yields in the more valuable pine sawtimber classes above 11 in. At age 30, almost all trees

TABLE 12-8. Volume Yields of Loblolly Pine Plantations in Relation to Hardwood Basal Area for the Thinomatic Optimum Regimes Derived Using an 8% Interest Rate

		Hardwood—Percentage of Stand Basal Area			
		0	10	30	50
Stand age (yr)	Rotation length (yr):	30	35	35	35
		ft³/acre removals			
10		379	258	—[a]	—[a]
15		178	732	—[a]	—[a]
20		1,175	465	1,169	698
25		1,115	832	272	549
30		2,090	622	929	617
35		—	2,287	2,379	2,253
Total yield (ft³/acre):		4,937	5,196	4,749	4,117
Mean annual increment (MAI) (ft³/acre):		164.6	148.5	135.7	117.6
Reduction in MAI (%):		—	10	18	29

[a]Hardwoods only removed.

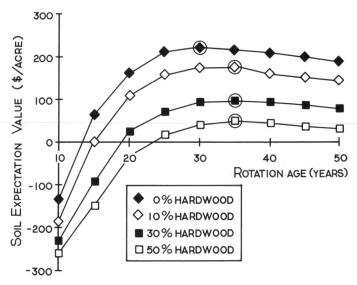

Figure 12-1. Soil expectation value at 8% interest rate in relation to hardwood percentage and Thinomatic rotation age for loblolly pine. Circled points indicate optimal regimes for each initial percentage of hardwood basal area.

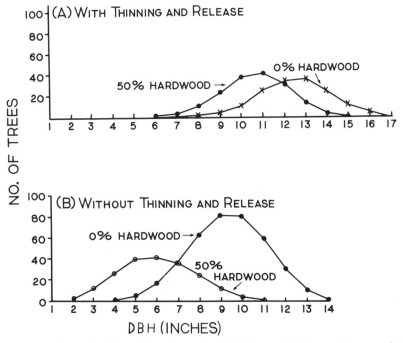

Figure 12-2. Effect of hardwood basal area (0 and 50%) on loblolly pine diameter distribution at age 30 (A) with and (B) without thinning and release.

are in this category for the thinned and released stand, whereas the stand with 50% hardwood that remains unthinned has virtually none.

The hardwood-loblolly model developed by Valsta and Brodie (1985) provides much flexibility for analysis by operating in either an optimization or simulation mode. A manager who is concerned about thinning at both ages 10 and 15 in the preceding example can eliminate the age 10 "precommercial thinning" in the simulation process or plant fewer trees in the optimization process. Elements such as grass competition at wider spacing are not included in the model and may justify the denser planting.

ASSESSING VEGETATION MANAGEMENT TREATMENTS AT THE FORESTWIDE ALLOWABLE-CUT LEVEL

The previous analyses for Douglas-fir and loblolly pine have assessed the impact of vegetation management treatments at the individual stand level by comparing treated and untreated individual acres. These analyses imply that each stand will be harvested at the most efficient point in time and ignore the role that these acres might play in sustaining a balanced harvest flow from a large forest ownership. If every stand in a forest is harvested at its most efficient point in time, then the impacts assessed at the stand and the forest level will be identical. If a stand is harvested before its optimal rotation age or rationed out beyond its optimal rotation age to sustain a relatively even long-term harvest flow until the conditions of a regulated forest (i.e., an even acreage distribution of age classes among site classes) are achieved, then the stand-level and forest-level impacts will be different. The annual harvest level established to sustain long-term timber production (but not necessarily an even flow) is called the "allowable cut." Fraser (1985) describes procedures for calculating the allowable cut and discusses the effect that investments in forest management can have on its determination.

To demonstrate the role of vegetation management in affecting levels of allowable cut, we have constructed two hypothetical forest age structures (an old-growth forest and a young-growth forest) with two different types of rules (rigid and flexible) for determining the allowable cut and two types of vegetation management impacts: (1) site preparation and rehabilitation treatments that expand, or in their absence, contract the land base; and (2) growth increase or decrease in regenerated stands resulting from control or failure to control competing vegetation, respectively.

Differences of these impacts in the various situations are known as allowable-cut effects (ACE), and divergent results from identical stand-level vegetation management activities arise from (1) differences in rules or constraints for determining allowable cuts; and (2) differences in the acreage-age class distribution between the two forests.

Examples of Harvest Scheduling and Allowable-Cut Situations

The initial harvest scheduling situations examined are a Douglas-fir old-growth forest and a young-growth forest, each 1000 acres in size. The standard yield for each forest is derived from DFSIM (Curtis et al. 1981) using Site Index 112 (ft, 50-year basis). Under the standard yield function, the young-growth forest cannot immediately sustain a harvest equal to the long-run sustained yield, whereas the old-growth forest could sustain a higher cut for an interim. This is because the old-growth forest has accumulated an inventory of standing volume in excess of the standard yield function.

Area-age class distributions, yields, and stumpage values for the two forests are displayed in Table 12-9. In addition to the standard yield table, there is a reduced yield table representing the hypothetical impact of competing vegetation in regenerated stands. These yields are designated to be 20% less at every age, and in addition, a 2.0 MCF (thousand cubic feet)/acre thinning at age 30 is assumed to be unavailable, resulting in only 67% of the standard yield over a 70-year rotation. Table 12-10 provides the stand-level analysis for the standard and reduced yield tables assuming a 4% interest rate, a \$200/acre regeneration cost, and yields and values from Table 12-9. The reduction to 67% of standard yield results in a reduction to 31% of present net worth for rotation lengths of 70 years.

An additional vegetation management impact that will be demonstrated is the impact of site rehabilitation to augment the forest land base by converting brushfields and noncommercial forest types to coniferous plantations. This is accomplished by adding 200 acres (20% of the current land base) to each forest during the first decade of analysis. These acres will not be available for harvest until the second rotation, but their presence will influence the levels of harvest calculated during the first rotation.

To demonstrate the impact of reduced growth or expanded land base on the old-growth and the young-growth forests, we chose two different harvest scheduling rules implemented with the computer program SHRUB—an expanded version of the HARVEST program (Barber 1983).

The first method used was nondeclining even flow (NDEF), a technique that maximizes harvest over a 240-year planning horizon in our cases, subject to each period's harvest being equal to or greater than the previous period's harvest. We thus arrive at the maximum harvest that can be obtained in the first period subject to no future reductions. The minimum harvest age is 70, and the length of each period is 10 years.

In the second set of harvest scheduling rules that we label "flexible,"

TABLE 12-9. Structure of Age Classes for Old- and Young-Growth Forests of Douglas-fir, with Associated Yields and Stumpage Values

| Age class (yr) | Structure of Age Classes | | Standard Yield (MCF/acre)[b] | | Reduced Yield[a] (MCF/acre)[b] | | Stumpage Value ($/MCF)[b] |
	Old-growth forest (acres)	Young-growth forest (acres)	Harvest	Thin	Harvest	Thin	
10	0	200	0	0	0	0	0
20	0	100	0	0	0	0	0
30	0	200	0	2	0	0	373
40	0	100	4.76	0	3.81	0	427
50	100	100	6.90	0	5.52	0	480
60	100	100	8.82	0	7.06	0	544
70	100	100	10.50	0	8.40	0	635
80	200	100	11.92	0	9.54	0	762
90	200	0	13.23	0	10.60	0	863
100	200	0	14.30	0	11.44	0	965
110	100	0	15.29	0	12.23	0	1067
120	0	0	16.08	0	12.86	0	1162
130	0	0	16.90	0	13.52	0	1245
140	0	0	17.50	0	14.00	0	1353
150	0	0	18.15	0	14.52	0	1422

[a]Harvest yields have been reduced 20% from the standard harvest yields, and no thinning yield is obtained.
[b]MCF = thousand cubic feet.

387

TABLE 12-10. Stand-Level Analysis for the Harvest Scheduling Examples Involving Douglas-fir[a]

Vegetation Management Situation	PNW ($/acre)	SE ($/acre)	Mean Annual Increment (ft³/acre/year)	Relative Yield (%)	Relative Value (%)
Standard yield for a 70-year rotation	458	490	178.6	100	100
Reduced yield for a 70-year rotation	143	152	120.0	67	31

[a]Interest rate is 4%, regeneration cost is $200/acre; yields and values are given in Table 12-9.

we do not require the initial level of cut to be sustainable for the full 240-year cycle but rather only for one 70-year rotation. To determine the cut in the second period (i.e., second decade), we only require that it be sustainable for 70 years, and so forth in a sequential look-ahead process. This procedure allows the cut to increase in the case of a vigorous young-growth forest or decrease in a decadent old-growth forest. A 70-year minimum harvest age forces convergence toward a fully regulated equilibrium (i.e., an equal number of acres and volumes harvested each year) as the length of the analysis period is increased.

The combination of two age-class distributions, two harvest scheduling rules and three vegetation management situations—standard yield, reduced growth and yield, and land-base expansion—result in 12 different harvest schedules. These harvest schedules are summarized in Figure 12-3 and in Table 12-11.

If we compare the standard yields for the old-growth forest under NDEF and flexible harvest scheduling rules (Examples 1 and 2 in Table 12-11), we find that NDEF suppresses the harvest by 21% in the first decade, increases harvest by 5% in the last decade, and reduces average harvest over 24 decades by only 3% in the old-growth forest. The impact on present net worth is a 13% decrease for NDEF. In contrast, in the young-growth forest, NDEF has virtually no impact on present net worth or first period harvest and results in a 4% reduction in last period and average harvests (Examples 7 and 8 in Table 12-11). The reason for the lesser impact of NDEF in the young-growth forest is that harvest is already restricted by the scarcity of merchantable timber so that the even-flow constraint further restricts availability by a lesser amount. Examples employing NDEF give substantially greater vegetation management impacts, and because this is a constraint often employed by public agencies, it is an important consideration.

The examples involving rehabilitation, which increase the land base,

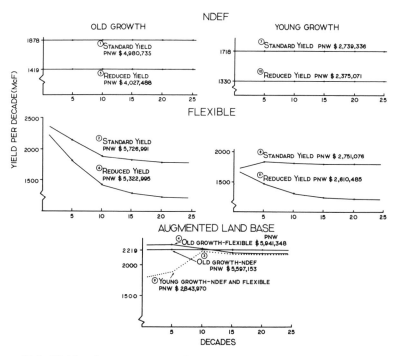

Figure 12-3. Yield and present net worth (PNW) for old- and young-growth Douglas-fir forests under nondeclining even flow (NDEF) and flexible harvest schedules, given standard yields, reduced yields (33% below standard), and augmented land base (20% increase in acreage). Circled numbers correspond to the examples in Table 12-11.

eventually approximate the full 20% increase in harvest toward the end of the scheduling cycle (Examples 3, 4, and 9 in Table 12-11). Because the benefit of the increased harvest is postponed to the second rotation, the benefit to present net worth is only 3 or 4%, except for old-growth NDEF where it is 12% (Examples 1 and 3 in Table 12-11).

In the case of the reduced growth in the second rotation examples, the NDEF examples average the harvest reduction over the earlier and later periods, whereas the flexible alternatives make minor harvest adjustments in the earlier periods, converging to the full adjustment in the later periods. Hence the impact on present net worth in the NDEF cases is substantial and more than double the relative impact in the flexible examples.

Allowable-Cut Effects Versus Stand Level Impacts

Table 12-10 can be used to derive the soil expectation value (and thereby present net worth) of 200 rehabilitated acres added to the forest land base. Alternatively, Table 12-10 can be used to determine the reduction

TABLE 12-11. Comparisons of Present Net Worth and Harvest Schedules for Old- and Young-Growth Douglas-fir Forests under Various Scenarios

| | | | | | Absolute Values | | | | Relative Values[f] | | | |
| | | | | | | Annual Periodic Harvest[e] | | | | Annual Periodic Harvest[e] | | |
Example	Forest Type[a]	Vegetation Management Situation[b]	Harvest Rule[c]	PNW[d] ($/forest)	1st decade (MCF)	Last decade (MCF)	Average (MCF)	PNW (%)	1st decade (%)	Last decade (%)	Average (%)
1.	Old growth	Standard yield	NDEF	4,980,735	187.78	187.78	187.78	100 (87)[g]	100 (79)[g]	100 (105)[g]	100 (97)[g]
2.	Old growth	Standard yield	Flexible	5,726,991	237.19	179.12	193.93	100	100	100	100
3.	Old growth	Augmented land base	NDEF	5,597,153	221.90	221.90	221.90	112	118	118	118
4.	Old growth	Augmented land base	Flexible	5,941,348	242.60	214.83	225.37	104	102	120	116
5.	Old growth	Reduced yield	NDEF	4,027,488	141.94	141.94	141.94	81	76	76	76
6.	Old growth	Reduced yield	Flexible	5,322,995	221.33	121.54	147.95	93	93	68	76
7.	Young growth	Standard yield	NDEF	2,739,336	171.80	171.80	171.80	100 (99.6)[g]	100 (100)[g]	100 (96)[g]	100 (96)[g]

			PNW[d]	\multicolumn{3}{c}{Annual periodic harvests[e]}		\multicolumn{4}{c}{}

No.	Age class[a]	Vegetation management[b]	Harvest rule[c]	PNW[d]							
8.	Young growth	Standard yield	Flexible	2,751,076	171.81	178.63	178.30	100	100	100	100
9.	Young growth	Augmented land base	NDEF or Flexible[h]	2,843,970	180.32	214.53	208.41	103	105	120	117
10.	Young growth	Reduced yield	NDEF	2,375,071	132.97	132.97	132.97	87	77	77	77
11.	Young growth	Reduced yield	Flexible	2,610,485	165.60	120.74	133.15	95	96	68	75

[a] Age-class distributions for the old- and young-growth forests are displayed in Table 12-9.

[b] Vegetation management situations include the following three scenarios: (1) standard yields as forecast by DFSIM for a 70-yr rotation; (2) yields reduced by 20% and no commercial thinnings as a result of weed competition; and (3) land base increased by 20% due to rehabilitation of brushfields and noncommercial forest types.

[c] Two sustained yield harvest rules are followed: (1) nondeclining even flow (NDEF), which requires a uniform harvest level over the long run; and (2) flexible, which permits accelerated harvest of old growth, provided it is later compensated for by young-growth accretion.

[d] Present net worth (PNW) is derived from information presented in Tables 12-9 and 12-10 and assumes a real interest rate of 4% over a 240-yr cycle of harvests.

[e] Annual periodic harvests represent the volume in thousand cubic feet (MCF) removed annually from each forest during (1) the first decade of the 240-year cycle; (2) the last decade of the 240-year cycle; and (3) the average for the 240-year cycle.

[f] Except where indicated, based on comparisons between the values for standard yield and corresponding values for augmented land base or reduced yield.

[g] Based on comparisons between the values for NDEF and flexible harvest rules for the standard yield situation.

[h] Because NDEF and flexible rules give almost identical results in young-growth forests with an augmented land base, these two cases have been combined in the table.

TABLE 12-12. Comparison of Stand-Level and Forest-Level Impacts for Various Vegetation Management Situations Involving Old- and Young-Growth Douglas-fir Forests

Vegetation Management Situation[a]	Analysis Level[b]	Forest Type[c]	Harvest Rule[d]	Addition to or Subtraction from Present Net Worth[e] ($/forest)	Allowable-Cut Effect[f] (%)
Augmented forest land base	Stand	—	—	97,926	100
	Forest	Old growth	NDEF	616,418	629
	Forest	Old growth	Flexible	214,357	219
	Forest	Young growth	NDEF or flexible	92,894	95
Reduced yield	Stand	—	—	−337,300	100
	Forest	Old growth	NDEF	−953,247	283
	Forest	Old growth	Flexible	−403,996	120
	Forest	Young growth	NDEF	−364,265	108
	Forest	Young growth	Flexible	−140,591	42

[a]Vegetation management situations consist of: (1) forest land base increased by 200 acres due to rehabitation of brushfields and noncommercial forest types; and (2) yield reduced to 67% of current yield in second rotation.

[b]Analysis based on either individual stands or entire forest property.

[c]Age-class distributions for the old- and young-growth forests are displayed in Table 12-9.

[d]Two sustained-yield harvest rules are followed: (1) nondeclining even flow (NDEF), which requires a uniform harvest level over the long run; and (2) flexible, which permits accelerated harvest of old growth, provided it is later compensated for by young-growth accretion.

[e]Values are derived from PNW computations using data provided in Tables 12-9 through 12-11 as the basis.

[f]Impact relative to stand-level impact.

in soil expectation value (and present net worth) in the second rotation as a result of reduced yield on the 1000-acre forest. These two values are the impact of the vegetation management assumptions assessed at the stand level. By comparing these values with the change in value of the different harvest schedules when these management impacts are introduced, it is possible to get a relative measure of the allowable-cut effect (ACE) to the stand-level effect. In Table 12-12 it is apparent that the introduction of 200 rehabilitated acres has more than six times the stand-level impact in the old-growth forest under NDEF, whereas under the flexible policy, it is slightly more than double. In both these instances the old-growth surplus inventory allows a substantial increase in harvest in the first decade rather than waiting the 70 years for the rehabilitated acres to mature. In the case of the young-growth forest, only slight near-term increases in harvest are available, and the ACE is slightly less than the stand-level value due to the difficulty in metering this large lump of initially nonproductive inventory into the harvest flow.

The reduced yield ACE impacts in Table 12-12 are greater than the stand-level impacts for each of the old-growth forest cases. In the case of the young-growth forest, the ACE loss is less than half the stand-level impact in the flexible case as losses are gradually metered in over two rotations rather than beginning immediately. In the NDEF case, the stand-level and ACE evaluations are very close. This is because second rotation yield reductions require immediate harvest adjustments in the first rotation.

SUMMARY

Examples of stand-level investment analysis have been presented using yield tables and simulation in the case of Douglas-fir and optimization in the case of loblolly pine. An alternate type of analysis involving both stand-level analysis and forest-level analysis has been presented, indicating that the allowable-cut effect (ACE) can be substantially greater or less than the corresponding stand-level impact, depending on forest age-class structure, harvest scheduling rules, and the type of impact a silvicultural activity has—for example, growth changing or land-base expansion. The stand-level analysis has the advantage of being invariant across forest and policy contexts. It measures simple investment efficiency of forest practices. If, on the other hand, macroeconomic regional production and employment analyses are to be undertaken, then the ACE approach, taking into account current and projected inventories and present and potential resource utilization and conservation policies, is an appropriate tool.

REFERENCES

Barber, R.L. 1983. A user's manual for HARVEST: an online interactive harvest scheduling simulator for even-aged forests. For. Res. Lab., Oregon State Univ., Corvallis, OR. 30 p.

Bruce, D., D.J. DeMars, and D.L. Reukema. 1977. Douglas-fir managed yield simulator—DFIT user's guide. USDA Forest Service, Pacific Northwest Forest and Range Experiment Station, Portland, OR. Gen. Tech. Rep. PNW-57. 26 p.

Burk, T.E., H.E. Burkhart, and Q.V. Cao. 1984. PCWTHIN. Version 1.0 users's manual. School of Foresty and Wildlife Resources, Virginia Polytech. Inst. and State Univ., Blacksburg, VA. (Mimeo). 23 p.

Burkhart, H.E. and P.T. Sprinz. 1984. A model for assessing hardwood competition effects on yields of loblolly pine plantations. School of Forestry and Wildlife Resources, Virginia Polytech. Inst. and State Univ., Blacksburg, VA. Publ. FWS-3-84. 55 p.

Cao, Q.V., H.E. Burkhart, and R.C. Lemin. 1982. Diameter distributions and yields of thinned loblolly pine plantations. School of Forestry and Wildlife Resources, Virginia Polytech. Inst. and State Univ., Blacksburg, VA. Publ. FWS-1-82. 62 p.

Curtis, R.O., G.W. Clendenen, and D.J. Demars. 1981. A new stand simulator for coast Douglas-fir: DFSIM user's guide. USDA Forest Service, Pacific Northwest Forest and Range Experiment Station, Portland, OR. Gen. Tech. Rep. PNW-128. 79 p.

Fraser, G.A. 1985. Benefit-cost analysis of forestry investments. Pacific Forestry Centre, Canadian Forestry Service, Victoria, BC. Information Rep. BC-X-275. 20 p.

Green, K. 1983. Forests, herbicides and people. A case study of phenoxy herbicides in western Oregon. Council on Economic Priorities. New York, NY. 203 p.

McArdle, R.E., W.H. Meyer, and D. Bruce. 1961. The yield of Douglas-fir in the Pacific Northwest. U. S. Dept. Agr., Washington, DC. Tech. Bull. 201. 72 p.

Roberts, C.A. 1982. Cooperative study on the long-term silvicultural benefits of chemical brush control. Interim Report. Corvallis, OR. 13 p. plus tables. (Report on file at the Forest Research Laboratory, College of Forestry, Oregon State University, Corvallis, OR).

Row, C. 1976. System MULTIPLOY: a computer language to simulate and evaluate investments in forestry. Part 1. Introduction and basic manual. USDA Forest Service, Washington, DC. (Mimeo); Rev. (76).

Sessions, J. 1979. Effects of harvesting technology upon optimal stocking regimes of forest stands in mountainous terrain. Ph.D. thesis, Oregon State Univ., Corvallis, OR. 259 p.

Stavins, R.N., D.L. Galt, and K.L. Eckhouse. 1981. An economic analysis of alternative vegetation management practices in commercial forests of the Pacific Coast region. Cooperative Extension and Giannini Foundation of Agricultural Economics, Univ. California, Berkeley, CA. Project Rep. 2. 66 p.

Stewart, R.E., L.L. Gross, and B.H. Honkala. 1984. Effects of competing vegetation on forest trees: a bibliography with abstracts. USDA Forest Service, Washington, DC. Gen. Tech. Rep. WO-43. 260 p.

2,4,5-T Assessment Team. 1979. The biologic and economic assessment of 2,4,5-T. Cooperative Impact Assessment Report, U.S. Dept. Agr., Washington, DC. Tech. Bull. 1671. 445 p. plus supplement.

Valsta, L.T. and J.D. Brodie. 1985. Joint optimization of thinning rotation age and vegetation management for loblolly pine plantations, a whole rotation approach. Proc., Soc. Amer. Foresters, Systems Analysis Working Group, Athens, GA.

Walstad, J.D., J.D. Brodie, B.G. McGinley, and C.A. Roberts. 1986. Silvicultural value of chemical brush control in the management of Douglas-fir. Western J. Appl. Forestry 1:69-73.

IV

SYNTHESIS

13

Principles of Silvicultural Prescriptions for Vegetation Management

JOHN C. TAPPEINER II
ROBERT G. WAGNER

INTRODUCTION

This text has covered the fundamental ecological, mensurational, and economic principles of vegetation management in silviculture. In this chapter, we discuss the application of such principles to silvicultural prescriptions for the management of individual forest stands. Briefly, we will cover (1) silvicultural systems and vegetation management; (2) setting objectives for stand and vegetation management; (3) evaluating the need for vegetation management; (4) treatment selection; (5) prioritizing stands for treatment; (6) treatment implementation; and (7) evaluating treatment effects. Our purpose is not to tell readers what treatments to use to manage forest vegetation; instead, we will outline some of the basic considerations in conducting vegetation management programs.

Forest vegetation management may be done for a variety of purposes including timber production, wildlife habitat management, forage production, watershed management, recreation and aesthetics, soil stability, and roadside maintenance. Although this chapter focuses on the management of competing vegetation for timber production, many of the concepts presented are applicable to these other uses of vegetation management.

We make several assumptions in this chapter regarding the purpose and implementation of vegetation management as a part of forest management. First, we assume that an array of tools are available, including fire, herbicides, manual and mechanical methods, and grazing animals as well as combinations of these. We assume that the goals of forest management are clearly defined. Finally, we assume that the forest stand is the basic unit of prescription, implementation, and evaluation of vegetation management activities. Thus we are not concerned with forest-level planning and analysis of silvicultural activities. This chapter will concentrate on the process of applying vegetation management to specific stands.

SILVICULTURAL SYSTEMS AND VEGETATION MANAGEMENT

Because most conifer management is practiced on an even-aged basis, this chapter will concentrate on that approach. As mentioned in Chapter 6, however, many of the problems, techniques, and principles applicable to even-aged silvicultural systems also are applicable to uneven-aged systems.

Even-aged systems of silviculture are conveniently displayed as a cycle (Figure 13-1), which includes a planned array of treatments for the regeneration, maintenance, improvement, and harvest of a forest stand. This cycle also can be considered a description of secondary succession

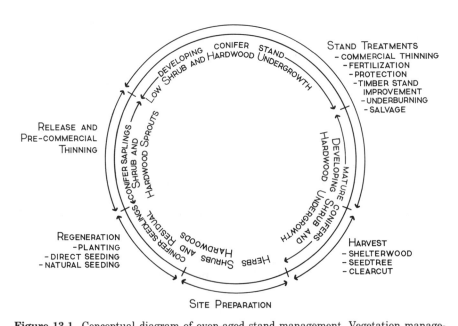

Figure 13-1. Conceptual diagram of even-aged stand management. Vegetation management considerations and opportunities exist throughout the cycle.

following the disturbance of a forest stand, with the treatments used to direct succession toward forestry goals. The potential rate and course of succession vary widely among forest types and can be significantly altered by the nature of forest management activities.

Two important points arise when viewing vegetation management in the context of silvicultural systems. First, vegetation management treatments that are applied during the period of site preparation and release are only a small part of the total silvicultural system. Although they may be intensive and extremely important in determining stand development, they occur over a relatively short period and are frequently no more significant than harvesting, thinning, or other silvicultural treatments. Second, forest vegetation is affected by all silvicultural treatments, or lack of them, not just by site preparation and release. For example, a sequence of heavy precommercial and commercial thinnings could result in more shrubs and hardwoods in the understory. Depending on the forest management objectives, an increase in understory vegetation could be viewed as beneficial (e.g., wildlife habitat or aesthetics) or detrimental (e.g., flammable fuels or competition with the conifer overstory). Viewing vegetation management within the context of a silvicultural system may reveal alternative management strategies and provide opportunities for managing vegetation to enhance a variety of forest resources and values.

SETTING OBJECTIVES FOR STAND AND VEGETATION MANAGEMENT

In forestry, vegetation management is done within the context of a silvicultural prescription. A silvicultural prescription is a plan for managing a forest stand. In the prescription, objectives for the stand are stated and a series of treatments outlined that will meet the objectives. The specific justifications for the treatment also are included in the prescription, as based on ecological, managerial, and social grounds (Daniel et al. 1979). Using an integrative approach, the silviculturist predicts the effects of various treatments on stand development and selects the practices that will best achieve the forest management objectives. An excellent example of prescription development for the regeneration phase of forest management is provided by Cleary et al. (1986).

Given our current knowledge of forest ecosystems and the realities of forest management, a silvicultural prescription may be considered a "working hypothesis" (Smith 1962). Prescriptions are developed for a wide variety of stands and purposes. Forest ecosystems vary considerably among stands, and there is often large variation within stands as well. Forest rotations span considerable time during which unforeseen events such as windthrow, disease, insect outbreaks, wildfire, and other problems are inherent. Added to these are a variety of forest policies, administrative constraints, social attitudes, and economic fluctuations. Consequently, silvicultural prescriptions need to be site-specific, flexible, and reevaluated periodically throughout the life of the stand.

The objectives for silvicultural prescriptions (including both stand and vegetation management practices) are set by combining the forest management goals with the characteristics of the vegetation and the environmental variables of particular stands. Each stand contributes to the output of resources or values from the forest as a whole. The prescription is a plan that will produce a stand with a particular set of characteristics (e.g., species composition, stand structure, stand density or stocking, tree size, stand volume, wildlife habitat) within a specified time while protecting the basic soil resource and other environmental values. These characteristics must be clearly specified to develop a workable silvicultural prescription.

It is important that the characteristics of the desired stand be quantified, if only in broad terms. For example, the objective might be a stand of conifers of approximately 200 trees/acre with an average stem diameter at breast height (DBH) of 12 to 14 in. at 35 years of age. In order to provide for several wildlife species, there should be approximately one group of hardwoods per acre (approximately 0.1 acre of four to eight trees, 6 to 10 in. DBH). Objectives such as these provide a reasonably clear description of the desired stand. The prescription then outlines the treatments (including vegetation management) and their timing needed to produce this stand. There is no one set of parameters suitable for describing all stands. The measures should be convenient, understandable, and facilitate the implementation of treatments (Table 13-1).

Once the desired stand parameters have been defined, an analysis is needed to determine if the existing stand conditions or variables (such as microclimate, pathogens, animals, soil) might preclude producing such a stand. Similarly, the costs of the treatments required to produce the stand can be compared to the income or resource values that the stand may produce or protect. Several iterations of objective setting and analysis may be required before developing the final prescription.

EVALUATING THE NEED FOR VEGETATION MANAGEMENT

Evaluating the need for vegetation management in a forest stand is an integral part of the silvicultural prescription. Failure to identify and reduce significant levels of vegetative competition early in stand development can have a substantial negative effect on the rate of development or the final yield. Further, treating well-developed vegetation problems

TABLE 13-1. Some Commonly Used Vegetation Measures in Silvicultural Prescriptions

Trees	Shrubs, Forbs, Grasses
Abundance or Size	
Number of individuals	Number of individuals
Number of stems	Number of stems
Basal area	Percentage of cover
Stem volume	Leaf area index
Stem diameter at breast height (DBH)	Height
Height	Biomass
Biomass	Crown volume
Leaf area index	
Stand density index	
Productivity or Vigor	
Site index (height at a specified age)	Height/age
Periodic annual increment	Primary production
(cubic volume/unit area/yr)	(biomass production/unit area/yr)
Mean annual increment	Stem increment
(cubic volume/unit area/yr)	Rates of invasion or establishment
Rings per inch	Seed production
Tree classes (vigor and risk rating)	Height growth rate
Live crown ratio	Animal unit months
Crown classes	
Height growth rate	
Seed production	
Structure (trees, shrubs, forbs, and grasses combined)	
Species composition by layer or groups	
Density by species, layer or groups	
Number of layers	
Number and type of groups	
Vertical profiles	
Horizontal arrangement	
Age classes	
Down logs, snags, and other dead material	

is often more expensive and less effective than preventive measures taken early in stand development. Conversely, investments in vegetation management treatments that are unnecessary or ineffective are a waste of money and effort.

Because most foresters manage stands of various ages, site quality, species composition, and in many cases silvicultural objectives, evaluating the need for vegetation management can be a challenging task. The stands that offer the greatest potential gains through vegetation management must be identified so that the often scarce resources available for forest management can be used most effectively.

Predicting the Effects of Vegetative Competition on Stand Development

Evaluating the need for vegetation management at any point in stand development requires that the effects of competing vegetation on future stand development be determined. In order to assess the potential for competing vegetation to influence stand development, several predictions must be made:

1. The growth and development of the competing species.
2. The effect of various types and amounts of competing vegetation on the survival and growth of the crop trees.
3. The effect of possible treatments on the competing species present in a stand and on the potential invasion of other species from adjacent stands or residual seed.

Based on these predictions, several questions about the rate and course of stand development can be asked:

1. Will the desired stand develop in the allotted time under projected levels of competition?
2. Will the effects of competition reduce growth but allow the desired stand to eventually develop?
3. Will competition cause a reduction in both growth and final yield of the stand?
4. Will competition cause serious mortality and growth reductions such that a manageable stand will not develop?

Figure 13-2 illustrates these possibilities, and several case examples are given in Chapter 9. Curve B represents normal stand development as described by commonly used yield tables or growth models that have been developed with unknown levels of vegetative competition. Curve C depicts a delayed but normal stand yield after a competition-induced growth reduction early in stand development. This delay may occur on a site where pines overcome and suppress a cover of grass that slows their early growth but does not cause high mortality. A similar pattern with a delay of 30 years or more can occur as true firs overcome early growth suppression by evergreen shrubs. In Case D, competition reduces both stand growth and final yield. This often occurs where persistent, unmerchantable hardwoods cause mortality and growth reductions of conifers, resulting in a stand that is sparsely stocked with merchantable trees. Curve E represents a case where nearly complete conifer mortality results and no merchantable stand develops. This can occur on dry sites where grass or shrub competition causes severe tree mortality. Finally, under inten-

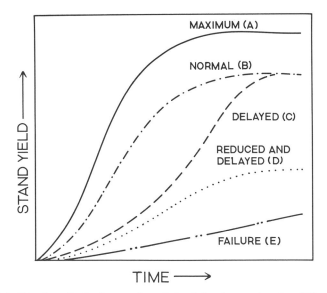

Figure 13-2. Five hypothetical scenarios of stand development under different kinds of vegetative competition: (A) maximum site productivity under low levels of vegetative competition; (B) normal rate of stand development and final yield as determined by commonly used yield tables or growth models; (C) effects of competition that reduce the rate of stand growth but not the final yield as compared to normal stands; (D) effects of competition that reduce both the rate of development and the amount of final yield; and (E) severe effects of competition that cause high mortality of desired species, thereby precluding development of a manageable stand.

sive management or very low levels of vegetative competition, a higher than normal rate of stand growth and perhaps final yield may be possible (Curve A). This curve represents the upper limit of growth and biomass accumulation for a particular tree species, genotype, and site.

Although the curves in Figure 13-2 provide a conceptual basis from which to evaluate the potential course of stand development under the influence of competing vegetation, it is not always possible in practice to accurately predict the growth and yield of a particular stand. Accurate predictions are most difficult in young stands where the long-term effects of vegetative competition or other variables have not yet become apparent. Predictions in older stands also can be difficult in that unforeseen events (e.g., windstorms, insect or disease outbreaks, wildfire, adverse climatic fluctuations) can alter stand development.

Evaluation at Different Stages of Stand Development

There are four stages in even-aged stand development when the need for vegetation management should be evaluated: (1) before harvest; (2) after harvest and before site preparation; (3) after site preparation and during stand establishment; and (4) after stand establishment. Existing or potential vegetation problems can be identified during each of these stages (McDonald and Tappeiner 1986). At each stage, there is an array of vegetation management objectives, treatment options, and constraints that should be considered.

1. *Before Harvest.* Entering a stand just before harvest can provide a valuable opportunity to identify and prevent many vegetation problems from arising when regenerating the next stand. Frequently, potential competitors are more apparent before a stand is harvested than at any other time until they appear in the next stand. The following items should be considered for each stand before harvest:

    a. Presence of undesirable shrub and tree species with high sprouting potential. Sprout development and future site occupancy for some hardwoods can be quantitatively estimated from stand tables or vegetation descriptions before harvest (Harrington et al. 1984, Tappeiner and McDonald 1984, Tappeiner et al. 1984).

    b. Availability of seed from undesirable species whose germination and survival are favored by the disturbances associated with harvesting and site preparation activities (e.g., mechanical treatment, prescribed burning) (Tappeiner et al. 1986).

    c. Presence of animals, insects, or pathogens that could be detrimental to young stands and that could be controlled with vegetation manipulation.

Identification of potential vegetation problems before harvest will allow for the prescription of preharvest treatments (such as understory burning or herbicide treatments), which can reduce the occurrence of these problems in the next stand. It also will facilitate selection of suitable harvesting and site preparation methods.

2. *After Harvest and before Site Preparation.* Soon after harvest, many of the effects of the logging and preharvest vegetation management treatments will become apparent. At this stage, many of the competitors with potential to occupy the next stand are present. Site preparation treatments may offer the best opportunity to prevent these competitors from becoming established in the next stand. Each newly harvested site should be carefully surveyed before site preparation to determine:

    a. Composition, abundance, and distribution of unwanted sprouting species from residual stumps and root systems.

    b. Presence of seedlings of undesirable species, if germination has occurred.

   c. Potential seed sources of undesirable species from adjacent stands or residual seed whose germination is favored by proposed site preparation treatments.

   d. Presence of damaging animals, insects, and pathogens that can be managed by site preparation treatments.

   e. Need for logging-debris removal to improve site access for tree planting or reduce fire hazard.

   f. Need for seedbed preparation if conifers are to be naturally regenerated.

3. *After Site Preparation and during Stand Establishment.* The first several years following site preparation when regeneration is becoming established are critical to stand development. The structure and species composition of a stand initiated during the early years of establishment often determine a long-term trajectory that can facilitate or preclude accomplishing the silvicultural objectives. Therefore, manipulating early stand structure and species composition with release treatments is an important consideration in most silvicultural prescriptions.

If the only objective is wood production, then the purpose of vegetation management at this stage is to ensure that each crop tree occupies its allocated growing space in the shortest time that is economically feasible. If wildlife habitat or grazing forage also are objectives, then encouraging desired forage and cover species at the proper time in combination with ensuring the eventual space occupancy of each tree may be the vegetation management objectives.

Most vegetation problems in the early years of stand establishment will usually be apparent within the first few growing seasons after site preparation, and frequent evaluation is needed during this period. Early identification of vegetation problems is critical in young stands because early losses in tree survival and growth cannot be recovered and replanting is often expensive and unsuccessful. In addition, release treatments for controlling well-established plants are usually more expensive and less effective than when plants are younger. When surveying young stands consider:

   a. Abundance, distribution, and size of undesirable shrub and tree species, and determine whether they are from sprout or seed origin. Recognizing the origin of the undesirable species is helpful in predicting their growth rates and ability to compete with the desired tree species. For most species, sprouts grow much faster than seedlings.

   b. Abundance of herbaceous vegetation on sites where competition for soil moisture can cause severe mortality or growth losses to tree seedlings. Identifying these sites is most important before conifers

are regenerated. Control of competitive herbaceous vegetation usually should be done before or within the first growing season after
trees are planted or naturally regenerated.

c. Presence of undesirable species that may be low in abundance on
   the site but are capable of rapid expansion upon release or that have
   seed sources in adjacent stands. Treatments should be considered
   that will minimize their expansion or invasion.

d. Presence of vertebrate or insect pests. Many animal and insect problems can be reduced by manipulating vegetation to alter their habitat. Failure to adequately control animal or insect damage to young
   trees can quickly eliminate any benefits gained by reducing vegetative competition.

e. Evidence that tree growth has been increased or decreased by previous treatments or other factors. It is important to determine the
   effect of previous treatments so that stands can be retreated or
   future treatments can be modified if necessary.

4. *After Stand Establishment.* After a stand is established, the silvicultural emphasis generally shifts from manipulating associated vegetation (interspecific competition) to manipulating the crop trees
(intraspecific competition). This may be at or near the point of crown
closure for some forest stands and well after crown closure for others.

There may be several objectives for vegetation management after stand
establishment. Examples include efforts to improve the form and species
composition of the stand, increase stand growth, improve forage, and/or
prevent vegetation problems in the next rotation. The treatments to accomplish these objectives can often be done during thinning or timber
stand improvement.

The following conditions should be evaluated periodically after a stand
is established:

a. Presence of undesirable trees that are dominant or are affecting the
   growth or form of crop trees.

b. Abundance of understory vegetation on sites where it can limit the
   growth of the desired overstory. Understory vegetation can sometimes seriously reduce the growth of the overstory and in some cases
   eliminate the benefits of thinning (Wilde et al. 1968, Barrett 1982,
   Oliver 1984). If understory vegetation is being managed for wildlife
   or livestock, then managing for desired forage and cover species also
   should be considered at this time.

c. Effect of previous thinning or timber stand improvement treatments
   on the development of undesirable species. These treatments can
   often stimulate the development of undesirable plant species.

d. Need for understory burning or other treatments to reduce understory vegetation and fuel loads for fire protection.

Vegetation Surveys

Vegetation surveys at each stage of stand development provide information necessary to evaluate the need for vegetation management. They provide a description of vegetation in a stand that can be used to predict the effects of vegetative competition on the rate and course of stand development.

1. *Kinds of Vegetation Surveys.* Vegetation surveys can be classified as either subjective or objective. A *subjective survey* is conducted by making a qualitative description of the species present and their relative abundance, distribution, and size within a stand. In contrast, an *objective survey* usually requires a random or systematic location of sample points across a stand. Vegetation parameters are measured and recorded at each point. An inventory of the species present and their abundance, distribution, and size within the stand are determined by a quantitative analysis of the data collected from the sample points.

The kind of survey used depends on the detail of information required to determine whether vegetation management is needed. For example, a subjective survey of a uniform cover of herbaceous vegetation prior to planting pine seedlings may provide sufficient information to determine the need for a preplanting weed control treatment. In contrast, a young pine plantation in which there are patches of sprouting shrubs and hardwoods may require a more detailed objective survey to delineate the specific areas needing release and the most appropriate treatments.

Subjective and objective vegetation surveys are both appropriate in different situations, and each has several advantages over the other. The advantages of *subjective* vegetation surveys are that they generally:

   a. Can be done quickly so that a decision to treat a stand can be made promptly in the field, thus allowing more stands to be surveyed in a given amount of time.
   b. Are less complicated and generally cost less to conduct and interpret.

The advantages of *objective* vegetation surveys are that they generally:

   a. Provide an unbiased and consistent measure of vegetation conditions.
   b. Provide an accurate, permanent record of vegetation conditions for later consideration or comparison following prescribed treatments.
   c. Standardize the method of stand descriptions and thereby facilitate comparisons and interpretations among different stands.

These advantages pertain to vegetation surveys conducted from the ground. Recent developments in remote sensing technology, however, are beginning to indicate potential for aerial surveys in vegetation management. For example, McCreight (1983) was able to demonstrate, using ground-based infrared spectrometry, that shrub species in a young Douglas-fir plantation in southwest Oregon had different spectral reflectance characteristics that could be used to quantify their abundance, distribution, and size. The research also showed that the relative effectiveness of herbicide applications could be determined from measurements of spectral reflectance. Therefore, advances in remote sensing technology may offer the potential for more cost-effective vegetation surveys of forest stands.

2. *Aims of Vegetation Surveys.* Surveys before harvest or site preparation describe the abundance, distribution, and origin of undesirable species to provide a basis for selecting preharvest or site preparation treatments. The information collected for this purpose is used for a simple vegetation description and may be gathered from subjective or objective surveys. Mueller-Dombois and Ellenberg (1974) provide thorough coverage of most objective vegetation survey techniques for this purpose. Randomly or systematically located plots (fixed, variable, strip, or line-intercept) are placed throughout a stand to record the size, density, cover, and frequency of each plant species.

Vegetation surveys to determine the need for release or timber stand improvement treatments describe the presence of undesirable species in a manner that will provide a meaningful estimate of their potential to reduce tree survival or growth. Vegetation surveys for this purpose are generally more complex than those before harvest or site preparation.

Subjective surveys to determine the potential influence of vegetation surrounding individual trees have been the most common methods employed to determine the need for release treatments in young stands. The amount of overtopping a tree is experiencing by undesirable shrubs and trees is the most frequently used criterion in deciding whether a stand is in need of release. Smith (1962) suggested that the area encompassing an imaginary inverted cone projected from the top of a desirable tree should be kept clear of undesirable trees (Figure 13-3). The magnitude of the cone angle is set according to the relative growth rates of the desirable tree and surrounding undesirable vegetation and the extent to which the tree is suppressed. The main limitation of the inverted-cone method is that it ignores vegetation outside of the cone that may influence the growth of the desired tree. The growth of young conifers often can be severely inhibited by the presence of herbaceous vegetation (Preest 1977, Knowe et al. 1985, Petersen and Newton 1985) or low-growing shrubs (Barrett 1982, Tappeiner and Radosevich 1982, Oliver 1984) that do not intersect the inverted cone.

The concept of crop trees being "free to grow" also has been a subjective standard used in deciding whether young stands are in need of competition release. There have been many attempts to clearly define a "free-to-grow" tree. The main limitation to most subjective methods of deter-

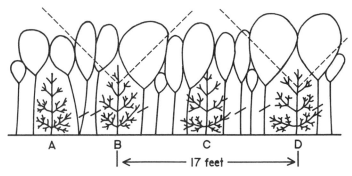

Figure 13-3. An example of how the intensity of cleaning (release) might be regulated in freeing a stand of conifers from overtopping hardwoods. The objective chosen here is to remove all hardwoods that project upward into an inverted cone with an apex that is 2 ft below the tops of the crop trees and has an angle of 90°. The trees to be removed are marked by dashes. Trees B and D, which are spaced to give a stand of about 150 conifers per acre, are the only trees deliberately released. Trees A and C are ignored. In a heavier cleaning, the angle would be increased or the apex of the imaginary cone lowered. The extent of release would depend on the relative growth rates of the different species present and the amount of time that would be allowed to elapse before another cleaning. (*Source:* From Smith, D.M. 1962. The practice of silviculture. 7th ed. Copyright © 1962 by John Wiley and Sons, Inc. New York, NY. 578 p.)

mining the competitive status of a tree is that they have not generally been linked to tree survival or growth and cannot be used to predict quantitative losses in stand development. An exception is the Virginia Division of Forestry's Free-To-Grow Classification (Table 13-2), which was found to be correlated with the subsequent height growth of loblolly pine (Zutter et al. 1984).

Most attempts to develop objective methods of measuring vegetation in young stands for the purpose of predicting losses in tree survival and growth have been restricted to research studies. The various methods of quantifying competing vegetation in forest stands can be divided into descriptions of general stand conditions and those surrounding individual trees (Table 13-3). Although these approaches have been somewhat successful in building static models of tree growth reductions under various levels of vegetative competition, most have not been able to project the long-term effects of the competition measures on stand development. A notable exception is the work by Burkhart and Sprinz (1984), who found that the percentage of hardwood basal area in loblolly pine stands at any time after crown closure (age 11) was highly correlated with pine yield at age 24. Using this relationship, they were able to develop a predictive model for loblolly pine yield based on the hardwood basal area at crown closure.

As new survey techniques and competition models to determine the

TABLE 13-2. The Virginia Division of Forestry's Free-To-Grow
Classification Developed by T.A. Dierauf and J.W. Garner, Division of
Forestry, Charlottesville, Virginia. (From Zutter et al. 1984).

Four classes are used to describe a pine seedling's potential for (1) capturing a place in the crown canopy; and (2) diameter growth up to the time of full crown closure. These classes are determined by the size and vigor of the pine seedlings compared to the size, vigor, and species of nearby hardwoods (and pines). This system can be used for pine reproduction of any age prior to full crown closure. Larger residual hardwoods are not considered; they should be eliminated during site preparation. Also root competition from hardwoods is not considered.

Class 1

Free to grow without significant hardwood competition. Class 1 trees are judged to have better than a 90% chance of capturing a place in the crown canopy. Release will *not* benefit these trees.

Class 2

Also free to grow, but with more hardwood competition than Class 1 seedlings. Most of the hardwood competition is side shading. Like Class 1 trees, Class 2 trees are judged to have better than 90% chance of capturing a place in the crown canopy. The separation into Class 1 or Class 2 is arbitrarily based on whether nearby hardwoods can throw shade above the midpoint of the pine seedling. The method for determining the height of shading is to measure the total height of the hardwood, then rotate a straight line of that length from the base of the hardwood to the point where it touches the pine stem (in practice, the hardwood is usually bent over). If this point is below one-half the total height of the pine, the pine is Class 1. If above one-half the total height of the pine, the pine is Class 2. Release will benefit Class 2 pines primarily by increasing diameter growth.

Class 3

Questionable trees, judged to have between 10 and 90% chance of capturing a place in the crown canopy. Even for pine that eventually make it into the crown canopy, competition will greatly reduce diameter growth. It is assumed that without release, half of the pines will not capture a place in the crown canopy.

Class 4

Not free to grow. Judged to have less than a 10% chance of capturing a place in the crown canopy because of suppression by overtopping hardwoods (or pines). Release will benefit Class 4 trees *only* at very young ages (see notes).

Notes

1. In deciding whether a seedling is Class 1 or 2, *side* shading by nearby pines is not considered (release from hardwoods would have no effect on such competition).

2. Overtopping or potential overtopping by nearby pines, however, *must* be considered if it will prevent a seedling from capturing a place in the canopy. In other words, a seedling can be Class 3 or 4 because of competition from nearby pine.

3. In deciding whether a seedling is Class 2 or 3, or Class 3 or 4, the vigor of the seedling is often as important as the amount of hardwood competition. The previous year's leader growth and the length and density of the needles are indicators of vigor.

4. Class 4 seedlings cannot be released successfully after age 2 or 3, in most cases, because nearby Class 1 and 2 seedlings will usually be so much taller that they will often suppress them. For the same reason, Class 3 seedlings cannot be released successfully after age 3 or 4, in most cases.

TABLE 13-3. Measures Used to Quantify Vegetation in Forest Stands for Determining the Effects of Vegetative Competition on Tree Survival and Growth

Vegetation Parameter	Author(s)
A. Stand Measures	
1. Percentage of cover	Kirchner et al. 1978, Oliver 1984
2. Crown volume	Bentley et al. 1971, Lanini and Radosevich 1986
3. Basal area	Brinkman and Liming 1961, Benzie 1977
4. Basal area ratios	Walstad 1976, Burkhart and Sprinz 1984
5. Biomass	Ross et al. 1986
B. Individual Tree Measures	
1. Percentage of overtopping and encroachment, visible sky	Chan 1984, Howard and Newton 1984
2. Competitor height to tree height ratio	Lewis 1981, Powers and Oliver 1984
3. Crown volume to distance ratio	Wagner 1984
4. Basal area to distance ratio, total height, and density	Glover 1982
5. Inverse proximity, relative height, percentage of cover, and foliage density	Brand 1985

need for release and timber stand improvement are developed, their usefulness should be evaluated by their ability to help accomplish four objectives:

1. Determine the probable short- and long-term mortality and growth reduction if current or projected levels of vegetative competition are allowed to develop.
2. Rank stands according to the severity of vegetative competition (or the potential gains from eliminating such competition) in order to facilitate selection of the highest priority stands for treatment.
3. Rank the principal competing species according to their relative importance in order to assist in the selection of treatments.
4. Determine the efficacy of treatments after they have been applied.

Regardless of advances made in competition modeling and vegetation survey techniques, one of the best tools will continue to be the observational skills of the forester. An example (presented in Figure 13-4), shows

Figure 13-4. Three Douglas-fir stands in the central Oregon Coast Range at several stages of development: (1) a 6-year-old stand that contains many large, sprouting bigleaf maple clumps; (2) a 1-year-old stand with numerous small bigleaf maple clumps; and (3) a newly harvested site on which the bigleaf maple stumps are beginning to sprout. The older stand (1) provides an example of what the younger stands will look like unless the bigleaf maple clumps are controlled.

three Douglas-fir stands at different stages of development. Stand 1 is a 6-year-old Douglas-fir plantation in which sprouts from bigleaf maple stumps are dominating the stand. Stand 2 is 1 year old and also has abundant stump sprouts. Stand 3 was harvested and burned several weeks before the photograph was taken and was planted with Douglas-fir a few months later. The untreated stumps in Stand 3 will look like those in Stand 2 in 1 year and like those in Stand 1 within 6 years. Using simple observational skills, a forester managing Stand 3 can anticipate the development of competing vegetation in that stand for the next 6 years and thereby assess the need for vegetation management. Control of bigleaf maple sprout clumps in all three stands will be required to prevent a reduced and delayed yield of Douglas-fir (Figure 13-2, Curve D).

Stratifying within Stands for Vegetation Management

It often is necessary to stratify a stand into smaller vegetation management units when some parts of the stand require different treatments.

Difficulty generally arises when deciding how small the units should be. The units must be small enough to ensure that each portion of the stand receives the appropriate treatment, yet large enough to prevent treatment costs from becoming greater than the benefits gained from stratifying the stand.

The minimum size of a vegetation management unit in any stand will generally vary with a number of factors: (1) site productivity and stand value; (2) treatment method and costs; (3) age and size of stand and competing vegetation; (4) access to the stand; and (5) topography. The minimum size of a unit will generally be large in stands of low productivity or on steep, relatively inaccessible sites. Conversely, stands of high productivity or those on flat, accessible land may have smaller units.

The treatments proposed also will help determine the minimum size of a unit. A unit may be less than an acre if manual cutting, backpack spraying, or stem injection of herbicide are proposed treatments. Efficient aerial application of herbicides or the use of large ground equipment requires larger vegetation management units.

TREATMENT SELECTION

Once it is determined that competing vegetation is an obstacle to achieving the desired stand, selection of an appropriate vegetation management treatment is considered. Treatment selection is an integral step in the prescription process but does not necessarily mean that a treatment should be implemented. Ideally, the decision to select a treatment is made when the cost of the treatment is less than the predicted loss to the stand. That is to say, the economic threshold (see Chapters 1 and 12) for controlling competing vegetation must be determined. However, in cases where reforestation is required by law and vegetation control is needed for successful reforestation, the decision to prescribe a treatment may be based on selecting the safest and most cost-effective treatment necessary to meet legal reforestation standards. The concept of treatment cost also must be extended beyond the direct cost of treatment application to include indirect costs of the treatment. As discussed in Chapter 11, indirect costs can include such things as administrative difficulty or losses to soil productivity, water quality, and wildlife habitat.

Although there is often accurate information on the direct cost and short-term efficacy of various treatments to reduce competing vegetation, accurate models to make long-term predictions of the effects of competition on stand growth and yield are generally not available. Consequently, it is difficult to determine economic thresholds for vegetative competition for most stands. Foresters must generally use their experience and professional judgment to determine whether the estimated gain can justify the cost of treatment.

Unit: __Smith Creek #6__   Operation: __Site Preparation__

I. Vegetation Management Objectives and Constraints

A. Projected Stand Loss if Untreated: __8-year delay in final harvest and a 30%__ __reduction in total stand yield.__

B. Maximum Allowable Expenditure to Prevent Loss: __$190 per acre (direct cost)__

C. Vegetation Manipulation Goal: __Achieve adequate site preparation to ensure__ __satisfactory stand establishment and growth.__

   1. Initial reduction: __No more than 15% cover remaining in the first__ __growing season following treatment.__
   2. Acceptable recovery: __No more than 30% cover for 5 years following__ __treatment.__

D. Other Treatment Goals: __Removal of logging debris__

II. Effects on Present Vegetation and Economic Efficiency of Treatment Alternatives

A. Effects on Present Vegetation

		TREATMENT ALTERNATIVES							
		A Manually cut and Broadcast burn		**B** Glyphosate @ 3 lb. per acre and Broadcast burn		**C** Glyphosate @ 3 lb. per acre		**D** Tractor scarification with brushrake	
PRESENT UNDESIRABLE SPECIES	ABUNDANCE (% COVER)	PROB. % KILL OR INJURY	AMOUNT OF REDUC-TION	PROB. % KILL OR INJURY	AMOUNT OF REDUC-TION	PROB. % KILL OR INJURY	AMOUNT OF REDUC-TION	PROB. % KILL OR INJURY	AMOUNT OF REDUC-TION
SALMONBERRY	60	55	33	95	57	95	57	80	48
RED ALDER	20	65	13	80	16	65	13	90	18
HAZEL	10	40	4	75	8	75	8	90	9
VINE MAPLE	5	40	2	90	5	75	4	90	5
TOTAL	95		52		86		82		80

1. Absolute abundance after treatment:[a/]   43   9   13   15

2. Percent reduction of original abundance:[b/]   55   91   86   84

3. Estimated years until acceptable recovery
   level is reached: 1   6   5   7

B. Economic Efficiency

   1. Direct cost per acre: $100 $175 $75 $80

   2. Direct cost per acre for each
      percent reduction of original abundance:[c/] $1.82 $1.92 $0.87 $0.95

   3. Direct cost per acre per year until
      acceptable recovery level is reached:[d/] $100 $29.17 $15.00 $11.43

Calculations: [a/] Total abundance - total reduction for treatment.
   [b/] Total reduction for treatment/total abundance.
   [c/] B.1./A.2.
   [d/] B.1./A.3.

Figure 13-5. Example of a Treatment Evaluation Worksheet for a hypothetical stand.

416

III. Treatment Effects On Potential Invading Species

TREATMENT ALTERNATIVES

POTENTIAL INVADING SPECIES	A Manually CUT and broadcast burn	B Glyphosate @ 3 lb. per acre and broadcast burn	C Glyphosate @ 3 lb per acre	D Tractor scarification with brush blade
Red alder seed source on north edge of unit	Potential seed-bed from hot fire ; possible alder problem	Potential seed-bed from hot fire ; possible alder problem	Minimal invasion; no soil disturbance	Creates good seed bed ; likely alder problem
Heavy grass cover on adjacent unit	Other herbs favored over grass	Other herbs favored over grass	Minimal Invasion	Favors invasion

IV. Other Treatment Effects

TREATMENT ALTERNATIVES[e/]

ITEM	PRIORITY	A	B	C	D
Worker Safety	1	−	−	−	−
Removal of Logging Debris	2	+	+	−	+
Water quality	3	−	−	0	−
Air quality	4	−	−	0	0
Soil Properties	5	−	−	0	−
WILDLIFE HABITAT	6	+	+	+	+
GRAZING	7	+	+	+	+
Aesthetics/Recreation	8	−	−	−	−
Administrative Difficulty	9	−	−	−	0

TREATMENT SELECTED: _Treatment B because of its potential effectiveness and the need for slash disposal._

[e/]Code: + = Positive effect, 0 = No effect, − = Negative effect.

Figure 13-5 (*Continued*)

Assuming an economic analysis (see Chapter 12) or practical experience indicates that a vegetation management treatement would be beneficial, there are several quantitative approaches to selecting the best treatment from an array of treatment alternatives (Talerico et al. 1978, Hirsch et al. 1979, Knapp et al. 1984). A discussion of these approaches to selecting the most cost-effective treatment is beyond the scope of this chapter. Nevertheless, we will illustrate one systematic method of evaluating the potential effects and costs of several vegetation management treatments that can assist in selection of the best treatment (or treatment combination) for a particular stand.

Treatment Evaluation Worksheet

The Treatment Evaluation Worksheet presented in Figure 13-5 provides a conceptual approach to comparing several treatment alternatives for a stand, based on technical information and professional experience. The worksheet consists of four parts:

1. Part I defines the vegetation management objectives and contraints under which the treatment alternatives will be evaluated.
2. Part II is used to quantitatively compare the potential efficacy and economic efficiency of treatments in suppressing established undesirable species.
3. Part III is used to assess the potential for treatments to encourage the invasion of undesirable species from adjacent stands or residual seed.
4. Part IV is used to compare the possible effect of the treatments on other forest resources and values, as well as off-site impacts.

The information from all four parts of the worksheet must be combined to select the best treatment alternative.

The Treatment Evaluation Worksheet has been completed for site preparation of a hypothetical stand (Smith Creek #6) to illustrate the approach in selecting the best treatment. Other types of vegetation management treatments such as pre-harvest, pre-planting, release, or timber stand improvement also may be evaluated in this way.

1. Vegetation Management Objectives and Constraints (Part I).
    a. The first step is to determine the projected loss to the stand if no vegetation management treatments were applied. The loss must be estimated by predicting the effects of competing vegetation on stand development. In the example, the forester used research combined with experience and professional judgment to determine that untreated vegetation on the site would cause an 8-year delay in final harvest and a 30% reduction in total yield.
    b. Using the predicted loss, an economic analysis can help determine the maximum amount that can be spent on the treatment (see Chapter 12). Alternatively, budget constraints may dictate the amount that can be spent. In the example, it was assumed that a maximum of $190/acre could be spent, provided that the vegetation management goal is achieved.
    c. The next step is to define the vegetation manipulation goal. The goal should state both the initial level of vegetation reduction desired and the maximum acceptable rate of vegetation recovery following the treatment. This goal should reflect the level of competition reduction necessary to accomplish the stand management objectives. In the example, the forester decided that the cover of the undesirable shrub and hardwood species on the site

should be reduced by the site preparation treatment so that less than 15% is remaining within the first growing season following treatment. Another goal was that recovery of the undesirable shrub and hardwood species should not exceed 30% cover during the 5 years following treatment.

d. Other goals of the treatment also are stated on the chart. For example, removal of logging debris is an additional site-preparation objective in this example.

2. Treatment Effects on Present Vegetation and Economic Efficiency of Treatment Alternatives (Part II).

a. Effects on Present Vegetation.

i. A list of the undesirable species present in the stand and a quantitative measure of their abundance is listed on the left side of the chart. This information can be collected from an objective or subjective vegetation survey of the stand. It also is important to include species that are minor components of the stand but have the potential to proliferate if other species are removed. Several measures may be used to quantify the abundance of the plant species (Table 13-1). Percentage of cover is used in the example.

ii. The various treatment alternatives to be compared are then listed across the top of the chart. Though the example compares only four treatments, any number may be evaluated. For simplicity, the number of treatments should be confined to those considered to be the best candidates.

iii. The probable percent kill or injury for each species found in the first growing season following treatment is then recorded. Such information may be found in technical bulletins and research papers or estimated from previous experience. In the case illustrated, an estimated 55% of the salmonberry is likely to be killed or injured with a manual cutting and broadcast burn treatment (A) within the first season following these treatments. In contrast, 95% kill or injury would result from the glyphosate treatment (B).

iv. The probable kill or injury value is then multiplied by the abundance value for each species to estimate the probable reduction for a given species and treatment. For example, under Treatment A, multiplying the 55% probable kill or injury by the 60% cover of salmonberry indicates that cover will be reduced by approximately 33%. The total vegetation reduction for a given treatment is then determined by adding the reductions for each species. In the example, there would be an estimated 52% total cover reduction from the manual cutting and broadcast burn treatment (A). Subtracting the

52% total cover reduction for Treatment A from the 95% total abundance for the stand provides a 43% estimate of total shrub and hardwood cover remaining in the first growing season following treatment. The 55% reduction of the original abundance for Treatment A is determined by dividing the 52% total cover reduction by the 95% total abundance value.

v.   The estimated number of years until the acceptable recovery level is reached is then recorded. This information also may be found in technical bulletins and research papers, or estimated from previous experience. In the example, the glyphosate and broadcast burn treatment (B) is estimated to keep shrub and hardwood recovery under the 30% level of cover for a minimum of six years. However, the manual cutting and broadcast burn treatment (A) is estimated to keep the target species cover under 30% for only one year following treatment.

b. Economic Efficiency.

The relative economic efficiency of each treatment on the initial reduction and subsequent recovery of the undesirable species is then determined from the calculations in Part II A. First, the estimated direct cost per acre of each treatment alternative is recorded. Dividing this direct cost per acre by the percentage of reduction of the original abundance provides a direct cost per acre for each percentage of reduction of the original species abundance. For example, $100/acre for Treatment A divided by 55% equals $1.82/acre for each percentage of reduction of shrub and hardwood abundance. The economic efficiency of each treatment in minimizing recovery of the undesirable species is determined by dividing the direct treatment cost per acre by the estimated number of years until the recovery exceeds the acceptable level. For example, the $29.17/acre/year for treatment B is calculated by dividing $175/acre by 6 years.

3. Treatment Effects on Potential Invading Species (Part III).

The purpose of Part III is to compare the anticipated effect of each treatment on the invasion of undesirable species that have been identified as having an available source of seed in the area. Frequently, the germination of seed from adjacent stands or residual seed in the soil is favored by a particular treatment. Examples include grasses, red alder, willow, birch, and cottonwood that readily colonize newly disturbed mineral soil, and also species of ceanothus and manzanita, which are stimulated to germinate following a prescribed fire or mechanical scarification. In the example, seed sources of red alder and grass from adjacent stands have the potential to invade following treatment.

4. Other Treatment Effects (Part IV).
   Treatments also should be evaluated by their potential effects on
   other forest values. Treatments efficient for controlling undesirable
   species may conflict with other forest management objectives or
   constraints. Part IV can be used to compare various other treatment
   effects in their relative order of importance. In the example, the
   forester prioritized important considerations for Smith Creek #6.
   The impact of each treatment on a given factor has been evaluated
   by using a positive sign for a beneficial effect, a zero for a negligible
   effect, and a negative sign for a detrimental effect. For example,
   use of fire and scarification (Treatments A, B, and D) are considered
   to have detrimental effects on the soil, whereas the glyphosate-only
   treatment (C) is anticipated to have a negligible effect. Alternatively, the magnitude of the effects could be indicated by an arbitrary numerical scale.
      The priority of these factors in decision making will change from
   site to site depending on the management objectives and constraints.
   For example, a stand located in a municipal watershed may have
   the highest priority for water quality, whereas another stand may
   have grazing or wildlife as the highest priority. Other factors not
   listed in the example also may deserve consideration.

Selecting the Best Treatment from the Treatment Evaluation Worksheet

By utilizing Part II, it is possible to select the most appropriate treatment
that will accomplish the vegetation manipulation goals identified in Part
I. For example, the manual cutting and broadcast burn treatment (A)
would be rejected because the initial reduction goal of leaving no more
than 15% cover in the first growing season could not be achieved; Treatments B, C, and D could achieve the goal. However, Treatment C could
accomplish the initial reduction goal for the lowest cost. None of the
treatment alternatives could be rejected for exceeding the maximum allowable expenditure.

Another vegetation manipulation consideration in treatment selection
is the length of time before the acceptable recovery level is reached. A
more expensive treatment might be selected if it successfully retards
recovery of the undesirable species for a longer period of time. Treatment
D is more expensive than Treatment C but also gives an estimated 2
years of additional control over Treatment C. Treatment D also can minimize the recovery for less cost per year than the other treatments.

Part III assists further in selecting among Treatments B, C, and D by
identifying new vegetation problems that may be created by the treatments. Treatment D would probably be rejected as an alternative due to
the high potential for red alder or grass invasion. Treatment C would

minimize the likelihood of invasion by either species. Treatment B presents some possibility of invasion but may be acceptable.

Further evaluation of Treatments B and C in Part IV shows that there are some potential negative effects on soil, water, and air quality with Treatment B due to the use of fire. However, if removal of logging debris is necessary to facilitate planting and reduce the fire hazard, Treatment B would probably be selected over Treatment C because broadcast burning will accomplish this objective. The final treatment selected and a brief justification for the choice is specified at the bottom of the worksheet.

The purpose of the Treatment Evaluation Worksheet is to provide a conceptual framework from which to evaluate many of the effects and costs of various vegetation management alternatives. It may be impractical to complete a worksheet of this type for every treatment prescribed, but periodic documentation of treatment selection in representative stands will help foresters develop analytical and decision-making skills, specify the reasons for treatment selection, and provide a record of predicted treatment effects for later evaluation.

PRIORITIZING STANDS FOR VEGETATION MANAGEMENT

Because vegetation management treatments must frequently compete for funds and personnel with other projects, some stands will be selected over others for treatment. Therefore, stands must be prioritized based on their need for vegetation management to ensure that limited funds are used most effectively.

There is no standard method to prioritize stands for treatment. As with most silvicultural activities, priority depends on conditions within the stand (such as age and value of the stand) and external considerations (such as funding, site access, and equipment availability). We suggest the following points be considered when prioritizing stands:

1. Is the treatment crucial for seedling survival, or will it favor increased growth rates? Referring to Figure 13-2, for example, will lack of treatment result in the development of Stand E or C? The current rates of seedling survival and growth are key considerations along with the current and potential rates of shrub, herb, or hardwood invasion.

2. How will the current treatment or lack of it affect other variables in the stand? For example, the treatment of grass in a 1-year-old plantation may not directly affect seedling survival, but it may retard the development of pocket gopher populations that damage 3- to 10-year-old plantations.

3. If treatment is postponed, how effective are future treatments likely to be and what will they cost? For example, broadcast foliar application of herbicides to 2-year-old hardwoods is generally cheaper than stem injection of older hardwoods.

4. What are the effects on other resources? For example, postponing a site preparation treatment might require the use of heavy equipment or result in an intense burn that could cause soil erosion or nutrient losses.

5. Will the necessary labor and material be available in the future, and will access to the stands change?

6. Which stands, if treated, will give the best return on investment?

IMPLEMENTING VEGETATION MANAGEMENT TREATMENTS

Proper implementation of treatments is crucial to successful vegetation management. A mistake during this stage can be costly. Improperly applied treatments may be ineffective, resulting in lost funds and additional costs for retreatment, or damage crop trees and other forest resources. Attention to detail at the implementation stage is important, and the number of details to consider is large (Table 13-4). Administrative concerns can obscure the silvicultural considerations. When this occurs, good prescriptions inadvertently may be compromised for administrative ease. Although we discuss treatment selection and implementation separately, both must be considered simultaneously when developing prescriptions.

The need for close attention to detail becomes apparent when considering all that is involved in successful implementation. Close supervision is generally needed to ensure worker safety, treatment effectiveness, and resource protection. For example, a prescription may call for treatment application when competing species are susceptible and the crop trees are least likely to be damaged. This condition is often judged by the phenology of the competing and crop species or by measures such as plant moisture stress. The treatment "window" may occur within a 2- to 3-week period and can be narrowed by factors such as crew and supervisory availability, the number of stands to treat, equipment breakdown, adverse weather, and road conditions.

A detailed discussion of the legal and administrative aspects of vegetation management is beyond the scope of this chapter. Laws and regulations vary considerably by state and, in some instances, by local jurisdiction. Those needing to pursue this subject in more detail should consult their local or state governments, university extension office, and professional forestry organizations.

Depending upon the size and structure of an organization and the

TABLE 13-4. Some Considerations in Implementing Vegetation Management Treatments

Ordinances and Regulations

Forest practice regulations
Federal and state pesticide label requirements
Applicator licensing
Pesticide handling, storage, and disposal requirements
Air quality standards (smoke management)
Water quality standards
Accident insurance and worker's compensation requirements
Compliance with NEPA and other environmental statutes

Administrative and Contractual Items

Adequate supervision
Clear end product and technique specifications
Availability of qualified contractors or trained crews
Availability of required equipment and qualified operators
Flexibility to react to changes in site-specific weather, vegetation development,
    soil conditions, and other factors
Safety awareness and training
Familiarity with ordinances, regulations, and precautions
Public notification
Security of personnel, materials, and equipment
Accurate record keeping
Cost (both direct and indirect)
Labor union considerations

Site-Specific Considerations

Local weather—wind, temperature, precipitation, relative humidity
Soil, fuel, and plant moisture status
Slope configuration
Stage of vegetation development—size, age, phenology
Daily fire danger risk
Access to the project site
Sensitive areas or conditions:
    Presence of humans
    Presence of livestock and wildlife
    Nearby residences
    Location of streams and water sources
    Historic or archaeological sites
    Threatened or endangered plants and animals

degree of centralized control of forestry operations, the procedures for treatment implementation may vary considerably. On small forest tracts, treatment selection and implementation may be under the direct control of one person. In large organizations, foresters who analyze and prescribe treatments may not be directly involved with their implementation. Furthermore, the entire prescription process may be conducted by an inter-disciplinary team of specialists. In these cases, thorough communication of the intent and desired outcome of the treatments and implementation instructions is required.

When carrying out vegetation management treatments for the first time, the following may help ensure success:

1.. Consult experienced personnel who can recommend appropriate treatments and identify potential problems (e.g., silviculturists, extension foresters, forest practice officers, equipment operators, crew bosses, chemical specialists, certified consultants).

2. Consult qualified forest managers and regulatory officials for information on legal requirements, local policy, administrative requirements, public concerns, and agreements with neighbors.

3. Acquire the training necessary to prescribe and implement vegetation management prescriptions safely and effectively (e.g., state licensing, continuing education programs, technical workshops, professional meetings).

4. Review the current literature for information on treatment effectiveness and experience in implementation (e.g., technical journals, extension bulletins, workshop manuals, treatment records).

5. Test new treatments on a small area first in order to allow adjustments before undertaking large projects.

6. Anticipate problems and have contingency plans in mind. Forecasting for unexpected events may prevent some problems from ever occurring, and being prepared will certainly help deal with them should they arise.

These steps are not unique to vegetation management but are ones that a professional should take prior to beginning any new program.

EVALUATING EFFECTS OF VEGETATION MANAGEMENT TREATMENTS

Evaluating the short- and long-term effects of vegetation management treatments is the final step in the prescription process. It is often overlooked. Systematic observations following treatment can provide valuable insight in determining whether it was successful. Ideally, the observed treatment effects should be stated in quantitative terms (e.g., diameter growth of crop trees or initial cover reduction and recovery of undesirable species). Increases in stem diameter of most conifer species are generally good short-term indicators of significant competition reduction because such increases usually occur before increases in height growth can be observed (see Chapter 7). Total height or height growth alone generally appears to be a poor short-term indicator of competitive stress. The original information from a Treatment Evaluation Worksheet (Figure 13-5) can be compared to the vegetation several years after treatment to provide a basis for evaluation.

The experience and information gained from treatments applied to stands of various sites, ages, and species composition can be a valuable aid to improving future treatment selection and implementation. However, careful treatment evaluation and record keeping are needed to capture this experience and make it available for future use. Although frequent, detailed measurements of treatment effects may not be practical following all treatments, they should be made on a periodic basis on at least some of the treated stands. This information will provide an excellent source of practical knowledge that, coupled with research information, should provide better site-specific guides to vegetation management. Some forestry organizations routinely leave untreated (control) plots for later comparison with treated areas to evaluate treatment effectiveness (Owston et al. 1986).

SUMMARY

Vegetation management is applied to individual stands within the context of a silvicultural system. The prescription should clearly define the stand management objectives in quantitative terms and outline a series of site-specific treatments that will meet the objectives. Vegetation management can occur frequently during a rotation, including just before or after final harvest, during stand establishment, or well after a stand is established.

Accurate quantitative models that forecast the long-term effects of competing vegetation on stand development are generally not available. Therefore, foresters must rely primarily on their experience and professional judgment when evaluating the need for vegetation management in individual stands. Proper use of vegetation surveys to identify current and potential vegetation problems can facilitate successful vegetation management.

Treatments should be evaluated by their (1) ability to suppress the vegetation and prevent the invasion of undesirable species; (2) effects on crop trees; (3) cost-effectiveness; and (4) protection of forest resources and other values. A systematic method using a Treatment Evaluation Worksheet is presented as one way to select the most appropriate vegetation management treatment.

Many regulatory, contractual, administrative, and site factors must be considered when implementing any silvicultural treatment. Small oversights in planning and implementation can often result in treatment failure or other problems. Care also must be taken that administrative expedience does not override silvicultural considerations.

Evaluation of vegetation management treatments should be done during application, immediately after application, and for several years following treatment. Documentation of treatment effects will assist in determining whether the silvicultural objectives have been achieved and will improve the prescription and implementation of future vegetation management treatments.

REFERENCES

Barrett, J.W. 1982. Twenty-year growth of ponderosa pine saplings thinned to five spacings in central Oregon. USDA Forest Service, Pacific Northwest Forest and Range Experiment Station, Portland, OR. Res. Pap. PNW-301. 18 p.

Bentley, J.R., S.B. Carpenter, and D.A. Blakeman. 1971. Early brush control promotes growth of ponderosa pine planted on bulldozed site. USDA Forest Service, Pacific Southwest Forest and Range Experiment Station, Berkeley, CA. Res. Note PSW-238. 6 p.

Benzie, J.W. 1977. Manager's handbook for red pine in the north central states. USDA Forest Service, North Central Forest Experiment Station, St. Paul, MN. Gen. Tech. Rep. NC-33. 23 p.

Brand, D.G. 1985. Early growth and development of Douglas-fir in relation to interspecific competition. Ph.D thesis, Univ. British Columbia, Vancouver, BC. 168 p.

Brinkman, K.A. and F.G. Liming. 1961. Oak and pine reproduction responds to overhead release. J. Forestry 59:341-346.

Burkhart, H.E. and P.T. Sprinz. 1984. A model for assessing hardwood competition effects on yields of loblolly pine plantations. School of Forestry and Wildlife Resources, Virginia Polytechnic Institute and State Univ., Blacksburg, VA. Publ. No. FWS-3-84. 55 p.

Chan, S.S. 1984. Competitive effects of overtopping vegetation on Douglas-fir morphology in the Oregon Coast Range. M.S. thesis, College of Forestry, Oregon State Univ., Corvallis, OR. 49 p.

Cleary, B.D., B.R. Kelpsas, and D.R. DeYoe. 1986. Five steps to successful regeneration planning. Forest Res. Lab., Oregon State Univ., Corvallis, OR. Spec. Pub. 1 (rev). 32 p.

Daniel, T.W., J.A. Helms, and F.S. Baker. 1979. Principles of silviculture. 2nd ed. McGraw-Hill Book Co., Inc., New York, NY. 500 p.

Glover, G.R. 1982. Evaluation of competing vegetation effects on growth of young loblolly pine (*Pinus taeda* L.) plantations in the Alabama piedmont. Ph.D. thesis, Virginia Polytechnic Institute and State Univ., Blacksburg, VA. 138 p.

Harrington, T.B., J.C. Tappeiner II, and J.D. Walstad. 1984. Predicting leaf area and biomass of 1- to 6-year-old tanoak (*Lithocarpus densiflorus*) and Pacific madrone (*Arbutus menziesii*) sprout clumps in southwestern Oregon. Can. J. Forest Res. 14:209-213.

Hirsch, S.N., G.F. Meyer, and D.L. Radloff. 1979. Choosing an activity fuel treatment for southwest ponderosa pine. USDA Forest Service, Rocky Mountain Forest and Range Experiment Station, Fort Collins, CO. Gen. Tech. Rep. RM-67. 15 p.

Howard, K.M. and M. Newton. 1984. Overtopping by successional Coast-Range vegetation slows Douglas-fir seedlings. J. Forestry 84:178-180.

Kirchner, W., B. Bradley, and S. Griffin. 1978. The effect of brush competition on conifer plantation growth on the Sequoia National Forest and recommended release schedules. USDA Forest Service, Sequoia National Forest, Porterville, CA.

Knapp, W.H., T.C. Turpin, and J.H. Beuter. 1984. Vegetation control for Douglas-fir regeneration on the Siuslaw National Forest: a decision analysis. J. Forestry 82:168-173.

Knowe, S.A., L.R. Nelson, D.H. Gjerstad, B.R. Zutter, G.R. Glover, P.J. Minogue, and J.H. Dukes, Jr. 1985. Four-year growth and development of planted loblolly pine on sites with competition control. South. J. Appl. Forestry 9:11-14.

Lanini, W.T. and S.R. Radosevich. 1986. Response of three conifer species to site preparation and shrub control. Forest Sci. 32:61-77.

Lewis, R.A. 1981. Silvicultural strategies and weed populations in western conifers. pp. 62-71. *In* Holt, H.A. and B.C. Fischer (eds.) Weed Control in forest Management. Proc., John S. Wright Forestry Conference. Dept. Forestry and Natural Resources, Purdue Univ., West Lafayette, IN. 305 p.

McCreight, R.W. 1983. Detection of 2,4-D herbicide damage using ground-based measurements: implications for remote sensing. M.S. thesis, College of Forestry, Oregon State Univ., Corvallis, OR. 33 p.

McDonald, P.M. and J.C. Tappeiner II. 1986. Weeds. J. Forestry 84(10):33-37.

Mueller-Dombois, D., and H. Ellenberg. 1974. Aims and methods of vegetation ecology. John Wiley and Sons, Inc., New York, NY. 547 p.

Oliver, W.W. 1984. Brush reduces growth of thinned ponderosa pine in northern California. USDA Forest Service, Pacific Southwest Forest and Range Experiment Station, Berkeley, CA. Res. Pap. PSW-172. 7 p.

Owston, P.W., M. Greenup, and V.A. Davis. 1986. A method for assessing the silvicultural effects of releasing young trees from competition. USDA Forest Service, Pacific Northwest Research Station, Portland, OR. Gen Tech. Rep. PNW-191. 18 p.

Petersen, T.D. and M. Newton. 1985. Growth of Douglas-fir following control of snowbrush and herbaceous vegetation in Oregon. Dow Chemical USA, Midland, MI. Down to Earth 41(1):21-25.

Powers, R.F. and W.W. Oliver. 1984. Ponderosa pine plantation growth in northern California: brush competition and response to release, p. 122-125. *In* Proc., Western Forestry Conference, Portland, OR.

Preest, D.S. 1977. Long-term growth response of Douglas-fir to weed control. New Zealand J. Forest Sci. 7:329-332.

Ross, D.W., W. Scott, R.L. Heninger, and J.D. Walstad. 1986. Effects of site preparation on ponderosa pine (*Pinus ponderosa*), associated vegetation, and soil properties in south central Oregon. Can. J. For. Res. 16:612-618.

Smith, D.M. 1962. The practice of silviculture. 7th ed. John Wiley and Sons, Inc., New York, NY. 578 p.

Talerico, R.L., C.M. Newton, and H.T. Valentine. 1978. Pest-control decisions by decision-tree analysis. J. Forestry 76:16-19.

Tappeiner, J.C. II, T.B. Harrington, and J.D. Walstad. 1984. Predicting recovery of tanoak (*Lithocarpus densiflorus*) and Pacific madrone (*Arbutus menziesii*) after cutting and burning. Weed Sci. 32:413-417.

Tappeiner, J.C. II and P.M. McDonald. 1984. Development of tanoak understories in conifer stands. Can. J. Forest Res. 14:271-277.

Tappeiner, J.C., P.M. McDonald, and T.F. Hughes 1986. Survival of tanoak (*Lithocarpus densiflorus*) and Pacific madrone (*Arbutus menziesii*) seedlings in forests of southwestern Oregon. New Forests 1:43-55.

Tappeiner, J.C. II, and S.R. Radosevich. 1982. Effect of bearmat (*Chamaebatia folisa*) on soil moisture and ponderosa pine (*Pinus ponderosa*) growth. Weed Sci. 30:98-101.

Wagner, R.G. 1984. A survey of competing vegetation in five young Douglas-fir plantations in the Western Oregon Cascades: a new approach. Department of Forest Science, College of Forestry, Oregon State Univ., Corvallis, OR. Project Report. 28 p.

Walstad, J.D. 1976. Weed control for better southern pine management. Southern Forestry Research Center, Weyerhaeuser Company, Hot Springs, AR. Forestry Paper 15. 44 p.

Wilde, S.A., B.H. Shaw, and A.W. Fedkenheuer. 1968. Weeds as a factor depressing forest growth. Weed Res. 8:196-204.

Zutter, B.R., G.R. Glover, and D.F. Dickins. 1984. Competing vegetation assessment systems in young southern pine plantations. Silvicultural Herbicide Cooperative, Auburn University, Auburn, AL. Res. Note 84-12. 8 p.

14

Seeing the Forest for the Weeds: A Synthesis of Forest Vegetation Management

RONALD E. STEWART

INTRODUCTION

The ecological dynamics and competitive relationships within the developing forest are at the core of the principles and practices of vegetation management. But much remains to be discovered before this silvicultural practice can move from an empirical base to a firm scientific foundation. This chapter focuses on the key biological concepts of vegetation management and highlights opportunities for enhancing forest productivity through sound application of current knowledge. To conclude, recommendations are offered that are designed to sustain progress in this aspect of silviculture.

About 483 million acres of commercial forest land are distributed throughout the United States. Only about half of this acreage may actually be available for timber production because of changing management objectives of the landowner; set-asides for wilderness, wildlife, and recreation; and changing land use patterns, for example, from forest land to agriculture, rights-of-way, or urban development. Low net energy requirements in the extraction (harvesting and transportation) and manufacture of forest products, coupled with the renewable nature of the forest, increase the long-range importance of wood in relation to more energy-intensive, nonrenewable materials.

Timber management research throughout the nation shows that productivity on suitable sites—compared with natural, unmanaged forests—

can be greatly increased by prompt reforestation to obtain fully stocked stands and by application of intensive cultural practices. Such practices may include site preparation, planting of genetically improved seedlings, competition release, protection from tree-damaging animals, early control of plantation spacing and species composition, fertilization, and commercial thinning.

The forest is most vulnerable to the effects of competing vegetation during the regeneration stage and extending to the sapling stage when young trees are 2 to 4 in. in diameter at breast height (DBH). The regeneration stage consists of an interdependent series of events; therefore, decisions at one point affect the outcome and options later in the process (Cleary and Greaves 1974). Reforestation begins by selecting the appropriate harvesting and silvicultural system and culminates in a well-stocked stand of free-growing trees of desirable species. What is important is that silvicultural practices applied during the regeneration stage have the most profound effect on the forest's future: its composition, development, growth, and product yield.

PRINCIPLES OF VEGETATION MANAGEMENT

The fundamental ecological principles of forest vegetation management (see Chapter 5) can be grouped into four major topics: population or individual plant interactions with the environment (e.g., autecology); interactions among plant populations (e.g., competition); community or ecosystem dynamics (e.g., succession); and patterns of tree growth and stand development (e.g., biometrics). These topics focus on eight key concepts: (1) the principle of limiting factors; (2) the principle of the holocoenotic environment; (3) the principle of trigger factors; (4) the operative environment; (5) the law of constant final yield; (6) competition and niche separation; (7) plant succession; and (8) resilience and inertia in ecosystems.

Plant Interactions with the Environment

As described in Chapter 5, resources are environmental factors that are directly used by plants, such as light, water, nutrients, and carbon dioxide. Conditions are factors that influence the survival and growth of plants but are not directly used by them such as temperature, soil permeability, and animal grazing. The resources available to an individual tree and the physical conditions it faces comprise its microenvironment. The manner by which plants experience and respond to the microenvironment determines species distribution patterns, size, and abundance on a site.

Several principles govern plant-environment relationships, three of which are of major importance: the principle of limiting factors, the principle of the holocoenotic environment, and the principle of trigger factors. Plants and other organisms respond to many environmental stimuli. Each process and each environmental factor has a minimum or threshold value below which the process does not function, an optimum value at which the process proceeds at the fastest or best rate, and a maximum value above which the rate of the process declines or ceases. The range of tolerance—the difference between maximum and minimum—of an environmental factor can vary at any stage of plant development. For example, many conifer species often are more tolerant of shade and less tolerant of high temperatures when seedlings than at later stages.

In 1855, the German organic chemist Justus von Liebig developed the *concept of limiting factors* while studying the response of plants to fertilizers. The rate of growth of an organism was originally thought to be controlled by that factor available in the smallest amount relative to its minimum requirement. However, we now know that growth rates can be increased by changes in the supply of more abundant factors that can compensate for the so-called limiting factor. The original concept is still valid; more broadly interpreted, it implies that one or more factors are often more important than others in the overall success or failure of plants in a particular environment. It is also true that whenever an environmental factor approaches minimum, its relative effect becomes very great.

Recent studies of forest fertilization provide examples of the principle of limiting factors. In general, response to fertilization is greatest when combined with thinning to reduce competition for light and moisture as well as the added nutrients. The same can be shown for fertilization combined with weed control in young stands. In California, for example, 200 lb of nitrogen/acre increased 5-year volume growth of ponderosa pine nearly 30%, and response was greater on sites where topsoil had been displaced during site preparation (McColl and Powers 1984, Powers 1983). However, trees under strong competition from brush responded only marginally to fertilization unless freed from competition. In fact, some of the added nutrients may have been utilized by the competing vegetation, resulting in increased growth and competitive ability of these species. On a droughty site, needle weight increased 129% over unreleased controls when fertilization was combined with weeding, compared with only 20 and 79% increases for fertilization and weeding applied separately (Powers and Jackson 1978). Combining fertilization with weeding improved 5-year height growth by 242%, compared with only 10 and 105%, respectively, for these practices applied singly (Powers 1983). In this example, the supply of soil moisture was more limiting than nutrient supply, thereby constraining the response to fertilization. However, once moisture stress was relieved through control of competing vegetation, the trees responded to an increased supply of nutrients.

The height growth of ponderosa pine on a droughty northern California site suggests only limited response to fertilization in the absence of weed control (Figure 14-1). Volume growth was 12 times greater on the poor site and nearly 3 times greater on a better site (McColl and Powers 1984). Combined treatments may lead to additive growth effects on better sites and synergistic effects on poorer sites. On shallow or rocky, skeletal soils, shrub competition aggravates stress from climatic drought and may block fertilization response even where nitrogen deficiency is severe.

This example of forest fertilization also illustrates that one limiting factor may quickly replace another that has been removed. Once the effect of moisture stress was removed, growth became limited by nutrient deficiency. Thus the effects of various environmental factors are often interconnected, reflecting the *principle of the holocoenotic environment*: it is virtually impossible to isolate and control a single factor or organism without affecting the remaining ecosystem.

Removal of a limiting factor can create a far-reaching chain reaction and occasionally leads to the replacement of one ecosystem by another.

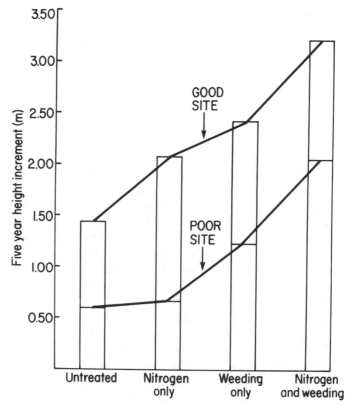

Figure 14-1. Height growth of ponderosa pine following nitrogen fertilization and weeding on a good site (SI 30 m at 50 yr) and a poor site (SI 15 m at 50 yr). (*Source:* Powers 1983)

The factor thus changed becomes a trigger factor that initiates the change. The *trigger factor principle* is a corollary to and depends upon the holo-coenotic principle, which in turn is based on the chain reaction set off by trigger factors. Because many trigger factors are actually limiting factors, all three principles are interrelated.

Limiting factors simplify the complex environment to the factor or set of factors that actually limit survival, growth, or development at the time and place of interest. This *operative environment* is of particular concern to the forester. With regard to competing vegetation, the operative environment consists of available soil moisture, sunlight, nutrients, or a combination of these three factors.

The local site resources are largely fixed and finite; therefore, the long-term biological potential or productivity of a site is considered to have a maximum that is characteristic of that site. For a fully occupied site, total yield per unit of area is largely independent of density. In such cases, the yield per unit area is approximately equivalent over a broad range of densities because the amount of growth by individual plants decreases proportionately as density increases (see Chapter 7, Figure 7-13). At low densities, the yield of the population is determined by the number of individuals. Eventually, the site becomes fully occupied and the resource-supplying power of the environment becomes limiting, thereby determining ultimate yield. Such a relationship between density and productivity—similar in all plant species and mixtures of species—is termed the *law of constant final yield*. The forest manager can affect the rate of production and its distribution among the various components of the forest community during its lifetime by manipulation of the vegetation.

A ponderosa pine spacing study conducted in central Oregon (Barrett 1970, 1973, 1982) illustrates these principles. The study was installed in a 40- to 70-year-old sapling-sized stand that had developed under an old-growth overstory of about 20 trees/acre. After removal of the overstory, replicated plots were thinned to 62, 125, 250, 500, and 1000 trees/acre. Soil moisture is thought to be the most critical factor limiting growth in this area, and measurements showed an increase in the availability of soil moisture following removal of the overstory and thinning of the sapling stand.

Increased availability of moisture (the trigger and limiting factor) resulted in increased biomass production. However, some of this production occurred in understory shrubs on thinned plots where trees did not fully capture the site resources. The degree of understory shrub response increased as tree overstory density was reduced, tending toward a constant total biomass (law of constant field yield), with allocation of productivity between overstory and understory varying by intensity of thinning.

Understory vegetation was removed from half of the plots for each treatment and the response of pines 20 yr after thinning and brush control

TABLE 14-1. Response of Ponderosa Pine to Control of Spacing and Understory Shrubs over a 20-Year Period

	Trees per Acre				
	1000	500	250	125	62
No understory shrubs controlled					
Quadratic mean DBH (in.)	4.7	5.5	6.7	8.3	9.2
Basal area (ft²/acre)	115.5	80.8	60.1	47.2	28.5
Average height (ft)	21.3	21.6	25.2	30.4	31.2
Net yield (ft³/acre)	980.0	740.0	600.0	540.0	320.0
Understory shrubs controlled					
Quadratic mean DBH (in.)	4.7	5.9	7.7	9.0	11.7
Basal area (ft²/acre)	120.7	93.8	78.5	62.6	45.9
Average height (ft)	20.5	23.5	29.8	32.2	36.9
Net yield (ft³/acre)	1140.0	920.0	900.0	840.0	600.0

Source: Barrett (1982).

was measured (Table 14-1). Where shrubs were not controlled, yields decreased drastically as pine density decreased; presumably the shrubs got a larger and larger proportion of the available site resources as pine density decreased. Where shrubs were controlled, yields also fell as pine density decreased, but to a lesser extent than when shrubs were present; presumably the pines were able to capture a greater share of the available site resources as evidenced by their greater heights and diameters at lower densities. Regardless of the presence or absence of shrubs, the greatest yields occurred at the highest pine density, commensurate with the well-known influence of stocking level on stand yield.

Overstory removal combined with thinning resulted in more than one environmental change; in addition to soil moisture supply, air and soil temperature and light quality and quantity within the canopy were increased. These changes in turn affected more than just the target trees. This multifaceted response demonstrates the principle of the holocoenotic environment.

Population Interactions

If two species were simultaneously introduced into the same environment, the rate of growth of one species would be modified by the extent to which the other species utilized the same resources. The interaction that arises between two or more species populations is known as *competition*. Competition between two species populations has two possible results: one species alone survives, or the two species coexist.

Successful competitors in young conifer stands generally have one or more characteristics that result in their rapid colonization of the site and domination over slower growing conifer seedlings. Reproductive strategies that contribute to rapid colonization include frequent seed crops amenable to dissemination by wind or animals; heavy, long-lived seeds stored in the soil and surface litter; and reproduction and spread from sprouts, suckers, tubers, and rhizomes. Other characteristics that may be associated with successful competitors are rapid juvenile growth rates, shade tolerance, and the ability of seeds to germinate in forest litter.

Plant communities that have attained an equilibrium in their environment exhibit two characteristics: (1) some means of population regulation; and (2) some means of coexistence with other species in the same habitat because no population exists in isolation as a pure culture under natural conditions. Coexistence takes many forms such as alternating food or energy utilization in different seasons or in different portions of the environmental space.

In mature forest communities, nearly all ecological niches are occupied. Individuals tend to be organized in the stand to minimize competitive effects. This process occurs initially through intense competition during early stand development. Individuals that cannot usurp scarce resources from neighbors are eliminated, and the resources are redistributed among the survivors. This process of competition-induced niche separation occurs at all stages of stand development but is most intense during the initial years following a disturbance that creates unoccupied space. Selection pressure drives species within a community to exploit different parts of the environment—the *concept of niche separation.*

Competition can be between species or between individuals of the same species. Often these two types of competition interact. For example, results from spacing trials initiated at planting suggest that, at least on dry sites, competition from shrubs and grasses may exert a greater influence on tree growth than does competition from nearby trees of the same age and species. McDonald and Oliver (1984) reported that ponderosa pine in California showed steeper response surfaces along the brush cover axis than along the tree spacing axis (Figure 14-2). On the poor site (the lower response surface in Figure 14-2), the diameter growth of pines at all densities was similar until brush cover was reduced below 30%. This suggests that the pines had not developed sufficiently to compete with one another except where the brush cover was quite low. Consequently, it appears that the brush, even at relatively low levels of cover, was consuming most of the available resources on this comparatively poor site. On the better site (the upper response surface in Figure 14-2), the diameter growth of pines was affected by their density throughout the range of brush cover. This indicates that sufficient site resources were available for the pines to develop and compete with one another regardless of the presence of brush. Even in this case, however, the greatest responses in pine growth occurred where brush cover was reduced below 30%. Thus the trees were not exploiting the site's resources to the extent that brush was.

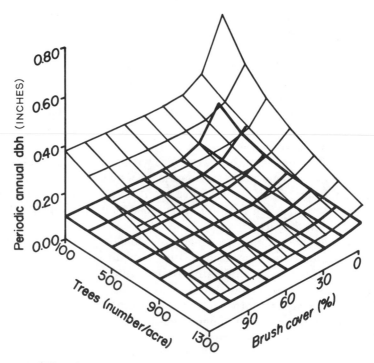

Figure 14-2. Effect of brush competition and tree spacing on periodic annual DBH growth of planted ponderosa pine saplings and poles on a poor site on the Mendocino National Forest (lower surface) and on a good site on the Challenge Experimental Forest (upper surface). (*Source:* McDonald and Oliver 1984)

Timing of release treatments is a key factor in determining tree survival and growth. Ample evidence shows that trees should be released (i.e., freed of competing vegetation) early; delays in controlling competing vegetation result in reduced survival or growth (Liming 1946, Muntz 1951, Roe 1952, Walker 1954, Shoulders 1955, Harrington 1960, Brinkman and Liming 1961, Hatchell 1964, Boyer 1975, Newton and White 1983). Longer periods of release are required if, at the time of treatment, trees show signs of suppression—thin crowns, spindly stems and branches, short or sparse needles, and limited leader growth. Suppressed trees have a higher ratio of older, less photosynthetically efficient foliage than trees that are not suppressed. Production of new, more photosynthetically active foliage must occur before rapid crown expansion and stem growth can resume.

Release of individual trees is usually more effective if the clearings are large rather than small because small clearings are rapidly reinvaded and roots of competing species surrounding such openings deplete soil moisture. This problem seems especially acute when the competing species are rhizomaceous. For example, studies of herbaceous vegetation around ponderosa pine seedlings (Hall, 1971) found that 4-ft-diameter scalps were about twice as effective as 2-ft scalps on east-facing slopes. In a study of alternative methods for releasing ponderosa pine and Douglas-fir, Fiddler and McDonald (1984) found that clearings less than 6 ft in radius around each tree were not as effective as broadcast chemical control.

Long-term studies (15 or more years) suggest that differences in growth due to release observed at early ages persist or increase with time at least until crown closure (Russell 1969, Balmer et al. 1978, Sander and Rogers 1979, Bengtson and Smart 1981, Tiarks 1983, Boyer 1985). For example, Roy (personal communication, 1984) found that differences in total height of released and unreleased Douglas-fir were 0.01 ft in the year of treatment, 6.9 ft after 10 years, and 12.4 ft after 17 years. Differences in yields between stands treated to control competition and those left untreated may increase through time (Figure 14-3). If the yield of untreated stands were to increase in relation to treated stands, the slopes of the curves in Figure 14-3 would be negative. If the initial differences in yield were maintained through time, the slopes would be 0—a horizontal line.

After crown closure, intertree competition begins to control growth. Regulation of stand density by thinning helps to prolong the effects of early reduction in interspecific competition.

Community Dynamics

The *process of plant succession* focuses on changes in the ecological community through time and space. Change occurs over the short as well as the long term. For example, a common successional sequence on coniferous forest lands following logging is (1) grasses and forbs; (2) shrubs or sprouting hardwoods; (3) young trees; (4) young mature forest; (5) mature forest; and (6) old-growth forest containing an overstory of large declining, dying, and dead trees with an understory of tolerant shrubs and young climax tree species.

The composition of early successional communities is largely a function of the nature and extent of disturbance, local environment, availability of colonizing species, and chance. The movement toward climax is largely governed by long-term climatic and edaphic conditions. Each stage blends into the next, with intermixtures of many dominants from the preceding stage persisting for several years or decades. The changes following disturbance are at first rapid, then decline as the early species are replaced by more tolerant climax species that can reproduce without the aid of disturbance. The shrub stage in particular can be prolonged if regeneration of desirable tree species is delayed and residual vegetation after logging is composed of aggressive sprouting shrubs and weed trees.

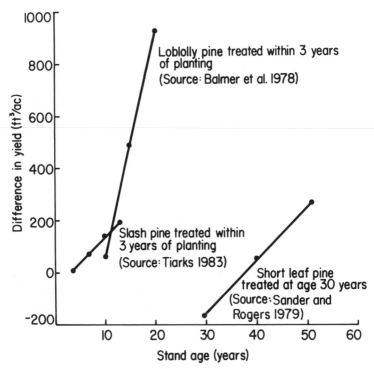

Figure 14-3. Difference in yield over time between weeded and unweeded southern pine stands.

Many early successional shrub and weed tree species on cutover sites are sprouters or require mineral soil seedbeds for seed germination. Some species, such as those in the genus *Ceanothus*, require heat from wildfire or slash burning to stimulate germination of buried seed (Gratkowski 1962, 1973a, 1973b, 1974). Other species, such as those in the genus *Rubus*, seem to need only the removal of surface litter and exposure of the soil to sunlight to germinate and emerge (Ruth 1970, Stewart 1978). Early successional shrub species also tend to be intolerant of shade and persist in abundance only until crown closure of the forest overstory. However, opening the tree canopy through thinnings and intermediate harvests can stimulate development of understory species (Ruth 1970). Such practices could result in less growth response in the remaining overstory (Barrett 1982, Grano 1970) or difficult site preparation problems following final harvest. Many climax or subclimax conifer species may also become established early in the life of the developing forest. These species may persist and attain large size. Periodic disturbance tends to maintain some elements of early and late successional overstory and understory species throughout the forest.

These biological facts suggest some possibilities for site preparation that would reduce the likelihood of weed problems. Each of the following practices has been tried, with success under appropriate conditions:

1. Applying effective herbicides on residual vegetation to achieve good root kill, followed by planting without additional disturbance to the soil surface. The herbicides reduce problems from sprouting shrubs. Invasion by herbs and shrub seedlings is reduced in undisturbed litter or even eliminated on summer-dry sites.

2. Piling logging slash without broadcast burning where the presence of buried seeds of fire-adapted germinants is expected. Although the soil is disturbed in such cases, brush seedlings may not dominate the site. Invading species can be limited to grasses and forbs.

3. Conducting preharvest application of systemic herbicides or burning to control understory shrubs and hardwoods and to stimulate germination of problem brush species. Direct control measures can then be taken against the germinants, or the overstory can be retained long enough to eliminate the intolerant brush seedlings. Frequency and seasonal timing of burns are key factors in achieving the desired results.

4. Using large cutting units and controlling nearby seed sources of competitors to reduce the rate of invasion of some species.

The resilience of ecosystems is important when manipulating vegetation. *Resilience* is the ability of a natural ecosystem to restore its structure following acute or chronic disturbance (Westman 1978). In contrast, *inertia* is the ability of a system to resist displacement in structure or function when subjected to a disturbing force. These two concepts and the four properties of resilience—elasticity, amplitude, hysteresis, and malleability (or plasticity)—are defined in Table 14-2.

A key feature of succession is that disturbance favors species that are resistant or adapted to disturbance (Newton 1967). These species account for a greater proportion of the postdisturbance community. Many foresters can recount treating a shrub-dominated community with a phenoxy herbicide only to release a scattered grass understory that rapidly expanded in response to the release of site resources. Pretreatment detection of species in the community that are both resistant to the chosen treatment and have the capacity to respond more rapidly than the desired trees to the increased availability of sunlight and soil moisture is essential to achieve vegetation management objectives (see Chapter 13, Figure 13-5).

Four environmental resources—light energy, carbon dioxide, nutrients, and water—are fundamental to every forest ecosystem. Therefore, the relative success of any species in a seral stage depends on its ability

TABLE 14-2. Key Concepts and Properties of Disturbed Ecosystems

Characteristic	Definition
Inertia	Resistance to change
Resilience	Ability to restore structure or function following disturbance
Elasticity	Rapidity of restoration of a stable state following disturbance (time needed for restoration)
Amplitude	Zone from which the system will return to a stable state (the degree of brittleness)
Hysteresis	Degree to which path of restoration is an exact reversal of path of degradation
Malleability (plasticity)	Degree to which stable state after disturbance differs from the original steady state (the case in which the system can become permanently altered)

Source: Westman, W.E. 1978. Measuring the inertia and resilience of ecosystems. BioScience 28(11): Table 1, p. 706. Copyright © 1978 by the American Institute of Biological Sciences. Reproduced by permission of the author and *BioScience.*

to survive environmental site conditions and preempt limited resources. Success of a species depends on the resource requirements of that species, the availability of resources during periods of demand, and adaptations to partitioning of resources in time and space relative to other species in the community to minimize competition.

Principles of Tree Growth and Stand Development

The general principles and patterns of tree growth and stand development have been discussed in Chapter 7. Knowledge of these principles permits the development of biologically sound forest growth and yield simulators for species such as loblolly pine (see Chapter 8), Pacific Coast Douglas-fir (see Chapter 9), and mixed conifers of the northern Rocky Mountains and Inland Northwest (see Chapter 10). Further, integration of basic ecological principles into growth and yield simulators will ultimately permit prediction of stand response to control of competing vegetation.

Tree growth is the result of the division, elongation, and thickening of plant cells. Specific rates and activities in the growth process vary widely among species, but the general pattern of growth is consistent. When expressed as a cumulative function, increase in size of a plant part or whole plant assumes a characteristic sigmoid-shaped curve (see Chapter 7, Figure 7-1a). This pattern is the same for all tree dimensions and periods of time, whether measured over a season or a lifetime. The Chapman-Richards logistic growth curve that expresses this pattern can be used to derive maximum tree size, maximum growth rate, and size at the maximum growth rate.

Because the rate of growth changes with tree size, absolute growth rate is not always a good measure of performance. Relative growth rate (RGR = 1/plant dimension × rate of change in the plant dimension) may be a better measure because it evaluates the efficiency of production of a given unit of plant size, thus standardizing the effect of tree size (see Chapters 5 and 7). The value of relative growth rate decreases as trees age.

Species vary widely in height growth and maximum height. Western conifers with long lifespans, like Douglas-fir and redwood, grow to heights exceeding 200 ft and maintain relatively rapid height growth for over 100 years. In contrast, loblolly pine—a southeastern species—rarely exceeds 140 ft and completes most of its height growth before age 50. Regardless of this extreme variation, certain chronological patterns in conifer height growth are consistent and can be classified into the following stages: seedling, sapling, pole, thrifty-mature, and mature (see Chapter 7, Figure 7-4).

Both planted and natural seedlings exhibit slow initial height growth compared with later stages. After outplanting, conifer seedlings can experience planting shock, which results from stress and root damage during lifting, handling, and planting. Thus newly planted trees may have slower relative growth rates when compared to natural trees of the same age or size growing under similar conditions. Nevertheless, planting has generally proven to be the most reliable method of reforestation, and planting shock can be minimized or eliminated by proper care of nursery stock. Trees are considered seedlings until the period of slow initial height growth is completed. Intolerant pioneer conifer species grow out of this stage quickly in the absence of competition. Some tolerants tend to prolong the seedling stage regardless of the level of competition, whereas others have the same growth pattern as intolerant species if competition is removed.

The sapling stage is characterized by a rapid acceleration of height growth. As in the seedling stage, some tolerants tend to lag behind intolerants in acceleration, although others, such as western hemlock, may respond more rapidly. Intense competition extends the sapling stage for both tolerants and intolerants, the latter having a much higher probability of mortality the longer that height growth is suppressed. Conifers intermediate in tolerance often maintain height growth and may even increase height growth under moderate levels of competition—usually, however, at the expense of diameter and root growth.

The pole stage is characterized by an almost linear increase in tree height. Growth rates from 2 to 5 ft/yr are common during this stage. No consistent difference between tolerants and intolerants is evident. Dominant and codominant conifer height growth in the pole stage is generally little affected by competing vegetation.

In the thrifty-mature stage, conifers still increase their height but at a slower rate; the relative height growth rate declines sharply. This period can span several decades, as usually occurs with long-lived tolerants or may be only a few years in short-lived intolerants.

The rate of height growth again slows during the mature stage. In some cases, tree height may actually decline due to top dieback or breakage. In the mature stage, tree height approaches an asymptote representing the upper limit of growth capable for the species under a given set of site conditions. Physiological controls of moisture transport, interacting with soil moisture availability and atmospheric demand, are thought to be the major determinants of the height asymptote.

Height growth is dependent on the size and number of cells produced by the apical meristem of the terminal shoot. When conifers are under moisture stress, their stomata close, thus reducing the uptake and fixation of carbon and, therefore, the amount of material available to produce new cells and thicken existing cell walls. Perhaps more profound, moisture stress reduces cell elongation.

Light and nutrients affect height growth mainly by the efficiency and amount of photosynthesis. As light intensifies, photosynthate production increases per unit of chlorophyll or leaf area per unit time if the tree is not under nutritional or water stress. Increasing nutrient availability augments the chlorophyll content of individual leaves and total leaf area of individual trees. Both conditions increase the amount of photosynthate produced; thus more material is available for cell production and growth.

Diameter growth results from cell division and thickening in the cambium. As with height, diameter growth rates differ widely among coniferous species. Diameter growth is determined by the number and diameter of individual cells produced. Individual cell diameter is inversely proportional to moisture stress and directly proportional to nutrient and light availability. Unlike height, diameter growth is more evenly distributed throughout the growing season in all conifers.

Although the general pattern of diameter growth follows the sigmoid shape, diameter increment decreases rapidly with age. Although an equal or greater amount of wood may be produced each year during the pole stage, that wood is distributed over an ever increasing surface area. The distribution of diameter increment follows Pressler's (1864) hypothesis: the cross-sectional area of a tree ring is directly proportional to the quantity of foliage above it and inversely proportional to stem length. Thus diameter increment is maximized at a point in the lower crown and decreases downward because the same cross-sectional area must be spread over a larger initial diameter.

The shape, size, and development of conifer crowns are important determinants of height and diameter growth. Conifers growing under ex-

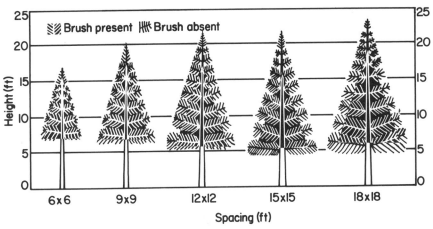

Figure 14-4. Influence of spacing and brush on size of planted ponderosa pine, age 14 years. (*Source:* U.S. Department of Agriculture 1982)

treme moisture stress develop small shrublike crowns—the result of early loss of apical control (Brown 1977). In contrast, conifers that are stressed by low light intensities typically increase apical control to the point of producing columnar crowns. Nutrient stress has no consistent effect on crown form, but deficiencies greatly reduce the density and distribution of leaves in the crown. Increased nutrient availability aids the retention and continued function of needles 2 years old or more. Tolerants tend to maintain their crown form and needle density under stress better than intolerants. Both intra- and interspecific competition result in reductions in crown width and length (Figure 14-4). Needle retention is less, and individual needles are shorter, thereby reducing the photosynthetic capacity of the tree and its long-term ability to grow.

Two distinct patterns of crown development have been identified in conifers: fixed growth, in which preformed primordia overwinter in the bud and elongate the following spring; and free growth, in which primordia elongate in the same growing season that they are formed. Some species, mostly southern yellow pines, exhibit both fixed and free growth during their entire life span. They set an overwintering bud that breaks dormancy in early spring but also set buds and flush as many as six times during summer. For other conifers, like Douglas-fir, true firs, red pine, white pines, ponderosa pine, and lodgepole pine, fixed growth is the norm.

These differences in crown development have important ramifications in the response of conifers to competition, particularly where moisture stress is the most limiting factor for growth. The annual shoot growth of conifers exhibiting fixed growth is closely related to the competition and growth environment of the previous year. The number of cells in the apical and terminal buds and the amount of carbohydrate necessary for cell expansion were determined during the previous growing season. The moisture necessary for cell elongation is readily available in early spring due to the recharge of soil moisture during winter. For fixed-and-free-growth conifers, a large proportion of the annual shoot growth often comes from the free-growth portion. Therefore, crown development in these species is most influenced by the competition and growth environment during the concurrent growing season. In terms of relative height growth, fixed-and-free-growth conifers may be more responsive than fixed-only species to control of competition under conditions of late summer moisture stress. Fixed-growth conifers predominate in regions with shorter growing seasons limited by frost or drought, whereas fixed-and-free-growth conifers are more common in humid, wet, summer climates with longer growing seasons.

A relationship of plant size or weight to density, recognized in many species, is known as the $-3/2$ power law of self-thinning (Yoda et al. 1963). When tree size versus density data are regressed against one another for many different species, the intercept varies, but the slope constant is usually close to $-3/2$. It seems logical that competing species have many attributes of excess stocking; thus a similar negative effect on tree size (see Figures 14-2 and 14-4).

Conifer stands under some density control treatment exhibit what is commonly referred to as *accelerated growth*, especially in diameter. This accelerated growth is a response to the release of site resources that were controlled by the vegetation removed (Hall and Curtis 1970, Newton 1973). Intraspecific density can be reduced by thinning conifers; interspecific density can be reduced by release treatments that remove or suppress noncommercial species.

Accelerated stand height growth occurs in intolerants at least in the seedling and sapling stage and perhaps later. Height growth is a function of site quality, the summation of total site resources available or that can be made more available to the trees following release. For example, note the increased height growth response of ponderosa pine 60 years old or more in central Oregon to both thinning and understory shrub control found by Barrett (1982) (Table 14-1) or the diameter growth response of young ponderosa pine in northern California to initial plantation spacing and brush control reported by McDonald and Oliver (1984) (Figure 14-2).

Accelerated height growth is generally less conspicuous than mean tree basal area or diameter growth immediately after release from competition. The acceleration in mean tree basal area growth may not be immediate. Trees respond to the release of site resources by building their crowns and stem strength and increasing their diameters just above-ground in response to increased mechanical stress. Increased diameter growth at breast height may not be evident for several years after density is reduced. Young trees may exhibit a rapid diameter growth response, perhaps reflecting increased cell expansion and a prolonged period of cell division if soil moisture is available for a longer period in spring. Older trees, especially those suppressed for some time, may even display slower growth rates. This deceleration, called *thinning shock* or *release shock*, is generally attributed to the failure of shade-grown crowns to tolerate increased light intensities and atmospheric moisture demands.

Conifer stand dynamics can be predicted through direct or indirect methods. The most common direct method is stand-table projection. This method requires a current stand table showing the number of trees in each diameter class. Future growth is predicted from past growth obtained from increment cores. A future stand table is developed from the predicted accretion, ingrowth, and expected mortality. Although useful for many different purposes, stand-table projection is not suitable for predicting growth and yield response from vegetation management. Inferences from past growth are limited to the conditions under which that growth occurred; moreover, conditions can change dramatically as a result of vegetation control. Indirect methods that are more suitable are made through yield tables, predictive equations, and computer simulations.

The indirect approaches to growth and yield prediction can be divided into three model classes that differ in their level of resolution (presented here in order of increasing detail): whole stand models, for example, the DFSIM model for Douglas-fir (Curtis et al. 1981) (see Chapter 9); size-class distribution models, for example, the loblolly pine competition model (Burkhart and Sprinz 1984) (see Chapter 8); and individual tree models, for example, the prognosis model (Stage 1973, Wykoff et al. 1982) (see Chapters 7 and 10).

Modifying an existing model to reflect various silvicultural treatments requires biological paradigms of how treatment might affect growth, mathematical models of those paradigms, and evaluation of the resultant predictions against conventional wisdom and experimental data. As additional data from treated stands become available, this information can be used to evaluate the appropriateness of the original models and to refine coefficients. The approach used to incorporate silvicultural treatment effects in growth and yield models is determined by the type of model(s) and the extent and nature of available data on treatment effects. A simple model of weed control effects following a release treatment would show accelerated stand closure, fewer voids within the stand, and growth rates characteristic of fully occupied sites once crown closure occurs.

Treatments may affect many aspects of tree growth and stand development. Nor are changes in one factor necessarily independent of other factors. Thus it is unrealistic to assume a simple change in diameter or height growth and no corresponding change in factors such as tree form, wood quality, and mortality rate.

Due to the lack of uniformity and difficulties in maintaining program-level quality control, yield improvement on a stand- or forest-level basis is rarely as good as predicted by results from small experimental research plots (Bruce 1977). If predictor variables differ significantly such as site, species composition, treatment effectiveness, or stand density for a given area, the area should be stratified into reasonably homogeneous units and predictions made separately. Nonproductive areas and other anomalies should be deducted before expanding yield estimates to an area basis. Allowance should be made for variable treatment effectiveness, logging breakage, and other losses incurred before or during harvest. Adjustments to predicted values from growth and yield models must often be made in order to approximate volumes likely to be realized under actual conditions.

BENEFITS OF VEGETATION MANAGEMENT

An extensive review of published and unpublished studies (Stewart et al. 1984) on the effects of competing vegetation on forest trees of the United States and Canada shows that forest trees respond markedly to good site preparation for reforestation and to release from competing vegetation in established stands. Increased volume growth of from 40 to 100% or more in the short term following treatment is common (Table 14-3). Further, response tends to be directly related to degree of vegetation control (Table 14-4). The trend of increased survival and growth following reduction in competition is remarkably consistent despite the wide range of environmental conditions, vegetation types, conifer species, and stand conditions represented in existing studies. This is not surprising, however, given that the same factors—soil moisture, light, and nutrients—often limit forest growth throughout the United States and Canada.

The relationship between tree or stand growth and degree of competition often can be represented by a simple model. Differences in model attributes and accuracy seem to be related to factors such as tree species, competing species, site productivity, stand age at time of release, quality of the data set, and the growth parameter and measure of competition chosen. Some examples of models are:

1. Ponderosa pine model by Barrett (1979): $y = 6.55 - 0.0352\,x$, where y = 10-year diameter growth in inches of 19- to 36-year-old trees in central Oregon and x = cover of shrubs, grass, and forbs in percentage. The coefficient of determination (r^2) for this relationship was 0.62.

2. Ponderosa pine model by Oliver (1979): $y = 0.629 + 0.0166\,x$, where y = diameter growth loss in years at age 12 for seedlings planted on a highly productive site in the northern Sierra Nevada of California and x = crown cover of brush in percentage. The coefficient of determination for the relationship was 0.48.

TABLE 14-3. Forest Tree Response to Site Preparation or Release

Region/ Tree Species	Practice	Vegetation Type	Stand Age at Treatment (years)	Stand Age at Measurement (years)	Mean or Periodic Annual Increment[a] Untreated (ft³/acre/yr)	Treated (ft³/acre/yr)	Relative Growth Increase (%)	Source
North								
Red pine	Release	Weed tree	15–17	33–35	73	111	52	Roe (1952)
			1–10	46	73	190	160	Stone (1976)
		Herbaceous	0–1	31	35	89	155	Wilde et al. (1968)
			0–1	27	28	84	198	Wittenkamp and Wilde (1964)
White pine	Release	Weed tree	28	50	8	59	649	Buckman and Lundgren (1962)
			19	44	35	70	100	
			35	53	26	39	51	
South								
Loblolly pine	Site preparation	Mixed	0	15	247	281	14	Cain (1978)
		Weed tree	0	22	1	267	166	Glover et al. (1981)
		Herbaceous	0	15	146	148	1	Haywood (1980)
		Weed tree	0	10	75	74	0	Pehl and Bailey (1983)
	Release	Herbaceous	7	12	31	41	32	Clason (1978)
		Weed tree	7	12	31	46	45	
		Mixed	7	12	31	51	63	
		Weed tree	9	15	78	94	20	
			5	14	14	52	276	Dierauf[b]
			5	14	65	83	27	
			4	13	40	87	116	
			2	13	30	73	145	

TABLE 14-3. Forest Tree Response to Site Preparation or Release (Continued)

Region/ Tree Species	Practice	Vegetation Type	Stand Age at Treatment (years)	Stand Age at Measurement (years)	Mean or Periodic Annual Increment[a] Untreated (ft³/acre/yr)	Treated (ft³/acre/yr)	Relative Growth Increase (%)	Source
Slash pine	Site preparation	Mixed	0	15	246	246	0	Cain (1978)
		Herbaceous	0	14	86	126	46	Campbell and Mann (1971)
		Weed tree	0	17	45	80	83	Haines (1981)
			0	17	85	109	27	
		Herbaceous	0	15	163	195	19	Haywood (1980)
		Mixed	0	10	15	30	99	May et al. (1973)
			0	10	28	58	105	Outcalt (1983)
			0	10	34	70	104	
			0	10	120	135	12	Tiarks (1983)
		Herbaceous	0	13	47	66	40	Bengtson and Smart (1981)
Longleaf pine	Release	Weed tree	—[c]	20+	36	51	40	Michael (1980)
Shortleaf pine	Release	Weed tree	30	51	89	96	8	Sander and Rogers (1979)
			30	51	83	88	6	
			13	37	21	66	210	Sander[d]
			13	37	21	66	210	
Pacific Coast								
Douglas-fir	Release	Mixed	—[c]	6+	0.4[e]	0.6[e]	50	Allan et al. (1978)
					0.4[e]	0.8[e]	100	
					0.4[e]	0.7[e]	75	

Species	Treatment	Type						Reference
Ponderosa pine	Release	Shrub	5	9	2805.0[f]	7241.0[f]	158	Peterson and Newton (1982)
		Mixed	5	9	2805.0[f]	11616.0[f]	314	Barrett (1982)
		Shrub	10	14	17553.0[f]	22672.0[f]	29	
		Mixed	10	14	17553.0[f]	31200.0[f]	78	
		Shrub	40–70	60–90	16	30	87	
					27	42	56	
					30	45	50	
		Shrub	4	16	21	5	111	McDonald[g]
					21	7	165	
		Shrub	2,4	16	35	1	45	Oliver (1979)
					36	53	48	
					21	43	108	
					10	30	203	
					13	30	132	
			11	16	9	22	152	Oliver (1984)
					21	29	35	
					13	37	194	
					26	53	100	

[a]Calculated from total volume/stand age or total growth during the period/yr in the period. Conversion factors from the original units of measure were 1 cord = 22 ft³, 1 bd ft = 0.2 ft³, 1 m³/ha = 0.1588 cords/acre.

[b]Dierauf, T.A. Research studies on response to release in the Commonwealth of Virginia. Unpublished report on file. Department of Conservation and Economic Development, Division of Forestry, Commonwealth of Virginia, Charlottesville, VA.

[c]Stand age at time of treatment was not specified.

[d]Sander, I.L. The long-term effects of releasing underplanted shortleaf pine from hardwood competition with 2,4,5-T and silvex. Unpublished report on file. USDA Forest Service, North Central Forest Experiment Station, Columbia, MO.

[e]Expressed as average volume per tree in ft³.

[f]Expressed as a stem volume index in cm³.

[g]McDonald, P. Brushfield ecology and growth of planted pine. Unpublished report on file. USDA Forest Service, Pacific Southwest Forest and Range Experiment Station, Redding, CA.

TABLE 14-4. Influence of Degree of Release on Tree Growth Response

| Tree Species | Competitive Species | Age When Released and (Period of Record) (yr) | Degree of Release | Tree Growth | | | Source |
				Height (ft)	Diameter (in.)	Volume (cords)	
Red pine	Aspen, paper birch	19	None	—	5.9	16.8	Buckman and Lundgren (1962)
		(25)	Moderate	—	7.8	25.4	
			Full	—	8.2	33.6	
Red pine	Oak, maple	40	None	1.3	—	—	Ralston (1953)
		(3)	Half	2.3	—	—	
			Full	3.4	—	—	
Red pine	Aspen	15–17	None	—	—	14.3	
		(18)	Partial	—	—	18.0	
			Full	—	—	21.8	
Eastern white pine	Aspen, paper birch	28	None	—	5.3	4.3	Buckman and Lundgren (1962)
		(22)	Moderate	—	6.9	14.4	
			Full	—	8.6	32.2	
Eastern white pine-red pine	Aspen, paper birch	35	None	—	—	14.9	
		(18)	Moderate	—	—	22.6	
Shortleaf pine	Oak	0	None	—	—	—	Brinkman and Liming (1961)
		(11)	One-third	3.1	—	—	
			Two-thirds	6.2	—	—	
			Full	15.0	—	—	
Shortleaf pine	Oak-hickory	0	None	1.4	—	—	Liming (1946)
		(4)	One-third	1.6	—	—	
			Two-thirds	2.7	—	—	
			Full	5.4	—	—	
Ponderosa pine	Manzanita	0	None	—	0.24	—	Oliver (1979)
		(2)	Half	—	0.32	—	
			Full	—	0.48	—	

3. Ponderosa pine model by Powers and Oliver (1985): $R = 180 \, (H_t/H_b)^{-139}$, where R = increase in mean 5-yr height growth after release in percentage and H_t/H_b = ratio of initial tree and brush heights. The coefficient of determination was 0.97.

4. Loblolly pine model by Grano (1961): $y = 18.19 + 0.9303 \, x$, where y = seedling mortality in percentage 24 months after planting and x = original hardwood cover in percentage. The coefficient of determination was 0.74.

5. Loblolly pine model by Langdon and Trousdell (1974): $y = 3.801 - 0.533 \, x$, where y = log of merchantable yield in ft^3/acre at age 20 for pines growing in the Southeast Piedmont and Atlantic Coastal Plain and x = log of hardwood basal area in ft^2/acre at age 10. The coefficient of determination for this relationship was 0.75.

6. A loblolly pine model by Burkhart and Sprinz (1984) in which a computer program (HDWD) is used to forecast the impact of various percentages of hardwood basal area on subsequent loblolly pine yield. Validation of the model against an independent data set indicated close agreement between predicted and observed yields (see Chapter 8, Figure 8-7).

Reduction of competing vegetation over several years has been observed to improve one or more of the following stand attributes: tree survival, diameter growth, height growth, basal area growth, individual tree and stand volume, crown length and width, needle color and length, tree vigor, and resistance to damage from insects. Where one or more site resources may be at or near critical supply, even low levels of competing plant cover may be detrimental to forest development (Oliver 1979, 1984). Where competing vegetation threatens regeneration establishment or growth, site preparation and release are often worthwhile silvicultural practices.

Control of understory vegetation can result in substantial increases in overstory forest growth, but responses are highly variable and dependent upon local climate and soil conditions (Stewart and Row 1981, Stewart et al. 1984). For example, under the conditions of limited soil moisture in central Oregon, Barrett (1973, 1982) found that understory shrubs reduced overstory ponderosa pine volume by 47% after 20 years at low stand densities (62 trees/acre) where shrub development was greatest, but volume was reduced only 14% at a stand density of 1000 trees/acre (Figure 14-5). Control of understory hardwoods in two loblolly-shortleaf pine stands in Arkansas resulted in growth advantages of 200 ft^3/acre and 358 ft^3/acre after 14 and 11 years, respectively (Grano 1970).

Numerous direct and indirect benefits from weed control are possible (see Chapter 6, Table 6-1). Tangible benefits to wood production are the easiest to identify and measure, including (1) increased volume at harvest because of better stocking, height, or diameter growth of trees; (2) in-

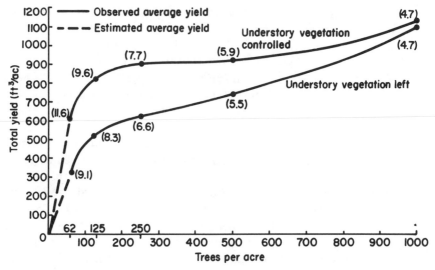

Figure 14-5. Yield of suppressed ponderosa pine saplings 20 yr after thinning to five densities, with vegetation allowed to develop naturally or vegetation controlled. Average diameters for each density (inches DBH) shown in parentheses. (*Source:* Barrett 1982)

creased stand value because of improved species composition; (3) higher value at the mill and lower felling, harvesting, and transportation costs because of larger and more uniform stem diameters; and (4) earlier return on investment from commercial thinning and final harvest because of increased diameter growth. Other positive benefits that are more difficult to quantify include the value of easier and more accurate stocking surveys because trees are more visible, earlier opportunities for fertilization and greater fertilizer efficiency, more rapid entry of the stand into a fire resistant stage, increased water yields to downstream users, improved habitat for some game and nongame species, and improved livestock carrying capacity resulting from better grass production following shrub control on forested ranges.

Certain nonmarket benefits involving environmental and visual resources can also accrue from weed control. These benefits include more rapid establishment of postharvest forest cover, resulting in better visual appearance of clearcuts; improved visibility within established forest stands; and reduction in noxious and poisonous plants or tree-damaging animals due to changes in habitat.

Response to weed control treatment can also negatively impact timber or other resource outputs (see Chapter 6, Table 6-1). For example, localized soil compaction resulting from heavy equipment for site preparation can cause reduced soil productivity; some treatments can damage crop trees and reduce their capacity to respond to release; removal of surface litter during broadcast burning or scarification can reduce soil productivity or water quality due to erosion; and removal of protective cover can expose seedlings to greater temperature extremes. In warmer climates with summer rains, substantial removal of vegetation can mobilize nutrients and cause leaching. Nutrient mobilization does not seem to be a problem in summer-dry climates. Weed control practices can reduce habitat for some wildlife species. Negative impacts on recreational and visual quality values may also occur by reducing desirable plants with showy flowers or edible fruit or by creation of unsightly "brownout." Control of palatable grasses and forbs in young plantations reduces range forage values and returns from grazing allotments. If herbicides or fire are used, damage to off-site crops or property due to chemical drift or escaped prescribed fire can reduce the benefits of weed control.

DECISION MAKING IN VEGETATION MANAGEMENT

A key factor in decision making is the expected benefit of weed control in terms of the increased value of timber produced relative to the costs of treatment. Two types of decisions are encountered in forest vegetation management: strategic and tactical (see Chapter 12, Stewart and Row 1981). Strategic decisions evaluate the effects of alternative management regimes and silvicultural or reforestation systems on both the need for and cost of weed control. Strategic evaluations examine the impact of weed populations on the entire production cycle. These evaluations permit the manager to select forest management regimes that minimize the development of weed populations or maximize present net value for the entire forest management regime.

Tactical evaluations help the manager to select weed control practices at various points in the stand management cycle, within the scope of existing strategic decisions. Tactical decision making focuses on treatment selection and application methods that produce responses compatible with the strategic analysis. In turn, strategic decision making requires insight into the response and costs of stand management and weed control tactics. However, the tactical evaluation may cast doubt on the strategic decision and prompt a reevaluation of long-term stand management policy.

The sequence of silvicultural practices or activities for a single rotation is called a *management regime*. The complexity and duration of forest production require an equally complex analysis of alternatives and estimated impacts due to changes in the production process. Vegetation management consists of a highly interdependent sequence: changes in practice at one stage may affect later options and the outcome of subsequent stages. Forest managers, therefore, need to anticipate the effect of practices within the scope of the management sequence and to modify or mitigate particular weed control practices as required. Entire management regimes or closely linked segments must often be considered even when making tactical decisions. Applying the concept of integrated pest management to weed control in forestry demonstrates the process of strategic and tactical analysis (see Chapter 1).

Economic decision making compares costs in the production cycle (for most vegetation management treatments, costs are incurred within the first 10 to 15 yr after harvesting the previous stand) with benefits that accrue when the stand is harvested. The methodologies for determining costs and benefits and for conducting appropriate economic analyses have been described (see Chapters 11 and 12). An overview of that process follows.

Unlike much agricultural production, the expenses and revenues from growing a single stand or block of timber do not occur in a single year. Instead, they extend in complex and variable patterns over many years from regeneration to harvest. Timber production is an investment in which the substantial expenses of regeneration and stand management are not returned from harvest revenues for many years, and additional growth or protection from loss is needed to compensate the owner for additional funds invested.

The economic analysis of this process should compare benefits and costs over time by discounting all future values to the present (Duerr 1960, Gregory 1972). The appropriate discount rate for the analysis is an important factor that affects the outcome. For public lands and many industrial ownerships, a discount rate equal to the opportunity cost of capital in the industrial sector of the economy seems appropriate (Row et al. 1981, Stewart and Row 1981). If costs and future timber values are calculated in real terms (i.e., corrected for the rate of inflation), then a real discount rate should also be used.

The costs of treatment should include all direct and indirect costs. If negative effects can be anticipated and quantified, they should be included in the analysis as costs. For strategic decision making, long-term average costs corrected for any inflationary trends may be used. For tactical decison making, site specific costs must be estimated. Many costs of stand management are sensitive to size and proximity of treatment areas and to the difficulty of the terrain and vegetative cover conditions. Large areas and units close together generally have lower unit fixed costs. As the terrain becomes more complex and steep and as vegetation becomes larger and denser, treatment costs increase. Therefore, records of past treatment costs should include information on these factors so that professional judgment can more accurately estimate expected costs of future treatments on specific areas. Professional judgment must also estimate the variability in expected treatment effectiveness. The analyst should not assume 100% effectiveness of any treatment over a unit or for a program involving many units.

Benefits of vegetation management are most often considered in terms of increased timber yields at harvest, requiring estimates of the additional timber volume produced and the stumpage value of this volume. The volume may be estimated from two sources—direct and indirect. In some cases, the increased timber production resulting from specific treatments has been studied. This information can be used directly after adjusting for differences between study and operational conditions. Considerable judgment is necessary in making such adjustments. Where study results are reported in terms other than timber volume, indirect estimates are necessary. For example, changes in height growth might be assumed equivalent to a change in site index, and the difference in volume produced for the two site conditions could be used as the measure of benefit. Use of stand growth simulators that include effects of competing vegetation such as described by Burkhart and Sprinz (1984), or Stage (1973) and Wycoff et al. (1982) are most useful for estimating effects of treatment on growth.

Benefits to the landowner are generally based on stumpage price—the price at the mill minus harvesting and transportation costs plus a profit margin for the logging contractor. Timber value and harvesting costs depend to some degree on tree size and variability. In general, vegetation control results in production of larger, more uniformly sized trees at harvest. Therefore, determining value must include a measure of the product mix; that is, the ratio of sawlogs to pulpwood and other timber products of differing value. Further, current stumpage values must be projected to rotation age. Nominal stumpage values have increased over the past 30 years at an irregular rate above inflation (see Chapter 11, Figure 11-6). At the same time, price indexes for lumber and wood products over the same period have increased little in real value. Thus, although some increase in real stumpage prices is expected in the future, it could occur at a much slower rate than in the past. Current prices may be estimated from regional price series that are published regularly. Future values can be estimated by projecting current values using forecasting techniques such as the spatial market-equilibrium method of Haynes and Adams (1985), corrected for any expected changes in product mix.

In addition to the more easily measured benefits from increased wood production, an economic analysis should consider the value of benefits to other resources if they can be quantified or reasonably estimated. Further, the schedules of benefits and costs should include allowances for losses from fire and pests and for costs of protection.

A number of measures of economic efficiency are commonly used in decision making (see Chapter 12): (1) present net value (PNV) or present net worth (PNW), the sum of the discounted benefits less the sum of the discounted costs; (2) the benefit-cost ratio (B/C), the ratio of discounted benefits to discounted costs; and (3) the internal rate of return (IRR), the interest rate at which the sum of the discounted benefits equals the sum of the discounted costs. Present net value is usually the preferred measure for vegetation management decision making.

Decisions based strictly on economic criteria are not always prudent. For example, an economic assessment of the effects of canceling use of the herbicide 2,4,5-T in forestry suggested that substitution of alternatives for site preparation and release in southern pine management would result in a higher present net value (U.S. Department of Agriculture 1979). The analysis indicated that economically rational landowners would substitute intensive mechanical site preparation on areas where this herbicide had been used. This would have resulted in heavy soil disturbance on steeper slopes, with likely increases in erosion. Many southern pine sites are found on former agricultural lands that were abandoned due to loss of productivity from severe erosion. Thus alternatives in an analysis must be environmentally sound and appropriate for the local conditions in order for the economic decision to be valid.

VEGETATION MANAGEMENT PRACTICES

Forest vegetation management is designed to improve the seedling or young tree environment, and in some cases to improve forage or wildlife values. The supply of essential environmental factors—sunlight, soil moisture, temperature, soil nutrients, and growing space—is fixed for any given site by climatic and soil conditions largely beyond the control of forest managers. The manager can, however, affect the allocation of these factors through manipulation of forest vegetation (see Chapter 6).

Measures to control vegetation are undertaken to achieve specific forest management objectives via seven silvicultural practices (presented here in approximate order of decreasing degree of disturbance or degree of vegetation control generally needed to attain the objective):

1. *Rehabilitation or species conversion* to allow establishment of desirable tree species (usually more valuable or faster growing species) in existing stands of weed trees, shrubs, or herbaceous vegetation.
2. *Reproduction cutting or harvesting* of the existing forest to reproduce a new forest stand.
3. *Site preparation* to allow establishment of desirable tree species on recently harvested areas dominated by residual vegetation.
4. *Tree release or cleaning* to increase survival and growth of young trees overtopped or threatened by competing vegetation.
5. *Commercial thinning or intermediate harvesting* to reduce competition between mechantable-sized trees; to concentrate the growth potential on fewer, more valuable stems; and to provide an earlier return on the investment in stand establishment.

6. *Precommercial thinning* to control spacing of trees and increase diameter and, in some species, height growth in sapling-sized stands. Noncommercial hardwoods competing with conifers may also be controlled during this operation.
7. *Timber stand improvement* to concentrate growth on more desirable species by removing low-value and poorly formed trees.

In addition to these seven practices, weed control is often necessary to produce high-quality planting stock in forest tree nurseries and seed in seed orchards.

Target species for control include herbs, shrubs, and weed trees for rehabilitation, site preparation, and release; weed trees and conifers of the same or different species as the crop trees for reproduction cutting, commercial thinning, precommercial thinning, and timber stand improvement; and grasses and forbs in forest tree nurseries and seed orchards. The most important competitors in various regions were previously described in Chapters 2, 3, and 4. A knowledge of the ways these species originate or develop as important competitors of conifers is essential for sound vegetation management. As indicated in Tables 2-3, 3-2, and 4-2, many of them have more than one means of reproduction. Knowing the adaptations of competitive plant species can help the forester select silvicultural practices that minimize vegetation problems. Avoiding hot, broadcast site preparation burns on sites prone to ceanothus and other fire-adapted shrubs is one example.

Vegetation control requirements for each silvicultural practice are somewhat different, depending on the severity of the weed problem. For example, more thorough, complete control is needed to establish small seedlings in well-developed brushfields than in new clearcuts. A high degree of root kill of competing species and prevention of weed establishment are also desirable for establishing trees on newly harvested areas. Here, though, competing vegetation is often initially less vigorous due to damage during logging, and satisfactory control may be achieved with less drastic measures. In both rehabilitation and site preparation, it is better to achieve a high degree of initial vegetation control with a minimum of soil disturbance to minimize sprouting and reinvasion by new seedlings of competing species. This combination is not often possible, so that a follow-up treatment to control sprouting residuals or seedlings of invaders is sometimes required.

Rehabilitation and site preparation practices must often accomplish several objectives: clearing logging slash or other debris to reduce fire hazard, reducing temporarily the habitat of tree-damaging animals, preparing mineral soil seed beds, reducing compaction or improving drainage of surface and upper soil horizons, creating more favorable microsites on harsh sites, controlling disease, and providing better access for planting crews or planting machines.

Reproduction cuttings so profoundly influence the character and management of new stands that silvicultural systems are generally named after them. The major systems for reproducing stands of essentially one age-class (i.e., even-aged systems) are clearcutting, seed-tree, and shelterwood (Daniel et al. 1979, Society of American Foresters 1981). Single-tree and group selection systems that produce and maintain stands containing many ages are termed *uneven-aged systems*. Each system includes reproduction cutting to establish seedlings and intermediate treatments to culture the developing stand.

The objective of stand release is not to kill brush or other vegetation but to increase the amount of light reaching young trees within the stand canopy or in the understory and to decrease competition for soil moisture and nutrients. Often, it is necessary only to obtain a high percentage of defoliation, a fair amount of topkill, and minimum resprouting. The precise level of control needed for a given situation (i.e., the "economic threshold" described in Chapter 1) is not generally known given the current level of knowledge. In principle, more complete control is needed where the degree to which the competitors overtop the trees is large, where trees are severely suppressed and require several years to recover after treatment, where soil moisture is especially limiting, and where competitors are capable of rapid recovery through resprouting or invasion. Ultimately, the response in terms of additional value gained when the trees are harvested must be balanced against the additional costs of more thorough treatments.

Given 3 to 5 years of improved light and moisture, young trees on many sites outgrow their damaged competitors and become permanently released. Additional treatments may be necessary on other sites, where recovery of competing vegetation may threaten to again overtop the crop trees. Resprouting plants and seedlings may be more susceptible to treatment than large, mature plants. As a rule, follow the initial site preparation or release treatment with an appropriate retreatment within 2 to 3 years, if needed and economically justified, to keep the trees in a "free-to-grow" condition and maximize growth. Waiting until the trees are overtopped before scheduling treatment results in some growth loss and mechanical damage.

Removal of overstory trees during precommerical thinning, commercial thinning, or timber stand improvement results in some increase in understory shrubs and herbs (Ruth 1970, Colorado State University Experiment Station 1983). In precommercial or commercial thinning, overstory composition changes little. Significant shifts in species composition can occur during timber stand improvement operations only if the stands contain several tree species of widely different value or form and if removals are relatively heavy. The total impact of either practice on ecosystem structure and function is relatively minor compared with reproduction cutting, rehabilitation, and site preparation.

Vegetation control is no more effective than the condition of the forest stand that must respond to the release of site resources. Healthy, vigorous seedlings benefit the most from treatment and result in the best value from both planting and weed control.

VEGETATION MANAGEMENT METHODS

Vegetation can be controlled by using one or more methods alone or in combination: mechanical equipment, prescribed burning, herbicides, manual cutting or pulling, insects and diseases, or grazing (see Chapter 6 and also McCormack 1985, Newton 1985, and Shoulders et al. 1985). Problems can be prevented or minimized in some situations by properly selecting cultural practices that discourage establishment of competitors or increase the competitive advantage of desirable trees. For example, empirical and experimental evidence suggest that good site preparation followed by prompt planting of high-quality planting stock can eliminate the need for later release treatments. Each year's delay in planting can result in as much as a one-third loss in survival of planted trees (Baron 1962, Newton and White 1983).

Selection of individual methods depends on (1) the objective of treatment; (2) the species, size, and relative position in the canopy and stocking of desirable trees; (3) the composition and structure of the ground cover; (4) physical factors such as terrain, exposure, soil type and condition, erosion hazard, size of treatment area, and accessibility; (5) climatic and weather conditions; (6) availability of labor and equipment; (7) financial resources; and (8) external contraints, including government rules and regulations, and proximity to sensitive areas, such as waterways and dwellings. Because of these factors and the complex mosaic of vegetation, topography, soils, and climate that are characteristic of most forest ownerships, treatment prescriptions must be site-specific; there is no substitute for good judgment in selecting treatments. Frequently, the chosen method is uniquely suited to the local combination of site conditions. Substitutes may not exist or, if they do exist, result in increased environmental impact, reduced effectiveness, or higher cost.

Some key advantages and disadvantages of the more common vegetation control methods are summarized in Chapter 6, Table 6-1.

VEGETATION MANAGEMENT PRESCRIPTIONS

The silvicultural practices in vegetation management are firmly grounded in basic ecological principles (Chapter 5). To ignore those principles in managing a forested tract is to court disaster. All operations that manipulate and shape the forest comprise vegetation management, whether by logger's axe, herbicide, tractor, or drip torch. Because these silvicultural practices are interrelated, stand development and management options are largely determined by the operations that precede them. Vegetation management prescription must, therefore, begin before the current stand is harvested. On-the-ground experience often allows the silviculturist to predict probable consequences of planned actions. By beginning the management process before a single tree is harvested, problems can be anticipated, proposed operations can be modified, and the impact of undesirable consequences can be minimized or averted.

Forest management is designed to accomplish specific objectives set by the landowner (see Chapter 13). The nature of these objectives profoundly influences the type and intensity of silvicultural practices applied to a given stand. A prescription is valid only in reference to these objectives, so the process must begin by setting management objectives for each stand.

The prescription is a hypothesis that needs to be continually evaluated against the reality of the developing stand. The prescription needs to be flexible and site specific; treatments should be carefully conceived and then updated throughout the life of the stand. Prescription objectives are based upon an assessment of forest management goals in light of the vegetation characteristics and environmental features of the stand. Therefore, at the core of prescription writing is a set of clearly defined goals: a plan that specifies the desired stand structure, stocking, tree size, and product yield within a specified period.

Next, the silvicultural system (even- or uneven-aged) and reproduction cutting method (clearcut, shelterwood, seed tree, individual tree selection, or group selection) are determined. Factors that should be considered at this time are the influence of the silvicultural system and cutting method on site preparation, reforestation practices and seedling stocking, competing vegetation and need for release, and populations of tree-damaging animals, insects, and disease organisms. Administrative concerns sometimes obscure purely silvicultural considerations, compromising what would otherwise be a good prescription in the interest of administrative ease or expediency. Care should be taken to prevent short-term issues from undermining sound, long-term silvicultural plans.

It is at the planning stage that potential problems with competing vegetation may be reduced or eliminated. The stand should be initially examined to determine the condition, distribution, and composition of both the understory and overstory. It is especially important to identify the presence, abundance, and distribution of species that may be resistant to common alternative treatments and that can rapidly invade the space created by treatment. For example, even a small amount of bracken fern—a species that can invade newly created openings rapidly from extensive, deep rhizome systems—may suggest future problems. The same caution should be exercised with species that sprout rapidly from stumps, roots, or root crowns.

On the basis of previous experience in a specific area, the silviculturist may be able to anticipate the presence of buried seeds that will germinate in response to overstory removal or prescribed burning. In forest types with species whose seeds germinate after fire, it may be possible to eliminate broadcast burning and reduce the need for release. In any case, the site preparation method should minimize sprouting of undesirable species and the germination of buried seed, while discouraging the invasion of undesirable species from nearby stands. Where this is not possible, the plan should call for early release of the seedlings from competing vegetation.

Once the sequence and schedule of practices are determined, the plan is implemented. Plan implementation requires periodic examination of the stand to determine the need for action and to select the appropriate practice. Such examinations should be more frequent during the early years of a stand and can decrease following stand closure.

Tree response to various levels of competing vegetation is important in determining when, where, and how much vegetation control is needed. Treatment guidelines are available for some species by region, timber type, and type of competing vegetation (Table 14-5); however, the limitations of the data presented in those references should be recognized.

Attention to detail is particularly critical during plan implementation. Sloppy or careless work can exacerbate a problem and lead to high direct costs for additional treatments or reduced stand yields.

The period just after site preparation and establishment of desirable species on a site is one of the most critical stages of stand development. It is during this period that conditions can deteriorate rapidly. Failure to detect problems early can result in losing the plantation or, at best, necessitating more expensive measures to correct the problem. Finally, a posttreatment examination is needed to determine if treatment objectives have been met or additional measures are necessary.

The experience and information gained from earlier treatments to stands of various sites, ages, and conditions are valuable aids in improving treatment selection and implementation. It is important to capture this information in some systematic way. Careful treatment evaluation and systematic record keeping are needed to document this experience and make it available for use. Frequent, detailed measurements of treatment effects on mortality, growth of crop trees and competitors, pest problems, and other important variables should be made on stands that serve as bench marks, representing the range of sites and forest types within the ownership. Such information provides a practical resource and better site-specific guides to vegetation management. In much of the western United States, silvicultural interpretations are possible within the framework of

TABLE 14-5. Key to Locating Data for Developing Brush Control Treatment Guidelines

Region	Timber Type	Type of Competing Vegetation	Reference	Measurement Period (yr)	Response Measured
Northeast and Lake States	White pine	Aspen/birch	Shirley (1941)	5, 10	Stocking, height, basal area
			Stoeckeler and Limstrom (1950)	9	Survival, height
	Jack pine	Aspen/birch	Stoeckeler and Limstrom (1950)	9	Survival, height
	Red pine	Aspen/birch	Stoeckeler and Limstrom (1950)	9	Survival, height
		Oak/maple	Benzie (1977)	2–40	Volume
			Ralston (1953)	3	Height
	Shortleaf pine	Oak/hickory	Brinkman and Liming (1961)	11	Survival, height
		Oak/hickory	Liming (1946)	4	Height
South	Shortleaf pine	Oak/hickory	Bower and Ferguson (1968)	5	Basal area
	Loblolly pine	Hardwoods	Langdon and Trousdell (1974)	10	Volume
		Hardwoods	Burkhart and Sprinz (1984)	Variable	Volume
		Hardwoods	Grano (1961)	2	Survival
	Mixed pine	Hardwoods	Smalley (1974)	19	Volume
		Hardwoods	Walstad (1976)	Variable	Height, diameter, basal area, volume
Northwest	Ponderosa pine	Manzanita/ceanothus	Carter and Holt (1978)	2	Height
		Manzanita/ceanothus	Bentley et al. (1971)	7	Height
		Manzanita/ceanothus	Oliver (1979)	12	Diameter
		Manzanita/ceanothus	Barrett (1979)	10	Diameter
		Manzanita	Powers and Oliver (1985)	5	Height

ecological site classification systems (Bailey et al. 1978, Pfister and Arno 1980). Ecologically based systems generally classify land units having similar climax vegetation, microclimate, soils, and other key features. Presumably, stands classified within the same habitat type will respond in like manner to the same silvicultural treatment.

INCREASING FOREST PRODUCTIVITY IN THE NORTHEAST, LAKE STATES, SOUTH, AND PACIFIC NORTHWEST AND SOUTHWEST

As part of its responsibilities under the Renewable Resources Planning Act of 1974, the USDA Forest Service periodically analyzes timber resources in the United States. The agency reviews current forest inventories, projects supply and demand, and analyzes opportunities for increasing timber supplies. The most recent assessment (USDA Forest Service 1982) identified economic opportunities (returns of at least 4% in constant dollars on the investment) for increasing supplies on 168 million acres of commercial timberland, some 35% of the national total. With treatment of these areas, net annual timber growth could be increased by 12.9 billion ft^3, a volume equal to the total timber harvest in 1976 (Table 14-6). However, given periodic downturns in predicted stumpage values, the estimated acres meeting the economic criteria in the assessment and summarized next may be optimistic.

About three-quarters of the treatment opportunities on an area basis involve reforestation or type conversion of existing stands, opportunities that most often require measures to control competing vegetation. This category includes regenerating nonstocked acres, harvesting mature stands and regenerating the tract, converting existing stands to more desired species, and release. Treatment of these reforestation/conversion opportunities alone would require an investment of $13.5 billion and increase net annual growth by 11.6 billion ft^3 (Table 14-6).

The following information taken from the Forest Service timber assessment report (USDA Forest Service 1982), except where noted, summarizes treatment opportunities in the six geographic areas where benefits are the greatest: Northeast, North Central (including the Lake states), Southeast, South Central, Pacific Northwest, and Pacific Southwest. The boundaries of these areas are described in the timber assessment report. The critical vegetation types involved have been previously discussed in Chapters 2 through 4.

The greatest economic opportunity for increasing softwood timber supplies in the Northeast is release of 3 million acres of spruce/fir seedling and sapling stands. Opportunities also exist for thinning another 2 million acres of softwoods, mostly pine. If all economic opportunities were im-

TABLE 14-6. Economic Opportunities for Increasing Timber Supplies in the United States, by Region and Treatment Opportunity[a]

Region and Treatment Opportunity	Total Area (million acres)	Cost of Treatment (million $)	Net Annual Growth Increment (million ft³)
Northeast			
Reforestation/type conversion[b]	0.2	10.9	8.5
Stocking control[c]	16.1	609.6	435.1
Total	16.3	620.5	443.6
North Central (includes Lake States)			
Reforestation/type conversion[b]	14.3	1,662.0	895.6
Stocking control[c]	4.2	81.7	231.7
Total	18.5	1,743.7	1,127.3
Southeast			
Reforestation/type conversion[b]	52.6	4,933.8	4,463.2
Stocking control[c]	0.6	19.8	23.7
Total	53.2	4,953.6	4,486.9
South Central			
Reforestation/type conversion[b]	44.1	4,591.6	4,180.0
Stocking control[c]	19.5	541.8	425.9
Total	63.6	5,133.4	4,605.9
Rocky Mountain			
Reforestation/type conversion[b]	0.1	22.3	5.0
Stocking control[c]	0.1	3.5	3.2
Total	0.2	25.7	8.2
Pacific Northwest			
Reforestation/type conversion[b]	6.0	1,613.0	1,355.6
Stocking control[c]	2.8	220.1	125.8
Total	8.8	1,833.1	1,481.3
Pacific Southwest			
Reforestation/type conversion[b]	4.2	691.5	667.1
Stocking control[c]	3.4	92.6	93.4
Total	7.7	784.1	760.5
United States			
Reforestaton/type conversion[b]	121.5	13,525.0	11,574.0
Stocking control[c]	46.7	1,569.1	1,339.7
Total	168.3	15,094.1	12,913.7

Source: USDA Forest Service (1982).

[a]Includes those opportunities that would yield 4% or more in constant dollars on the investment. Note: Data may not add to totals because of rounding.

[b]Includes regeneration of nonstocked acres, regeneration of areas as mature stands are harvested, and conversion of existing stands to more desired species.

[c]Includes precommercial and commercial thinning.

plemented, net annual softwood growth in the Northeast could be increased by about 138 million ft³.

Similar investments in the North Central (including the Lake states) region of the United States include seeding and planting on 1.3 million acres of nonstocked land, regenerating poorly stocked or mature stands on 2.3 million acres, and converting of 10.5 million acres of oak/hickory, maple/beech/birch, or aspen/birch on low-to-medium sites to red pine. Together, these investments could increase net growth by 931 million ft³/yr of softwood timber. However, unstable market conditions and undesirable lumber properties reduce the incentive for private investment in red pine.

The bulk of opportunities to increase timber supplies in these two regions is on nonindustrial private forest lands. Unfortunately, owners of these lands are not likely to undertake large capital expenditures in forest management. Low-cost site preparation, reforestation, and plantation release practices along with tax incentives, landowner assistance and extension education programs, and subsidies will be needed if these forests are to attain anywhere near their potential productivity.

Throughout the Northeast and Lake states/provinces region, harvesting without deliberate reforestation has been the rule for the 100- to 200-year period of forest exploitation (see Chapter 4). The systematic removal of valuable species and the better individuals of all species has left the forest with very poor growing stock and, consequently, current growth rates and stand composition are not good indicators of potential. Of all the forested regions of the United States and Canada, the Northeast and Lake states/provinces region has the lowest proportion of private owners that seem to want to use their lands for forest production. Even industrial lands have been largely managed on a custodial basis because much of the land regenerates naturally to low value but marketable species. Thus the degree to which the 300 million acres of potential conifer type will be reclaimed or intensively managed for conifers is unknown.

Shortfalls in softwood timber supplies are likely in the Pacific Northwest by 1990. In anticipation, many forest products firms are expanding operations in the South where the rapid growth and short rotations of southern pines provide attractive investments. However, over a 10-year period, the southern United States experienced a net loss of about 7 million acres in pine forests due to inadequate site preparation and reforestation practices, especially on nonindustrial private lands. In many areas, hardwoods replaced pines on about half the acreage harvested.

Up through the early 1960s, the reversion of idle and abandoned farmlands to pine forests compensated for the loss of existing pine stands through inadequate postharvest reforestation (Boyce and Knight 1979, Knight 1977, 1978). Thus statistics showed upward trends in both pine acreage and timber volume. Since then, this source of new forest acreage and added pine timber has diminished significantly.

Adequate pine regeneration requires an investment in site preparation and planting. Many individuals, particularly owners of small tracts, are not making these investments. Because nonindustrial private landowners control 70% of the South's timberland, their help is central to solving the problem (Knight 1978).

Even planting does not guarantee a pine stand. In the Southeast, hardwoods dominate stocking on 5% of the old-field plantations, 13% of the plantations established following harvest, and 21% following oak/hickory stand conversion (Knight 1977). These percentages suggest that site preparation on cutover forest land has not been nearly as effective as alternating land use (from farming to forestry) in controlling hardwood encroachment. Competing hardwoods have been virtually eliminated from formerly intensively farmed lands. However, hardwoods invade readily under the relatively open crowns of southern pines during the first cycle after planting or natural seeding, thus ensuring the need for hardwood control in subsequent pine rotations.

An analysis of economic opportunities for forest management suggests that softwood timber supplies could be increased by 4.5 billion ft^3/yr in the Southeast through investment on 53 million acres, more than half of the commercial timberland in the region. Almost 99% of the opportunities, on an area basis, involve stand conversion or reforestation. For example, conversion of 28 million acres of oak/hickory and oak/pine to southern pines would increase net annual softwood growth by an estimated 2.3 billion ft^3.

Economic opportunities also exist for planting on about 4.2 million acres of nonstocked commercial timberland and 3.2 million acres of idle cropland in the Southeast. Opportunities for timber stand improvement are limited, amounting to only 0.6 million acres of young pine plantations overrun by brush and hardwoods; however, the potential returns from the investment are high—18%—if brush control costs remain low.

Economic opportunities are greatest in the South Central region where investment on 63.6 million acres—almost two-thirds of the region's commercial timberland—would increase net annual softwood growth by 4.6 billion ft^3. As in the Southeast, the largest opportunities are in reforestation and stand conversion. This includes clearing, site preparation, and planting to pine on 28 million acres, which would increase net annual softwood growth by an estimated 3.6 billion ft^3. About 20 million acres, constituting 71% of this area, require conversion of oak/hickory stands growing on low productivity sites to faster growing pines.

In contrast to the Southeast, substantial economic opportunities—27 million acres—exist for timber stand improvement in the South Central region. These acres are in pine or oak/pine stands, and investment could increase softwood supplies by 0.6 billion ft^3/yr.

The largest economic opportunity for increasing softwood timber supplies in the Pacific Northwest is reforestation of 2.7 million acres of lands nonstocked or poorly stocked with hardwoods in the Douglas-fir subregion of western Oregon and Washington. Implementing this practice could increase net annual growth by 727 million ft^3. In the ponderosa pine subregion, rehabilitation of 685 thousand acres of nonstocked or brush-covered lands could add 24 million ft^3/yr of softwood timber.

Brush problems are important in most forest types, but a recent survey suggests that they are acute in western Oregon:

> There are 13.5 million acres of timberlands in western Oregon, and only 8 million of them support merchantable stands of conifers. The remaining 5.5 million acres will not contribute to timber supply for at least 30 years, but they will become increasingly important thereafter. The size of the timber yield from these young stands and nonstocked areas will depend on the silviculture investment made during the next few years. The fate of 2.2 million acres of timber that do not now support a suitable conifer stand will be particularly important. These acres are not totally unproductive, since about 900,000 of them are growing hardwood stands and the other 1.4 million support scattered conifers and hardwoods. Still, the potential growing stock is but a fraction of the 250 million ft^3 per year of timber that could be grown if the area were fully stocked with conifers...The large areas of brushland, "junk conifer," and hardwoods in western Oregon represent a substantial opportunity to increase future timber supply through investment in site preparation, stand conversion, and planting...

> In the long run, timber supply will depend on regeneration success on the 300,000 acres of recent cutover and on the new cutover lands that are created each year. Present backlogs of unregenerated land attest to the inadequacy of past efforts. (MacLean 1980, p. 28-29)

Vegetation management will play an important role in forestry in the Pacific Northwest because control of competition is often needed to achieve successful reforestation and to maintain desired growth rates in young plantations. Herbs, shrubs, and hardwoods will continue to be problems due to their reproductive strategies and rapid early growth potentials. Light-seeded species and those disseminated by animals will likely increase, whereas heavy-seeded species, such as oak, tanoak, chinkapin, laurel, and ceanothus, may diminish in importance (Chapter 2). Careful regulation of stand density, preharvest control of understory species, and proper site preparation practices should prevent heavy-seeded and slower growing competitors from dominating future plantations.

As in most regions, reforestation opportunities in the Pacific Southwest (California) have a great potential for raising net annual growth while realizing high return on investment. Harvest, site preparation, and planting of 2.1 million acres of mature redwood/Douglas-fir, coastal Douglas-fir, and interior mixed conifers could increase net annual growth by 308 million ft^3. Rehabilitation, site preparation, and planting of 2.2 million acres of brush-covered forest lands could add 339 million ft^3 of net growth annually. Finally, release of redwood/Douglas-fir, coastal Douglas-fir, and interior mixed conifers could add another 11.9 million ft^3/yr of softwood growth.

VEGETATION MANAGEMENT RESEARCH NEEDS

Although significant advances have been made on many fronts, more research is needed on vegetation management to reduce the need for treatment, to target treatments to those areas where needed at the minimum intensity, and to provide a broad array of treatment alternatives to achieve a full range of forest management objectives. The needed research program has three major phases: treatment development and evaluation, treatment decision criteria, and problem prevention.

Treatment Development and Evaluation

The objectives of forest management range from preservation of rare or unique plant communities, to extensive management for wildlife or recreation, to intensive management to maximize timber or fiber production. Moreover, the combination of ownership patterns, forest types, stand conditions, topographic and soil conditions, and microclimates creates a mosaic across the landscape. At the same time, public concerns about health and environmental quality continue to constrain the use of some common silvicultural tools such as herbicides, prescribed fire, and tractors. Forest managers need many alternatives for manipulating forest vegetation to meet these varying conditions. Of course, emphasis in the silvicultural prescription and planning stage is designed to prevent or eliminate problems with competing vegetation where possible, but the silviculturist must be prepared to undertake direct control when needed.

Research is needed in three broad areas as follows:

1. *Develop Alternative Treatments for Direct Control of Competing Vegetation for Site Preparation and Plantation Release.* Research should include testing and evaluation of new herbicides. But with the continued likelihood of litigation and restrictions on their use, more effort is needed in seeking viable alternatives, including evaluation of their efficacy and environmental and health impacts. Silviculturists need more effective, broad-spectrum herbicides for site preparation to obtain good control of existing vegetation without disturbing the soil surface and litter layer. Chemicals or combinations of chemicals that control both woody and herbaceous weeds are needed to prevent shifts in composition of the competing vegetation after treatment. More selective herbicides are needed for plantation release and for better targeting of treatment against the key species that are the actual competitors. Concern about smoke pollution from prescribed fire is also likely to result in more limited use of

this tool unless research can better predict and identify weather conditions that disperse the smoke or develop low-moisture fuel preparation techniques that decrease emission of particulates.

We know that sheep, cattle, and goats can consume woody and herbaceous weeds in plantations. The keys seem to be intensive herd management and use of properly preconditioned livestock. Additional study of timing and intensity of grazing, placement of water and salt, methods for preventing plantation damage, interactions with wildlife and fish habitat, effects on water quality, and evaluation of effectiveness are needed. The possibility of a 2-year grazing period before planting deserves attention as a rotation system where hardwoods and shrubs typically survive logging.

Although the development of equipment that operates on steep terrain is appealing, the indiscriminate extension of mechanical clearing to unstable ground is not advisable. What is needed is equipment adapted to gentle topography that works faster, at less cost, with less downtime, and with lighter ground pressures to reduce compaction potential. Combinations of treatments, such as herbicidal spraying followed by crushing, should be tested to better utilize the strengths of the individual methods while minimizing their weaknesses.

2. *Evaluate Treatment Cost and Effectiveness.* Costs of weed control occur early in the rotation, whereas the benefits in terms of increased stand yield are deferred until the stand is harvested. Thus a significant effort is needed to find the lowest cost treatments or combinations of treatments. Ultimately, these costs must be evaluated in terms of additional stand yield expected. Because quantified long-term benefits are often lacking, evaluations are necessarily made on the basis of degree of control achieved per dollar invested until better data are available.

3. *Identify Biological and Physical Factors Affecting Treatment Effectiveness and Use.* The influence of various biological and physical factors on the suitability and effectiveness of treatment is reasonably well known for herbicides and fire under common operating conditions; mechanical and manual methods have received less attention. However, with the development of new tools and the extension of old ones into new areas, a continuing effort in understanding the limitations and long-term effects of specific treatments is desirable. Some areas that should be evaluated include the effect of treatment on short- and long-term site productivity from soil loss or compaction and from changes in nutrient cycling or mobilization; the effect of soil physical conditions on herbicide effectiveness; and the effect of climate and age, density, and composition of the weed community on treatment response and degree of control. Better information on environmental and personal safety is also needed for all methods, especially for mechanical and manual treatments.

Results of this research will provide a range of environmentally safe, cost-effective alternatives for direct control of competing vegetation. In addition, better information on the short- and long-term impacts of individual treatments on site productivity and better guidelines for treatment selection will be available.

Treatment Decision Criteria

Research on treatment decision criteria is needed in four areas as follows:

1. *Develop Relationships between Tree and Stand Growth and Weed Population Density.* The effect of weeds on stand growth and development is needed for a full range of population densities, including "free-to-grow" conditions. Pure populations and representative mixtures of species should be evaluated. Among the more theoretical approaches, researchers should examine the validity of the law of constant final yield using replacement series studies and other appropriate designs (see Chapter 5 and Radosevich and Holt 1984). At a more practical level, research designs such as the Coordinated Research on Alternative Forestry Treatments and Systems (CRAFTS) competition studies (Walstad and Wagner 1982) can be used to evaluate the response to release of young conifer stands.

2. *Evaluate the Influence of Treatment Timing on Plantation Performance and Degree of Control Needed.* Some research suggests that early control of competing vegetation is best. However, optimum timing for different weed communities and tree species is often unknown. Timing depends on management objectives, often requiring a compromise between maximizing tree growth and maintaining desirable cover for other resource values or site protection. Better guidelines for treatment timing for a range of objectives are desirable.

3. *Link Growth and Yield Simulators to Regeneration and Young Stand Development, Incorporating the Effects of Competing Vegetation and Low Stand Densities.* To properly evaluate the economic impact of weed control in young stands, the benefits of increased survival, height growth, and diameter growth must be projected to rotation age. Most stand growth and yield simulators initiate projections at an age when trees begin to reach merchantable size for the local markets of interest. This means that additional research is needed to link the growth and development of young stands to existing simulation models, such as has been done for the Prognosis model (see Chapter 10).

Because one of the effects of competing vegetation is to reduce stand density, silviculturists may need to evaluate the trade-offs between allowing stands with low stocking to grow to rotation versus incurring the costs of clearing and planting. Most growth and yield simulators only accurately project yields for stands that are at least moderately stocked. Some additional calibration is necessary to allow their extension to stands with lower levels of stocking.

4. *Conduct Basic Studies of Competitive Interactions between Forest Trees and Weed Species.* Silviculturists must better understand the mech-

anisms of competition and the relative competitiveness of different species to properly target treatment. This research must include identification of the specific site resources that are involved and the influence of individual species on the allocation of these resources. Because competitive interactions can involve chemical interference between species, called allelopathy, studies should extend beyond the concern for allocation of water, light, and nutrients.

The results from this phase of research can be used in preparation of guidelines for determining when, where, and how much vegetation control is needed. Moreover, these guidelines will be firmly based on sound biological and economic criteria.

Problem Prevention

In the long run, the most economic and biologically sound approach to vegetation management will likely be through the prevention or minimization of weed problems. This approach will require a more thorough understanding of the interaction between silvicultural practices and forest community dynamics than is now available. It is impossible to obtain this information for each specific forest type and condition; therefore, the emphasis must be on the fundamental physical and biological principles governing stand dynamics and on development of useful predictive models. Research on problem prevention is needed in two broad areas as follows:

1. *Evaluate Complete Reforestation and Stand Management Systems (e.g., Choice of Silvicultural System; Preharvest Treatment; Harvest Method; Site Preparation; Planting Stock Species, Size, and Type; Release; and Control of Animal Damage) to Reduce or Eliminate Weed Problems.* The individual steps and practices in stand management are interrelated—each one passes on its outcome in terms of stand condition to the next stage in development. Therefore, decisions made at one point influence decisions and outcomes later. With sufficient knowledge, it should be possible to predict the effect of different management strategies on the development of weed problems. If so, it also should be possible to modify those strategies to eliminate or mitigate the problem. Important areas for study include evaluating the effects of rotation length, intermediate harvesting, no-till site preparation, and control of weed species seed sources on weed management needs.

2. *Conduct Basic Studies of Weed Biology and Ecology, Especially Ecesis (the Establishment of a Plant in a New Habitat) and the Role of Early Seral Species in Nutrient Cycling, Nutrient Retention, and Maintenance of Long-Term Productivity.* By understanding how weed species become established, it may be possible to modify silvicultural practices to create conditions unfavorable for population buildup. For example, discovery of the mechanism of heat-induced germination of buried ceanothus seeds

has resulted in modified logging slash disposal practices such as pile and burn or lop and scatter to meet fire hazard reduction needs without causing a brush problem.

Successful completion of this phase of research will lead to a reduction in stand establishment costs, a reduction in the use of chemicals and other vegetation management tools, and attainment of stand management objectives without creating problems with competing vegetation.

These three phases of research (treatment alternatives, treatment decision criteria, and treatment prevention) are generally considered important by scientists and land managers. Most university, federal, and forest industry research organizations are addressing various aspects of the described needs. However, given the complexity of the field of research and limitations of individual organizations in conducting a broadly based program, development of cooperative approaches to pool resources is likely and desirable.

REFERENCES

Allan, G.G., J.W. Beer, and M.J. Cousin. 1978. Controlled release pesticides. 9. Growth enhancement of a juvenile conifer forest six years after application of a controlled release herbicide. Internat. Pest Control J. 20:6-13.

Bailey, R.G., R.G. Pfister, and J.A. Henderson. 1978. Nature of land and resource classification—a review. J. Forestry 76:650-655.

Balmer, W.E., K.A. Utz, and O.G. Langdon. 1978. Financial returns from cultural work in natural loblolly pine stands. South. J. Appl. Forestry 2:111-117.

Baron, F.J. 1962. Effects of different grasses on ponderosa pine seedling establishment. USDA Forest Service, Pacific Southwest Forest and Range Experiment Station, Berkeley, CA. Res. Note 199. 8 p.

Barrett, J.W. 1970. Ponderosa pine saplings respond to control of spacing and understory vegetation. USDA Forest Service, Pacific Northwest Forest and Range Experiment Station, Portland, OR. Res. Pap. PNW-106. 16 p.

Barrett, J.W. 1973 Latest results from the Pringle Falls ponderosa pine spacing study. USDA Forest Service, Pacific Northwest Forest and Range Experiment Station, Portland, OR. Res. Note PNW-209. 21 p.

Barrett, J.W. 1979. Silviculture of ponderosa pine in the Pacific Northwest: state of our knowledge. USDA Forest Service, Pacific Northwest Forest and Range Experiment Station, Portland, OR. Gen. Tech. Rep. PNW-97. 106 p.

Barrett, J.W. 1982. Twenty-year growth of ponderosa pine saplings thinned to five spacings in central Oregon. USDA Forest Service, Pacific Northwest Forest and Range Experiment Station, Portland, OR. Res. Pap. PNW-301. 18 p.

Bengtson, G.W. and G.C. Smart, Jr. 1981. Slash pine growth and response to fertilizer after application of pesticides to the planting site. Forest Sci. 27:487-502.

Bentley, J.R., S.B. Carpenter, and D.A. Blakeman. 1971. Early brush control promotes growth of ponderosa pine planted on bulldozed site. USDA Forest

Service, Pacific Southwest Forest and Range Experiment Station, Berkeley, CA. Res. Note PSW-238. 6 p.

Benzie, J.W. 1977. Manager's handbook for red pine in the north central states. USDA Forest Service, North Central Forest Experiment Station, St. Paul, MN. Gen. Tech. Rep. NC-33. 22 p.

Bower, D.R. and E.R. Ferguson. 1968. Understory removal improves shortleaf pine growth. J. Forestry 66:421-422.

Boyce, S.G. and H.A. Knight. 1979. Prospective ingrowth of southern pine beyond 1980. USDA Forest Service, Southeastern Forest Experiment Station, Asheville, NC. Res. Pap. SE-200. 48 p.

Boyer, W.D. 1975. Timing overstory removal in longleaf pine. J. Forestry 73:578-580.

Boyer, W.D. 1985. Timing of longleaf pine seedling release from overtopping hardwoods: a look 30 years later. South. J. Appl. Forestry 9:114-116.

Brinkman, K.A. and F.G. Liming. 1961. Oak and pine reproduction responds to overhead release. J. Forestry 59:341-346.

Brown, C.L. 1977. Growth and form, p. 125-168. *In* Zimmerman, M.H. and C.L. Brown (eds.) Trees: structure and function. Springer-Verlag, New York, N.Y. 336 p.

Bruce, D. 1977. Yield differences between research plots and managed forests. J. Forestry 75:14-17.

Buckman, R.E. and A.L. Lundgren. 1962. Three pine release experiments in northern Minnesota. USDA Forest Service, Lake States Forest Experiment Station, St. Paul, MN. Pap. 97. 9 p.

Burkhart, H.E. and P.T. Sprinz. 1984. A model for assessing hardwood competition effects on yields of loblolly pine plantations. School of Forestry and Wildlife Resources, Virginia Polytechnic Institute and State Univ., Blacksburg, VA. Publ. No. FWS-3-84. 55 p.

Cain, M.D. 1978. Planted loblolly and slash pine response to bedding and flat disking on a poorly drained site—an update. USDA Forest Service, Southern Forest Experiment Station, New Orleans, LA. Res. Note SO-237. 6 p.

Campbell, T.E. and W.F. Mann, Jr. 1971. Site preparation boosts growth of direct-seeded slash pine. USDA Forest Service, Southern Forest Experiment Station, New Orleans, LA. Res. Note SO-115. 4 p.

Carter, M.C. and H.A. Holt. 1978. Alternative methods of vegetation management for timber production, p. 125-145. *In* Ketcham, D.E. (coordinator) Proc., Symposium on the Use of Herbicides in Forestry, Feb. 21-22, 1978, Arlington, VA. U.S. Dept. Agr. and U.S. Environ. Prot. Agency, Washington, DC. 213 p.

Clason, T.R. 1978. Removal of hardwood vegetation increases growth and yield of a young loblolly pine stand. South. J. Appl. Forestry 2:96-97.

Cleary, B. and R. Greaves. 1974. Harvesting and reforestation...are they compatible?, p. 32-33. *In* Loggers Hbk., Vol. 34, Pacific Logging Congr., Vancouver, BC., Canada.

Colorado State University Experiment Station. 1983. Overstory-understory relationships in western forests. Colorado State Univ. Western Regional Res. Publ. 1. 37 p.

Curtis, R.O., G.W. Clendenen, and D.J. DeMars. 1981. A new stand simulator for coast Douglas-fir: DFSIM user's guide. USDA Forest Service, Pacific Northwest Forest and Range Experiment Station, Portland, OR. Gen. Tech. Rep. PNW-128. 79 p.

Daniel, T.W., J.A. Helms, and F.S. Baker. 1979. Principles of silviculture. McGraw-Hill Book Co. New York, NY. 500 p.

Duerr, W.A. 1960. Fundamentals of forestry economics. McGraw-Hill Book Co. New York, NY. 579 p.

Fiddler, G.O. and P.M. McDonald. 1984. Alternatives to herbicides in vegetation management: a case study, p. 115-126. *In* Proc., Fifth Annu. Forest Vegetation Management Conf., Nov. 2-3, 1983, Sacramento, CA. 162 p.

Glover, G.R., S.A. Knowe, and D.H. Gjerstad. 1981. Fayette site preparation study—22 year results. Dept. Forestry, Auburn Univ., Auburn, AL. Silvicultural Herbicide Cooperative Res. Note 1. 8 p.

Grano, C.X. 1961. Mortality of loblolly pine planted under small hardwoods. Tree Planters' Notes 48:1-2.

Grano, C.X. 1970. Small hardwoods reduce growth of pine overstory. USDA Forest Service, Southern Forest Experiment Station, New Orleans, LA. Res. Pap. SO-55. 9 p.

Gratkowski, H.J. 1962. Heat as a factor in germination of seeds of *Ceanothus veluntinus* var. *laevigatus* T. & G. Ph.D. thesis. Oregon State Univ., Corvallis, OR. 131 p.

Gratokwski, H.J. 1973a. Ecology of deerbrush ceanothus seeds. West. Soc. Weed Sci., Res. Prog. Rep. 1973:45.

Gratkowski, H.J. 1973b. Pregermination treatments for redstem ceanothus seeds. USDA Forest Service, Pacific Northwest Forest and Range Experiment Station, Portland, OR. Res. Pap. PNW-156. 10 p.

Gratkowski, H.J. 1974. Origin of mountain whitethorn brushfields on burns and cuttings in Pacific Northwest forests. 1974 Proc., West. Soc. Weed Sci. 27:5-8.

Gregory, G. R. 1972. Forest resource economics. McGraw-Hill Book Co., New York, NY. 548 p.

Haines, L.W. 1981. Integrated pest management and competing forest vegetation, p. 1-9. *In* Holt, H.A. and B.C. Fischer (eds.) Weed control in forest management. 1981 John S. Wright Forestry Conf., Proc., Dept. Forestry and Natur. Resour., Purdue Univ., West Lafayette, IN. 305 p.

Hall, D.O. 1971. Ponderosa pine planting techniques, survival, and height growth in the Idaho Batholith. USDA Forest Service, Intermountain Forest and Range Experiment Station, Ogden, UT. Res. Pap. INT-104. 28 p.

Hall, D.O. and J.D. Curtis. 1970. Planting method affects height growth of ponderosa pine in central Idaho. USDA Forest Service, Intermountain Forest and Range Experiment Station, Ogden, UT. Res. Note INT-125. 8 p.

Harrington, T.A. 1960. Immediate release pays off. USDA Forest Service, Southern Forest Experiment Station, New Orleans, LA. South. Forestry Notes 127. 4 p.

Hatchell, G.E. 1964. Immediate release needed for maximum growth of seeded loblolly pine. Tree Planters' Notes 66:19-22.

Haynes, R. and D.M. Adams. 1985. Simulations of the effects of alternative assumptions on demand-supply determinants on the timber situation in the United States. USDA Forest Service, Forest Resources Economics Research, Washington, DC. 113 p.

Haywood, J.D. 1980. Planted pines do not respond to bedding on an Acadia-Beauregard-Kolin Loam site. USDA Forest Service, Southern Forest Experiment Station, New Orleans, LA. Res. Note. SO-259. 4 p.

Knight, H.A. 1977. The southern pine is losing ground. Alabama Forest Prod. 20(9):4-6.

Knight, H.A. 1978. The South is losing its pines. Forest Farmer 38(2):10-12.

Langdon, O.G. and K.B. Trousdell. 1974. Increasing growth and yield of natural loblolly pine by young stand management, p. 288-296. *In* Proc., Symposium on Management of Young Pines, Oct. 22-24, 1974, Alexandria, LA and Dec. 3-5, 1974, Charleston, SC. USDA Forest Service, Southeastern Area, State and Private Forestry, Atlanta, GA. 349 p.

Liming, F.G. 1946. Response of planted shortleaf pine to overhead release. USDA Forest Service, Central States Forest Experiment Station, Columbus, OH. Tech. Pap. 105. 20 p.

MacLean, C.D. 1980. Opportunities for silvicultural treatment in western Oregon. USDA Forest Service, Pacific Northwest Forest and Range Experiment Station, Portland, OR. Resour. Bull. PNW-90. 35 p.

May, J.T., S. Rahman, and R.H. Worst. 1973. Effects of site preparation and spacing on planted slash pine. J. Forestry 71:333-335.

McColl, J.G. and R.F. Powers. 1984. Consequences of forest management on soil-tree relationships, p. 379-412. *In* Bowen, G.D. and E.K.S. Nambiar (eds.) Nutrition of plantation forests, Academic Press, London. 516 p.

McCormack, M.L., Jr. 1985. Vegetation management in plantations — Northeast, U.S.A., p 240-244. *In* Proc., 1984 Soc. Amer. Foresters Annu. Conv., Forest Resources Management—the Influence of Policy and Law. Soc. Amer. Foresters, Washington, DC.

McDonald, P.M. and W.W. Oliver. 1984. Woody shrubs retard growth of ponderosa pine seedlings and saplings, p. 65-89. *In* Proc., Fifth Annu. Forest Vegetation Management Conf., Nov. 2-3, 1983, Sacramento, CA. 162 p.

Michael, J.L. 1980. Long-term impact of aerial application of 2,4,5-T to longleaf pine (*Pinus palustris*). Weed Sci. 28:255-257.

Muntz, H.H. 1951. Converting scrub oak areas to pine plantations. J. Forestry 49:714-715.

Newton, M. 1967. Response of vegetation communities to manipulation, p. 83-87. *In* Newton, M. (ed.) Proc., Herbicides and Vegetation Management in Forests, Ranges, and Noncrop Lands. School of Forestry, Oregon State Univ., Corvallis, OR. 356 p.

Newton, M. 1973. Environmental management for seedling establishment. Forest Research Laboratory, Oregon State Univ., Corvallis. Res. Pap. 16. 5 p.

Newton, M. 1985. Vegetation management in plantations of the Pacific Northwest, p 250-257. *In* Proc., 1984 Soc. Amer. Foresters Annu. Conv., Forest Resources Management—the Influence of Policy and Law. Soc. Amer. Foresters, Washington, DC.

Newton, M. and D.E. White. 1983. Effect of salmonberry on growth of planted conifers. 1983 Proc., West. Soc. Weed Sci. 36:59-64.

Oliver, W.W. 1979. Early response of ponderosa pine to spacing and brush: observations in a 12-year-old plantation. USDA Forest Service, Pacific Southwest Forest and Range Experiment Station, Berkeley, CA. Res. Note PSW-341. 7 p.

Oliver, W.W. 1984. Brush reduces growth of thinned ponderosa pine in northern California. USDA Forest Service, Pacific Southwest Forest and Range Experiment Station, Berkeley, CA. Res. Pap. PSW-172. 7 p.

Outcalt, K.W. 1983. Mechanical site preparation improves growth of genetically improved and unimproved slash pine on a Florida flatwoods site, p. 11-13. *In* Jones, E.P., Jr., (ed.) Proc., Second Biennial Southern Silvicultural Research Conference, Nov. 4-5, 1982, Atlanta, GA. USDA Forest Service, Southeastern Forest Experiment Station, Asheville, NC. Gen. Tech. Rep. SE-24. 514 p.

Pehl, C.E. and R.L. Bailey. 1983. Performance to age ten of a loblolly pine plantation on an intensively prepared site in the Georgia Piedmont. Forest Sci. 29:96-102.

Petersen, T.D. and M. Newton. 1982. Growth of Douglas-fir following release from snowbrush and forbs—implications for vegetation management of brushfields. Research and Development, Rocky Mountains Timberlands, Champion International Corp., Milltown, MT. Res. Note RM 82-8. 9 p.

Pfister, R.D. and S.F. Arno. 1980. Classifying forest habitat types based on potential climax vegetation. Forest Sci. 26:52-70.

Powers, R.F. 1983. Forest fertilization research in California, p. 388-397. *In* Ballard, R. and S.P. Gessel, (eds.) I.U.F.R.O. Symposium on Forest Site and Continuous Productivity, Aug. 22-28, 1982, Seattle, WA. USDA Forest Service, Pacific Northwest Forest and Range Experiment Station, Portland, OR. Gen Tech. Rep. PNW-163. 406 p.

Powers, R.F. and G.D. Jackson. 1978. Ponderosa pine response to fertilization: influence of brush removal and soil type. USDA Forest Service, Pacific Southwest Forest and Range Experiment Station, Berkeley, CA. Res. Pap. PSW-132. 9 p.

Powers, R.F. and W.W. Oliver. 1985. Ponderosa pine plantation growth in northern California...brush competition and response to release, p. 122-125. *In* Executive Summaries, Proc., 1984 Western Forestry Conference. West. Forestry and Conserv. Assoc., Portland, OR.

Pressler, M.R. 1864. Das Gesetz der Stamanbildung und dessen forstwirthschaftliche Bedeutung, insbesondere fuer den Waldbau hoechsten Reinertrags. Arnoldische Buchhandlung, Leipzig. 153 p.

Radosevich, S.R. and J.S. Holt. 1984. Ecology of Weeds. John Wiley and Sons, Inc. New York, NY. 265 p.

Ralston, R.A. 1953. Red pine suppressed for forty years responds to release. USDA Forest Service, Lake States Forest Experiment Station, St. Paul, MN. Tech. Note No. 408. 2 p.

Roe, E.I. 1952. Understory balsam fir responds well to release. USDA Forest Service, Lake States Forest Experiment Station, St. Paul, MN. Tech. Notes 377. 1 p.

Row, C., H.F. Kaiser, and J. Sessions. 1981. Discount rate for long-term Forest Service investments. J. Forestry 79:367-369.

Roy, D.F. 1984. Personal communication. Pacific Southwest Forest and Range Experiment Station, Redding, CA.

Russell, T.E. 1969. Underplanting shortleaf pine. Forest Farmer 29:10, 17, 18.

Ruth, R.H. 1970. Effect of shade on germination and growth of salmonberry. USDA Forest Service, Pacific Northwest Forest and Range Experiment Station, Portland, OR. Res. Pap. PNW-96. 10 p.

Sander, I.L. and R. Rogers. 1979. Growth and yield of shortleaf pine in Missouri: 21-year results from a thinning study, p. 14-27. *In* Proc., Symposium for the Management of Pines in the Interior South, Univ. Tennessee, Knoxville, TN.

Shirley, H.L. 1941. Restoring conifers to aspen lands in the Lake States. U.S. Dept. Agr., Tech. Bull. 763. 36 p.

Shoulders, E. 1955. Release underplanted loblolly early. USDA Forest Service, Southern Forest Experiment Station, New Orleans, LA. Southern Forest Notes 100. 4 p.

Shoulders, E., J.D. Haywood, A.E. Tiarks, and J.D. Burton. 1985. Vegetation management in southern pine plantations, p. 245-249. *In* Proc., 1984 Soc. Amer. Foresters Annu. Conv., Forest Resources Management—the Influence of Policy and Law. Soc. Amer. Foresters, Washington, DC.

Smalley, G.W. 1974. Development of pine-hardwood stands in north Alabama following improvement cuttings. USDA Forest Service, Southern Forest Experiment Station, New Orleans, LA. Res. Pap. SO-100. 9 p.

Society of American Foresters. 1981. Choices in silviculture for American forests. Soc. Amer. Foresters, Washington, DC. 80 p.

Stage, A.R. 1973. Prognosis model for stand development. USDA Forest Service, Intermountain Forest and Range Experiment Station, Ogden, UT. Res. Pap. INT-137. 32 p.

Stewart, R.E. 1978. Origin and development of vegetation after spraying and burning in a coastal Oregon clearcut. USDA Forest Service, Pacific Northwest Forest and Range Experiment Station, Portland, OR. Res. Note PNW-317. 11 p.

Stewart, R.E., L.L. Gross, and B.H. Honkala. 1984. Effects of competing vegetation on forest trees: a bibliography with abstracts. USDA Forest Service, Washington, DC. Gen. Tech. Rep. WO-43. 260 p.

Stewart, R.E. and C. Row. 1981. Assessing the economic benefits of weed control in forest management, p. 26-53. *In* Holt, H.A. and B.C. Fischer (eds.) Weed control in forest management. John S. Wright Forestry Conf. Proc., Dept. Forestry and Natur. Resour., Purdue Univ., West Lafayette, IN. 305 p.

Stoeckeler, J.H. and G.A. Limstrom. 1950. Reforestation research findings in northern Wisconsin and upper Michigan. USDA Forest Service, Lake States Forest Experiment Station, St. Paul, MN. Pap. 23. 34 p.

Stone, D.M. 1976. Growth of red pine planted on a northern hardwood site. USDA Forest Service, North Central Forest Experiment Station, St. Paul, MN. Res. Note NC-210. 4 p.

Tiarks, A.E. 1983. Effect of site preparation and fertilization on slash pine growing on a good site, p. 34-39. *In* Jones, E.P., Jr. (ed.) Proc., Second Biennial Southern

Silvicultural Research Conference, Nov. 4-5, 1982, Atlanta, GA. USDA Forest Service, Southeastern Forest Experiment Station, Asheville, NC. Gen. Tech. Rep. SE-24. 514 p.

U.S. Department of Agriculture. 1979. The biologic and economic assessment of 2,4,5-T. U.S. Dept. Agr. Tech. Bull. 1671. 445 p.

U.S. Department of Agriculture. 1982. 1983 Budget Explantory Notes for Committee on Appropriations—Forest Service. Washington, D.C.

USDA Forest Service. 1982. An analysis of the timber situation in the United States 1952-2030. USDA Forest Service, Forest Resour. Rep. 23. 499 p.

Walker, L.C. 1954. Early scrub-oak control helps longleaf pine seedlings. J. Forestry 52:939-940.

Walstad, J.D. 1976. Weed control for better southern pine management. Southern Forestry Research Center, Weyerhaeuser Company, Hot Springs, AR. Forestry Pap. 15. 44 p.

Walstad, J.D. and R.G. Wagner. 1982. CRAFTS experimental design for B-level studies: release of young conifer stands from uniformly distributed brush competition. College of Forestry, Oregon State Univ., Corvallis, OR. 39 p. study plan.

Westman, W.E. 1978. Measuring the inertia and resilience of ecosystems. BioSci. 28:705-710.

Wilde, S.A., B.H. Shaw, and A.W. Fedkenheuer. 1968. Weeds as a factor depressing forest growth. Weed Res. 8:196-204.

Wittenkamp, R. and S.A. Wilde. 1964. Effect of cultivation on the growth of red pine plantations. J. Forestry 62:35-37.

Wykoff, R.W., N.L. Crookston, and A.R. Stage. 1982. User's guide to the stand prognosis model. USDA Forest Service, Intermountain Forest and Range Experiment Station, Ogden, UT. Gen. Tech. Rep. INT-133. 112 p.

Yoda, K., T. Kira, H. Ogawa, and K. Hozumi. 1963. Intraspecific competition among higher plants. XI. Self-thinning in over-crowded pure stands under cultivated and natural conditions. Osaka City Univ., Japan. J. Biology 14:107-129.

List of Common and Scientific Names of Plant Species[a]

COMMON NAME	SCIENTIFIC NAME
Coniferous Tree Species	
Alaska-cedar	*Chamaecyparis nootkatensis* (D. Don) Spach
Douglas-fir	*Pseudotsuga menziesii* (Mirb.) Franco
Douglas-fir, bigcone	*P. macrocarpa* (Vasey) Mayr
Fir	
Balsam	*Abies balsamea* (L.) Mill.
California red	*A. magnifica* A. Murr.
California white	*A. concolor* var. *lowiana* (Gord.) Lemm.
Fraser	*A. fraseri* (Pursh) Poir.
Grand	*A. grandis* (Dougl. ex D. Don) Lindl.
Noble	*A. procera* Rehd.

[a]Scientific names are primarily from:
Fernald, M.L. 1950. Gray's manual of botany. 8th ed. American Book Co., New York, NY. 1,632 p.
Hitchcock, C.L. and A. Cronquist. 1973. Flora of the Pacific Northwest. Univ. Washington Press, Seattle, WA. 730 p.
Little, E.L., Jr. 1979. Checklist of United States trees (native and naturalized). U.S. Dept. Agr., Washington, DC. Agr. Hbk. 541. 375 p.

COMMON NAME	SCIENTIFIC NAME

Coniferous Tree Species

Fir (*Continued*)

Pacific silver	*A. amabalis* Dougl. ex Forbes
Shasta red	*A. magnifica* var. *shastensis* Lemm.
Subalpine	*A. lasiocarpa* (Hook.) Nutt.
White	*A. concolor* (Gord & Glend.) Lindl. ex Hildebr.

Hemlock

Eastern	*Tsuga canadensis* (L.) Carr.
Mountain	*T. mertensiana* (Bong.) Carr.
Western	*T. heterophylla* (Raf.) Sarg.
Incense-cedar	*Libocedrus decurrens* Torr.

Juniper

Common	*Juniperus communis* L.
Western	*J. occidentalis* Hook.

Larch

Eastern (tamarack)	*Larix laricina* (Du Roi) K. Koch
Subalpine	*L. lyallii* Parl.
Western	*L. occidentalis* Nutt.

Pine

Bishop	*Pinus muricata* D. Don
Bristlecone	*P. aristata* Engelm.
Coulter	*P. coulteri* D. Don
Digger	*P. sabiniana* Dougl.
Eastern white	*P. strobus* L.
Foxtail	*P. balfouriana* Grev. & Balf.
Jack	*P. banksiana* Lamb.
Jeffrey	*P. jeffreyi* Grev. & Balf.
Knobcone	*P. attenuata* Lemm.
Limber	*P. flexilis* James
Loblolly	*P. taeda* L.
Lodgepole	*P. contorta* Dougl. ex Loud.
Longleaf	*P. palustris* Mill.
Monterey	*P. radiata* D. Don
Pinyon	*P. edulis* Engelm.
Pitch	*P. rigida* Mill.
Pond	*P. serotina* Michx.

COMMON NAME	SCIENTIFIC NAME

Coniferous Tree Species

Pine (*Continued*)

Ponderosa	*P. ponderosa* Dougl. ex Laws.
Red	*P. resinosa* Ait.
Sand	*P. clausa* (Chapm. ex Engelm.) Vasey ex Sarg.
Shortleaf	*P. echinata* Mill.
Slash	*P. elliottii* Engelm. var. *elliottii*
Sugar	*P. lambertiana* Dougl.
Virginia	*P. virginiana* Mill.
Western white	*P. monticola* Dougl. ex D. Don
Whitebark	*P. albicaulis* Engelm.
Port-Orford-cedar	*Chamaecyparis lawsoniana* (A. Murr.) Parl.

Redcedar

Eastern	*Juniperus virginiana* L.
Western	*Thuja plicata* Donn ex D. Don
Redwood, coast	*Sequoia sempervirens* (D. Don) Endl.

Spruce

Black	*Picea mariana* (Mill.) B.S.P.
Blue	*P. pungens* Engelm.
Engelmann	*P. engelmannii* Parry ex Engelm.
Red	*P. rubens* Sarg.
Sitka	*P. sitchensis* (Bong.) Carr.
White	*P. glauca* (Moench) Voss
Torreya, California	*Torreya californica* Torr.
White-cedar, northern (eastern)	*Thuja occidentalis* L.
Yew, Pacific	*Taxus brevifolia* Nutt.

Hardwood Tree Species

Alder, red	*Alnus rubra* Bong.

Ash

Black	*Fraxinus nigra* Marsh.
Green	*F. pennsylvanica* Marsh.

COMMON NAME	SCIENTIFIC NAME

Hardwood Tree Species

Ash (*Continued*)

Oregon	*F. latifolia* Benth.
White	*F. americana* L.
Mountain, Greene	*Sorbus scopulina* Greene

Aspen

Bigtooth	*Populus grandidentata* Michx.
Quaking (trembling)	*P. tremuloides* Michx.

Basswood

American	*Tilia americana* L.
White	*T. heterophylla* Vent.

Beech, American — *Fagus grandifolia* Ehrh.

Birch

Gray (wire)	*Betula populifolia* Marsh.
Paper	*B. papyrifera* Marsh.
Sweet (black)	*B. lenta* L.
White (northwestern paper)	*B. papyrifera* var. *subcordata* (Rydb.) Sarg.
Yellow	*B. alleghaniensis* Britton

California-laurel (Oregon myrtle) — *Umbellularia californica* (Hook. & Arn.) Nutt.

Cascara buckthorn — *Rhamnus purshiana* DC.

Cherry

Bitter	*Prunus emarginata* Dougl. ex Eaton
Black	*P. serotina* Ehrh.
Pin	*P. pensylvanica* L. f.

Chinkapin, golden (giant) — *Castanopsis chrysophylla* (Dougl.) A. DC.

Cottonwood

Black	*Populus trichocarpa* Torr. & Gray
Eastern	*P. deltoides* Bartr. ex Marsh. var. *deltoides*

Dogwood, flowering — *Cornus florida* L.

Elm

Slippery	*Ulmus rubra* Muhl.
Winged	*U. alata* Michx.

Hickory

Black	*Carya texana* Buckl.

COMMON NAME	SCIENTIFIC NAME

Hardwood Tree Species

Hickory (*Continued*)

Mockernut	*C. tomentosa* (Poir.) Nutt.
Pignut	*C. glabra* (Mill.) Sweet
Sand	*C. pallida* (Ashe) Engl. & Graebn.
Shagbark	*C. ovata* (Mill.) K. Koch
Locust, black	*Robinia pseudoacacia* L.
Magnolia, southern	*Magnolia grandiflora* L.

Maple

Bigleaf	*Acer macrophyllum* Pursh
Red	*A. rubrum* L.
Silver	*A. saccharinum* L.
Sugar	*A. saccharum* Marsh.
Mulberry	*Morus* spp.

Oak

Black	*Quercus velutina* Lam.
Blackjack	*Q. marilandica* Muenchh.
Bluejack	*Q. incana* Bartr.
California black	*Q. kelloggii* Newb.
California white (valley)	*Q. lobata* Nee
Chestnut	*Q. prinus* L.
Laurel	*Q. laurifolia* Michx.
Live	*Q. virginiana* Mill.
Northern red	*Q. rubra* L.
Oregon white	*Q. garryana* Dougl. ex Hook.
Overcup	*Q. lyrata* Walt.
Post	*Q. stellata* Wangenh.
Scarlet	*Q. coccinea* Muenchh.
Southern red	*Q. falcata* Michx.
Turkey	*Q. laevis* Walt.
Water	*Q. nigra* L.
White	*Q. alba* L.
Willow	*Q. phellos* L.
Pacific madrone	*Arbutus menziesii* Pursh.
Persimmon, common	*Diospyros virginiana* L.
Poplar, balsam	*Populus balsamifera* L.

COMMON NAME	SCIENTIFIC NAME

Hardwood Tree Species

Redbud, eastern	*Cercis canadensis* L.
Sassafras	*Sassafras albidum* (Nutt.) Nees
Serviceberry, western	*Amelanchier alnifolia* (Nutt.) Nutt.
Sourwood	*Oxydendrum arboreum* (L.) DC.
Sweetgum	*Liquidambar styraciflua* L.
Sycamore	*Platanus occidentalis* L.
Tanoak	*Lithocarpus densiflorus* (Hook. & Arn.) Rehd.
Tupelo, black (blackgum)	*Nyssa sylvatica* Marsh.
Willow, Scouler (upland)	*Salix scoulerana* Barratt ex Hook.
Yellow-poplar	*Liriodendron tulipifera* L.

Shrub Species

Alder	
Sitka (thinleaf)	*Alnus sinuata* (Regel) Rydb.
Speckled	*A. rugosa* (Du Roi) Spreng.
Baccharis	
Chapparral broom	*Baccharis pilularis* DC.
Eastern (sea-myrtle)	*B. halimifolia* L.
Bayberry, southern (waxmyrtle)	*Myrica cerifera* L.
Bearmat (bear clover, Mountain misery)	*Chamaebatia foliolosa* Benth.
Beautyberry, American	*Callicarpa americana* L.
Berry	
Himalayan blackberry	*Rubus procerus* Muell.
Raspberry	*R.* spp.
Salmonberry	*R. spectabilis* Pursh
Thimbleberry	*R. parviflorus* Nutt.
Trailing blackberry	*R. ursinus* Cham. & Schlecht
Bitterbrush	*Purshia tridentata* (Pursh) DC.
Blueberry	*Vaccinium* spp.
Boxwood	*Pachistima myrsinites* (Pursh) Raf.
Buffalo berry	*Shepherdia canadensis* (L.) Nutt.

COMMON NAME   SCIENTIFIC NAME

Shrub Species

Ceanothus
  Blueblossom   *Ceanothus thyrsiflorus* Esch.
  Buckbrush   *C. cuneatus* (Hook.) D. & G.
   (wedgeleaf)
  Deerbrush   *C. integerrimus* H. & A.
  Littleleaf   *C. parvifolius* (Wats.) Trel.
  Mountain whitethorn   *C. cordulatus* Kell.
  Redstem   *C. sanguineus* Pursh
  Snowbrush (slickleaf)   *C. velutinus* var. *velutinus* Dougl. ex
                               Hook.
  Squaw carpet   *C. prostratus* Benth.
  Varnishleaf   *C. velutinus* var. *laevigatus* (Hook.) T. &
                               G.
Chinkapin, Sierra   *Castanopsis sempervirens* (Kell.) Dudl.
 (bush)
Devils-walkingstick   *Aralia spinosa* L.
 (Devil's club)
Dogwood, Pacific   *Cornus nutallii* Audubon
Elderberry
  Blue   *Sambucus cerulea* Raf.
  Pacific red   *S. callicarpa* Greene
Gallberry, low   *Ilex glabra* (L.) Gray
Gooseberry (currant)
  Sierra   *Ribes roezlii* Rehd.
  Sticky currant   *R. viscosissimum* Pursh
Hackberry   *Celtis occidentalis* L.
Hawthorn   *Crataegus* spp.
Hazel
  American   *Corylus americana* Walt.
  Beaked   *C. cornuta* Marsh.
  California   *C. cornuta* var. *californica* (A DC.) Sharp
Holly   *Ilex* spp.
Hornbeam, American   *Carpinus caroliniana* Walt.
Huckleberry
  Big   *Vaccinium membranaceum* Dougl. ex
                            Hook.

COMMON NAME	SCIENTIFIC NAME

Shrub Species

Huckleberry (*Continued*)

Evergreen	*V. ovatum* Pursh
Red	*V. parvifolium* Smith
False	*Menziesia ferruginea* Smith
Lyonia	*Lyonia* spp.
Manzanita	
Greenleaf	*Arctostaphylos patula* Greene
Hairy	*A. columbiana* Piper
Whiteleaf	*A. viscida* Parry
Maple	
Mountain	*Acer spicatum* Lam.
Rocky Mountain	*A. glabrum* Torr.
Striped	*A. pensylvanicum* L.
Vine	*A. circinatum* Pursh
Mountain-laurel	*Kalmia latifolia* L.
Mountain mahogany	*Cercocarpus ledifolius* Nutt. in T. & G.
Ninebark, mallow	*Physocarpus malvaceus* (Greene) Kuntze
Oak	
Canyon live	*Quercus chrysolepis* Liebm.
Sadler	*Q. sadleriana* R. Br.
Oceanspray	*Holodiscus discolor* (Pursh) Maxim.
Oregon grape	*Berberis repens* Lindl.
Palmetto, cabbage	*Sabal palmetto* (Walt.) Lodd.
Poison oak	*Rhus diversiloba* T. & G.
Privet	*Ligustrum* spp.
Rabbit brush	*Chrysothamnus nauseosus* (Pall.) Brit.
Rhododendron	
Pacific	*Rhododendron macrophyllum* G. Don
Rosebay	*R. maximum* L.
Rose	*Rosa* spp.
Sagebrush, big	*Artemisia tridentata* Nutt.
Salal	*Gaultheria shallon* Pursh
Scotch broom	*Cytisus scoparius* (L.) Link
Snowberry	*Symphoricarpos* spp.
Spirea	*Spiraea betulifolia* Pall. var. *lucida* (Dougl.) C. L. Hitchc.

COMMON NAME	SCIENTIFIC NAME

Shrub Species

Sugarberry	*Celtis laevigata* Willd.
Sumac	
Smooth	*Rhus glabra* L.
Staghorn	*R. typhina* L.
Winged (shining)	*R. copallina* L.
Swamp cyrilla (titi)	*Cyrilla racemiflora* L.
Sweetbay magnolia	*Magnolia virginiana* L.
Sweet-fern	*Comptonia peregrina* (L.) Coult.
Twinberry, red (honeysuckle)	*Lonicera utahensis* Wats.
Viburnum	*Viburnum* spp.
Witch-hazel	*Hamamelis virginiana* L.
Yaupon	*Ilex vomitoria* Ait.

Vine Species

Blackberry (dewberry)	*Rubus* spp.
Greenbriar	*Smilax* spp.
Honeysuckle, Japanese	*Lonicera japonica* Thunb.
Kudzu	*Pueraria lobata* (Willd.) Ohwi
Morningglory	*Ipomoea* spp.
Peppervine	*Ampelopsis arborea* (L.) Koehne
Poison-ivy	*Rhus radicans* L.
Trumpetcreeper	*Campsis radicans* (L.) Seem.

Herbaceous Species

Aster	*Aster* spp.
Bedstraw	*Galium* spp.
Cocklebur, common	*Xanthium pensylvanicum* Wallr.
Cotton	*Gossypium hirsutum* L.
Croton, woolly	*Croton capitatus* Michx.
Dandelion	*Taraxacum officinale* Webber
Dock	*Rumex* spp.
Dogfennel	*Eupatorium capillifolium* (Lam.) Small
Elder, American	*Sambucus canadensis* L.
Goldenrod	*Solidago* spp.

COMMON NAME	SCIENTIFIC NAME

Herbaceous Species

Grasses

Barnyardgrass	*Echinochloa crus-galli* (L.) Beauv.
Bermudagrass	*Cynodon dactylon* (L.) Pers.
Blue-joint	*Calamagrostis canadensis* (Michx.) Nutt.
Bluestem (broomsedge)	*Andropogon* spp.
Brome	*Bromus* spp.
Common beargrass	*Xerophyllum tenax* (Pursh) Nutt.
Corn	*Zea mays* L.
Crabgrass	*Digitaria* spp.
Fescue	*Festuca* spp.
Giant foxtail	*Setaria faberii* Herrm.
Green foxtail	*S. viridis* (L.) Beauv.
Johnsongrass	*Sorghum halepense* (L.) Pers.
Lovegrass	*Eragrostis* spp.
Nutsedge	*Cyperus* spp.
Panicum	*Panicum* spp.
Paspalum	*Paspalum* spp.
Pine grass	*Calamagrostis rubescens* Buckl.
Quackgrass	*Agropyron repens* (L.) Beauv.
Rice	*Oryza sativa* L.
Short husk grass	*Brachelytrum erectum* (Schreb.) Beauf.
Switchcane	*Arundinaria* spp.
Wheat	*Triticum aestivum* L.
Wild oat	*Avena fatua* L.
Wood reedgrass	*Cinna latifolia* (Trev.) Griseb.

Fern

Bracken	*Pteridium aquilinum* (L.) Kuhn
Hayscented	*Dennstaedtia punctilobula* (Michx.) Moore
New York	*Dryopteris noveboracensis* (L.) Gray
Sword	*Polystichum munitum* (Kaulf.) Presl
Fireweed	*Epilobium* spp.
Horseweed	*Conyza canadensis* (L.) Cronq.
Klamath weed (St. John's-wort)	*Hypericum perforatum* L.
Kochia	*Kochia scoparia* (L.) Roth

COMMON NAME	SCIENTIFIC NAME

Herbaceous Species

Lambsquarters	*Chenopodium* spp.
Lespedeza	*Lespedeza* spp.
Meadow-beauty	*Rhexia* spp.
Milkweed	*Asclepias* spp.
Mustard, wild	*Brassica kaber* (DC.) L.C. Wheeler
Nightshade, black	*Solanum nigrum* L.
Partridgepea	*Cassia fasciculata* Michx.
Pea	*Pisum sativum* L.
Pigweed	*Amaranthus* spp.
Pokeweed, common	*Phytolacca americana* L.
Poorjoe	*Diodia teres* Walt.
Pusley, Florida	*Richardia scabra* L.
Ragweed	
Common	*Ambrosia artemisifolia* L.
Giant	*A. trifida* L.
Sedges	*Carex* spp. and *Cyperus* spp.
Sicklepod	*Cassia obtusifolia* L.
Smartweed	*Polygonum* spp.
Soybean	*Glycine max* Merr.
Spurge	*Euphorbia* spp.
Sugarbeet	*Beta vulgaris* L.
Sweet Cicely	*Osmorhiza* spp.
Tansy ragwort	*Senecio jacobea* L.
Thistle	*Cirsium* spp.
Thoroughwort	*Eupatorium* spp.
Vetch	*Vicia* spp.
Violet	*Viola* spp.
Woodsorrel	*Oxalis* spp.

English-to-Metric Conversion Factors

Length

in. × 2.54 = cm

ft × 0.305 = m

breast height (4.5 ft) = 1.4 m

mi. × 1.61 = km

Area

in.^{2} × 6.45 = cm^2

ft^2 × 0.093 = m^2

ft^2/acre × 0.23 = m^2/ha

yd^2 × 0.837 = m^2

acre × 0.405 = ha

Volume—solid

in.^{3} × 16.4 = cm^3

ft^3 (CF) × 0.0283 = m^3

ft^3/acre × 0.07 = m^3/ha

cunit (100 ft^3, CCF) × 2.83 = m^3

cunit/acre × 7.0 = m^3/ha

bd ft^a (BF) $\times$ 0.00236 = m^3

thousand bd ft^a (MBF) $\times$ 2.36 = m^3/ha

bd ft^a/acre $\times$ 0.0058 = m^3/ha

thousand bd ft^a (MBF)/acre $\times$ 5.8 = m^3/ha

cord^b $\times$ 3.62 = m^3

cord^b/acre $\times$ 8.96 = m^3/ha

Volume—liquid

fl oz $\times$ 28.4 = ml

qt $\times$ 0.95 = liter

U.S. gal $\times$ 3.785 = liter

Imperial gal $\times$ 4.546 = liter

Mass

oz $\times$ 31.1 = g

lb $\times$ 0.454 = kg

lb/acre $\times$ 1.12 = kg/ha

Miscellaneous

bar $\times$ 100 = kPa

degree Fahrenheit (°F):

  0.555 (°F − 32) = degree Celsius (°C)

Costs and values

$/acre $\times$ 2.47 = $/ha

$/ft^3 $\times$ 35.3 = $/m^3

$/cunit $\times$ 0.353 = $/m^3

$/MCF $\times$ 0.0353 = $/m^3

$/BF^a $\times$ 423.7 = $/m^3

$/MBF^a $\times$ 0.424 = $/m^3

$/cord^b $\times$ 0.276 = $/m^3

---

[a]Based on nominal measurement (1 in. $\times$ 1 ft $\times$ 1 ft), not actual measurement derived from scaling.
[b]Based on 128 ft^3 of stacked roundwood (4 ft $\times$ 4 ft $\times$ 8 ft).

Formulas and Equations for Present Net Worth Evaluations

The purpose of this appendix is to indicate how economic analysis of silvicultural treatments such as vegetation control is accomplished and to provide for changes in cost, revenue, interest rate, and time assumptions.

1. Net Revenue (NR_t): For a harvest operation, net stumpage revenue is FOB-mill price minus haul cost and stump-to-truck cost. Thus it represents the financial return to growing timber. A t subscript denotes the year of occurrence.

2. Present Net Worth (PNW_t): Present net worth is derived from the sum of the discounted net revenues and costs for a series of silvicultural operations. A subscript denotes the year basis for the PNW. In this study, all values were based at time zero or the beginning of the rotation (PNW_0).

$$PNW_0 = -RC_0 + \frac{-C_{t_1}}{(1+i)^{t_1}} + \frac{-C_{t_2}}{(1+i)^{t_2}}$$

$$+ \frac{NR_{t_3}}{(1+i)^{t_3}} + \frac{NR_{t_4}}{(1+i)^{t_4}} + \frac{NR_{t_r}}{(1+i)^{t_r}} \quad (1)$$

where t_1, t_2 ...t_r represent ages of treatment with r representing the rotation or final harvest age; C represents a year with net costs and NR represents a year with net revenues; and i represents interest rate.

495

3. Soil expectation value (*SE*) is the value based at time zero of an infinite series of identical silvicultural sequences (rotations).

$$SE = PNW_0 \frac{(1+i)^r}{(1+i)^r - 1} \tag{2}$$

The preceding multiplier is known as the infinite series multiplier and can be used to transform a present net worth element in a single rotation to an element in an infinite series of rotations. The inverse can be used to transform an element in an infinite series of rotations to an element in a single rotation.

4. The present net worth of a stand at an intermediate point in a rotation (*r*); for example, at the time the thinning at t_3 is about to be taken (see Formula 1):

$$PNW_{t_3} = NR_{t_3} + \frac{NR_{t_4}}{(1+i)^{(t_4 - t_3)}} + \frac{NR_{t_r}}{(1+i)^{(t_r - t_3)}} \tag{3}$$

Costs and revenues occurring prior to t_3 are irrelevant to the calculation, but are embodied in the current physical condition of the stand. The calculation is essentially the present net worth of the value of the trees on the land plus the use of the land for the remainder of the rotation.

5. The soil expectation value of a stand at an intermediate point in a rotation can be determined by:

$$SE_{t_3} = NR_{t_3} + \frac{NR_{t_4}}{(1+i)^{(t_4 - t_3)}} + \frac{NR_{t_r}}{(1+i)^{(t_r - t_3)}} + \frac{SE_0}{(1+i)^{(t_r - t_3)}} \tag{4}$$

The calculation is essentially the purchase of an existing partial rotation and all future rotations. The future rotations are discounted to account for the remainder of the current rotation so that the infinite series of rotations will be postponed.

6. The maximum justified amount to be spent on one or two treatments at known times, given that the results of the "with treatment" and "without treatment" regimes are known, can be determined as follows: Calculate ΔPNW_0 with and without treatment. The $\Delta PNW_0 = PNW$ with, minus *PNW* without, for one treatment at time t_1 is given by the following equation:

$$C_{t_1} = \Delta PNW_0 (1+i)^{t_1} \tag{5}$$

For two or more treatments at t_1 and t_2

$$C_{t_1,t_2} = \Delta PNW_0 \div \left[\frac{1}{(1+i)^{t_1}} + \frac{1}{(1+i)^{t_2}}\right] \tag{6}$$

The preceding formula assumes C_1 and C_2 are equal. If they are not equal, then only one of the elements can be solved and the other or others must be known.

7. Delay cost, where a rotation is delayed D years can be measured in present net worth terms using the following equations:

$$PNW_D = \frac{PNW_0}{(1+i)^D} \tag{7}$$

$$PNW \text{ cost} = PNW_0 - PNW_D \tag{8}$$

$$\text{Annual cost of delay} = SE_0(i) \tag{9}$$

8. Replacement of a 5-yr-old stand of low stocking with a higher cost protected stand can be analyzed as follows:

$$S = [PNW_{LS} + RC](1+i)^5 + \frac{SE_{pt}}{(1+i)^{t_r-5}} \tag{10}$$

where SE_{pt} = Value of ∞ series of protected stands *now*;
 S = value of low stocked single rotation with protected series at end of first rotation. The regeneration cost is added back in because it is embedded in the PNW_{LS} but is sunk with respect to the retention decision.

If $SE_{pt} > S$, then replacement of the stand is the better alternative.

Index